TABLE OF LAPLACE TRANSFORMS

$f(t)$	Property	$F(s)$
$f(t)$	Definition	$\int_0^\infty f(t)e^{-st}\,dt$
$f_1(t) + f_2(t)$	Linearity	$\mathbf{F}_1(s) + \mathbf{F}_2(s)$
$Kf(t)$	Linearity	$K\mathbf{F}(s)$
$\dfrac{df(t)}{dt}$	Differentiation	$s\mathbf{F}(s) - f(0)$
$\dfrac{d^n f(t)}{dt^n}$	Differentiation	$s^n\mathbf{F}(s) - s^{n-1}f(0) - \cdots - \dfrac{d^{n-1}f(0)}{dt^{n-1}}$
$\int_0^t f(t)\,dt$	Integration	$\dfrac{1}{s}\mathbf{F}(s)$
$tf(t)$	Complex differentiation	$-\dfrac{d\mathbf{F}(s)}{ds}$
$e^{-at}f(t)$	Complex translation	$\mathbf{F}(s + a)$
$f(t-a)u(t-a)$	Real translation	$e^{-sa}\mathbf{F}(s)$
$f(t)$	Periodic function	$\dfrac{\mathbf{F}_1(s)}{1 - e^{-sT}}$
$\int_0^t x(\tau)h(t-\tau)\,d\tau$	Convolution	$\mathbf{H}(s)\mathbf{X}(s)$
$\delta(t)$		1
$u(t)$		$\dfrac{1}{s}$
$e^{-at}u(t)$		$\dfrac{1}{s+a}$
$\sin \beta t\, u(t)$		$\dfrac{\beta}{s^2 + \beta^2}$
$\cos \beta t\, u(t)$		$\dfrac{s}{s^2 + \beta^2}$
$e^{-\alpha t}\sin \beta t\, u(t)$		$\dfrac{\beta}{(s+\alpha)^2 + \beta^2}$
$e^{-\alpha t}\cos \beta t\, u(t)$		$\dfrac{s+\alpha}{(s+\alpha)^2 + \beta^2}$
$tu(t)$		$\dfrac{1}{s^2}$
$t^n u(t)$		$\dfrac{n!}{s^{n+1}}$
$te^{-at}u(t)$		$\dfrac{1}{(s+a)^2}$
$t^n e^{-at}u(t)$		$\dfrac{n!}{(s+a)^{n+1}}$

D0022594

ELEMENTARY LINEAR CIRCUIT ANALYSIS

**HRW
Series in
Electrical
Engineering**

M. E. Van Valkenburg, Series Editor Electrical Engineering

SECOND EDITION

ELEMENTARY LINEAR CIRCUIT ANALYSIS

Leonard S. Bobrow

UNIVERSITY OF MASSACHUSETTS, AMHERST

Holt, Rinehart and Winston, Inc.
New York   Chicago   San Francisco   Philadelphia
Montreal   Toronto   London   Sydney   Tokyo
Mexico City   Rio de Janeiro   Madrid

Acquisitions Editor: Deborah L. Moore
Production Manager: Paul Nardi
Project Editor: Bob Hilbert
Interior Design: Rita Naughton
Cover Illustration: Marc Cohen
Cover Design: Andrea DaRif
Illustrations: J&R Services

Copyright © 1987 CBS College Publishing
All rights reserved
Address correspondence to:
383 Madison Avenue, New York, NY 10017

Library of Congress Cataloging-in-Publication Data

Bobrow, Leonard S.
  Elementary linear circuit analysis.

  (HRW series in electrical engineering)
  Includes index.
  1. Electric circuits, Linear.   2. Electric networks.
I. Title. II. Series.
TK454.B58   1987   621.319′2   86-22935
ISBN 0-03-007298-0

Printed in the United States of America
Published simultaneously in Canada
  8 9   016   9 8 7 6 5 4 3

Holt, Rinehart and Winston
The Dryden Press
Saunders College Publishing

For My Mother and Father

Contents

Preface

This text is written for sophomore-level courses in beginning electric circuits and systems. I have found that there is sufficient material in the first seven chapters and the appendix for the first semester's course, and the next five chapters could form the basis for the second semester's course. Perhaps a school whose students allow a faster pace could include one or both of the last two chapters. As an alternative, an institution that is on the quarter system could complete the book in three quarters.

The text begins with such traditional topics as voltage, current, sources, resistors, and Ohm's law. It is assumed that the reader has had a course in high school or college freshman physics in which the concepts of the physics of electricity and magnetism (e.g., electric charge, electric potential, and magnetic fields) were introduced and discussed at an elementary level. Higher-level exposure to these topics, though illuminating, is not necessary since a more axiomatic approach to the subject matter can be taken if desired. Furthermore, it is assumed that the reader has had one or more courses in elementary calculus in which the topics of differentiation and integration were included.

Nowadays many students have already had experience with matrix notation, matrix arithmetic, and some applications of determinants (such as Cramer's rule) by the time they study this subject matter. The appendix on matrices and determinants will be a review for such people. For schools having a majority of students who are not familiar with these topics, the material in the appendix should be introduced before or during the study of Chapter 2, in which circuit analysis techniques are discussed.

Rather than devote a separate chapter to network topology, I have introduced various topological concepts throughout the text where needed as part of their application to circuit analysis.

Many circuits texts seem to neglect nonsinusoidal signals and waveforms by postponing their introduction or avoiding much of the subject. In this book, the topic is made an integral part of the discussion of inductors and capacitors. Also studied, at an even earlier stage, is the increasingly important subject of operational amplifiers. Op-amp circuits appear frequently throughout the subsequent portion of the text.

The coverage of first- and second-order circuits is traditional and self-contained with regard to the solving of linear differential equations with constant coefficients. The notion of describing circuits by differential equations is expanded to matrix formulations in the chapter on computer-aided circuit analysis. There, however, it is the numerical solution via a digital computer that is stressed.

The transformation from the time domain to the frequency domain takes place in the chapter on sinusoidal analysis. The resulting concepts see application in the subsequent chapter on power, and they are later generalized with the notion of complex frequency. This is followed by the study of the Laplace transform and its application to electric circuits and systems. The following chapter on two-port networks begins with a discussion of the concept of mutual inductance and investigates ideal as well as nonideal transformers. The subject of two-port parameters is also included in this chapter.

The book concludes with two chapters on Fourier analysis. Fourier series in both the trigonometric and exponential forms are studied as is the Fourier transform.

This edition contains several improvements over the first edition of this book. A second color has been added to emphasize the differences between variables and given quantities and to distinguish waveforms from coordinate axes. The 213 worked examples have been numbered for easy reference, and 192 drill exercises have been added to reinforce a student's understanding of the material being discussed. All the text's problems are located at the ends of their respective chapters, and answers to approximately half of these 750 problems are located at the back of the book. The instructor's manual for this text contains the worked-out solutions for all of the book's drill exercises and problems. (In this manual the chapter sections of the problems are identified for the instructor.) Chapter 4 contains a section on the evaluation of initial conditions, and phasor diagrams are included in Chapters 8 and 9. Furthermore, Chapter 10 has a section on Bode plots. The chapter on the Laplace transform has been moved up so as to allow for an earlier general treatment of circuit analysis. A second appendix has been added. The subject of this appendix is the circuit-analysis computer program SPICE.

The material in the text increases in difficulty as the subject matter progresses. A second-term student has already had the experience of one term, whereas the student in the first term is almost totally unsophisticated—and there is quite a difference between the two cases.

It is my philosophy that a text include many examples, and that these examples be worked in sufficient detail so that the reader can follow each example from beginning to end. I find phrases such as "It can be shown that . . ." unpleasant, for although I may be able to show it, maybe the reader cannot. Under this circumstance, if I don't show it to the reader (and the reader can't or won't show it), then the result under consideration will not be as meaningful. Of course, there are those rare occasions when, for practical reasons, I have to let a result appear without formal justification.

Rather than approach a topic initially from a general point of view, I prefer to start with an example that a student can understand, and then have it naturally evolve into something new or simply suggest something new. Generalizations are, of course, necessary, but they should appear after a student has seen some specifics (if possible). Seeing examples solved in detail gives readers a certain amount of feeling for the problem-solving process and subject material. It is then easier for them to grasp more general concepts. Inasmuch as this book has been written primarily for people to whom the material is new, and they are trying to learn it for the first time, I feel such an approach is pedagogically superior.

An extremely important part of the learning process involves solving problems. Even if a student can follow every line of every example in this book, that doesn't mean that he or she can solve problems unaided. In order to gain confidence and agility (and insight), the reader must work out many problems. In this book, drill exercises are given throughout the text and problems are presented at the ends of chapters. A number of problems have been chosen so that their values, as well as topology, are typical of real situations. However, since the stress of this text is on the concepts of circuit analysis and not on numerical computation, most circuits (even those with practical configurations) have numerically simple element values.

The writing style of this book may seem to be a little more casual than for a typical text. But, as the object of any book is to convey information and ideas, I feel that it is important that a text be written in a way that makes a reader (who will be spending a lot of time with it) feel comfortable. I personally think that informality tends to make students feel less intimidated.

I would like to express my appreciation to the many people who have contributed to the second edition of this book. Many discussions with my friend and colleague Dr. Donald Scott have proven to be invaluable. I wish to thank Mr. Jan Narkiewicz and Ms. Lisa Chandler for their contribution to the instructor's manual of this text, and Ms. Patricia Moriarty for her secretarial skills. I am also grateful to the reviewers of this book for their many excellent comments and suggestions. The first edition and the manuscript for its revision have been reviewed in whole or in part by:

Prof. Vernon D. Albertson, University of Minnesota
Prof. Bennett L. Basore, Oklahoma State University
Prof. Nihat Bilgutay, Drexel University
Prof. James F. Delansky, Pennsylvania State University
Prof. William C. Duesterhoeft, University of Texas
Prof. A.L. Duke, Clemson University

Prof. John A. Fleming, Texas A&M University
Prof. Ronald Hoelzeman, University of Pittsburgh
Prof. Carl Hozlinger, Lehigh University
Prof. K. Ross Johnson, Michigan Technological University
Prof. Michael Lightner, University of Colorado—Boulder
Prof. Pen-Min Lin, Purdue University
Prof. David C. Munson, Jr., University of Illinois
Prof. Burks Oakley, II, University of Illinois
Prof. Bernhard M. Schmidt, University of Dayton
Prof. David A. Seamans, Washington State University
Prof. Charles V. Stephenson, Vanderbilt University
Prof. Arthur T. Tiedemann, University of Wisconsin
Prof. Leonard J. Weber, Oregon State University
Prof. Charles Yakomoto, Indiana Purdue University
Prof. Robert E. Yantorno, Temple University

Finally, I would like to thank Mr. Bob Hilbert for his production work, and my editor Ms. Deborah Moore for her encouragement and enthusiasm.

Leonard S. Bobrow

ELEMENTARY LINEAR CIRCUIT ANALYSIS

CHAPTER 1

Basic Elements and Laws

● INTRODUCTION

The study of electric circuits is fundamental in electrical engineering education, and can be quite valuable in other disciplines as well. The skills acquired not only are useful in such electrical engineering areas as electronics, communications, microwaves, control, and power systems but also can be employed in other seemingly different fields.

By an **electric circuit** or **network** we mean a collection of electrical devices (for example, voltage and current sources, resistors, inductors, capacitors, transformers, amplifiers, and transistors) that are interconnected in some manner. The various uses of such circuits, though important, is not the major concern of this text. Instead, our prime interest will be with the process of determining the behavior of a given circuit—which is referred to as **analysis**.

We begin our study by discussing some basic electric elements and the laws that describe them. It is assumed that the reader has been introduced to the concepts of electric charge, potential, and current in various science and physics courses in high school and college.

1.1 IDEAL SOURCES

Electric charge[†] is measured in **coulombs** (abbreviated C) in honor of the French scientist Charles de Coulomb (1736–1806); the unit of work or energy—the **joule**

[†] An electron has a negative charge of 1.6×10^{-19} C.

(J)—is named for the British physicist James P. Joule (1818–1889). Although the unit for energy expended on electric charge is J/C, we give it the special name **volt** (V) in honor of the Italian physicist Alessandro Volta (1745–1827), and we way that it is a measure of **electric potential difference** or **voltage**. These units are part of the **Système International d'Unités** (International System of Units). Units of this system are referred to as **SI** units. Unless indicated to the contrary, SI units are the units used in this book.

An **ideal voltage source**, which is represented in Fig. 1.1, is a device that produces a voltage or potential difference of v volts across its terminals *regardless of what is connected to it.*

For the device shown in Fig. 1.1, terminal 1 is marked plus (+) and terminal 2 is marked minus (−). This denotes that terminal 1 is at an electric potential that is v volts higher than that of terminal 2. (Alternatively, the electric potential of terminal 2 is v volts lower than that of terminal 1.)

The quantity v can have either a positive or a negative value. For the latter case, it is possible to obtain an equivalent source with a positive value. For suppose that $v = -5$ V for the voltage source shown in Fig. 1.1. Then the potential at terminal 1 is -5 V higher than that of terminal 2. However, this is equivalent to saying that terminal 1 is at a potential of $+5$ V lower than terminal 2. Consequently, the two ideal voltage sources shown in Fig. 1.2 are equivalent.

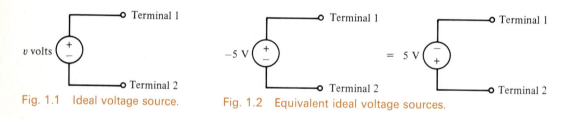

Fig. 1.1   Ideal voltage source.   Fig. 1.2   Equivalent ideal voltage sources.

In the discussion above, we may have implied that the value of an ideal voltage source is constant, that is, it does not change with time. Such a situation is plotted in Fig. 1.3 for the case that $v = 3$ V. For occasions such as this, an ideal voltage source is commonly represented by the equivalent notation shown in Fig. 1.4. We refer to such a device as an ideal **battery**. Although an actual battery is not ideal, there are many circumstances under which an ideal battery is a very good approximation. One

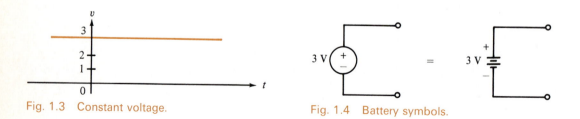

Fig. 1.3   Constant voltage.   Fig. 1.4   Battery symbols.

such example is the 9-V battery that you use for your portable transistor radio—or you may have the type that uses four or six C or D $1\frac{1}{2}$-V batteries. A 12-V automobile storage battery is another case in point. In general, however, the voltage produced by an ideal voltage source will be a function of time. A few of the multitude of possible voltage waveforms are shown in Fig. 1.5.

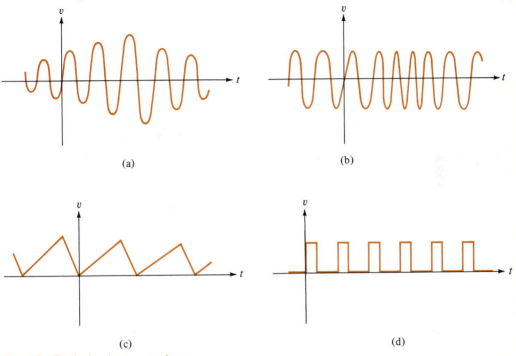

(a)

(b)

(c)

(d)

Fig. 1.5   Typical voltage waveforms.

Since the voltage produced by a source is, in general, a function of time, say $v(t)$, then the most general representation of an ideal voltage source is that shown in Fig. 1.6. There should be no confusion if the units "volts" are not included in the representation of the source. Thus, the ideal voltage source in Fig. 1.7 is identical to the one in Fig. 1.6 with "volts" being understood.

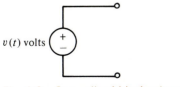

Fig. 1.6   Generalized ideal voltage source.

Fig. 1.7   Equivalent generalized ideal voltage source.

DRILL EXERCISE 1.1

An ideal voltage source has a value of $v(t) = 10e^{-t}$ V. What is the voltage produced by this source when (a) $t = 0$ seconds, (b) $t = 1$ second, (c) $t = 2$ seconds, (d) $t = 3$ seconds, and (e) $t = 4$ seconds?
Answer: (a) 10 V; (b) 3.68 V; (c) 1.35 V; (d) 0.498 V; (e) 0.183 V

Placing an electric potential difference (voltage) across some material generally results in a flow of electric charge. Negative charge (in the form of electrons) flows from a given electric potential to a higher potential. Conversely, positive charge tends to flow from a given potential to a lower potential. Charge is usually denoted by q, and since this quantity is generally time dependent, the total amount of charge that is present in a given region is designated by $q(t)$.

We define **current**, denoted $i(t)$, to be the flow rate of the charge; that is,

$$i(t) = \frac{dq(t)}{dt}$$

is the current in the region containing $q(t)$. Following the convention of Benjamin Franklin (a positive thinker), the direction of current has been chosen to be opposite to the direction of electron flow. The units of current (coulombs per second, or C/s) are referred to as **amperes** (A) or **amps** for short, in honor of the French physicist André Ampère (1775–1836).

An **ideal current source**, represented as shown in Fig. 1.8, is a device which, *when connected to anything*, will always move I amperes in the direction indicated by the arrow.

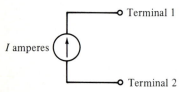

Fig. 1.8   Ideal current source.

As a consequence of the definition, it should be quite clear that the ideal current sources in Fig. 1.9 are equivalent.

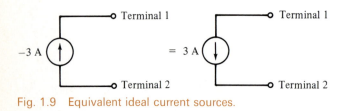

Fig. 1.9   Equivalent ideal current sources.

Fig. 1.10   Generalized ideal current source.

Again, in general, the amount of current produced by an ideal source will be a function of time. Thus, the general representation of an ideal current source is shown in Fig. 1.10, where the units "amperes" are understood.

DRILL EXERCISE 1.2

The total charge in some region is described by the function $q(t) = 3e^{-4t} + 0.02 \sin 120\pi t$ C. Find the magnitude of the current in this region.

Answer: $-12e^{-4t} + 7.54 \cos 120\pi t$ A

1.2 RESISTORS AND OHM'S LAW

Suppose that some material is connected to the terminals of an ideal voltage source $v(t)$ as shown in Fig. 1.11. Suppose that $v(t) = 1$ V. Then the electric potential at the top of the material is 1 V above the potential at the bottom. Since an electron has a negative charge, electrons in the material will tend to flow from bottom to top. Therefore, we say that current tends to go from top to bottom through the material. Hence, for the given polarity, when $v(t)$ is a positive number, $i(t)$ will be a positive number with the direction indicated. If $v(t) = 2$ V, again the potential at the top is greater than at the bottom, so $i(t)$ will again be positive. However, because the potential is now twice as large as before, the current will be greater. (If the material is a "linear" element, the current will be twice as great.) Suppose now that $v(t) = 0$ V. Then the potentials at the top and the bottom of the material are the same. The result is no flow of electrons and, hence, no current. In this case, $i(t) = 0$ A. But suppose that $v(t) = -2$ V. Then the top of the material will be at a potential lower than at the bottom of the material. A current from bottom to top will result, and $i(t)$ will be a negative number. Due to the physical law of the conservation of electric charge, $i(t)$ goes through the voltage source as indicated.

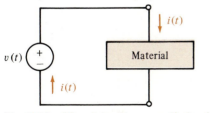

Fig. 1.11   Material with an applied voltage.

If in Fig. 1.11 the resulting current $i(t)$ is always directly proportional to the voltage for any function $v(t)$, then the material is called a **linear resistor**, or **resistor** for short.

Since voltage and current are directly proportional for a resistor, there exists a proportionality constant R, called **resistance**, such that

$$v(t) = Ri(t)$$

In dividing both sides of this equation by $i(t)$, we obtain

$$R = \frac{v(t)}{i(t)}$$

The units of resistance (volts per ampere) are referred to as **ohms**[†] and are denoted by the capital Greek letter omega, Ω. The accepted circuit symbol for a resistor whose resistance is R ohms is shown in Fig. 1.12. A plot of voltage versus current for a (linear) resistor is given in Fig. 1.13.

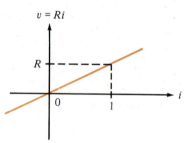

Fig. 1.13   Plot of voltage versus current for a resistor.

Fig. 1.12   Circuit symbol for a resistor.

It was Ohm who discovered that if a resistor R has a voltage $v(t)$ *across* it and a current $i(t)$ *through* it, then if one is the cause, the other is the effect. Furthermore, if the polarity of the voltage and the direction of the current are as shown in Fig. 1.14, then it is true that

$$v(t) = Ri(t)$$

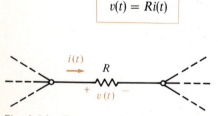

Fig. 1.14   Current and voltage convention for Ohm's law.

[†] Named for the German physicist Georg Ohm (1787–1854).

This equation is often called **Ohm's law**. From it, we may immediately deduce that

$$R = \frac{v(t)}{i(t)}$$ and $$i(t) = \frac{v(t)}{R}$$

These last two equations are also referred to as Ohm's law.

EXAMPLE 1.1

For the resistor given in Fig. 1.14, suppose that $R = 10\ \Omega$. When $i(t) = 2$ A, then $v(t) = Ri(t) = 10(2) = 20$ V.

But, now consider the case that $i(t) = -3$ A. Under this circumstance, $v(t) = Ri(t) = 10(-3) = -30$ V. This can be represented either as shown in Fig. 1.15(a), or alternatively, as shown in Fig. 1.15(b), where $i_1(t) = -i(t)$.

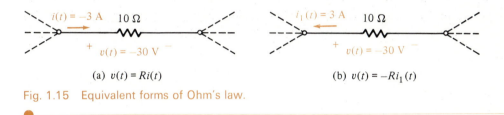

(a) $v(t) = Ri(t)$ (b) $v(t) = -Ri_1(t)$

Fig. 1.15   Equivalent forms of Ohm's law.

From Example 1.1, we see that because of the use of negative numbers, we can have situations where currents are indicated going through resistors from + to − as depicted in Fig. 1.14, or going from − to + as in Fig. 1.16. For the former case, Ohm's law is $v(t) = Ri(t)$. However, for the latter case, since Fig. 1.17 is equivalent to Fig. 1.16, and since Fig. 1.17 is in the form of Fig. 1.14, we use Ohm's law to write its alternative version

$$v_1(t) = R[-i_1(t)]$$

or

$$v_1(t) = -Ri_1(t)$$

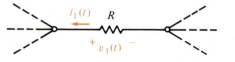

Fig. 1.16   Situation requiring negative sign for Ohm's law.

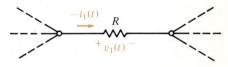

Fig. 1.17   Equivalent form of Fig. 1.16.

EXAMPLE 1.2

Consider the circuit shown in Fig. 1.18. We use the letter "k" to represent the prefix "kilo," which indicates a value of 10^3. Following is a table of the more common symbols.

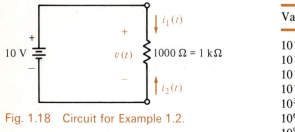

Fig. 1.18   Circuit for Example 1.2.

Value	Prefix	Symbol
10^{-12}	pico	p
10^{-9}	nano	n
10^{-6}	micro	μ
10^{-3}	milli	m
10^3	kilo	k
10^6	mega	M
10^9	giga	G

For the circuit in Fig. 1.18, the voltage across the 1-kΩ resistor is, by the definition of an ideal voltage source, $v(t) = 10$ V. Thus, by Ohm's law, we get

$$i_1(t) = \frac{v(t)}{R} = \frac{10}{1000} = \frac{1}{100} = 0.01 \text{ A} = 10 \text{ mA}$$

and

$$i_2(t) = -\frac{v(t)}{R} = -\frac{10}{1000} = -\frac{1}{100} = -0.01 \text{ A} = -10 \text{ mA}$$

Note that $i_2(t) = -i_1(t)$ as expected.

For the circuit shown in Fig. 1.19, by the definition of an ideal current source, $i(t) = 25 \ \mu\text{A} = 25 \times 10^{-6}$ A. By Ohm's law, we have that

$$v(t) = -Ri(t) = -(2 \times 10^6)(25 \times 10^{-6}) = -50 \text{ V}$$

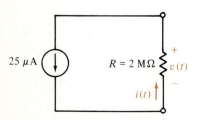

Fig. 1.19.   Another circuit for Example 1.2.

DRILL EXERCISE 1.3

For the circuit shown in Fig. DE1.3, find (a) v_1, (b) v_2, (c) i_3, (d) i_4, and (e) R.
Answer: (a) -1 V; (b) 6 V; (c) -2 mA; (d) 2 mA; (e) 3 kΩ

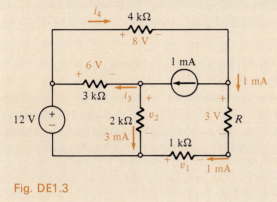

Fig. DE1.3

Given a resistor R connected to an ideal voltage source $v(t)$ as shown in Fig. 1.20, we conclude the following. Since $i(t) = v(t)/R$ for any particular ideal source $v(t)$, the amount of current $i(t)$ that results can be made to be any finite value by choosing the appropriate value for R (e.g., to make $i(t)$ large, make R small). Thus, we see that an ideal voltage source is capable of supplying *any* amount of current, and that amount depends on what is connected to the source—only the voltage is constrained to be $v(t)$ volts at the terminals.

Fig. 1.20   Current through a voltage source.

Fig. 1.21   Voltage across a current source.

If $v(t)$ is positive, then for the circuit shown in Fig. 1.21, the current comes out of the + side of the voltage source (assuming a positive resistance, or course). However, as we shall see later, when other types of elements are connected to a voltage source, the current through the voltage source can be in either direction—the direction depends on what exactly is connected to the source.

When a resistor R is connected to an ideal current source as in Fig. 1.21, we know that $v(t) = Ri(t)$. Therefore, for a given current source $i(t)$, the voltage $v(t)$ that results can be made to be any finite value by appropriately choosing R[e.g., to make $v(t)$ large, make R large]. Hence, we conclude that an ideal current source is capable of producing *any* amount of voltage across its terminals, and that amount depends on what is connected to the source—only the current is constrained to be $i(t)$ amperes through the source.

For the circuit in Fig. 1.21, if $i(t)$ is positive, then the polarity of the (positive-valued) voltage $v(t)$ is as indicated. In general, however, the polarity (as well as the magnitude) of the voltage across a current source depends on what exactly is connected to the source.

Physical (nonideal) sources do not have the ability to produce unlimited currents and voltages. As a matter of fact, an actual source may approximate an ideal source only for a limited range of values.

Now consider the two ideal voltage sources whose terminals are connected as shown in Fig. 1.22. By definition of an ideal 3-V source, $v(t)$ must be 3 V. However, by the definition of a 5-V ideal voltage source, $v(t) = 5$ V. Clearly, both conditions cannot be satisfied simultaneously. (Note that connecting a resistor, or anything else, for that matter, to the terminals will not alleviate this problem.) Therefore, to avoid this paradoxical situation, we will insist that two ideal voltage sources never have their terminals connected together as in Fig. 1.22; the only exception is two sources with the same value and the same polarity.

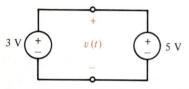

Fig. 1.22   Example of nonallowable connection of ideal voltage sources.

Now consider a resistor whose value is zero ohms. An equivalent representation, called a **short circuit**, of such a resistance is given in Fig. 1.23. By Ohm's law, we have that

$$v(t) = Ri(t) = 0i(t) = 0 \text{ V}$$

Thus, no matter what finite value $i(t)$ has, $v(t)$ will be zero. Hence, we see that *a zero-ohm resistor is equivalent to an ideal voltage source whose value is zero volts,* provided that the current through it is finite. Therefore, for a zero resistance to be synonymous with a constraint of zero volts (and to avoid the unpleasantness of infinite currents), we will insist that we never be allowed to place a short circuit directly

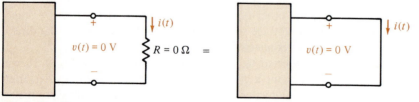

Fig. 1.23   Short-circuit equivalents.

across a voltage source. In actuality, the reader will be spared a lot of grief by never attempting this in a laboratory or field situation.

Next consider a resistor having infinite resistance. An equivalent representation, called an **open circuit**, of such a situation is depicted in Fig. 1.24. By Ohm's law,

$$i(t) = \frac{v(t)}{R} = 0 \text{ A}$$

as long as $v(t)$ has a finite value. Thus, we may conclude that *an infinite resistance is equivalent to an ideal current source whose value is zero amperes.* Furthermore, we will always assume that an ideal current source has something connected to its terminals.

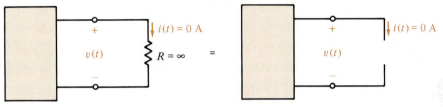

Fig. 1.24   Open-circuit equivalents.

1.3 KIRCHHOFF'S CURRENT LAW (KCL)

It is a consequence of the work of the German physicist Gustav Kirchhoff (1824–1887) that enables us to analyze an interconnection of any number of elements (voltage sources, current sources, and resistors, as well as elements not yet discussed). We will refer to any such interconnection as a **circuit** or a **network**.

For a given circuit, a connection of two or more elements[†] shall be called a **node**. An example of a node is depicted in the partial circuit shown in Fig. 1.25. In

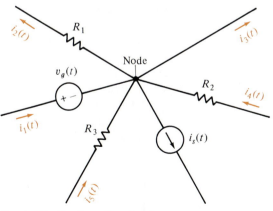

Fig. 1.25   Portion of a circuit.

[†] One element can be an open circuit.

addition to using a solid dot, we may also indicate a node by a hollow dot, as was done for a terminal. Conversely, we may use a solid dot for the terminal of a device.

We now present the first of Kirchhoff's two laws, his current law (KCL), which is essentially the law of conservation of electric charge.

KCL: At any node of a circuit, at every instant of time, the sum of the currents into the node is equal to the sum of the currents out of the node.

Specifically for the portion of the network shown in Fig. 1.25, by applying KCL we obtain the equation

$$i_1(t) + i_4(t) + i_5(t) = i_2(t) + i_3(t) + i_s(t)$$

Note that one of the elements [the one in which $i_3(t)$ flows] is a short circuit—KCL holds regardless of the kinds of elements in the circuit.

An alternative, but equivalent, form of KCL can be obtained by considering currents directed into a node to be positive in sense and currents directed out of a node to be negative in sense (or vice versa). Under this circumstance, the alternative form of KCL can be stated as follows:

KCL: At any node of a circuit, the currents algebraically sum to zero.

Applying this form of KCL to the node in Fig. 1.25 and considering currents directed in to be positive in sense, we get

$$i_1(t) - i_2(t) - i_3(t) + i_4(t) - i_s(t) + i_5(t) = 0$$

A close inspection of the last two equations, however, reveals that they are the same!

From this point on, we will simplify our notation somewhat by often abbreviating functions of time t such as $v(t)$ and $i(t)$ as v and i, respectively. For instance, we may rewrite the last two equations, respectively, as

$$i_1 + i_4 + i_5 = i_2 + i_3 + i_s$$

and

$$i_1 - i_2 - i_3 + i_4 - i_s + i_5 = 0$$

It should always be understood, however, that lowercase letters such as v and i, in general, represent time-varying quantities.[†]

[†] A constant is a special case of a function of time.

EXAMPLE 1.3

Let us find the voltage v in the two-node circuit given in Fig. 1.26 in which the directions of i_1, i_2, and i_3 and the polarity of v were chosen arbitrarily. (The directions of the 2-A and 13-A sources are given.)

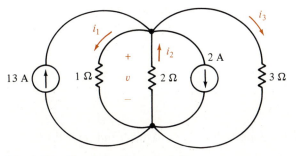

Fig. 1.26 Circuit for Example 1.3.

By KCL (at either of the two nodes), we have

$$13 - i_1 + i_2 - 2 - i_3 = 0 \qquad (1.1)$$

From this we can write

$$i_1 - i_2 + i_3 = 11$$

By Ohm's law,

$$i_1 = \frac{v}{1} \qquad i_2 = -\frac{v}{2} \qquad i_3 = \frac{v}{3}$$

Substituting these into the preceding equation yields

$$\frac{v}{1} - \left(-\frac{v}{2}\right) + \frac{v}{3} = 11$$

from which

$$v = 6 \text{ V}$$

Having solved for v, we now find that

$$i_1 = \frac{v}{1} = \frac{6}{1} = 6 \text{ A} \qquad i_2 = -\frac{v}{2} = -\frac{6}{2} = -3 \text{ A} \qquad i_3 = \frac{v}{3} = \frac{6}{3} = 2 \text{ A}$$

Note that a reordering of the circuit elements, as shown in Fig. 1.27, will result in the same equation (1.1) when KCL is applied. Since Ohm's law remains unchanged, the same answers are obtained.

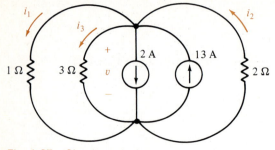

Fig. 1.27   Circuit equivalent to Fig. 1.26.

DRILL EXERCISE 1.4

For the circuit shown in Fig. DE1.4, suppose that $i_s = 10$ mA. Find (a) v, (b) i_1, (c) i_2, (d) i_3, and (e) i_4.

Answer: (a) 4.8 V; (b) -4.8 mA; (c) 2.4 mA; (d) -1.6 mA; (e) 1.2 mA

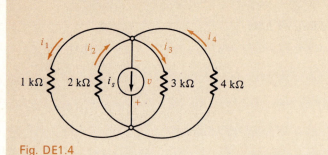

Fig. DE1.4

Just as KCL applies to any node of a circuit (i.e., to satisfy the physical law of conservation of charge, the current going in must equal the current coming out), so must KCL hold for any closed region.

For the circuit shown in Fig. 1.28, three regions have been arbitrarily identified. Applying KCL to Region 1, we get

$$i_1 + i_4 + i_5 = i_2$$

Applying KCL to Region 2, we obtain

$$i_5 + i_6 + i_7 = 0$$

and by applying KCL to Region 3, we get

$$i_2 + i_7 = i_4 + i_g$$

Note that Region 3 apparently contains two nodes. However, since they are connected by a short circuit, there is no difference in voltage between these two points.

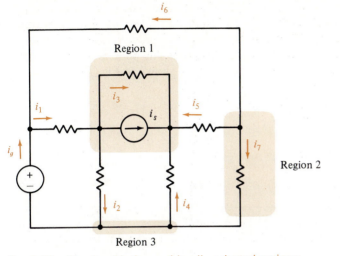

Fig. 1.28   Circuit with three arbitrarily selected regions.

Therefore, we can shrink the short circuit so as to coalesce the two points into a single node without affecting the operation of the circuit. Applying KCL at the resulting node again yields $i_2 + i_7 = i_4 + i_g$.

The converse process of expanding a node into apparently different nodes interconnected by short circuits also does not affect the operation of a circuit. For example, the portion of a circuit shown in Fig. 1.25 has the equivalent form shown in Fig. 1.29. Applying KCL to the region indicated results in the same equation as is obtained when KCL is applied to the node shown in Fig. 1.25. Thus, although it may appear that there are four distinct nodes in the region depicted in Fig. 1.29, they actually constitute a single node.

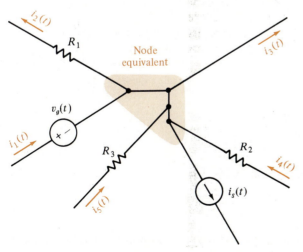

Fig. 1.29   Equivalent of circuit portion in Fig. 1.25.

It is because of the foregoing that we can redraw the circuit given in Fig. 1.26 in the equivalent form shown in Fig. 1.30(a). Even though it may not appear so at first glance, the circuit shown in Fig. 1.30(a) has two distinct nodes—they are indicated by the depicted regions. With this fact in mind, from this point on we shall draw such a circuit without the indication of regions, as is shown in Fig. 1.30(b).

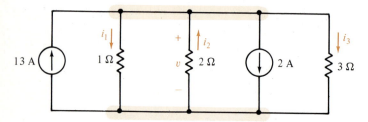

Fig. 1.30(a)   Equivalent form of circuit in Fig. 1.26.

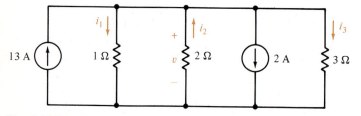

Fig. 1.30(b)   Circuit in Fig. 1.30(a) with region indications omitted.

DRILL EXERCISE 1.5

For the circuit shown in Fig. DE1.5, find i_1, i_2, and i_3 when (a) $i_s = 10$ A and (b) $i_s = 7$ A.

Answer: (a) 6 A, 3 A, 1 A; (b) 6 A, 3 A, −2 A

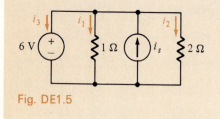

Fig. DE1.5

Current Division

We now consider the circuit given in Fig. 1.31. For this circuit, let us express the current i in terms of R_1, R_2, and v. Clearly, the voltage across each resistor is v.

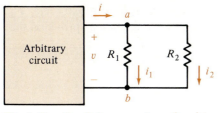

Fig. 1.31   Parallel connection of resistors.

By Ohm's law, we can write

$$i_1 = \frac{v}{R_1} \quad \text{and} \quad i_2 = \frac{v}{R_2}$$

Applying KCL (at either node), we get

$$i = i_1 + i_2 = \frac{v}{R_1} + \frac{v}{R_2} = v\left(\frac{1}{R_1} + \frac{1}{R_2}\right) \tag{1.2}$$

Note that resistors R_1 and R_2 are connected to the same pair of nodes (nodes a and b). We call this a **parallel connection**. Specifically, we say that two elements are **connected in parallel** if they are connected to the same pair of nodes, regardless of what else is connected to those two nodes. This definition holds not only for two elements, but for three or four, or more, as well. As a consequence of the definition, we see that elements connected in parallel all have the same voltage across them.

As far as the arbitrary circuit in Fig. 1.31 is concerned, there is a resistance R between nodes a and b. But how is this value related to R_1 and R_2? From Equation (1.2), by Ohm's law, we have

$$\frac{i}{v} = \frac{1}{R} = \frac{1}{R_1} + \frac{1}{R_2}$$

Thus, we see that the parallel connection of resistors R_1 and R_2 is equivalent to a single resistor R, provided that

$$\boxed{\frac{1}{R} = \frac{1}{R_1} + \frac{1}{R_2}}$$

From this equation,[†]

$$\frac{1}{R} = \frac{R_1 + R_2}{R_1 R_2} \quad \Rightarrow \quad \boxed{R = \frac{R_1 R_2}{R_1 + R_2}}$$

[†] The symbol $\Rightarrow$ means "implies."

Using reasoning as in the above discussion, we deduce that m resistors $R_1, R_2,$ $R_3, \ldots, R_m$ connected in parallel are equivalent to a single resistor R, provided that

$$\frac{1}{R} = \frac{1}{R_1} + \frac{1}{R_2} + \cdots + \frac{1}{R_m}$$

In the discussion above, the reciprocal of a resistance appeared a number of times. It is because of the frequent occurrence of the quantity $1/R$ that we denote it by a separate symbol. Given an R-ohm resistor, we define its **conductance** G to be

$$G = \frac{1}{R}$$

In SI units, conductance is measured in **siemens**[†] (S). (Formerly, the unit **mho**— designated $\mho$—was used for conductance.) Figure 1.32 shows two equivalent ways of representing the same element. The equivalent forms of Ohm's law are

$$v = Ri = \frac{1}{G} i \qquad i = \frac{1}{R} v = Gv$$

$$R = \frac{v}{i} = \frac{1}{G} \qquad G = \frac{i}{v} = \frac{1}{R}$$

Note that when combining resistors in parallel, to obtain an equivalent resistor, we add conductances. This fact is demonstrated in Fig. 1.33.

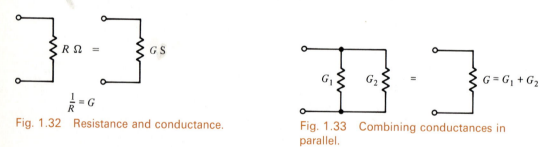

Fig. 1.32   Resistance and conductance.

Fig. 1.33   Combining conductances in parallel.

Now consider the circuit given in Fig. 1.34. We ask the question that has been haunting scientists for a long time: "If you were an ampere, where would you go?" To answer this question, we simply replace the parallel connection of R_1 and R_2 by its

---

[†] Named for the British inventor William Siemens (1823–1883).

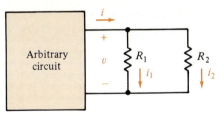

Fig. 1.34   Current division.

Fig. 1.35   Equivalent resistance of parallel connection.

equivalent resistance as shown in Fig. 1.35. We then have

$$v = Ri = \frac{R_1 R_2}{R_1 + R_2} i$$

Since this is the same v that appears in Fig. 1.34, we conclude that

$$i_1 = \frac{v}{R_1} \quad \text{and} \quad i_2 = \frac{v}{R_2}$$

Thus,

$$i_1 = \frac{R_2}{R_1 + R_2} i \quad \text{and} \quad i_2 = \frac{R_1}{R_1 + R_2} i$$

Since, by KCL, $i_1 + i_2 = i$, the above two boxed formulas described how the current i is divided by the resistors. For this reason, a pair of resistors in parallel is often referred to as a **current divider**. Note that if R_1 and R_2 are both positive, and if R_1 is greater than R_2, then i_2 is greater than i_1. In other words, a larger amount of current will go through the smaller resistor—amperes tend to take the path of least resistance!

For the circuit shown in Fig. 1.36, since $G_1 = 1/R_1$ and $G_2 = 1/R_2$, then by the current-divider formula for i_1, we have

$$i_1 = \frac{R_2}{R_1 + R_2} i = \frac{1/G_2}{(1/G_1) + (1/G_2)} i = \frac{1/G_2}{(G_1 + G_2)/G_1 G_2} i = \frac{G_1}{G_1 + G_2} i$$

Similarly,

$$i_2 = \frac{G_2}{G_1 + G_2} i$$

Thus, we also have current-divider formulas in terms of conductances.

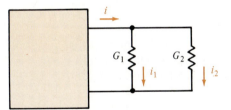

Fig. 1.36   Conductances in parallel.

EXAMPLE 1.4

For the circuit given in Fig. 1.37, let us determine the currents indicated by using current division.

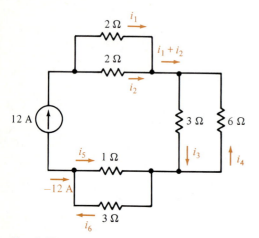

Fig. 1.37   Example of current division.

The current that is to be divided by the two 2-Ω resistors is 12 A. By the current-division formulas,

$$i_1 = i_2 = \frac{2(12)}{2 + 2} = 6 \text{ A}$$

The current that is to be divided by the 3-Ω and 6-Ω resistors is $i_1 + i_2 = 12$ A. By the current-division formulas, we have

$$i_3 = \frac{6(12)}{3 + 6} = 8 \text{ A}$$

and

$$-i_4 = \frac{3(12)}{3 + 6} = 4 \text{ A} \qquad \Rightarrow \qquad i_4 = -4 \text{ A}$$

Finally, the current that is to be divided by the 1-Ω and 3-Ω resistors is -12 A. Thus, by current division,

$$i_5 = \frac{3(-12)}{1 + 3} = -9 \text{ A}$$

and

$$-i_6 = \frac{1(-12)}{1 + 3} = -3 \text{ A} \qquad \Rightarrow \qquad i_6 = 3 \text{ A}$$

DRILL EXERCISE 1.6

Given the circuit shown in Fig. DE1.6, (a) use current-divider formulas to determine i_1, i_2, and i_3; (b) find i_s.

Answer: (a) 1.5 A, 4.5 A, 9 A; (b) -4 A

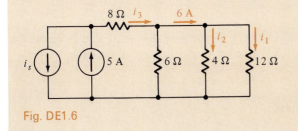

Fig. DE1.6

1.4 KIRCHHOFF'S VOLTAGE LAW (KVL)

We now present the second of Kirchhoff's laws—the voltage law. To do this, we must introduce the concept of a "loop."

Starting at any node n in a circuit, we form a **loop** by traversing through elements (open circuits included!) and returning to the starting node n, and never encountering any other node more than once. As an example, consider the partial circuit shown in Fig. 1.38. In this circuit, the 1-Ω, 2-Ω, 3-Ω, and 6-Ω resistors, along with the 2-A current source, constitute the loop a, b, c, e, f, a. A few (but not all) of the other loops are: (1) a, b, c, d, e, f, a; (2) c, d, e, c; (3) d, e, f, d; (4) a, b, c, e, d, f, a; (5) a, b, e, f, a; (6) b, c, e, b.

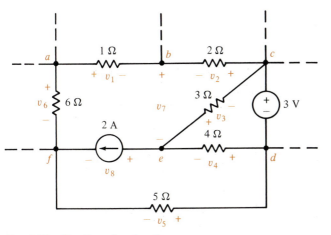

Fig. 1.38   Portion of a circuit.

We now can present Kirchhoff's voltage law (KVL):

KVL: In traversing any loop in any circuit, at every instant of time, the sum of the voltages having one polarity equals the sum of the voltages having the opposite polarity.[†]

For the partial circuit shown in Fig. 1.38, suppose that the voltages across the elements are as shown. Then by KVL around loop a, b, c, e, f, a, we have

$$v_1 + v_8 = v_2 + v_3 + v_6$$

and around loop b, c, d, e, b, we have

$$v_2 + v_7 = 3 + v_4$$

In this last loop, one of the elements traversed (the element between nodes b and e) is an open circuit—KVL holds regardless of the nature of the elements in the circuit.

Since voltage is energy (or work) per unit charge, then KVL is another way of stating the physical law of the conservation of energy.

An alternative statement of KVL can be obtained by considering voltages across elements that are traversed from plus to minus to be positive in sense and voltages across elements that are traversed from minus to plus to be negative in sense (or vice versa). Under this circumstance, KVL has the following alternative form.

KVL: Around any loop in a circuit, the voltages algebraically sum to zero.

By applying this form of KVL to the partial circuit shown in Fig. 1.38, and selecting a traversal from plus to minus to be positive in sense, around loop a, b, c, e, f, a, we get

$$v_1 - v_2 - v_3 + v_8 - v_6 = 0$$

and around loop b, c, d, e, b, we get

$$-v_2 + 3 + v_4 - v_7 = 0$$

These two equations are the same, respectively, as the preceding two equations.

[†] Another form of this statement is: The sum of the voltage rises equals the sum of the voltage drops, where traversing a voltage from minus to plus is a voltage rise and from plus to minus is a voltage drop.

EXAMPLE 1.5

Let us find the current i in Fig. 1.39(a), where the polarities of v_1, v_2, v_3 and the direction of i were chosen arbitrarily.

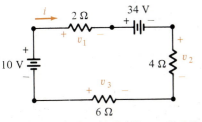

Fig. 1.39(a)   Circuit for Example 1.5.

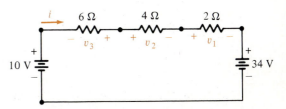

Fig. 1.39(b)   Circuit with elements reordered.

Applying KVL, we get

$$v_1 + 34 + v_2 - v_3 - 10 = 0$$

Thus,

$$v_1 + v_2 - v_3 = -24$$

From Ohm's law,

$$v_1 = 2i \qquad v_2 = 4i \qquad v_3 = -6i$$

Substituting these into the preceding equation yields

$$(2i) + (4i) - (-6i) = -24$$

from which

$$i = -2 \text{ A}$$

Having solved for i, we now find that

$$v_1 = 2i = 2(-2) = -4 \text{ V} \qquad v_2 = 4i = 4(-2) = -8 \text{ V}$$
$$v_3 = -6i = (-6)(-2) = 12 \text{ V}$$

Note that a reordering of the Fig. 1.39(a) circuit elements as shown in Fig. 1.39(b) will result in the same equation when KVL is applied. Since Ohm's law remains unchanged, the same answers are obtained.

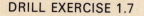

DRILL EXERCISE 1.7

For the circuit shown in Fig. DE1.7, find v when (a) $v_s = 4$ V, (b) $v_s = 9$ V, and (c) $v_s = 10$ V.

Answer: (a) 5 V; (b) 0 V; (c) -1 V

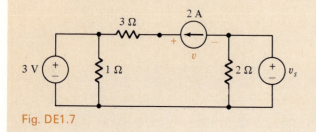

Fig. DE1.7

Voltage Division

Now consider the circuit given in Fig. 1.40. For this circuit, let us express the voltage v in terms of R_1, R_2, and i. By Ohm's law, we can write

$$v_1 = R_1 i \quad \text{and} \quad v_2 = R_2 i$$

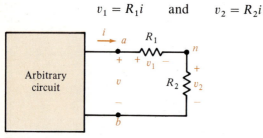

Fig. 1.40   Series connection of resistors.

Applying KVL, we get

$$v = v_1 + v_2 = R_1 i + R_2 i = (R_1 + R_2)i \tag{1.3}$$

Note that resistors R_1 and R_2 have a node in common (node n), and no other element is connected to this node. This is known as a **series connection**. Specifically, we say that two elements are **connected in series** if they have a node in common and no other element is connected to this common node. In general, if m elements are connected together such that each resulting node joins no more than two of the elements, then these elements are connected in series. As a consequence of the definition, we see that elements connected in series all have the same current through them.

As far as the arbitrary circuit in Fig. 1.40 is concerned, there is a resistance R between nodes a and b. From Equation (1.3), by Ohm's law, we have

$$\frac{v}{i} = R = R_1 + R_2$$

Thus, we see that the series connection of resistors R_1 and R_2 is equivalent to a single resistor R, provided that

$$R = R_1 + R_2$$

Using reasoning as above, we deduce that m resistors $R_1, R_2, R_3, \ldots, R_m$ connected in series are equivalent to a single resistor R, provided that

$$R = R_1 + R_2 + R_3 + \cdots + R_m$$

EXAMPLE 1.6

Let us find i in the circuit shown in Fig. 1.41. To find i, we can replace series and parallel connections of resistors by their equivalent resistances. We begin by noting that the 1-Ω and 3-Ω resistors are in series. Upon combining them, we get the circuit in Fig. 1.42(a).

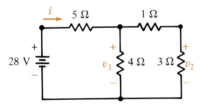

Fig. 1.41   Series-parallel circuit.

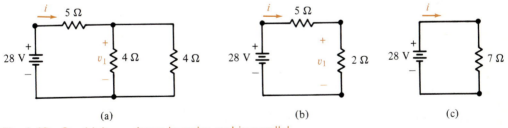

Fig. 1.42   Combining resistors in series and in parallel.

Note that it is not possible to display the voltage v_2 given in Fig. 1.41 in the circuit in Fig. 1.42(a). Since the two 4-Ω resistors are connected in parallel, we can further simplify the circuit as shown in Fig. 1.42(b). Here the 5-Ω and 2-Ω resistors are in series, so we may combine them and obtain the circuit in Fig. 1.42(c). Hence, by Ohm's law, we have

$$i = \tfrac{28}{7} = 4 \text{ A}$$

Furthermore, we can say that the resistance "seen" by the voltage source is 7 Ω.

DRILL EXERCISE 1.8

Combine resistances in parallel and series in order to determine the resistance between terminals a and b for the connection of resistors given in Fig. DE1.8.
Answer: $4.8\ \Omega$

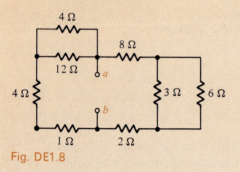

Fig. DE1.8

Now consider the circuit given in Fig. 1.43(a). To determine how the voltage v is divided between R_1 and R_2, we express i in terms of R_1, R_2, and v by replacing the series connection of the resistors by its equivalent resistance as shown in Fig. 1.43(b). By Ohm's law,

$$i = \frac{v}{R} = \frac{v}{R_1 + R_2}$$

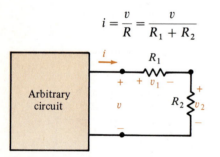

Fig. 1.43(a)   Voltage division.

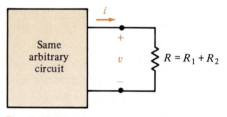

Fig. 1.43(b)   Equivalent resistance of series connection.

Thus, for the circuit in Fig. 1.43(a), we have

$$v_1 = R_1 i \quad \text{and} \quad v_2 = R_2 i$$

so

$$v_1 = \frac{R_1}{R_1 + R_2} v \quad \text{and} \quad v_2 = \frac{R_2}{R_1 + R_2} v$$

and the two boxed formulas describe how the voltage v is divided by the resistors. Because of this, a pair of resistors in series is often called a **voltage divider**. Note that for positive-valued resistors, if R_1 is greater than R_2, then v_1 is greater than v_2. In other words, a larger voltage will be maintained across the larger resistor.

EXAMPLE 1.7

Let us find the voltage v_2 in the circuit given in Fig. 1.41. Combining the series connection of the 1-Ω and 3-Ω resistors, we obtain the circuit shown in Fig. 1.42(a). The resulting pair of 4-Ω resistors in parallel can be combined as shown in Fig. 1.42(b). By voltage division, we have

$$v_1 = \frac{2(28)}{2 + 5} = \frac{56}{7} = 8 \text{ V}$$

Returning to the original circuit (Fig. 1.41) and applying voltage division again yields

$$v_2 = \frac{3v_1}{3 + 1} = \frac{3(8)}{4} = 6 \text{ V}$$

DRILL EXERCISE 1.9

For the circuit given in Fig. DE1.8, suppose that a voltage $v_{ab} = 12$ V is applied between terminals a and b (with + at terminal a). Use the voltage-divider formulas to determine the voltages across the 1-Ω and 2-Ω resistors (with − at terminal b).
Answer: 1.5 V; 2 V

1.5 DEPENDENT SOURCES

Up to this point, we have been considering voltage and current sources whose values are, in general, time dependent. However, these values were given to be independent of the behavior of the circuits to which the sources belonged. For this reason, we say that such sources are **independent**.

We now consider an ideal source, either voltage or current, whose value depends upon some variable (usually a voltage or current) in the circuit to which the source belongs. We call such an ideal source a **dependent** (or **controlled**) **source**, and represent it as shown in Fig. 1.44. Note that a dependent source is represented by a diamond-shaped symbol so as not to confuse it with an independent source.

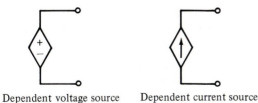

Dependent voltage source   Dependent current source

Fig. 1.44   Circuit symbols for dependent sources.

EXAMPLE 1.8

Consider the circuit shown in Fig. 1.45 in which the value of the dependent current source depends on the current i_1 in the 3-Ω resistor. Thus, we say that it is a **current-dependent current source**. Specifically, the value of the dependent source is $4i_1$, and the units are amperes, of course. (This implies that the constant 4 is dimensionless.)

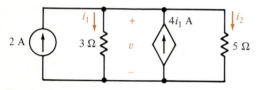

Fig. 1.45   Circuit with current-dependent current source.

Hence, if the current through the 3-Ω resistor is $i_1 = 2$ A, then the dependent current source has a value of $4i_1 = 8$ A; if the current is $i_1 = -3$ A, then the dependent current source has a value of $4i_1 = -12$ A; and so on. To find the actual quantity i_1, we proceed as follows:

Applying KCL (at either node), we can write

$$i_1 + i_2 = 4i_1 + 2$$

Simplifying this equation, we have

$$-3i_1 + i_2 = 2$$

By Ohm's law,

$$i_1 = \frac{v}{3} \quad \text{and} \quad i_2 = \frac{v}{5}$$

Therefore,

$$-3\left(\frac{v}{3}\right) + \frac{v}{5} = 2 \quad \Rightarrow \quad v = -\tfrac{10}{4} = -\tfrac{5}{2} \text{ V}$$

Hence, we see that in actuality

$$i_1 = \frac{v}{3} = -\frac{5}{6} \text{ A}$$

so that the value of the dependent current source is

$$4i_1 = -\tfrac{20}{6} = -\tfrac{10}{3} \text{ A}$$

Remember, if the independent source has a different value, then the quantity $4i_1$ will in general be different from $-\tfrac{10}{3}$ A.

DRILL EXERCISE 1.10

For the circuit shown in Fig. DE1.10, find (a) i, (b) v, (c) i_s, and (d) v_s.
Answer: (a) 2 A; (b) -9 V; (c) -3 A; (d) 3 V

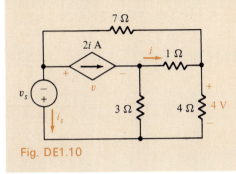

Fig. DE1.10

EXAMPLE 1.9

Let us now consider the circuit given in Fig. 1.46. In this circuit, the value of the dependent current source is specified by a voltage! In other words, the value of the source is $4v$ amperes, where v is the *amount* of voltage across the 3-Ω resistor (also the 5-Ω resistor in this case). This implies that the constant 4 has as units A/V, or siemens—so it is a conductance. Such a device is a **voltage-dependent current source**.

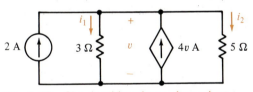

Fig. 1.46   Circuit with voltage-dependent current source.

To solve for v, we apply KCL, and obtain

$$i_1 + i_2 = 4v + 2$$

Thus,

$$\frac{v}{3} + \frac{v}{5} = 4v + 2 \quad \Rightarrow \quad v = -\tfrac{15}{26} \text{ V}$$

Consequently, the numerical value of the dependent current source is

$$4v = -\tfrac{30}{13} \text{ A}$$

Again, we will point out that if the independent source has a value other than 2 A, then the dependent source's value of $4v$ amperes will be something other than $-\tfrac{30}{13}$ A.

The other variables in this circuit are

$$i_1 = \frac{v}{3} = -\frac{5}{26} \text{ A} \quad \text{and} \quad i_2 = \frac{v}{5} = -\frac{3}{26} \text{ A}$$

DRILL EXERCISE 1.11

For the circuit shown in Fig. DE1.11 find (a) v, (b) i, and (c) v_d.
Answer: (a) 7.5 V; (b) 0.5 A; (c) 0.5 V

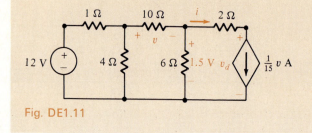

Fig. DE1.11

EXAMPLE 1.10

The circuit shown in Fig. 1.47 contains a **current-dependent voltage source**. The value of this dependent voltage source is determined by the loop current i. In this case, the constant 4 has as its units V/A, or ohms—so it is a resistance.

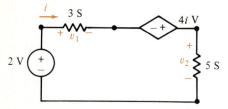

Fig. 1.47   Circuit with current-dependent voltage source.

Before we analyze this circuit, let us compare it with the circuit given in Fig. 1.46. What is a parallel connection there is a series connection here; what is a voltage (v) there, is a current (i) here; what is a current there (2 A, $i_1, i_2, 4v$ amperes) is a voltage here (2 V, $v_1, v_2, 4i$ volts, respectively), and what is a resistance there (3 Ω, 5 Ω) is a conductance here (3 S, 5 S, respectively). For this reason, we say that this circuit is the **dual** of the previous circuit (and vice versa). Once a circuit has been analyzed, its dual is analyzed automatically. A more formal discussion of the concept of duality is given in Chapter 4. However, for the time being, let us verify it for this particular case.

By KVL,

$$v_1 - 4i + v_2 = 2$$

By Ohm's law,

$$v_1 = \frac{i}{3} \quad \text{and} \quad v_2 = \frac{i}{5}$$

Thus

$$\frac{i}{3} - 4i + \frac{i}{5} = 2$$

from which

$$i = -\tfrac{15}{26} \text{ A}$$

which is the numerical value for v in volts in the dual circuit (Fig. 1.46). Therefore, the value of the dependent source is

$$4i = 4(-\tfrac{15}{26}) = -\tfrac{30}{13} \text{ V}$$

Furthermore,

$$v_1 = \frac{i}{3} = -\frac{5}{26} \text{ V} \quad \text{and} \quad v_2 = \frac{i}{5} = -\frac{3}{26} \text{ V}$$

which are the respective values for i_1 and i_2 in the dual circuit.

DRILL EXERCISE 1.12

For the circuit shown in Fig. DE1.12, find (a) i, (b) v, and (c) i_d.
Answer: (a) 4 A; (b) 6 V; (c) 1 A

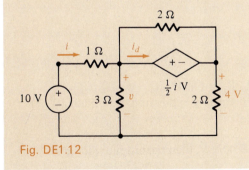

Fig. DE1.12

The concept of dependent sources is not introduced simply for abstraction; rather, it is precisely this type of source that models the behavior of such important electronic devices as transistors and amplifiers.

EXAMPLE 1.11

The circuit of Fig. 1.48 is a single field-effect transistor (FET) amplifier in which the input is v_1 and the output is v_2. The colored portion of the circuit is an approximate model of an FET. Let us find the output voltage v_2 in terms of the input voltage v_1.

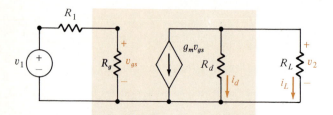

Fig. 1.48   FET amplifier.

By voltage division,

$$v_{gs} = \frac{R_g v_1}{R_g + R_1}$$

Applying KCL to the right-hand portion of the circuit, we get

$$g_m v_{gs} + i_d + i_L = 0$$

Substituting the preceding expression for v_{gs}, we get

$$g_m \left(\frac{R_g v_1}{R_g + R_1} \right) + \frac{v_2}{R_d} + \frac{v_2}{R_L} = 0$$

Thus,

$$v_2 \left(\frac{1}{R_d} + \frac{1}{R_L} \right) = \frac{-g_m R_g v_1}{R_g + R_1}$$

from which

$$v_2 = \frac{-g_m R_d R_g R_L v_1}{(R_g + R_1)(R_L + R_d)}$$

Typical values for such an amplifier are $g_m = 5$ mS, $R_1 = 600 \ \Omega$, $R_g = 1$ MΩ, $R_d = 10$ kΩ, and $R_L = 10$ kΩ. Substituting these into the preceding expression, we obtain[†]

$$v_2 \approx -25 v_1$$

so, for example, if the input voltage is $v_1(t) = 0.1 \cos 2000\pi t$ V, then the output voltage is $v_2(t) \approx -2.5 \cos 2000\pi t$ V.

[†] The symbol $\approx$ means "approximately equal to."

DRILL EXERCISE 1.13

For the FET amplifier given in Example 1.11, change R_L to 20 kΩ and calculate the ratio v_2/v_1 (called the "voltage gain") for the amplifier.
Answer: -33.3

From Example 1.11, you may think that practical circuit analysis is simple. It is—especially when you analyze a simple circuit.

EXAMPLE 1.12

The circuit shown in Fig. 1.49 is a single bipolar junction transistor (BJT) amplifier. The portion in the colored box is an approximate T-model of a BJT. Let us find v_2 in terms of v_1, and v_2 in terms of v_b.

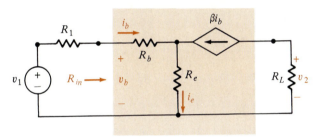

Fig. 1.49   BJT amplifier.

By KVL,

$$v_1 = R_1 i_b + R_b i_b + R_e i_e$$

By KCL,

$$i_e = i_b + \beta i_b = (1 + \beta)i_b$$

Thus,

$$v_1 = R_1 i_b + R_b i_b + R_e(1 + \beta)i_b = [R_1 + R_b + (1 + \beta)R_e]i_b$$

from which

$$i_b = \frac{v_1}{R_1 + R_b + (1 + \beta)R_e}$$

Thus,

$$v_2 = -R_L \beta i_b = \frac{-R_L \beta v_1}{R_1 + R_b + (1 + \beta)R_e}$$

Typical values for such a circuit are $\beta = 50$, $R_L = 1.5 \text{ k}\Omega$, $R_e = 25 \ \Omega$, $R_b = 150 \ \Omega$, and $R_1 = 75 \ \Omega$. Using these values, we get

$$v_2 = \frac{-(1500)(50)v_1}{75 + 150 + (51)25} = -50v_1$$

The voltage across the input of the transistor is

$$v_b = R_b i_b + R_e i_e = R_b i_b + R_e(1 + \beta)i_b = [R_b + (1 + \beta)R_e]i_b$$

Thus, the resistance R_{in} looking into the input of the transistor is

$$R_{in} = \frac{v_b}{i_b} = R_b + (1 + \beta)R_e = 150 + (51)25 = 1425 \ \Omega$$

The resistance R_{eq} seen by the voltage source is

$$R_{eq} = R_1 + R_{in} = 75 + 1425 = 1500 \ \Omega$$

The voltage v_b across the input of the transistor is, by voltage division,

$$v_b = \frac{R_{in}v_1}{R_{in} + R_1} = \frac{1425v_1}{1425 + 75} = 0.95v_1$$

From the fact that $v_2 = -50v_1$, then $v_1 = -v_2/50$. Thus,

$$v_b = 0.95\left(\frac{-v_2}{50}\right) \quad \Rightarrow \quad v_2 = -\frac{50}{0.95}v_b = -52.63v_b$$

This result can also be obtained from the fact that

$$i_b = \frac{v_b}{R_b + (1 + \beta)R_e}$$

and

$$v_2 = -R_L\beta i_b = \frac{-R_L\beta v_b}{R_b + (1 + \beta)R_e} = \frac{-(1500)(50)v_b}{150 + (51)25} = -52.63v_b$$

DRILL EXERCISE 1.14

For the BJT amplifier given in Example 1.12, change R_L to 3 kΩ and calculate the voltage gain v_2/v_1 for the amplifier.
Answer: -100

Comments about Circuit Elements

Certain types of nonideal circuit elements, such as physical resistors, come in a wide variety of values and are readily available in the form of discrete components. For many situations, the assumption that an actual resistor behaves as an ideal resistor is a reasonable one.

With a few exceptions, however, this is not the case with independent voltage and current sources. Although an actual battery often can be modeled by an ideal voltage source, other nonideal independent sources are approximated by a combination of circuit elements (some of which will be discussed later). Among these elements are the dependent sources, which are not discrete components as are many resistors and batteries, but are in a sense part of electronic devices such as transistors and operational amplifiers (which consist of numerous transistors and resistors). But don't try to peel open a transistor's metal can (for those that are constructed that way) so that you can see a little diamond-shaped object. The dependent source is an ideal element that is used to help describe or model the behavior of various electric devices.

In summary, although ideal circuit elements are not off-the-shelf circuit components, their importance lies in the fact that they can be interconnected (on paper or on a computer) to approximate actual circuits that consist of nonideal elements and assorted electrical components—thus allowing for the analysis of such circuits.

1.6 INSTANTANEOUS POWER

Recall that electrons flow through a resistor from a given potential to a higher potential, and hence (positive-valued) current goes from a given potential to a lower one. Potential difference or voltage is a measure of work per unit charge (i.e., joules per coulomb). To obtain a current through an element, as shown in Fig. 1.50, it takes a certain amount of work or energy—and we say that this energy is absorbed by the element. By taking the product of voltage (energy per unit charge) and current (charge per unit time), we get a quantity that measures energy per unit time. Such a term is known as **power**. It is for this reason that we define $p(t)$, the **instantaneous power absorbed** by an element as in Fig. 1.50, as the product of voltage and current. That is,

$$p(t) = v(t)i(t)$$

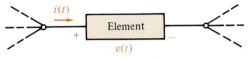

Fig. 1.50   Arbitrary element with conventional current direction and voltage polarity.

The unit of power (joules per second) is called the **watt**[†] (W). Given an expression for instantaneous power absorbed $p(t)$, to determine the power absorbed at time t_o, simply substitute the number t_o into the expression.

[†] Named for the Scottish inventor James Watt (1736–1819).

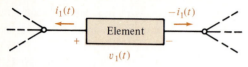

Fig. 1.51 Nonconventional current direction with respect to voltage polarity.

As with Ohm's law, when using the formula for power absorbed, we must always be conscious of both the voltage polarity and the current direction. For example, for the situation shown in Fig. 1.51, going back to the definition for instantaneous power absorbed, we have in this case that

$$p_1(t) = -v_1(t)i_1(t)$$

Since power absorbed in a given element can be either a positive or a negative quantity (depending on the relationship between voltage and current for the element), we can say that the element absorbs x watts, or equivalently, that it **supplies** or **delivers** $-x$ watts.

DRILL EXERCISE 1.15

The voltage across a 100-Ω resistor is $v(t) = 163 \cos 120\pi t$ V. Find the instantaneous power absorbed by this resistor (a) as a function of time, (b) at time $t = 0$ s, (c) at time $t = \frac{1}{240}$ s, and (d) at time $t = \frac{1}{120}$ s.
Answer: (a) $265.7 \cos^2 120\pi t$ W; (b) 265.7 W; (c) 0 W; (d) 265.7 W

● **EXAMPLE 1.13**

Consider the circuit in Fig. 1.52. Let us determine the power absorbed by each of the elements for the case that $I = 10$ A. Note that the voltage across each of the elements is 6 V, since all the elements are connected in parallel. Therefore, by Ohm's law,

$$i_1 = \tfrac{6}{1} = 6 \text{ A}, \qquad i_2 = \tfrac{6}{2} = 3 \text{ A}, \qquad i_3 = \tfrac{6}{3} = 2 \text{ A}$$

and the power absorbed by the 1-Ω, 2-Ω, and 3-Ω resistors is

$$p_1 = 6i_1 = 36 \text{ W}, \qquad p_2 = 6i_2 = 18 \text{ W}, \qquad p_3 = 6i_3 = 12 \text{ W}$$

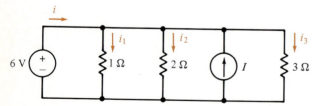

Fig. 1.52 Circuit for Example 1.13.

respectively, or a total of

$$p_R = p_1 + p_2 + p_3 = 36 + 18 + 12 = 66 \text{ W}$$

absorbed by the resistors. By KCL,

$$i + 10 = i_1 + i_2 + i_3 = 6 + 3 + 2 = 11$$

or

$$i = 11 - 10 = 1 \text{ A}$$

Thus, the power absorbed by the voltage source is

$$p_V = -6i = -6 \text{ W}$$

Also note that the power absorbed by the current source is

$$p_I = -6(10) = -60 \text{ W}$$

Hence, the total power absorbed is

$$p_R + p_V + p_I = 66 - 6 - 60 = 0 \text{ W}$$

Recalling from elementary physics that power is work (energy) per unit time, we see that the fact that the total power absorbed is zero is equivalent to saying that the principle of the conservation of energy is satisfied in this circuit (as it is in any circuit). In this case, the two sources supply all the power and the resistors absorb it all.

Now, however, consider the situation in which $I = 12$ A. Under this circumstance,

$$i_1 = 6 \text{ A} \qquad i_2 = 3 \text{ A} \qquad i_3 = 2 \text{ A}$$

and

$$p_1 = 36 \text{ W} \qquad p_2 = 18 \text{ W} \qquad p_3 = 12 \text{ W} \qquad \Rightarrow \qquad p_R = p_1 + p_2 + p_3 = 66 \text{ W}$$

as before. But by KCL,

$$i + 12 = i_1 + i_2 + i_3 \qquad \Rightarrow \qquad i = 11 - 12 = -1 \text{ A}$$

Therefore,

$$p_V = 6(1) = 6 \text{ W} \qquad \text{and} \qquad p_I = -6(12) = -72 \text{ W}$$

so that the total power absorbed is

$$p_R + p_V + p_I = 66 + 6 - 72 = 0 \text{ W}$$

and again energy (power) is conserved. However, in this case, not only do the resistors absorb power, but so does the voltage source.[†] It is the current source that supplies all the power absorbed in the circuit.

[†] In practical terms, the voltage source (battery) is being charged.

DRILL EXERCISE 1.16

For the circuit given in Fig. DE1.12 on p. 31, find the power absorbed by the (a) 1-Ω resistor, (b) 3-Ω resistor, (c) independent voltage source, and (d) dependent voltage source.
Answer: (a) 16 W; (b) 12 W; (c) −40 W; (d) 2 W

In all the examples worked so far, the reader may have noted that the power absorbed in every (positive-valued) resistor was a nonnegative[†] number. As we now shall see, this is always the case; consider Fig. 1.53. By definition, the power absorbed by the resistor is $p = vi$. But by Ohm's law, $v = Ri$. Thus, $p = (Ri)i$, or

$$p = Ri^2$$

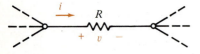

Fig. 1.53   Resistor with conventional current direction and voltage polarity.

Also, $i = v/R$, so that $p = v(v/R)$, or

$$p = \frac{v^2}{R}$$

and both formulas for calculating the power absorbed by a resistor R demonstrate that p is always a nonnegative number when R is positive.

EXAMPLE 1.14

For the transistor amplifier circuit given in Example 1.12 (p. 33), the power absorbed by the load resistor R_L is

$$p_2 = \frac{v_2^2}{R_L} = \frac{v_2^2}{1500}$$

[†] A **positive number** is a number that is greater than zero; a **nonnegative number** is a number that is greater than or equal to zero

and the power supplied by the independent voltage source is

$$p_1 = v_1 i_b = v_1 \left(\frac{v_1}{R_1 + R_b + (1 + \beta)R_e} \right) = \frac{v_1^2}{R_1 + R_b + (1 + \beta)R_e} = \frac{v_1^2}{1500}$$

(Also note that p_1 is the power absorbed by R_{eq}.)

However, since $v_2 = -50v_1$, then

$$p_2 = \frac{(-50v_1)^2}{1500} = \frac{2500v_1^2}{1500}$$

We call the ratio p_2/p_1 the **power gain** from source to load. For this example it is

$$\frac{p_2}{p_1} = \frac{2500v_1^2}{1500} \left(\frac{1500}{v_i^2} \right) = 2500$$

DRILL EXERCISE 1.17

For the FET amplifier given in Example 1.11 (p. 32), find the power gain p_2/p_1 from source to load, where p_1 is the power supplied by the independent voltage source v_1 and p_2 is the power absorbed by the load $R_L = 10 \text{ k}\Omega$.
Answer: 62,500

Physical Resistors

A (positive-valued) resistor always absorbs power. In a physical resistor, this power is dissipated as heat. In some types of resistors (e.g., an incandescent lamp or bulb, a toaster, or an electric space heater), this property is desirable in that the net result may be light or warmth. In other types of resistors, such as those in electronic circuits, the heat dissipated by a resistor may affect the operation of its circuit. In this case, heat dissipation cannot be ignored.

The common carbon resistor comes in values that range from less than $10 \ \Omega$ to more than $10 \ \text{M}\Omega$. The physical size of such resistors will determine the amount of power that they can safely dissipate. These amounts are referred to as **power ratings**. Typical power ratings of electronic-circuit carbon resistors are $\frac{1}{8}, \frac{1}{4}, \frac{1}{2}$, 1, and 2 W. The dissipation of power that exceeds the rating of a resistor can damage the resistor physically. When an application requires the use of a resistor that must dissipate more than 2 W, another type—the wire-wound resistor—is often used. Metal-film resistors, although more expensive to construct, can have higher power ratings than carbon resistors and are more reliable and more stable. In addition to the lumped circuit elements such as carbon, wire-wound, and metal-film resistors, there are resistors in integrated-circuit (IC) form. These types of resistors, which dissipate only small amounts of power, are part of the countless ICs employed in present-day electronics.

● **SUMMARY**

1. An ideal voltage source is a device that produces a specific (not necessarily constant with time) electric potential difference across its terminals regardless of what is connected to it.

2. An ideal current source is a device that produces a specific (not necessarily constant with time) current through it regardless of what is connected to it.

3. A (linear) resistor is a device in which the voltage across it is directly proportional to the current through it. If we write the equation (Ohm's law) describing this as $v = Ri$, then the constant of proportionality R is called resistance. If we write $i = Gv$, then G is known as conductance. Thus, $R = 1/G$.

4. An open circuit is an infinite resistance and a short circuit is a zero resistance. The former is equivalent to an ideal current source whose value is zero; the latter is equivalent to an ideal voltage source whose value is zero.

5. At any node of a circuit, the currents algebraically sum to zero—Kirchhoff's current law (KCL).

6. Around any loop in a circuit, the voltages algebraically sum to zero—Kirchhoff's voltage law (KVL).

7. Current going into a parallel connection of resistors divides among them—the smallest resistance has the most current through it.

8. Voltage across a series connection of resistors divides among them—the largest resistance has the most voltage across it.

9. Resistances in series behave as a single resistance whose value equals the sum of the individual resistances.

10. Conductances in parallel behave as a single conductance whose value equals the sum of the individual conductances.

11. Voltage and current sources can be dependent as well as independent.

12. A dependent source is a voltage or current source whose value depends on some other circuit variable.

13. The power absorbed by an element (with the conventional current direction and voltage polarity) is the product of the current through it and the voltage across it.

● PROBLEMS FOR CHAPTER 1

1.1 An ideal voltage source has a value of $v(t) = (3t + 2)e^{-2t}$ V. Give the value of this voltage source when (a) $t = 0$ seconds; (b) $t = 1$ second; (c) $t = 2$ seconds; (d) $t = 3$ seconds; (e) $t = 4$ seconds.

1.2 Repeat Problem 1.1 for the case $v(t) = 5\sin(\pi/2)t$ volts.

1.3 Repeat Problem 1.1 for the case $v(t) = 3e^{-t}\cos(\pi/2)t$ volts.

1.4 The total charge in some region is described by the function $q(t) = 4e^{-2t}$ coulombs. Find the current in this region.

1.5 Repeat Problem 1.4 for the case that $q(t) = 3\sin \pi t$ coulombs.

1.6 Repeat Problem 1.4 for the case that $q(t) = 6e^{-t}\cos 2\pi t$ coulombs.

1.7 Repeat Problem 1.1 for the case that $v(t)$ is described by the function shown in Fig. P1.7.

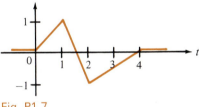

Fig. P1.7

1.8 The total charge $q(t)$ in some region is described by the function given in

Problem 1.7. Sketch the current $i(t)$ in this region.

1.9 Consider the circuit shown in Fig. P1.9.
(a) Given $i_1 = 4$ A, find v_1.
(b) Given $i_2 = -2$ A, find v_2.
(c) Given $i_3 = 2$ A, find v_3.
(d) Given $i_4 = -2$ A, find v_4.

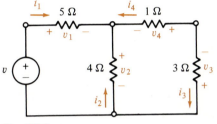

Fig. P1.9

1.10 Consider the circuit in Fig. P1.10.
(a) Given $v_1 = -\frac{2}{3}$ V, find i_1.
(b) Given $v_2 = \frac{8}{3}$ V, find i_2.
(c) Given $v_3 = \frac{11}{9}$ V, find i_3.
(d) Given $v_4 = \frac{7}{3}$ V, find i_4.
(e) Given $v_5 = -\frac{14}{9}$ V, find i_5.

1.11 Consider the circuit shown in Fig. P1.11.
(a) Given $i_1 = -2$ A, find v_1.
(b) Given $v_2 = -\frac{11}{7}$ V, find i_2.
(c) Given $i_3 = \frac{30}{7}$ A, find v_3.
(d) Given $v_4 = 2$ V, find i_4.

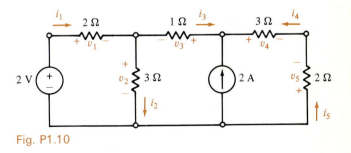

Fig. P1.10

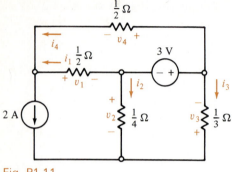

Fig. P1.11

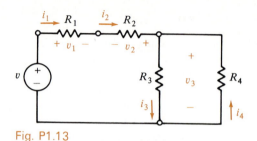

Fig. P1.13

1.12 Consider the circuit given in Fig. P1.9.
  (a) Find $i_1(t)$ for the case $v_1(t) = 20$ V.
  (b) Find $i_2(t)$ for the case $v_2(t) = 3e^{-2t}$ V.
  (c) Find $v_3(t)$ for the case $i_3(t) = 6 \sin 2t$ A.
  (d) Find $v_4(t)$ for the case $i_4(t) = -e^{-t} \cos 5t$ A.

1.13 Consider the circuit in Fig. P1.13.
  (a) Given $i_1 = 2$ A and $v_1 = 4$ V, find R_1.
  (b) Given $i_2 = 2$ A and $v_2 = -12$ V, find R_2.
  (c) Given $i_3 = -\frac{4}{3}$ A and $v_3 = -4$ V, find R_3.
  (d) Given $i_4 = -\frac{2}{3}$ A and $v_3 = 4$ V, find R_4.

1.14 Consider the circuit shown in Fig. P1.13.
  (a) Given $i_1(t) = -e^{-2t}$ and $v_1(t) = -2e^{-2t}$, find R_1.
  (b) Given $i_2(t) = -e^{-2t}$ and $v_2(t) = 6e^{-2t}$, find R_2.

  (c) Given $i_3(t) = \frac{2}{3}e^{-2t}$ and $v_3(t) = 2e^{-2t}$, find R_3.
  (d) Given $i_4(t) = \frac{1}{3}e^{-2t}$ and $v_3(t) = -2e^{-2t}$, find R_4.

1.15 For the circuit shown in Fig. P1.15, find v for the case that (a) $i = 1$ A, (b) $i = 2$ A, and (c) $i = 3$ A.

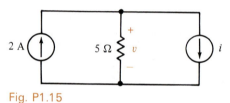

Fig. P1.15

1.16 For the circuit given in Fig. P1.16, find i for the case that (a) $v = 1$ V, (b) $v = 2$ V, and (c) $v = 3$ V.

1.17 For the circuit given in Fig. P1.17, find v_1 for the case that (a) $v = 2$ V, (b) $v = 4$ V, and (c) $v = 6$ V.

1.18 For the circuit shown in Fig. P1.18, assuming $i_1 = 5$ A, determine $i_2, i_3, i_4,$ and i_5.

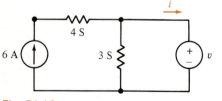

Fig. P1.16

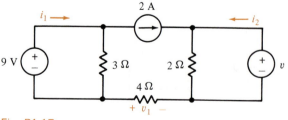

Fig. P1.17

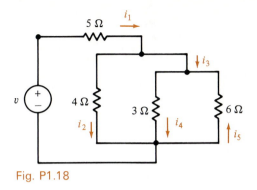

Fig. P1.18

1.19 For the circuit given in Fig. P1.18, suppose that $i_4 = 4$ A. Find $i_1, i_2, i_3,$ and i_5.

1.20 For the circuit given in Fig. P1.18, suppose that $i_5 = 4$ A. Find $i_1, i_2, i_3,$ and i_4.

1.21 For the circuit given in Fig. P1.18, suppose that $i_2(t) = 6 \cos 5t$ A. Find $i_1(t)$, $i_3(t)$, $i_4(t)$, and $i_5(t)$.

1.22 Given the circuit shown in Fig. P1.22, suppose that $i_1 = 2$ A. Find v for the case that (a) $i_2 = 1$ A, (b) $i_2 = 2$ A, and (c) $i_2 = 3$ A.

1.23 For the circuit given in Fig. P1.22, suppose that $i_1(t) = 3 \cos 2t$ A. Find $v(t)$ for the case that $i_2(t) = 5 \cos 2t$ A.

1.24 Repeat Problem 1.23 for the case that $i_2(t) = 5 \sin 2t$ A.

1.25 For the circuits given in Fig. P1.25, what values of v are permissible? Is the circuit of part (b) a series or parallel connection?

1.26 For the circuits shown in Fig. P1.26, what values of i are permissible?

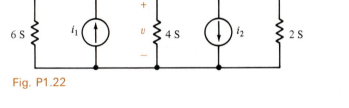

Fig. P1.22

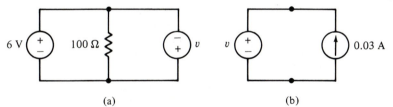

(a)   (b)

Fig. P1.25

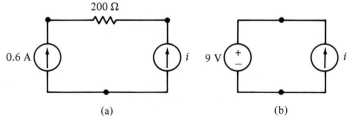

(a)   (b)

Fig. P1.26

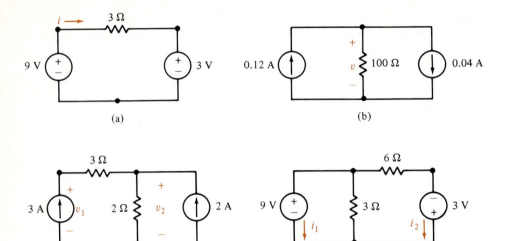

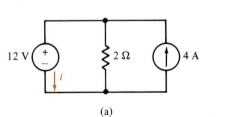

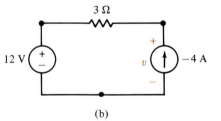

(c)   (d)

Fig. P1.27

1.27 For the circuits given in Fig. P1.27, find the variables indicated.

1.28 For the circuits shown in Fig. P1.28, find the variables indicated.

1.29 For the circuits given in Fig. P1.29, find the variables indicated.

1.30 For the circuit shown in Fig. P1.30, find the variables indicated for (a) $R = 2\,\Omega$ and (b) $R = 4\,\Omega$.

1.31 Repeat Problem 1.30 for the circuit shown in Fig. P1.31.

1.32 For the series-parallel circuit given in Fig. P1.32, find v and i.

1.33 Repeat Problem 1.32 for the circuit shown in Fig. P1.33.

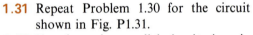

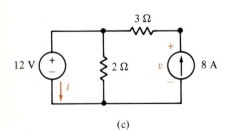

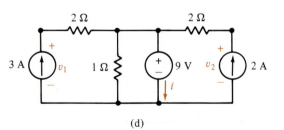

Fig. P1.28

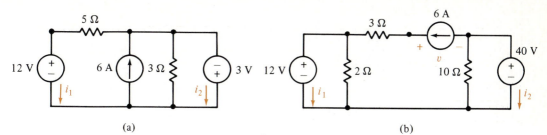

(a)

(b)

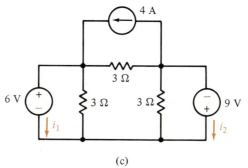

(c)

Fig. P1.29

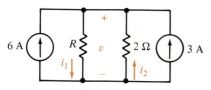

Fig. P1.30

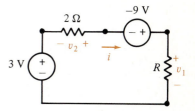

Fig. P1.31

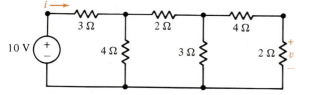

Fig. P1.32

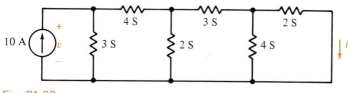

Fig. P1.33

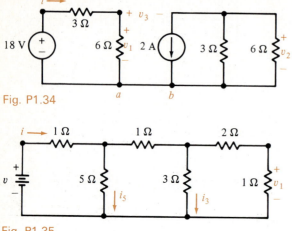

Fig. P1.34

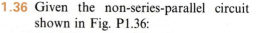

Fig. P1.35

1.34 Given the circuit shown in Fig. P1.34:
(a) Find i, v_1, v_2, and v_3.
(b) Remove the short circuit between a and b (erase it). Find i, v_1, and v_2. (Don't try to find v_3—it can't be done!)

1.35 Given the series-parallel circuit shown in Fig. P1.35:
(a) If $v_1 = 2$ V, what is v?
(b) If $i_3 = 3$ A, what is v?
(c) If $i_5 = 4$ A, what is v?
(d) What is the resistance $R_{eq} = v/i$ seen by the battery for part (a)? For part (b)? For part (c)?

1.36 Given the non-series-parallel circuit shown in Fig. P1.36:
(a) When $R = \frac{1}{2}\Omega$, then $v_1 = 6$ V. What is the resistance $R_{eq} = v/i$ seen by the battery?
(b) When $R = 4\Omega$, then $v_1 = 4$ V. What is R_{eq}?
(c) When $v_1 = 3$ V, what is R and R_{eq}?

1.37 The non-series-parallel circuit shown in Fig. P1.37 is known as a **twin-T network**.
(a) Suppose that $R_1 = 1\,\Omega$, $R_2 = 3\,\Omega$, and $v_2 = 3$ V. Find the resistance $R_{eq} = v/i$ seen by the battery.
(b) Suppose that $R_2 = \frac{2}{7}\Omega$ and $v_2 = 1$ V. Find R_1 and R_{eq}.

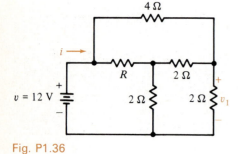

Fig. P1.36

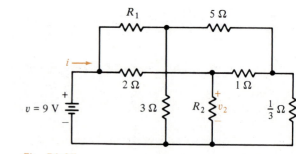

Fig. P1.37

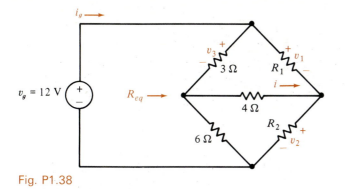

Fig. P1.38

1.38 Shown in Fig. P1.38 is a non-series-parallel connection known as a **bridge circuit**.

  (a) Given that $R_1 = 6\,\Omega$, $R_2 = 3\,\Omega$, and $v_1 = 7$ V, find v_2, i, v_3, and the resistance $R_{eq} = v_g/i_g$ seen by the voltage source.

  (b) Repeat part (a) for the case $R_1 = 3\,\Omega$, $R_2 = 6\,\Omega$, and $v_1 = 4$ V.

  (c) When the current $i = 0$, we say that the bridge is **balanced**. Under what condition (find an expression relating R_1 and R_2) will this bridge be balanced?

1.39 Given the circuit shown in Fig. P1.39, find i_1 for (a) $K = 2$, (b) $K = 3$, and (c) $K = 4$.

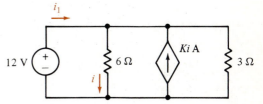

Fig. P1.39

1.40 The circuit given in Fig. P1.40 contains a **voltage-dependent voltage source** as well as a current-dependent current source. Repeat Problem 1.39 for this circuit.

1.41 Consider the circuit shown in Fig. P1.41. Find v for (a) $K = 2$ and (b) $K = 4$.

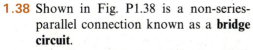

Fig. P1.40

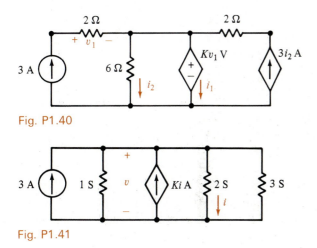

Fig. P1.41

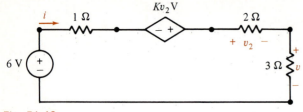

Fig. P1.42

1.42 Repeat Problem 1.41 for the circuit given in Fig. P1.42.

1.43 For the circuit shown in Fig. P1.43, find the output voltage v_2 in terms of the input voltage v_1. Also find $R_{eq} = v_1/i_1$.

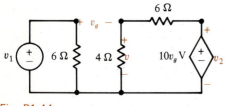

Fig. P1.43

1.44 Consider the circuit given in Fig. P1.44.
 (a) Use voltage division to find v in terms of v_g.
 (b) Find the output voltage v_2 in terms of the input voltage v_1.

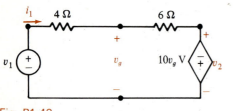

Fig. P1.44

1.45 Given the circuit shown in Fig. P1.45:
 (a) Find i_s.
 (b) Find the resistance $R_{eq} = v_s/i_s$ seen by the current source.

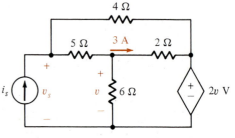

Fig. P1.45

1.46 For the circuit given in Fig. P1.45, change the 3-Ω resistor to a 5-Ω resistor and repeat Problem 1.45.

1.47 Given the circuit shown in Fig. P1.47:
 (a) Find v_s.
 (b) Find the resistance $R_{eq} = v_s/i_s$ seen by the voltage source.

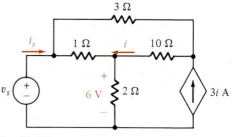

Fig. P1.47

1.48 For the circuit given in Fig. P1.47, change the 10-Ω resistor to an 8-Ω resistor and repeat Problem 1.47.

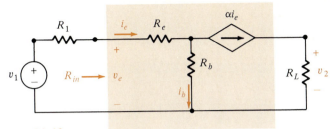

Fig. P1.49

1.49 The circuit in Fig. P1.49 is another single BJT amplifier. The portion of the circuit in the colored box is an alternative model of a BJT.

(a) Find i_e in terms of the various resistors, α, and the input voltage v_1.

(b) Find v_2 in terms of the resistors, α, and v_1.

(c) Given that $R_1 = 40 \ \Omega$, $R_e = 27 \ \Omega$, $R_b = 150 \ \Omega$, $R_L = 1.5 \ k\Omega$, and $\alpha = 0.98$, find the voltage gain v_2/v_1.

1.50 Consider the circuit given in Problem 1.49 and the values given in part (c).

(a) Find the resistance $R_{eq} = v_1/i_e$ seen by the voltage source.

(b) Find the resistance $R_{in} = v_e/i_e$ at the input of the amplifier.

(c) Find the voltage gain v_2/v_e.

1.51 For the circuit in Fig. 1.45 (p. 28), find the power absorbed by each element.

1.52 For the circuit in Fig. 1.46 (p. 29), find the power absorbed by each element.

1.53 For the circuit in Fig. 1.47 (p. 30), find the power absorbed by each element.

1.54 For the circuit given in Fig. P1.41, find the power absorbed by each element for (a) $K = 2$ and (b) $K = 4$.

1.55 For the circuit given in Fig. P1.42, find the power absorbed by each element for (a) $K = 2$ and (b) $K = 4$.

1.56 For the single BJT amplifier given in Problem 1.49, find the power gain p_2/p_1 from source to load, where p_1 is the power supplied by the independent voltage source v_1 and p_2 is the power absorbed by the load $R_L = 1.5 \ k\Omega$.

Circuit Analysis Techniques

● INTRODUCTION

The process by which we determine a variable (either voltage or current) of a circuit is called **analysis**. Up to this point we have been analyzing circuits that were not very complicated. Don't be fooled, though; some very simple circuits can be quite useful. We have already come across some simple single-stage amplifier circuits whose analysis was accomplished by applying the basic principles covered to date—Ohm's law, KCL, and KVL. Nonetheless, we must also be able to analyze more complicated circuits—those in which it is simply not possible to conveniently write and solve a single equation having only one unknown. Instead, we shall have to write and solve a set of linear algebraic equations. To obtain such equations, we again utilize Ohm's law, KCL, and KVL.

There are several distinct approaches that we can take. In one we write a set of simultaneous equations in which the variables are voltages; this is known as **nodal analysis**. In another we write a set of simultaneous equations in which the variables are currents; this is known as **mesh analysis**. Although nodal analysis can be used for all circuits, this is not the case for mesh analysis. A class of circuits known as "nonplanar networks" cannot be handled with mesh analysis. However, a similar approach—**loop analysis**—can be used. Here the variables are also currents.

Although in this chapter we shall consider **resistive circuits**—those containing only resistors and sources, both independent and dependent—we shall see later that the same techniques are applicable to networks that contain other types of elements as well.

2.1 NODAL ANALYSIS

Given a circuit to be analyzed, the first step in employing nodal analysis is the arbitrary choice of one of the nodes of the circuit as the **reference** (or **datum**) **node**. Although this node can be indicated by any of the three symbols shown in Fig. 2.1, we will use the symbol depicted in Fig. 2.1(a) exclusively.

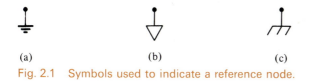

(a)   (b)   (c)

Fig. 2.1   Symbols used to indicate a reference node.

We can label any node in a circuit with its potential with respect to the reference node in the following manner.

Suppose that the voltages between nodes a, b, c, and the reference node are as shown in Fig. 2.2. Then, Fig. 2.3 indicates how the nodes are labeled. Of course, since the potential difference between the reference node and itself must be zero volts, we can mark the reference node "0 V" if we wish—but this is redundant.

Fig. 2.2   Some node voltages.   Fig. 2.3   Node-voltage designations.

It is possible, and easy, to express the voltage between any pair of nodes in terms of the potentials (with respect to the reference node) of those two nodes. Suppose that we wish to determine the voltage v_{ac} between nodes a and c, with the plus at node a and the minus at node c, in terms of v_a and v_c. This situation is depicted in Fig. 2.4(a). Since the labeling in Fig. 2.4(b) is equivalent to Fig. 2.4(a), by KVL, we have that $v_{ac} = v_a - v_c$. Similarly, the voltage v_{ca} between nodes a and c, with the plus at node c and the minus at node a, is $v_{ca} = v_c - v_a$. With reference to Fig. 2.3, we see that the voltage v_{ab} between nodes a and b (plus at node a and minus at node b) is $v_{ab} = v_a - (-v_b) = v_a + v_b$. Also, v_{bc}, the voltage between nodes b and c (plus at node b and minus at node c), is $v_{bc} = -v_b - v_c$.

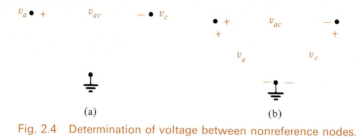

(a)   (b)

Fig. 2.4   Determination of voltage between nonreference nodes.

EXAMPLE 2.1

For the circuit in Fig. 2.5(a), the voltage across each element is indicated. If node *b* is selected as the reference node, then the node voltages are as shown in Fig. 2.5(b). Similarly, if node *c* is the reference node, then the node voltages are as shown in Fig. 2.5(c); while if node *d* is the reference node, then the node voltages are as shown in Fig. 2.5(d). Regardless of the node that is chosen to be the reference, the voltage across each element is as indicated in Fig. 2.5(a). Furthermore, the current through each element is not affected by the choice of a reference node.

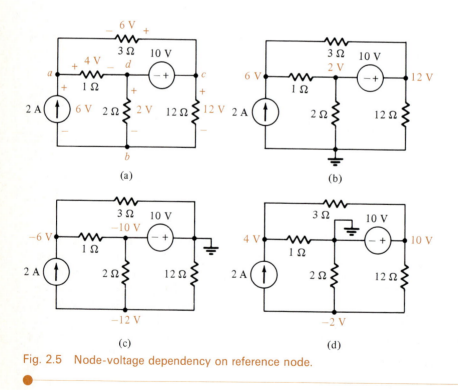

Fig. 2.5   Node-voltage dependency on reference node.

DRILL EXERCISE 2.1

For the circuit shown in Fig. DE2.1, find the node voltages when the reference is chosen to be (a) node a, (b) node b, (c) node c, and (d) node d.

Answer: (a) 12 V, 9 V, 1.5 V, 0.5 V; (b) -12 V, -3 V, -10.5 V, -11.5 V; (c) -9 V, 3 V, -7.5 V, -8.5 V; (d) -1.5 V, 10.5 V, 7.5 V, -1 V

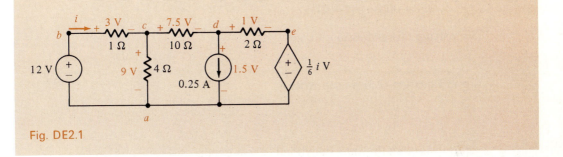

Fig. DE2.1

With the preceding discussion in mind, let us see how to employ nodal analysis for the circuit shown in Fig. 2.6. After choosing the reference node arbitrarily, the two nonreference nodes are labeled v_1 and v_2. The next step is to indicate currents (the names and directions are arbitrary) through elements that do not already have currents indicated through them. For this example, the values and directions of the current sources are given, whereas i_1, i_2, and i_3 were chosen arbitrarily.

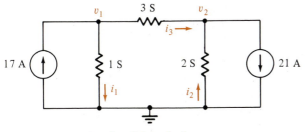

Fig. 2.6 Example of nodal analysis.

Now apply KCL at the node labeled v_1. The result is

$$i_1 + i_3 = 17 \tag{2.1}$$

By Ohm's law,

$$i_1 = 1v_1 \qquad i_2 = -2v_2 \qquad i_3 = 3(v_1 - v_2)$$

Substituting into Equation (2.1) yields

$$1v_1 + 3(v_1 - v_2) = 17$$

from which

$$4v_1 - 3v_2 = 17 \tag{2.2}$$

When we apply KCL at node v_2 (i.e., the node labeled v_2), we obtain

$$i_2 + i_3 = 21$$

and by Ohm's law, this equation becomes

$$-2v_2 + 3(v_1 - v_2) = 21$$

Simplifying this expression, we get

$$3v_1 - 5v_2 = 21 \tag{2.3}$$

From Equation (2.3) we can write

$$v_2 = \frac{3v_1 - 21}{5}$$

and substituting this into Equation (2.2) we obtain

$$4v_1 - 3\left(\frac{3v_1 - 21}{5}\right) = 17$$

Solving this equation for v_1 yields

$$v_1 = 2 \text{ V}$$

Substituting this value into either Equation (2.2) or (2.3) results in

$$v_2 = -3 \text{ V}$$

Having determined the values of v_1 and v_2, it is a simple matter to determine i_1, i_2, and i_3. By Ohm's law,

$$i_1 = 1v_1 = 2 \text{ A} \qquad i_2 = -2v_2 = 6 \text{ A} \qquad i_3 = 3(v_1 - v_2) = 15 \text{ A}$$

In the procedure just discussed, we applied KCL at node v_1 and again at node v_2. In both cases, we used the form of KCL that says, "the sum of the currents going into a node is equal to the sum of the currents coming out of that node." Instead, however, now let us use the version of KCL which states, "the currents algebraically sum to zero," and let us pick the positive sense to be out of the node. In other words, for KCL we'll use the statement that, "all the currents coming out of a node sum to zero." Applying this form of KCL at node v_1, we get

$$i_1 + i_3 - 1 = 0$$

which again results in Equation (2.2). However, for node v_2, we obtain

$$-i_2 - i_3 + 2 = 0$$

and by Ohm's law,

$$-(-2v_2) - 3(v_1 - v_2) + 21 = 0$$

Simplifying this equation yields

$$-3v_1 + 5v_2 = -21 \tag{2.4}$$

Equation (2.4) is equivalent to Equation (2.3)—one can be obtained from the other by multiplying both sides of one equation by the constant -1. But why even bother to use the alternative form of KCL to obtain Equation (2.4) instead of Equation (2.3)? Here's why.

Equations (2.2) and (2.4) can be written in matrix form as

$$\begin{bmatrix} 4 & -3 \\ -3 & 5 \end{bmatrix} \begin{bmatrix} v_1 \\ v_2 \end{bmatrix} = \begin{bmatrix} 17 \\ -21 \end{bmatrix} \tag{2.5}$$

For this matrix equation, we can form the determinants

$$\Delta = \begin{vmatrix} 4 & -3 \\ -3 & 5 \end{vmatrix} = 20 - 9 = 11 \qquad \Delta_1 = \begin{vmatrix} 17 & -3 \\ 21 & 5 \end{vmatrix} = 85 - 63 = 22$$

$$\Delta_2 = \begin{vmatrix} 4 & 17 \\ -3 & -21 \end{vmatrix} = -84 + 51 = -33$$

Therefore, by Cramer's rule,

$$v_1 = \frac{\Delta_1}{\Delta} = \frac{22}{11} = 2 \text{ V} \qquad \text{and} \qquad v_2 = \frac{\Delta_2}{\Delta} = \frac{-33}{11} = -3 \text{ V}$$

and these results were obtained previously by using algebraic manipulations.

The matrix equation (2.5) is in the form $\mathbf{Gv} = \mathbf{i}$, where

$$\mathbf{G} = \begin{bmatrix} 4 & -3 \\ -3 & 5 \end{bmatrix} \qquad \mathbf{v} = \begin{bmatrix} v_1 \\ v_2 \end{bmatrix} \qquad \mathbf{i} = \begin{bmatrix} 17 \\ -21 \end{bmatrix}$$

Thus, we see that Equation (2.5) is just a matrix form of Ohm's law. Therefore, the 2×2 matrix $\mathbf{G}$ is called a **conductance matrix**, $\mathbf{v}$ is a voltage matrix, and the current matrix $\mathbf{i}$ contains entries that arise from the independent current sources in the circuit.

The reason why currents are summed coming out of nodes for nodal analysis is so that, for circuits containing only resistances (or conductances) and independent current sources, all of the main-diagonal entries of the corresponding conductance matrix $\mathbf{G}$ will be positive.

In the process of nodal analysis, therefore, it is not even necessary to designate currents such as i_1, i_2, and i_3 in Fig. 2.6 in order to apply KCL. However, if a specific current variable is to be determined, of course that variable will be designated.

Now that we have seen an example of the application of nodal analysis, we can state the rules for nodal analysis for circuits that do not contain voltage sources. We will discuss the case of circuits with voltage sources immediately thereafter.

> ## NODAL ANALYSIS—NO VOLTAGE SOURCES
>
> **Given a circuit with n nodes and no voltage sources, proceed as follows:**
>
> 1. **Select any node as the reference node.**
>
> 2. **Label the remaining $n - 1$ nodes (e.g., $v_1, v_2, \ldots, v_{n-1}$).**
>
> 3. **Apply KCL at each nonreference node by summing the currents out of the nodes. Use Ohm's law to express the currents through resistors in terms of the node voltages.**
>
> 4. **Solve the resulting set of $n - 1$ simultaneous equations for the node voltages.**

EXAMPLE 2.2

For the circuit shown in Fig. 2.7, the reference node, as indicated, has already been selected, and the nonreference nodes have been labeled. Let us solve for v_1, v_2, and v_3 by using nodal analysis.

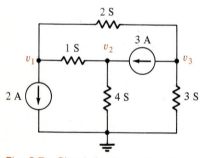

Fig. 2.7   Circuit for Example 2.2.

Since $i = Gv$, by KCL (summing currents out of node v_1),

$$1(v_1 - v_2) + 2(v_1 - v_3) + 2 = 0 \tag{2.6}$$

from which

$$3v_1 - v_2 - 2v_3 = -2 \tag{2.7}$$

By KCL at node v_2,

$$1(v_2 - v_1) + 4v_2 - 3 = 0$$

from which

$$-v_1 + 5v_2 = 3 \tag{2.8}$$

Finally, by KCL at node v_3,

$$2(v_3 - v_1) + 3v_3 + 3 = 0$$

from which

$$-2v_1 + 5v_3 = -3 \tag{2.9}$$

Writing Equations (2.7), (2.8), and (2.9) in matrix form we have

$$\begin{bmatrix} 3 & -1 & -2 \\ -1 & 5 & 0 \\ -2 & 0 & 5 \end{bmatrix} \begin{bmatrix} v_1 \\ v_2 \\ v_3 \end{bmatrix} = \begin{bmatrix} -2 \\ 3 \\ -3 \end{bmatrix}$$

Thus,

$$\Delta = \begin{vmatrix} 3 & -1 & -2 \\ -1 & 5 & 0 \\ -2 & 0 & 5 \end{vmatrix} = 75 - 20 - 5 = 50$$

$$\Delta_1 = \begin{vmatrix} -2 & -1 & -2 \\ 3 & 5 & 0 \\ -3 & 0 & 5 \end{vmatrix} = -50 - 30 + 15 = -65$$

$$\Delta_2 = \begin{vmatrix} 3 & -2 & -2 \\ -1 & 3 & 0 \\ -2 & -3 & 5 \end{vmatrix} = 45 - 6 - 12 - 10 = 17$$

$$\Delta_3 = \begin{vmatrix} 3 & -1 & -2 \\ -1 & 5 & 3 \\ -2 & 0 & -3 \end{vmatrix} = -45 + 6 - 20 + 3 = -56$$

and by Cramer's rule,

$$v_1 = \frac{\Delta_1}{\Delta} = -\frac{65}{50} = -1.30 \text{ V} \qquad v_2 = \frac{\Delta_2}{\Delta} = \frac{17}{50} = 0.34 \text{ V}$$

$$v_3 = \frac{\Delta_3}{\Delta} = -\frac{56}{50} = -1.12 \text{ V}$$

The nodal analysis for this circuit is now complete—all of the node voltages have been determined. With these node voltages, we can easily calculate any circuit variable. For example, the voltage across the 2-S conductance, where the + is on the left side, is

$$v_1 - v_3 = -1.30 - (-1.12) = -0.18 \text{ V}$$

and the current, directed to the right, through the 2-S conductance is

$$i_2 = 2(v_1 - v_3) = 2(-0.18) = -0.36 \text{ A}$$

DRILL EXERCISE 2.2

Use nodal analysis to find the node voltages v_1, v_2, and v_3 for the circuit shown in Fig. DE2.2.

Answer: -2 V; 1 V; 0.5 V

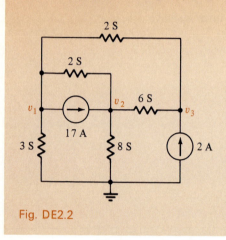

Fig. DE2.2

Having used nodal analysis to analyze a circuit with independent current sources, let us now consider a circuit that contains a dependent current source. Specifically, let us analyze a more practical circuit—a simple transistor amplifier.

EXAMPLE 2.3

The circuit shown in Fig. 2.8 is a more accurate version[†] of the BJT amplifier given in Fig. 1.49 on p. 33. (Note the additional 15-kΩ resistor.) Let us use nodal analysis to calculate the voltage gain v_3/v_1 for the circuit in Fig. 2.8.

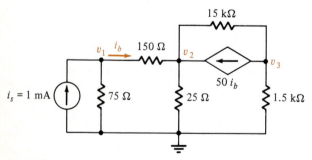

Fig. 2.8   Transistor amplifier.

[†] Why the voltage source v_1 in series with $R_1 = 75$ Ω is equivalent to a current source i_s in parallel with 75 Ω will be discussed in Chapter 3.

At node v_1, by KCL,

$$\frac{v_1 - v_2}{150} + \frac{v_1}{75} - 10^{-3} = 0$$

from which

$$3v_1 - v_2 = 0.15 \tag{2.10}$$

At node v_2, by KCL,

$$-i_b - 50i_b + \frac{v_2}{25} + \frac{v_2 - v_3}{15 \times 10^3} = 0$$

Since $i_b = (v_1 - v_2)/150$, then

$$-51\left(\frac{v_1 - v_2}{150}\right) + \frac{v_2}{25} + \frac{v_2 - v_3}{15 \times 10^3} = 0$$

Simplifying yields

$$-5100v_1 + 5701v_2 - v_3 = 0 \tag{2.11}$$

At node v_3, by KCL,

$$50\left(\frac{v_1 - v_2}{150}\right) + \frac{v_3}{1.5 \times 10^3} + \frac{v_3 - v_2}{15 \times 10^3} = 0$$

from which we obtain

$$5000v_1 - 5001v_2 + 11v_3 = 0 \tag{2.12}$$

Writing Equations (2.10), (2.11), and (2.12) in matrix form, we have

$$\begin{bmatrix} 3 & -1 & 0 \\ -5100 & 5701 & -1 \\ 5000 & -5001 & 11 \end{bmatrix} \begin{bmatrix} v_1 \\ v_2 \\ v_3 \end{bmatrix} = \begin{bmatrix} 0.15 \\ 0 \\ 0 \end{bmatrix}$$

Calculating determinants, we obtain

$$\Delta = \begin{vmatrix} 3 & -1 & 0 \\ -5100 & 5701 & -1 \\ 5000 & -5001 & 11 \end{vmatrix} = 188,133 + 5000 - 15,003 - 56,100 = 122,030$$

$$\Delta_1 = \begin{vmatrix} 0.15 & -1 & 0 \\ 0 & 5701 & -1 \\ 0 & -5001 & 11 \end{vmatrix} = 9406.65 - 750.15 = 8656.5$$

$$\Delta_2 = \begin{vmatrix} 3 & 0.15 & 0 \\ -5100 & 0 & -1 \\ 5000 & 0 & 11 \end{vmatrix} = -750 + 8415 = 7665$$

$$\Delta_3 = \begin{vmatrix} 3 & -1 & 0.15 \\ -5100 & 5701 & 0 \\ 5000 & -5001 & 0 \end{vmatrix} = 3,825,765 - 4,275,750 = -449,985$$

and by Cramer's rule,

$$v_1 = \frac{\Delta_1}{\Delta} = \frac{8656.5}{122,030} = 0.071 \text{ V} \qquad v_2 = \frac{\Delta_2}{\Delta} = \frac{7665}{122,030} = 0.063 \text{ V}$$

$$v_3 = \frac{\Delta_3}{\Delta} = \frac{-449,985}{122,030} = -3.69 \text{ V}$$

The voltage gain for this amplifier is

$$\frac{v_3}{v_1} = -51.98$$

The gain that was calculated in Example 1.12 by ignoring the 15-kΩ resistor in Fig. 2.8 (removing it) was -52.63, which is roughly a 1 percent difference from this result. Thus, the inclusion of the 15-kΩ resistor (i.e., using the more accurate model of the transistor) does not significantly change the result obtained.

The resistance R_{eq} seen by the independent current source is

$$R_{eq} = \frac{v_1}{i_s} = \frac{0.071}{0.001} = 71 \ \Omega$$

In the above analysis, exact numerical values were used. In practice, however, approximations are the rule rather than the exception. For this example, 5701 and 5001 would be replaced by 5700 and 5000, respectively. Using these approximations we get $\Delta = 122,000$, $\Delta_1 = 8650$, $\Delta_2 = 7660$, and $\Delta_3 = -450,000$. Thus, $v_3/v_1 \approx -52$.

DRILL EXERCISE 2.3

For the circuit shown in Fig. DE2.3, use nodal analysis to find the node voltages v_1, v_2, and v_3.
Answer: 12 V; 6 V; -4 V

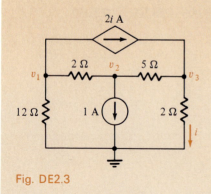

Fig. DE2.3

2.2 NODAL ANALYSIS FOR CIRCUITS WITH VOLTAGE SOURCES

The circuit depicted in Example 2.3 contains a current-dependent current source. A voltage-dependent current source is treated in a similar manner. However, when using nodal analysis for circuits with voltage sources—either independent or dependent—we slightly modify the procedure for nodal analysis. In some cases, the new procedure is actually simpler than the original, and in other cases, it turns out to be no more complex than the original.

We will begin our look at nodal analysis for circuits with voltage sources by considering a circuit with a voltage source connected between a nonreference node and the reference node.

●

EXAMPLE 2.4

The circuit shown in Fig. 2.9 contains an independent voltage source in addition to a voltage-dependent current source. Let us determine the node voltages v_1, v_2, and v_3 via nodal analysis.

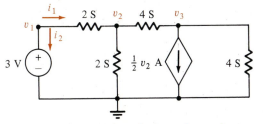

Fig. 2.9   Circuit with an independent voltage source.

By KCL at node v_1,

$$i_1 + i_2 = 0 \tag{2.13}$$

Clearly, $i_1 = 2(v_1 - v_2)$. But, what is i_2 in terms of the node voltages? The 3-V source is not a resistance (or conductance) and Ohm's law does not apply to it. The current through an ideal voltage source can be anything—the current magnitude and direction depend on what is connected to the voltage source. Of course, $i_2 = -i_1 = -2(v_1 - v_2)$. But, substituting this expression for i_2 and the above expression for i_1 into Equation (2.13) results in the trivial identity $0 = 0$.

This discussion indicates simply that we do not apply KCL at node v_1. Instead, however, note that by the definition of an ideal voltage source (or by KVL) we must have

$$v_1 = 3 \text{ V}$$

and this is the equation obtained at node v_1.

In general, when an independent voltage source is connected between a non-reference node and the reference node, the voltage of the nonreference node is constrained by the voltage source and therefore is obtained by inspection.

To determine the remaining voltage variables v_2 and v_3, we proceed as before. By KCL at node v_2,

$$2(v_2 - v_1) + 2v_2 + 4(v_2 - v_3) = 0$$

Using the fact that $v_1 = 3$ V, simplifying this expression results in

$$8v_2 - 4v_3 = 6 \qquad (2.14)$$

At node v_3, by KCL,

$$4(v_3 - v_2) + \tfrac{1}{2}v_2 + 4v_3 = 0$$

from which

$$-7v_2 + 16v_3 = 0 \qquad (2.15)$$

(Note the simplicity of dealing with the voltage-dependent current source.)

Solving Equations (2.14) and (2.15) results in

$$v_2 = 0.96 \text{ V} \qquad \text{and} \qquad v_3 = 0.42 \text{ V}$$

Since $i_1 = 2(v_1 - v_2) = 2(3 - 0.96) = 4.08$ A, then the conductance seen by the voltage source is

$$G_{eq} = \frac{i_1}{v_1} = \frac{4.08}{3} = 1.36 \text{ S}$$

Furthermore, now we can use KCL at node v_1 to determine i_2. Specifically,

$$i_2 = -i_1 = -4.08 \text{ A}$$

A dependent voltage source that is connected between the reference node and a nonreference node is treated similarly to that for an independent voltage source. Specifically, the value and polarity of the dependent source determines, by inspection, the equation for that nonreference node—KCL is not applied at that node. However, after the nodal analysis of the circuit is completed, KCL can be applied at that nonreference node in order to determine the current through the dependent voltage source.

DRILL EXERCISE 2.4

For the circuit shown in Fig. DE2.4, find the node voltages v_1, v_2, v_3, and v_4. In addition, find the conductance seen by the independent voltage source and the current going down through the dependent voltage source.
Answer: 25 V; 3 V; −6 V; −1 V; 0.88 S; 20 A

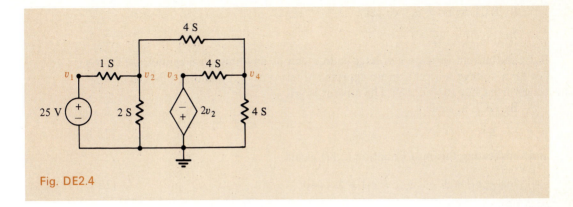

Fig. DE2.4

Now let us consider the situation that a circuit contains a voltage source that is connected between two nonreference nodes.

EXAMPLE 2.5

The circuit shown in Fig. 2.10 has an independent voltage source connected between two nonreference nodes. Let us determine the node voltages v_1, v_2, and v_3 by using nodal analysis.

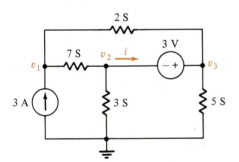

Fig. 2.10   Circuit with voltage source connected between nonreference nodes.

By KCL at node v_1 we get

$$7(v_1 - v_2) + 2(v_1 - v_3) - 3 = 0$$

from which

$$9v_1 - 7v_2 - 2v_3 = 3 \tag{2.16}$$

and this is the first of the three equations needed to solve for the three voltage variables v_1, v_2, and v_3.

By KCL at node v_2, we get

$$7(v_2 - v_1) + 3v_2 + i = 0 \tag{2.17}$$

But i, the current through a voltage source, can be anything—we cannot use Ohm's law for a voltage source! Can we express i in terms of v_1, v_2, and v_3 other than what we get from Equation (2.17)? The answer is yes.

By KCL at node v_3,

$$i = 2(v_3 - v_1) + 5v_3 \tag{2.18}$$

and substituting this into Equation (2.17) yields

$$7(v_2 - v_1) + 3v_2 + 2(v_3 - v_1) + 5v_3 = 0 \tag{2.19}$$

from which

$$-9v_1 + 10v_2 + 7v_3 = 0 \tag{2.20}$$

and this is the second of the three equations needed to solve for v_1, v_2, and v_3.

So far we have applied KCL at all three nonreference nodes, and we only have two equations [Equations (2.16) and (2.20)] to show for it. Where is the third equation?

It was the voltage source that required us to combine two equations [Equations (2.17) and (2.18)] into a single equation [Equation (2.20)] in order to get an expression that does not include i. Yet, it is the voltage source that gives us the third needed equation. Specifically, by KVL,

$$v_3 - v_2 = 3 \tag{2.21}$$

Solving Equations (2.16), (2.20), and (2.21), we get $\Delta = 72$, $\Delta_1 = -36$, $\Delta_2 = -108$, and $\Delta_3 = 108$. Therefore,

$$v_1 = \frac{\Delta_1}{\Delta} = \frac{-36}{72} = -0.5 \text{ V} \quad v_2 = \frac{\Delta_2}{\Delta} = \frac{-108}{72} = 1.5 \text{ V} \quad v_3 = \frac{\Delta_3}{\Delta} = \frac{108}{72} = 1.5 \text{ V}$$

Now that nodal analysis is complete, we can determine i if we so desire. By KCL at node v_3,

$$i = 2(v_3 - v_1) + 5v_3 = 2(1.5 + 0.5) + 5(1.5) = 11.5 \text{ A}$$

Alternatively, by KCL at node v_2,

$$i = 7(v_1 - v_2) - 3v_2 = 7(-0.5 + 1.5) - 3(-1.5) = 11.5 \text{ A}$$

DRILL EXERCISE 2.5

For the circuit shown in Fig. DE2.5, use nodal analysis to find the node voltages v_1, v_2, and v_3. Use these results to determine i_1 and i_2.
Answer: -4 V; 6 V; 8 V; 4 A; 0 A

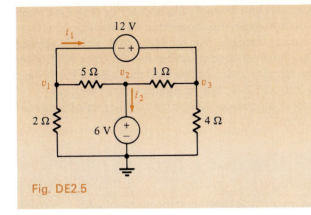

Fig. DE2.5

Supernodes

For the circuit given in Fig. 2.10, because there is a voltage source connected between the two nonreference nodes labeled v_2 and v_3, we designated a current i through the voltage source. Having applied KCL to the node labeled v_2, we obtained an equation [Equation (2.17)] with i in it. Having applied KCL to the node labeled v_3, we got another equation [Equation (2.18)] with i in it. We then combined the two equations to get an expression [Equation (2.19)] that does not contain i. But note that Equation (2.19) is the expression that is obtained by applying KCL to the region, shown in Fig. 2.11, which surrounds the 3-V source and the nodes to which it is connected. This region is referred to as a **supernode**.

When employing nodal analysis on a circuit with a voltage source (either independent or dependent) that is connected between two nonreference nodes, either a current through the voltage source can be designated or a region (supernode) can

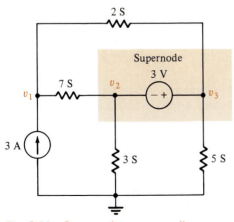

Fig. 2.11 Supernode corresponding to voltage source.

be indicated around the voltage source and its adjoining nodes. For the former case, KCL is applied individually to both nonreference nodes and the resulting equations are combined to eliminate the current variable. For the latter case, KCL is applied to the supenode. Both approaches yield the same equation. In both cases, KVL gives the relationship between the nonreference node voltages and the value of the voltage source. (For the circuit in Figs. 2.10 and 2.11, this relationship is $v_3 - v_2 = 3$.)

If a circuit has two (or more) supernodes that intersect, they can be merged into a single larger supernode.

EXAMPLE 2.6
The circuit shown in Fig. 2.12 looks quite formidable—it contains one current source and three voltage sources. Let us see what is involved to determine the node voltages v_1, v_2, v_3, and v_4.

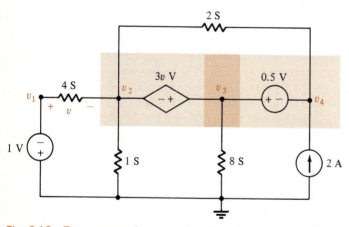

Fig. 2.12   Two supernodes merged to form larger supernode.

By inspection, the 1-V source establishes that

$$v_1 = -1 \text{ V}$$

Merging the supernodes associated with the dependent voltage source and the 0.5-V independent voltage source gives the larger region shown. Applying KCL to this region yields

$$4(v_2 - v_1) + 1v_2 + 2(v_2 - v_4) + 8v_3 + 2(v_4 - v_2) - 2 = 0 \tag{2.22}$$

Note that the current $2(v_2 - v_4)$ directed out of the node labeled v_2 comes out of the large region. The current $2(v_4 - v_2)$ directed out of the node labeled v_4 also comes out of the large region. The net effect is that these terms, which are both in Equation (2.22), cancel out each other. Substituting $v_1 = -1$ V into Equation (2.22), we get

$$5v_2 + 8v_3 = -2 \tag{2.23}$$

For the given circuit, we now use the values of the voltage sources to get the remaining equations. Specifically, for the dependent voltage source, by KVL, we get

$$v_3 - v_2 = 3v$$

Since $v = v_1 - v_2 = -1 - v_2$, then

$$v_3 - v_2 = 3(-1 - v_2) = -3 - 3v_2$$

from which

$$2v_2 + v_3 = -3 \qquad\qquad (2.24)$$

The solution to Equations (2.23) and (2.24) is

$$v_2 = -2 \text{ V} \qquad \text{and} \qquad v_3 = 1 \text{ V}$$

For the 0.5-V independent voltage source, by KVL,

$$v_3 - v_4 = 0.5 \qquad \Rightarrow \qquad v_4 = v_3 - 0.5 = 1 - 0.5 = 0.5 \text{ V}$$

This completes the nodal analysis of the circuit in Fig. 2.12.

DRILL EXERCISE 2.6

For the circuit shown in Fig. DE2.6, use nodal analysis to find the node voltages v_1, v_2, and v_3.
Answer: -1 V; 2 V; 5 V

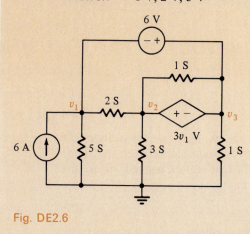

Fig. DE2.6

Consider the case that a supernode (or a region of merged supernodes) includes a nonreference node for which that node is at one end of a voltage source, and the other end of the voltage source is connected to the reference. For such a situation, when using nodal analysis, KCL is not applied to the supernode (or to the region of merged supernodes).

EXAMPLE 2.7

For the circuit shown in Fig. 2.13, let us determine v_1, v_2, v_3, and v_4 via nodal analysis.

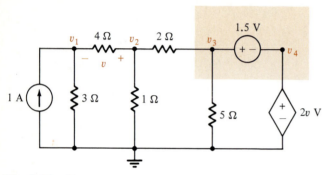

Fig. 2.13   Circuit for Example 2.7.

By KCL at node v_1,

$$-1 + \frac{v_1}{3} + \frac{v_1 - v_2}{4} = 0$$

from which

$$7v_1 - 3v_2 = 12 \tag{2.25}$$

By KCL at node v_2,

$$\frac{v_2 - v_1}{4} + \frac{v_2}{1} + \frac{v_2 - v_3}{2} = 0$$

from which

$$-v_1 + 7v_2 - 2v_3 = 0 \tag{2.26}$$

However, since the indicated region associated with the 1.5-V source includes the node labeled v_4, and since there is a voltage source connected between that node and the reference, we do not apply KCL to the indicated region. Instead, we use the fact that

$$v_3 - v_4 = 1.5 \tag{2.27}$$

The final equation is obtained from the dependent voltage source by inspection. Specifically,

$$v_4 = 2v = 2(v_2 - v_1) = 2v_2 - 2v_1$$

from which

$$2v_1 - 2v_2 + v_4 = 0 \tag{2.28}$$

Thus, we have four equations [Equations (2.25), (2.26), (2.27), and (2.28)] and four unknowns. Instead of solving these equations directly, let us substitute $v_4 = 2v_2 - 2v_1$ into Equation (2.27). The result is

$$2v_1 - 2v_2 + v_3 = 1.5 \tag{2.29}$$

For Equations (2.25), (2.26), and (2.29), it is a routine matter to show that

$$v_1 = \frac{\Delta_1}{\Delta} = \frac{45}{30} = 15 \text{ V} \quad v_2 = \frac{\Delta_2}{\Delta} = \frac{-15}{30} = -0.5 \text{ V} \quad v_3 = \frac{\Delta_3}{\Delta} = \frac{-75}{30} = -2.5 \text{ V}$$

It follows that

$$v_4 = 2v = 2(v_2 - v_1) = 2(-0.5 - 1.5) = -4 \text{ V}$$

DRILL EXERCISE 2.7

For the circuit shown in Fig. DE2.7, use nodal analysis to find v_1, v_2, and v_3.
Answer: 6 V; 9 V; 10 V

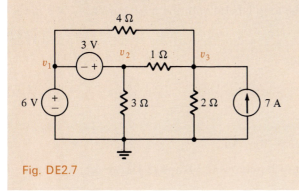

Fig. DE2.7

2.3 MESH ANALYSIS

Having discussed one technique for analyzing a circuit, that being nodal analysis, we are now in a position to introduce another. Suppose that we wish to analyze the circuit shown in Fig. 2.14. Clearly, it would be a simple matter to proceed by nodal

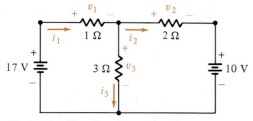

Fig. 2.14 Circuit to be analyzed.

analysis. Instead, however, note that if we can determine i_1 and i_2, then any other variable can be determined. By KCL,

$$i_3 = i_1 - i_2$$

By Ohm's law,

$$v_1 = 1i_1 \qquad v_2 = 2i_2 \qquad v_3 = 3i_3$$

Since the current going "down" through the 3-Ω resistor is i_3, and since $i_3 = i_1 - i_2$, this current can be broken up into its component parts: i_1 going down and $-i_2$ going down. However, since $-i_2$ going down is identical to the condition of i_2 going up, we can represent i_3 equivalently by the two currents in the circuit as shown in Fig. 2.15. Note that the actual current going down through the 3-Ω resistor is still $i_1 - i_2 = i_3$. By applying KCL at the other nodes in the circuit, we see that the current going up through the 17-V battery is i_1, whereas the current going down through the 10-V source is i_2. These situations are also indicated in the circuit. It is because of this that in the loop on the left we can imagine that there is a current i_1 circulating clockwise, and in the loop on the right there is a current i_2 also circulating clockwise. We represent this pictorially in Fig. 2.16. We refer to i_1 and i_2 as **mesh currents**. For this circuit, let us apply KVL to loop i_1—the loop labeled with the mesh current i_1. We have

$$v_1 + v_3 - 17 = 0 \tag{2.30}$$

For loop i_2, applying KVL yields

$$v_2 + 10 - v_3 = 0 \tag{2.31}$$

By Ohm's law,

$$v_1 = 1i_1 \qquad v_2 = 2i_2 \qquad v_3 = 3(i_1 - i_2)$$

Substituting these expressions into Equations (2.30) and (2.31), we get

$$4i_1 - 3i_2 = 17 \tag{2.32}$$

and

$$-3i_1 + 5i_2 = -10 \tag{2.33}$$

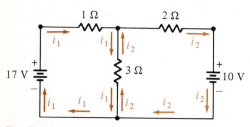

Fig. 2.15   Equivalent form of circuit in Fig. 2.14.

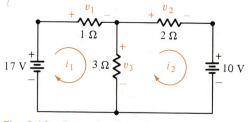

Fig. 2.16   Example of mesh analysis.

respectively. From Equation (2.32), $i_2 = (4i_1 - 17)/3$. Substituting this into Equation (2.33) yields

$$-3i_1 + 5\left(\frac{4i_1 - 17}{3}\right) = -10 \quad \Rightarrow \quad i_1 = 5 \text{ A}$$

Substituting this value into either Equation (2.32) or (2.33) results in

$$i_2 = 1 \text{ A}$$

Having determined the values of the mesh currents i_1 and i_2, it is a simple matter to determine v_1, v_2, and v_3. Specifically,

$$v_1 = 1i_1 = 5 \text{ V} \qquad v_2 = 2i_2 = 2 \text{ V} \qquad v_3 = 3(i_1 - i_2) = 12 \text{ V}$$

Writing Equations (2.32) and (2.33) in matrix form, we have

$$\begin{bmatrix} 4 & -3 \\ -3 & 5 \end{bmatrix} \begin{bmatrix} i_1 \\ i_2 \end{bmatrix} = \begin{bmatrix} 17 \\ -10 \end{bmatrix} \tag{2.34}$$

Forming determinants and using Cramer's rule, we get

$$\Delta = \begin{vmatrix} 4 & -3 \\ -3 & 5 \end{vmatrix} = 20 - 9 = 11$$

$$\Delta_1 = \begin{vmatrix} 17 & -3 \\ -10 & 5 \end{vmatrix} = 85 - 30 = 55 \quad \Rightarrow \quad i_1 = \frac{\Delta_1}{\Delta} = 5 \text{ A}$$

$$\Delta_2 = \begin{vmatrix} 4 & 17 \\ -3 & -10 \end{vmatrix} = -40 + 51 = 11 \quad \Rightarrow \quad i_2 = \frac{\Delta_2}{\Delta} = 1 \text{ A}$$

The matrix equation (2.34) is in the form $\mathbf{Ri} = \mathbf{v}$, where

$$\mathbf{R} = \begin{bmatrix} 4 & -3 \\ -3 & 5 \end{bmatrix} \qquad \mathbf{i} = \begin{bmatrix} i_1 \\ i_2 \end{bmatrix} \qquad \mathbf{v} = \begin{bmatrix} 17 \\ -10 \end{bmatrix}$$

Thus, we see that Equation (2.34) is also a matrix form of Ohm's law. The 2×2 matrix $\mathbf{R}$ is a **resistance matrix**, $\mathbf{i}$ is a current matrix, and $\mathbf{v}$ is a voltage matrix.

In the procedure just described, when we applied KVL around the loop labeled with the mesh current i_2, we obtained Equation (2.31), which is

$$v_2 + 10 - v_3 = 0 \tag{2.31}$$

Since $v_3 = 3(i_1 - i_2)$, then $-v_3 = -3(i_1 - i_2) = 3(i_2 - i_1)$. Hence, from Equation (2.31) we get

$$2i_2 + 10 + 3(i_2 - i_1) = 0$$

where $i_2 - i_1$ is the current directed up through the 3-Ω resistor.

This discussion indicates that it is not even necessary to designate voltages such as v_1, v_2, and v_3 in Fig. 2.16 when applying KVL to each loop. All we have to do is use Ohm's law to express resistor voltages in terms of mesh currents (and resistances), and in doing so we employ resistor currents that have the same directions as the directions of loop traversals. In particular, for the circuit given in Fig. 2.16, for a clockwise traversal of the loop on the left, we use the current directed down through the 3-Ω resistor (i.e., $i_1 - i_2$). By doing this, KVL yields

$$1i_1 + 3(i_1 - i_2) - 17 = 0$$

and from this expression we get Equation (2.32). Furthermore, for a clockwise traversal of the loop on the right, we use the current directed up through the 3-Ω resistor (i.e., $i_2 - i_1$). In this case, KVL gives

$$10 + 3(i_2 - i_1) + 2i_2 = 0$$

from which we get Equation (2.33).

By taking such an approach, we can avoid cluttering a circuit diagram, and for circuits containing only resistances (or conductances) and independent sources, all of the main-diagonal entries of the corresponding resistance matrix **R** will be positive.

Planar and Nonplanar Circuits

What we have just seen is an example of the technique known as **mesh analysis**. Before listing the rules for applying this method of analysis, we must mention that the set of rules that will follow shortly, unlike that for nodal analysis, will not be valid for all types of circuits. A general procedure, which can be applied to any circuit, will be discussed in Section 2.5 on loop analysis. We shall now specify those types of circuits to be considered in this section.

For the circuit shown in Fig. 2.17, note that the 4-Ω and 5-Ω resistors are not connected, but that one "crosses over" the other. This situation, however, can be avoided simply by redrawing the circuit as in Fig. 2.18. This circuit, which is identical to the preceding one, is displayed in a manner in which no element crosses over another. Such a circuit is said to be **planar**; that is, a planar circuit is one which may be drawn in the plane such that there is no element that crosses over another.

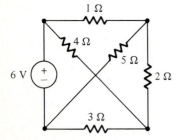

Fig. 2.17 Circuit which appears to be nonplanar.

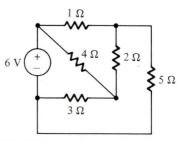

Fig. 2.18 Demonstration that the circuit in Fig. 2.17 is planar.

For the ten-element circuit (one voltage source and nine resistors) shown in Fig. 2.19, no matter how you try, there is no way of redrawing this circuit so that none of the elements cross. This, therefore, is an example of a **nonplanar** circuit.

A second example of a nonplanar circuit is shown in Fig. 2.20. This circuit has nine elements: one voltage source and eight resistors. There is no nonplanar circuit having less than nine elements; that is, any circuit with eight or fewer elements must be planar.

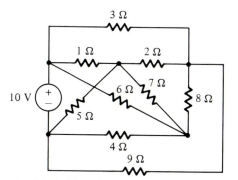

Fig. 2.19   Nonplanar circuit with ten elements.

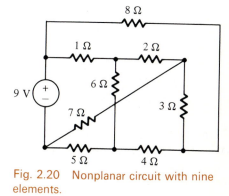

Fig. 2.20   Nonplanar circuit with nine elements.

In the discussion of mesh analysis that follows immediately, we shall deal only with planar circuits. Note that in a planar circuit, the elements partition the plane into regions called **meshes**. For example, in Fig. 2.21 the three finite meshes are explicitly indicated. The infinite region that surrounds the circuit will be ignored. With this in mind, we now present the rules for analyzing a planar circuit having m meshes and no current sources via mesh analysis. The situation for circuits containing current sources will be discussed shortly thereafter.

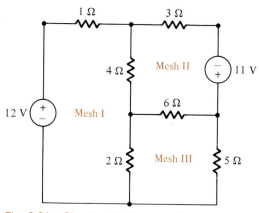

Fig. 2.21   Circuit with three meshes.

MESH ANALYSIS—NO CURRENT SOURCES

Given a planar circuit with m meshes and no current sources, proceed as follows:

1. **Place clockwise mesh currents (e.g., $i_1, i_2, \ldots, i_m$) in the m (finite) meshes.**

2. **Apply KVL to each of the m meshes by traversing each mesh in the clockwise direction. Use Ohm's law to express the voltages across resistors in terms of the mesh currents.**

3. **Solve the resulting set of m simultaneous equations for the mesh currents.**

EXAMPLE 2.8

For the circuit given in Fig. 2.21, let us use mesh analysis to determine the mesh currents i_1, i_2, and i_3 which are indicated in Fig. 2.22.

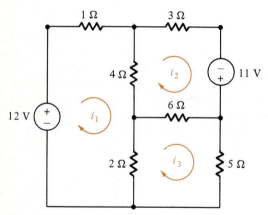

Fig. 2.22   Preceding circuit with mesh currents indicated.

By KVL around mesh i_1 (i.e., the mesh indicated by the mesh current i_1),

$$1i_1 + 4(i_1 - i_2) + 2(i_1 - i_3) - 12 = 0$$

from which

$$7i_1 - 4i_2 - 2i_3 = 12 \tag{2.35}$$

For mesh i_2, by KVL,

$$3i_2 - 11 + 6(i_2 - i_3) + 4(i_2 - i_1) = 0$$

from which

$$-4i_1 + 13i_2 - 6i_3 = 11 \qquad (2.36)$$

Finally, for mesh i_3, by KVL,

$$5i_3 + 2(i_3 - i_1) + 6(i_3 - i_2) = 0$$

from which

$$-2i_1 - 6i_2 + 13i_3 = 0 \qquad (2.37)$$

Equations (2.35), (2.36), and (2.37) can be written in matrix form as

$$\begin{bmatrix} 7 & -4 & -2 \\ -4 & 13 & -6 \\ -2 & -6 & 13 \end{bmatrix} \begin{bmatrix} i_1 \\ i_2 \\ i_3 \end{bmatrix} = \begin{bmatrix} 12 \\ 11 \\ 0 \end{bmatrix}$$

Calculating determinants results in

$$\Delta = 575 \qquad \Delta_1 = 2300 \qquad \Delta_2 = 1725 \qquad \Delta_3 = 1150$$

Therefore, by Cramer's rule,

$$i_1 = \frac{\Delta_1}{\Delta} = 4 \text{ A} \qquad i_2 = \frac{\Delta_2}{\Delta} = 3 \text{ A} \qquad i_3 = \frac{\Delta_3}{\Delta} = 2 \text{ A}$$

Given the mesh currents, it is now a simple matter to determine any current or voltage in the circuit. For example, the current, directed to the right, through the 1-Ω resistor is $i_1 = 4$ A. The current, directed to the right, through the 6-Ω resistor is $i_3 - i_2 = 2 - 3 = -1$ A. The current, directed down, through the 2-Ω resistor is $i_1 - i_3 = 4 - 2 = 2$ A. Figure 2.23 shows all the element currents for the circuit.

Using the current through a resistor and Ohm's law, we can find the voltage across that resistor. Figure 2.23 also shows the given circuit with a reference node and

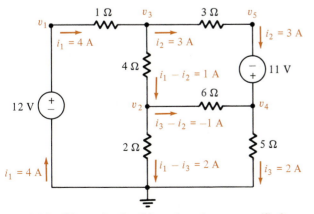

Fig. 2.23   Given circuit with node voltages specified.

nonreference node voltages indicated. By inspection, $v_1 = 12$ V. By Ohm's law, $v_2 = 2(i_1 - i_3) = 2(4 - 2) = 4$ V. Also, $v_4 = 5i_3 = 5(2) = 10$ V. By KVL, $v_5 = -11 + v_4 = -11 + 10 = -1$ V. Furthermore, $v_3 = 4(i_1 - i_2) + v_2 = 4(4 - 3) + 4 = 8$ V. Alternatively, $v_3 = 3i_2 + v_5 = 3(3) + (-1) = 8$ V.

DRILL EXERCISE 2.8

For the circuit shown in Fig. DE2.8, find the mesh currents i_1, i_2, and i_3. Use these currents to find v_1 and v_2.
Answer: 2 A; 4 A; 2 A; -4 V; 8 V

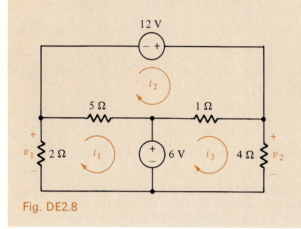

Fig. DE2.8

Mesh analysis for a circuit which contains a dependent voltage source is no more complicated than for circuits with independent voltage sources.

EXAMPLE 2.9

The circuit shown in Fig. 2.24 contains a dependent voltage source. Let us use mesh analysis to find the mesh currents i_1, i_2, and i_3.

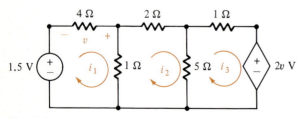

Fig. 2.24   Circuit with a dependent voltage source.

By KVL around mesh i_1,

$$4i_1 + 1(i_1 - i_2) - 1.5 = 0$$

from which

$$5i_1 - i_2 = 1.5 \tag{2.38}$$

By KVL around mesh i_2,

$$2i_2 + 5(i_2 - i_3) + 1(i_2 - i_1) = 0$$

from which

$$-i_1 + 8i_2 - 5i_3 = 0 \tag{2.39}$$

Finally, by KVL around mesh i_3,

$$1i_3 + 2v + 5(i_3 - i_2) = 0$$

Since $v = -4i_1$, then substituting this expression for v into the preceding equation and simplifying yields

$$-8i_1 - 5i_2 + 6i_3 = 0 \tag{2.40}$$

Writing Equations (2.38), (2.39), and (2.40) in matrix form we obtain

$$\begin{bmatrix} 5 & -1 & 0 \\ -1 & 8 & -5 \\ -8 & -5 & 6 \end{bmatrix} \begin{bmatrix} i_1 \\ i_2 \\ i_3 \end{bmatrix} = \begin{bmatrix} 1.5 \\ 0 \\ 0 \end{bmatrix}$$

for which

$$\Delta = 69 \qquad \Delta_1 = 34.5 \qquad \Delta_2 = 69 \qquad \Delta_3 = 103.5$$

By Cramer's rule,

$$i_1 = \frac{\Delta_1}{\Delta} = 0.5 \text{ A} \qquad i_2 = \frac{\Delta_2}{\Delta} = 1 \text{ A} \qquad i_3 = \frac{\Delta_3}{\Delta} = 1.5 \text{ A}$$

and this completes the mesh analysis.

By Ohm's law

$$v = -4i_1 = -4(0.5) = -2 \text{ V}$$

If the node common to both voltage sources is chosen to be the reference, then the node voltages—reading them from left to right—are

$$v_1 = 1.5 \text{ V} \qquad v_2 = 1(i_1 - i_2) = 1(0.5 - 1) = -0.5 \text{ V}$$

$$v_3 = 5(i_2 - i_3) = 5(1 - 1.5) = -2.5 \text{ V} \qquad v_4 = 2v = 2(-2) = -4 \text{ V}$$

For the circuit given in Fig. 2.24, the resistance seen by the 1.5-V independent voltage source is

$$R_{eq} = \frac{1.5}{i_1} = \frac{1.5}{0.5} = 3 \, \Omega$$

78
CIRCUIT ANALYSIS TECHNIQUES

DRILL EXERCISE 2.9

Find the mesh currents i_1, i_2, and i_3 for the circuit shown in Fig. DE2.9. Determine the resistance R_{eq} seen by the 4-V independent voltage source.
Answer: 6 A; 7 A; 4 A; $\frac{2}{3}$ Ω

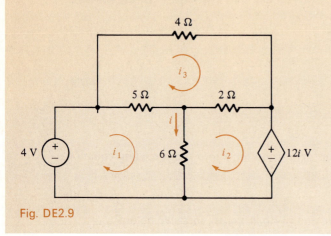

Fig. DE2.9

2.4 MESH ANALYSIS FOR CIRCUITS WITH CURRENT SOURCES

As suggested before, we must modify the procedure for utilizing mesh analysis when dealing with circuits containing current sources—either independent or dependent. Fortunately, however, analyzing circuits that contain current source via mesh analysis is actually no more complicated than the procedure already described, and in certain cases it is even simpler.

EXAMPLE 2.10

For the circuit shown in Fig. 2.25, let us find the mesh currents i_1, i_2, and i_3. Furthermore, let us determine the resistance R_{eq} seen by the current source.

Applying KVL to mesh i_1, we get

$$1(i_1 - i_2) + 2(i_1 - i_3) - v = 0 \tag{2.41}$$

Since v is the voltage across a current source—and such a voltage can be anything—and since Ohm's law is not valid for a current source (or a voltage source, either), we cannot make a substitution for v using information from mesh i_1 other than that obtained from Equation (2.41) itself. However, we can avoid using Equation (2.41) altogether for mesh analysis by noting that the current directed up through the current source (-2 A) must equal the mesh current i_1. Thus,

$$i_1 = -2 \text{ A}$$

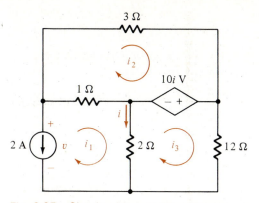

Fig. 2.25   Circuit with an independent current source.

and this is the equation for mesh i_1. Thus, the first mesh equation is obtained by inspection.

For mesh i_2, by KVL,

$$3i_2 + 10i + 1(i_2 - i_1) = 0$$

Substituting the fact that $i = i_1 - i_3$ and $i_1 = -2$ A into this equation results in

$$4i_2 - 10i_3 = 18 \tag{2.42}$$

For mesh i_3,

$$12i_3 + 2(i_3 - i_1) - 10i = 0$$

Again substituting $i = i_1 - i_3 = -2 - i_3$ into this equation and simplifying yields

$$i_3 = -1 \text{ A}$$

From Equation (2.42),

$$i_2 = \frac{18 + 10i_3}{4} = \frac{18 + 10(-1)}{4} = 2 \text{ A}$$

This completes the mesh analysis for the given circuit.

We can now apply KVL to determine the voltage v across the current source. From Equation (2.41),

$$v = 1(i_1 - i_2) + 2(i_1 - i_3) = 1(-2 - 2) + 2(-2 + 1) = -6 \text{ V}$$

Therefore, the resistance seen by the 2-A current source is

$$R_{eq} = \frac{v}{-2} = \frac{-6}{-2} = 3 \ \Omega$$

DRILL EXERCISE 2.10

For the circuit shown in Fig. DE2.10, find the mesh currents i_1, i_2, and i_3. Determine the resistance R_{eq} seen by the independent current source.

Answer: 2 A; 0.5 A; -1 A; 6 Ω

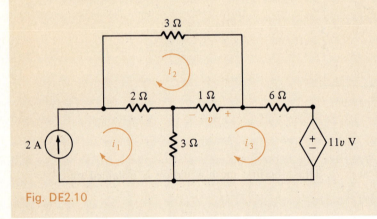

Fig. DE2.10

The circuit given in Fig. 2.25 has an independent current source that borders one mesh only—specifically, it borders mesh i_1. A dependent current source that borders only one mesh is treated in a manner similar to that done in Example 2.10.

DRILL EXERCISE 2.11

For the circuit shown in Fig. DE2.11, find the mesh currents i_1, i_2, and i_3.

Answer: -1 A; -2 A; -4 A

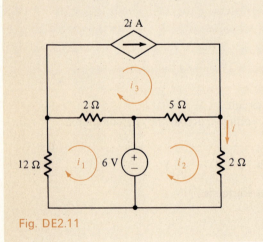

Fig. DE2.11

So far our discussion of mesh analysis for circuits with current sources has considered the case of a current source that borders only a single mesh. Let us now consider the case that a current source borders two meshes.

EXAMPLE 2.11

The circuit shown in Fig. 2.26 contains a current source which borders both mesh i_2 and mesh i_3. Let us see how to determine i_1, i_2, and i_3 via mesh analysis.

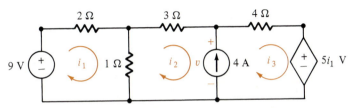

Fig. 2.26 Current source which borders two meshes.

By KVL for mesh i_1,

$$2i_1 + 1(i_1 - i_2) - 9 = 0$$

from which

$$3i_1 - i_2 = 9 \qquad (2.43)$$

For mesh i_2, by KVL,

$$1(i_2 - i_1) + 3i_2 + v = 0 \qquad (2.44)$$

But, the voltage v across the current source can be anything—we cannot make a substitution as is done for a resistor with Ohm's law. However, a similar situation will occur when we apply KVL to mesh i_3. Specifically, by KVL

$$v = 4i_3 + 5i_1 \qquad (2.45)$$

Substituting this expression into Equation (2.44), we obtain

$$1(i_2 - i_1) + 3i_2 + 4i_3 + 5i_1 = 0 \qquad (2.46)$$

and this simplifies to

$$i_1 + i_2 + i_3 = 0 \qquad (2.47)$$

In summary, therefore, applying KVL to mesh i_2 and mesh i_3, because of the current source we get two equations—each containing the voltage variable v. These two expressions are then combined so as to eliminate the voltage variable, and Equation (2.47) results.

So far, applying KVL to all three meshes has yielded only two equations [Equations (2.43) and (2.47)] in the three current variables i_1, i_2, and i_3. Where is the third equation?

It was the current source that required us to combine the equations obtained for mesh i_2 and mesh i_3. It is also the current source which gives us the third and final equation. Specifically, the current directed up through the current source is 4 A. In terms of mesh currents, the current directed up through the current source is $i_3 - i_2$. Hence, we have that

$$-i_2 + i_3 = 4 \tag{2.48}$$

For Equations (2.43), (2.47), and (2.48), $\Delta = 7$, $\Delta_1 = 14$, $\Delta_2 = -21$, and $\Delta_3 = 7$. Therefore, the mesh currents are

$$i_1 = \frac{\Delta_1}{\Delta} = 2 \text{ A} \qquad i_2 = \frac{\Delta_2}{\Delta} = -3 \text{ A} \qquad i_3 = \frac{\Delta_3}{\Delta} = 1 \text{ A}$$

and the mesh analysis of the circuit is complete.

We may now determine the voltage v across the current source. By KVL [Equation (2.45)],

$$v = 4i_3 + 5i_1 = 4(1) + 5(2) = 14 \text{ V}$$

DRILL EXERCISE 2.12

For the circuit shown in Fig. DE2.12, find the mesh currents i_1, i_2, and i_3. In addition, find v.

Answer: -1 A; -2 A; -4 A; 6 V

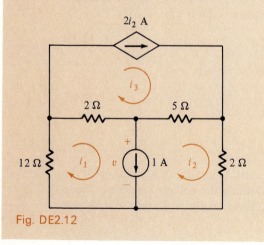

Fig. DE2.12

Supermeshes

For the circuit given in Fig. 2.26, because there is a current source which is common to two meshes, we designated a voltage v across the current source. Having applied KVL to the mesh labeled i_2, we obtained an equation [Equation (2.44)] with v in it. Having applied KVL to the mesh labeled i_3, we got another equation [Equation (2.45)] with v in it. We then combined the two equations to get an expression [Equation (2.46)] that does not contain v. But note that Equation (2.46) is the expression that is obtained by applying KVL to the loop, indicated with dashes in Fig. 2.27, formed by combining the meshes labeled i_2 and i_3. This loop is called a **supermesh**, although strictly speaking it is not a mesh but a loop.

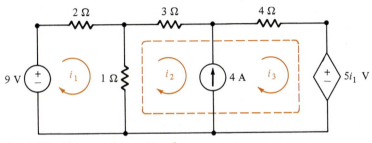

Fig. 2.27   Supermesh resulting from current source.

When employing mesh analysis on a circuit with a current source (either independent or dependent) that borders two meshes, either a voltage across the current source can be designated or a loop (supermesh) can be indicated around the appropriate meshes. For the former case, KVL is applied individually to both meshes and the resulting equations are combined to eliminate the voltage variable. For the latter case, KVL is applied to the supermesh. Both approaches yield the same equation. In both cases, the value of the current source is related to the mesh currents to produce the additional needed equation. (For the circuit in Figs. 2.26 and 2.27, this equation is $i_3 - i_2 = 4$.)

If a circuit has two (or more) supermeshes that intersect, they can be combined into a larger supermesh.

EXAMPLE 2.12

The circuit shown in Fig. 2.28 has four mesh currents: i_1, i_2, i_3, and i_4. Let us find these circuit variables.

For mesh i_1, by inspection,

$$i_1 = 2 \text{ A}$$

Since mesh i_2 and mesh i_3 have the same independent current source in common, these two meshes define a supermesh consisting of the 3-Ω resistor, the 6-Ω resistor, and the dependent current source. However, the dependent current source borders

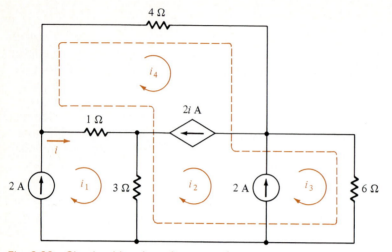

Fig. 2.28 Circuit with enlarged supermesh.

both mesh i_2 and mesh i_4, so these two meshes define another supermesh consisting of the 1-Ω resistor, the 3-Ω resistor, the 4-Ω resistor, and the 2-A current source on the right. Since these two supermeshes intersect, they can be combined into the larger supermesh indicated with dashes. Applying KVL to this larger supermesh, we get

$$4i_4 + 6i_3 + 3(i_2 - i_1) + 1(i_4 - i_1) = 0$$

from which

$$3i_2 + 6i_3 + 5i_4 = 4i_1 = 4(2) = 8 \tag{2.49}$$

For the independent source common to mesh i_2 and mesh i_3,

$$-i_2 + i_3 = 2 \tag{2.50}$$

For the dependent current source,

$$2i = i_4 - i_2$$

Since $i = i_1 - i_4$, then

$$2(i_1 - i_4) = i_4 - i_2$$

from which

$$-i_2 + 3i_4 = 2i_1 = 2(2) = 4 \tag{2.51}$$

Solving Equations (2.49), (2.50), and (2.51), we get

$$i_2 = -1 \text{ A} \qquad i_3 = 1 \text{ A} \qquad i_4 = 1 \text{ A}$$

and from above, $i_1 = 2$ A. This completes the mesh analysis for the given circuit.

DRILL EXERCISE 2.13

For the circuit shown in Fig. DE2.13, use mesh analysis to find i_1, i_2, and i_3.
Answer: 2 A; -1 A; 3 A

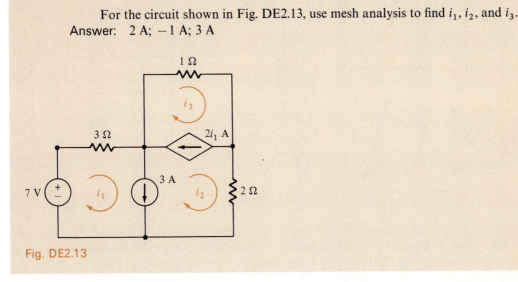

Fig. DE2.13

2.5 LOOP ANALYSIS

In our discussions of nodal analysis and mesh analysis, we established rules to follow which enabled us to systematically analyze circuits. In the case of nodal analysis, the technique presented is valid for all circuits—both planar and nonplanar. However, for the case of mesh analysis, the technique presented is valid only for planar circuits. Nonplanar circuits can be analyzed via a technique known as loop analysis, which is quite similar to mesh analysis. In order to study this technique, we must first introduce some concepts from the mathematical discipline known as **graph theory**.

Perhaps you have referred to a plot of some function $f(x)$ versus x as a "graph." This is precisely the notion that we are *not* referring to when we speak about a graph. A **graph** is merely a collection of points and lines. The points are called **nodes**, and the lines are called **edges**. Each end of an edge is connected to a node, and both ends of an edge may be connected to the same node. As a matter of convention, the edges are drawn by smooth—but not necessarily straight—lines. A few examples of graphs are shown in Fig. 2.29. In a graph, two or more edges can meet only at a node. Edges can be drawn "crossing over" each other, but this does not mean that they intersect.

Having introduced the concept of a graph, we shall now proceed to represent circuits as graphs so that we may discuss loop analysis.

As we mentioned earlier, a node in a circuit is determined by the connection of two or more circuit elements—excluding short circuits and open circuits. Given a circuit, we can form a graph by replacing each circuit element (of course, excluding short circuits and open circuits) by an edge.

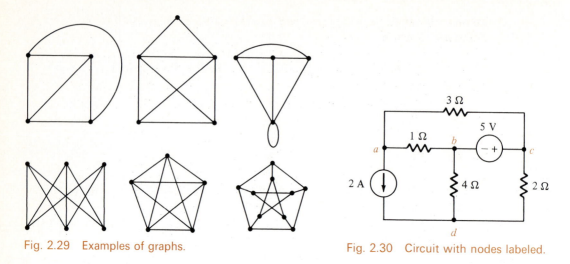

Fig. 2.29   Examples of graphs.

Fig. 2.30   Circuit with nodes labeled.

As an example, for the circuit shown in Fig. 2.30 the nodes are labeled a, b, c, and d. Replacing each element by a single edge, we get the corresponding graph shown in Fig. 2.31. In this graph, edges e_3 and e_4 correspond to the voltage and current sources, respectively. The remaining edges correspond to the resistors. Figure 2.31 is an example of a **connected graph**, that is, a graph in which any node can be reached from any other node by traversing the edges. An example of an **unconnected** or **disconnected graph** is shown in Fig. 2.32. In this graph, for example, there is no way of getting from node b to node g by traversing the edges.

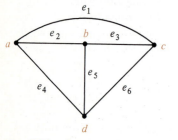

Fig. 2.31   Graph corresponding to circuit shown in Fig. 2.30.

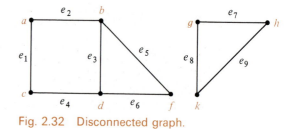

Fig. 2.32   Disconnected graph.

Given a set of n nodes, what is the fewest number of edges required to connect all the nodes? Clearly, one edge placed between any pair of nodes, say n_1 and n_2, will connect them. A second edge placed between n_3 and either n_1 or n_2 will connect the three nodes: n_1, n_2, n_3. A third edge placed between n_4 and either n_1 or n_2 or n_3 will connect the four nodes: n_1, n_2, n_3, n_4. Continuing in this manner, we see that $n - 1$ edges (and no fewer) can be used to connect n nodes. We call a connected graph with n nodes and $n - 1$ edges a **tree**. Examples of trees with four, five, and six nodes are shown in Fig. 2.33.

Fig. 2.33   Examples of trees.

Since $n - 1$ is the fewest number of edges required to connect n nodes, a connected graph having n nodes contains a minimum of $n - 1$ edges. In other words, a connected n-node graph that is not a tree will contain a number of n-node trees called **spanning trees**. Each edge of a spanning tree is called a **branch**.

EXAMPLE 2.13

Consider the four-node connected graph in Fig. 2.31. This graph contains 16 spanning trees. They are shown in Fig. 2.34.

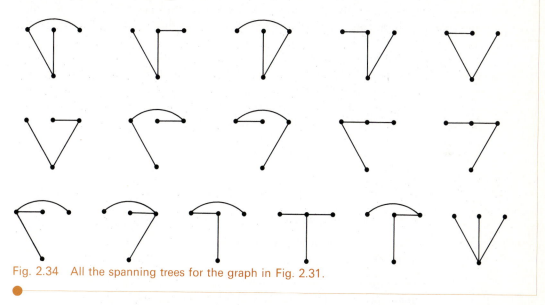

Fig. 2.34   All the spanning trees for the graph in Fig. 2.31.

Given an n-node connected graph, unfortunately there is no simple way of determining the number of spanning trees contained in the graph. Given a graph, let us select some node n_1. Suppose that we start at n_1 and traverse some of the edges of the graph such that we finish at n_1. If we do not traverse any edge more than once and if we do not encounter any node except n_1 more than once and n_1 exactly twice, then the resulting set of edges traversed is called a **loop**.

EXAMPLE 2.14

For the graph given in Fig. 2.31, the set of edges e_1, e_2, e_3 forms a loop, as does the set e_3, e_5, e_6. Actually, all the loops of this graph are depicted in Fig. 2.35.

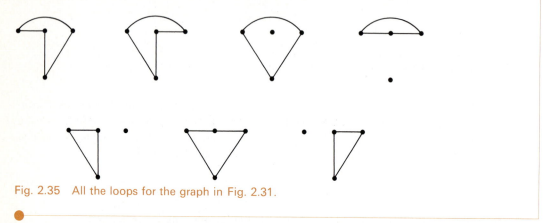

Fig. 2.35   All the loops for the graph in Fig. 2.31.

Given a graph, unfortunately there is no simple way of determining the number of loops contained in the graph. Note that a tree cannot contain any loops, since any edge in a loop can be removed without disconnecting the nodes connected by that loop.

In our previous discussion of mesh analysis, we placed a mesh current in each window or mesh of a planar circuit. However, we could not extend this idea to nonplanar circuits for it is not apparent where to place the appropriate mesh currents in such cases. Loop analysis, though, tells us how to select appropriate loop currents for nonplanar, as well as planar, circuits. The technique is now outlined.

LOOP ANALYSIS

1. **Given a (connected) circuit, form the corresponding graph of the circuit.**

2. **For the resulting (connected) graph, select any spanning tree.**

3. **Choose any edge not in the spanning tree—that is, any edge that is not a branch.**

4. **Determine the unique loop that consists of the edge chosen in step 3 and appropriate tree branches. This is called a *fundamental loop*.**

5. **Repeat this process until all of the edges not in the spanning tree have been chosen in step 3.**

6. **Establish clockwise loop currents in the given circuit that correspond to the fundamental loops determined above. Then proceed as for mesh analysis.**

Following these steps, for each edge not in the selected spanning tree, we get a unique loop. If the graph has n nodes and e edges, since there are $n-1$ branches in a spanning tree, there are $e-(n-1)=e-n+1$ edges not in the tree. Hence, for loop analysis, we write $e-n+1$ loop equations.[†]

EXAMPLE 2.15
Suppose that the corresponding graph of a circuit is the graph shown in Fig. 2.31. Furthermore, suppose that the spanning tree selected is the one indicated by the edges in color (e_2, e_3, e_5) in Fig. 2.36.

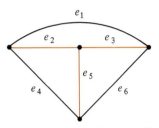

Fig. 2.36   Spanning tree formed by edges e_2, e_3, and e_5.

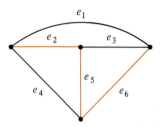

Fig. 2.37   Another tree for the given graph.

Choosing edge e_1 results in the fundamental loop e_1, e_2, e_3, whereas choosing e_4 results in the fundamental loop e_4, e_2, e_5. Finally, choosing e_6 yields e_6, e_3, e_5. Thus, for the tree selected, we obtain the loops that would result by using mesh analysis. Therefore, let us select the tree depicted in Fig. 2.37. Choosing e_1, we get (fundamental) loop e_1, e_2, e_5, e_6: choosing e_3 yields loop e_3, e_5, e_6; and choosing e_4 results in loop e_2, e_4, e_5. Referring to the original circuit (Fig. 2.30) that corresponds to Fig. 2.37, the loop currents resulting from the given tree are shown in Fig. 2.38.

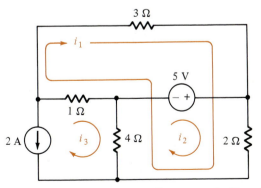

Fig. 2.38   Loops corresponding to tree indicated in Fig. 2.37.

[†] This is the number of mesh equations as well if the circuit is planar.

For loop i_1 (i.e., the loop labeled i_1), by KVL,

$$3i_1 + 2(i_1 + i_2) + 4(i_1 + i_2 - i_3) + 1(i_1 - i_3) = 0$$

from which

$$10i_1 + 6i_2 - 5i_3 = 0 \tag{2.52}$$

For loop i_2, by KVL,

$$2(i_1 + i_2) + 4(i_1 + i_2 - i_3) - 5 = 0$$

from which

$$6i_1 + 6i_2 - 4i_3 = 5 \tag{2.53}$$

However, for loop i_3, by inspection we have that

$$i_3 = -2 \text{ A}$$

Substituting this value into Equations (2.52) and (2.53), we get

$$10i_1 + 6i_2 = -10 \tag{2.54}$$

and

$$6i_1 + 6i_2 = -3 \tag{2.55}$$

respectively. Subtracting Equation (2.55) from Equation (2.54), we get

$$4i_1 = -7 \quad \Rightarrow \quad i_1 = -1.75 \text{ A}$$

Substituting this value into either Equation (2.54) or (2.55), we obtain

$$i_2 = 1.25 \text{ A}$$

This completes the loop analysis of the circuit.

Having determined the indicated loop currents for the circuit, it is now a simple matter to determine either the voltage or the current for any element in the circuit. For example, the voltage v_s across the 2-A source (+ on top), by KVL, is

$$\begin{aligned} v_s &= 1(i_3 - i_1) + 4(i_3 - i_1 - i_2) \\ &= 1(-2 + 1.75) + 4(-2 + 1.75 - 1.25) = -6.25 \text{ V} \end{aligned}$$

The current, directed to the right, through the 5-V source is

$$i_2 = 1.25 \text{ A}$$

The current, directed down, through the 2-Ω resistor is

$$i_1 + i_2 = -1.75 + 1.25 = -0.5 \text{ A}$$

The voltage v_4 across the 4-Ω resistor (+ on top) is

$$v_4 = 4(i_3 - i_1 - i_2) = 4(-2 + 1.75 - 1.25) = -6 \text{ V}$$

By selecting another (spanning) tree for the circuit given in Fig. 2.30, we get an alternative set of loops. In general, a different set of loops will result in different-valued loop currents. Of course, however, the current through and the voltage across each element does not change.

EXAMPLE 2.16

Instead of the tree depicted in Fig. 2.37, let us now select the one indicated in Fig. 2.39.

Choosing e_1 yields the loop e_1, e_4, e_6. Choosing e_2 results in the loop e_2, e_4, e_5, and choosing e_3 gives the loop e_3, e_5, e_6. With respect to the original circuit, the loop currents, therefore, are as shown in Fig. 2.40.

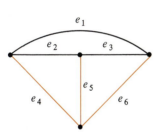

Fig. 2.39 Alternative tree for circuit in Fig. 2.30.

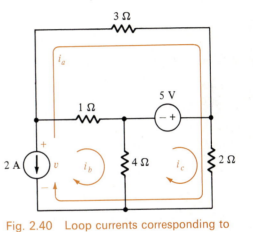

Fig. 2.40 Loop currents corresponding to tree in Fig. 2.39.

For loop i_a, by KVL

$$3i_a + 2(i_a + i_c) - v = 0 \qquad (2.56)$$

In addition, for loop i_b, by KVL

$$v = 1i_b + 4(i_b - i_c) \qquad (2.57)$$

Substituting this expression for v into Equation (2.56), we get

$$3i_a + 2(i_a + i_c) - 1i_b - 4(i_b - i_c) = 0 \qquad (2.58)$$

[Note that Equation (2.58) can be obtained by applying KVL to the loop formed by the 1-Ω, 2-Ω, 3-Ω, and 4-Ω resistors.] Simplifying Equation (2.58), we obtain

$$5i_a - 5i_b + 6i_c = 0 \qquad (2.59)$$

Expressing the value of the current source in terms of loop currents, we have that

$$i_a + i_b = -2 \qquad (2.60)$$

Finally, for loop i_c, by KVL,

$$-5 + 2(i_a + i_c) + 4(i_c - i_b) = 0$$

from which

$$2i_a - 4i_b + 6i_c = 5 \tag{2.61}$$

Writing Equations (2.59), (2.60), and (2.61) in matrix form, we obtain

$$\begin{bmatrix} 5 & -5 & 6 \\ 1 & 1 & 0 \\ 2 & -4 & 6 \end{bmatrix} \begin{bmatrix} i_a \\ i_b \\ i_c \end{bmatrix} = \begin{bmatrix} 0 \\ -2 \\ 5 \end{bmatrix} \tag{2.62}$$

and we see that for loop analysis, as well as mesh analysis, we get a matrix equation of the form $\mathbf{v} = \mathbf{R}\mathbf{i}$. Solving matrix equation (2.62), yields

$$\Delta = 24 \qquad \Delta_a = -42 \qquad \Delta_b = -6 \qquad \Delta_c = 30$$

from which

$$i_a = -1.75 \text{ A} \qquad i_b = -0.25 \text{ A} \qquad i_c = 1.25 \text{ A}$$

The voltage v across the 2-A source is, by KVL,

$$v = 1i_b + 4(i_b - i_c) = 1(-0.25) + 4(-0.25 - 1.25) = -6.25 \text{ V}$$

The current, directed to the right, through the 5-V source is

$$i_c = 1.25 \text{ A}$$

The current, directed down, through the 2-Ω resistor is

$$i_a + i_c = -1.75 + 1.25 = -0.5 \text{ A}$$

The voltage v_4 across the 4-Ω resistor (+ on top) is

$$v_4 = 4(i_b - i_c) = 4(-0.25 - 1.25) = -6 \text{ V}$$

DRILL EXERCISE 2.14

For the circuit shown in Fig. DE2.14, choose the tree which corresponds to 1-Ω, 2-Ω, and 3-Ω resistors. Find the resulting loop currents.
Answer: 2 A; 1 A; -10 A

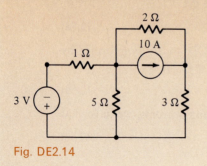

Fig. DE2.14

For certain circuits, two different trees may result in the same set of loop equations. For example, Fig. 2.41(a) shows a graph with a tree designated and the resulting fundamental loops. Figure 2.41(b) shows the same graph with a different tree designated, but the set of fundamental loops is the same.

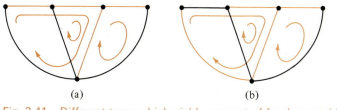

(a)   (b)

Fig. 2.41   Different trees which yield same set of fundamental loops.

For certain circuits, the fundamental loops that result for a particular tree correspond to the set of meshes for the circuit—for example, see Fig. 2.36. Even two different trees can yield the set of meshes for the corresponding circuit, as is demonstrated by Fig. 2.42. However, for some circuits, there exists no tree for which the resulting fundamental loops are the set of meshes. For instance, for the graph shown in Fig. 2.43, no matter what tree is selected, the resulting set of fundamental loops will not be the same as the set of meshes. Therefore, although loop analysis is more general than mesh analysis—more general, since loop analysis can be applied to nonplanar as well as planar circuits—loop analysis is not a generalization or extension of mesh analysis.

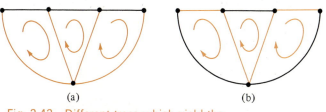
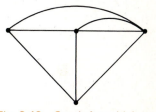

(a)   (b)

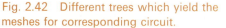

Fig. 2.42   Different trees which yield the meshes for corresponding circuit.

Fig. 2.43   Graph for which no tree yields all the meshes for corresponding circuit.

● **SUMMARY**

1. To use nodal analysis, apply KCL at each nonreference node, express the resulting equations in terms of the node voltages, and solve.

2. A set of node equations can be expressed as a single matrix equation of the form **Gv = i**.

3. To use mesh analysis (on planar circuits), apply KVL around each finite mesh, express the resulting equations in terms of the mesh currents, and solve.

4. A set of mesh equations can be expressed as a single matrix equation of the form **Ri** = **v**.

5. To use loop analysis (on planar or nonplanar circuits) apply KVL around each loop formed from one nonbranch edge and branches, express the resulting equations in terms of the loop currents, and solve.

6. A set of loop equations can be expressed as a single matrix equation of the form **Ri** = **v**.

● PROBLEMS FOR CHAPTER 2

2.1 For the circuit shown in Fig. P2.1, select node a to be the reference node. (a) Use nodal analysis to find the nonreference node voltages. (b) Find i_1, i_2, i_3, and i_4.

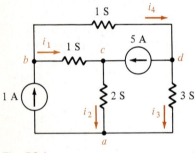

Fig. P2.1

2.2 Repeat Problem 2.1 using node b as the reference node.

2.3 Repeat Problem 2.1 using node c as the reference node.

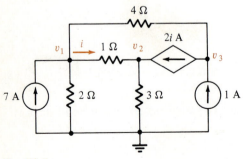

Fig. P2.5

2.4 Repeat Problem 2.1 using node d as the reference node.

2.5 Find the node voltages v_1, v_2, and v_3 for the circuit shown in Fig. P2.5.

2.6 Find the node voltages v_1, v_2, and v_3 for the circuit shown in Fig. P2.6.

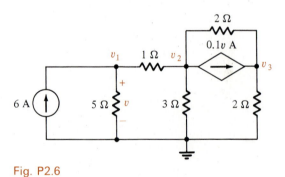

Fig. P2.6

2.7 For the circuit shown in Fig. P2.7, find (a) the node voltages v_1, v_2, v_3, and v_4, (b) i_s, and (c) the conductance $G_{eq} = i_s/v_s$ seen by the voltage source.

2.8 Repeat Problem 2.7 for the circuit shown in Fig. P2.8.

2.9 Find the node voltages v_1, v_2, v_3, and v_4 for the circuit shown in Fig. P2.9.

2.10 Find the node voltages v_1, v_2, v_3, and v_4 for the circuit shown in Fig. P2.10.

2.11 For the circuit shown in Fig. P2.11, find the node voltages v_1, v_2, and v_3.

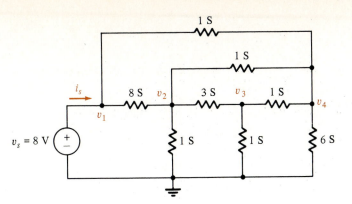

Fig. P2.7

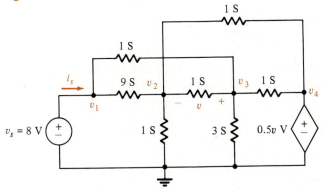

Fig. P2.8

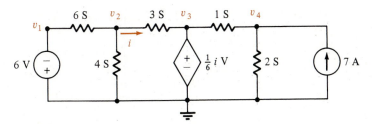

Fig. P2.9

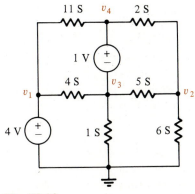

Fig. P2.10

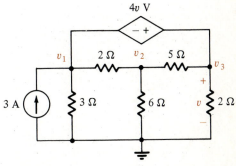

Fig. P2.11

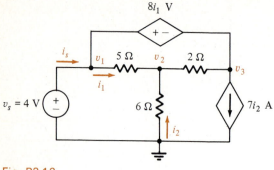

Fig. P2.12

2.12 For the circuit shown in Fig. P2.12, find (a) the node voltages v_1, v_2, v_3, (b) i_s, and (c) the resistance $R_{eq} = v_s/i_s$ seen by the independent voltage source.

2.13 Find the node voltages v_1, v_2, and v_3 for the circuit shown in Fig. P2.13.

2.14 For the circuit shown in Fig. P2.14, find (a) the node voltages v_1, v_2, v_3, (b) v_s, and (c) the resistance $R_{eq} = v_s/i_s$ seen by the independent current source.

2.15 Find the node voltages v_1, v_2, v_3, and v_4 for the circuit shown in Fig. P2.15.

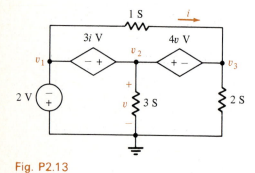

Fig. P2.13

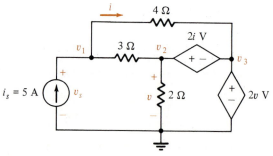

Fig. P2.14

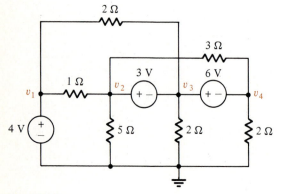

Fig. P2.15

2.16 For the circuit shown in Fig. P2.16, find (a) the node voltages v_1, v_2, v_3, v_4, (b) i_s, and (c) the resistance $R_{eq} = v_s/i_s$ seen by the voltage source.

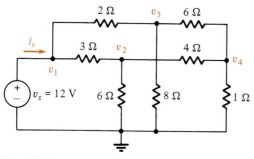

Fig. P2.16

2.17 In the simple transistor amplifier circuit shown in Fig. P2.17 the portion in the colored box is the **hybrid** or **h-parameter model** of a bipolar junction transistor (BJT). Note that h_i is a resistance and h_o is a conductance. Use nodal analysis to find (a) the voltage gain v_2/v_1 and (b) the resistance $R_{eq} = v_1/i_1$.

2.18 The circuit in Fig. P2.18 is a simple BJT amplifier with "feedback." The portion of the circuit in the colored box is an approximate T-model of the transistor. Use nodal analysis to find (a) the voltage gain v_2/v_1 and (b) the resistance $R_{eq} = v_1/i_1$.

2.19 The circuit shown in Fig. P2.19 is a simple BJT amplifier. The portion of the circuit in the colored box is another T-model of a transistor. Use nodal analysis to find (a) the voltage gain v_2/v_1 and (b) the resistance $R_{eq} = v_1/i_e$.

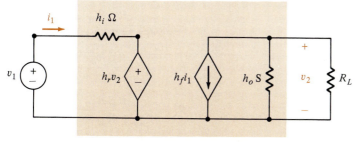

Fig. P2.17

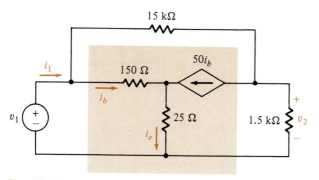

Fig. P2.18

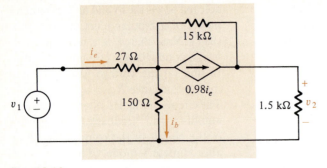

Fig. P2.19

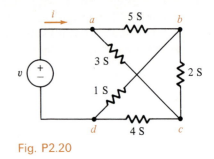

Fig. P2.20

2.20 For the circuit shown in Fig. P2.20, use nodal analysis to determine $G = i/v$.

2.21 Suppose that a circuit contains the colored box shown on the left in Fig. P2.21(a). Without affecting the remainder of the circuit, the box on the left can be replaced by the box on the right provided that

$$G_{AB} = \frac{G_A G_B}{G_A + G_B + G_C}$$

$$G_{AC} = \frac{G_A G_C}{G_A + G_B + G_C}$$

$$G_{BC} = \frac{G_B G_C}{G_A + G_B + G_C}$$

Such a process is called a **Y-Δ(wye-delta) transformation**.

The circuit in Fig. P2.21(b) is identical to the circuit given in Problem 2.20. Use a Y-Δ transformation on the 1-S, 2-S, and 5-S conductances, and then combine elements in series and parallel to determine $G = i/v$.

2.22 With reference to Problem 2.21, the formulas for a **Δ-Y (delta-wye) transformation** are

$$R_A = \frac{R_{AB}R_{AC}}{R_{AB} + R_{AC} + R_{BC}}$$

$$R_B = \frac{R_{AB}R_{BC}}{R_{AB} + R_{AC} + R_{BC}}$$

$$R_C = \frac{R_{AC}R_{BC}}{R_{AB} + R_{AC} + R_{BC}}$$

where $R = 1/G$.

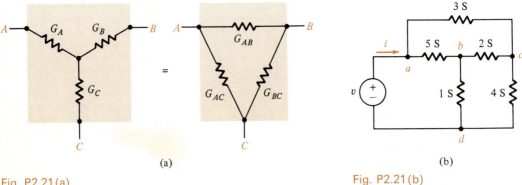

(a)

Fig. P2.21(a)

(b)

Fig. P2.21(b)

The circuit shown in Fig. P2.22 is identical to the circuit given in Problem 2.20. Use a Δ-Y transformation on the 2-S, 3-S, and 5-S conductances, and then combine elements in series and parallel to determine $G = i/v$.

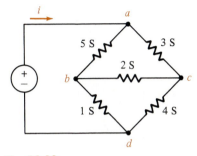

Fig. P2.22

2.23 For the circuit shown in Fig. P2.23, use mesh analysis to find (a) the current, directed down, through the 3-V source, (b) the current, directed to the right, through the 9-V source, and (c) v.

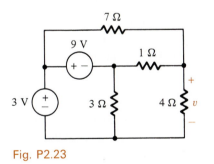

Fig. P2.23

2.24 For the circuit shown in Fig. P2.24, use mesh analysis to find (a) the current, directed to the right, through the 12-V source and (b) the current, directed down, through the 6-V source.

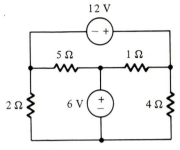

Fig. P2.24

2.25 For the circuit shown in Fig. P2.25, use mesh analysis to find (a) the resistance seen by the voltage source and (b) v.

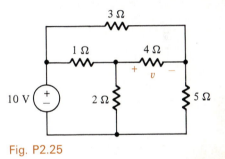

Fig. P2.25

2.26 For the circuit given in Fig. P2.25, change the 5-Ω resistor to 6 Ω and repeat Problem 2.25.

2.27 Use mesh analysis to find the resistance seen by the current source for the circuit shown in Fig. P2.27.

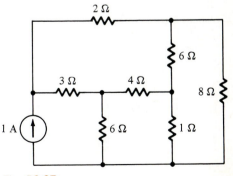

Fig. P2.27

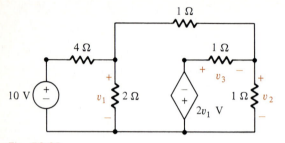

Fig. P2.28

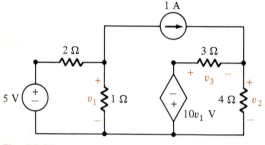

Fig. P2.29

2.28 Use mesh analysis to find v_1, v_2, and v_3 for the circuit shown in Fig. P2.28.

2.29 Repeat Problem 2.28 for the circuit shown in Fig. P2.29.

2.30 Repeat Problem 2.28 for the circuit shown in Fig. P2.6.

2.31 Repeat Problem 2.28 for the circuit shown in Fig. P2.5.

2.32 Find the resistance seen by the 1-A current source for the circuit shown in Fig. P2.32.

2.33 For the circuit given in Fig. P2.32, change the 5-Ω resistor to 3 Ω and repeat Problem 2.32.

2.34 Find the resistance seen by the 1-V voltage source for the circuit shown in Fig. P2.34.

2.35 For the circuit given in Fig. P2.34, change the 10-Ω resistor to 8 Ω and repeat Problem 2.34.

2.36 The simple transistor amplifier in Fig. P2.36 incorporates an alternative *h*-parameter model of a transistor. Use mesh analysis to find (a) the voltage gain v_2/v_1 and (b) the resistance $R_{eq} = v_1/i_1$.

2.37 For the transistor amplifier circuit in Fig. P2.37, use mesh analysis to find (a) the voltage gain v_2/v_1 and (b) the resistance $R_{eq} = v_1/i_e$.

2.38 For the transistor amplifier circuit shown in Fig. P2.38, use mesh analysis to find (a) the voltage gain v_2/v_1 and (b) the resistance $R_{eq} = v_1/i_b$.

2.39 For the circuit shown in Fig. P2.39, find the loop currents for the tree corresponding to the 1-Ω, 2-Ω, 3-Ω, and 4-Ω resistors. Determine the resistance seen by the 3-V source.

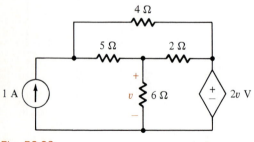

Fig. P2.32

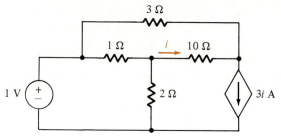

Fig. P2.34

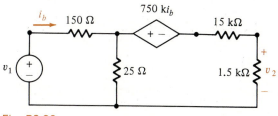

Fig. P2.36

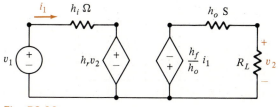

Fig. P2.37

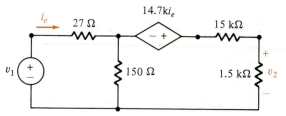

Fig. P2.38

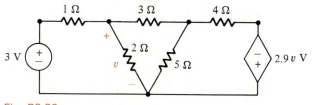

Fig. P2.39

2.40 Repeat Problem 2.39 for the tree corresponding to the 1-Ω, 3-Ω, 4-Ω resistors, and the 3-V source.

2.41 For the circuit shown in Fig. P2.32, find the loop currents for the tree corresponding to the 4-Ω, 5-Ω, and 6-Ω resistors. Determine the resistance seen by the 1-A source.

2.42 Repeat Problem 2.41 for the tree corresponding to the 5-Ω resistor and the two sources.

2.43 For the circuit shown in Fig. P2.28, find the loop currents for the tree corresponding to the 4-Ω and three 1-Ω resistors.

2.44 For the circuit shown in Fig. P2.27, find the loop currents for the tree corre-

sponding to the 2-Ω, 3-Ω, and two 6-Ω resistors. Determine the resistance seen by the 1-A source.

2.45 For the circuit shown in Fig. P2.45, find the loop currents for the tree corresponding to the 1-Ω, 2-Ω, and 3-Ω resistors.

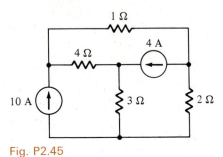

Fig. P2.45

Important Circuit Concepts

● INTRODUCTION

An increasingly important circuit element is the operational amplifier. Because of the evolution of integrated-circuit (IC) technology, the operational amplifier (or op amp) is both small in size and inexpensive. Its versatility and usefulness have made it extremely popular. In this chapter, we study the operational amplifier from the point of view of an ideal circuit element, and a number of applications are presented.

   Up to this point we have assumed that all the elements under consideration were ideal. Although nothing is ideal, including voltage and current sources, a combination of ideal elements may accurately describe the behavior of an actual source. The subject of nonideal sources will be discussed in this chapter. Included are the conditions for which a nonideal voltage source and a nonideal current source are equivalent.

   A very important circuit concept is Thévenin's theorem. This result says, in essence, that an arbitrary circuit behaves as an appropriately valued voltage source in series with an appropriately valued resistance to the outside world. A major consequence of this fact is the determination of the maximum power that can be delivered to a load and the condition for which this occurs.

   When a circuit contains more than one independent source, a response (a voltage or a current) of the circuit can be obtained by finding the response to each individual independent source, and then summing these individual responses. This notion, known as the **principle of superposition**, is another important circuit concept that is frequently used.

Although in this chapter we consider **resistive circuits**—that is, circuits that contain only resistors and sources (both independent and dependent)—we will see later that the same techniques are applicable to networks that contain other types of elements as well.

3.1 THE OPERATIONAL AMPLIFIER

Of fundamental importance in the study of electric circuits is the **ideal voltage amplifier**. Such a device, in general, has two inputs, v_1 and v_2, and one output, v_o. The relationship between the output and the inputs is given by $v_o = A(v_2 - v_1)$, where A is called the **gain** of the amplifier. The ideal amplifier is modeled by the circuit shown in Fig. 3.1(a), which contains a dependent voltage source. Note that since the input resistance $R = \infty$, when such an amplifier is connected to any circuit, no current will go into the input terminals. Also, since the output v_o is the voltage across an ideal source, we have that $v_o = A(v_2 - v_1)$ regardless of what is connected to the output. For the sake of simplicity, the ideal amplifier having gain A is often represented as shown in Fig. 3.1(b). (Note that the reference node is not explicitly displayed in this figure.) We refer to the input terminal labeled "$-$" as the **inverting input** and the input terminal labeled "$+$" as the **noninverting input**.

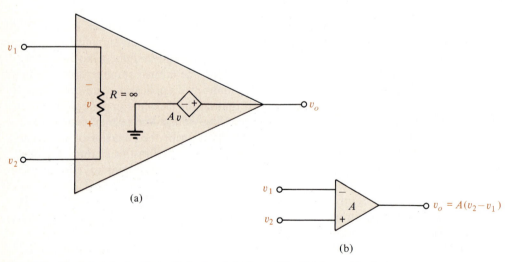

Fig. 3.1   Model and circuit symbol of an ideal amplifier having gain A.

For the circuit given in Fig. 3.2(a) the noninverting input is at the reference potential, that is, $v_2 = 0$ V. Furthermore, since node v_s and node v_o are constrained by voltage sources (independent and dependent, respectively), in using nodal analysis we need only sum currents at node v_1. Since the amplifier inputs draw no current,

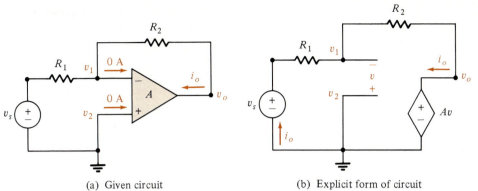

(a) Given circuit   (b) Explicit form of circuit

Fig. 3.2. Ideal-amplifier circuit.

by KCL at the inverting input,

$$\frac{v_1 - v_s}{R_1} + \frac{v_1 - v_o}{R_2} = 0$$

from which

$$-R_2 v_s + R_2 v_1 - R_1 v_o + R_1 v_1 = 0$$

or

$$R_2 v_s = (R_1 + R_2)v_1 - R_1 v_o \tag{3.1}$$

But, due to the amplifier, $v_o = A(v_2 - v_1) = -Av_1$, so

$$v_1 = -\frac{v_o}{A} \tag{3.2}$$

and substituting this into Equation (3.1), we get

$$R_2 v_s = (R_1 + R_2)(-v_o/A) - R_1 v_o = -[(1/A)(R_1 + R_2) + R_1]v_o$$

Thus,

$$v_o = \frac{-R_2}{R_1 + (1/A)(R_1 + R_2)} v_s \tag{3.3}$$

For the case that $A = 200,000$, $R_1 = 1\,\text{k}\Omega$, and $R_2 = 10\,\text{k}\Omega$, from Equation (3.3) we get

$$v_o = \frac{-10 \times 10^3}{1 \times 10^3 + (1/[2 \times 10^5])(1 \times 10^3 + 10 \times 10^3)} v_s = -10.0 v_s$$

Therefore, the amplifier-circuit gain (that is, the gain of the amplifier circuit as opposed to the gain of the ideal amplifier itself) is

$$\frac{v_o}{v_s} = -10.0$$

When $v_s = 1$ V, then $v_o = -10.0$ V. Furthermore, from Equation (3.2),

$$v_1 = -\frac{v_o}{A} = \frac{10.0}{2 \times 10^5} = 5.0 \times 10^{-5} \text{ V}$$

so

$$i_o = \frac{v_1 - v_o}{10 \times 10^3} = \frac{5.0 \times 10^5 + 10.0}{10 \times 10^3} = 1.0 \times 10^{-3} = 1.0 \text{ mA}$$

Since $i_o = 1$ mA, then a current of 1 mA goes into the output terminal of the amplifier. Since the input terminals draw no current, the circuit in Fig. 3.2(a) appears to violate KCL—it seems that 1 mA is going in and nothing is coming out! The apparent discrepancy is due to the fact that the circuit in Fig. 3.2(a) uses the amplifier circuit symbol shown in Fig. 3.1(b). Although this is a convenient way to represent an ideal amplifier, it should be remembered that Fig. 3.1(a) is the actual model of the amplifier. By using this model, we get the circuit shown in Fig. 3.2(b), so we see explicitly that the current i_o which goes into the output terminal of the amplifier passes through the dependent voltage source and then goes through the independent voltage source followed by resistors R_1 and R_2—so KCL is not violated.

Since the inputs of an ideal amplifier draw no current, then the power absorbed by the ideal amplifier is the power absorbed by the dependent voltage source. Specifically, for the numbers above, the power absorbed by the ideal amplifier is

$$p_a = v_o i_o = (-10.0)(1.0 \times 10^{-3}) = -10.0 \text{ mW}$$

In other words, the ideal amplifier supplies 10.0 mW of power.

The power absorbed by the voltage source $v_s = 1$ V is

$$p_s = v_s(-i_o) = 1(-1.0 \times 10^{-3}) = -1.0 \text{ mW}$$

so the voltage source also supplies power, in particular, 1.0 mW.

The power absorbed by the resistor $R_1 = 1$ kΩ is

$$p_1 = R_1 i_o^2 = (1 \times 10^3)(1.0 \times 10^{-3})^2 = 1.0 \times 10^{-3} = 1.0 \text{ mW}$$

and the power absorbed by the resistor $R_2 = 10$ kΩ is

$$p_2 = R_2 i_o^2 = (10 \times 10^{-3})(1.0 \times 10^{-3})^2 = 10.0 \text{ mW}$$

DRILL EXERCISE 3.1

For the ideal amplifier circuit shown in Fig. DE3.1, suppose that $A = 200{,}000$, $R_1 = 1$ kΩ, $R_2 = 9$ kΩ, and $v_s = 1$ V. Find (a) v_o, (b) v_1, and (c) the power absorbed by the ideal amplifier, the 1-V voltage source, the 1-kΩ resistor, and the 9-kΩ resistor.

Answer:　(a) 10.0 V; (b) 1.0 V; (c) -10.0 mW, 0 W, 1.0 mW, 9.0 mW

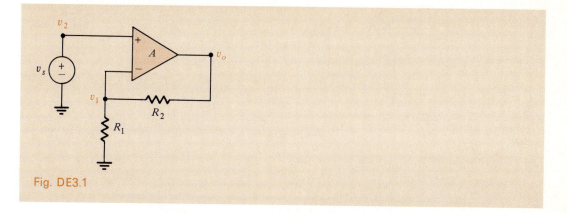

Fig. DE3.1

For a circuit such as that in Fig. 3.2, let us consider the case that the gain A becomes arbitrarily large. We can rewrite Equation (3.3) as

$$v_o = \frac{-R_2/R_1}{1 + (1/A)(1 + R_2/R_1)} \, v_s$$

Therefore, when $A \to \infty$, in the limit

$$v_o = -\frac{R_2}{R_1} v_s$$

We see that although the gain of the amplifier is infinite, for a finite input voltage v_s, the output voltage v_o is finite (provided, of course, that $R_1 \neq 0$). Inspection of Equation (3.2) indicates why the output voltage remains finite—as $A \to \infty$, then $v_1 = -v_o/A \to 0$. This result occurs because there is a resistor connected between the output and the inverting input. Such a connection is called **negative feedback**.

For the circuit shown in Fig. 3.2, we have just seen that when the gain A of the ideal amplifier is infinite, then the potential at the inverting input is 0 V—the reference potential. Although the inverting input of the amplifier has the same potential as the reference, this input is not directly connected to the reference. (It is the noninverting input that is connected directly to the reference.) Because the reference of a circuit is commonly referred to as "ground," we say that the inverting input is a **virtual ground**. As a consequence, $v_1 = 0$ V.

An ideal amplifer having gain $A = \infty$ is known as an **operational amplifier**, or **op amp**. In an op-amp circuit, because of the infinite gain property, we must have a feedback resistor and must not connect a voltage source directly between the amplifier's input terminals. For the circuit given in Fig. 3.2, the corresponding op-amp circuit is usually drawn as shown in Fig. 3.3. Using the (virtual ground) fact that $v_1 = 0$ V, by KCL at node v_1, we have that

$$-\frac{v_s}{R_1} - \frac{v_o}{R_2} = 0 \quad \Rightarrow \quad v_o = -\frac{R_2}{R_1} v_s$$

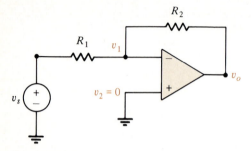

Fig. 3.3   Op-amp circuit—an inverting amplifier.

and the gain of the overall circuit is

$$\frac{v_o}{v_s} = -\frac{R_2}{R_1}$$

This circuit is called an **inverting amplifier**.

Notice how simple the analysis of the op-amp circuit in Fig. 3.3 is when we use the fact that $v_1 = 0$ V. Although this result was originally deduced from Equation (3.3), the combination of infinite gain and negative feedback constrains the voltage between the inputs of the op-amp (between terminals v_1 and v_2) to be zero. In other words, we must have that $v_1 = v_2$.

EXAMPLE 3.1

Consider the op-amp circuit with feedback in Fig. 3.4. Again, the inputs of the op amp draw no current, and so in applying KCL at node v_1, we have

$$\frac{v_1}{R_1} + \frac{v_1 - v_o}{R_2} = 0$$

Since the input voltage to the op amp is zero, or equivalently, since both input

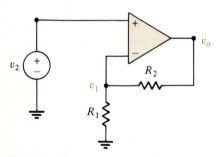

Fig. 3.4   Noninverting amplifier.

terminals must be at the same potential, then $v_1 = v_2$, and by KCL,

$$\frac{v_2}{R_1} + \frac{v_2 - v_o}{R_2} = 0$$

from which

$$R_2 v_2 + R_1 v_2 - R_1 v_o = 0 \qquad \Rightarrow \qquad (R_1 + R_2) v_2 = R_1 v_o$$

Hence,

$$v_o = \frac{R_1 + R_2}{R_1} v_2 = \left(1 + \frac{R_2}{R_1}\right) v_2$$

The overall gain of this circuit is therefore

$$\frac{v_o}{v_2} = \frac{R_1 + R_2}{R_1} = 1 + \frac{R_2}{R_1}$$

This circuit is called a **noninverting amplifier**.

Since the inverting input of the op amp draws no current, we can apply the voltage-divider formula to resistors R_1 and R_2. Specifically, by voltage division,

$$v_1 = \frac{R_1}{R_1 + R_2} v_o \qquad \Rightarrow \qquad \frac{v_o}{v_1} = \frac{R_1 + R_2}{R_1} = 1 + \frac{R_2}{R_1}$$

as was obtained above.

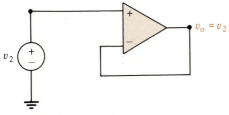

Fig. 3.5   Voltage follower.

Note that if $R_2 = 0$, then $v_o = v_2$. Under this circumstance, R_1 is superfluous and may be removed. The resulting op-amp circuit shown in Fig. 3.5 is known as a **voltage follower**. This configuration is used to isolate or buffer one circuit from another.

●

DRILL EXERCISE 3.2

For the op-amp circuit shown in Fig. DE3.2, find (a) v_o and (b) the power absorbed by the op amp.

Answer: (a) -2.1 V; (b) -0.63 mW

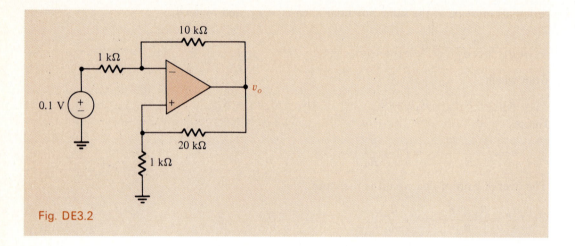

Fig. DE3.2

Opertional-amplifier circuits can be quite useful in some situations in which there is more than a single input.

EXAMPLE 3.2

For the op-amp circuit shown in Fig. 3.6, since $v_2 = 0$ V, then $v_1 = 0$ V. Thus, by KCL at the inverting input of the op amp (i.e., at node v_1),

$$-\frac{v_a}{R_1} - \frac{v_b}{R_1} - \frac{v_o}{R_2} = 0 \quad \Rightarrow \quad v_o = -\frac{R_2}{R_1}(v_a + v_b)$$

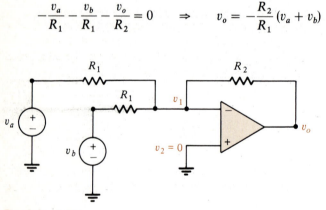

Fig. 3.6   Adder.

Since the output v_o is the sum of the voltages v_a and v_b (multiplied by the constant $-R_2/R_1$), this circuit is called an **adder** (or **summer**). A common application of such a circuit is as an "audio mixer," where, for example, the inputs are voltages attributable to two separate microphones and the output voltage is their sum.

DRILL EXERCISE 3.3

Find v_o for the **difference-amplifier** circuit shown in Fig. DE3.3 when $R_3 = R_1$ and $R_4 = R_2$.

Answer: $\dfrac{R_2}{R_1}(v_b - v_a)$

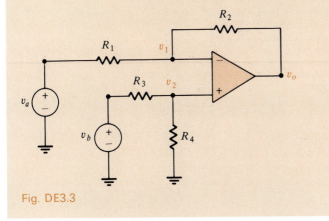

Fig. DE3.3

Analyzing circuits containing two op amps is not much more complicated than analyzing a circuit with a single op amp. As was done for the preceding op-amp circuits, the analytical procedure that is used is nodal analysis. Since a dependent source is connected between an op amp's output and the reference, when employing nodal analysis, we do not apply KCL at the output of an op amp. (After the nodal analysis is done, KCL is used to determine the current coming out of or going into the output terminal of the op amp—if this quantity is to be determined.) Instead, we apply KCL at the appropriate input terminals of op amps and at other nodes of the circuit (if required).

EXAMPLE 3.3

Consider the circuit shown in Fig. 3.7, which contains two operational amplifiers. Let us determine v_o in terms of the conductances G, G_1, G_2, G_3, G_4, and the applied voltage v_s.

By KCL at the inverting input of the op amp on the left we get

$$G_1 v_s + G_4 v_o = -Gv$$

and, by KCL at the inverting input of the other op amp,

$$G_2 v_s + G_3 v_o = -Gv$$

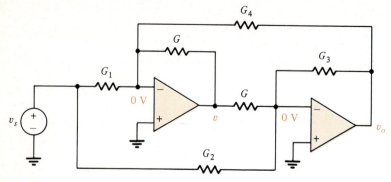

Fig. 3.7   Circuit with two op amps.

Combining these two equations, we get

$$G_1 v_s + G_4 v_o = G_2 v_s + G_3 v_o \qquad \Rightarrow \qquad (G_1 - G_2) v_s = (G_3 - G_4) v_o$$

from which

$$v_o = \frac{G_1 - G_2}{G_3 - G_4} v_s$$

DRILL EXERCISE 3.4

For the op-amp circuit shown in Fig. DE3.4, suppose that $G_1 = 1$ S, $G_2 = 2$ S, $G_3 = 3$ S, $G_4 = 4$ S, and $G_5 = 5$ S. Find v_o in terms of v_s.

Answer: $-0.75 v_s$

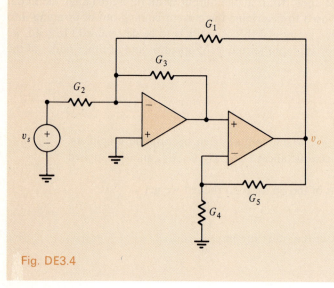

Fig. DE3.4

For a physical operational amplifier, the gain and the input resistance are large, but not infinite. A more practical model of an actual op amp is to have a resistance R_o (called the **output resistance**) in series with the dependent voltage source. Yet, assuming that an op amp is ideal often yields a simple analysis with very accurate results.

Although its usefulness is great, the physical size of an op amp typically is small. This is a result of the fact that op amps are commonly available on IC chips, which normally contain between one and four of them. In our discussions above, we depicted the op amp as a three-terminal device. In actuality, a package containing one or more op amps typically has between 8 and 14 terminals. As we have seen, three of the terminals are the inverting input, the noninverting input, and the output. However, there are also terminals for applying dc voltages (power supplies) to "bias" the numerous transistors comprising an op amp, for frequency compensation, and for other reasons discussed in electronics courses. One of the important practical electronic considerations for proper op-amp operation is that when there is feedback between the output and only one input terminal, the input terminal should be the inverting input.

EXAMPLE 3.4

Shown in Fig. 3.8 is a simple practical amplifier that uses the popular 741 op amp. For this circuit, terminal (pin) 4 is the inverting input, terminal 5 is the noninverting input, and terminal 10 is the output. Furthermore, pin 6 has a voltage of -15 V applied to it and pin 11 a voltage of $+15$ V. The 741 op amp typically has a gain of $A = 200{,}000$, an input resistance of $R = 2$ MΩ, and an output resistance of $R_o = 75$ Ω.

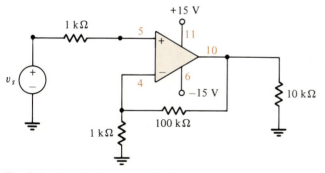

Fig. 3.8   Practical op-amp circuit.

Suppose that v_j is the voltage at terminal j, where $j = 1, 2, 3, \ldots$. Assuming that the op amp is ideal, then $v_5 = v_s$, since the (ideal) op amp inputs draw no current. Also, due to feedback, $v_4 = v_5 = v_s$, and by KCL at terminal 4,

$$\frac{v_s - v_{10}}{100{,}000} + \frac{v_s}{1000} = 0 \quad \Rightarrow \quad v_{10} = 101 v_s$$

We can get a more accurate result by not assuming that the op amp is ideal. To do this, which requires a much greater analysis effort (try it and see), yields

$$v_{10} \approx 100 v_s$$

which is not significantly different from the simple approach taken above.

3.2 NONIDEAL SOURCES

We know that an ideal voltage source is capable of supplying any amount of current. The amount supplied depends on what is connected to the voltage source. However, actual physical voltage sources do not have this capability in that there is a limit as to the amount of current they can supply. A more practical representation of a real voltage source is shown in Fig. 3.9. That is, an actual voltage source *behaves* more as an ideal voltage source v_s in series with a resistance R_s than just as an ideal source. Do not in any way infer that a practical voltage source is constructed from an ideal source and a resistor. (Practical sources may be constructed from transistors, resistors, capacitors, diodes, and so on.) It is simply that the behavior of certain practical sources may be better described or modeled by an ideal voltage source in series with a resistor.

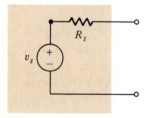

Fig. 3.9   Nonideal voltage-source model.

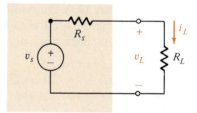

Fig. 3.10   Load resistor connected to nonideal voltage source.

Suppose that we connect some resistor R_L, called a **load resistor**, to the nonideal source shown in Fig. 3.9. The result is shown in Fig. 3.10. We see that, by Ohm's law,

$$i_L = \frac{v_s}{R_s + R_L}$$

and, by voltage division,

$$v_L = \frac{R_L v_s}{R_s + R_L}$$

Thus, we find that the current and the voltage reaching the load is affected by the resistance R_s—called the **internal resistance** or the **source resistance** of the (nonideal) voltage source. Furthermore, the amount of load current and load voltage is less than would be the case if R_s were equal to zero, assuming of course that R_s is nonnegative.

If we extend the preceding discussion of voltage sources to the case of current sources, we would deduce that a more realistic representation of a practical current source is as shown in Fig. 3.11. In this case, the internal resistance of the source is labeled R_g. For a practical voltage source, the closer the internal resistance is to zero, the closer the source is to being ideal. However, for a practical current source, the larger R_g is, the closer the source is to being ideal.

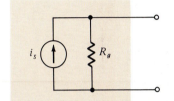

Fig. 3.11   Nonideal current-source model.

We may now ask whether or not a voltage source and a current source can exhibit the same behavior. For the case of an ideal voltage source and an ideal current source, due to their definitions, the answer is no. However, this is not the case for nonideal voltage and current sources. To see this, let us indicate precisely what we mean by the phrase "exhibit the same behavior."

Suppose that two sources are connected to the same circuit—called a **load**. If the effect on that load is the same, then the two sources are said to be equivalent with respect to that given load. If two sources are equivalent with respect to all possible loads, then they are said to be **equivalent**.

With this definition of equivalence, let us consider the two circuits shown in Fig. 3.12. Assuming that the nonideal voltage source and the nonideal current source are equivalent, they will produce the same voltage v across the load and, hence, the same current i. For Fig 3.12(a), by KVL

$$v = -R_s i + v_s \tag{3.4}$$

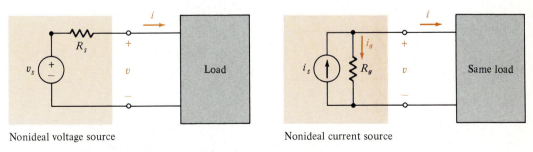

Nonideal voltage source   Nonideal current source

(a)   (b)

Fig. 3.12   Equivalent nonideal voltage and current sources.

For Fig. 3.12(b),

$$v = R_g i_s = R_g(i_s - i)$$

or

$$v = -R_g i + R_g i_s \qquad (3.5)$$

The conditions for Equations (3.4) and (3.5) to be the same are

$$v_s = R_g i_s \quad \text{or} \quad i_s = \frac{v_s}{R_g} \qquad \text{and} \qquad R_s = R_g$$

Thus, these two conditions will result in the nonideal voltage source and the nonideal current source having the same effect on any arbitrary load. (If you're not convinced of this, assume that the load is the resistor R_L, and calculate the resulting load current or voltage given that $R_s = R_g$ and $v_s = R_g i_s$.) To summarize, the sources shown in Fig. 3.13 are equivalent. Alternatively, we have the equivalence shown in Fig. 3.14.

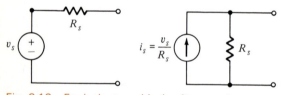

Fig. 3.13   Equivalent nonideal voltage and current sources.

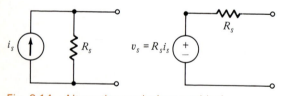

Fig. 3.14   Alternative equivalent nonideal current and voltage sources.

Source Transformations

For a given circuit, replacing a (nonideal) source by an equivalent (nonideal) source, as depicted in Fig. 3.13 or Fig. 3.14, is known as a **source transformation**. Performing a source transformation will not change the operation of the remainder of the circuit.

EXAMPLE 3.5

Let us use source transformations to determine the voltage v between nodes a and b for the circuit shown in Fig. 3.15.

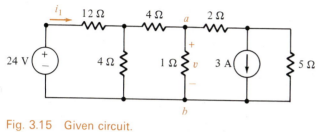

Fig. 3.15   Given circuit.

Performing a source transformation on the 24-V voltage source in series with the 12-Ω resistance, we get a $\frac{24}{12} = 2$-A current source in parallel with a 12-Ω resistance. Furthermore, performing a source transformation on the 3-A current source in parallel with the 5-Ω resistance, we obtain a $5(3) = 15$-V voltage source in series with a 5-Ω resistance. The resulting circuit is shown in Fig. 3.16.

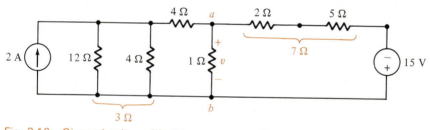

Fig. 3.16   Given circuit modified by source transformations.

For the modified circuit in Fig. 3.16, the 12-Ω and 4-Ω resistances, which are connected in parallel, can be replaced with a 3-Ω resistance. The parallel combination of this 3-Ω resistance and the 2-A current source can be transformed into a $3(2) = 6$-V voltage source in series with a 3-Ω resistance. Furthermore, the 2-Ω and 5-Ω resistances, which are connected in series, can be replaced with a 7-Ω resistance. The series connection of this 7-Ω resistance and the 15-V voltage source can be transformed into a $\frac{15}{7}$-A current source in parallel with a 7-Ω resistance. The resulting circuit is shown in Fig. 3.17.

For the additionally modified circuit in Fig. 3.17, the 3-Ω and 4-Ω resistances, which are connected in series, can be replaced with a 7-Ω resistance. The series combination of this 7-Ω resistance and the 6-V voltage source can be transformed into a $\frac{6}{7}$-A current source in parallel with a 7-Ω resistance. The resulting circuit is shown

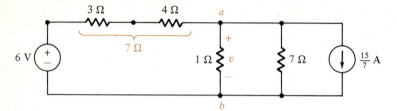

Fig. 3.17   Circuit after additional modifications.

in Fig. 3.18. Since the current sources are connected in parallel, they can be combined into a single current source. (Why?) In addition, the two 7-Ω resistances can be combined into a single $\frac{7}{2}$-Ω resistance. The circuit that results is shown in Fig. 3.19.

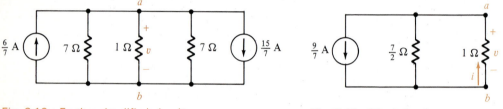

Fig. 3.18   Further simplified circuit.

Fig. 3.19   Final circuit.

With an additional source transformation, we can replace the $\frac{9}{7}$-A current source in parallel with the $\frac{7}{2}$-Ω resistance with a $(\frac{7}{2})(\frac{9}{7}) = \frac{9}{2}$-V voltage source in series with a $\frac{7}{2}$-Ω resistance. However, this transformation is not necessary, since for the circuit shown in Fig. 3.19 it is immediately evident by current division that

$$i = \frac{7/2}{7/2 + 1}\left(\frac{9}{7}\right) = \frac{7/2}{9/2}\left(\frac{9}{7}\right) = 1 \text{ A}$$

and by Ohm's law,

$$v = -1i = -1 \text{ V}$$

Note that when a source transformation is performed, a variable (or variables) may disappear. For instance, in the original circuit, i_1 is the current through the series 12-Ω resistor; note, however, that after the first transformation, this is not necessarily the same as the current through the parallel 12-Ω resistor. Although a source transformation does not change the behavior of the remainder of the circuit, whatever was transformed is, needless to say, no longer the same.

DRILL EXERCISE 3.5

Use source transformations to reduce the circuit shown in Fig. DE3.5. Find v from this simplified circuit.

Answer: -2 V

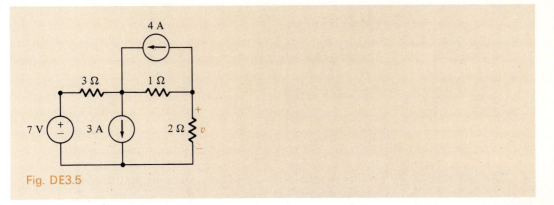

Fig. DE3.5

Not only can source transformations be used for independent sources, they can be used for dependent sources as well. Care must be taken, however, to keep the dependent variable intact. Specifically, the dependent voltage source in series with the resistance R_s shown in Fig. 3.20(a) can be transformed into the dependent current source in parallel with R_s as depicted in Fig. 3.20(b). Here, K_s is a constant, and f is either a voltage variable or a current variable. Alternatively, the dependent current source in parallel with the resistance R_p shown in Fig. 3.21(a) can be transformed into the dependent voltage source in series with R_p as depicted in Fig. 3.21(b). Here, K_p is a constant, and g is either a voltage variable or a current variable.

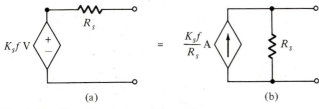

(a)   (b)

Fig. 3.20   Transformation of dependent source.

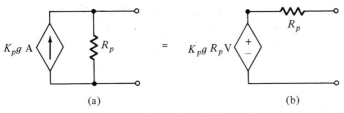

(a)   (b)

Fig. 3.21   Alternative transformation of dependent source.

EXAMPLE 3.6

The circuit shown in Fig. 3.22 was analyzed previously via nodal analysis (see Problem 2.28). Let us use source transformations to determine the current i and the voltages v_1 and v_2.

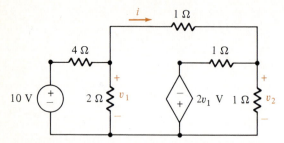

Fig. 3.22   Circuit with independent and dependent sources.

Transforming the 10-V source in series with the 4-Ω resistance, we get a current source of value $\frac{10}{4} = \frac{5}{2}$ A in parallel with a 4-Ω resistance. Transforming the $2v_1$-V dependent voltage source in series with a 1-Ω resistance, we get a dependent current source of value $2v_1/1 = 2v_1$ A in parallel with a 1-Ω resistance. The resulting circuit is shown in Fig. 3.23.

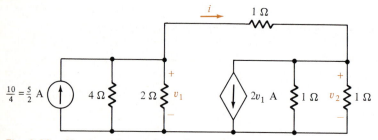

Fig. 3.23   Circuit with transformed sources.

Combining the 2-Ω and 4-Ω resistances, which are connected in parallel, we obtain a $(2)(4)/(2 + 4) = \frac{4}{3}$-$\Omega$ resistance. Furthermore, the parallel connection of the two 1-Ω resistances can be replaced by a $\frac{1}{2}$-Ω resistance. Performing additional source transformations, we get the single-loop circuit shown in Fig. 3.24.

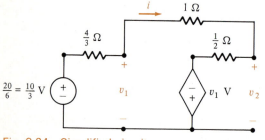

Fig. 3.24   Simplified circuit.

For this circuit, by KVL,

$$\frac{4}{3}i + 1i + \frac{1}{2}i - v_1 - \frac{10}{3} = 0 \qquad (3.6)$$

Substituting the fact that

$$v_1 = -\tfrac{4}{3}i + \tfrac{10}{3}$$

(3.7)

into Equation (3.6), we get that

$$i = \tfrac{8}{5}\,\text{A}$$

Substituting this value into Equation (3.7) yields

$$v_1 = -\tfrac{4}{3}(\tfrac{8}{5}) + \tfrac{10}{3} = -\tfrac{32}{15} + \tfrac{50}{15} = \tfrac{6}{5} = 1.2\,\text{V}$$

Furthermore, by KVL,

$$v_2 = \tfrac{1}{2}i - v_1 = \tfrac{1}{2}i - (-\tfrac{4}{3}i + \tfrac{10}{3}) = \tfrac{11}{6}i - \tfrac{10}{3} = \tfrac{11}{6}(\tfrac{8}{5}) - \tfrac{10}{3} = -\tfrac{2}{5} = -0.4\,\text{V}$$

DRILL EXERCISE 3.6

Use source transformations on the circuit shown in Fig. DE3.6 to obtain a circuit consisting of a single loop, and use this single-loop circuit to determine v.
Answer: 6 V

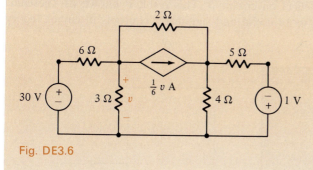

Fig. DE3.6

3.3 THÉVENIN'S THEOREM

Suppose that a load resistor R_L is connected to an arbitrary (in the sense that it contains only elements discussed previously) circuit as shown in Fig. 3.25. What value of the load R_L will absorb the maximum amount of power? Knowing the particular circuit, we can use nodal or mesh analysis to obtain an expression for the power absorbed by R_L, then take the derivative of this expression to determine what value of R_L results in maximum power. The effort required for such an approach can be quite great. Fortunately, though, a remarkable and important circuit theory concept states that as far as R_L is concerned, the arbitrary circuit shown in Fig. 3.25 behaves as though it is a single independent voltage source in series with a single resistance. Once we determine the values of this source and this resistance, we simply apply the results on maximum power transfer, which follows shortly, to find the appropriate value of R_L and the resulting maximum power.

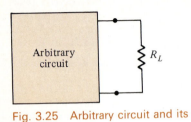

Fig. 3.25 Arbitrary circuit and its associated load.

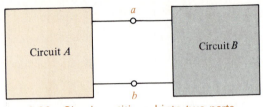

Fig. 3.26 Circuit partitioned into two parts.

Suppose we are given an arbitrary circuit containing any or all of the following elements: resistors, voltage sources, current sources. (The sources can be dependent as well as independent.) Let us identify a pair of nodes, say node a and node b, such that the circuit can be partitioned into two parts as shown in Fig. 3.26. Furthermore, suppose that circuit A contains no dependent source that is dependent on a variable in circuit B, and vice versa. Then we can replace circuit A by an appropriate independent voltage source, call it v_{oc}, in series with an appropriate resistance, call it R_o, and the effect on circuit B is the same as that produced by circuit A. This voltage source and resistance series combination is called the **Thévenin equivalent** of circuit A. In other words, circuit A in Fig. 3.26 and the circuit in the colored box in Fig. 3.27 have the same effect on circuit B. This result is known as **Thévenin's theorem,**[†] and is one of the more useful and significant concepts in circuit theory.

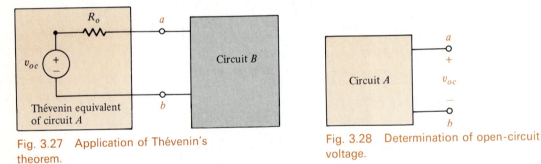

Fig. 3.27 Application of Thévenin's theorem.

Fig. 3.28 Determination of open-circuit voltage.

To obtain the voltage v_{oc}—called the **open-circuit voltage**—remove circuit B from circuit A, and determine the voltage between nodes a and b. This voltage, as shown in Fig. 3.28, is v_{oc}.

To obtain the resistance R_o—called the **Thévenin-equivalent resistance** or the **output resistance** of circuit A—again remove circuit B from circuit A. Next, set all independent sources in circuit A to zero. Leave the dependent sources as is! (A zero voltage source is equivalent to a short circuit, and a zero current source is equivalent to an open circuit.) Now determine the resistance between nodes a and b—this is R_o—as shown in Fig. 3.29.

[†] Named for the French engineer M.L. Thévenin (1857–1926).

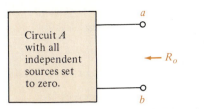

Fig. 3.29   Determination of Thévenin-equivalent (output) resistance.

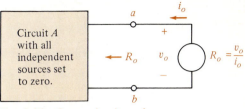

Fig. 3.30   Determination of output resistance.

If circuit A contains no dependent sources, when all independent sources are set to zero, the result may be simply a series-parallel resistive network. In this case, R_o can be found by appropriately combining resistors in series and parallel. In general, however, R_o can be found by applying an independent source between nodes a and b and then by taking the ratio of voltage to current. This procedure is depicted in Fig. 3.30. For the most part it doesn't matter whether v_o is applied and i_o is calculated or vice versa. (Exceptions to this rule are special cases which will be discussed later.)

In applying Thévenin's theorem, circuit B (which is often called the **load**) may consist of many circuit elements, a single element (e.g., a load resistor), or no elements (that is, circuit B already may be an open circuit).

EXAMPLE 3.7

Let us find the voltage v_L across the 3-Ω load resistor for the circuit shown in Fig. 3.31 by replacing circuit A by its Thévenin equivalent.

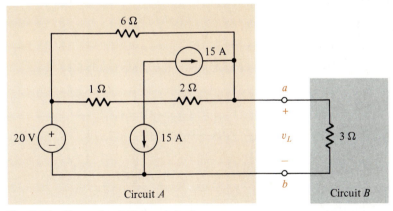

Fig. 3.31   Example of Thévenin's theorem.

First, we remove the 3-Ω load resistor and calculate v_{oc} from the circuit shown in Fig. 3.32. Summing the currents out of node v, by KCL, we get

$$\frac{v-20}{1} + \frac{v-v_{oc}}{2} + 15 + 15 = 0$$

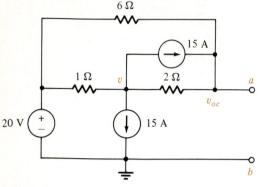

Fig. 3.32   Determination of open-circuit voltage.

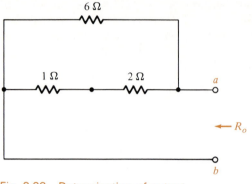

Fig. 3.33   Determination of output resistance.

Summing the currents out of node v_{oc}, by KCL, we get

$$\frac{v_{oc} - v}{2} + \frac{v_{oc} - 20}{6} - 15 = 0$$

Solving these equations for v_{oc} yields $v_{oc} = 30$ V.

To find the Thévenin equivalent resistance R_o, set the independent sources to zero. The resulting circuit is given in Fig. 3.33. Since the 1-Ω and 2-Ω resistors are in series, their combined resistance is 3 Ω. But this resulting 3-Ω resistance is in parallel with 6 Ω. Thus, $R_o = (3)(6)/(3 + 6) = 2\,\Omega$.

In replacing circuit A by its Thévenin equivalent, we get the circuit shown in Fig. 3.34(a). By voltage division, we have that

$$v_L = \frac{3}{3 + 2}(30) = 18 \text{ V}$$

Direct analysis of the circuit given in Fig. 3.31, of course, yields the same result for v_L—try it and see!

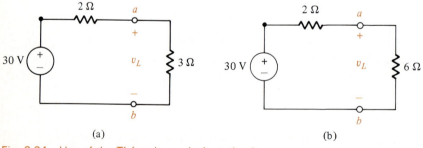

(a)   (b)

Fig. 3.34   Use of the Thévenin-equivalent circuit.

For the circuit given in Fig. 3.31, using the Thévenin equivalent of circuit A was no real bargin for the purpose of calculating the voltage across the 3-Ω resistor—

after all, we had to analyze two circuits (Figs. 3.32 and 3.33). However, once the Thévenin equivalent has been determined, it is a simple matter to see what the effect is on different loads. For example, suppose that the load in Fig. 3.31 is doubled from 3 Ω to 6 Ω. Rather than analyzing the resulting new circuit, we may use the Thévenin equivalent as indicated by Fig. 3.34(b). For this circuit, by voltage division, the new load voltage is

$$v_L = \frac{6}{6+2} (30) = 22.5 \text{ V}$$

This demonstrates one of the important uses of Thévenin's theorem—determining the effect that a given circuit has on different loads.

DRILL EXERCISE 3.7

For the circuit shown in Fig. DE3.7, (a) replace the portion of the circuit to the left of terminals a and b by its Thévenin equivalent and (b) use the resulting circuit to calculate v.

Answer: (a) 6 V, 3 Ω; (b) 3.75 V

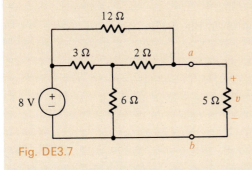

Fig. DE3.7

In calculating R_o for a particular circuit, it may be that there are no resistances connected either in series or in parallel. For such a circuit, R_o can be determined by applying a voltage and calculating the resulting current (or vice versa), and then taking the ratio of voltage to current.

DRILL EXERCISE 3.8

Determine the Thévenin equivalent of the circuit shown in Fig. DE3.8.
Answer: 2 V; 4 Ω

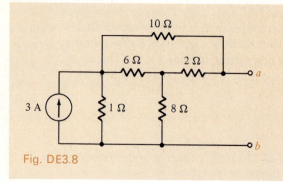

Fig. DE3.8

Circuits with Dependent Sources

So far we have studied Thévenin's theorem by considering circuits which contain just resistors and independent sources. Now let us apply Thévenin's theorem to circuits which contain dependent sources as well. We will again be required to calculate both v_{oc} and R_o—that is, we will again have to analyze two circuits in order to obtain the Thévenin equivalent of a given circuit. However, when a circuit contains a dependent source, it is not possible to obtain R_o for that circuit simply by combining resistances in series and parallel.

EXAMPLE 3.8

Let us find the Thévenin equivalent of the circuit given in Fig. 3.35.

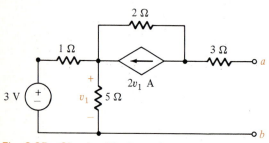

Fig. 3.35   Circuit with dependent source.

First we determine v_{oc} by analyzing the circuit shown in Fig. 3.36. Note that since there is no current going through the 3-Ω resistor, the voltage across that resistor is 0 V. Hence, $v_2 = v_{oc}$.

By KCL at node v_1,

$$\frac{v_1 - 3}{1} + \frac{v_1}{5} + \frac{v_1 - v_{oc}}{2} - 2v_1 = 0$$

from which

$$-3v_1 - 5v_{oc} = 30 \tag{3.8}$$

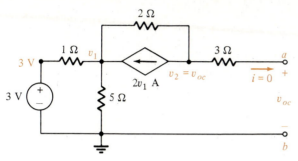

Fig. 3.36   Calculation of v_{oc}.

By KCL at node $v_2 = v_{oc}$,

$$2v_1 + \frac{v_{oc} - v_1}{2} = 0$$

from which

$$3v_1 + v_{oc} = 0 \tag{3.9}$$

Solving Equations (3.8) and (3.9) we get

$$v_1 = 2.5 \text{ V} \quad \text{and} \quad v_{oc} = -7.5 \text{ V}$$

We determine R_o by analyzing the circuit shown in Fig. 3.37. Here we will apply a voltage source v_o and calculate the resulting current i_o. Specifically, if we make $v_o = 1$ V, then

$$R_o = \frac{v_o}{i_o} = \frac{1}{i_o}$$

By KCL at node v_1,

$$\frac{v_1}{1} + \frac{v_1}{5} + \frac{v_1 - v_2}{2} - 2v_1 = 0$$

from which

$$-3v_1 - 5v_2 = 0 \tag{3.10}$$

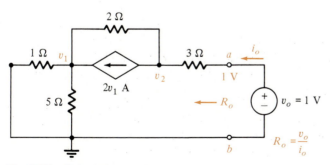

Fig. 3.37   Calculation of R_o.

By KCL at node v_2,

$$2v_1 + \frac{v_2 - v_1}{2} + \frac{v_2 - 1}{3} = 0$$

from which

$$9v_2 + 5v_2 = 2 \qquad\qquad (3.11)$$

Solving Equations (3.10) and (3.11), we get

$$v_1 = \tfrac{1}{3} \text{ V} \qquad \text{and} \qquad v_2 = -\tfrac{1}{5} \text{ V}$$

Thus,

$$i_o = \frac{v_o - v_2}{3} = \frac{1 + 1/5}{3} = \frac{2}{5} = 0.4 \text{ A}$$

and

$$R_o = \frac{v_o}{i_o} = \frac{1}{0.4} = 2.5 \text{ } \Omega$$

Hence, the Thévenin equivalent of the circuit given in Fig. 3.35 is either of the circuits shown in Fig. 3.38.

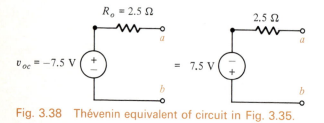

Fig. 3.38   Thévenin equivalent of circuit in Fig. 3.35.

DRILL EXERCISE 3.9

Find the Thévenin equivalent of the circuit shown in Fig. DE3.9.
Answer: 24 V; 2.4 Ω

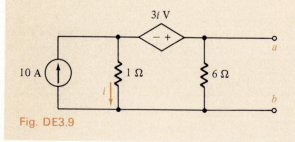

Fig. DE3.9

The reader may have noticed, that for the circuit shown in Fig. 3.37, the output resistance R_o is the series connection of a 3-Ω resistance and a resistance R', where R' is the resistance indicated by Fig. 3.39.

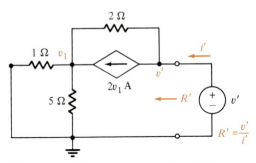

Fig. 3.39   Realization of negative resistance.

For the circuit in Fig. 3.39, by KCL at node v_1,

$$\frac{v_1}{1} + \frac{v_1}{5} + \frac{v_1 - v'}{2} - 2v_1 = 0 \qquad \Rightarrow \qquad v_1 = -\frac{3}{5}v'$$

By KCL,

$$i' = 2v_1 + \frac{v' - v_1}{2} = \frac{3}{2}v_1 + \frac{1}{2}v' = \frac{3}{2}\left(-\frac{5}{3}v'\right) + \frac{1}{2}v' = -2v'$$

Thus,

$$R' = \frac{v'}{i'} = -0.5\ \Omega$$

which is a negative resistance. And, as was determined in Example 3.8, $R_o = 3 + R' = 3 - 0.5 = 2.5\ \Omega$.

But, what is a negative resistance? A negative resistance is like a positive resistance in that $v = Ri$. For a positive resistance, (positive-valued) current goes from a given potential to a lower potential. However, for a negative resistance, (positive-valued) current goes from a given potential to a higher potential. It takes power (energy) for this to happen, and since resistors only absorb power, it is the dependent source which supplies the necessary power. Therefore, the circuit shown in Fig. 3.39 is an example of how a negative resistance is simulated by using resistors and a dependent source.

The resistance of a connection of resistors and a dependent source or sources may be positive or negative—or even zero. The value of the resistance depends on the values of the resistors and the dependent sources, and the way in which the elements are interconnected.

DRILL EXERCISE 3.10

For the circuit given in Fig. DE3.9, reverse the polarity of the dependent source and repeat Drill Exercise 3.9.
Answer: -30 V; -3 Ω

Having applied Thévenin's theorem to circuits that contain dependent sources in addition to resistors, let us now consider an op-amp circuit.

EXAMPLE 3.9

Let us now find the Thévenin equivalent of the op-amp circuit (with no load) shown in Fig. 3.40. We have already seen (Fig. 3.3 on p. 108) that

$$v_{oc} = -\frac{R_2}{R_1} v_s$$

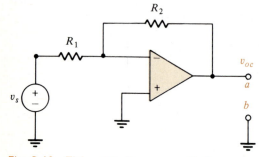

Fig. 3.40   Thévenin's theorem applied to an op-amp circuit.

To find the output resistance R_o, we set v_s to zero and take the ratio $R_o = v_o/i_o$ as depicted in Fig. 3.41. By KCL

$$\frac{0}{R_1} - \frac{v_o}{R_2} = 0 \quad \Rightarrow \quad v_o = 0 \text{ V}$$

Hence,

$$R_o = v_o/i_o = 0 \,\Omega$$

and the Thévenin equivalent of the op-amp circuit given in Fig. 3.40 is the (ideal) voltage source shown in Fig. 3.42.

In this case, we determined R_o by applying a current source i_o between terminals a and b, and then calculating the voltage v_o that results. Since $v_o = 0$, then $R_o = v_o/i_o = 0 \,\Omega$.

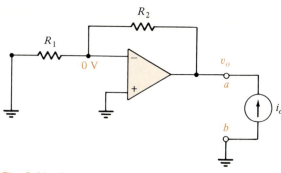

Fig. 3.41   Determination of output resistance.

Fig. 3.42   Thévenin-equivalent circuit.

It is not possible, however, to determine R_o for the given circuit by applying a voltage source $v_o \neq 0$ between terminals a and b. For doing so would be tantamount to connecting two voltage sources in parallel—and this is not allowed. Of course, if we did not know that the Thévenin equivalent of the given circuit is a voltage source, and we tried to apply a voltage source $v_o \neq 0$ between terminals a and b, we would develop contradictory results. For example, applying $v_o \neq 0$ to terminals a and b implies that there is a current v_o/R_2 directed to the left through R_2 and R_1. Furthermore, a current through R_1 implies that there is a voltage across R_1, and hence, there is a nonzero voltage at the inverting input of the op amp—a contradiction to the fact that this voltage is 0 V. Thus, we conclude that it is not possible to apply a nonzero voltage between terminals a and b for the circuit in Fig. 3.41—so a current source must be used to determine R_o.

DRILL EXERCISE 3.11

Find the Thévenin equivalent of the circuit shown in Fig. DE3.11.

Answer: $\left(1 + \dfrac{R_2}{R_1}\right) v_s; \ 0 \ \Omega$

Fig. DE3.11

3.4 NORTON'S THEOREM

Suppose that for the Thévenin-equivalent circuit in Fig. 3.43(a) we perform a source transformation. The result is shown in Fig. 3.43(b). Since, in the application of Thévenin's theorem, circuit B can be any load, consider the case that the load is a short circuit. If the resulting current is denoted i_{sc}, then the two equivalent situations shown in Fig. 3.44 yield i_{sc}. From the circuit on the right, we see that

$$i_{sc} = \frac{v_{oc}}{R_o} \qquad (3.12)$$

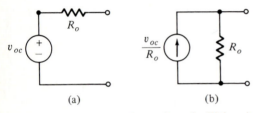

(a)   (b)

Fig. 3.43   Source transformation of a Thévenin-equivalent circuit.

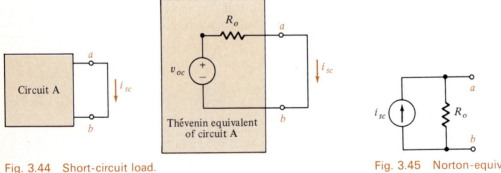

Fig. 3.44   Short-circuit load.

Fig. 3.45   Norton-equivalent circuit.

Thus a circuit equivalent to the Thévenin equivalent is shown in Fig. 3.45, where i_{sc} is the current that results when a short circuit is placed between nodes a and b. This result is known as **Norton's theorem**,[†] and the circuit in Fig. 3.45 is called the **Norton equivalent** of circuit A.

From Equation (3.12), we have that

$$R_o = \frac{v_{oc}}{i_{sc}} \qquad (3.13)$$

[†] Named for the American engineer Edward L. Norton.

Hence, Equation (3.13) is an alternative for obtaining R_o. Instead of calculating R_o directly as described previously, both v_{oc} and i_{sc} are determined individually, and then the ratio of v_{oc} to i_{sc} is found.

To obtain the Norton equivalent of circuit A without first finding the Thévenin equivalent, determine the short-circuit current i_{sc} by placing a short circuit between nodes a and b and then calculate the resulting current through it. The output resistance R_o can be found as was done for the Thévenin-equivalent circuit. Alternatively, v_{oc} can be determined as was done for the Thévenin-equivalent circuit, and then the formula $R_o = v_{oc}/i_{sc}$ employed.

EXAMPLE 3.10

For the circuit shown in Fig. 3.46, let us find the voltage across the $\frac{1}{4}$-Ω resistor by replacing the remainder of the circuit by its Norton equivalent.

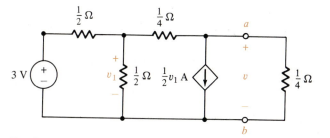

Fig. 3.46 Example of the use of the Norton-equivalent circuit.

First, replace the $\frac{1}{4}$-Ω resistor between nodes a and b with a short circuit, and calculate i_{sc} as shown in Fig. 3.47. Summing the currents out of node v_1, by KCL we obtain

$$\frac{v_1 - 3}{1/2} + \frac{v_1}{1/2} + \frac{v_1}{1/4} = 0$$

Solving this equation for v_1 yields $v_1 = \frac{3}{4}$ V. By KCL,

$$i_{sc} = \frac{v_1}{1/4} - \frac{v_1}{2} = \frac{7}{2}v_1 = \frac{21}{8} \text{ A}$$

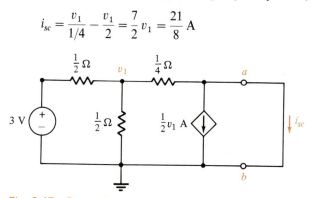

Fig. 3.47 Determination of short-circuit current.

To find R_o, we remove the $\frac{1}{4}$-Ω load resistor, set the independent source to zero, and calculate $R_o = v_o/i_o$ between nodes a and b as depicted in Fig. 3.48. Summing the currents out of node v_1, we get

$$\frac{v_1}{1/2} + \frac{v_1}{1/2} + \frac{v_1 - v_o}{1/4} = 0$$

from which $v_1 = v_o/2$. By KCL,

$$i_o = \frac{1}{2}v_1 + \frac{v_o - v_1}{1/4} = \frac{1}{2}\left(\frac{v_o}{2}\right) + 4\left(v_o - \frac{v_o}{2}\right) = \frac{9}{4}v_o$$

Hence,

$$R_o = \frac{v_o}{i_o} = \frac{4}{9}\,\Omega$$

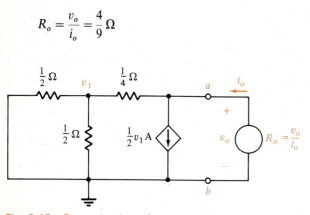

Fig. 3.48   Determination of output resistance.

An alternative procedure for finding R_o is to remove the $\frac{1}{4}$-Ω resistor from the circuit in Fig. 3.46, and calculate the open-circuit voltage v_{oc} between nodes a and b. Doing so results in $v_{oc} = \frac{7}{6}$ V. Thus, we also have that

$$R_o = \frac{v_{oc}}{i_{sc}} = \frac{7/6}{21/8} = \frac{4}{9}\,\Omega$$

as was determined above.

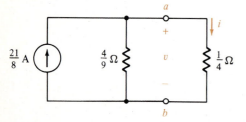

Fig. 3.49   Use of the Norton-equivalent circuit.

To determine the voltage v indicated in Fig. 3.46, we may replace the portion of the circuit to the left of nodes a and b by its Norton equivalent. This is illustrated by Fig. 3.49. Using the current-divider formula, we get

$$i = \frac{4/9}{4/9 + 1/4}\left(\frac{21}{8}\right) = \frac{42}{25}\,A \quad \Rightarrow \quad v = \frac{1}{4}\left(\frac{42}{25}\right) = 0.42\,V$$

DRILL EXERCISE 3.12

Find the Norton equivalent of the circuit shown in Fig. DE3.12.
Answer: 8 A; 1 Ω

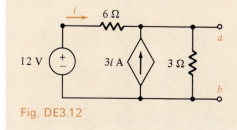

Fig. DE3.12

Special Cases

In the preceding example, we mentioned that R_o can be determined by finding v_{oc} and i_{sc} and using $R_o = v_{oc}/i_{sc}$ rather than taking the direct approach shown in Fig. 3.30. However, $R_o = v_{oc}/i_{sc}$ cannot be employed if neither v_{oc} nor i_{sc} exists. For instance, the op-amp circuit given in Fig. 3.40 is equivalent to an ideal voltage source (Fig. 3.42). This means that i_{sc} does not exist for this circuit. In other words, an ideal voltage source cannot be equivalent to a current source in parallel with a resistance. Nor can an ideal current source be equivalent to a voltage source in series with a resistance. This means that for a circuit that is equivalent to an ideal current source, v_{oc} does not exist.

EXAMPLE 3.11

Let us demonstrate that the circuit shown in Fig. 3.50 is equivalent to an ideal 1-A current source by finding the Norton equivalent of the circuit.

First we determine i_{sc} using mesh analysis for the circuit shown in Fig. 3.51. For mesh i_1, by KVL,

$$-1 + 1i_1 + 3(i_1 - i_{sc}) + 8(i_1 - i_2) = 0$$

from which

$$12i_1 - 8i_2 - 3i_{sc} = 1 \tag{3.14}$$

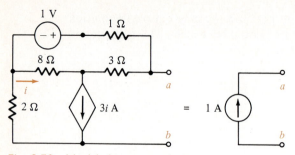

Fig. 3.50   Ideal 1-A current source.

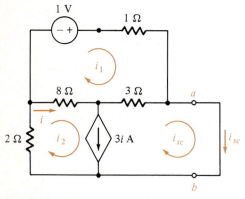

Fig. 3.51   Determination of i_{sc}.

For the supermesh consisting of mesh i_2 and mesh i_{sc}, by KVL,

$$2i_2 + 8(i_2 - i_1) + 3(i_{sc} - i_1) = 0$$

from which

$$-11i_1 + 10i_2 + 3i_{sc} = 0 \tag{3.15}$$

Finally, for the dependent current source,

$$i_2 - i_{sc} = 3i = 3(i_2 - i_1)$$

from which

$$-3i_1 + 2i_2 + i_{sc} = 0 \tag{3.16}$$

Solving Equations (3.14), (3.15), and (3.16), we get

$$i_1 = 0.5 \text{ A} \qquad i_2 = 0.25 \text{ A} \qquad i_{sc} = 1 \text{ A}$$

We determine R_o from the circuit shown in Fig. 3.52. For node v_1, by KCL,

$$\frac{v_1}{2} + \frac{v_1 - v_2}{8} + \frac{v_1 - v_o}{1} = 0$$

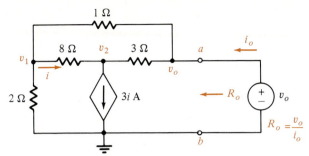

Fig. 3.52   Determination of output resistance.

from which

$$13v_1 - v_2 = 8v_o \qquad (3.17)$$

For node v_2, by KCL

$$-i + 3i + \frac{v_2 - v_o}{3} = 0 \qquad \Rightarrow \qquad 2i + \frac{v_2 - v_o}{3} = 0$$

Substituting the fact that $i = (v_1 - v_2)/8$ into this equation yields

$$3v_1 + v_2 = 4v_o \qquad (3.18)$$

Solving Equations (3.17) and (3.18), we obtain

$$v_1 = 0.75v_o \qquad \text{and} \qquad v_2 = 1.75v_o$$

Thus, by KCL,

$$i_o = \frac{v_o - v_1}{1} + \frac{v_o - v_2}{3} = \frac{v_o - 0.75v_o}{1} + \frac{v_o - 1.75v_o}{3} = 0.25v_o - 0.25v_o = 0 \text{ A}$$

and, therefore,

$$R_o = \frac{v_o}{i_o} = \frac{v_o}{0} = \infty$$

Hence, the Norton-equivalent circuit, which is a 1-A current source in parallel with an infinite resistance (an open circuit), is just a 1-A current source—as indicated in Fig. 3.50. Consequently, the given circuit does not have a Thévenin equivalent.

DRILL EXERCISE 3.13

Find the Norton equivalent of the circuit shown in Fig. DE3.13.
Answer: -3 A; $R_o = \infty$

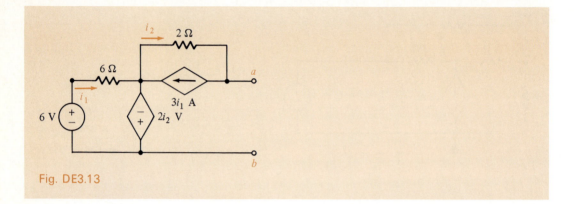

Fig. DE3.13

There are circuits whose Thévenin and Norton equivalents are identical. For example, in general, a circuit that contains no independent sources will have $v_{oc} = 0$ and $i_{sc} = 0$. This means that the Thévenin and Norton equivalents simply consist of the output resistance R_o. Of course, in such a case, the formula $R_o = v_{oc}/i_{sc}$ cannot be used to find R_o. However, there are the exceptional circuits with nonzero independent sources that also have Thévenin and Norton equivalent circuits consisting only of a resistance (see Problem 3.55).

EXAMPLE 3.12

Let us find the Norton equivalent of the circuit shown in Fig. 3.53.

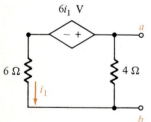

Fig. 3.53   Circuit with no independent source.

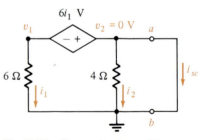

Fig. 3.54   Determination of i_{sc}.

We first determine i_{sc} from the circuit in Fig. 3.54. Since

$$v_1 = -6i = -6\left(\frac{v_1}{6}\right) = -v_1$$

then

$$2v_1 = 0 \qquad \Rightarrow \qquad v_1 = 0 \text{ V}$$

By KCL,

$$i_{sc} = -i_1 - i_2 = -\frac{v_1}{6} - \frac{v_2}{4} = -\frac{0}{6} - \frac{0}{4} = 0 \text{ A}$$

Of course, since the circuit contains no independent source, we must have that $i_{sc} = 0$ A—so analysis of the circuit is superfluous.

We next determine R_o from the circuit shown in Fig. 3.55. For the dependent voltage source,

$$v_o - v_1 = 6i_1 = 6\left(\frac{v_1}{6}\right) = v_1$$

from which

$$v_o = 2v_1 \qquad \Rightarrow \qquad v_1 = \tfrac{1}{2}v_o$$

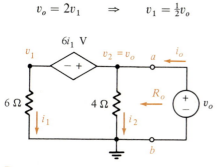

Fig. 3.55   Determination of R_o.

By KCL,

$$i_o = i_1 + i_2 = \frac{v_1}{6} + \frac{v_2}{4} = \frac{(1/2)v_o}{6} + \frac{v_o}{4} = \frac{v_o}{12} + \frac{v_o}{4} = \frac{v_o + 3v_o}{12} = \frac{v_o}{3}$$

Hence,

$$R_o = \frac{v_o}{i_o} = 3 \, \Omega$$

Therefore, the Norton equivalent of the circuit shown in Fig. 3.53 is just the resistance $R_o = 3 \, \Omega$ as depicted in Fig. 3.56.

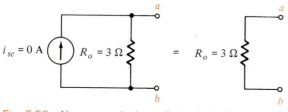

Fig. 3.56   Norton equivalent of circuit in Fig. 3.53.

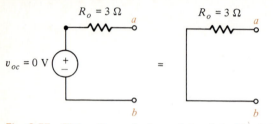

Fig. 3.57   Thévenin equivalent of circuit in Fig. 3.53.

Note, too, that for the circuit in Fig. 3.53, we must have that $v_{oc} = 0$ V, and therefore, the Thévenin equivalent of the circuit is again just the resistance $R_o = 3$ Ω as depicted in Fig. 3.57. (A source transformation will also give the same result.)

DRILL EXERCISE 3.14

Find the Norton equivalent of the circuit shown in Fig. DE3.14.
Answer: 0 A; 2 Ω

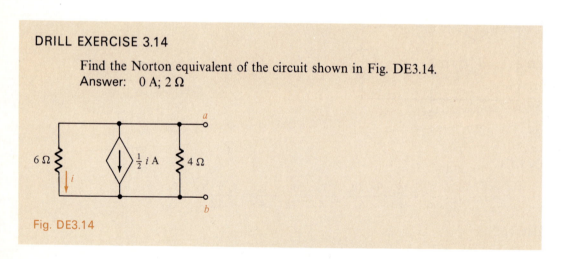

Fig. DE3.14

Most circuits have both a Thévenin and Norton equivalent circuit, and in such a case knowing one is tantamount to knowing the other, since one can be obtained from the other simply by a source transformation.

Maximum Power Transfer

We may now answer the question that was posed at the beginning of Section 3.3. For the situation depicted in Fig. 3.25 (p. 122), we wish to determine the value of the load R_L that will absorb the maximum amount of power. By Thévenin's theorem, we can replace the arbitrary circuit by its Thévenin equivalent and the effect on R_L will be the same. Doing so, we obtain Fig. 3.58. Since the power absorbed by the load is $p = i^2 R_L$, it may be tempting to believe that to increase the power absorbed, we simply increase the load resistance R_L. This reasoning, however, is invalid since an

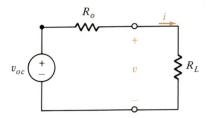

Fig. 3.58   Determination of maximum power transfer.

increase in R_L will result in a decrease in i. To find the value for which maximum power is delivered to the load, we proceed as follows:

By Ohm's law,

$$i = \frac{v_{oc}}{R_o + R_L}$$

The (instantaneous) power absorbed by the load is

$$p = i^2 R_L = \left(\frac{v_{oc}}{R_o + R_L} \right)^2 R_L = \frac{v_{oc}^2 R_L}{(R_o + R_L)^2} \tag{3.19}$$

Thus, we have an expression for the power in terms of the variable R_L. For what value of R_L is the power a maximum? From introductory calculus we know that if we have a function $f(x)$ of the real variable x, then maxima occur for the values of x where the derivative of $f(x)$ is equal to zero. Thus, let us take the derivative of p with respect to the variable R_L. Using the fact that

$$\frac{d}{dx} \left[\frac{f(x)}{g(x)} \right] = \frac{g(x)\, df(x)/dx - f(x)\, dg(x)/dx}{[g(x)]^2}$$

we obtain

$$\frac{dp}{dR_L} = \frac{(R_o + R_L)^2\, d(v_{oc}^2 R_L)/dR_L - v_{oc}^2 R_L\, d(R_o + R_L)^2/dR_L}{[(R_o + R_L)^2]^2}$$

Simplifying this expression yields

$$\frac{dp}{dR_L} = \frac{(R_o - R_L)v_{oc}^2}{(R_o + R_L)^3}$$

Clearly, $dp/dR_L = 0$ when the numerator $(R_o - R_L)v_{oc}^2 = 0$. Furthermore, given that v_{oc} is a nonzero source, then $dp/dR_L = 0$ when

$$R_o - R_L = 0 \qquad \text{or} \qquad R_o = R_L$$

Therefore, when $R_o = R_L$, the power absorbed by the load [Equation (3.19)] becomes

$$p_m = \frac{v_{oc}^2}{4R_o} = \frac{v_{oc}^2}{4R_L} \tag{3.20}$$

and this quantity is either a maximum or a minimum. However, since we can make the expression for power absorbed by the load arbitrarily small by making R_L arbitrarily small, the quantity $v_{oc}^2/4R_o$ cannot be a minimum. We may also verify that $p_m = v_{oc}^2/4R_o$ is maximum by taking the second derivative of p, setting $R_o = R_L$, and obtaining a negative quantity.

In summary, for the situation depicted in Fig. 3.25 (or Fig. 3.58), the maximum power that can be delivered to a resistive load R_L is obtained when $R_L = R_o$, and that power is given by Equation (3.20).

EXAMPLE 3.13

For the circuit given in Fig. 3.31 (p. 123), we have already seen (Example 3.7) that the voltage across the 3-Ω load resistor is $v_L = 18$ V. Thus, the power absorbed by this load resistor is

$$p_L = \frac{v_L^2}{3} = \frac{(18)^2}{3} = 108 \text{ W}$$

However, this is not the maximum power that can be absorbed by a load connected to circuit A indicated in Fig. 3.31. Since $R_o = 2\,\Omega$ for circuit A, then the load that absorbs the maximum power is

$$R_L = R_o = 2\,\Omega$$

and the maximum power absorbed is

$$p_m = \frac{v_{oc}^2}{4R_o} = \frac{(30)^2}{4(2)} = 112.5 \text{ W}$$

DRILL EXERCISE 3.15

For the circuit shown in Fig. DE3.9 (p. 128), connect a load resistor R_L to terminals a and b. For what value of R_L will this load absorb the maximum amount of power? Determine this maximum power.
Answer: 2.4 Ω; 60 W

3.5 THE PRINCIPLE OF SUPERPOSITION

Given a circuit that contains two or more independent sources (voltage or current or both), as we have seen, one way to determine the value of a specific variable (either voltage or current) is by the direct use of nodal, mesh or loop analysis. An alternative, however, is to find that portion of the value attributable to each independent source, and then sum these up. This concept is known as the **principle of superposition**.

The justification for the principle of superposition is based on the concept of linearity. Specifically, let us first consider the relationship between voltage and current for a resistor (i.e., Ohm's law). Suppose that a current i_1 (the **excitation** or **input**) is applied to a resistor, R. Then the resulting voltage v_1 (the **response** or **output**) is $v_1 = Ri_1$. Similarly, if i_2 is applied to R, then $v_2 = Ri_2$ results. But if $i = i_1 + i_2$ is applied, the response is

$$v = Ri = R(i_1 + i_2) = Ri_1 + Ri_2 = v_1 + v_2$$

In other words, the response to a sum of inputs is equal to the sum of the individual responses (Condition I).

In addition, if v is the response to i (i.e., $v = Ri$), then the response to Ki is

$$R(Ki) = K(Ri) = Kv$$

In other words, if the input is scaled by the constant K, then the response is also scaled by K (Condition II).

Because Conditions I and II are satisfied, we say that the relationship between current (input) and voltage (output) is **linear** for a resistor. Similarly, by using the alternative form of Ohm's law $i = v/R$, we can show that the relationship between voltage (input) and current (output) is also linear for a resistor.

Although the relationships between voltage and current for a resistor are linear, the power relationships $p = Ri^2$ and $p = v^2/R$ are not. For instance, if the current through a resistor is i_1, then the power absorbed by the resistor R is $p_1 = Ri_1^2$, while if the current is i_2, then the power absorbed is $p_2 = Ri_2^2$. However, the power absorbed due to the current $i_1 + i_2$ is

$$p_3 = R(i_1 + i_2)^2 = Ri_1^2 + Ri_2^2 + 2Ri_1i_2 \quad \Rightarrow \quad p_3 \neq p_1 + p_2$$

Hence, the relationship $p = Ri^2$ is **nonlinear**.

Since the relationships between voltage and current are linear for resistors, we say that a resistor is a **linear element**. A dependent source (either current or voltage) whose value is directly proportional to some voltage or current is also a linear element. Because of this, we say that a circuit consisting of independent sources, resistors, and linear dependent sources (as well as other linear elements to be introduced later) is a **linear circuit**. All of the circuits dealt with so far have been linear circuits.

We now return to the simple case of a resistor R connected to a voltage source v. If the voltage is v_1, then the current is $i_1 = v_1/R$, while if v_2 is applied, then $i_2 = v_2/R$ results. By linearity, we have that for the input $v_1 + v_2$, the response is $i_1 + i_2$. However, we can represent this situation as shown in Fig. 3.59. But each component (i_1 and i_2) of the response can be determined as shown in Fig. 3.60. This is a very special case showing how it is possible to obtain the response due to two independent voltage sources by calculating the response to each one separately and then summing the responses. However, for any linear circuit, we can take the same approach: find the response to each independent source (both voltage and current) separately, and then sum the responses. A formal general proof of this principle is much more involved, but utilizes analogous ideas.

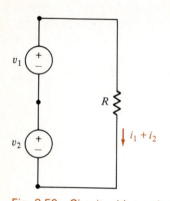

Fig. 3.59   Circuit with two independent voltage sources.

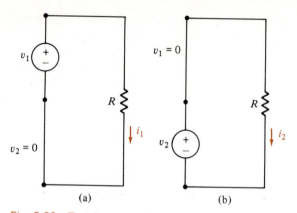

(a)   (b)

Fig. 3.60   Treating each independent source separately.

For demonstration purposes, consider the linear circuit given in Fig. 3.61, which contains three independent sources. By KCL, at node v,

$$\frac{v}{6} + \frac{v - v_g}{3} + i_y - i_x = 0$$

from which

$$3v = 2v_g + 6i_x - 6i_y \qquad (3.21)$$

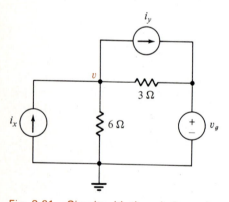

Fig. 3.61   Circuit with three independent sources.

Suppose that when $i_x = i_y = 0$, the resulting node voltage is v_1. Thus, we have the equality

$$3v_1 = 2v_g + 6(0) - 6(0) \qquad (3.22)$$

For the case that $v_g = 0$ and $i_y = 0$, let the resulting node voltage be v_2. This yields the equality

$$3v_2 = 2(0) + 6i_x - 6(0) \tag{3.23}$$

Finally, let v_3 be the node voltage that results when $v_g = 0$ and $i_x = 0$. This gives us the equality

$$3v_3 = 2(0) + 6(0) - 6i_y \tag{3.24}$$

Adding the three equalities (3.22), (3.23), and (3.24) produces the equality

$$3(v_1 + v_2 + v_3) = 2v_g + 6i_x - 6i_y$$

which means that $v_1 + v_2 + v_3$ is the solution to Equation (3.21).

We now formally state the principle of superposition:

> **Given a linear circuit with independent sources $s_1, s_2, \ldots, s_n$, let r be the response (either voltage or current) of this circuit. If r_i is the response of the circuit to source s_i with all other independent sources set to zero (dependent sources are left as is), then**
>
> $$r = r_1 + r_2 + \cdots + r_n.$$

EXAMPLE 3.14

The circuit given in Fig. 3.62 contains three independent sources. To find the voltage v by using the principle of superposition, we first find that portion of v, call it v_a, due to the independent voltage source. Thus, we set the two independent current sources to zero, as shown in Fig. 3.63. Note that the 1-Ω and 2-Ω resistors are in series, and the resulting equivalent 3-Ω resistance is in parallel with the 6-Ω resistor. These three

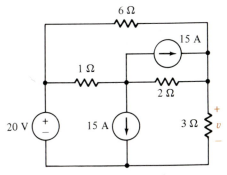

Fig. 3.62   Example of the principle of superposition.

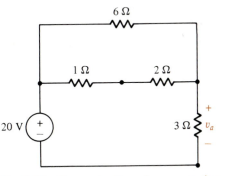

Fig. 3.63   Determination of response due to 20-V source.

resistors, therefore, are equivalent to a 2-Ω resistance. By voltage division,

$$v_a = \frac{3}{3+2}(20) = 12 \text{ V}$$

To find the voltage v_b due solely to the lower 15-A current source, set the other current source and the voltage source to zero as shown in Fig. 3.64. In this circuit, the 6-Ω resistor is in parallel with the 3-Ω resistor. We can redraw the circuit as shown in Fig. 3.65. The 3-Ω and 6-Ω resistors in parallel are equivalent to a 2-Ω resistor—and this is in series with a 2-Ω resistor. The combination is effectively a 4-Ω resistance that is in parallel with the 1-Ω resistor. By current division,

$$i_2 = \frac{1}{1+4}(-15) = -3 \text{ A}$$

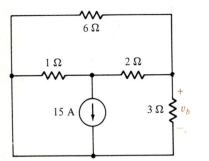

Fig. 3.64   Determination of response due to one 15-A source.

Fig. 3.65   Equivalent circuit for calculating v_b.

Having determined i_2, we can use current division again to get

$$i_3 = \frac{6}{6+3}i_2 = -2 \text{ A} \qquad \Rightarrow \qquad v_b = 3i_3 = -6 \text{ V}$$

To find the voltage v_c due to the upper 15-A current source, set the other two independent sources to zero. The resulting circuit is shown in Fig. 3.66. Since the 6-Ω and 3-Ω resistors are in parallel, we can redraw the circuit as in Fig. 3.67. Suppose for this circuit that we apply a source transformation to the 15-A source in parallel with the 2-Ω resistor. The result is a 15(2) = 30-V source (with the plus toward node n) in series with a 2-Ω resistor. Since the 3-Ω and 6-Ω resistors in parallel are an equivalent 2-Ω resistance, by voltage division we have that

$$v_c = \frac{2}{2+1+2}(30) = 12 \text{ V}$$

By the principle of superposition, we have

$$v = v_a + v_b + v_c = 12 - 6 + 12 = 18 \text{ V}$$

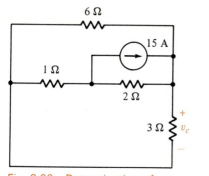

Fig. 3.66   Determination of response due to the other 15-A source.

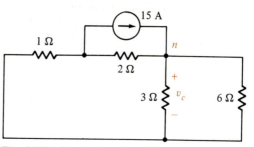

Fig. 3.67   Equivalent circuit for calculating v_c.

DRILL EXERCISE 3.16

For the circuit shown in Fig. DE3.16, use the principle of superposition to find v_1, v_2, and i.

Answer: -4 V; 8 V; 0 A

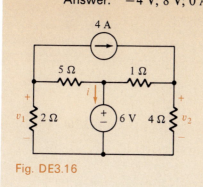

Fig. DE3.16

In the example just completed, all the sources in the circuit were independent sources. For the case in which dependent sources are also included, they are left as is; only independent sources are set to zero when applying the principle of superposition.

EXAMPLE 3.15

Let us use the principle of superposition to find the voltage v for the circuit shown in Fig. 3.68.

To find v_a, the portion of v due to the 3-V independent voltage source, we set the independent current source to zero (i.e., replace it with an open circuit). The resulting circuit is shown in Fig. 3.69. Using mesh analysis, we have for mesh i_1 that

$$-3 + 4i_1 + 2i_1 + 5(i_1 - i_2) = 0$$

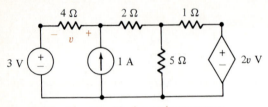

Fig. 3.68   Circuit with dependent source.

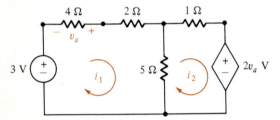

Fig. 3.69   Independent current source set to zero.

from which

$$11i_1 - 5i_2 = 3 \tag{3.25}$$

For mesh i_2,

$$5(i_2 - i_1) + 1i_2 + 2v_a = 0$$

Since $v_a = -4i_1$, this equation reduces to

$$-13i_1 + 6i_2 = 0 \tag{3.26}$$

The solution to Equations (3.25) and (3.26) is

$$i_1 = 18 \text{ A} \qquad \text{and} \qquad i_2 = 39 \text{ A}$$

Thus,

$$v_a = -4i_1 = -4(18) = -72 \text{ V}$$

To find v_b, the portion of v due to the 1-A independent current source, we set the independent voltage source to zero (i.e., replace it with a short circuit). The resulting circuit is shown in Fig. 3.70. Using nodal analysis, we have for node v_b,

$$\frac{v_b}{4} + \frac{v_b - v_1}{2} - 1 = 0$$

from which

$$3v_b - 2v_1 = 4 \tag{3.27}$$

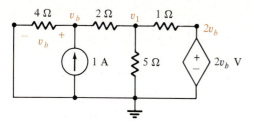

Fig. 3.70 Independent voltage source set to zero.

For node v_1,

$$\frac{v_1 - v_b}{2} + \frac{v_1}{5} + \frac{v_1 - 2v_b}{1} = 0$$

from which

$$-25v_b + 17v_1 = 0 \tag{3.28}$$

The solution to Equations (3.27) and (3.28) is

$$v_b = 68 \text{ V} \qquad \text{and} \qquad v_1 = 100 \text{ V}$$

Hence, the voltage v in the circuit shown in Fig. 3.68 is, by the principle of superposition,

$$v = v_a + v_b = -72 + 68 = -4 \text{ V}$$

DRILL EXERCISE 3.17

Use the principle of superposition to find v and i for the circuit shown in Fig. DE3.17.

Answer: -2 V; 2 A

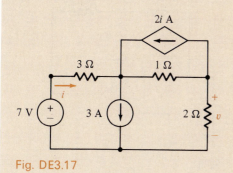

Fig. DE3.17

● SUMMARY

1. An (ideal) operational amplifier is an ideal amplifier with infinite gain. When used in conjunction with negative feedback, the input voltage to an op amp is constrained to be zero volts. The input terminals of an op amp draw no current.

2. Some nonideal voltage sources can be modeled as an ideal voltage source in series with a resistance, and certain nonideal current sources can be modeled as an ideal current source in parallel with a resistance.

3. A voltage source in series with a resistance behaves as a current source in parallel with that resistance, and vice versa.

4. The effect of an arbitrary circuit on a load is equivalent to an appropriate voltage source in series with an appropriate resistance (Thévenin's theorem) or an appropriate current source in parallel with that resistance (Norton's theorem).

5. An arbitrary circuit delivers maximum power to a resistive load R_L when $R_L = R_o$, where R_o is the Thévenin-equivalent (output) resistance of the arbitrary circuit.

6. The response of a circuit having n independent sources equals the sum of the n responses to each individual independent source (the principle of superposition).

● PROBLEMS FOR CHAPTER 3

3.1 For the ideal-amplifier circuit shown in Fig. DE3.1 (p. 107), (a) find an expression for v_o in terms of A, R_1, R_2, and v_s; (b) find an expression for v_1 in terms of A, R_1, R_2, and v_s; and (c) find an expression for the current directed out of the output terminal in terms of A, R_1, R_2, and v_s.

3.2 For the op-amp circuit shown in Fig. DE3.2 (p. 110), interchange the 10-kΩ and 20-kΩ resistors. Find (a) v_o; (b) the power absorbed by the op amp.

3.3 For the op-amp circuit given in Fig. DE3.3 (p. 111), find v_o.

3.4 For the op-amp circuit shown in Fig. P3.4, find the ratio v_o/i_s.

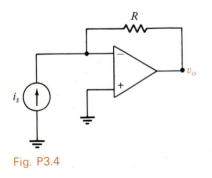

Fig. P3.4

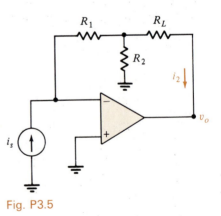

Fig. P3.5

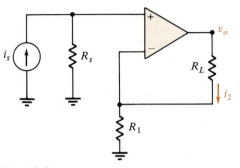

Fig. P3.6

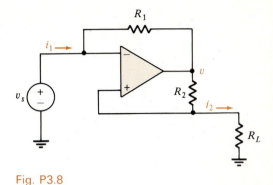

Fig. P3.8

3.5 For the op-amp circuit given in Fig. P3.5, (a) find the ratio v_o/i_s; (b) find the current gain i_2/i_s.

3.6 For the op-amp circuit shown in Fig. P3.6, find v_o/i_s.

3.7 For the op-amp circuit given in Fig. P3.6, find the current gain i_2/i_s.

3.8 For the op-amp circuit shown in Fig. P3.8, find (a) the voltage v; (b) the current gain i_2/i_1.

3.9 For the op-amp circuit given in Fig. P3.9, find the voltage gain v_o/v_s.

3.10 Find the voltage gain v_o/v_s for the op-amp circuit shown in Fig. P3.10.

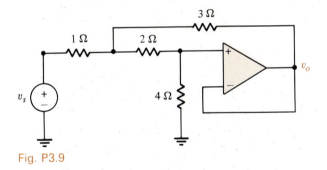

Fig. P3.9

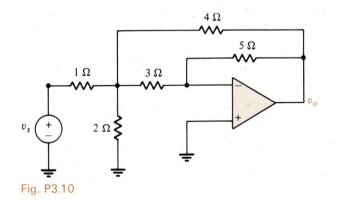

Fig. P3.10

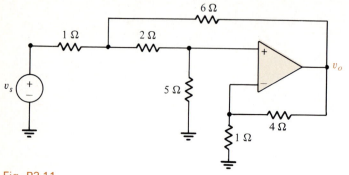

Fig. P3.11

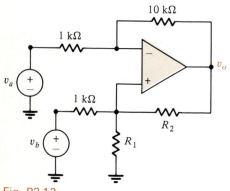

Fig. P3.12

3.11 For the op-amp circuit given in Fig. P3.11, find the voltage gain v_o/v_s.

3.12 For the op-amp circuit shown in Fig. P3.12, find v_o when $R_1 = 1\ \mathrm{k\Omega}$ and $R_2 = 10\ \mathrm{k\Omega}$.

3.13 Repeat Problem 3.12 for the case that $R_1 = \infty$ and $R_2 = 20\ \mathrm{k\Omega}$.

3.14 For the op-amp circuit given in Fig. P3.14, find the voltage gain v_o/v_s.

3.15 For the op-amp circuit given in Fig. P3.15, find the voltage gain v_o/v_s when (a) $R_1 = 4\ \Omega$, $R_2 = 5\ \Omega$ and (b) $R_1 = 5\ \Omega$, $R_2 = 4\ \Omega$.

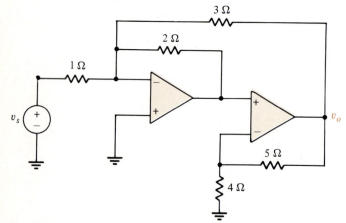

Fig. P3.14

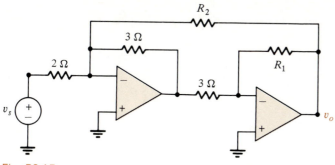

Fig. P3.15

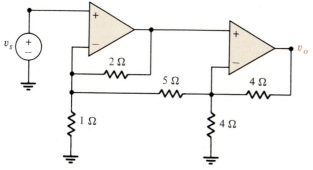

Fig. P3.16

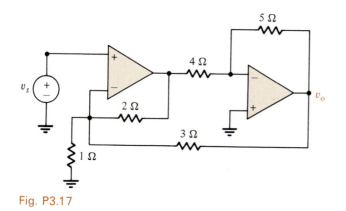

Fig. P3.17

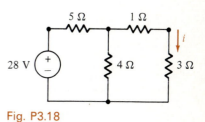

Fig. P3.18

3.16 For the op-amp circuit given in Fig. P3.16, find the voltage gain v_o/v_s.

3.17 For the op-amp circuit given in Fig. P3.17, find the voltage gain v_o/v_s.

3.18 For the circuit shown in Fig. P3.18, use source transformations to determine i.

3.19 Repeat Problem 3.18 for the circuit shown in Fig. P3.19.

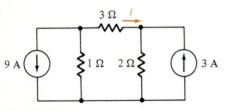

Fig. P3.19

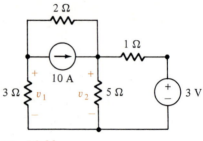

Fig. P3.20

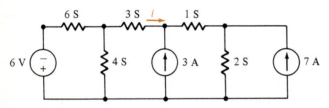

Fig. P3.21

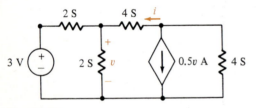

Fig. P3.22

3.20 For the circuit shown in Fig. P3.20, use source transformations to determine v_1 and v_2.

3.21 Repeat Problem 3.18 for the circuit shown in Fig. P3.21.

3.22 For the circuit shown in Fig. P3.22, use source transformations to determine i and v.

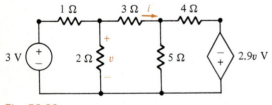

Fig. P3.23

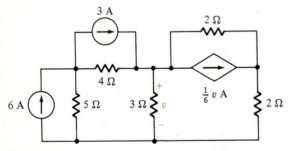

Fig. P3.24

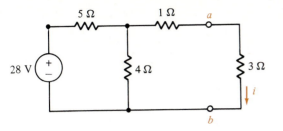

Fig. P3.25

3.23 Repeat Problem 3.22 for the circuit shown in Fig. P3.23.

3.24 For the circuit shown in Fig. 3.24, use source transformations to determine v.

3.25 Given the circuit shown in Fig. P3.25:
  (a) Find the Thévenin equivalent of the circuit to the left of terminals a and b.
  (b) Use the result of part (a) to find i.

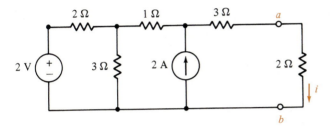

Fig. P3.26

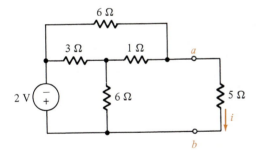

Fig. P3.27

3.26 Repeat Problem 3.25 for the circuit given in Fig. P3.26.

3.27 Repeat Problem 3.25 for the circuit shown in Fig. P3.27.

3.28 Repeat Problem 3.25 for the circuit shown in Fig. P3.28.

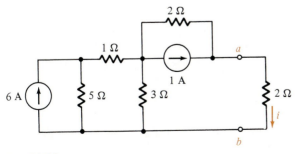

Fig. P3.28

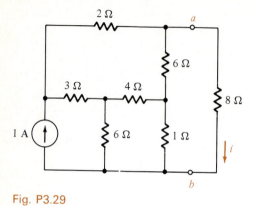

Fig. P3.29

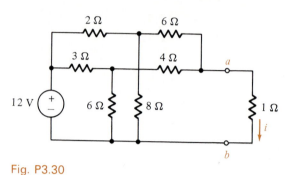

Fig. P3.30

3.29 Repeat Problem 3.25 for the circuit shown in Fig. P3.29.

3.30 Repeat Problem 3.25 for the circuit shown in Fig. P3.30.

3.31 Find the Thévenin equivalent of the circuit shown in Fig. P3.31.

3.33 For the circuit given in Fig. 3.35 (p. 126), change the 2-Ω resistor to a 1-Ω resistor. Find the Thévenin equivalent of the resulting circuit.

3.34 Find the Thévenin equivalent of the circuit shown in Fig. P3.34.

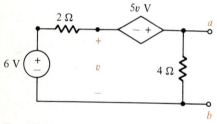

Fig. P3.31

3.32 Find the Thévenin equivalent of the circuit shown in Fig. P3.32.

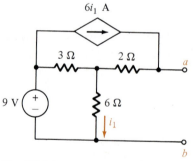

Fig. P3.34

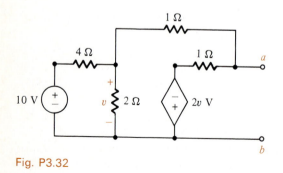

Fig. P3.32

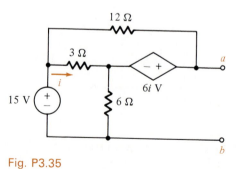

Fig. P3.35

3.35 Find the Thévenin equivalent of the circuit shown in Fig. P3.35.

3.36 Find the Thévenin equivalent of the circuit shown in Fig. P3.36. (*Hint:* Use a current source i_o to determine R_o.)

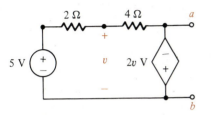

Fig. P3.36

3.37 Repeat Problem 3.36 for the circuit shown in Fig. P3.37.

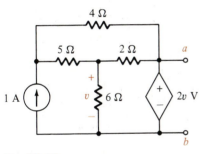

Fig. P3.37

3.38 Find the Thévenin equivalent of the op-amp circuit shown in Fig. P3.38.

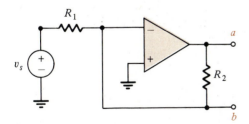

Fig. P3.38

3.39 Find the Thévenin equivalent of the op-amp circuit shown in Fig. P3.39.

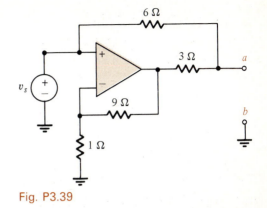

Fig. P3.39

3.40 For the circuit shown in Fig. 3.25 (p. 122), $v_{oc} = 9$ V. If the voltage across the load is 4 V when $R_L = 2\,\Omega$, find the output resistance R_o of the circuit.

3.41 For the circuit shown in Fig. 3.25 (p. 122), when $R_L = 1\,\Omega$ the voltage across R_L is 4 V, and when $R_L = 4\,\Omega$ the voltage across it is 8 V. Find the voltage across R_L when $R_L = 3\,\Omega$.

3.42 For the circuit given in Fig. P3.25, (a) find the Norton equivalent of the circuit to the left of terminals a and b and (b) use the Norton-equivalent circuit to determine i.

3.43 Repeat Problem 3.42 for the circuit shown in Fig. P3.26.

3.44 Repeat Problem 3.42 for the circuit shown in Fig. P3.27.

3.45 Repeat Problem 3.42 for the circuit shown in Fig. P3.28.

3.46 Repeat Problem 3.42 for the circuit shown in Fig. P3.29.

3.47 Repeat Problem 3.42 for the circuit shown in Fig. P3.30.

3.48 Find the Norton equivalent of the circuit shown in Fig. P3.31.

3.49 Find the Norton equivalent of the circuit shown in Fig. P3.32.

3.50 Find the Norton equivalent of the circuit shown in Fig. P3.34.

3.51 Find the Norton equivalent of the circuit shown in Fig. P3.35.

3.52 Find the Norton equivalent of the circuit shown in Fig. P3.38.

3.53 Find the Norton equivalent of the circuit shown in Fig. P3.39.

3.54 Find the Norton equivalent of the circuit shown in Fig. P3.54.

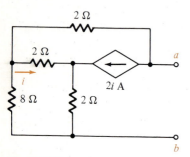

Fig. P3.54

3.55 Find the Norton equivalent of the circuit shown in Fig. P3.55.

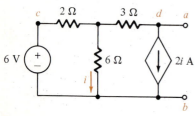

Fig. P3.55

3.56 For the circuit given in Fig. P3.55, connect a 4-Ω resistor between nodes *c* and *d*, and change the value of the dependent current source to $5i$ A. Find the

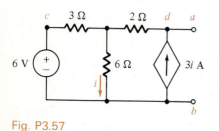

Fig. P3.57

Norton equivalent of the resulting circuit.

3.57 Find the Norton equivalent of the circuit shown in Fig. P3.57. (*Hint:* Use a voltage source v_o to determine R_o.)

3.58 For the circuit given in Fig. P3.57, connect a 4-Ω resistor between nodes *c* and *d*, and change the value of the dependent current source to $6i$ A. Find the Norton equivalent of the resulting circuit. (*Hint:* Use a voltage source v_o to determine R_o.)

3.59 For the circuit given in Fig. P3.27, to what value should the 5-Ω resistor be changed such that this new resistor will absorb maximum power? Determine this maximum power.

3.60 For the circuit given in Fig. P3.29, to what value should the 8-Ω resistor be changed such that this new resistor will absorb maximum power? Determine this maximum power.

3.61 Place a load resistor R_L between terminals *a* and *b* for the circuit given in Fig. P3.31. What value of R_L will absorb maximum power? Determine this power.

3.62 Repeat Problem 3.61 for the circuit given in Fig. P3.32.

3.63 For the circuit shown in Fig. P3.19, (a) use the principle of superposition to find *i* and (b) show that the principle of superposition does not hold for power.

3.64 Use the principle of superposition to find v_1 and v_2 for the circuit shown in Fig. P3.20.

3.65 Use the principle of superposition to find *i* for the circuit shown in Fig. P3.21.

3.66 Use the principle of superposition to find *v* for the circuit shown in Fig. P3.24.

3.67 For the circuit shown in Fig. P3.67 use the principle of superposition to find *i* and *v*.

3.68 Repeat Problem 3.67 for the circuit given in Fig. P3.68.

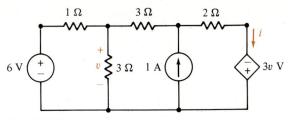

Fig. P3.67

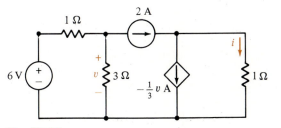

Fig. P3.68

3.69 Repeat Problem 3.67 for the circuit shown in Fig. P3.69.

3.70 Repeat Problem 3.67 for the circuit shown in Fig. P3.70 when (a) $i_s = 4$ A; (b) $i_s = 12$ A.

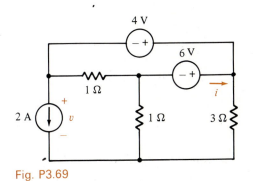

Fig. P3.69

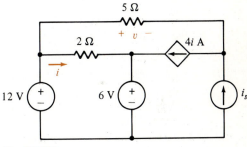

Fig. P3.70

CHAPTER 4

Energy-Storage Elements

● INTRODUCTION

The applications of electric circuits consisting of sources and resistors is quite limited indeed. Furthermore, sources that produce voltages or currents that vary with time can be extremely useful. Because of this, in the present chapter we introduce two circuit elements, the inductor and the capacitor, that have voltage-current relationships that are not simple direct proportionalities. Instead, the behavior of each element can be described by either a differential or an integral relationship. In addition, we define some basic, but important, nonconstant functions of time and examine their derivatives and integrals. Furthermore, we see how simple functions can be combined into more complicated functions and vice versa.

Although resistors dissipate power (or energy), inductors and capacitors store energy. The relationships describing this property are derived in this chapter. We shall also see how to deal with series and parallel connections of inductors and capacitors and how to write mesh and node equations for circuits containing inductors and capacitors. By using the concept of "duality," analysis of a planar circuit results in the automatic analysis of a second circuit. We shall also see how to handle inductors that have initial currents through them and capacitors that have initial charge (voltage across them).

4.1 THE INDUCTOR

In our high school science courses (or earlier), we learned that a current going through a conductor such as a wire produces a magnetic field around that conductor. Furthermore, winding such a conductor into a coil strengthens the magnetic field. For the resulting element, known as an **inductor**, the voltage across it is directly proportional to the time rate of change of the current through it. This fact is credited to the independent work of the American inventor Joseph Henry (1797–1878) and the English physicist Michael Faraday (1791–1867).

To signify a coil of wire, we represent an **ideal inductor** as shown in Fig. 4.1. The relationship between voltage and current (for the polarity and direction respectively indicated) for this element is given by

$$v = L\frac{di}{dt} \qquad\qquad (4.1)$$

where L is the **inductance** of the element, and its unit is the **henry** (abbreviated H) in honor of Joseph Henry. Remember that in the differential relationship just given, v and i represent the functions of time $v(t)$ and $i(t)$ respectively.

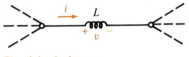

Fig. 4.1   Inductor.

EXAMPLE 4.1

Consider the circuit given in Fig. 4.2 in which the ideal source produces a constant current, called a **direct current** (abbreviated dc). From Equation (4.1), we have that

$$v = L\frac{di}{dt} = 2\frac{d}{dt}[5] = 0 \text{ V}$$

This example is an illustration of the fact that an (ideal) inductor behaves as a short circuit to dc.

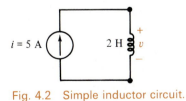

Fig. 4.2   Simple inductor circuit.

In the example just presented, the dc circuit analyzed was quite simple—so let us consider a more complicated situation.

EXAMPLE 4.2

Let us determine the current i in the circuit shown in Fig. 4.3. This circuit has one independent voltage source whose value is constant. For a resistive circuit, we would naturally anticipate that all voltages and currents are constant. However, this is not a resistive circuit. Yet our intuition suggests that the constant-valued voltage source (even if there were additional constant-valued independent sources, and dependent sources, too) produces constant-valued responses. This fact will be confirmed more rigorously later. In the meantime, we will use the result that a circuit containing only constant-valued sources is a dc circuit.

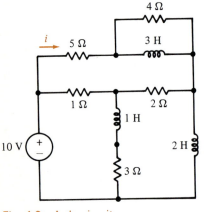

Fig. 4.3   A dc circuit.

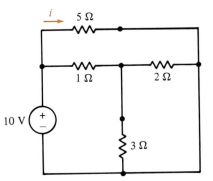

Fig. 4.4   Equivalent form of preceding dc circuit.

For the dc circuit given in Fig. 4.3, the inductors behave as short circuits. Thus, as far as the resistors are concerned, we have the circuit shown in Fig. 4.4. Note that in this circuit, the 4-Ω resistor does not appear. The reason is that a 4-Ω resistor in parallel with a short circuit (zero resistance) is equivalent to a short circuit. By KVL, the voltage across the 5-Ω resistor is 10 V (the plus is on the left). Therefore,

$$i = \tfrac{10}{5} = 2 \text{ A}$$

DRILL EXERCISE 4.1

For the circuit given in Fig. 4.3, find the current (a) directed down through the 1-H inductor, (b) directed down through the 2-H inductor, and (c) directed to the right through the 3-H inductor.
Answer: (a) 1.82 A; (b) 2 A; (c) 4.73 A

For the circuit given in Fig. 4.3, because of the dc source, we were able to simplify the analysis problem to that of analyzing a resistive circuit. But don't get the impression that the analysis of a circuit containing an inductor or inductors is a snap. Generally, circuits containing inductors have sources that are not simply constant valued.

EXAMPLE 4.3

For the simple circuit given in Fig. 4.2, let the current $i(t)$ that is produced by the source be described by the function of time shown in Fig. 4.5, which is described in analytical terms as follows:

$$i(t) = \begin{cases} 0 & \text{for } -\infty < t < 0 \\ t & \text{for } 0 \le t < 1 \\ -(t-2) & \text{for } 1 \le t < 2 \\ 0 & \text{for } 2 \le t < \infty \end{cases}$$

Then

$$v(t) = L\frac{di(t)}{dt} = 2\frac{di(t)}{dt} = \begin{cases} 0 & \text{for } -\infty < t < 0 \\ 2 & \text{for } 0 \le t < 1 \\ -2 & \text{for } 1 \le t < 2 \\ 0 & \text{for } 2 \le t < \infty \end{cases}$$

A sketch of $v(t)$ is shown in Fig. 4.6.

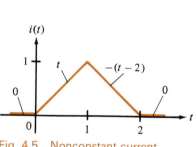

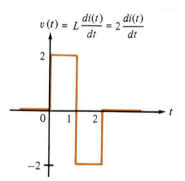

Fig. 4.5 Nonconstant current.

Fig. 4.6 Resulting inductor voltage.

We know that a resistor always absorbs power and the energy absorbed is dissipated as heat. But how about an inductor? For the inductor in the circuit shown in Fig. 4.2, the instantaneous power $p(t) = v(t)i(t)$ absorbed by the inductor is given by

$$p(t) = \begin{cases} 0 & \text{for } -\infty < t < 0 \\ 2t & \text{for } 0 \le t < 1 \\ 2(t-2) & \text{for } 1 \le t < 2 \\ 0 & \text{for } 2 \le t < \infty \end{cases}$$

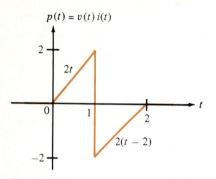

Fig. 4.7   Power absorbed by the inductor.

A sketch of $p(t)$ is shown in Fig. 4.7, in which we see that the power absorbed by the inductor is zero for $-\infty < t \leq 0$ and $2 \leq t < \infty$. For $0 < t < 1$ s, since $p(t)$ is a positive quantity, the inductor is absorbing power (which is produced by the source). However, for $1 < t < 2$ s, since $p(t)$ is a negative quantity, the inductor is actually supplying power (to the source)!

To get the energy absorbed by the inductor, we simply integrate the power absorbed over time. For this example, the energy absorbed increases from 0 to $\frac{1}{2}(1)(2) = 1$ J as time goes from $t = 0$ to $t = 1$ s. However, from $t = 1$ s to $t = 2$ s, the inductor supplies energy, such that at time $t = 2$ s, and thereafter, the energy absorbed by the inductor is zero. Since the energy absorbed by the inductor is not dissipated, but is eventually returned, we say that the inductor **stores** energy. The energy is stored in the magnetic field that surrounds the inductor.

DRILL EXERCISE 4.2

For the circuit shown in Fig. DE4.2, the current through the inductor is

$$i(t) = \begin{cases} 0 & \text{for } -\infty < t < 0 \\ 1 - e^{-2t} & \text{for } 0 \leq t < \infty \end{cases}$$

Find, for $t \geq 0$, (a) $v_L(t)$, (b) $v_R(t)$, (c) $v_s(t)$, and (d) the power absorbed by the inductor.

Answer: (a) $2e^{-2t}$ V; (b) $2(1 - e^{-2t})$ V; (c) 2 V; (d) $2(e^{-2t} - e^{-4t})$ W

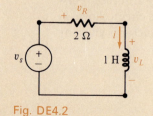

Fig. DE4.2

Given an expression for $p(t)$, the instantaneous power absorbed by an inductor, we can obtain an expression for $w_L(t)$, the energy stored in the inductor—we just sum up the power over time. In other words, the energy stored in an inductor at time t is

$$w_L(t) = \int_{-\infty}^{t} p(t) \, dt$$

However, rather than find the particular expression $w_L(t)$ for a specific example, let us derive a simple formula for the energy stored in an inductor. We proceed as follows:

For an inductor (see Fig. 4.1), since

$$p(t) = i(t)v(t) \quad \text{and} \quad v(t) = L \frac{di(t)}{dt}$$

then

$$p(t) = i(t) \left[L \frac{di(t)}{dt} \right] = Li(t) \frac{di(t)}{dt}$$

Thus, the energy absorbed by the inductor at time t is $w_L(t)$, where

$$w_L(t) = \int_{-\infty}^{t} p(t) \, dt = \int_{-\infty}^{t} Li(t) \frac{di(t)}{dt} \, dt$$

By using the chain rule of calculus, the variable of integration can be changed from t to $i(t)$. Changing the limits of integration appropriately results in

$$w_L(t) = \int_{i(-\infty)}^{i(t)} Li(t) \, di(t) = L \frac{i^2(t)}{2} \Big|_{i(-\infty)}^{i(t)} = \frac{1}{2} L[i^2(t) - i^2(-\infty)]$$

Assuming that you can go back sufficiently in time, there is a time when there was no current in the inductor. Thus, we adopt the convention that $i(-\infty) = 0$. The result is the following expression for the energy absorbed at time t by an inductor whose value is L henries:[†]

$$\boxed{w_L(t) = \tfrac{1}{2} Li^2(t)}$$

EXAMPLE 4.4

The energy stored in the inductor given in Example 4.3 is

$$w_L(t) = \tfrac{1}{2} Li^2(t) = i^2(t) = \begin{cases} 0 & \text{for } -\infty < t < 0 \\ t^2 & \text{for } 0 \le t < 1 \\ (t-2)^2 & \text{for } 1 \le t < 2 \\ 0 & \text{for } 2 \le t < \infty \end{cases}$$

A sketch of the energy stored in the inductor versus time is shown in Fig. 4.8.

[†] The plural of the unit "henry" is spelled either "henries" or "henrys."

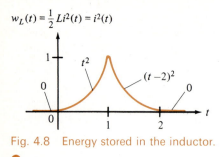

$$w_L(t) = \frac{1}{2}Li^2(t) = i^2(t)$$

Fig. 4.8   Energy stored in the inductor.

DRILL EXERCISE 4.3

Find the energy stored in the inductor described in Drill Exercise 4.2.
Answer: 0 J for $t < 0$, $\frac{1}{2}(1 - 2e^{-2t} + e^{-4t})$ J for $t \ge 0$

Unlike an ideal inductor, an actual inductor (an automobile ignition coil is an example) has some resistance associated with it. This arises from the fact that a physical inductor is constructed from real wire that may have a very small, but still nonzero resistance. For this reason, we model a physical inductor as an ideal inductor in series with a resistance. Practical inductors (also called "coils" and "chokes") range in value from about 10^{-6} H $= 1$ μH all the way up to around 100 H. To construct inductors having large values requires many turns of wire and iron cores, and consequently results in large-value series resistances. The series resistance is typically in the range from a fraction of an ohm to several hundred ohms.

4.2 THE CAPACITOR

Another extremely important circuit element is obtained when two conducting surfaces (called **plates**) are placed in proximity to one another, and between them is a nonconducting material called a **dielectric**. For the resulting element, known as a **capacitor** (formerly **condenser**), a voltage across the plates results in an electric field between them and the current through the capacitor is directly proportional to the time rate of change of the voltage across it. The **ideal capacitor** is depicted in Fig. 4.9 and the relationship between current and voltage (for the direction and polarity re-

Fig. 4.9   Capacitor.

spectively indicated) is given by[†]

$$i = C \frac{dv}{dt}$$

(4.2)

where C is the **capacitance** of the element, and its unit is the **farad** (abbreviated F) in honor of Michael Faraday.

EXAMPLE 4.5

Consider the simple circuit shown in Fig. 4.10. For the case that $v = 5$ V, the circuit in Fig. 4.10 is a dc circuit. Suppose that $C = 2$ F. From the differential relationship for the capacitor, we have

$$i = C \frac{dv}{dt} = 2 \frac{d}{dt} [5] = 0 \text{ A}$$

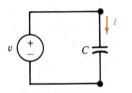

Fig. 4.10   Simple capacitor circuit.

We deduce, therefore, that a capacitor is an open circuit to dc. A more elaborate dc circuit is presented in the following example.

EXAMPLE 4.6

Suppose that we wish to find i in the dc circuit shown in Fig. 4.11(a). Using the fact that a capacitor behaves as an open circuit to dc—as well as the fact that an inductor behaves as a short circuit—we can determine the current i from the resistive circuit given in Fig. 4.11(b). By current division, we have that

$$i = \frac{4}{4 + 2} (6) = 4 \text{ A}$$

[†] For those who remember from elementary physics that $q = Cv$, where q is charge, C is capacitance, and v is voltage, by taking the derivative, we get

$$C \frac{dv}{dt} = \frac{dq}{dt} = i$$

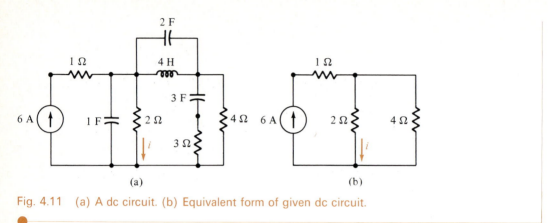

(a)   (b)

Fig. 4.11   (a) A dc circuit. (b) Equivalent form of given dc circuit.

DRILL EXERCISE 4.4

For the circuit given in Fig. 4.11(a), find the voltage (a) across the 1-F capacitor (+ on top), (b) across the 2-F capacitor (+ on the left), and (c) across the 3-F capacitor (+ on top).
Answer: (a) 8 V; (b) 0 V; (c) 24 V

Perhaps the fact that a capacitor acts as an open circuit to dc does not seem surprising since such an element has a nonconducting dielectric (material that will not allow the flow of charge) between its (conducting) plates. How, then, can there ever be any current through a capacitor? To answer this question, consider the simple circuit shown in Fig. 4.10. For the case that v is a constant, then indeed $i = 0$ (i.e., there is no current through the capacitor). However, there is a voltage v across the capacitor and a charge q on the plates. From elementary physics, we know that $q = Cv$. For the case that the voltage is not constant with time [let's explicitly write $v(t)$], the charge will vary with time, that is, $q(t) = Cv(t)$. Since the net charge on the plates fluctuates, and no charge crosses the dielectric, there must be a transfer of charge throughout the remaining portion of the circuit. Hence, when $v(t)$ is noncon-stant, there is a nonzero current $i(t) = C\,dv(t)/dt$. In summary, even though there is no flow of charge across the dielectric of a capacitor, the effect of alternate charging and discharging due to a nonconstant voltage results in an actual current outside of the dielectric.

EXAMPLE 4.7

For the circuit given in Fig. 4.10, suppose that $C = 2$ F and the voltage v is described by the function given in Fig. 4.12. Then the current through the capacitor is as given in Fig. 4.13. At this point, compare these results with those given in Figs. 4.2, 4.5, and

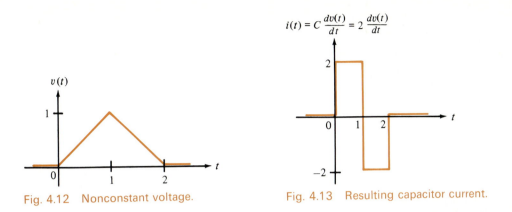

$$i(t) = C\frac{dv(t)}{dt} = 2\frac{dv(t)}{dt}$$

Fig. 4.12 Nonconstant voltage.

Fig. 4.13 Resulting capacitor current.

4.6. Calculating the instantaneous power absorbed by the capacitor in this example results in the same function $p(t)$ that was obtained in Fig. 4.7. As a consequence, a similar subsequent discussion leads us to the conclusion that a capacitor, like an inductor, is an energy-storage element.

For a capacitor, energy is stored in the electric field that exists between its plates. To obtain an expression for the energy stored in a capacitor, we proceed in a manner analogous to the case of the inductor. The result is that the energy absorbed by a capacitor of C farads at time t is

$$w_C(t) = \tfrac{1}{2}Cv^2(t)$$

DRILL EXERCISE 4.5

For the circuit shown in Fig. DE4.5, the voltage across the capacitor is

$$v(t) = \begin{cases} 0 & \text{for } -\infty < t < 0 \\ 1 - e^{-t/2} & \text{for } 0 \le t < \infty \end{cases}$$

Find, for $t \ge 0$, (a) $i_C(t)$, (b) $v_R(t)$, (c) $v_s(t)$, and (d) the energy stored by the capacitor.
Answer: (a) $0.5e^{-t/2}$ A; (b) $e^{-t/2}$ V; (c) 1 V; (d) $0.5(1 - 2e^{-t/2} + e^{-t})$ J

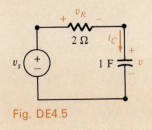

Fig. DE4.5

EXAMPLE 4.8

For the op-amp circuit shown in Fig. 4.14, because the inverting input is at a potential of zero volts, then $v_C = v$. Thus,

$$i = C\frac{dv_C}{dt} = 2\frac{dv}{dt}$$

Since the inputs of the op amp draw no current, $i_R = i$, and

$$v_R = \frac{1}{2}i_R = \frac{1}{2}i = \frac{1}{2}\left(2\frac{dv}{dt}\right) = \frac{dv}{dt}$$

Finally, by KVL we have that $v_o = -v_R$. Hence,

$$v_o = -\frac{dv}{dt}$$

In other words, the output voltage $v_o(t)$ is the derivative of the input voltage $v(t)$ (multiplied by the constant -1). Because of this, we call such a circuit a **differentiator**.

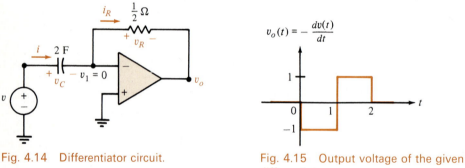

Fig. 4.14   Differentiator circuit.

Fig. 4.15   Output voltage of the given differentiator.

For the case that $v(t)$ is the function given in Fig. 4.12, the output voltage $v_o(t)$ is as given in Fig. 4.15.

DRILL EXERCISE 4.6

For the op-amp circuit shown in Fig. DE4.6, find $v_o(t)$ for the case that the voltage $v(t)$ is described by Fig. 4.12.

Answer: 0 for $-\infty < t < 0$; $t + 1$ for $0 \le t < 1$ s; $-t + 1$ for $1 \le t < 2$ s; 0 for $2 \le t < \infty$

Since no physical dielectric is perfect, an actual capacitor will allow a certain amount of current (perhaps extremely small), called **leakage current**, through it. For this reason, we can model a physical capacitor as an ideal capacitor in parallel with a resistance. This leakage resistance is inversely proportional to the capacitance. Depending on the construction of capacitors, values can range from a few picofarads (10^{-12} F) up to 10,000 μF and more. The product of leakage resistance and capacitance typically lies between 10 and 10^6 Ω-F. The **working voltage** of a capacitor—that is, the maximum voltage that can be applied to the capacitor without damaging it or breaking down the dielectric—can be anything from a few volts to hundreds, or even thousands, of volts.

The capacitor, like the operational amplifier and the resistor, has the valuable property of miniaturization—it can be made part of integrated circuits. On the other hand, because semiconductors do not possess the appropriate magnetic properties, and because of size limitations, inductors are not, in general, readily adaptable to IC form. This, however, does not diminish the importance of the inductor—your radio, television set, and various kinds of telecommunications equipment employ many of them.

Since the expressions for the energy stored in an inductor and a capacitor are, respectively,

$$w_L(t) = \tfrac{1}{2} Li^2(t) \qquad \text{and} \qquad w_C(t) = \tfrac{1}{2} Cv^2(t)$$

we see that regardless of the current through the inductor or the voltage across the capacitor, the energy stored is never negative. That is, these elements can supply energy, but never more than has been previously delivered to them. In other words, they can store and return energy, but not produce it. We refer to such elements as being **passive**. Since the power absorbed by a resistor is $i^2R = v^2/R$, the energy absorbed is always positive, and consequently a resistor is also a passive element.

An element that is capable of producing energy (e.g., an independent or dependent source) is called an **active** element. A circuit that consists only of passive elements is called a **passive circuit** or **network**, whereas one that contains one or more active elements is known as an **active circuit** or **network**.

In the foregoing discussion about resistors, inductors, and capacitors being passive, it was assumed that these elements were positive-valued. By using active elements (such as op amps), it is possible to construct or "simulate" negative-valued resistors, inductors, or capacitors. These types of resistors, inductors, and capacitors must necessarily be active elements. The remainder of this book will deal almost exclusively with positive-valued inductors, capacitors, and resistors.

4.3 RAMP AND STEP FUNCTIONS

In previous examples we encountered the function diagrammed in Fig. 4.16, which is described as follows:

$$f(t) = \begin{cases} 0 & \text{for } -\infty < t < 0 \\ t & \text{for } 0 \le t < 1 \\ -(t-2) & \text{for } 1 \le t < 2 \\ 0 & \text{for } 2 \le t < \infty \end{cases}$$

What we are doing here is specifying the function $f(t)$ by partitioning time into a number of intervals, and then describing $f(t)$ for each interval. However, this is not the only way in which a function can be specified. It is possible to express the above and many other functions as a sum of elementary functions which will be defined shortly. There are several reasons for doing this: (1) We get a one-line expression for $f(t)$ that is often more convenient to handle; (2) the mathematical juggling can be less involved; (3) we frequently may take analytical advantage of the linearity properties of circuits; and (4) we can easily decompose the response of a circuit, thereby getting a better understanding of its behavior.

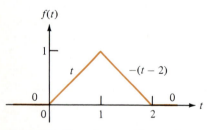

Fig. 4.16 Function used in previous examples.

We begin by considering the simple function $f(t) = t$. Clearly, $df(t)/dt = 1$. Plots of this function and its derivative are shown in Fig. 4.17.

We now define a similar function, the difference being that we want to constrain this new function to be zero for all $t < 0$. The **unit ramp function** $r(t)$ is defined as follows:

$$r(t) = \begin{cases} 0 & \text{for } -\infty < t < 0 \\ t & \text{for } 0 \le t < \infty \end{cases}$$

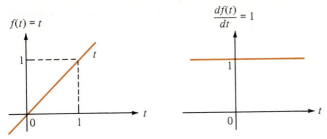

Fig. 4.17   Plots of the function $f(t) = t$ and its derivative.

Pictorially, the unit ramp function $r(t)$ is shown in Fig. 4.18(a). To take the derivative of this function, we proceed in two steps as follows:

$$\text{For } t < 0, \qquad \frac{d[r(t)]}{dt} = \frac{d[0]}{dt} = 0$$

$$\text{For } t \geq 0, \qquad \frac{d[r(t)]}{dt} = \frac{d(t)}{dt} = 1$$

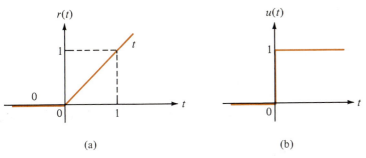

(a)   (b)

Fig. 4.18   (a) Unit ramp function. (b) Unit step function.

The result is a function, called the **unit step function**, that is denoted by $u(t)$. In other words,

$$\frac{d}{dt}[r(t)] = u(t) = \begin{cases} 0 & \text{for } -\infty < t < 0 \\ 1 & \text{for } 0 \leq t < \infty \end{cases}$$

A sketch of the unit step function versus time is shown in Fig. 4.18(b).

EXAMPLE 4.9

Multiplying a function $f(t)$ by a unit step function $u(t)$ results in the product $f(t)u(t)$. Since $u(t) = 0$ for $t < 0$ and $u(t) = 1$ for $t \geq 0$, then

$$f(t)u(t) = \begin{cases} 0 & \text{for } -\infty < t < 0 \\ f(t) & \text{for } 0 \leq t < \infty \end{cases}$$

Specifically, for $f(t) = t$, then

$$tu(t) = \begin{cases} 0 & \text{for } -\infty < t < 0 \\ t & \text{for } 0 \le t < \infty \end{cases}$$

Thus, from the definition of a unit ramp function, we see that

$$tu(t) = r(t)$$

Subtracting a unit step function $u(t)$ from some function $f(t)$ results in the difference $f(t) - u(t)$, where

$$f(t) - u(t) = \begin{cases} f(t) & \text{for } -\infty < t < 0 \\ f(t) - 1 & \text{for } 0 \le t < \infty \end{cases}$$

Specifically, for the constant function $f(t) = 1$, then

$$1 - u(t) = \begin{cases} 1 & \text{for } -\infty < t < 0 \\ 0 & \text{for } 0 \le t < \infty \end{cases}$$

A sketch of this function is shown in Fig. 4.19.

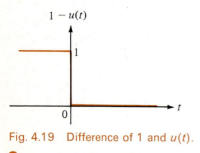

Fig. 4.19   Difference of 1 and $u(t)$.

DRILL EXERCISE 4.7

Sketch the following functions: (a) $1 + u(t)$, (b) $u(t) - 1$, (c) $r(t) - t$, (d) $tr(t)$, (e) $t^2 u(t)$, (f) $[r(t)]^2$

Answer: (a) 1 for $-\infty < t < 0$, 2 for $0 \le t < \infty$
(b) -1 for $-\infty < t < 0$, 0 for $0 \le t < \infty$
(c) $-t$ for $-\infty < t < 0$, 0 for $0 \le t < \infty$
(d) 0 for $-\infty < t < 0$, t^2 for $0 \le t < \infty$
(e) Same as (d)
(f) Same as (d)

Multiplying a unit ramp function $r(t)$ by a constant K results in the ramp function

$$Kr(t) = \begin{cases} 0 & \text{for } -\infty < t < 0 \\ Kt & \text{for } 0 \le t < \infty \end{cases}$$

while multiplying a unit step function $u(t)$ by K yields the step function

$$Ku(t) = \begin{cases} 0 & \text{for } -\infty < t < 0 \\ K & \text{for } 0 \le t < \infty \end{cases}$$

Of course,

$$\frac{d[Kr(t)]}{dt} = K\frac{d[r(t)]}{dt} = Ku(t)$$

Sketches of $Kr(t)$ and $Ku(t)$ are shown in Fig. 4.20.

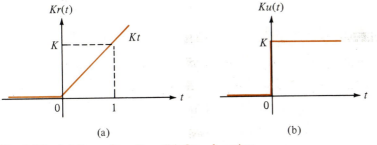

Fig. 4.20   (a) Ramp function. (b) Step function.

So far we have been discussing ramp and step functions which "start" at time $t = 0$. Let us now generalize our discussions by looking at functions which "start" at some time $t = a \neq 0$. Specifically, we define the ramp function

$$Kr(t - a) = \begin{cases} 0 & \text{for } -\infty < t < a \\ K(t - a) & \text{for } a \le t < \infty \end{cases}$$

Plotting the ramp function $Kr(t - a)$ versus t, we therefore obtain the plot in Fig. 4.21(a) when $a > 0$. Note that the plot of this ramp function can be obtained from the plot of the ramp function $Kr(t)$ simply by "shifting" the latter to the right by the amount a. Similarly, if $a < 0$, then the shift would be to the left by the amount a.

The discussion above is based on the fact that a plot of $f(t)$ versus t is identical to a plot of $f(t - a)$ versus $t - a$; and to obtain a plot of $f(t - a)$ versus t we merely

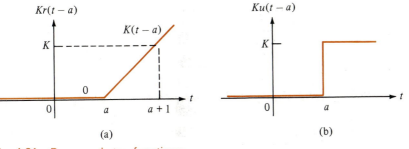

Fig. 4.21   Ramp and step functions.

add the amount a to every point on the horizontal axis in the plot of $f(t - a)$ versus $t - a$.

We may now differentiate the ramp function in the general form $Kr(t - a)$ to obtain $Ku(t - a)$, the general form of the step function. In other words,

$$\frac{d}{dt}[Kr(t - a)] = Ku(t - a) = \begin{cases} 0 & \text{for } -\infty < t < a \\ K & \text{for } a \leq t < \infty \end{cases}$$

a sketch of which is shown in Fig. 4.21(b).

EXAMPLE 4.10

Reconsider the circuit and current shown in Fig. 4.22. Let us analyze this circuit again by first expressing $i(t)$ as a sum of the elemental functions just discussed.

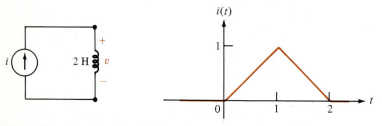

Fig. 4.22   Circuit and applied current.

To write an analytical expression for $i(t)$, note that for $t \leq 1$, $i(t)$ is described by the unit ramp function $r(t)$. However, for $t > 1$ this is no longer the case. Thus, to negate the effect of $r(t)$ for $t > 1$, we subtract a ramp of value $K = 1$ that is zero for $t < 1$; that is, we subtract $r(t - 1)$ from [add $-r(t - 1)$ to] $r(t)$. The result is shown in Fig. 4.23. Now, however, we would like to add a function to $r(t) - r(t - 1)$ such that the result is unchanged for $t \leq 1$ and has a slope of -1 when $t > 1$. This is accomplished simply by adding $-r(t - 1)$. The result, $r(t) - r(t - 1) - r(t - 1) = r(t) - 2r(t - 1)$, is shown in Fig. 4.24.

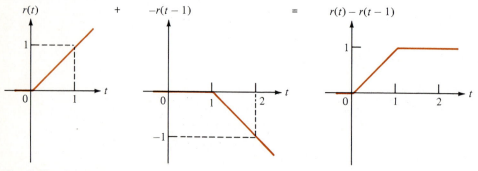

Fig. 4.23   Addition of two ramps.

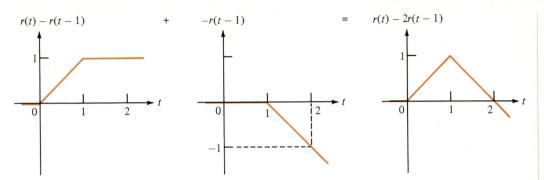

Fig. 4.24   Addition of another negative ramp.

We now see that $r(t) - 2r(t - 1)$ describes $i(t)$ so long as $t \le 2$. To obtain the function that describes $i(t)$ for all t, we simply add $r(t - 2)$ to $r(t) - 2r(t - 1)$. The result, $i(t) = r(t) - 2r(t - 1) + r(t - 2)$, is shown in Fig. 4.25.

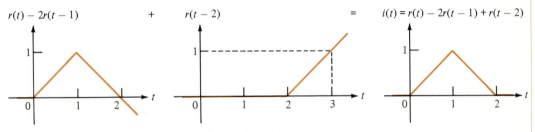

Fig. 4.25   Applied current as a sum of ramp functions.

Since $v = L \, di/dt$, for the given circuit we have that

$$v(t) = 2\frac{d}{dt}\left[r(t) - 2r(t - 1) + r(t - 2)\right]$$

However, since the derivative of a sum of functions is equal to the sum of the derivatives of the functions, we have

$$v(t) = 2\left(\frac{d}{dt}\left[r(t)\right] + \frac{d}{dt}\left[-2r(t - 1)\right] + \frac{d}{dt}\left[r(t - 2)\right]\right)$$

and since the derivative of a ramp is a step,

$$v(t) = 2u(t) - 4u(t - 1) + 2u(t - 2) \text{ V}$$

A sketch of $v(t)$ is obtained by adding the component step functions as shown in Fig. 4.26. Thus, we get the same sketch (naturally) of $v(t)$ as was obtained previously (see Fig. 4.6) by expressing $i(t)$ in terms of ramp functions and working directly with this analytical expression. In general, the approach that is simpler to employ will depend on the nature of the problem.

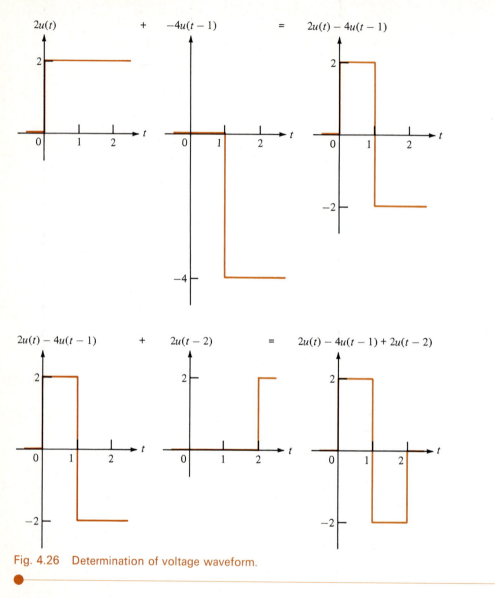

Fig. 4.26   Determination of voltage waveform.

DRILL EXERCISE 4.8

Find an expression for $v_o(t)$ in terms of ramp and step functions for the op-amp circuit and applied voltage $v(t)$ described in Drill Exercise 4.6 (p. 170).

Answer: $r(t) - 2r(t - 1) + r(t - 2) + u(t) - 2u(t - 1) + u(t - 2) \text{ V}$

The Sampling Pulse

Example 4.10 demonstrated an intuitive approach for expressing a function as a sum of elemental functions—specifically, the function $i(t)$ shown in Fig. 4.22 was written as a sum of ramp functions. With experience, the reader should be able to get the result by inspection without requiring the need for Figs. 4.23, 4.24, and 4.25. Yet there is an analytical approach which will yield the same result. Let us now describe how this is done.

By adding the step functions $u(t - a)$ and $-u(t - b)$, where $b > a > 0$, we get the **sampling pulse** $s(t) = u(t - a) - u(t - b)$ shown in Fig. 4.27. Since

$$s(t) = u(t - a) - u(t - b) = \begin{cases} 0 & \text{for } -\infty < t < a \\ 1 & \text{for } a \le t < b \\ 0 & \text{for } b \le t < \infty \end{cases}$$

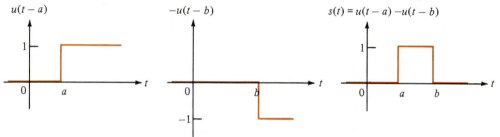

Fig. 4.27 Formation of sampling pulse.

then multiplying the functions $f(t)$ and $s(t)$, we get the product

$$f(t)s(t) = f(t)[u(t - a) - u(t - b)] = \begin{cases} 0 & \text{for } -\infty < t < a \\ f(t) & \text{for } a \le t < b \\ 0 & \text{for } b \le t < \infty \end{cases}$$

For example, if $a = 1$, $b = 2$, and $f(t) = t$, then a plot of the function $t[u(t - 1) - u(t - 2)]$ is obtained as shown in Fig. 4.28.

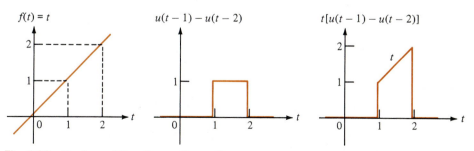

Fig. 4.28 Product of function and sampling pulse.

Let us now see how to express the product $t[u(t-1) - u(t-2)]$ as a sum of ramp and step functions.

In Example 4.9 we saw that $r(t) = tu(t)$. So, too, we have the more general form

$$Kr(t-a) = K(t-a)u(t-a)$$

Therefore

$$
\begin{aligned}
t[u(t-1) - u(t-2)] &= tu(t-1) - tu(t-2) \\
&= (t+0)u(t-1) - (t+0)u(t-2) \\
&= (t-1+1)u(t-1) - (t-2+2)u(t-2) \\
&= (t-1)u(t-1) + 1u(t-1) - (t-2)u(t-2) - 2u(t-2) \\
&= r(t-1) + u(t-1) - r(t-2) - 2u(t-2)
\end{aligned}
$$

which is a sum of ramp and step functions.

Basically, what we did was to convert a product such as $tu(t-a)$ to the sum of a ramp and a step function as follows:

$$
\begin{aligned}
tu(t-a) = (t+0)u(t-a) &= (t-a+a)u(t-a) \\
&= (t-a)u(t-a) + au(t-a) \\
&= r(t-a) + au(t-a)
\end{aligned}
$$

EXAMPLE 4.11

Let us express the function $f(t)$ described by Fig. 4.16 (p. 172) in terms of ramp and step functions by employing sampling pulses.

To do this, note that we can write that $f(t) = f_1(t) + f_2(t)$, where $f_1(t)$ and $f_2(t)$ are as depicted in Fig. 4.29. Since

$$
\begin{aligned}
f(t) = f_1(t) + f_2(t) &= t[u(t) - u(t-1)] - (t-2)[u(t-1) - u(t-2)] \\
&= tu(t) - tu(t-1) - (t-2)u(t-1) + (t-2)u(t-2) \\
&= tu(t) - (2t-2)u(t-1) + (t-2)u(t-2) \\
&= tu(t) - 2(t-1)u(t-1) + (t-2)u(t-2) \\
&= r(t) - 2r(t-1) + r(t-2)
\end{aligned}
$$

which was the result obtained in Example 4.10.

$f_1(t) = t[u(t) - u(t-1)]$ $f_2(t) = -(t-2)[u(t-1) - u(t-2)]$

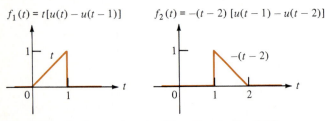

Fig. 4.29   Component parts of function in Fig. 4.16.

DRILL EXERCISE 4.9

Express the function described by Fig. DE4.9 in terms of ramp and step functions.

Answer: $u(t) - r(t) + r(t - 2) + u(t - 2) - 2u(t - 3)$

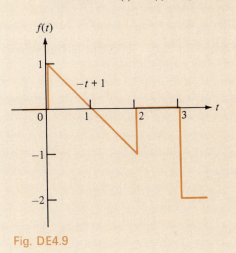

Fig. DE4.9

4.4 THE IMPULSE FUNCTION

Suppose that the function $f(t)$ given in Fig. DE4.9 describes the voltage $v(t)$ across a capacitor. Since $i(t) = C\,dv(t)/dt$ for a capacitor, we can determine the current through the capacitor by taking the derivative of the given function. In particular, for $t < 0$,

$$\frac{dv(t)}{dt} = \frac{df(t)}{dt} = \frac{d(0)}{dt} = 0$$

while for $0 < t < 2$ s,

$$\frac{dv(t)}{dt} = \frac{df(t)}{dt} = \frac{d(-t + 1)}{dt} = -1$$

and for $t > 2$ s,

$$\frac{dv(t)}{dt} = \frac{df(t)}{dt} = \frac{d(0)}{dt} = 0$$

We may be tempted to believe that we have determined $df(t)/dt = dv(t)/dt$ for all t. But what is the derivative of the given function at times $t = 0$ and $t = 2$ s where the function is discontinuous? In terms of the concept of slope, the derivative at a discontinuity should be infinite. How do we deal with this?

To answer this question, we introduce a new function. Just as we obtained a step function by taking the derivative of a ramp function, let us refer to the derivative of a step function as an **impulse function**. Specifically, we define the impulse function $K\delta(t - a)$ by

$$K\delta(t - a) = \frac{d}{dt}[Ku(t - a)]$$

To conform to the concept of slope, we represent $K\delta(t - a)$ pictorially as shown in Fig. 4.30.

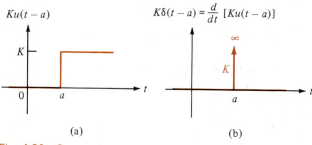

Fig. 4.30   Step and impulse functions.

Since the impulse function is designated by the Greek letter delta, we also refer to an impulse function as a **delta function**. Furthermore, for the special case that $K = 1$ and $a = 0$, we call the function $\delta(t)$ a **unit impulse function** or a **unit delta function**—this function is depicted in Fig. 4.31.

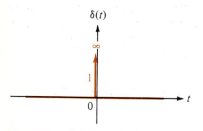

Fig. 4.31   Unit impulse function.

Note that the impulse function $K\delta(t - a)$ is zero everywhere except for $t = a$, where it is infinite. Since $K\delta(t - a)$ is obtained by taking the derivative of $Ku(t - a)$—a function with a discontinuity of value K at time $t = a$—then $Ku(t - a)$ results from taking the integral of $K\delta(t - a)$. This indicates that the K associated with $K\delta(t - a)$ represents the area under the impulse function. In other words, although an impulse function has infinite height and zero width, it has a finite area.

Defining the impulse function $K\delta(t - a)$ by taking the derivative of the step function $Ku(t - a)$—a function with a discontinuity of value K which occurs at time $t = a$—may seem somewhat forced. However, there are other ways of defining the impulse function $K\delta(t - a)$ which are mathematically more palatable.

Consider the function $f(t)$ and its derivative shown in Fig. 4.32. The pulse $df(t)/dt$ has height K/ε and width $a + \varepsilon - a = \varepsilon$. Thus, the area under this pulse is $(K/\varepsilon)(\varepsilon) = K$. If we take the limit as $\varepsilon \to 0$, then we see that in the limit, $f(t)$ becomes $Ku(t - a)$. Furthermore, the height of $df(t)/dt$ goes to infinity and the width goes to zero, but the area remains the constant value K. Hence, in the limit, $df(t)/dt$ becomes $K\delta(t - a)$.

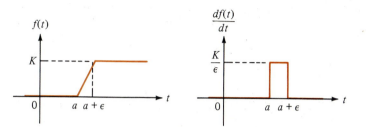

Fig. 4.32   Functions used to form step and impulse functions.

Needless to say, because of its zero width and infinite height, it is not possible physically to obtain a unit impulse function as either a voltage or a current. But don't get upset—it's not possible to construct ideal sources, ideal resistors, ideal inductors, and ideal capacitors either. Nor is it possible to get a unit step function—it is not physically possible to have a function (either voltage or current) change a specified amount in zero time.[†] However, we shall find the unit impulse function to be a convenient and very useful mathematical tool.

EXAMPLE 4.12

Suppose that the voltage across a 3-F capacitor is

$$v(t) = u(t) - r(t) + r(t - 2) + u(t - 2) - 2u(t - 3) \text{ V}$$

(see Fig. DE4.9 on p. 181). Then the current through the capacitor is

$$i(t) = C\frac{dv(t)}{dt} = 3\frac{d}{dt}\left[u(t) - r(t) + r(t - 2) + u(t - 2) - 2u(t - 3)\right]$$

$$= 3\frac{d}{dt}\left[u(t)\right] + 3\frac{d}{dt}\left[-r(t)\right] + 3\frac{d}{dt}\left[r(t - 2)\right] + 3\frac{d}{dt}\left[u(t - 2)\right]$$

$$+ 3\frac{d}{dt}\left[-2u(t - 3)\right]$$

$$= 3\delta(t) - 3u(t) + 3u(t - 2) + 3\delta(t - 2) - 6\delta(t - 3) \text{ A}$$

A sketch of this current is shown in Fig. 4.33.

[†] Physically, a unit step function can be approximated more accurately than can a unit impulse function.

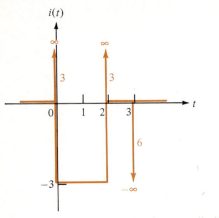

Fig. 4.33   Current resulting from applied voltage.

DRILL EXERCISE 4.10

The current through a 4-H inductor is $i(t) = u(t) - r(t) + 2r(t-1) - r(t-2)$ A. Find the voltage $v(t)$ across the inductor. Sketch $i(t)$ and $v(t)$.

Answer: $4\delta(t) - 4u(t) + 8u(t-1) - 4u(t-2)$ V

We now derive an important and useful property of impulse functions that we shall make use of many times in subsequent material. This property is based on the fact that $\delta(t-a) = 0$ for $t \neq a$.

Suppose that $f(t)$ is an arbitrary function that is defined at time $t = a$—i.e., the value $f(a)$ is finite. Forming the product $f(t)\delta(t-a)$, we have that

$$f(t)\delta(t-a) = \begin{cases} 0 & \text{for } t \neq a \\ f(a)\delta(t-a) & \text{for } t = a \end{cases}$$

Forming the product $f(a)\delta(t-a)$, we have that

$$f(a)\delta(t-a) = \begin{cases} 0 & \text{for } t \neq a \\ f(a)\delta(t-a) & \text{for } t = a \end{cases}$$

Therefore, we see that

$$f(t)\delta(t-a) = f(a)\delta(t-a)$$

and this is known as the **sampling property** of the impulse function (not to be confused with the concept of a sampling pulse as shown in Fig. 4.27).

EXAMPLE 4.13

The sampling property of the impulse function gives us the following identities:

1. $3t\delta(t - 2) = 3(2)\delta(t - 2) = 6\delta(t - 2)$
2. $(5t - 2)\delta(t - 4) = (5[4] - 2)\delta(t - 4) = 18\delta(t - 4)$
3. $(2t^2 + t - 1)\delta(t + 3) = (2[-3]^2 + [-3] - 1)\delta(t + 3) = 14\delta(t + 3)$
4. $6e^{-3t}\delta(t) = 6e^{-3(0)}\delta(t) = 6\delta(t)$
5. $(\cos 3t)\delta(t - \pi) = (\cos 3[\pi])\delta(t - \pi) = -\delta(t - \pi)$
6. $(1 - e^{-4t})\delta(t) = (1 - e^{-4(0)})\delta(t) = 0\delta(t)$

In this last case, we obtained an impulse function whose area is zero! Taking the integral of the zero impulse function $0\delta(t - a)$, we get the zero step function $0u(t - a)$. The derivative of this step function, which again is $0\delta(t - a)$, is clearly zero. Our conclusion is that an impulse function whose area is zero is equivalent to zero; that is,

$$0\delta(t - a) = 0$$

DRILL EXERCISE 4.11

Use the sampling property of the impulse function to simplify the following expressions: (a) $(2t - 5)\delta(t - 1)$; (b) $e^{-t/2}\delta(t + 3)$; (c) $(\sin \pi t)\delta(t - 1)$; (d) $3t\delta(t)$; (e) $4(1 - e^{-t})\delta(t + 1)$; (f) $4(1 - e^{-t})\delta(t - 1)$
Answer: (a) $-3\delta(t - 1)$; (b) $4.48\delta(t + 3)$; (c) 0; (d) 0; (e) $-6.87\delta(t + 1)$; (f) $2.53\delta(t - 1)$

4.5 INTEGRAL RELATIONSHIPS

Given any fixed value t_0, the integral

$$\int_{-\infty}^{t_0} f(t)\, dt$$

is a real number that represents the net area under the curve $f(t)$ for the segment of the t-axis which extends from $-\infty$ to t_0. Since t_0 can be any real number between $-\infty$ and ∞, let us instead use for the upper limit on the integral the variable t. In this way, the integral will not result in a specific number, but rather it will result in a function of the variable t. Let us call this function $g(t)$; that is, we define

$$g(t) = \int_{-\infty}^{t} f(t)\, dt$$

Specifically, then, the area under the curve $f(t)$ between $-\infty$ and t_0 is

$$g(t_0) = \int_{-\infty}^{t_0} f(t)\, dt$$

Therefore, for all $t > t_0$, we have that

$$g(t) = \int_{-\infty}^{t} f(t)\, dt = \int_{-\infty}^{t_0} f(t)\, dt + \int_{t_0}^{t} f(t)\, dt = g(t_0) + \int_{t_0}^{t} f(t)\, dt$$

Now let us return to the inductor. We know that $v = L\, di/dt$ (provided that i is directed through L from $+$ to $-$; otherwise, $v = -L\, di/dt$). This is the differential relationship between voltage and current for an inductor. From this we may now obtain an integral relationship between voltage and current for an inductor. To do this, first integrate both sides of this equation with respect to time, choosing t_0 and t as the lower and upper limits, respectively. Doing this we get

$$\int_{t_0}^{t} v(t)\, dt = \int_{t_0}^{t} L\, \frac{di(t)}{dt}\, dt$$

By the chain rule of calculus, we can change the variable of integration for the term on the right. Since $t = t_0$ implies that $i(t) = i(t_0)$, we have

$$\int_{t_0}^{t} v(t)\, dt = \int_{i(t_0)}^{i(t)} L\, di(t) = Li(t)\Big|_{i(t_0)}^{i(t)} = L[i(t) - i(t_0)]$$

Hence,

$$i(t) - i(t_0) = \frac{1}{L} \int_{t_0}^{t} v(t)\, dt \qquad \Rightarrow \qquad \boxed{i(t) = i(t_0) + \frac{1}{L} \int_{t_0}^{t} v(t)\, dt}$$

But as we have seen above, for $t > t_0$ we can write this last equation as

$$\boxed{i(t) = \frac{1}{L} \int_{-\infty}^{t} v(t)\, dt}$$

Since these last two equations are equivalent, either one is referred to as the integral relationship between voltage and current for an inductor.

Consider the step function $Ku(t - a)$. For $t < a$, we have that

$$\int_{-\infty}^{t} Ku(t - a)\, dt = \int_{-\infty}^{t} 0\, dt = 0$$

For $t \geq a$, however, we have that

$$\int_{-\infty}^{t} Ku(t - a)\, dt = \int_{-\infty}^{a} Ku(t - a)\, dt + \int_{a}^{t} Ku(t - a)\, dt$$

$$= \int_{-\infty}^{a} 0\, dt + \int_{a}^{t} K\, dt = 0 + Kt\Big|_{a}^{t} = K(t - a)$$

Thus,

$$\int_{-\infty}^{t} Ku(t - a)\, dt = K(t - a)u(t - a) = Kr(t - a)$$

That is, the integral of a step is a ramp. This result should be no surprise since the derivative of a ramp is a step. Hence, since the derivative of a step function is an impulse function, then it follows that

$$\int_{-\infty}^{t} K\delta(t - a)\,dt = Ku(t - a)$$

These results are sketched in Fig. 4.34.

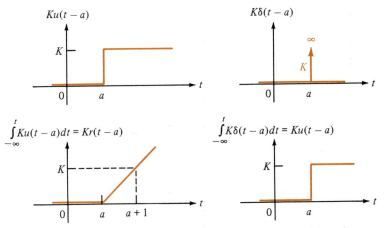

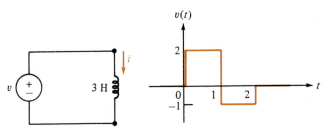

Fig. 4.34 Integral relationships between steps, ramps, and impulses.

We see from the sketch of the integral of the impulse function $K\delta(t - a)$ that although at the point $t = a$ the impulse function is infinite, the area under it is finite and is equal to K.

EXAMPLE 4.14

For the circuit and voltage v described in Fig. 4.35 let us find the inductor current i.

Fig. 4.35 Application of voltage across an inductor.

One way to determine i is to first express v in terms of step functions. To do this, we note that $v(t) = 2u(t) - 3u(t - 1) + u(t - 2)\,$V. Since

$$i(t) = \frac{1}{L}\int_{-\infty}^{t} v(t)\,dt$$

then

$$i(t) = \frac{1}{3} \int_{-\infty}^{t} \left[2u(t) - 3u(t-1) + u(t-2) \right] dt$$

$$= \frac{1}{3} \left[\int_{-\infty}^{t} 2u(t)\, dt + \int_{-\infty}^{t} -3u(t-1)\, dt + \int_{-\infty}^{t} u(t-2)\, dt \right]$$

$$= \tfrac{1}{3}\left[2r(t) - 3r(t-1) + r(t-2) \right] = \tfrac{2}{3}r(t) - r(t-1) + \tfrac{1}{3}r(t-2)\, \text{A}$$

A sketch of this current is shown in Figure 4.36.

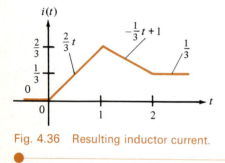

Fig. 4.36   Resulting inductor current.

DRILL EXERCISE 4.12

For the circuit shown in Fig. DE4.12, the current through the 1-Ω resistor is $i_R(t) = u(t) - u(t-1)$ A. Find (a) $v(t)$; (b) $i_L(t)$; and (c) $i_s(t)$. Sketch these functions.
Answer: (a) $u(t) - u(t-1)$ V; (b) $r(t) - r(t-1)$ A;
(c) $r(t) - r(t-1) + u(t) - u(t-1)$ A

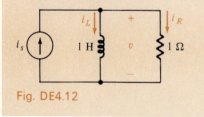

Fig. DE4.12

To return to the capacitor, we know that

$$i = C \frac{dv}{dt}$$

and this is the differential relationship between current and voltage. In a manner identical to that discussed for the inductor, we can obtain the equivalent integral relationships between voltage and current for a capacitor that are given by

$$v(t) = v(t_0) + \frac{1}{C} \int_{t_0}^{t} i(t) \, dt \qquad \text{and} \qquad v(t) = \frac{1}{C} \int_{-\infty}^{t} i(t) \, dt$$

● ───────

EXAMPLE 4.15

For the circuit shown in Fig. 4.37(a), let us determine v given that i is described by Fig. 4.37(b). In this case, let us consider three intervals of time.

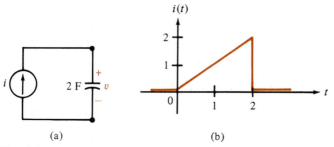

(a)   (b)

Fig. 4.37   (a) Circuit with a capacitor. (b) Applied current.

For $t \le 0$,

$$v(t) = \frac{1}{C} \int_{-\infty}^{t} i(t) \, dt = \frac{1}{2} \int_{-\infty}^{t} 0 \, dt = 0 \text{ V}$$

For $0 < t \le 2$ s,

$$v(t) = \frac{1}{C} \int_{-\infty}^{t} i(t) \, dt = v(0) + \frac{1}{C} \int_{0}^{t} i(t) \, dt = 0 + \frac{1}{2} \int_{0}^{t} t \, dt = \frac{1}{2} \left(\frac{t^2}{2} \right) \Big|_{0}^{t} = \frac{t^2}{4} \text{ V}$$

For $t > 2$ s,

$$v(t) = \frac{1}{C} \int_{-\infty}^{t} i(t) \, dt = v(2) + \frac{1}{2} \int_{2}^{t} i(t) \, dt$$

and since $v(t) = t^2/4$ for $0 < t \le 2$ s,

$$v(t) = \frac{2^2}{4} + \frac{1}{2} \int_{2}^{t} 0 \, dt = 1 \text{ V}$$

In summary, then, the voltage $v(t)$ is as shown in Fig. 4.38.

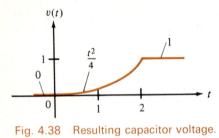

Fig. 4.38 Resulting capacitor voltage.

DRILL EXERCISE 4.13

For the circuit shown in Fig. DE4.13, the voltage across the 1-Ω resistor is $v_R(t) = e^{-t}$ V for $t \geq 0$. Given that $v_C(0) = 0$ V, find the following functions for $t \geq 0$:
(a) $i_R(t)$; (b) $v_C(t)$; and (c) $v_s(t)$.
Answer: (a) e^{-t} A; (b) $1 - e^{-t}$ V; (c) 1 V

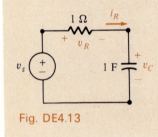

Fig. DE4.13

EXAMPLE 4.16

For the op-amp circuit shown in Fig. 4.39, since $v_1 = 0$, then $i = 2v_s$. Since the input terminals of the op amp draw no current,

$$i_C = i = 2v_s$$

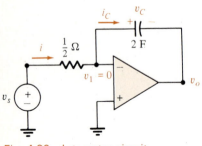

Fig. 4.39 Integrator circuit.

Thus,

$$v_c = \frac{1}{C} \int_{-\infty}^{t} i_C(t)\, dt = \frac{1}{2} \int_{-\infty}^{t} 2v_s(t)\, dt = \int_{-\infty}^{t} v_s(t)\, dt$$

By KVL, $v_o = -v_c$. Hence,

$$v_o(t) = -\int_{-\infty}^{t} v_s(t)\, dt$$

and the output voltage is the integral of the input voltage (multiplied by the constant -1). For this reason, such a circuit is known as an **integrator**. This type of circuit is extremely useful—it is the backbone of the analog computer.

4.6 IMPORTANT CIRCUIT CONCEPTS

Series and Parallel Connections

Just as resistors connected in series or parallel can be combined into an equivalent resistor, so can inductors and capacitors be combined. To see specifically how, we begin with a series connection of inductors as shown in Fig. 4.40.

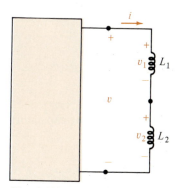

Fig. 4.40   Inductors connected in series.

Fig. 4.41   Combining inductors connected in series.

We find that

$$v = v_1 + v_2 = L_1 \frac{di}{dt} + L_2 \frac{di}{dt} = (L_1 + L_2)\frac{di}{dt} = L\frac{di}{dt}$$

where $L = L_1 + L_2$. Since the relationship between v and i is not changed, the series connection of L_1 and L_2 can be replaced by a single inductor of value $L = L_1 + L_2$ and the effect on the remainder of the network is the same. We depict this condition in Fig. 4.41.

For the case of two inductors in parallel, as shown in Fig. 4.42, by KCL,

$$i = i_1 + i_2 = \frac{1}{L_1} \int_{t_0}^{t} v \, dt + i_1(t_0) + \frac{1}{L_2} \int_{t_0}^{t} v \, dt + i_2(t_0)$$

$$= \left(\frac{1}{L_1} + \frac{1}{L_2} \right) \int_{t_0}^{t} v \, dt + i_1(t_0) + i_2(t_0) = \frac{1}{L} \int_{t_0}^{t} v \, dt + i(t_0)$$

where

$$\frac{1}{L} = \frac{1}{L_1} + \frac{1}{L_2} \quad \text{or} \quad L = \frac{L_1 L_2}{L_1 + L_2}$$

and

$$i(t_0) = i_1(t_0) + i_2(t_0)$$

Thus, the parallel combination of inductors L_1 and L_2 can be replaced by a single inductor L provided that $1/L = (1/L_1) + (1/L_2)$ and the initial current in L is equal to the sum of the initial currents in L_1 and L_2. This result is shown in Fig. 4.43.

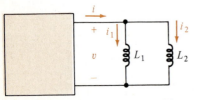

Fig. 4.42   Inductors connected in parallel.

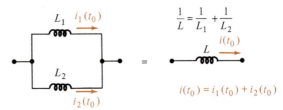

Fig. 4.43   Combining inductors connected in parallel.

Let us now consider capacitors in parallel. Specifically, for two capacitors in parallel (Fig. 4.44), by KCL,

$$i = i_1 + i_2 = C_1 \frac{dv}{dt} + C_2 \frac{dv}{dt} = (C_1 + C_2) \frac{dv}{dt} = C \frac{dv}{dt}$$

so that we obtain the result shown in Fig. 4.45.

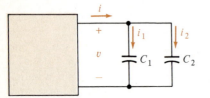

Fig. 4.44   Capacitors connected in parallel.

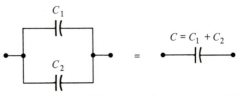

Fig. 4.45   Combining capacitors connected in parallel.

For capacitors in series, analogously to inductors in parallel, we get the result shown in Fig. 4.46.

$$\frac{1}{C} = \frac{1}{C_1} + \frac{1}{C_2} \left(\text{or } C = \frac{C_1 C_2}{C_1 + C_2} \right)$$

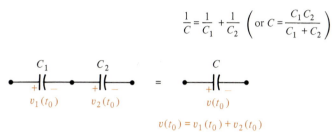

$$v(t_0) = v_1(t_0) + v_2(t_0)$$

Fig. 4.46   Combining capacitors connected in series.

In summary, inductors in series and parallel are treated like resistors, whereas capacitors are treated like conductances.

EXAMPLE 4.17

For the connection of inductors shown in Fig. 4.47, let us determine the value for L which results in the series-parallel connection having a value of L henries.

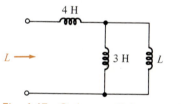

4 H

$L \longrightarrow$ 3 H L

Fig. 4.47   Series-parallel connection of inductors.

The parallel connection of a 3-H inductor and an L-henry inductor has a value of $3L/(3 + L)$. But this combination is in series with a 4-H inductor. Thus, we have that the overall inductance L is given by

$$L = 4 + \frac{3L}{3 + L}$$

Solving this equation for L results in a quadratic equation, the solution of which is $L = -2$ H and $L = 6$ H. Assuming positive-valued inductors, we deduce that

$$L = 6 \text{ H}$$

DRILL EXERCISE 4.14

For the circuit shown in Fig. DE4.14, the initial capacitor voltages are $v_1(0) = 6$ V and $v_2(0) = -2$ V. Find $v(t)$ for $t \geq 0$ given that

$$i(t) = \begin{cases} 1 & \text{for } 0 \leq t < 1 \text{ s} \\ 0 & \text{for } t \geq 1 \text{ s} \end{cases}$$

Answer: $4 + 0.5t$ V for $0 \leq t < 1$ s; 4.5 V for $t \geq 1$ s

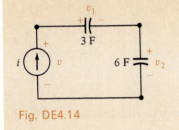

Fig. DE4.14

Node and Mesh Equations

Just as we analyzed resistive circuits with the use of node or mesh equations, we can write a set of equations for circuits that contain capacitors and inductors in addition to resistors and sources. The procedure is similar to that described for the resistive case—the difference being that for inductors and capacitors the appropriate relationships between voltage and current are used in place of Ohm's law.

EXAMPLE 4.18

Consider the circuit shown in Fig. 4.48. Let us write the node equations.

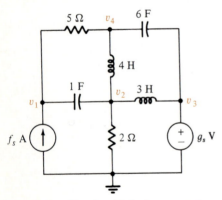

Fig. 4.48   Circuit with inductors and capacitors.

By KCL at node v_1,

$$1\frac{d}{dt}(v_1 - v_2) + \frac{1}{5}(v_1 - v_4) - f_s = 0$$

At node v_2, by KCL,

$$1\frac{d}{dt}(v_2 - v_1) + \frac{1}{4}\int_{-\infty}^{t}(v_2 - v_4)\,dt + \frac{1}{2}v_2 + \frac{1}{3}\int_{-\infty}^{t}(v_2 - v_3)\,dt = 0$$

At node v_3,

$$v_3 = g_s$$

At node v_4, by KCL,

$$\frac{1}{4}\int_{-\infty}^{t}(v_4 - v_2)\,dt + \frac{1}{5}(v_4 - v_1) + 6\frac{d}{dt}(v_4 - v_3) = 0$$

The equation, whose variables are voltages, obtained at node v_1 is called a **differential equation**, since it contains variables and their derivatives. The equations obtained at nodes v_2 and v_4 are called **integrodifferential equations**, since they contain integrals as well as derivatives.

DRILL EXERCISE 4.15

Write the node equations for the circuit shown in Fig. DE4.15.

Answer: $v_1 = v_s$; $\dfrac{v_2 - v_1}{1} + \dfrac{1}{5}\displaystyle\int_{-\infty}^{t} v_2\,dt + \dfrac{v_2 - v_3}{3} + 4\dfrac{d}{dt}(v_2 - v_3) = 0$;

$$\frac{v_3}{2} + \frac{v_3 - v_2}{3} + 4\frac{d}{dt}(v_3 - v_2) = 0$$

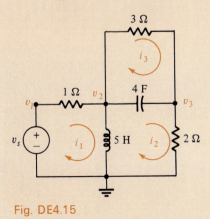

Fig. DE4.15

EXAMPLE 4.19

Referring to Fig. 4.49, we can write a set of mesh equations as follows:

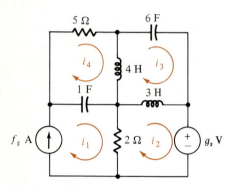

Fig. 4.49   Circuit with mesh currents designated.

For mesh i_1,

$$i_1 = f_s$$

For mesh i_2, by KVL,

$$g_s + 2(i_2 - i_1) + 3\frac{d}{dt}(i_2 - i_3) = 0$$

For mesh i_3, by KVL,

$$3\frac{d}{dt}(i_3 - i_2) + 4\frac{d}{dt}(i_3 - i_4) + \frac{1}{6}\int_{-\infty}^{t} i_3\, dt = 0$$

For mesh i_4, by KVL,

$$\frac{1}{1}\int_{-\infty}^{t}(i_4 - i_1)\, dt + 4\frac{d}{dt}(i_4 - i_3) + 5i_4 = 0$$

DRILL EXERCISE 4.16

Write the mesh equations for the circuit given in Fig. DE4.15.

Answer: $1i_1 + 5\dfrac{d}{dt}(i_1 - i_2) - v_s = 0;$

$$5\frac{d}{dt}(i_2 - i_1) + \frac{1}{4}\int_{-\infty}^{t}(i_2 - i_3)\, dt + 2i_2 = 0;$$

$$3i_3 + \frac{1}{4}\int_{-\infty}^{t}(i_3 - i_2)\, dt = 0$$

Writing the equations for a circuit, as in the preceding examples is not difficult. Finding the solution of equations like these, however, is another matter—it is no simple task. Thus, with the exception of some very simple circuits, we shall have to resort to additional concepts and techniques to be discussed later.

Duality

Let us formalize our discussion of "duality" which was mentioned briefly earlier (see Example 1.10 on p. 30). Consider the two circuits shown in Fig. 4.50.

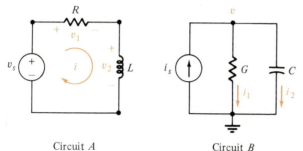

Circuit *A*   Circuit *B*

Fig. 4.50   Dual circuits.

Using mesh analysis for circuit *A* and nodal analysis for circuit *B*, we get the following results:

Circuit *A*	Circuit *B*
$v_s = v_1 + v_2$	$i_s = i_1 + i_2$
$v_s = Ri + L\dfrac{di}{dt}$	$i_s = Gv + C\dfrac{dv}{dt}$

In other words, both circuits are described by the same equations

$$x_s = x_1 + x_2$$

$$x_s = a_1 y + a_2 \frac{dy}{dt}$$

except that a variable that is a current in one circuit is a voltage in the other and vice versa. For these two circuits this result is not a coincidence, but rather is due to a concept known as **duality**, which has its roots in the subject of graph theory— a topic we discussed briefly previously.

In actuality, circuits *A* and *B* are **dual circuits** when the values $R = G$ and $L = C$ and the functions $v_s = i_s$, since the following roles are interchanged:

Series ↔ Parallel

Voltage ↔ Current

Resistance ↔ Conductance

Capacitance ↔ Inductance

In summary, the relationships between a circuit and its dual are as follows:

Circuit	Dual Circuit
Series connection	Parallel connection
Parallel connection	Series connection
Voltage of x volts	Current of x amperes
Current of x amperes	Voltage of x volts
Resistance of x ohms	Conductance of x siemens
Conductance of x siemens	Resistance of x ohms
Capacitance of x farads	Inductance of x henries
Inductance of x henries	Capacitance of x farads
KCL	KVL
KVL	KCL

The usefulness of duality lies in the fact that once a circuit is analyzed, its dual is in essence analyzed also—two for the price of one! Note that if circuit B is the dual of circuit A, then taking the dual of circuit B in essence results in circuit A. Not every circuit, however, has a dual. With the aid of graph theory it can be shown that a circuit has a dual if and only if it is a planar network.

Given a series-parallel network, its dual can be found by inspection using the list above. However, a circuit may not be series-parallel. We now present a technique for obtaining the dual of a planar circuit—regardless of whether or not it is a series-parallel network.

1. Inside of each mesh, including the infinite region surrounding the circuit, place a node.
2. Suppose two of these nodes, say nodes a and b, are in adjacent meshes. Then there is at least one element in the boundary common to these two meshes. Place the dual of each common element between nodes a and b.

In order to get the mesh equations of the original circuit to correspond to the node equations of the dual circuit, place clockwise mesh currents $i_1, i_2, \ldots, i_n$ in the finite regions. The corresponding nodes in the dual are labeled with the voltages $v_1, v_2, \ldots, v_n$, respectively. The reference node of the dual circuit corresponds to the infinite region of the original circuit.

EXAMPLE 4.20

For the circuit given in Fig. 4.49, the dual is shown in heavy lines in Fig. 4.51. The dual circuit is redrawn in Fig. 4.52 for simplicity.

To determine the voltage polarities and the current directions in the dual circuit, we employ the mesh currents of the original circuit. For this example, the mesh currents are indicated in Fig. 4.49 on p. 196.

The dual of the independent current source labeled f_s A is an independent voltage source labeled f_s V. Since the direction of the current source f_s A agrees with the

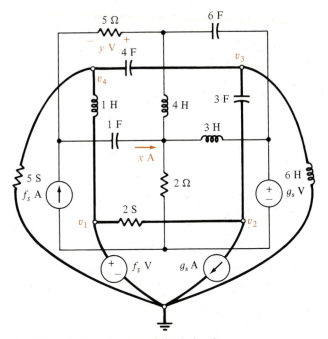

Fig. 4.51   Determination of dual circuit.

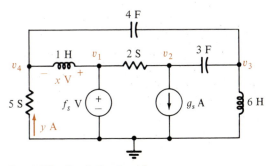

Fig. 4.52   Dual circuit redrawn.

direction of mesh current i_1, then in the dual circuit node v_1 is on the $+$ side of the voltage source f_s V.

The dual of the current x A going through the 1-F capacitor in the original circuit is a voltage of x V across the 1-H inductor in the dual circuit. Since the direction of x A agrees with the direction of mesh current i_1, then in the dual circuit node v_1 is on the $+$ side of the voltage x V. (Alternatively, since the direction of x A opposes the direction of mesh current i_4, then in the dual circuit node v_4 is on the $-$ side of the voltage x V.)

The dual of the independent voltage source labeled g_s V is an independent current source labeled g_s A. Since mesh current i_2 is directed from $+$ to $-$ for voltage source g_s V, then in the dual circuit the current g_s A is directed out of node v_2.

The dual of the voltage y V across the 5-Ω resistor in the original circuit is a current of y A through the 5-S conductance in the dual circuit. Since mesh current i_4 is directed from $-$ to $+$, then in the dual circuit the current y A is directed into node v_4.

Let us now write the node equations for the dual circuit shown in Fig. 4.52. For node v_1,

$$v_1 = f_s$$

At node v_2, by KCL,

$$g_s + 2(v_2 - v_1) + 3\frac{d}{dt}(v_2 - v_3) = 0$$

At node v_3, by KCL,

$$3\frac{d}{dt}(v_3 - v_2) + 4\frac{d}{dt}(v_3 - v_4) + \frac{1}{6}\int_{-\infty}^{t} v_3\,dt = 0$$

and, at node v_4, by KCL,

$$\frac{1}{1}\int_{-\infty}^{t}(v_4 - v_1)\,dt + 4\frac{d}{dt}(v_4 - v_3) + 5v_4 = 0$$

Note that these are the duals of the mesh equations that we obtained in Example 4.19.

DRILL EXERCISE 4.17

Fig. DE4.17 shows a circuit and its dual. In the given circuit are currents x_1 A, x_2 A, x_3 A, x_4 A, and voltages y_1 V, y_2 V, y_3 V, 6 cos $3t$ V. Determine the dual quantities of these currents and voltages.

Answer: x_1 V (a^+, c^-); x_2 V (a^+, b^-); x_3 V (c^+, b^-); x_4 V (d^+, b^-); y_1 A $(c \rightarrow d)$; y_2 A $(a \rightarrow b)$; y_3 A $(b \rightarrow d)$; 6 cos $3t$ A $(d \rightarrow a)$

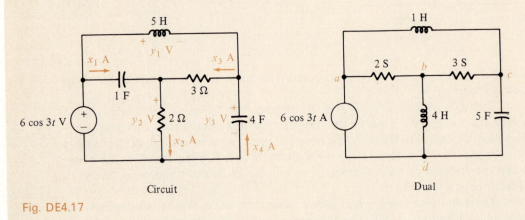

Circuit   Dual

Fig. DE4.17

4.7 INITIAL CONDITIONS

In the analysis of circuits in the future, we shall repeatedly make use of two very important properties—one for inductors and one for capacitors. Let us now derive these properties.

Again, consider an inductor. Since

$$i(t) = \frac{1}{L} \int_{-\infty}^{t} v(t)\, dt$$

then the current through the inductor at time $t = a$ is

$$i(a) = \frac{1}{L} \int_{-\infty}^{a} v(t)\, dt$$

For any positive number ε, the current through the inductor at time $t = a + \varepsilon$ is

$$i(a + \varepsilon) = \frac{1}{L} \int_{-\infty}^{a+\varepsilon} v(t)\, dt = \frac{1}{L} \int_{-\infty}^{a} v(t)\, dt + \frac{1}{L} \int_{a}^{a+\varepsilon} v(t)\, dt$$

$$= i(a) + \frac{1}{L} \int_{a}^{a+\varepsilon} v(t)\, dt$$

If ε gets arbitrarily small, then

$$\frac{1}{L} \int_{a}^{a+\varepsilon} v(t)\, dt$$

gets arbitrarily small and $i(a + \varepsilon)$ gets arbitrarily close to $i(a)$—provided that $v(t)$ does not contain an impulse at time $t = a$. We therefore conclude that *the current through an inductor cannot change instantaneously* unless there is an impulse of voltage present.

Since for a capacitor it is true that

$$v(t) = \frac{1}{C} \int_{-\infty}^{t} i(t)\, dt$$

proceeding in a manner as above we can deduce that *the voltage across a capacitor cannot change instantaneously* except for an impulse of current.

In practical terms, there is no such thing as an impulse function. So, practically speaking, we can say that the current through an inductor cannot change instantaneously nor can the voltage across a capacitor. However, the voltage across an inductor and the current through a capacitor *can* change instantaneously (theoretically) or in a very short period of time (practically) without the presence of an impulse function.

Let us see how we can use the above results to establish "initial conditions"—that is, the values of voltages and currents (and their derivatives) in a circuit at some particular time (typically at time $t = 0$).

EXAMPLE 4.21

For the circuit shown in Fig. 4.53, let us determine the initial conditions $i_L(0)$, $v_C(0)$, $i_C(0)$, $v_L(0)$, $di_L(0)/dt$, $dv_C(0)/dt$, $di_C(0)/dt$, and $dv_L(0)/dt$.

For $t < 0$, the applied voltage is $v_s(t) = 6$ V—a constant. Thus, for $t < 0$, we have a dc circuit—the capacitor behaves as an open circuit ($i_C = 0$ A) and the inductor behaves as a short circuit ($v_L = 0$ V). Thus,

$$i_L(t) = \frac{v_s(t)}{1 + 2} = \frac{6}{3} = 2 \text{ A} \qquad \text{for } t < 0$$

and

$$v_C(t) = 2i_L(t) + v_L(t) = 2(2) + 0 = 4 \text{ V} \qquad \text{for } t < 0$$

Furthermore, since $i_C(t) = 0$ A, then

$$i_1(t) = i_2(t) = i_L(t) = 2 \text{ A} \qquad \text{for } t < 0$$

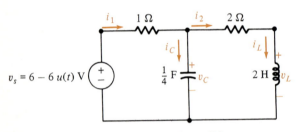

Fig. 4.53   Determination of initial conditions.

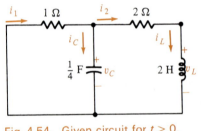

Fig. 4.54   Given circuit for $t \geq 0$.

However, at time $t = 0$, the applied voltage is $v_s(t) = 0$ V, i.e., $v_s(0) = 0$ V. Thus, for time $t = 0$ (and thereafter), the circuit is as shown in Fig. 4.54. Since the voltage across the capacitor cannot change instantaneously (except for an impulse of current),

$$v_C(0) = 4 \text{ V}$$

Also, the current through the inductor cannot change instantaneously (except for an impulse of voltage). Therefore,

$$i_L(0) = 2 \text{ A}$$

But, other voltages and currents can change instantaneously, since the applied voltage $v_s(t)$ changes instantaneously from 6 V to 0 V at time $t = 0$. By KCL,

$$i_C(t) = -i_1(t) + i_2(t) = \frac{v_C(t)}{1} + i_L(t) \tag{4.3}$$

Thus, at time $t = 0$,

$$i_C(0) = v_C(0) + i_L(0) = 4 + 2 = 6 \text{ A}$$

and we see that the current through the cacpacitor changes instantaneously. By KVL,

$$v_L(t) = -2i_L(t) + v_C(t) \tag{4.4}$$

Thus,

$$v_L(0) = -2i_L(0) + v_C(0) = -2(2) + 4 = 0 \text{ V}$$

and it is a special case that the voltage across the inductor does not change instantaneously—in general, the voltage across an inductor can change instantaneously even without the presence of an impulse.

Since

$$v_L(t) = L\frac{di_L(t)}{dt} = 2\frac{di_L(t)}{dt} \qquad \Rightarrow \qquad \frac{di_L(t)}{dt} = \frac{1}{2}v_L(t)$$

then

$$\frac{di_L(0)}{dt} = \frac{1}{2}v_L(0) = 0 \text{ A/s}$$

Furthermore, since

$$i_C(t) = C\frac{dv_C(t)}{dt} = \frac{1}{4}\frac{dv_C(t)}{dt} \qquad \Rightarrow \qquad \frac{dv_C(t)}{dt} = 4i_C(t)$$

then

$$\frac{dv_C(0)}{dt} = 4i_C(0) = 4(6) = 24 \text{ V/s}$$

Differentiating both sides of Equation (4.3), we get

$$\frac{di_C(t)}{dt} = \frac{dv_C(t)}{dt} + \frac{di_L(t)}{dt}$$

from which

$$\frac{di_C(0)}{dt} = \frac{dv_C(0)}{dt} + \frac{di_L(0)}{dt} = 24 + 0 = 24 \text{ A/s}$$

Differentiating both sides of Equation (4.4), we obtain

$$\frac{dv_L(t)}{dt} = -2\frac{di_L(t)}{dt} + \frac{dv_C(t)}{dt}$$

from which

$$\frac{dv_L(0)}{dt} = -2\frac{di_L(0)}{dt} + \frac{dv_C(0)}{dt} = -2(0) + 24 = 24 \text{ V/s}$$

In the above calculations, the notation $di_L(0)/dt$ means "the derivative $di_L(t)/dt$ evaluated at time $t = 0$"—it does not mean "the derivative with respect to time of the constant $i_L(0)$."

We will have to wait until we study the material in the next two chapters before we will be able to determine for time $t > 0$ any of the variables indicated in the given circuit.

DRILL EXERCISE 4.18

For the circuit shown in Fig. DE4.18, find the following initial conditions: $i_L(0)$, $v_C(0)$, $i_C(0)$, $v_L(0)$, $di_L(0)/dt$, $dv_C(0)/dt$, $di_C(0)/dt$, $dv_L(0)/dt$.

Answer: 0 A; 6 V; 0 A; −6 V; −2 A/s; 0 V/s; −2 A/s; 4 V/s

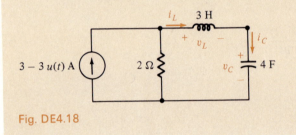

Fig. DE4.18

Switches

In Example 4.21, the applied voltage v_s is nonzero (6 V) for $t < 0$ and zero for $t \geq 0$. One way to produce such a voltage source as v_s is with a battery and a "switch." In particular, a **single-pole, single-throw (SPST) switch** is a two-terminal device that is either **closed** (i.e., a short circuit) or **open** (i.e., an open circuit). Figure 4.55(a) depicts a SPST switch that is closed, and Fig. 4.55(b) shows a SPST switch that is open. If a switch is to be opened or closed at a particular time, we shall indicate such an operation with a curved arrow that is labeled with the time of the opening or closing, as depicted in Fig. 4.56. For the switch in Fig. 4.56(a), the switch opens at time $t = t_1$, and for the switch in Fig. 4.56(b), the switch closes at time $t = t_2$. For the former case, the switch is closed for $t < t_1$ and open for $t \geq t_1$, while for the latter case, the switch is open for $t < t_2$ and closed for $t \geq t_2$.

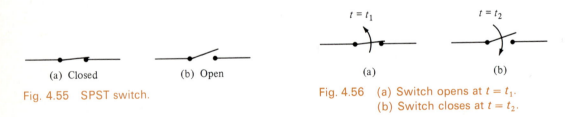

(a) Closed   (b) Open   (a)   (b)

Fig. 4.55   SPST switch.

Fig. 4.56   (a) Switch opens at $t = t_1$.
(b) Switch closes at $t = t_2$.

A **single-pole, double-throw (SPDT) switch** is shown in Fig. 4.57. Here a short circuit exists between a and b and an open circuit exists between a and c for $t < 0$, while an open circuit exists between a and b and a short circuit exists between a and c for $t \geq 0$.

Now consider the connection of a battery and a SPDT switch as shown in Fig. 4.58. For $t < 0$, there is a short circuit (an ideal voltage source of value 0 V) between terminals a and b. Furthermore, for $t \geq 0$, there is an ideal voltage source of value

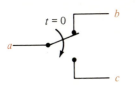

Fig. 4.57   SPDT switch.

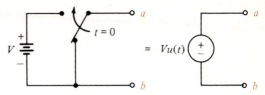

Fig. 4.58   Realization of a step-function voltage source.

V volts between terminals a and b. Since

$$Vu(t) = \begin{cases} 0 & \text{for } t < 0 \\ V & \text{for } t \geq 0 \end{cases}$$

we see that the battery-switch combination realizes an ideal voltage source described by the step function $Vu(t)$.

By using a battery and a SPDT switch as shown in Fig. 4.59, we can realize the function $V - Vu(t)$. This is because, for $t < 0$, there is an ideal voltage source of value V volts between terminals a and b, while for $t \geq 0$, there is a short circuit (an ideal voltage source of value 0 V) between terminals a and b. Since

$$V - Vu(t) = \begin{cases} V & \text{for } t < 0 \\ 0 & \text{for } t \geq 0 \end{cases}$$

then the switch-battery combination given in Fig. 4.59 realizes an ideal voltage source described by the function $V - Vu(t)$.

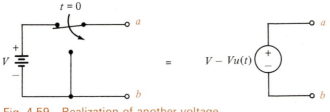

Fig. 4.59   Realization of another voltage source.

Let us now work an example of determining the initial conditions for a circuit which contains a switch.

EXAMPLE 4.22

For the circuit shown in Fig. 4.60, let us determine the initial conditions: $i_L(0)$, $v_C(0)$, $i_C(0)$, $v_L(0)$, $di_L(0)/dt$, and $dv_C(0)/dt$.

For $t < 0$, the circuit in Fig. 4.60 is a dc circuit. By KVL,

$$-6 + v_L + 2(i_C + i_L) = 0$$

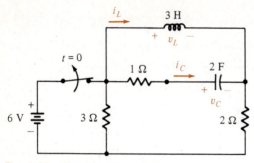

Fig. 4.60   Circuit with switch.

Since $i_C = 0$ A and $v_L = 0$ V for $t < 0$, we get

$$-6 + 0 + 2(0 + i_L) = 0 \qquad \Rightarrow \qquad i_L = 3 \text{ A} \qquad \text{for } t < 0$$

Also by KVL,

$$v_C = -1i_C + v_L = -1(0) + 0 = 0 \qquad \text{for } t < 0$$

For $t = 0$ (and thereafter), the switch is open and we have the circuit shown in Fig. 4.61. Since the current through the inductor and the voltage across the capacitor cannot change instantaneously,

$$i_L(0) = 3 \text{ A} \qquad \text{and} \qquad v_C(0) = 0 \text{ V}$$

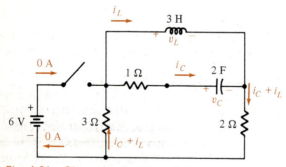

Fig. 4.61   Given circuit with switch open.

By KVL,

$$1i_C + v_C + 2(i_C + i_L) + 3(i_C + i_L) = 0 \qquad \Rightarrow \qquad i_C = -\tfrac{1}{2}i_L - \tfrac{1}{6}v_C$$

Thus,

$$i_C(0) = -\tfrac{1}{2}i_L(0) - \tfrac{1}{6}v_C(0) = -\tfrac{1}{2}(3) - \tfrac{1}{6}(0) = -1.5 \text{ A}$$

Also, by KVL,

$$v_L + 2(i_C + i_L) + 3(i_C + i_L) = 0 \qquad \Rightarrow \qquad v_L = -5i_C - 5i_L$$

Thus,

$$v_L(0) = -5i_C(0) - 5i_L(0) = -5(-1.5) - 5(3) = -7.5 \text{ V}$$

Since

$$v_L = 3\frac{di_L}{dt} \quad \Rightarrow \quad \frac{di_L}{dt} = \frac{1}{3}v_L$$

then

$$\frac{di_L(0)}{dt} = \frac{1}{3}v_L(0) = \frac{1}{3}(-7.5) = -2.5 \text{ A/s}$$

Also, since

$$i_C = 2\frac{dv_C}{dt} \quad \Rightarrow \quad \frac{dv_C}{dt} = \frac{1}{2}i_C$$

then

$$\frac{dv_C(0)}{dt} = \frac{1}{2}i_C(0) = \frac{1}{2}(-1.5) = -0.75 \text{ V/s}$$

DRILL EXERCISE 4.19

For the circuit shown in Fig. DE4.19, determine the initial conidtions: $i_L(0)$, $v_C(0)$, $i_C(0)$, $v_L(0)$, $di_L(0)/dt$, $dv_C(0)/dt$.
Answer: 2 A; 6 V; 0 A; -10 V; 0 V/s; -2 A/s

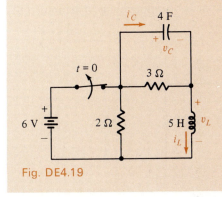

Fig. DE4.19

● SUMMARY

1. The voltage across an inductor is directly proportional to the derivative of the current through it.

2. An inductor behaves as a short circuit to direct current.

3. The current through a capacitor is directly proportional to the derivative of the voltage across it.

4. A capacitor behaves as an open circuit to direct current.

5. The derivative of a ramp function is a step function. The derivative of a step function is an impulse function.

6. The integral of an impulse function is a step function. The integral of a step function is a ramp function.

7. The current through an inductor is directly proportional to the integral of the voltage across it.

8. The voltage across a capacitor is directly proportional to the integral of the current through it.

9. The energy stored in an inductor is $Li^2/2$ joules; the energy stored in a capacitor is $Cv^2/2$ joules.

10. Inductors in series and parallel are combined in the same way as are resistances. Capacitors in series and parallel are combined in the same way as are conductances.

11. Writing node and mesh (or loop) equations for circuits containing inductors and capacitors is done as was for resistive circuits. Except for simple circuits, the solutions of equations in this form will be avoided.

12. A planar circuit and its dual are in essence described by the same equations.

13. The current through an inductor cannot change instantaneously except for an impulse of voltage. The voltage across a capacitor cannot change instantaneously except for an impulse of current.

● *PROBLEMS FOR CHAPTER 4*

4.1 For the circuit shown in Fig. DE4.2 (p. 164), suppose that the current through the inductor is

$$i(t) = \begin{cases} 0 & \text{for } -\infty < t < 0 \\ 1 - e^{-2t} & \text{for } 0 \le t < 1 \text{ s} \\ (e^2 - 1)e^{-2t} & \text{for } 1 \le t < \infty \end{cases}$$

Find (a) $v_L(t)$; (b) $v_R(t)$; and (c) $v_s(t)$.

4.2 For the circuit shown in Fig. P4.2, suppose that the current through the inductor is

$$i(t) = \begin{cases} 0 & \text{for } -\infty < t < 0 \\ 1 - e^{-2t} & \text{for } 0 \le t < \infty \end{cases}$$

Find (a) $v_L(t)$; (b) $i_R(t)$; and (c) $i_s(t)$.

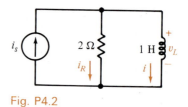

Fig. P4.2

4.3 Repeat Problem 4.2 for the current given in Problem 4.1.

4.4 For the circuit shown in Fig. DE4.2 (p. 164), suppose that the current through the inductor is as described in Example 4.3 (p. 163). Find (a) $v_L(t)$; (b) $v_R(t)$; and (c) $v_s(t)$. Sketch these functions.

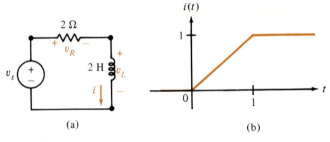

(a)

(b)

Fig. P4.6

4.5 Repeat Problem 4.2 for the current described in Example 4.3 (p. 163). Sketch the functions.

4.6 Given the circuit shown in Fig. P4.6(a), suppose that the current $i(t)$ is given by the function in Fig. P4.6(b). Sketch $v_L(t)$, $w_L(t)$, $p_R(t)$, $v_R(t)$, and $v_s(t)$.

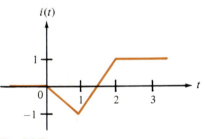

Fig. P4.7

4.7 Repeat Problem 4.6 for the current given by the function in Fig. P4.7.

4.8 Given the circuit shown in Fig. P4.2, suppose that the current $i(t)$ is given by the function in Fig. P4.6(b). Sketch $v_L(t)$, $w_L(t)$, $p_R(t)$, $i_R(t)$, and $i_s(t)$.

4.9 Repeat Problem 4.8 for the current given in Fig. P4.7.

4.10 For the circuit and current shown in Fig. P4.10(a) and P4.10(b), respectively, sketch $v_R(t)$, $v_L(t)$, and $v(t)$.

4.11 For the circuit shown in Fig. DE4.5 (p. 169), suppose that the voltage across the capacitor is

$$v(t) = \begin{cases} 0 & \text{for } -\infty < t < 0 \\ 1 - e^{-t/2} & \text{for } 0 \le t < 1 \text{ s} \\ (e^{1/2} - 1)e^{-t/2} & \text{for } 1 \le t < \infty \end{cases}$$

Find (a) $i_C(t)$; (b) $v_R(t)$; and (c) $v_s(t)$.

4.12 For the circuit shown in Fig. P4.12, suppose that the voltage across the capacitor is

$$v(t) = \begin{cases} 0 & \text{for } -\infty < t < 0 \\ 1 - e^{-t/2} & \text{for } 0 \le t < \infty \end{cases}$$

Find (a) $i_C(t)$; (b) $i_R(t)$; and (c) $i_s(t)$.

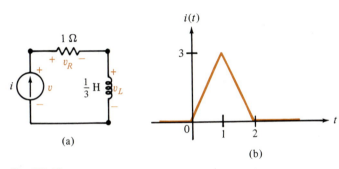

(a)

(b)

Fig. P4.10

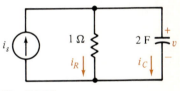

Fig. P4.12

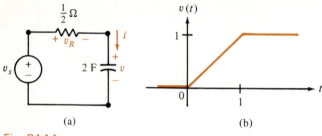

Fig. P4.14

4.13 Repeat Problem 4.12 for the voltage given in Problem 4.11.

4.14 Given the circuit and voltage shown in Fig. P4.14(a) and P4.14(b), respectively, sketch $i(t)$, $w_C(t)$, $p_R(t)$, $v_R(t)$, and $v_s(t)$.

4.15 Given the circuit shown in Fig. P4.12, suppose that the voltage $v(t)$ is described by the function given in Fig. P4.14(b). Find $i_C(t)$, $w_C(t)$, $p_R(t)$, $i_R(t)$, and $i_s(t)$, and sketch these functions.

4.16 Given the op-amp circuit shown in Fig. P4.16, suppose that $v(t)$ is described by the function given in Fig. P4.14(b). Sketch $i(t)$, $i_R(t)$, $v_R(t)$, $v_s(t)$, and $v_o(t)$.

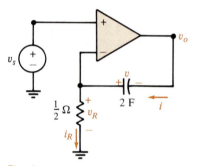

Fig. P4.18

4.20 Repeat Problem 4.16 for the op-amp circuit shown in Fig. P4.20.

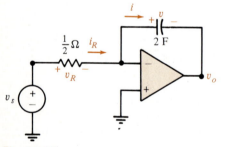

Fig. P4.16

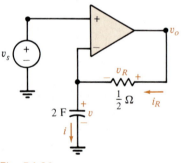

Fig. P4.20

4.17 Repeat Problem 4.16 for the case that there is an additional $\frac{1}{2}$-Ω resistor in parallel with the capacitor.

4.18 Repeat Problem 4.16 for the op-amp circuit shown in Fig. P4.18.

4.19 For the op-amp circuit given in Fig. P4.18, place an additional $\frac{1}{2}$-Ω resistor in parallel with the capacitor and repeat Problem 4.16.

4.21 For the op-amp circuit given in Fig. P4.20, place an additional $\frac{1}{2}$-Ω resistor in parallel with the capacitor and repeat Problem 4.16.

4.22 Verify the following:

(a) $[u(t)]^2 = u(t)$

(b) $[u(t - a)]^2 = u(t - a)$

(c) $[r(t)]^2 = t^2 u(t)$

(d) $[r(t - a)]^2 = (t - a)^2 u(t - a)$

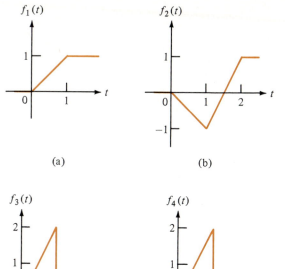

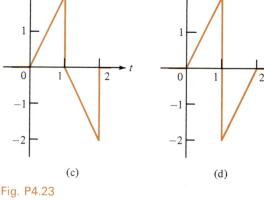

Fig. P4.23

4.23 Express the functions shown in Fig. P4.23 in terms of ramp and step functions.

4.24 For the circuit and current given in Fig. P4.6, express the following in terms of ramp and step functions: (a) $i(t)$; (b) $v_L(t)$; (c) $v_R(t)$; (d) $v_s(t)$. Sketch these functions.

4.25 For the circuit given in Fig. P4.2 and the current shown in Fig. P4.7, express the following in terms of ramp and step functions: (a) $i(t)$; (b) $v_L(t)$; (c) $i_R(t)$; (d) $i_s(t)$. Sketch these functions.

4.26 For the circuit and current shown in Fig. P4.10, express the following in terms of ramp and step functions: (a) $i(t)$; (b) $v_L(t)$; (c) $v_R(t)$; (d) $v(t)$. Sketch these functions.

4.27 For the circuit and voltage shown in Fig. P4.14, express the following in terms of ramp and step functions: (a) $v(t)$; (b) $i(t)$; (c) $v_R(t)$; (d) $v_s(t)$. Sketch these functions.

4.28 For the op-amp circuit given in Fig. P4.16 and the voltage shown in Fig. P4.14(b), express the following in terms of ramp and step functions: (a) $v(t)$; (b) $i(t)$; (c) $v_R(t)$; (d) $v_s(t)$; (e) $v_o(t)$. Sketch these functions.

4.29 Repeat Problem 4.28 for the op-amp circuit shown in Fig. P4.18.

4.30 Repeat Problem 4.28 for the op-amp circuit shown in Fig. P4.20.

4.31 Find the voltage $v(t)$ across a 2-H inductor given that the current $i(t)$

through the inductor is $i(t) = r(t) - 2u(t-1) - r(t-2)$ A. Sketch these functions.

4.32 Find the current $i(t)$ through a 2-F capacitor given that the voltage $v(t)$ across the capacitor is $v(t) = r(t) - 2r(t-1) - u(t-1) + r(t-2) + u(t-2)$ V. Sketch these functions.

4.33 For the circuit given in Fig. P4.2, suppose that the current $i(t)$ is as shown in Fig. P4.33. Express the following in terms of ramp, step, and impulse functions: (a) $i(t)$; (b) $v_L(t)$; (c) $i_R(t)$; (d) $i_s(t)$. Sketch these functions.

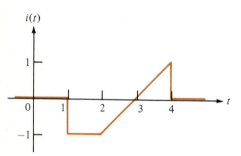

Fig. P4.33

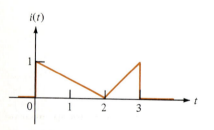

Fig. P4.34

4.34 For the circuit given in Fig. P4.6(a), suppose that the current $i(t)$ is as shown in Fig. P4.34. Express the following in terms of ramp, step, and impulse functions: (a) $i(t)$; (b) $v_L(t)$; (c) $v_R(t)$, (d) $v_s(t)$. Sketch these functions.

4.35 For the op-amp circuit given in Fig. P4.16, suppose that $v(t) = u(t) - u(t-1)$ V. Express the following in terms of step and impulse functions: (a) $i(t)$; (b) $v_s(t)$; (c) $v_o(t)$. Sketch these functions.

4.36 Repeat Problem 4.35 for the op-amp circuit given in Fig. P4.18.

4.37 For the op-amp circuit given in Fig. P4.20, suppose that $v_s(t) = u(t) - u(t-1)$ V. Express the following in terms of step and impulse functions: (a) $i(t)$; (b) $v_R(t)$; (c) $v_o(t)$. Sketch these functions.

4.38 Repeat Problem 4.37 for the op-amp circuit shown in Fig. P4.38.

4.39 The voltage $v(t)$ across a 2-F capacitor at time $t = 1$ s is $\frac{1}{4}$ V. Given that the current through the capacitor is $i(t) = t$ for $1 \le t \le 2$ s and $i(t) = 0$ for $2 < t < \infty$, find $v(t)$ for $t \ge 1$ s.

4.40 The current $i(t)$ through a 3-H inductor at time $t = 1$ s is $\frac{2}{3}$ A. Given that the voltage across the inductor is $v(t) = -1$ for $1 \le t \le 2$ s and $v(t) = 0$ for $2 < t < \infty$, find $i(t)$ for $t \ge 1$ s.

4.41 The voltage $v(t)$ across a $\frac{1}{3}$-H inductor is shown in Fig. P4.41. Sketch the cur-

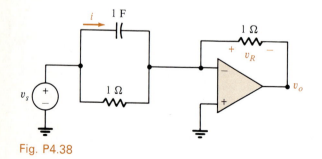

Fig. P4.38

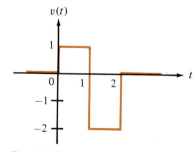

Fig. P4.41

rent $i(t)$ through the inductor. Express $v(t)$ and $i(t)$ in terms of ramp and step functions.

4.42 For the circuit shown in Fig. P4.42, suppose that $v(t) = u(t) - u(t - 1)$ V. Find (a) $i_R(t)$; (b) $i_L(t)$; (c) $i_C(t)$; and (d) $i_s(t)$. Sketch these functions.

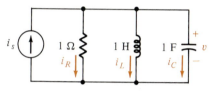

Fig. P4.42

4.43 For the circuit shown in Fig. P4.43, suppose that $i(t) = u(t) - u(t - 1)$ A. Find (a) $v_R(t)$; (b) $v_L(t)$; (c) $v_C(t)$; and (d) $v_s(t)$. Sketch these functions.

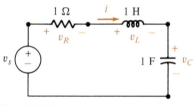

Fig. P4.43

4.44 For the circuit shown in Fig. P4.44, suppose that $v_L(t) = u(t) - u(t - 1)$ V. Find (a) $i_L(t)$; (b) $v_C(t)$; (c) $i_C(t)$; (d) $i_R(t)$; and (e) $v_s(t)$. Sketch these functions.

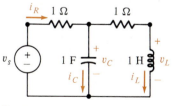

Fig. P4.44

4.45 For the op-amp circuit given in Fig. P4.16, suppose that $v_s(t) = u(t) -$

$u(t - 1)$ V. Find (a) $i_R(t)$; (b) $v(t)$; and (c) $v_o(t)$. Sketch these functions.

4.46 Repeat Problem 4.45 for the op-amp circuit given in Fig. P4.18.

4.47 For the circuit given in Fig. P4.16, connect a 2-F capacitor in parallel with the $\frac{1}{2}$-Ω resistor, and repeat Problem 4.45.

4.48 The integral of the ramp function $r(t - a)$ is the **parabola function** $p(t - a)$. Show that

$$p(t - a) = \int_{-\infty}^{t} r(t - a)\, dt$$

$$= \frac{1}{2}(t - a)^2 u(t - a)$$

$$= \frac{1}{2}[r(t - a)]^2$$

4.49 For the circuit shown in Fig. P4.49, derive the voltage divider formula

$$v_2(t) = \frac{L_2}{L_1 + L_2}\, v_s(t)$$

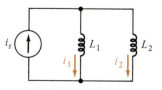

Fig. P4.49

4.50 For the circuit in Fig. P4.50, assume that $i_1(t_0) = i_2(t_0) = 0$. Derive the current divider formula

$$i_2(t) = \frac{L_1}{L_1 + L_2}\, i_s(t)$$

Fig. P4.50

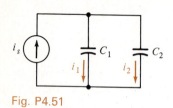

Fig. P4.51

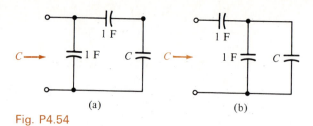

(a)   (b)

Fig. P4.54

4.51 With reference to Problem 4.49, use duality to obtain a current division formula for the circuit in Fig. P4.51.

4.52 With reference to Problem 4.50, use duality to obtain a voltage division formula for the circuit in Fig. P4.52.

4.53 For the connection of inductors in Fig. P4.53, find the equivalent inductance L.

4.54 For each of the circuits shown in Fig. P4.54, what value of C results in an equivalent capacitance of C farads?

4.55 Write the node equations for the circuit shown in Fig. P4.55.

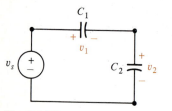

Fig. P4.52

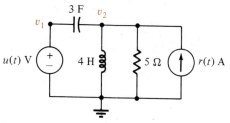

Fig. P4.55

4.56 Write the node equations for the circuit shown in Fig. P4.56.

4.57 Write the node equations for the circuit shown in Fig. P4.57.

4.58 Write the node equations for the circuit shown in Fig. P4.58.

4.59 For the circuit in Fig. P4.59, write the mesh equations.

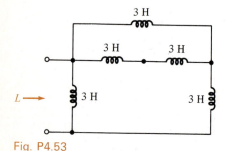

Fig. P4.53

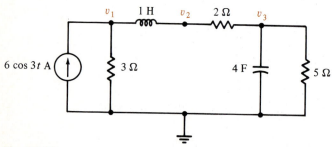

Fig. P4.56

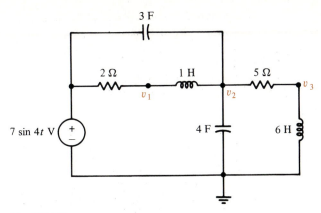

Fig. P4.57

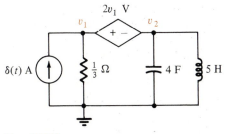

Fig. P4.58

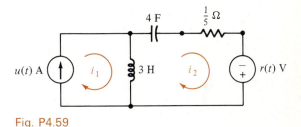

Fig. P4.59

4.60 For the circuit shown in Fig. P4.60, write the mesh equations.

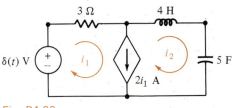

Fig. P4.60

4.61 Find the dual of the circuit given in Fig. P4.55.

4.62 Find the dual of the circuit given in Fig. P4.56.

4.63 Find the dual of the circuit given in Fig. P4.57.

4.64 Find the dual of the circuit given in Fig. P4.58.

4.65 Find the dual of the circuit given in Fig. P4.59.

4.66 Find the dual of the circuit given in Fig. P4.60.

4.67 For the circuit given in Fig. P4.6(a), suppose that $v_s(t) = 6 - 6u(t)$ V. Find (a) $i(0)$; (b) $v_L(0)$; (c) $di(0)/dt$; and (d) $dv_L(0)/dt$.

4.68 For the circuit given in Fig. P4.2, suppose that $i_s(t) = 2 - 2u(t)$ A. Find (a) $i(0)$; (b) $v_L(0)$; (c) $di(0)/dt$; and (d) $dv_L(0)/dt$.

4.69 For the circuit given in Fig. P4.14(a), suppose that $v_s(t) = 6 - 6u(t)$ V. Find (a) $v(0)$; (b) $i(0)$; (c) $dv(0)/dt$; and (d) $di(0)/dt$.

4.70 For the circuit given in Fig. P4.12, suppose that $i_s(t) = 2 - 2u(t)$ A. Find (a) $v(0)$; (b) $i_C(0)$; (c) $dv(0)/dt$; and (d) $di_C(0)/dt$.

4.71 For the op-amp circuit shown in Fig. P4.71, suppose that $v_s(t) = 3 - 3u(t)$ V. Find (a) $v_o(0)$; (b) $i_C(0)$; (c) $i_o(0)$; (d) $dv_o(0)/dt$; and (e) $di_C(0)/dt$.

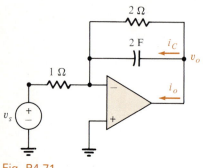

Fig. P4.71

4.72 For the op-amp circuit shown in Fig. P4.72, suppose that $v_s(t) = 3 - 3u(t)$ V. Find (a) $v_C(0)$; (b) $i_C(0)$; (c) $i_o(0)$; (d) $v_o(0)$; (e) $dv_C(0)/dt$; and (f) $di_C(0)/dt$.

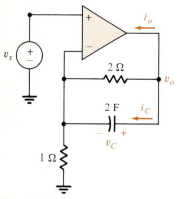

Fig. P4.72

4.73 Repeat Problem 4.68 for the case that $i_s(t) = 2 - 4u(t)$ A.

4.74 Repeat Problem 4.69 for the case that $v_s(t) = 6 - 3u(t)$ V.

4.75 For the circuit shown in Fig. P4.75, find (a) $v(0)$; (b) $i(0)$; (c) $dv(0)/dt$; and (d) $di(0)/dt$.

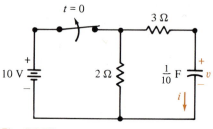

Fig. P4.75

4.76 For the circuit shown in Fig. P4.75, replace the $\frac{1}{10}$-F capacitor with a 5-H inductor and change the value of the voltage source from 10 V to 9 V. For the resulting circuit find (a) $i(0)$; (b) $v(0)$; (c) $di(0)/dt$; and (d) $dv(0)/dt$.

4.77 Repeat Problem 4.75 for the circuit shown in Fig. P4.77.

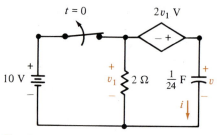

Fig. P4.77

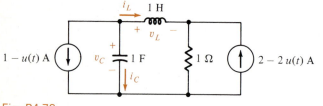

Fig. P4.78

4.78 For the circuit shown in Fig. P4.78, find (a) $i_L(0)$; (b) $v_C(0)$: (c) $i_C(0)$; (d) $v_L(0)$; (e) $di_L(0)/dt$; (f) $dv_C(0)/dt$; (g) $di_C(0)/dt$; and (h) $dv_L(0)/dt$.

4.79 Repeat Problem 4.78 for the circuit shown in Fig. P4.44, where $v_s(t) = 2 - 2u(t)$ V.

4.80 Repeat Problem 4.78 for the circuit shown in Fig. P4.80.

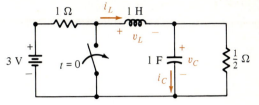

Fig. P4.80

First-Order Circuits

● INTRODUCTION

To analyze a resistive circuit, we can write a set of node or mesh or loop equations—which are algebraic equations—and solve them. However, for circuits with inductors and/or capacitors, not all the equations will be algebraic. To see how to analyze such circuits, we begin by considering simple networks that in addition to resistors contain a single inductor or capacitor.

We shall first consider the situation where an initial condition is present but an independent source is not (the zero-input case), and then the situation where an independent source is present but the initial condition is zero (the zero-state case). We shall also consider circuits that have both nonzero initial conditions and nonzero inputs. The analysis of such circuits requires the solution of simple "differential equations"—this topic being part of our study.

Once a few simple circuits have been analyzed we shall see that the use of various principles such as duality, linearity, and "time invariance" will enable us to handle more complicated situations without having to start from scratch.

5.1 THE ZERO-INPUT RESPONSE

We begin this section by considering the simple resistor-capacitor (RC) circuit shown in Fig. 5.1.

Suppose that at time $t = 0$, the voltage across the capacitor is known to be $v_C(0)$. (We shall see how this can occur shortly.) We can then determine $v_C(t)$ for all $t \geq 0$ as follows.

Fig. 5.1   Simple RC circuit.

By KCL,

$$i_C + i_R = 0 \quad \Rightarrow \quad C\frac{dv_C}{dt} + \frac{v_C}{R} = 0$$

and, dividing both sides of this equation by C, we get

$$\frac{dv_C}{dt} + \frac{1}{RC} v_C = 0 \tag{5.1}$$

In this equation there appears the function $v_C(t)$ we wish to determine, as well as its first derivative $dv_C(t)/dt$. For this reason we say that this equation is a **first-order differential equation**. Since the circuit shown in Fig. 5.1 is described by a first-order differential equation, we call it a **first-order circuit**. Since the variable v_C and its derivative are of the first power, we call the differential equation **linear**. Furthermore, since the right side is zero, we say that the equation is **homogeneous**. Note that the coefficients of v_C and its derivative are constants. In order to solve this equation—that is, find the function $v_C(t)$ that satisfies the equation and the initial (or boundary) condition $v_C(0)$, we proceed as follows:

From the given differential equation we have

$$\frac{dv_C}{dt} = -\frac{1}{RC} v_C$$

and dividing both sides by v_C (called **separating variables**), we get

$$\frac{1}{v_C}\frac{dv_C}{dt} = -\frac{1}{RC}$$

Integrating both sides of this equation with respect to time, we have

$$\int \frac{1}{v_C}\frac{dv_C}{dt}\, dt = \int \frac{dv_C}{v_C} = \int -\frac{1}{RC}\, dt$$

Integrating we get

$$\ln v_C(t) = -\frac{t}{RC} + K$$

where K is a constant of integration. From this equation, taking powers of e, the result is

$$v_C(t) = e^{-t/RC + K} = e^{-t/RC} e^{K} \tag{5.2}$$

Setting $t = 0$, we obtain

$$v_C(0) = e^0 e^K = e^K$$

Substituting this value of e^K into Equation (5.2) yields

$$v_C(t) = v_C(0)e^{-t/RC} \qquad \text{for} \quad t \geq 0 \tag{5.3}$$

Thus, this is the solution to the differential equation

$$\frac{dv_C(t)}{dt} + \frac{1}{RC}\, v_C(t) = 0 \tag{5.4}$$

subject to the initial condition that the voltage across the capacitor at $t = 0$ is $v_C(0)$.

Of course, the symbol of a variable is irrelevant—so even if we change the variable's name from $v_C(t)$ to $x(t)$, by going through the same routine we get the same results. In other words, the solution to the homogeneous, first-order, linear differential equation (with constant coefficients)

$$\frac{dx(t)}{dt} + ax(t) = 0 \tag{5.5}$$

subject to the initial (or boundary) condition $x(0)$ is the exponential function

$$\boxed{\; x(t) = x(0)e^{-at} \qquad \text{for} \quad t \geq 0 \;} \tag{5.6}$$

A sketch of the function $v_C(t)$ versus t for $t \geq 0$ is shown in Fig. 5.2. Note that the resistor current can now be determined for $t \geq 0$ since

$$i_R(t) = \frac{v_C(t)}{R} = \frac{v_C(0)}{R}\, e^{-t/RC}$$

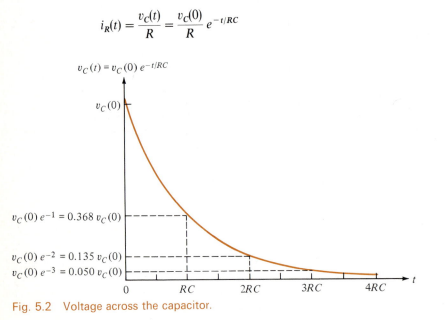

Fig. 5.2 Voltage across the capacitor.

Furthermore, the capacitor current for $t \geq 0$ is

$$i_C(t) = -i_R(t) = -\frac{v_C(0)}{R} e^{-t/RC}$$

or, alternatively,

$$i_C(t) = C\frac{dv_C(t)}{dt} = C\frac{d}{dt}\left[v_C(0)e^{-t/RC}\right] = C\left(\frac{-1}{RC}\right)v_C(0)e^{-t/RC} = -\frac{v_C(0)}{R}e^{-t/RC}$$

From these results we see that initially (at $t = 0$) the capacitor is charged to $v_C(0)$ volts, and for $t > 0$, the capacitor discharges through the resistor exponentially. From the formula $w_C(t) = \frac{1}{2}Cv_C^2(t)$, we see that the energy stored in the capacitor at $t = 0$ is $w_C(0) = \frac{1}{2}Cv_C^2(0)$. Since the voltage goes to zero as time goes to infinity, the energy stored in the capacitor also goes to zero as time goes to infinity. Where does this energy go?

The power absorbed by the resistor is

$$p_R(t) = Ri_R^2(t) = R\left(\frac{v_C(0)}{R}e^{-t/RC}\right)^2 = \frac{v_C^2(0)}{R}e^{-2t/RC}$$

and therefore the total energy absorbed by the resistor is

$$w_R = \int_0^\infty p_R(t)\,dt = \int_0^\infty \frac{v_C^2(0)}{R}e^{-2t/RC}\,dt = -\frac{RC}{2}\frac{v_C^2(0)}{R}e^{-2t/RC}\Big|_0^\infty$$

$$= -\frac{C}{2}v_C^2(0)[0-1] = \frac{1}{2}Cv_C^2(0) = w_C(0)$$

Thus, we see that the energy intially stored in the capacitor is eventually dissipated as heat by the resistor.

We see that the voltage and current in the circuit in Fig. 5.1 have the form

$$f(t) = Ke^{-t/\tau}$$

where K and τ are constants. The constant τ is called the **time constant** and, since the power of e should be a dimensionless number, the units of τ therefore are seconds. For the voltage and current expressions above, we have that the time constant is $\tau = RC$. Thus we see that the product of resistance and capacitance has as units seconds; that is, ohms × farads = seconds. This fact can be verified from $R = v/i$ and $C = q/v$, which have the respective units volts/ampere = volts/coulombs/second and coulombs/volt. Hence, the product RC has as its unit the second. For the circuit above, making R or C or both larger, increases the time constant. Conversely, making R or C or both smaller decreases the time constant.

A sketch of $f(t)$ versus t is shown in Fig. 5.3. For this exponential function we can see that as t goes to infinity, $f(t)$ goes to zero. Although $f(t)$ never identically equals zero for any finite value of t, when $t = 3\tau$ the value of $f(t)$ is down to only about 5 percent of the value of $f(t)$ at $t = 0$. Hence, after just a few time constants, the value of the function $f(t)$ is practically zero. Also note how the initial slope

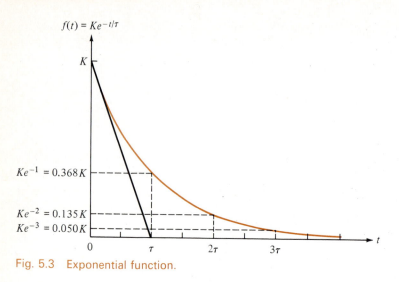

Fig. 5.3 Exponential function.

(i.e., the slope immediately after time 0—designated $t = 0^+$) of $f(t)$ is related to τ. Specifically,

$$\frac{df(t)}{dt} = -\frac{K}{\tau} e^{-t/\tau} \quad \Rightarrow \quad \left.\frac{df(t)}{dt}\right|_{t=0^+} = -\frac{K}{\tau}$$

Hence, the corresponding tangent line intersects the horizontal axis at $t = \tau$ as shown in Fig. 5.3.

In the circuit shown in Fig. 5.1 there was no independent source (that is, no input), only an initial condition (or initial state) of the circuit. For this reason, we say that the voltage and current that we determined are **zero-input** or **natural responses**. Now let us look at a situation in which a zero-input response occurs.

EXAMPLE 5.1

Let us begin this example by considering the circuit in Fig. 5.4, in which there is a switch that is closed for time $t < 0$, is opened at time $t = 0$, and stays open for all time $t > 0$. For this circuit, let us determine $v_C(t)$ for all values of t.

For $t < 0$, since the capacitor behaves as an open circuit for dc, we can determine $v_C(t)$ by simply using the voltage division formula

$$v_C(t) = \frac{RV}{R_1 + R} \quad \text{for} \quad t < 0$$

At time $t = 0$, the switch is opened. Since the voltage across a capacitor cannot change instantaneously (except for an impulse of current), we must have that

$$v_C(0) = \frac{RV}{R_1 + R}$$

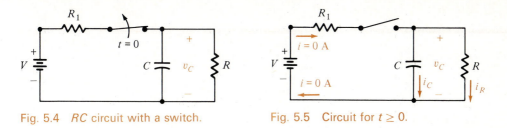

Fig. 5.4   *RC* circuit with a switch.   Fig. 5.5   Circuit for $t \geq 0$.

Next, for time $t \geq 0$, since the switch is then open, to determine $v_C(t)$ we consider the *RC* circuit shown in Fig. 5.5. Since $i_C + i_R = 0$, as for the circuit in Fig. 5.1, we get the differential equation (5.1), which has the solution

$$v_C(t) = v_C(0)e^{-t/RC} = \frac{RV}{R_1 + R} e^{-t/RC} \quad \text{for} \quad t \geq 0$$

A sketch of $v_C(t)$ versus t, for all values of t, is given in Fig. 5.6. Note that instead of writing the two-part expression

$$v_C(t) = \begin{cases} \dfrac{RV}{R_1 + R} & \text{for} \quad t < 0 \\[3mm] \dfrac{RV}{R_1 + R} e^{-t/RC} & \text{for} \quad t \geq 0 \end{cases}$$

we can equivalently write the single expression

$$v_C(t) = \frac{RV}{R_1 + R} - \frac{RV}{R_1 + R} u(t) + \frac{RV}{R_1 + R} e^{-t/RC} u(t)$$

$$= \frac{RV}{R_1 + R} - \frac{RV}{R_1 + R} (1 - e^{-t/RC}) u(t)$$

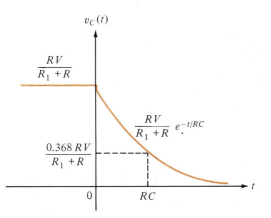

Fig. 5.6   Capacitor voltage for all time.

DRILL EXERCISE 5.1

For the circuit shown in Fig. DE5.1, find a single expression for all t for (a) $v_C(t)$ and (b) $i_C(t)$.

Answer: (a) $6 - 6(1 - e^{-4t})u(t)$ V; (b) $-2e^{-4t}$ A

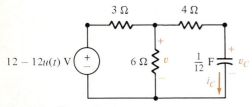

Fig. DE5.1

Having seen how to determine the natural response of a circuit consisting of one resistor and one capacitor (for $t \geq 0$), let us look at a circuit with more elements.

EXAMPLE 5.2

For the circuit shown in Fig. 5.7, let us determine $v_C(t)$, $i_C(t)$, and $v(t)$ for all time.

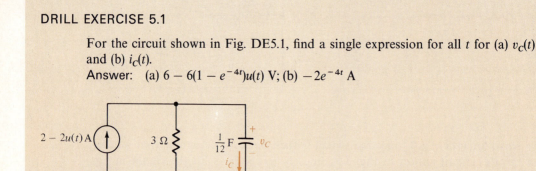

Fig. 5.7   Circuit for Example 5.2.

For $t < 0$, the circuit shown in Fig. 5.7 is equivalent to the dc circuit shown in Fig. 5.8(a). Since $i_C(t) = 0$ A, then $v_C(t) = v(t)$. But since no current goes through the 4-Ω resistor, we can determine $v(t)$ by using voltage division. Specifically,

$$v(t) = \frac{6}{6 + 3}(12) = 8 \text{ V} = v_C(t) \qquad \text{for} \quad t < 0$$

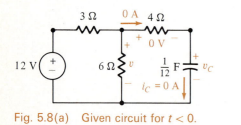

Fig. 5.8(a)   Given circuit for $t < 0$.

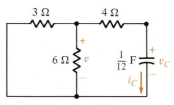

Fig. 5.8(b)   Given circuit for $t \geq 0$.

At time $t = 0$ the value of the independent source changes instantaneously from 12 V to 0 V. However, the voltage across the capacitor cannot change instantaneously. Thus, $v_C(0) = 8$ V.

For $t \geq 0$, the circuit given in Fig. 5.7 is as shown in Fig. 5.8(b). By using nodal analysis, we can write two equations in the variables v and v_C, and then combine these equations to write a single differential equation in the variable v_C. Doing so yields

$$\frac{dv_C}{dt} + 2v_C = 0$$

(Verify this result!) However, as far as the capacitor is concerned, the three resistors can be replaced by their equivalent resistance. Since the 3-Ω and 6-Ω resistors are connected in parallel, they can be combined into a 2-Ω resistance. This, in turn, is in series with 4 Ω. Thus, the equivalent resistance is $2 + 4 = 6\ \Omega$. Hence, the circuit in Fig. 5.8(b) can be put into the form of Fig. 5.1, where $R = 6\ \Omega$ and $C = \frac{1}{12}$ F. Substituting these values into the describing differential equation [Equation (5.1)] yields the above differential equation. Therefore,

$$v_C(t) = 8e^{-2t}\ \text{V} \qquad \text{for} \quad t \geq 0$$

Furthermore,

$$i_C(t) = \frac{1}{12}\frac{dv_C(t)}{dt} = \frac{1}{12}[8(-2)e^{-2t}] = -\frac{4}{3}e^{-2t}\ \text{A} \qquad \text{for} \quad t \geq 0$$

From Fig. 5.8(b), we see that the voltage $v(t)$ is across the parallel connection of 3 Ω and 6 Ω (i.e., 2 Ω). Thus, by voltage division, we have that

$$v(t) = \frac{2}{2+4}v_C(t) = \frac{1}{3}(8e^{-2t}) = \frac{8}{3}e^{-2t}\ \text{V} \qquad \text{for} \quad t \geq 0$$

Combining the functions for $t < 0$ and $t \geq 0$ into single expressions, we get

$$v_C(t) = 8 - 8u(t) + 8e^{-2t}u(t) = 8 - 8(1 - e^{-2t})u(t)\ \text{V}$$

$$i_C(t) = -\tfrac{4}{3}e^{-2t}u(t)\ \text{A}$$

$$v(t) = 8 - 8u(t) + \tfrac{8}{3}e^{-2t}u(t)\ \text{V}$$

DRILL EXERCISE 5.2

For the circuit shown in Fig. DE5.2, find an expression for all t for (a) $v_C(t)$, (b) $i_C(t)$, and (c) $v(t)$.

Answer: (a) $6 - 6(1 - e^{-5t})u(t)$ V; (b) $-3e^{-5t}u(t)$ A; (c) $12 - 12u(t) + 3e^{-5t}u(t)$ V

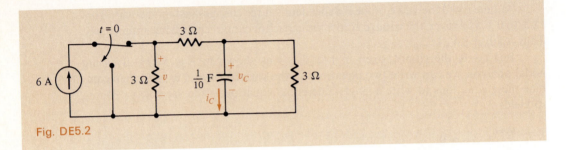

Fig. DE5.2

Now suppose that for the circuit in Fig. 5.4 (p. 223) the switch opens at some arbitrary time $t = t_0$. To find $v_C(t)$ we would proceed in a manner similar to that which yielded Equation (5.3). This time, however, the solution must satisfy the boundary condition $v_C(t_0)$. Proceeding as before results in

$$v_C(t) = v_C(t_0)e^{-(t-t_0)/RC} \qquad \text{for} \quad t \geq t_0$$

If $t_0 = 0$, then we obtain Equation (5.3). A plot of $v_C(t)$ versus t is shown in Fig. 5.9.

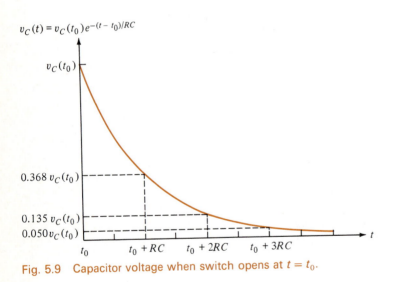

Fig. 5.9 Capacitor voltage when switch opens at $t = t_0$.

We now conclude that the solution to the general linear, homogeneous, first-order differential equation

$$\frac{dx(t)}{dt} + ax(t) = 0 \tag{5.7}$$

subject to the boundary condition $x(t_0)$ is

$$x(t) = x(t_0)e^{-a(t-t_0)} \qquad \text{for} \quad t \geq t_0 \tag{5.8}$$

RL Circuits

Now let us look at the simple resistor-inductor (*RL*) circuit shown in Fig. 5.10(a), where at time $t = 0$ the inductor current is $i_L(0)$.

We can determine $i_L(t)$ for $t \geq 0$ as follows: By KVL,

$$L \frac{di_L}{dt} + R i_L = 0$$

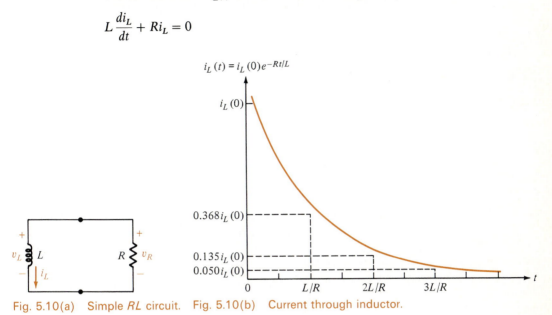

Fig. 5.10(a)   Simple *RL* circuit.   Fig. 5.10(b)   Current through inductor.

so that

$$\frac{di_L}{dt} + \frac{R}{L} i_L = 0 \qquad\qquad (5.9)$$

From Equations (5.5) and (5.6), we can write

$$i_L(t) = i_L(0)e^{-Rt/L} \qquad \text{for} \quad t \geq 0 \qquad\qquad (5.10)$$

A sketch of $i_L(t)$ versus t for $t \geq 0$ is shown in Fig. 5.10(b). Note that in this case the time constant is $\tau = L/R$. Thus, dividing inductance by resistance yields seconds.

The resulting inductor voltage is

$$v_L(t) = L \frac{di_L(t)}{dt} = L \frac{d}{dt} [i_L(0)e^{-Rt/L}] = L \left(\frac{-R}{L}\right) i_L(0)e^{-Rt/L}$$

$$= -R i_L(0)e^{-Rt/L} \qquad \text{for} \quad t \geq 0$$

and the resistor voltage is

$$v_R(t) = -R i_L(t) = -R i_L(0)e^{-Rt/L} \qquad \text{for} \quad t \geq 0$$

This, of course, verifies the fact that $v_L(t) = v_R(t)$, which we know by KVL.

The energy stored in the inductor initially (at $t = 0$) is determined from

$$w_L(t) = \tfrac{1}{2}Li_L^2(t) \qquad \Rightarrow \qquad w_L(0) = \tfrac{1}{2}Li_L^2(0)$$

and as time goes to infinity, since the current in the inductor goes to zero exponentially, the energy stored in the inductor also goes to zero.

The power absorbed by the resistor is

$$p_R(t) = Ri_L^2(t) = R[i_L(0)e^{-Rt/L}]^2 = Ri_L^2(0)e^{-2Rt/L}$$

and therefore the total energy absorbed by the resistor is

$$w_R = \int_0^\infty p_R(t)\,dt = \int_0^\infty Ri_L^2(0)e^{-2Rt/L}\,dt = -\frac{L}{2R}Ri_L^2(0)e^{-2Rt/L}\Big|_0^\infty$$

$$= -\frac{L}{2}i_L^2(0)[0 - 1] = \frac{1}{2}Li_L^2(0) = w_L(0)$$

Thus, we see that the energy initially stored in the inductor is eventually dissipated as heat by the resistor.

When we are given the boundary condition $i_L(t_0)$ instead of the initial condition $i_L(0)$ for the RL circuit in Fig. 5.10(a), then

$$i_L(t) = i_L(t_0)e^{-R(t-t_0)/L} \qquad \text{for} \quad t \geq t_0$$

We now present a situation in which a zero-input response like the one just discussed occurs.

EXAMPLE 5.3

For the circuit shown in Fig. 5.11, the switch is closed for time $t < 0$ and is open for time $t \geq 0$. Let us determine $i_L(t)$ for all t.

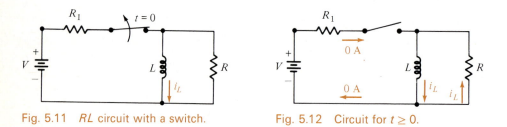

Fig. 5.11   *RL* circuit with a switch.   Fig. 5.12   Circuit for $t \geq 0$.

For $t < 0$, since the inductor acts as a short circuit to dc, the inductor current is simply

$$i_L(t) = \frac{V}{R_1} \qquad \text{for} \quad t < 0$$

At time $t = 0$, the switch is opened. Since the current through an inductor cannot change instantaneously (except for an impulse of voltage), we must have that

$$i_L(0) = \frac{V}{R_1}$$

Next for time $t \geq 0$, since the switch is open, to determine $i_L(t)$ we consider the RL circuit, shown in Fig. 5.12. Proceeding as for the simple RL circuit in Fig. 5.10(a), we get Equation (5.9). Thus, from Equation (5.10), we have that

$$i_L(t) = \frac{V}{R_1} e^{-Rt/L} \qquad \text{for} \quad t \geq 0$$

A sketch of $i_L(t)$ versus t for all t is identical to the sketch of $v_C(t)$ versus t in Fig. 5.6; only the constants are different.

Again, we may write either

$$i_L(t) = \begin{cases} \dfrac{V}{R_1} & \text{for} \quad t < 0 \\[2ex] \dfrac{V}{R_1} e^{-Rt/L} & \text{for} \quad t \geq 0 \end{cases}$$

or

$$i_L(t) = \frac{V}{R_1} - \frac{V}{R_1} u(t) + \frac{V}{R_1} e^{-Rt/L} u(t) = \frac{V}{R_1} - \frac{V}{R_1}(1 - e^{-Rt/L})u(t)$$

DRILL EXERCISE 5.3

For the circuit shown in Fig. DE5.3, find an expression for all t for (a) $i_L(t)$, (b) $v_L(t)$, and (c) $i(t)$.

Answer: (a) $2 - 2(1 - e^{-3t})u(t)$ A; (b) $-6e^{-3t}u(t)$ V; (c) $2 - 2u(t) + \frac{3}{2}e^{-3t}u(t)$ A

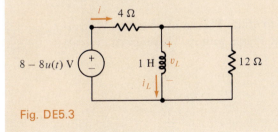

Fig. DE5.3

Now let us consider an example of a zero-input response for a first-order circuit that contains a dependent source.

EXAMPLE 5.4

The circuit shown in Fig. 5.13 has no independent source, but it does have a dependent current source. Let us find $i_L(t)$ for $t \geq 0$, given that $i_L(0) = 5$ A.

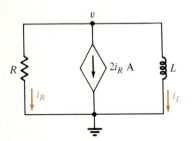

Fig. 5.13   *RL* circuit with a dependent current source.

By KCL,

$$i_R + 2i_R + i_L = 0 \qquad \Rightarrow \qquad 3i_R + i_L = 0$$

Since $i_R = v/R$, then

$$\frac{3v}{R} + i_L = 0$$

However, $v = L \, di_L/dt$. Thus

$$\frac{3L}{R}\frac{di_L}{dt} + i_L = 0 \qquad \Rightarrow \qquad \frac{di_L}{dt} + \frac{R}{3L}i_L = 0$$

The solution of this differential equation is

$$i_L(t) = i_L(0)e^{-Rt/3L} = 5e^{-Rt/3L} \qquad \text{for} \quad t \geq 0$$

Note that because of the presence of the dependent source, the time constant is not L/R but rather $3L/R$.

An alternative for analyzing this circuit is to utilize Thévenin's theorem. We can do this by replacing the resistor and dependent source with its Thévenin-equivalent circuit.

DRILL EXERCISE 5.4

For the circuit shown in Fig. DE5.4, find an expression for all t for (a) $i_L(t)$ and (b) $v_L(t)$.

Answer: (a) $2 - 2(1 - e^{-2t})u(t)$ A; (b) $-64e^{-2t}u(t)$ V

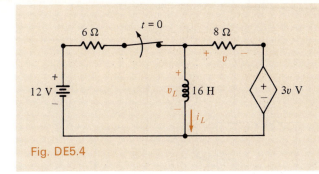

Fig. DE5.4

Additional First-Order Circuits

Let us now analyze a first-order op-amp circuit.

EXAMPLE 5.5

For the op-amp circuit shown in Fig. 5.14, let us determine $v_C(t)$, $i_C(t)$, and $v_o(t)$.

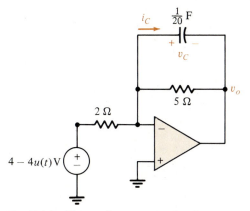

Fig. 5.14   First-order op-amp circuit.

For $t < 0$, we analyze the circuit shown in Fig. 5.15(a). By KCL,

$$\frac{4}{2} = \frac{v_C}{5} + i_C$$

Since $i_C(t) = 0$ A for $t < 0$ (the capacitor is an open circuit to dc), then

$$v_C(t) = \frac{4}{2}(5) = 10 \text{ V} \qquad \text{for} \quad t < 0$$

In addition,

$$v_o(t) = -v_C(t) = -10 \text{ V} \qquad \text{for} \quad t < 0$$

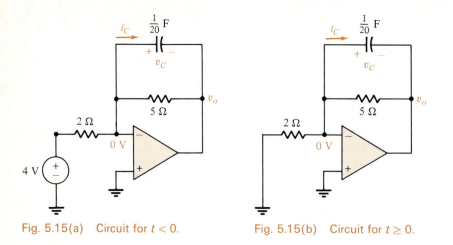

Fig. 5.15(a)   Circuit for $t < 0$.   Fig. 5.15(b)   Circuit for $t \geq 0$.

For $t \geq 0$, we have the circuit shown in Fig. 5.15(b), where $v_C(0) = 10$ V. By KCL,

$$\frac{0}{2} + \frac{1}{20}\frac{dv_C}{dt} + \frac{v_C}{5} = 0 \quad \Rightarrow \quad \frac{dv_C}{dt} + 4v_C = 0$$

The solution to this equation is

$$v_C(t) = v_C(0)e^{-4t} = 10e^{-4t} \text{ V} \qquad \text{for} \quad t \geq 0$$

Thus,

$$i_C(t) = \frac{1}{20}\frac{dv_C(t)}{dt} = \frac{1}{20}[10(-4)e^{-4t}] = -2e^{-4t} \text{ A} \qquad \text{for} \quad t \geq 0$$

Also,

$$v_o(t) = -v_C(t) = -10e^{-4t} \text{ V} \qquad \text{for} \quad t \geq 0$$

Hence, for all t

$$v_C(t) = 10 - 10u(t) + 10e^{-4t}u(t) = 10 - 10(1 - e^{-4t})u(t) \text{ V}$$

$$i_C(t) = -2e^{-4t}u(t) \text{ A}$$

$$v_o(t) = -10 + 10u(t) - 10e^{-4t}u(t) = -10 + 10(1 - e^{-4t})u(t) \text{ V}$$

DRILL EXERCISE 5.5

For the circuit shown in Fig. DE5.5, find an expression for all t for (a) $v_C(t)$, (b) $i_C(t)$, and (c) $v_o(t)$.
Answer: (a) $10 - 10(1 - e^{-4t})u(t)$ V; (b) $-2e^{-4t}u(t)$ A;
(c) $14 - 14u(t) + 10e^{-4t}u(t)$ V

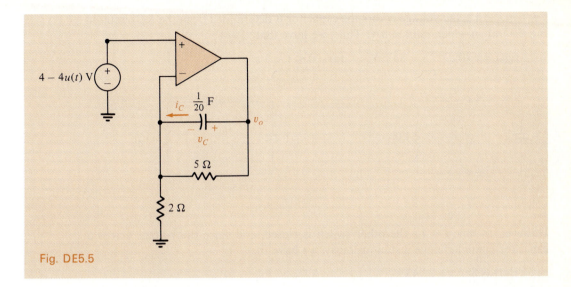

Fig. DE5.5

Now let us turn our attention to a circuit which has a more complicated arrangement of switches.

EXAMPLE 5.6

For the circuit shown in Fig. 5.16 there are two switches—one that opens at time $t = 0$ and one that closes at time $t = 1$ s. For this circuit, let us determine $v_C(t)$ and $i_C(t)$ for all t.

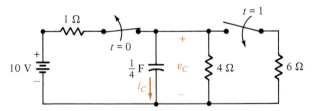

Fig. 5.16 *RC* circuit with two switches.

Since a capacitor acts as an open circuit to dc, for $t < 0$, by voltage division we have that

$$v_C(t) = \frac{4}{4 + 1}(10) = 8 \text{ V}$$

Since the voltage across a capacitor cannot change instantaneously, when the first switch is opened at time $t = 0$, we have

$$v_C(0) = 8 \text{ V}$$

For $0 \le t < 1$ s, the voltage across the capacitor is determined from the RC circuit in Fig. 5.17(a), in which $v_C(0) = 8$ V. Thus, we have that

$$v_C(t) = v_C(0)e^{-t/RC} = 8e^{-t} \text{ V} \qquad \text{for} \quad 0 \le t < 1 \text{ s}$$

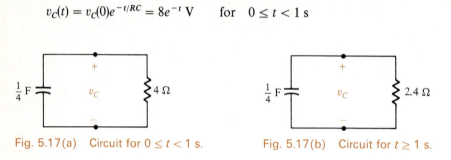

Fig. 5.17(a)   Circuit for $0 \le t < 1$ s.   Fig. 5.17(b)   Circuit for $t \ge 1$ s.

However, at time $t = 1$ s the other switch is closed, and since the voltage across a capacitor cannot change instantaneously, we have that

$$v_C(1) = 8e^{-1} = 2.943 \text{ V}$$

For $t \ge 1$ s, the 4-Ω and 6-Ω resistors are connected in parallel, and the effective resistance is

$$\frac{(4)(6)}{4 + 6} = \frac{12}{5} \Omega$$

We then therefore have the RC circuit shown in Fig. 5.17(b), in which $v_C(1) = 2.943$ V. From our previous discussion [see Equations (5.7) and (5.8)], we know that

$$v_C(t) = v_C(1)e^{-(t-1)/RC} = 2.943e^{-5(t-1)/3} \text{ V} \qquad \text{for} \quad t \ge 1 \text{ s}$$

In summary,

$$v_C(t) = \begin{cases} 8 \text{ V} & \text{for} \quad t < 0 \\ 8e^{-t} \text{ V} & \text{for} \quad 0 \le t < 1 \text{ s} \\ 2.943e^{-5(t-1)/3} \text{ V} & \text{for} \quad t \ge 1 \text{ s} \end{cases}$$

Furthermore, since $i_C = C \, dv_C/dt$, we also have that for $t < 0$,

$$i_C(t) = \frac{1}{4} \frac{d}{dt} (8) = 0 \text{ A}$$

For $0 \le t < 1$ s

$$i_C(t) = \frac{1}{4} \frac{d}{dt} (8e^{-t}) = -2e^{-t} \text{ A}$$

and, for $t \ge 1$ s

$$i_C(t) = \frac{1}{4} \frac{d}{dt} [2.94e^{-5(t-1)/3}] = \frac{1}{4}(2.94)\left(-\frac{5}{3}\right)e^{-5(t-1)/3} = -1.226e^{-5(t-1)/3} \text{ A}$$

In other words,

$$i_C(t) = \begin{cases} 0 \text{ A} & \text{for } t < 0 \\ -2e^{-t} \text{ A} & \text{for } 0 \le t < 1 \text{ s} \\ -1.226e^{-5(t-1)/3} \text{ A} & \text{for } t \ge 1 \text{ s} \end{cases}$$

Sketches of $v_C(t)$ and $i_C(t)$ are shown in Fig. 5.18. Note that although the voltage across the capacitor does not change instantaneously, the current through it does change instantaneously at time $t = 0$ and time $t = 1$ s. In this example, for $t < 0$ the capacitor is charged to 8 V. After the first switch is opened at $t = 0$, the capacitor begins to discharge through the 4-Ω resistor with a time constant of $\tau = RC = 4(1/4) = 1$ s. At $t = 1$ s, the capacitor has not completely discharged; there is still 2.943 V across it. At this time, the second switch is closed, and the capacitor begins to discharge through the parallel combination of the 4-Ω and 6-Ω resistors (effectively $\frac{12}{5}$ Ω) with a time constant of $\tau = (\frac{12}{5})(\frac{1}{4}) = \frac{3}{5}$ s.

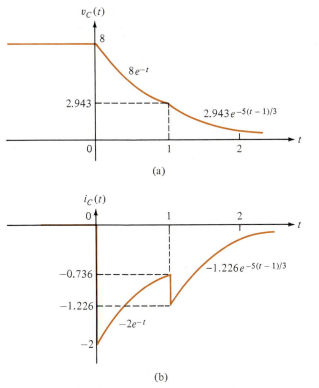

(a)

(b)

Fig. 5.18 (a) Voltage across capacitor. (b) Current through capacitor.

DRILL EXERCISE 5.6

For the circuit shown in Fig. DE5.6, one switch opens at $t = 0$ and the other closes at $t = 2$ s. Find $i_L(t)$ and $v_L(t)$ for all t.

Answer: 3 A for $t < 0$; $3e^{-2t}$ A for $0 \leq t < 2$ s; $0.055e^{-(t-2)/2}$ A for $t \geq 2$ s; 0 V for $t < 0$; $-36e^{-2t}$ V for $0 \leq t < 2$ s; $-0.165e^{-(t-2)/2}$ V for $t \geq 2$ s

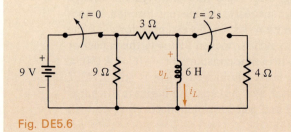

Fig. DE5.6

5.2 THE ZERO-STATE RESPONSE

Now that we have discussed the responses of first-order circuits that have no inputs (i.e., no independent sources) and nonzero initial (or boundary) conditions, let us next consider the case of responses to a nonzero input for a circuit in which all the initial conditions are equal to zero. Such a response is called a **zero-state response**.

We begin by determining the **step response** (i.e., the response that is due to a step function) for the series RC circuit shown in Fig. 5.19.

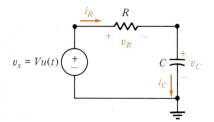

Fig. 5.19 Series RC circuit with voltage step input.

Before we determine the step response, say $v_C(t)$, mathematically, let us try to predict what will happen. Given that the capacitor is originally uncharged, for $t < 0$ the input voltage is zero. Thus, since there is no voltage to produce a current that will charge the capacitor, it should be obvious that $v_C(t) = 0$ for $t < 0$. At time $t = 0$ when the input voltage goes from 0 to V volts, since the voltage across the capacitor cannot change instantaneously (the capacitor acts as a short circuit to an instantaneous change of voltage), $v_C(0) = 0$. By KVL, $v_R(0) = V - 0 = V$ volts, and $i_R(0) = v_R(0)/R = V/R = i_C(0)$ amperes. Thus the voltage across the resistor changes instantaneously, as does the current through the resistor, which is the current through the capacitor.

The nonzero current through the capacitor begins to charge it to some nonzero value. Since the input voltage remains constant for $t > 0$, by KVL, an increase in the capacitor voltage means a decrease in the resistor voltage. This in turn means a reduction in the resistor current, which is the capacitor current, and therefore the capacitor charges at a slower rate than before. The charging process continues until the capacitor is completely charged. After a long, long time, the input voltage seems more and more like a constant (dc), so as time goes to infinity, the capacitor behaves as an open circuit. Therefore, the final voltage across the capacitor is V volts. For the case of a zero-input response we have seen that a capacitor discharges exponentially. So we can take an educated guess that it will charge up exponentially as well.

To summarize, for $t < 0$ and for $t = 0$, the voltage across the capacitor is zero. For $t > 0$, the voltage across the capacitor increases at a slower and slower rate until it is completely charged to V volts. By KVL, the voltage across the resistor is zero for $t < 0$, it jumps to V volts instantaneously at $t = 0$, and decreases exponentially to zero as time increases. Furthermore, the current through the resistor—which equals the current through the capacitor—is proportional to the voltage across the resistor.

Let us now confirm our intuition with a mathematical analysis. By KCL,

$$i_R = i_C \quad \Rightarrow \quad \frac{Vu(t) - v_C}{R} = C\frac{dv_C}{dt}$$

from which

$$\frac{dv_C}{dt} + \frac{1}{RC}v_C = \frac{V}{RC}u(t) \qquad (5.11)$$

Since

$$u(t) = \begin{cases} 0 & \text{for} \quad t < 0 \\ 1 & \text{for} \quad t \geq 0 \end{cases}$$

let us consider the above differential equation for the two time intervals $t < 0$ and $t \geq 0$.

First, for $t < 0$, the differential equation becomes

$$\frac{dv_C}{dt} + \frac{1}{RC}v_C = 0$$

Although it is a trivial solution, $v_C(t) = 0$ is clearly a solution of this equation. Since we want to find the response to the input under the circumstance that there is no initial voltage on the capacitor, and since the input is zero before time $t = 0$, this trivial solution is what we seek; that is,

$$v_C(t) = 0 \text{ V} \qquad \text{for} \quad t < 0$$

Next, for $t \geq 0$, Equation (5.11) becomes

$$\frac{dv_C}{dt} + \frac{1}{RC}v_C = \frac{V}{RC}$$

To solve this differential equation, we write

$$\frac{dv_C}{dt} = \frac{V}{RC} - \frac{1}{RC} v_C = \frac{V - v_C}{RC}$$

and, dividing by $(V - v_C)/RC$, we get

$$\frac{RC}{V - v_C} \frac{dv_C}{dt} = 1$$

Integrating both sides with respect to t, we get

$$\int \frac{RC}{V - v_C} \frac{dv_C}{dt}\, dt = \int dt = -RC \int \frac{-dv_C}{V - v_C}$$

which yields

$$-RC \ln(V - v_C) = t + K \tag{5.12}$$

where K is a constant of integration. Since $v_C(t) = 0$ for $t < 0$ and since the voltage across the capacitor cannot change instantaneously, $v_C(0) = 0$. Hence, substituting $t = 0$ in the above expression, we get

$$-RC \ln[V - v_C(0)] = 0 + K \qquad \Rightarrow \qquad -RC \ln V = K$$

which determines the value of K. Substituting this value into Equation (5.12), we obtain

$$-RC \ln(V - v_C) = t - RC \ln V$$

from which

$$RC[\ln V - \ln(V - v_C)] = t$$

or

$$RC \ln \frac{V}{V - v_C} = t \qquad \Rightarrow \qquad \frac{V}{V - v_C} = e^{t/RC}$$

from which

$$v_C = V - V e^{-t/RC}$$

Thus,

$$v_C(t) = V(1 - e^{-t/RC}) \qquad \text{for} \quad t \geq 0$$

which is the remainder of the solution. Hence, the solution is

$$v_C(t) = \begin{cases} 0 & \text{for } t < 0 \\ V(1 - e^{-t/RC}) & \text{for } t \geq 0 \end{cases}$$

which can be written as the single expression

$$v_C(t) = V(1 - e^{-t/RC})u(t) \qquad \text{for all } t$$

For the circuit given in Fig. 5.19, having determined the capacitor voltage we can now find the capacitor current (which is equal to the resistor current in this case) by using $i_C(t) = C\, dv_C(t)/dt$.

For $t < 0$, since $v_C(t) = 0$ V, then $i_C(t) = 0$ A. For $t \geq 0$,

$$i_C(t) = C\frac{d}{dt}\left[V(1 - e^{-t/RC})\right] = CV(-e^{-t/RC})\left(\frac{-1}{RC}\right) = \frac{V}{R}e^{-t/RC}$$

Thus

$$i_C(t) = \frac{V}{R}e^{-t/RC}u(t) \qquad \text{for all} \quad t$$

An alternative for determining $i_C(t)$ is to take the derivative of $v_C(t)$ for all t as follows:

$$i_C(t) = C\frac{d}{dt}\left[V(1 - e^{-t/RC})u(t)\right]$$

Since

$$\frac{d}{dt}\left[f(t)g(t)\right] = f(t)\frac{dg(t)}{dt} + \frac{df(t)}{dt}g(t)$$

then

$$i_C(t) = CV\left[(1 - e^{-t/RC})\delta(t) + (-e^{-t/RC})\left(\frac{-1}{RC}\right)u(t)\right]$$

By the sampling property of the impulse function,

$$CV(1 - e^{-t/RC})\delta(t) = CV(1 - e^0)\delta(t) = 0\delta(t) = 0$$

Hence, again we have that

$$i_C(t) = \frac{V}{R}e^{-t/RC}u(t) \qquad \text{for all} \quad t$$

Yet another way for finding i_C is to determine i_R since $i_C = i_R$. To do this, we can use KVL to write

$$v_R(t) = Vu(t) - v_C(t) = Vu(t) - V(1 - e^{-t/RC})u(t)$$
$$= Vu(t) - Vu(t) + Ve^{-t/RC}u(t) = Ve^{-t/RC}u(t)$$

from which

$$i_C(t) = i_R(t) = \frac{V}{R}e^{-t/RC}u(t)$$

Sketches of $v_C(t)$, $i_C(t)$, and $v_R(t)$ are shown in Fig. 5.20. These results confirm the predictions that were made earlier.

By using the concept of duality, we can immediately determine the step responses for the parallel *RL* circuit shown in Fig. 5.21. Since this circuit is the dual of the *RC*

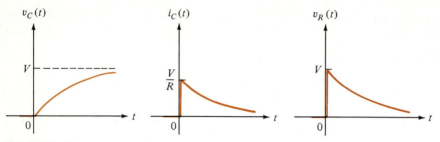

Fig. 5.20   Step responses for circuit in Fig. 5.19.

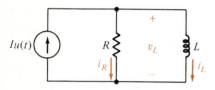

Fig. 5.21   Dual of circuit in Fig. 5.19.

circuit given in Fig. 5.19, by inspection, we have that

$$i_L(t) = I(1 - e^{-Rt/L})u(t) \qquad v_L(t) = IRe^{-Rt/L}u(t) \qquad i_R(t) = Ie^{-Rt/L}u(t)$$

Sketches of these functions are shown in Fig. 5.22.

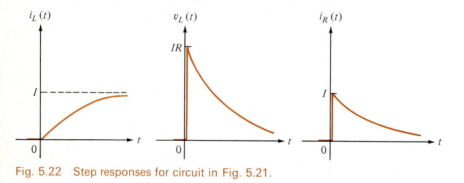

Fig. 5.22   Step responses for circuit in Fig. 5.21.

Time Invariance

Suppose that for the RC series circuit shown in Fig. 5.19 (p. 236) the input is a step of voltage in which the instantaneous change occurs at time $t = t_0$ rather than at time $t = 0$. In other words, suppose that we wish to find the zero-state step response to the input $Vu(t - t_0)$ volts. Then the differential equation describing the circuit becomes

$$\frac{dv_C}{dt} + \frac{1}{RC} v_C = \frac{V}{RC} u(t - t_0) \tag{5.13}$$

Proceeding in a manner similar to that done for Equation (5.11), we can determine that

$$v_C(t) = V(1 - e^{-(t-t_0)/RC})u(t - t_0) \qquad \text{for all} \quad t$$

After a bit of manipulation, we can get the following formulas:

$$i_C(t) = \frac{V}{R} e^{-(t-t_0)/RC} u(t - t_0) \qquad \text{for all} \quad t$$

$$v_R(t) = V e^{-(t-t_0)/RC} u(t - t_0) \qquad \text{for all} \quad t$$

Sketches of these functions are shown in Fig. 5.23. In these sketches t_0 is depicted as a positive quantity, but t_0 may be nonpositive as well.

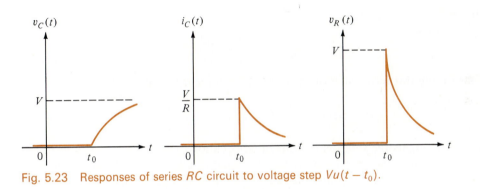

Fig. 5.23 Responses of series *RC* circuit to voltage step $Vu(t - t_0)$.

Notice that the only difference between these step responses and those due to the step input $Vu(t)$ volts is the "shift" of the response by t_0 seconds. In other words, the response is the same; only the time at which it starts is different—and this is because the input becomes nonzero at time $t = t_0$ rather than at time $t = 0$. A circuit such as this (that is, a circuit whose response is the same regardless of when the input is applied) is called a **time-invariant circuit**. For a time-invariant circuit, therefore, knowing the zero-state response $x(t)$ to an input $f(t)$, it is a simple matter to obtain the zero-state response to the input $f(t - t_0)$: It is simply $x(t - t_0)$. This fact is demonstrated for a first-order time-invariant circuit as follows.

Suppose that $y(t)$ is the solution of the first-order linear differential equation with constant coefficients

$$\frac{dx(t)}{dt} + ax(t) = f(t) \tag{5.14}$$

subject to the constraint that $x(0) = 0$. Then what is the solution of the differential equation

$$\frac{dx(t)}{dt} + ax(t) = f(t - t_0) \tag{5.15}$$

subject to the constraint that $x(t_0) = 0$? Since $y(t)$ is the solution of differential equation (5.14), we have the equality

$$\frac{dy(t)}{dt} + ay(t) = f(t)$$

Substituting $t - t_0$ for t in this equation, we get the equality

$$\frac{dy(t - t_0)}{d(t - t_0)} + ay(t - t_0) = f(t - t_0) \tag{5.16}$$

However, by the chain rule,

$$\frac{dy(t - t_0)}{dt} = \frac{dy(t - t_0)}{d(t - t_0)} \frac{d(t - t_0)}{dt}$$

But, since t_0 is a constant,

$$\frac{d(t - t_0)}{dt} = 1 \quad\Rightarrow\quad \frac{dy(t - t_0)}{dt} = \frac{dy(t - t_0)}{d(t - t_0)}$$

Substituting this into Equation (5.16), we obtain the equality

$$\frac{dy(t - t_0)}{dt} + ay(t - t_0) = f(t - t_0)$$

Thus, $y(t - t_0)$ is the solution of differential equation (5.15).

The time-invariance property just discussed results when differential equations have constant coefficients—and such equations, in turn, result from circuits composed of resistors, capacitors, and inductors whose values are constant.

Forced and Natural Responses

For the series RC circuit given in Fig. 5.19, the differential equation describing the voltage across the capacitor is

$$\frac{dv_C}{dt} + \frac{1}{RC} v_C = \frac{V}{RC} u(t)$$

and the solution of this equation is[†]

$$v_C(t) = V(1 - e^{-t/RC})u(t) = Vu(t) - Ve^{-t/RC}u(t)$$

Note that this last expression is the sum of two terms, one having the form of the input and the other having the form of the zero-input response. Is this always the case or is this the case only for this circuit? To answer this question, let us consider

---

[†] From now on, when it is apparent that an expression is valid for all time, the phrase "for all t" will be omitted.

the general first-order linear differential equation with constant coefficients:

$$\frac{dx(t)}{dt} + ax(t) = f(t) \tag{5.17}$$

In this case $f(t)$ arises from the input and $x(t)$ represents the response. Let us multiply both sides of this equation by e^{at}. We therefore have

$$e^{at} \frac{dx(t)}{dt} + e^{at}ax(t) = e^{at}f(t)$$

Since

$$\frac{d}{dt}\left[e^{at}x(t)\right] = e^{at}\frac{dx(t)}{dt} + e^{at}ax(t)$$

then

$$\frac{d}{dt}\left[e^{at}x(t)\right] = e^{at}f(t)$$

Integrating both sides of this equation with respect to t, we get

$$\int \frac{d\left[e^{at}x(t)\right]}{dt}\,dt = \int e^{at}f(t)\,dt \qquad \Rightarrow \qquad \int d\left[e^{at}x(t)\right] = \int e^{at}f(t)\,dt$$

from which

$$e^{at}x(t) = \int e^{at}f(t)\,dt + A$$

where A is a constant of integration. Multiplying both sides of this equation by e^{-at}, we obtain the solution

$$x(t) = e^{-at}\int e^{at}f(t)\,dt + Ae^{-at} \tag{5.18}$$

where the constant A is determined from an initial (boundary) condition. Thus, we see that in general the solution [Equation (5.18)], called the **complete response**, of the differential equation (5.17) consists of the sum of two parts. The first part is

$$e^{-at}\int e^{at}f(t)\,dt$$

which basically is determined by the function $f(t)$. Since $f(t)$ results from the input of a circuit, we call this part of the solution the **forced response** (also known as the **steady-state response**), and we refer to $f(t)$ as the **forcing function**. The other part of the solution is

$$Ae^{-at}$$

which we recognize has the form of the zero-input response or natural response. (It is also called the **transient response**.) Unlike the forced response, the form of the natural response does not depend on the forcing function, but instead is dependent upon the circuit's configuration and element values.

Now let us be specific and consider the case that the forcing function is a constant, say b. Then the differential equation (5.17) is

$$\frac{dx(t)}{dt} + ax(t) = b \tag{5.19}$$

The forced response $x_f(t)$ is

$$x_f(t) = e^{-at} \int e^{at}b\,dt = e^{-at}\left(\frac{1}{a}e^{at}\right)b = \frac{b}{a}$$

which is a constant. The natural response $x_n(t)$ has the form

$$x_n(t) = Ae^{-at}$$

Thus, the complete response [i.e., the solution to Equation (5.19)] is

$$x(t) = x_f(t) + x_n(t) = \frac{b}{a} + Ae^{-at} \tag{5.20}$$

where the constant A is determined from a boundary condition.

Let us now use the above result to find the zero-state step response for the series RL circuit shown in Fig. 5.24. Before analyzing this circuit, let us predict its behavior.

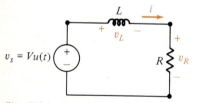

Fig. 5.24 Series *RL* circuit with voltage step input.

For $t < 0$ the input voltage is zero, as are all the inductor and resistor voltages and currents. At time $t = 0$ the input voltage becomes V volts. Since the current through an inductor cannot change instantaneously, the mesh current $i(0) = 0$. Thus, the voltage across the resistor is also zero. By KVL the voltage across the inductor at $t = 0$ is V volts. (The inductor acts as an open circuit to instantaneous current changes.) Since $v_L = L\,di_L/dt$, a voltage across the inductor means a positive rate of change of the current. Thus, the current starts to increase. This results in an increasing voltage across the resistor and, since the input voltage remains constant, a decreasing voltage across the inductor. The consequence of this is a positive rate of change of current that is less than before; that is, the current is still increasing but at a slower rate. This process continues until, after a long time, the input acts as a dc source. At that point, the inductor behaves as a short circuit, so $v_L = 0$, $i = V/R$ amperes, and $v_R = V$ volts. Because of the exponential nature of the RL zero-input circuit studied previously, we can anticipate this type of behavior.

Let us now proceed with a formal analysis. By KVL,

$$L\frac{di}{dt} + Ri - Vu(t) = 0 \quad \Rightarrow \quad \frac{di}{dt} + \frac{R}{L}i = \frac{V}{L}u(t)$$

For $t < 0$, this equation becomes

$$\frac{di}{dt} + \frac{R}{L}i = 0$$

Since the input is zero for $t < 0$, and since the circuit is in the zero state intially, the solution to this equation which satisfies the boundary condition is the trivial solution $i = 0$. Thus,

$$i(t) = 0 \text{ A} \quad \text{for} \quad t < 0$$

For $t \geq 0$, the differential equation becomes

$$\frac{di}{dt} + \frac{R}{L}i = \frac{V}{L}$$

which has the form of Equation (5.19), where $x(t) = i(t)$, $a = R/L$, and $b = V/L$. Thus, the forced response is

$$i_f(t) = \frac{b}{a} = \frac{V/L}{R/L} = \frac{V}{R}$$

and the natural response has the form

$$i_n(t) = Ae^{-at} = Ae^{-Rt/L}$$

Hence, the complete response is

$$i(t) = i_f(t) + i_n(t) = \frac{V}{R} + Ae^{-Rt/L}$$

Since $i(t) = 0$ for $t < 0$, and since the current through an inductor cannot change instantaneously, $i(0) = 0$. Thus, substituting $t = 0$ into the preceding equation we get

$$i(0) = \frac{V}{R} + Ae^0 = 0 \quad \Rightarrow \quad A = -\frac{V}{R}$$

Therefore,

$$i(t) = \frac{V}{R} - \frac{V}{R}e^{-Rt/L} \quad \text{for} \quad t \geq 0$$

Consequently, the final expression for the current is

$$i(t) = \left(\frac{V}{R} - \frac{V}{R}e^{-Rt/L}\right)u(t) = \frac{V}{R}(1 - e^{-Rt/L})u(t) \qquad (5.21)$$

Furthermore,

$$v_R(t) = Ri(t) = V(1 - e^{-Rt/L})u(t)$$

In addition, by KVL,

$$v_L(t) = Vu(t) - v_R(t) = Vu(t) - V(1 - e^{-Rt/L})u(t) = Ve^{-Rt/L}u(t)$$

Alternatively, we could have determined $v_L(t)$ as follows:

$$v_L(t) = L\frac{di(t)}{dt} = L\frac{d}{dt}\left[\frac{V}{R}(1 - e^{-Rt/L})u(t)\right]$$

$$= \frac{LV}{R}\left[(1 - e^{-Rt/L})\delta(t) + (-e^{-Rt/L})\left(-\frac{R}{L}\right)u(t)\right]$$

and since $(1 - e^{-Rt/L})\delta(t) = 0$, we have that

$$v_L(t) = \frac{LV}{R}\left(\frac{R}{L}e^{-Rt/L}\right)u(t) = Ve^{-Rt/L}u(t)$$

Sketches of these step responses are shown in Fig. 5.25.

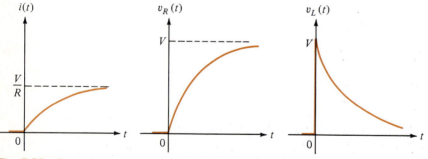

Fig. 5.25   Step responses for series *RL* circuit.

DRILL EXERCISE 5.7

For the circuit shown in Fig. DE5.7, suppose that $v_s(t) = 12u(t)$ V. Find the step responses (a) $i_L(t)$, (b) $v_L(t)$, and (c) $v(t)$.
Answer: (a) $2(1 - e^{-3t})u(t)$ A; (b) $12e^{-3t}u(t)$ V; (c) $(4 + 8e^{-3t})u(t)$ V

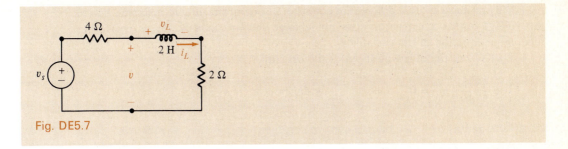

Fig. DE5.7

To determine the step responses of the parallel *RC* circuit shown in Fig. 5.26, with reference to the preceding example, we can apply the concept of duality to write

$$v(t) = IR(1 - e^{-t/RC})u(t) \qquad i_R(t) = I(1 - e^{-t/RC})u(t) \qquad i_C(t) = Ie^{-t/RC}u(t)$$

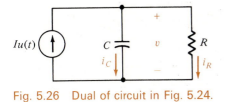

Fig. 5.26 Dual of circuit in Fig. 5.24.

EXAMPLE 5.7

For the op-amp circuit shown in Fig. 5.27, suppose that $v_s(t) = u(t)$ V. Let us find the (unit) step responses $v_C(t)$, $i_C(t)$, and $v_o(t)$.

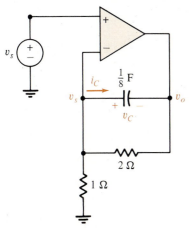

Fig. 5.27 Op-amp circuit.

We first must write a differential equation in one of the circuit variables. Since the voltage across a capacitor does not change instantaneously, let us write the differential equation in the variable v_C.

By KCL at the inverting input of the op amp,

$$\frac{v_s}{1} + \frac{1}{8}\frac{dv_C}{dt} + \frac{v_C}{2} = 0 \qquad \Rightarrow \qquad \frac{dv_C}{dt} + 4v_C = -8v_s = -8u(t)$$

For $t < 0$,

$$\frac{dv_C}{dt} + 4v_C = 0$$

and the solution we seek is $v_C(t) = 0$ V. For $t \geq 0$,

$$\frac{dv_C}{dt} + 4v_C = -8$$

Since this differential equation has the form of Equation (5.19), the solution is given by Equation (5.20). In particular,

$$v_C(t) = \frac{-8}{4} + Ae^{-4t} = -2 + Ae^{-4t}$$

Since $v_C(t) = 0$ V for $t < 0$, then $v_C(0) = 0$ V. Thus,

$$v_C(0) = -2 + Ae^{-0} = 0 \qquad \Rightarrow \qquad A = 2$$

Hence,

$$v_C(t) = -2 + 2e^{-4t} = -2(1 - e^{-4t}) \text{ V} \qquad \text{for} \quad t \geq 0$$

Thus, for all t,

$$v_C(t) = -2(1 - e^{-4t})u(t) \text{ V}$$

In addition,

$$i_C(t) = \frac{1}{8}\frac{dv_C(t)}{dt} = \frac{1}{8}\frac{d}{dt}\left[-2(1 - e^{-4t})u(t)\right]$$

$$= -\tfrac{2}{8}\left[(1 - e^{-4t})\delta(t) + 4e^{-4t}u(t)\right]$$

$$= -\tfrac{1}{4}\left[0\delta(t) + 4e^{-4t}u(t)\right] = -e^{-4t}u(t) \text{ A}$$

and by KVL,

$$v_o(t) = -v_C(t) + u(t) = 2(1 - e^{-4t})u(t) + u(t)$$

$$= 3u(t) - 2e^{-4t}u(t) = (3 - 2e^{-4t})u(t) \text{ V}$$

DRILL EXERCISE 5.8

For the op-amp circuit shown in Fig. DE5.8, suppose that $v_s(t) = u(t)$ V. Find the step responses (a) $v_C(t)$, (b) $i_C(t)$, and (c) $v_o(t)$.

Answer: (a) $2(1 - e^{-4t})u(t)$ V; (b) $e^{-4t}u(t)$ A; (c) $-2(1 - e^{-4t})u(t)$ V

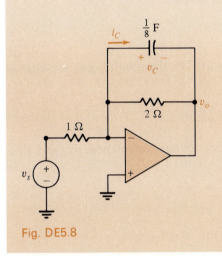

Fig. DE5.8

Response to a Pulse

Let us now consider the zero-state response $v_C(t)$ for the circuit shown in Fig. 5.28(a), where the input is the voltage pulse $v_s(t) = Vu(t) - Vu(t - t_0)$. A sketch of the input is given in Fig. 5.28(b).

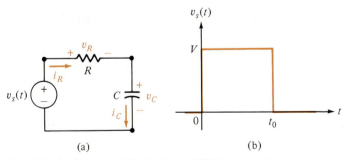

Fig. 5.28   (a) Series *RC* circuit and (b) input pulse.

Writing the differential equation for the circuit, we get

$$\frac{dv_C}{dt} + \frac{1}{RC} v_C = \frac{V}{RC} [u(t) - u(t - t_0)]$$

For $t < 0$, this equation becomes

$$\frac{dv_C}{dt} + \frac{1}{RC} v_C = 0$$

and since the voltage across the capacitor is initially zero, we have $v_C(t) = 0$ V for $t < 0$. For $0 \le t < t_0$, the differential equation becomes

$$\frac{dv_C}{dt} + \frac{1}{RC} v_C = \frac{V}{RC}$$

Since this equation has the form of Equation (5.19), the solution has the form of Equation (5.20). Specifically,

$$v_C(t) = \frac{V/RC}{1/RC} + Ae^{-t/RC} = V + Ae^{-t/RC}$$

Since the voltage across the capacitor cannot change instantaneously, and since $v_C(t) = 0$ for $t < 0$, then $v_C(0) = 0$. Hence

$$v_C(0) = V + Ae^{-0} = 0 \qquad \Rightarrow \qquad A = -V$$

Thus,

$$v_C(t) = V - Ve^{-t/RC} = V(1 - e^{-t/RC}) \qquad \text{for} \quad 0 \le t < t_0$$

Now, for $t \ge t_0$, the differential equation again becomes

$$\frac{dv_C}{dt} + \frac{1}{RC} v_C = 0$$

But, since the voltage across the capacitor cannot change instantaneously,

$$v_C(t_0) = V(1 - e^{-t_0/RC})$$

and the solution to this differential equation [see Equations (5.7) and (5.8)] is, for $t \ge t_0$,

$$v_C(t) = v_C(t_0)e^{-(t-t_0)/RC} = V(1 - e^{-t_0/RC})e^{-(t-t_0)/RC}$$

Therefore,

$$v_C(t) = \begin{cases} 0 & \text{for} \quad t < 0 \\ V(1 - e^{-t/RC}) & \text{for} \quad 0 \le t < t_0 \\ V(1 - e^{-t_0/RC})e^{-(t-t_0)/RC} & \text{for} \quad t \ge t_0 \end{cases}$$

or, in terms of a single expression,

$$v_C(t) = V(1 - e^{-t/RC})[u(t) - u(t - t_0)] + V(1 - e^{-t_0/RC})e^{-(t-t_0)/RC}u(t - t_0)$$
$$= V(1 - e^{-t/RC})u(t) - V(1 - e^{-(t-t_0)/RC})u(t - t_0)$$

A sketch of $v_C(t)$ is obtained as shown in Fig. 5.29.

For the circuit in Fig. 5.28(a), the capacitor is initially uncharged. For $0 \le t < t_0$, the input voltage is V volts, and the capacitor begins to charge up as was the case

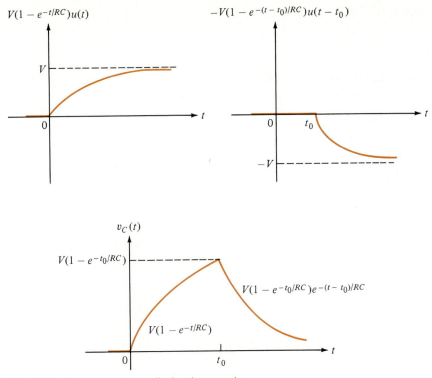

Fig. 5.29   Response to applied voltage pulse.

for a step input studied previously. However, for $t \geq t_0$, the input voltage is again zero. Since the voltage source then acts as a short circuit, a zero-input circuit results, and the capacitor discharges through the resistor.

DRILL EXERCISE 5.9

For the series RL circuit shown in Fig. 5.24 (p. 244), find the zero-state response $i(t)$ to the voltage pulse $v_s(t) = Vu(t) - Vu(t - t_0)$.

Answer: 0 for $t < 0$; $\dfrac{V}{R}(1 - e^{-Rt/L})$ for $0 \leq t \leq t_0$; $\dfrac{V}{R}(1 - e^{-Rt_0/L})e^{-R(t - t_0)/L}$

for $t \geq t_0$

5.3 LINEARITY AND SUPERPOSITION

There is an alternative to the analysis of the series RC circuit shown in Fig. 5.28. What we can do instead is consider the input to be a sum of functions and then use the property of linearity, which we shall now justify.

Consider the first-order differential equation

$$\frac{dx(t)}{dt} + ax(t) = f(t) \tag{5.22}$$

subject to the initial condition $x(0) = 0$. Suppose that $y_1(t)$ is the solution of this equation for the case that $f(t) = f_1(t)$. Then we have the equality

$$\frac{dy_1(t)}{dt} + ay_1(t) = f_1(t)$$

where $y_1(0) = 0$. Furthermore, suppose that $y_2(t)$ is the solution of Equation (5.22) for the case that $f(t) = f_2(t)$. Then we also have the equality

$$\frac{dy_2(t)}{dt} + ay_2(t) = f_2(t)$$

where $y_2(0) = 0$. Adding these two equalities, we get the following equalities:

$$\frac{dy_1(t)}{dt} + ay_1(t) + \frac{dy_2(t)}{dt} + ay_2(t) = f_1(t) + f_2(t)$$

or

$$\frac{d}{dt}[y_1(t) + y_2(t)] + a[y_1(t) + y_2(t)] = f_1(t) + f_2(t)$$

where $y_1(0) + y_2(0) = 0 + 0 = 0$. This last equality means that $y_1(t) + y_2(t)$ is the solution of Equation (5.22) for the case that $f(t) = f_1(t) + f_2(t)$ and subject to the constraint that $x(0) = 0$.

Based upon the discussion above, we can now conclude that if we know the zero-state response to $f_1(t)$ and the zero-state response to $f_2(t)$, it is a trivial matter to determine the zero-state response to $f_1(t) + f_2(t)$; it is simply the sum of the individual zero-state responses.

Clearly, this result can be extended to the case of inputs of the form $f_1(t) + f_2(t) + f_3(t) + \cdots + f_n(t)$. The zero-state response to such an input is simply the sum of the individual zero-state responses.

Furthermore, it should be clear that if $y(t)$ is the zero-state response to $f(t)$, then $Ky(t)$ is the zero-state response to $Kf(t)$.

EXAMPLE 5.8

Let us again find the zero-state response $v_C(t)$ for the series RC circuit given in Fig. 5.28.

Since we can write

$$v_s(t) = v_1(t) + v_2(t)$$

where $v_1(t) = Vu(t)$ and $v_2(t) = -Vu(t - t_0)$, suppose that $v_a(t)$ is the zero-state response to $v_1(t)$ and $v_b(t)$ is the zero-state response to $v_2(t)$. Then the zero-state response to $v_s(t)$ is

$$v_C(t) = v_a(t) + v_b(t)$$

From previous discussions we know that

$$v_a(t) = V(1 - e^{-t/RC})u(t) \quad \text{and} \quad v_b(t) = -V(1 - e^{-(t - t_0)/RC})u(t - t_0)$$

Thus,

$$v_C(t) = V(1 - e^{-t/RC})u(t) - V(1 - e^{-(t - t_0)/RC})u(t - t_0)$$

which agrees with our previous analysis (albeit more complicated) of this circuit.

The expression for the voltage across the resistor can be obtained from KVL as follows:

$$\begin{aligned} v_R(t) &= v_s(t) - v_C(t) \\ &= [Vu(t) - Vu(t - t_0)] - [V(1 - e^{-t/RC})u(t) - V(1 - e^{-(t - t_0)/RC})u(t - t_0)] \\ &= Ve^{-t/RC}u(t) - Ve^{-(t - t_0)/RC}u(t - t_0) \end{aligned}$$

A sketch of $v_R(t)$ is shown in Fig. 5.30; a sketch of $v_C(t)$ was given previously in Fig. 5.29. Of course, we can obtain $i_C(t) = i_R(t)$ by using either $i_C(t) = C\, dv_C(t)/dt$ or $i_R(t) = v_R(t)/R$. In either case,

$$i_C(t) = i_R(t) = \frac{V}{R}e^{-t/RC}u(t) - \frac{V}{R}e^{-(t - t_0)/RC}u(t - t_0)$$

The two sketches of $v_C(t)$ and $v_R(t)$ in Figs. 5.29 and 5.30 were typical. Let us now look at some extreme cases. First, suppose that the time constant $\tau = RC$ is small relative to t_0. In this case, the capacitor has enough time essentially to completely charge before it discharges. The resulting plots are shown in Fig. 5.31.

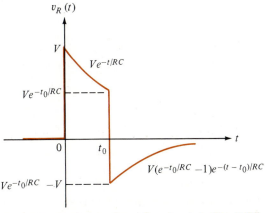

Fig. 5.30   Resistor voltage for circuit in Fig. 5.28.

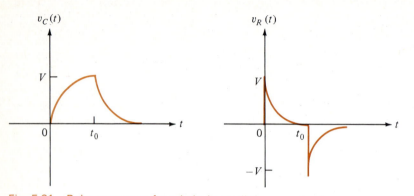

Fig. 5.31 Pulse responses for relatively small time constant.

Next suppose that $\tau = RC$ is large compared to t_0. In this case, the capacitor barely charges up before the input becomes zero. Although charging occurs at an exponential rate, the very beginning of the exponential curve approximates a straight line. Typical plots are shown in Fig. 5.32.

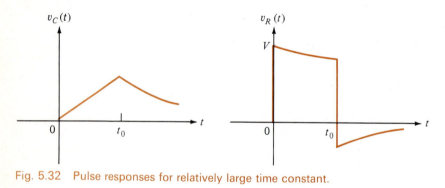

Fig. 5.32 Pulse responses for relatively large time constant.

DRILL EXERCISE 5.10

For the series RL circuit shown in Fig. 5.24 (p. 244), find a single expression for the zero-state response $i(t)$ to $v_s(t) = Vu(t) - Vu(t - t_0)$.

Answer: $\dfrac{V}{R}(1 - e^{-Rt/L})u(t) - \dfrac{V}{R}(1 - e^{-R(t-t_0)/L})u(t - t_0)$

Even though the series RC circuit in the preceding example is very simple in structure, it is quite useful. Specifically, consider the case where the output is the resistor voltage as shown in Fig. 5.33. Suppose that the input voltage is a "square-wave" function as that given in Fig. 5.34(a). If $\tau = RC$ is much less than t_0 (written $\tau \ll t_0$), the resulting output voltage is as shown in Fig. 5.34(b). The "spikes" in the

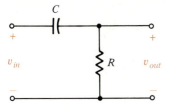

Fig. 5.33 Simple differentiator.

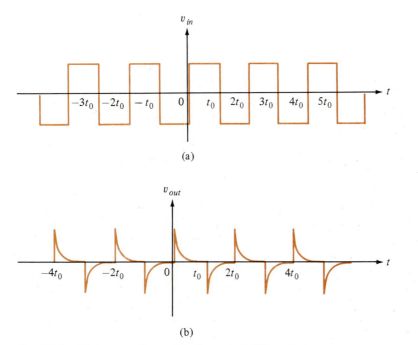

Fig. 5.34 (a) Input voltage. (b) Output of differentiator.

output voltage waveform are by no means impulses, but they do suggest them. In other words, the output voltage approximates the derivative of the input voltage. For this reason we call this circuit a (nonideal) **differentiator**.

Now consider the case where the output is the capacitor voltage as shown in Fig. 5.35(a). If $\tau = RC$ is much greater than t_0 (written $\tau \gg t_0$), for the input voltage in Fig. 5.34(a), the resulting output voltage is as shown in Fig. 5.35(b). Because of the large time constant, the line segments are approximately straight. Since the output voltage has the rough form of the integral of the input voltage, we call the circuit in Fig. 5.35(a) an (nonideal) **integrator**.[†]

[†] Even though such an integrator is useful, the op-amp integrator considered previously is a much more accurate device.

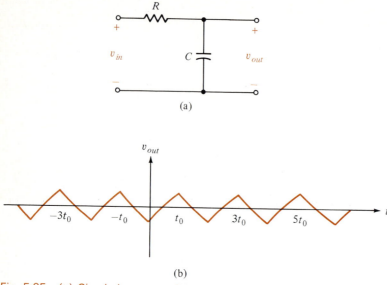

(a)

(b)

Fig. 5.35   (a) Simple integrator. (b) Output of integrator.

Both of the above simple circuits are used in the standard television set. Part of a TV video signal is a sequence or "train" of pulses, which provides the information used for horizontal and vertical synchronization. The video signal goes to a circuit called the "sync separator," which removes the pulse train, and this is then applied to both a differentiator and an integrator. The output of the differentiator "triggers" the horizontal synchronization, while the output of the integrator is applied to the vertical oscillator for vertical synchronization purposes.

Nonzero Initial Conditions

In general, analyzing circuits with nonzero initial conditions is no more difficult than analyzing circuits with zero initial conditions.

EXAMPLE 5.9

Let us determine the voltage $v(t)$ across the capacitor for the circuit shown in Fig. 5.36(a), where the input current

$$i_s(t) = \begin{cases} 2\,\text{A} & \text{for} \quad -\infty < t < 0 \\ -4\,\text{A} & \text{for} \quad 0 \le t < \infty \end{cases}$$

is shown in Fig. 5.36(b).

By KCL at node v',

$$\frac{v' - v}{5} = i + 2i = 3i = 3\left(\frac{v_s - v'}{3}\right)$$

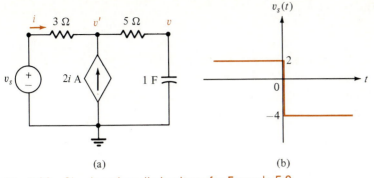

(a)   (b)

Fig. 5.36   Circuit and applied voltage for Example 5.9.

from which

$$v' = \tfrac{1}{6}(v + 5v_s)$$ (5.23)

By KCL at node v,

$$\frac{v - v'}{5} + 1\frac{dv}{dt} = 0$$

Substituting Equation (5.23) into this expression and simplifying, results in

$$\frac{dv}{dt} + \frac{1}{6}v = \frac{1}{6}v_s$$

For $t < 0$, this differential equation becomes

$$\frac{dv}{dt} + \frac{1}{6}v = \frac{1}{3}$$

Since the circuit is a dc circuit for $t < 0$, the solution to this equation is a constant, K. Substituting K into the equation, we get

$$\frac{dK}{dt} + \frac{1}{6}K = \frac{1}{3} \qquad \Rightarrow \qquad K = 2$$

Hence,

$$v(t) = 2 \text{ V} \qquad \text{for} \quad t < 0$$

For $t \geq 0$, the differential equation becomes

$$\frac{dv}{dt} + \frac{1}{6}v = -\frac{2}{3}$$

and since the voltage across the capacitor cannot change instantaneously, $v(0) = 2$ V. The solution to this differential equation is

$$v(t) = \frac{-2/3}{1/6} + Ae^{-t/6} = -4 + Ae^{-t/6}$$

Setting $t = 0$ in this expression, we have

$$v(0) = -4 + Ae^0$$

$$2 = -4 + A \quad \Rightarrow \quad A = 6$$

Thus,

$$v(t) = -4 + 6e^{-t/6} \text{ V} \qquad \text{for} \quad t \geq 0$$

Hence, we can write

$$v(t) = \begin{cases} 2 & \text{for} \quad t < 0 \\ -4 + 6e^{-t/6} & \text{for} \quad t \geq 0 \end{cases}$$

or the single expression

$$v(t) = 2 - 2u(t) + [-4 + 6e^{-t/6}]u(t)$$
$$= 2 - 6u(t) + 6e^{-t/6}u(t) = 2 - 6(1 - e^{-t/6})u(t) \text{ V}$$

A sketch of $v(t)$ is shown in Fig. 5.37.

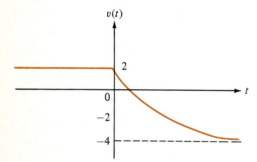

Fig. 5.37   Voltage across 1-F capacitor.

DRILL EXERCISE 5.11

For the op-amp circuit given in Fig. 5.27 (p. 247), change the value of the capacitor to $\frac{1}{4}$ F. Find $v_C(t)$ for the case that the applied voltage is $v_s(t) = 1$ V for $t < 0$ and 3 V for $t \geq 0$.

Answer: -2 V for $t < 0$; $-6 + 4e^{-2t}$ V for $t \geq 0$

An alternative to finding $v(t)$ by the direct method discussed in Example 5.9 is to use the property of linearity. The key to this approach is to note that we can write the input voltage as $v_s(t) = 2 - 6u(t) = v_a(t) + v_b(t)$.

If $v_1(t)$ is the response to $v_a(t) = 2$ V, then $v_1(t)$ is the solution to the equation

$$\frac{dv_1}{dt} + \frac{1}{6}v_1 = \frac{1}{6}v_a(t) = \frac{1}{3} \qquad \text{for all} \quad t$$

and, as we have seen in Example 5.9,

$$v_1(t) = 2 \text{ V} \qquad \text{for all} \quad t$$

If $v_2(t)$ is the response to $v_b(t) = -6u(t)$ V, then $v_2(t)$ is the solution to

$$\frac{dv_2}{dt} + \frac{1}{6}v_2 = \frac{1}{6}v_b(t) = -u(t)$$

For $t < 0$, $v_2(t) = 0$ V. For $t \geq 0$, $v_2(t)$ satisfies

$$\frac{dv_2}{dt} + \frac{1}{6}v_2 = -1$$

Thus,

$$v_2(t) = \frac{-1}{1/6} + Ae^{-t/6} = -6 + Ae^{-t/6}$$

from which

$$v_2(0) = -6 + A$$

$$0 = -6 + A \qquad \Rightarrow \qquad A = 6$$

Hence,

$$v_2(t) = (-6 + 6e^{-t/6})u(t) = -6(1 - e^{-t/6})u(t) \text{ V}$$

By linearity, we have that

$$v(t) = v_1(t) + v_2(t) = 2 - 6(1 - e^{-t/6})u(t) \text{ V}$$

as was obtained previously.

DRILL EXERCISE 5.12

For the op-amp circuit given in Fig. 5.27 (p. 247), change the value of the capacitor to $\frac{1}{4}$F and use the fact that $v_s(t) = v_a(t) + v_b(t)$, where $v_a(t) = 1$ V and $v_b(t) = 2u(t)$ V, and the property of linearity to find $v_C(t)$.
Answer: $-2 - 4(1 - e^{-2t})u(t)$ V

Because we are dealing with linear circuits, we can employ the principle of superposition. In essence, we did this above when we expressed a forcing function as a sum of two other functions. For the case of a voltage source $v_s(t) = v_a(t) + v_b(t)$, a single voltage source whose value is $v_s(t)$ is equivalent to the series connection of two voltage sources—one whose value is $v_a(t)$ and the other whose value is $v_b(t)$. To apply the principle of superposition, set one voltage source to zero (replace it by a short circuit) and find the response due to the other source—then vice versa. The sum of these two responses is equal to the response due to $v_s(t)$.

5.4 SOME OTHER FORCING FUNCTIONS

Suppose now that we would like to determine zero-state responses that are due to inputs other than step functions. If the inputs are ramps or impulses, the responses can be determined by a simple operation on the step response. To see this, suppose that $y(t)$ is the solution to the differential equation

$$\frac{dx(t)}{dt} + ax(t) = f(t) \tag{5.24}$$

Then we have the following equality:

$$\frac{dy(t)}{dt} + ay(t) = f(t)$$

Differentiating both sides of this equation, we get the equality

$$\frac{d\left[\dfrac{dy(t)}{dt}\right]}{dt} + a\frac{dy(t)}{dt} = \frac{df(t)}{dt}$$

Hence, we see that for the differential equation

$$\frac{dx(t)}{dt} + ax(t) = \frac{df(t)}{dt}$$

the solution is $dy(t)/dt$. In other words, if $y(t)$ is the zero-state response to $f(t)$, then $dy(t)/dt$ is the zero-state response to $df(t)/dt$. Since the impulse function $\delta(t)$ is the derivative of the step function $u(t)$, then the derivative of the zero-state response to $u(t)$ is equal to the zero-state response to $\delta(t)$.

Repeating the same argument as above and using integration instead of differentiation, since the integral of a step is a ramp, we conclude that the integral of the zero-state response to $u(t)$ is equal to the zero-state response to $r(t)$.

EXAMPLE 5.10

Let us find the impulse responses for the parallel RC circuit shown in Fig. 5.38(a).

From our previous discussion (see Fig. 5.28 on p. 249), we know that the voltage across the capacitor due to an input of $Iu(t)$ is

$$v_s(t) = IR(1 - e^{-t/RC})u(t)$$

Therefore, the zero-state response due to the impulse input is

$$v(t) = \frac{dv_s(t)}{dt} = \frac{d}{dt}\left[IR(1 - e^{-t/RC})u(t)\right]$$

$$= IR(1 - e^{-t/RC})\delta(t) + IR(-e^{-t/RC})\left(\frac{-1}{RC}\right)u(t)$$

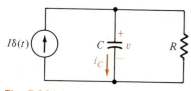

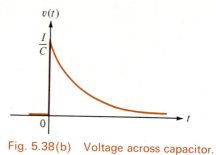

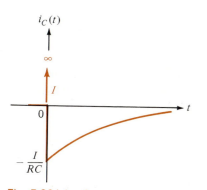

Fig. 5.38(a)   Parallel *RC* circuit.   Fig. 5.38(b)   Voltage across capacitor.

Fig. 5.38(c)   Current through capacitor.

and since $(1 - e^{-t/RC})\delta(t) = 0$, the impulse response is

$$v(t) = \frac{I}{C} e^{-t/RC} u(t)$$

A sketch of $v(t)$ is shown in Fig. 5.38(b). Note that in this circuit the voltage across the capacitor does change instantaneously (at time $t = 0$). This is because an impulse of current is produced by the source.

The current through the capacitor for this circuit is

$$i_C(t) = C \frac{dv(t)}{dt} = C \frac{d}{dt}\left[\frac{I}{C} e^{-t/RC} u(t)\right] = Ie^{-t/RC}\delta(t) + Ie^{-t/RC}\left(\frac{-1}{RC}\right)u(t)$$

By the sampling property of the impulse function, $e^{-t/RC}\delta(t) = \delta(t)$. Hence,

$$i_C(t) = I\delta(t) - \frac{I}{RC} e^{-t/RC} u(t)$$

A sketch of $i_C(t)$ is shown in Fig. 5.38(c).

DRILL EXERCISE 5.13

For the op-amp circuit shown in Fig. 5.27 (p. 247), find the zero-state responses $v_C(t)$, $i_C(t)$, and $v_o(t)$ due to a unit impulse input voltage of $v_s(t) = \delta(t)$ V.
Answer: $-8e^{-4t}u(t)$ V; $-\delta(t) + 4e^{-4t}u(t)$ A; $\delta(t) + 8e^{-4t}u(t)$ V

EXAMPLE 5.11

Let us find the zero-state responses $i_L(t)$ and $v_L(t)$ for the parallel RL circuit shown in Fig. 5.39.

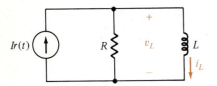

Fig. 5.39   Parallel RL circuit with ramp input.

We mentioned previously (see Fig. 5.21) that the zero-state response of the inductor current for an input of $Iu(t)$ is

$$i_s(t) = I(1 - e^{-Rt/L})u(t)$$

Therefore, the zero-state ramp response is

$$i_L(t) = \int_{-\infty}^{t} i_s(t)\, dt = \int_{-\infty}^{t} I(1 - e^{-Rt/L})u(t)\, dt$$

$$= \int_{-\infty}^{t} Iu(t)\, dt - \int_{-\infty}^{t} Ie^{-Rt/L}u(t)\, dt \qquad (5.25)$$

We already know that the integral of a step is a ramp. Thus, for the first integral on the right side of Equation (5.25), we have that

$$\int_{-\infty}^{t} Iu(t)\, dt = Ir(t) \qquad (5.26)$$

Let us now evaluate the second integral on the right side of Equation (5.25).
First, for $t < 0$,

$$\int_{-\infty}^{t} Ie^{-Rt/L}u(t)\, dt = \int_{-\infty}^{t} 0\, dt = 0$$

And, for $t \ge 0$,

$$\int_{-\infty}^{t} Ie^{-Rt/L}u(t)\, dt = \int_{-\infty}^{0} Ie^{-Rt/L}(0)\, dt + \int_{0}^{t} Ie^{-Rt/L}(1)\, dt$$

$$= 0 + I \int_{0}^{t} e^{-Rt/L}\, dt = -\frac{L}{R} Ie^{-Rt/L} \Big|_{0}^{t}$$

$$= -\frac{L}{R} I(e^{-Rt/L} - e^{0}) = \frac{LI}{R}(1 - e^{-Rt/L})$$

Combining these results for $t < 0$ and $t \geq 0$, we have that for all t,

$$\int_{-\infty}^{t} Ie^{-Rt/L}u(t)\,dt = \frac{LI}{R}(1 - e^{-Rt/L})u(t) \tag{5.27}$$

Substituting Equations (5.26) and (5.27) into Equation (5.25) results in

$$i_L(t) = Ir(t) - \frac{LI}{R}(1 - e^{-Rt/L})u(t)$$

and this is the inductor current that is due to the applied current ramp. Furthermore, the inductor voltage is

$$v_L(t) = L\frac{di_L(t)}{dt} = L\frac{d}{dt}\left[\int_{-\infty}^{t} i_s(t)\,dt\right] = Li_s(t) = LI(1 - e^{-Rt/L})u(t)$$

DRILL EXERCISE 5.14

For the op-amp circuit shown in Fig. 5.27 (p. 247), find the zero-state ramp responses $v_C(t)$ and $i_C(t)$ due to a unit ramp input voltage of $v_s(t) = r(t)$ V.
Answer: $-2r(t) + \frac{1}{2}(1 - e^{-4t})u(t)$ V; $-\frac{1}{4}(1 - e^{-4t})u(t)$ A

Exponential Forcing Functions

Since we have seen many examples of how exponential functions arise, let us now consider circuits for which the forcing functions are exponentials.

EXAMPLE 5.12

The parallel *RL* circuit shown in Fig. 5.40 has an exponential forcing function. Let us find the zero-state responses $i_L(t)$ and $v_L(t)$ given that $i_s(t) = 2e^{-4t}u(t)$ A.

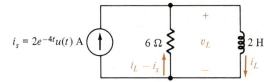

$i_s = 2e^{-4t}u(t)$ A $\quad$ 6 Ω $\quad$ v_L $\quad$ 2 H

$i_L - i_s$ $\qquad$ i_L

Fig. 5.40   Circuit with exponential forcing function.

By KVL,

$$2\frac{di_L}{dt} + 6(i_L - i_s) = 0$$

from which

$$\frac{di_L}{dt} + 3i_L = 3i_s = 6e^{-4t}u(t) \tag{5.28}$$

For $t < 0$, the solution of this equation is $i_L(t) = 0$ A. For $t \geq 0$, Equation (5.28) is

$$\frac{di_L}{dt} + 3i_L = 6e^{-4t} \tag{5.29}$$

and since the current through an inductor cannot change instantaneously, we have that $i_L(0) = 0$ A.

Since differential equation (5.29) has the form of Equation (5.17), which is

$$\frac{dx(t)}{dt} + ax(t) = f(t) \tag{5.17}$$

then the solution is given by Equation (5.18), which is

$$x(t) = e^{-at} \int e^{at} f(t)\, dt + Ae^{-at} \tag{5.18}$$

Comparing Equations (5.17) and (5.29), we have that $a = 3$, $f(t) = 6e^{-4t}$, and $x(t) = i_L(t)$. Thus, the solution to Equation (5.29) is

$$i_L(t) = e^{-3t} \int e^{3t}(6e^{-4t})\, dt + Ae^{-3t} = 6e^{-3t} \int e^{3t-4t}\, dt + Ae^{-3t}$$

$$= 6e^{-3t} \int e^{-t}\, dt + Ae^{-3t} = -6e^{-3t}e^{-t} + Ae^{-3t}$$

$$= -6e^{-4t} + Ae^{-3t}$$

Setting $t = 0$, since $i_L(0) = 0$ A, then

$$i_L(0) = -6e^{-0} + Ae^{-0} = 0 \qquad \Rightarrow \qquad A = 6$$

Thus,

$$i_L(t) = -6e^{-4t} + 6e^{-3t} = 6(e^{-3t} - e^{-4t})\ \text{A} \qquad \text{for} \quad t > 0$$

Hence, the inductor current for the given circuit is

$$i_L(t) = 6(e^{-3t} - e^{-4t})u(t)\ \text{A}$$

Therefore,

$$v_L(t) = 2\frac{di_L(t)}{dt} = 2\frac{d}{dt}\left[6(e^{-3t} - e^{-4t})u(t)\right]$$

$$= 12\left[(e^{-3t} - e^{-4t})\delta(t) + (-3e^{-3t} + 4e^{-4t})u(t)\right]$$

$$= 12(4e^{-4t} - 3e^{-3t})u(t)\ \text{V}$$

Alternatively,

$$v_L(t) = 6[i_s(t) - i_L(t)] = 6[2e^{-4t}u(t) - 6(e^{-3t} - e^{-4t})u(t)]$$
$$= 12e^{-4t}u(t) - 36e^{-3t}u(t) + 36e^{-4t}u(t)$$
$$= 48e^{-4t}u(t) - 36e^{-3t}u(t) = 12(4e^{-4t} - 3e^{-3t})u(t) \text{ V}$$

DRILL EXERCISE 5.15

For the circuit given in Fig. 5.36(a) (p. 257), suppose that the applied voltage is $v_s(t) = 18e^{-t/2}u(t)$ V. Find the zero-state responses $v(t)$ and $i(t)$.

Answer: $9(e^{-t/6} - e^{-t/2})u(t)$ V; $3(\frac{1}{2}e^{-t/2} - \frac{1}{6}e^{-t/6})u(t)$ A

Let us now consider the special case that for the differential equation (5.17) the forcing function has the form $f(t) = Ke^{-at}$. (This case occurs when the forcing function and the natural response have the same exponent.) Under this circumstance, by Equation (5.18),

$$x(t) = e^{-at} \int e^{at}(Ke^{-at})\, dt + Ae^{-at} = e^{-at} \int K\, dt + Ae^{-at}$$

$$= Kte^{-at} + Ae^{-at} = (Kt + A)e^{-at} \tag{5.30}$$

and this is the solution to

$$\frac{dx(t)}{dt} + ax(t) = Ke^{-at} \tag{5.31}$$

EXAMPLE 5.13

For the circuit given in Fig. 5.40, let us find the zero-state responses $i_L(t)$ and $v_L(t)$ when the input voltage is changed to $i_s(t) = 2e^{-3t}u(t)$ A.

Just as we obtained Equation (5.28), we have that

$$\frac{di_L}{dt} + 3i_L = 3i_s = 6e^{-3t}u(t) \tag{5.32}$$

For $t < 0$, the solution is $i_L(t) = 0$ A. For $t \geq 0$, Equation (5.32) is

$$\frac{di_L}{dt} + 3i_L = 6e^{-3t} \tag{5.33}$$

Comparing this equation with Equation (5.31), we have that $a = 3$ and $K = 6$. Thus, by Equation (5.30), the solution to Equation (5.33) is

$$i_L(t) = 6te^{-3t} + Ae^{-3t}$$

Setting $t = 0$, since $i_L(0) = 0$ A, then

$$i_L(0) = 6(0)e^{-0} + Ae^{-0} = 0 \quad \Rightarrow \quad A = 0$$

Thus,

$$i_L(t) = 6te^{-3t} \text{ A} \quad \text{for} \quad t \geq 0$$

Hence, the inductor current is

$$i_L(t) = 6te^{-3t}u(t) \text{ A}$$

Furthermore,

$$v_L(t) = 6[i_s(t) - i_L(t)] = 6[2e^{-3t}u(t) - 6te^{-3t}u(t)]$$
$$= 12e^{-3t}u(t) - 36te^{-3t}u(t) = 12(1 - 3t)e^{-3t}u(t) \text{ V}$$

Of course, we could have also determined the voltage across the inductor by employing $v_L = L\,di_L/dt$—try it and see.

DRILL EXERCISE 5.16

For the op-amp circuit given in Fig. 5.27 (p. 247), find the zero-state responses $v_C(t)$ and $i_C(t)$ for the case that $v_s(t) = 2e^{-4t}u(t)$ V.
Answer: $-16te^{-4t}u(t)$ V; $2(4t - 1)e^{-4t}u(t)$ A

● SUMMARY

1. A circuit containing either a single inductor or a single capacitor is described by a first-order differential equation.

2. If no independent source is present, the equation is homogeneous and the solution is called the zero-input or natural response.

3. If the initial condition is zero and the equation nonhomogeneous, the solution is called the zero-state response.

4. The complete response is the sum of two terms: One is the forced response and the other has the form of the natural response.

5. A time-invariant circuit is one in which the zero-state response to a delayed input can be obtained by delaying the zero-state response to the corresponding undelayed input.

6. In a linear circuit the zero-state response to a sum of inputs equals the sum of the individual zero-state responses.

7. In a linear circuit if the input is scaled, then the zero-state response is scaled by the same factor.

8. In a linear circuit if the input is differentiated, then the zero-state output is differentiated; if the input is integrated, so is the output.

9. Zero-state step responses for *RL* and *RC* series and parallel circuits are summarized in Table 5.1.

Table 5.1 SUMMARY OF SERIES AND PARALLEL
RC AND *RL* CIRCUIT STEP RESPONSES

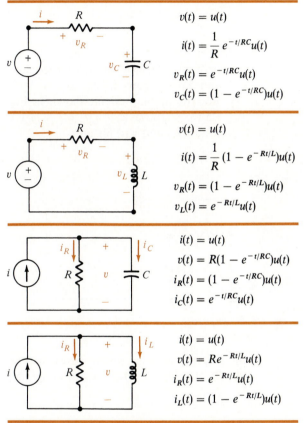

$$v(t) = u(t)$$
$$i(t) = \frac{1}{R} e^{-t/RC} u(t)$$
$$v_R(t) = e^{-t/RC} u(t)$$
$$v_C(t) = (1 - e^{-t/RC}) u(t)$$

$$v(t) = u(t)$$
$$i(t) = \frac{1}{R} (1 - e^{-Rt/L}) u(t)$$
$$v_R(t) = (1 - e^{-Rt/L}) u(t)$$
$$v_L(t) = e^{-Rt/L} u(t)$$

$$i(t) = u(t)$$
$$v(t) = R(1 - e^{-t/RC}) u(t)$$
$$i_R(t) = (1 - e^{-t/RC}) u(t)$$
$$i_C(t) = e^{-t/RC} u(t)$$

$$i(t) = u(t)$$
$$v(t) = Re^{-Rt/L} u(t)$$
$$i_R(t) = e^{-Rt/L} u(t)$$
$$i_L(t) = (1 - e^{-Rt/L}) u(t)$$

● *PROBLEMS FOR CHAPTER 5*

5.1 For the circuit shown in Fig. P5.1, the switch is opened when $t = 0$. Find $v(t)$ and $i(t)$ for all t. Sketch these functions.

5.2 For the circuit shown in Fig. P5.1, replace the capacitor with a 5-H inductor and repeat Problem 5.1.

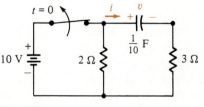

Fig. P5.1

5.3 For the circuit shown in Fig. P5.3, suppose that $v_s(t) = 15 - 15u(t)$ V. Find $v(t)$ and $i(t)$ for all t. Sketch these functions.

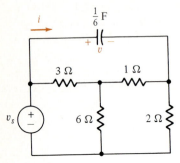

Fig. P5.3

5.4 For the circuit in Fig. P5.3, replace the capacitor with an 8-H inductor, change the 1-Ω resistor to 6 Ω, and suppose that $v_s(t) = 8 - 8u(t)$ V; then repeat Problem 5.3.

5.5 For the circuit given in Fig. DE5.2 (p. 226), replace the capacitor with a 10-H inductor. Find the current through the inductor and the voltage across the inductor for all t.

5.6 For the circuit shown in Fig. P5.6, find $v(t)$ and $i(t)$ for all t.

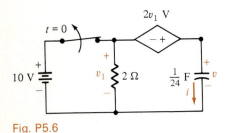

Fig. P5.6

5.7 For the circuit given in Fig. P5.6, connect a 6-Ω resistor in parallel with the capacitor, and repeat Problem 5.6.

5.8 For the circuit shown in Fig. P5.8, suppose that $v_s(t) = 9 - 9u(t)$ V. Find $i(t)$ and $v(t)$ for all t.

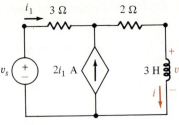

Fig. P5.8

5.9 For the circuit given in Fig. P5.8, replace the inductor with a 3-F capacitor, and repeat Problem 5.8.

5.10 For the op-amp circuit shown in Fig. P5.10, suppose that $i_s(t) = 1 - u(t)$ A. Find $v_C(t)$ and $v_o(t)$ for all t.

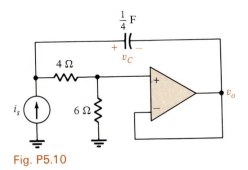

Fig. P5.10

5.11 For the op-amp circuit shown in Fig. P5.10, connect a 4-Ω resistor in parallel

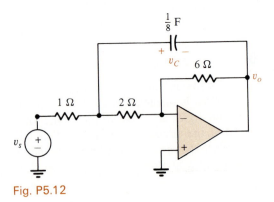

Fig. P5.12

with the capacitor, and repeat Problem 5.10.

5.12 For the op-amp circuit shown in Fig. P5.12, suppose that $v_s(t) = 3 - 3u(t)$ V. Find $v_C(t)$ and $v_o(t)$ for all t.

5.13 For the op-amp circuit shown in Fig. P5.12, connect an 8-Ω resistor in parallel with the capacitor, and repeat Problem 5.12.

5.14 For the circuit shown in Fig. P5.14, find $v(t)$ and $i(t)$ for all t. Sketch these functions.

5.15 For the circuit given in Fig. P5.14, change the value of the $\frac{1}{12}$-F capacitor to $\frac{1}{3}$ F and repeat Problem 5.14.

5.16 For the circuit given in Fig. P5.14, replace the $\frac{1}{6}$-F capacitor by a 12-H inductor and repeat Problem 5.14.

5.17 For the circuit given in Fig. P5.14, replace the $\frac{1}{6}$-F capacitor by a 1.5-H inductor and repeat Problem 5.14.

5.18 In the circuit shown in Fig. P5.18, both switches open when $t = 0$. Find $i(t)$ and $v(t)$ for all time. Sketch these functions.

5.19 Repeat Problem 5.18 for the circuit in Fig. P5.19.

5.20 For the circuit shown in Fig. P5.20, one switch opens at $t = 0$ and the other switch closes at $t = 2$ s. Find $v(t)$ and $i(t)$ for all t. Sketch these functions.

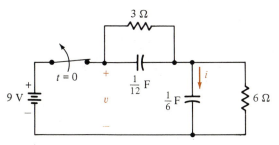

Fig. P5.14

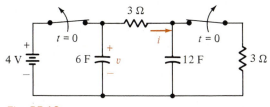

Fig. P5.18

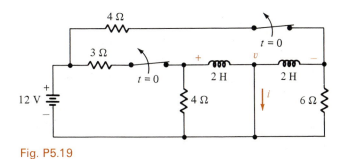

Fig. P5.19

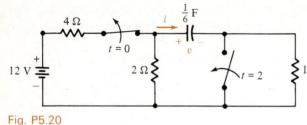

Fig. P5.20

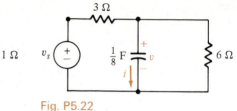

Fig. P5.22

5.21 For the circuit given in Fig. DE5.6 (p. 236), replace the 4-Ω resistor with a 3-H inductor, and repeat Drill Exercise 5.6.

5.22 For the circuit shown in Fig. P5.22, suppose that $v_s(t) = u(t)$ V. Find the zero-state step responses $v(t)$ and $i(t)$.

5.23 For the circuit shown in Fig. P5.22, replace the capacitor with a $\frac{1}{8}$-H inductor, and repeat Problem 5.22.

5.24 For the circuit given in Fig. P5.3, suppose that $v_s(t) = u(t)$ V. Find the zero-state step responses $v(t)$ and $i(t)$.

5.25 For the circuit given in Fig. P5.8, suppose that $v_s(t) = u(t)$ V. Find the zero-state step responses $i(t)$ and $v(t)$.

5.26 For the circuit given in Fig. P5.8, replace the inductor with a 3-F capacitor, and repeat Problem 5.25.

5.27 For the circuit shown in Fig. P5.27, suppose that $v_s(t) = 7u(t)$ V. Find the zero-state response $v(t)$.

5.28 For the op-amp circuit given in Fig. P5.10, suppose that $i_s(t) = u(t)$ A. Find

the zero-state step responses $v_C(t)$ and $v_o(t)$.

5.29 For the op-amp circuit given in Fig. P5.12, suppose that $v_s(t) = u(t)$ V. Find the zero-state step responses $v_C(t)$ and $v_o(t)$.

5.30 For the op-amp circuit shown in Fig. P5.10, connect a 4-Ω resistor in parallel with the capacitor. Suppose that $i_s(t) = u(t)$ A. Find the zero-state step responses $v_C(t)$ and $v_o(t)$.

5.31 For the op-amp circuit shown in Fig. P5.12, connect an 8-Ω resistor in parallel with the capacitor. Suppose that $v_s(t) = u(t)$ V. Find the zero-state step responses $v_C(t)$ and $v_o(t)$.

5.32 For the op-amp circuit in Fig. P5.32, suppose that $R_1 = R_2 = R_3 = R$. Find the zero-state step response $v_o(t)$.

5.33 For the circuit given in Fig. P5.32, interchange capacitor C and resistor R_3 and repeat Problem 5.32.

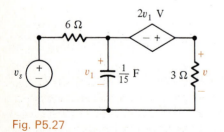

Fig. P5.27

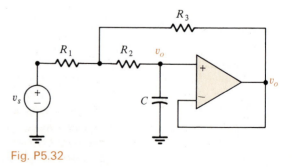

Fig. P5.32

5.34 For the circuit shown in Fig. P5.34, suppose that $i_s(t) = r(t)$ A. Find the zero-state ramp response $i(t)$.

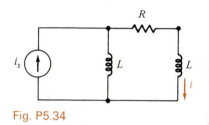

Fig. P5.34

5.35 For the circuit shown in Fig. P5.35, suppose that $v_s(t) = r(t)$ V. Find the zero-state ramp response $v(t)$.

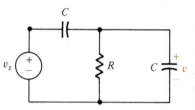

Fig. P5.35

5.36 For the circuit given in Fig. P5.22, suppose that $v_s(t) = -3 + 4u(t)$ V. Find $v(t)$ for all t.

5.37 For the circuit given in Fig. P5.22, replace the capacitor with a $\frac{1}{8}$-H inductor. Suppose that $v_s(t) = 3 - 4u(t)$ V. Find $i(t)$ for all t.

5.38 For the circuit given in Fig. P5.8, suppose that $v_s(t) = 9 - 10u(t)$ V. Find $i(t)$ and $v(t)$ for all t.

5.39 For the circuit given in Fig. P5.27, suppose that $v_s(t) = 7 + 7u(t)$ V. Find $v(t)$ for all t.

5.40 Find $v(t)$ and $i(t)$ for all t for the circuit shown in Fig. P5.40.

5.41 For the circuit given in Fig. P5.40, replace the capacitor with a $\frac{1}{9}$-H inductor, and repeat Problem 5.40.

5.42 Find $v(t)$ and $i(t)$ for all t for the circuit shown in Fig. P5.42.

5.43 For the circuit given in Fig. P5.42, replace the capacitor with a 1-H inductor, and repeat Problem 5.42.

5.44 For the circuit given in Fig. DE5.7 (p. 247), find the unit impulse responses [i.e., $v_s(t) = \delta(t)$ V] (a) $i_L(t)$, (b) $v_L(t)$, and (c) $v(t)$.

5.45 For the circuit given in Fig. DE5.7 (p. 247), find the unit ramp responses [i.e., $v_s(t) = r(t)$ V] (a) $i_L(t)$ and (b) $v_L(t)$.

5.46 For the op-amp circuit given in Fig. DE5.8 (p. 249), find the unit impulse responses [i.e., $v_s(t) = \delta(t)$ V] (a) $v_C(t)$, (b) $i_C(t)$, and (c) $v_o(t)$.

5.47 For the op-amp circuit given in Fig. DE5.8 (p. 249), find the unit ramp responses [i.e., $v_s(t) = r(t)$ V] (a) $v_C(t)$ and (b) $i_C(t)$.

5.48 For the circuit given in Fig. DE5.7 (p. 247), suppose that $v_s(t) = 12e^{-2t}u(t)$ V.

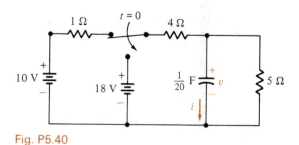

Fig. P5.40

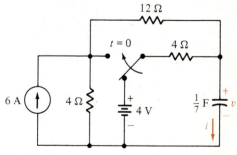

Fig. P5.42

Find the zero-state responses (a) $i_L(t)$, (b) $v_L(t)$, and (c) $v(t)$.

5.49 Repeat Problem 5.48 for the case that $v_s(t) = 12e^{-3t}u(t)$ V.

5.50 For the op-amp circuit given in Fig. 5.27 (p. 247), suppose that $v_s(t) = e^{-2t}u(t)$ V. Find the zero-state responses (a) $v_C(t)$, (b) $i_C(t)$, and (c) $v_o(t)$.

5.51 For the op-amp circuit given in Fig. DE5.8 (p. 249), suppose that $v_s(t) = e^{-2t}u(t)$ V. Find the zero-state responses (a) $v_C(t)$, (b) $i_C(t)$, and (c) $v_o(t)$.

5.52 For the op-amp circuit given in Fig.

DE5.8 (p. 249), suppose that $v_s(t) = e^{-4t}u(t)$ V. Find the zero-state responses (a) $v_C(t)$, (b) $i_C(t)$, and (c) $v_o(t)$.

5.53 For the op-amp circuit given in Fig. 5.27 (p. 247), suppose that $v_s(t) = (1 - e^{-4t})u(t)$ V. Find the zero-state responses (a) $v_C(t)$ and (b) $i_C(t)$.

5.54 For the series RC circuit given in Fig. 5.19 (p. 236), suppose that $R = 2\,\Omega$, $C = \frac{1}{2}$ F, and $v_s(t) = \cos t\, u(t)$ V. Find the zero-state response $v_C(t)$. [*Hint*: $\int e^t \cos t\, dt = \frac{1}{2}e^t(\cos t + \sin t).$]

Second-Order Circuits

● INTRODUCTION

Having dealt with circuits containing either a single inductor or capacitor, we shall now consider the case of two energy storage elements in a circuit. Most such networks, called **second-order circuits**, are described by second-order linear differential equations—the solution of which takes three forms.

As with first-order circuits, we start by considering the zero-input case, follow it with the situation in which there is an input present and the initial conditions (states) are zero (the zero-state case), and then proceed to circuits having both nonzero inputs and initial conditions.

We shall see that the complexity of analysis increases significantly when compared to that encountered with first-order circuits. It is because of this fact that we do not extend such an approach to higher-order circuits but, instead, take different points of view in the subsequent chapters.

6.1 THE SERIES *RLC* CIRCUIT

Suppose that for the zero-input series *RLC* circuit shown in Fig. 6.1, the inital current through the inductor is $i(0)$ and the initial voltage across the capacitor is $v(0)$. By KVL, we get the integrodifferential equation

$$Ri + L\frac{di}{dt} + \frac{1}{C}\int_0^t i\,dt + v(0) = 0$$

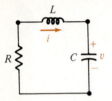

Fig. 6.1   Series *RLC* circuit with no input
applied.

Taking the derivative of this equation and dividing by L yields the second-order, homogeneous, linear differential equation with constant coefficients

$$\frac{d^2 i}{dt^2} + \frac{R}{L} \frac{di}{dt} + \frac{1}{LC} i = 0 \tag{6.1}$$

Again, from the circuit, by KVL,

$$L \frac{di}{dt} + Ri + v = 0$$

Substituting the fact that $i = C\, dv/dt$ into this equation, after dividing by LC, we also get the second-order differential equation

$$\frac{d^2 v}{dt^2} + \frac{R}{L} \frac{dv}{dt} + \frac{1}{LC} v = 0 \tag{6.2}$$

Both Equations (6.1) and (6.2) have the form

$$\frac{d^2 y(t)}{dt^2} + K_1 \frac{dy(t)}{dt} + K_2 y(t) = 0$$

so let us concentrate on solving this equation. Experience has shown that it is more convenient to use the constant 2α in place of K_1, and the constant ω_n^2 in place of K_2. In other words, consider the equation

$$\frac{d^2 y(t)}{dt^2} + 2\alpha \frac{dy(t)}{dt} + \omega_n^2 y(t) = 0 \tag{6.3}$$

We have seen that the solution to a first-order, homogeneous differential equation is

$$y(t) = Ae^{st}$$

where A and s are constants. However, is this a solution to the second-order homogeneous equation (6.3)? In order to find out, substitute this expression into the equation. The result is

$$\frac{d^2}{dt^2} (Ae^{st}) + 2\alpha \frac{d}{dt} (Ae^{st}) + \omega_n^2 (Ae^{st}) = 0 \tag{6.4}$$

from which

$$s^2 Ae^{st} + 2\alpha s Ae^{st} + \omega_n^2 Ae^{st} = 0$$

Dividing both sides by Ae^{st} yields

$$s^2 + 2\alpha s + \omega_n^2 = 0 \tag{6.5}$$

If this equality holds, then so does the one given in Equation (6.4). By the quadratic formula, this equality holds when

$$s = \frac{-2\alpha \pm \sqrt{4\alpha^2 - 4\omega_n^2}}{2} = -\alpha \pm \sqrt{\alpha^2 - \omega_n^2}$$

In other words, the two values of s that satisfy Equation (6.5) are

$$\boxed{s_1 = -\alpha - \sqrt{\alpha^2 - \omega_n^2} \qquad \text{and} \qquad s_2 = -\alpha + \sqrt{\alpha^2 - \omega_n^2}}$$

Thus, $A_1 e^{s_1 t}$ and $A_2 e^{s_2 t}$ satisfy Equation (6.3). That is,

$$\frac{d^2}{dt^2}(A_1 e^{s_1 t}) + 2\alpha \frac{d}{dt}(A_1 e^{s_1 t}) + \omega_n^2(A_1 e^{s_1 t}) = 0$$

and

$$\frac{d^2}{dt^2}(A_2 e^{s_2 t}) + 2\alpha \frac{d}{dt}(A_2 e^{s_2 t}) + \omega_n^2(A_2 e^{s_2 t}) = 0$$

Adding these two equations results in the equality

$$\frac{d^2}{dt^2}(A_1 e^{s_1 t} + A_2 e^{s_2 t}) + 2\alpha \frac{d}{dt}(A_1 e^{s_1 t} + A_2 e^{s_2 t}) + \omega_n^2(A_1 e^{s_1 t} + A_2 e^{s_2 t}) = 0$$

Therefore we see that, in addition to $A_1 e^{s_1 t}$ and $A_2 e^{s_2 t}$, their sum

$$\boxed{y(t) = A_1 e^{s_1 t} + A_2 e^{s_2 t}} \tag{6.6}$$

satisfies Equation (6.3). Since this is the most general expression (it contains both $A_1 e^{s_1 t}$ and $A_2 e^{s_2 t}$) that satisfies Equation (6.3), it is the solution.

In this solution, A_1 and A_2 are arbitrary constants. However, if we are given the initial conditions $y(0)$ and $dy(0)/dt$, then using the fact that

$$y(t) = A_1 e^{s_1 t} + A_2 e^{s_2 t} \qquad \text{and} \qquad \frac{dy(t)}{dt} = s_1 A_1 e^{s_1 t} + s_2 A_2 e^{s_2 t}$$

we can determine the constants A_1 and A_2 from the two simultaneous equations

$$y(0) = A_1 + A_2 \qquad \text{and} \qquad \frac{dy(0)}{dt} = s_1 A_1 + s_2 A_2$$

Note that depending on the relative values of α and ω_n, the values of s_1 and s_2 can be either real or complex numbers. If $\alpha > \omega_n$, then $\alpha^2 - \omega_n^2 > 0$ so s_1 and s_2

are real numbers. This condition is referred to as the **overdamped** case. If $\alpha < \omega_n$, then $\alpha^2 - \omega_n^2 < 0$ (equivalently $\omega_n^2 - \alpha^2 > 0$), and therefore s_1 and s_2 are complex numbers. In particular,

$$s_1 = -\alpha - \sqrt{\alpha^2 - \omega_n^2} = -\alpha - \sqrt{-(\omega_n^2 - \alpha^2)} = -\alpha - j\omega_d$$

$$s_2 = -\alpha + \sqrt{\alpha^2 - \omega_n^2} = -\alpha + \sqrt{-(\omega_n^2 - \alpha^2)} = -\alpha + j\omega_d$$

where $j = \sqrt{-1}$ and $\omega_d = \sqrt{\omega_n^2 - \alpha^2}$. This condition is referred to as the **underdamped** case. Finally, the special case that $\alpha = \omega_n$, called the **critically damped** case, results in $s_1 = s_2 = -\alpha$. For this condition,

$$y(t) = A_1 e^{s_1 t} + A_2 e^{s_2 t} = A_1 e^{-\alpha t} + A_2 e^{-\alpha t} = (A_1 + A_2)e^{-\alpha t} = Ae^{-\alpha t}$$

which cannot be the solution to Equation (6.3), since in general it is impossible to satisfy the two initial conditions $y(0)$ and $dy(0)/dt$ with the single constant A. The solution of Equation (6.3) for this special case will be discussed shortly. Let us now discuss these three cases in detail.

Returning to the series *RLC* circuit, we have for the second-order current differential equation (6.1), as well as the voltage equation (6.2),

$$2\alpha = \frac{R}{L} \quad \Rightarrow \quad \alpha = \frac{R}{2L}$$

and

$$\omega_n^2 = \frac{1}{LC} \quad \Rightarrow \quad \omega_n = \frac{1}{\sqrt{LC}}$$

Let us now do a numerical example of a series *RLC* circuit.

EXAMPLE 6.1

Let us find $i(t)$ and $v(t)$ for the circuit shown in Fig. 6.2.

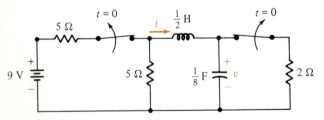

Fig. 6.2 *RLC* circuit for Example 6.1.

For $t < 0$, the inductor behaves as a short circuit and the capacitor behaves as an open circuit. The equivalent circuit is shown in Fig. 6.3(a). Since the parallel combination of $2\,\Omega$ and $5\,\Omega$ is $(2)(5)/(2 + 5) = \frac{10}{7}\,\Omega$, then by voltage division,

$$v = \frac{10/7}{10/7 + 5}(9) = 2\text{ V}$$

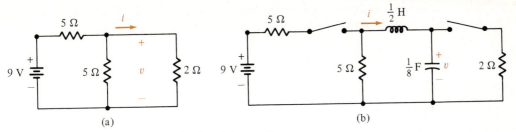

Fig. 6.3   (a) Circuit for $t < 0$. (b) Circuit for $t \geq 0$.

and by Ohm's law,

$$i = \frac{v}{2} = \frac{2}{2} = 1 \text{ A}$$

For $t \geq 0$, the circuit is as shown in Fig. 6.3(b), and we have that $i(0) = 1$ A and $v(0) = 2$ V. By KVL,

$$5i + \frac{1}{2}\frac{di}{dt} + v = 0 \qquad \Rightarrow \qquad v = -\frac{1}{2}\frac{di}{dt} - 5i \qquad (6.7)$$

Thus,

$$i = \frac{1}{8}\frac{dv}{dt} = \frac{1}{8}\frac{d}{dt}\left(-\frac{1}{2}\frac{di}{dt} - 5i\right) = -\frac{1}{16}\frac{d^2i}{dt^2} - \frac{5}{8}\frac{di}{dt}$$

from which

$$\frac{d^2i}{dt^2} + 10\frac{di}{dt} + 16i = 0 \qquad (6.8)$$

[Note that we can get this equation by substituting $R = 5\ \Omega$, $L = \frac{1}{2}$ H, and $C = \frac{1}{8}$ F into Equation (6.1).] But Equation (6.8) has the form of Equation (6.3), where

$$2\alpha = 10 \qquad \Rightarrow \qquad \alpha = 5 \qquad \text{and} \qquad \omega_n^2 = 16 \qquad \Rightarrow \qquad \omega_n = 4$$

Since $\alpha > \omega_n$, and the circuit is overdamped. Since

$$s_1 = -\alpha - \sqrt{\alpha^2 - \omega_n^2} = -8 \qquad \text{and} \qquad s_2 = -\alpha + \sqrt{\alpha^2 - \omega_n^2} = -2$$

then the expression for the current $i(t)$ has the form

$$i(t) = A_1 e^{-8t} + A_2 e^{-2t}$$

Setting $t = 0$ and using the initial condition $i(0) = 1$ A, we get

$$1 = A_1 + A_2 \qquad (6.9)$$

Taking the derivative of $i(t)$ yields

$$\frac{di(t)}{dt} = -8A_1 e^{-8t} - 2A_2 e^{-2t} \qquad (6.10)$$

The second initial condition given is $v(0) = 2$ V, not a value for $di(0)/dt$. However, from Equation (6.7) we have that

$$\frac{di}{dt} = -10i - 2v$$

Setting $t = 0$ yields

$$\frac{di(0)}{dt} = -10i(0) - 2v(0) = -10(1) - 2(2) = -14$$

Hence, setting $t = 0$ in Equation (6.10) results in

$$-14 = -8A_1 - 2A_2 \tag{6.11}$$

The solution of the simultaneous Equations (6.9) and (6.11) is

$$A_1 = 2 \quad \text{and} \quad A_2 = -1$$

Thus, the solution of Equation (6.8) is

$$i(t) = 2e^{-8t} - e^{-2t} \text{ A} \quad \text{for} \quad t \geq 0$$

From Equation (6.7), we have that

$$v(t) = -\frac{1}{2}\frac{di(t)}{dt} - 5i(t) = -\frac{1}{2}(-16e^{-8t} + 2e^{-2t}) - 5(2e^{-8t} - e^{-2t})$$

$$= -2e^{-8t} + 4e^{-2t} \text{ V} \quad \text{for} \quad t \geq 0$$

From our expressions for $i(t)$ and $v(t)$, setting $t = 0$, we get

$$i(0) = 2e^{-0} - e^{-0} = 2 - 1 = 1 \text{ A}$$

and

$$v(0) = -2e^{-0} + 4e^{-0} = -2 + 4 = 2 \text{ V}$$

as required. Plots of $v(t)$ and $i(t)$ for $t \geq 0$ are shown in Figs. 6.4(a) and (b), respectively.

The initial current in the inductor, and hence through each element, is a clockwise current. The initial voltage across the capacitor is a positive value with the polarity indicated. The capacitor, therefore, tends to discharge by producing a counterclockwise current. The net effect is that, due to the inductor current, the capacitor will first charge to a greater voltage before it begins to discharge. The current through the inductor goes to zero when $t \approx 0.116$ s, at which time the capacitor is charged to its maximum value of approximately 2.38 V. Aftter this time the current becomes counterclockwise (negative in value) and the energy stored is eventually dissipated in the resistor as heat. Note that if the direction of the initial current had the opposite direction (or if the polarity of the initial voltage was opposite) the capacitor would not have charged to a greater value before it discharged.

For this example, the energy stored in the inductor at $t = 0$ is

$$w_L(0) = \tfrac{1}{2}Li^2(0) = \tfrac{1}{2}(\tfrac{1}{2})(1)^2 = \tfrac{1}{4} \text{ J}$$

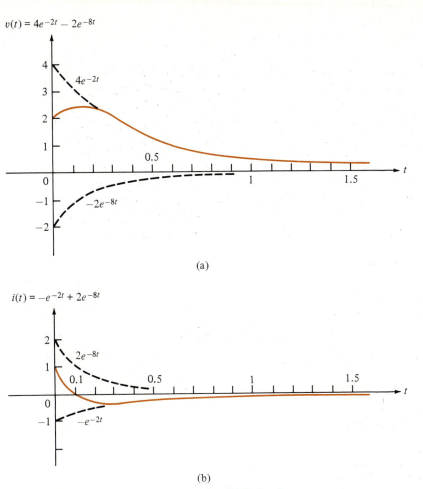

(a)

(b)

Fig. 6.4   Zero-input responses for series *RLC* circuit.

and the energy stored in the capacitor at $t = 0$ is

$$w_C(0) = \tfrac{1}{2}Cv^2(0) = \tfrac{1}{2}(\tfrac{1}{8})(2)^2 = \tfrac{1}{4} \text{ J}$$

so that the total energy stored at $t = 0$ is $\tfrac{1}{2}$ J. The power absorbed by the resistor is

$$p_R(t) = Ri^2(t) = 5(-e^{-2t} + 2e^{-8t})^2 = 5(e^{-4t} - 4e^{-10t} + 4e^{-16t})$$

Thus, the energy absorbed by the resistor is

$$w_R = \int_0^\infty p_R(t)\,dt = \int_0^\infty 5(e^{-4t} - 4e^{-10t} + 4e^{-16t})\,dt$$

$$= 5(-\tfrac{1}{4}e^{-4t} + \tfrac{4}{10}e^{-10t} - \tfrac{4}{16}e^{-16t})\Big|_0^\infty = \tfrac{1}{2} \text{ J}$$

as it should be.

DRILL EXERCISE 6.1

For the circuit shown in Fig. DE6.1, find $v(t)$ and $i(t)$ for $t \geq 0$.

Answer: $-e^{-6t} + 3e^{-2t}$ V; $2e^{-6t} - 2e^{-2t}$ A

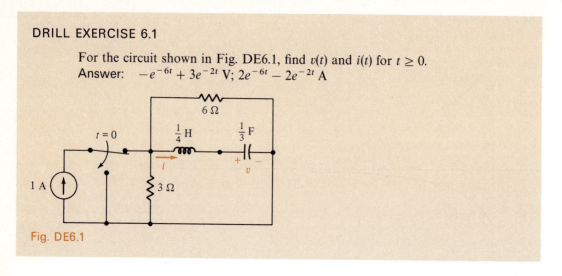

Fig. DE6.1

In the second of the three cases (underdamping) to be considered next, we shall see quite different waveforms than for the overdamped case. Of course, we could change the values of R, L, and C in the series RLC circuit to get the underdamped case ($\omega_n > \alpha$); the initial conditions $v(0)$ and $i(0)$ have no effect on the damping of a circuit. However, let us discuss the underdamped case with a different circuit.

6.2 THE PARALLEL *RLC* CIRCUIT

For the zero-input parallel RLC circuit shown in Fig. 6.5, the initial conditions (state) of the circuit are $i(0)$ and $v(0)$. From

$$v = L\frac{di}{dt} \qquad \text{and} \qquad \frac{v}{R} + i + C\frac{dv}{dt} = 0$$

we get

$$\frac{d^2i}{dt^2} + \frac{1}{RC}\frac{di}{dt} + \frac{1}{LC}i = 0 \tag{6.12}$$

which has the form of Equation (6.3), where

$$\alpha = \frac{1}{2RC} \qquad \text{and} \qquad \omega_n = \frac{1}{\sqrt{LC}}$$

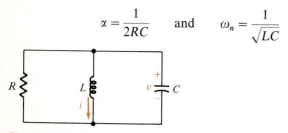

Fig. 6.5   Parallel *RLC* circuit with no input applied.

(Note that these results could have been obtained from the series *RLC* zero-input circuit by duality.)

EXAMPLE 6.2

Let us find $i(t)$ and $v(t)$ for the circuit shown in Fig. 6.6.

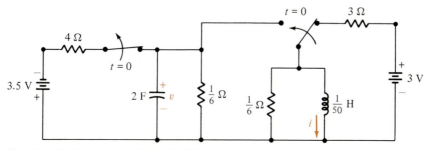

Fig. 6.6 *RLC* circuit for Example 6.2.

For $t < 0$, the equivalent circuit is shown in Fig. 6.7. By voltage division,

$$v = \frac{1/6}{1/6 + 4}(-3.5) = \frac{1}{1 + 24}(-3.5) = -0.14 \text{ V}$$

Furthermore, by Ohm's law,

$$i = \frac{3}{3} = 1 \text{ A}$$

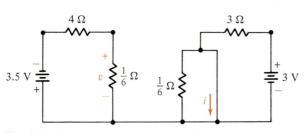

Fig. 6.7 Equivalent circuit for $t < 0$.

For $t \geq 0$, the equivalent circuit is as shown in Fig. 6.8, where $v(0) = -0.14$ V and $i(0) = 1$ A. Combining the two $\frac{1}{6}$-Ω resistors into a $\frac{1}{12}$-Ω resistor, we then get a parallel *RLC* connection. Therefore, substituting $R = \frac{1}{12}\Omega$, $L = \frac{1}{50}$ H, and $C = 2$ F into Equation (6.12), we get

$$\frac{d^2i}{dt^2} + 6\frac{di}{dt} + 25i = 0$$

Comparing this with Equation (6.3), we have that

$$2\alpha = 6 \quad \Rightarrow \quad \alpha = 3 \quad \text{and} \quad \omega_n^2 = 25 \quad \Rightarrow \quad \omega_n = 5$$

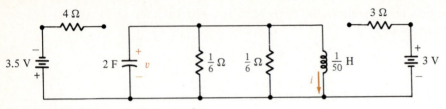

Fig. 6.8 Equivalent circuit for $t \geq 0$.

or, we could use the fact that for a parallel *RLC* circuit

$$\alpha = \frac{1}{2RC} \quad \text{and} \quad \omega_n = \frac{1}{\sqrt{LC}}$$

In either case, $\alpha = 3 < \omega_n = 5$ and the circuit is underdamped. Since

$$\omega_d = \sqrt{\omega_n^2 - \alpha^2} = \sqrt{25 - 9} = 4$$

then

$$s_1 = -\alpha - j\omega_d = -3 - j4 \quad \text{and} \quad s_2 = -\alpha + j\omega_d = -3 + j4$$

and the expression for the current $i(t)$ has the form

$$i(t) = A_1 e^{(-3-j4)t} + A_2 e^{(-3+j4)t} = A_1 e^{-3t} e^{-j4t} + A_2 e^{-3t} e^{j4t}$$
$$= e^{-3t}(A_1 e^{-j4t} + A_2 e^{j4t})$$

Using **Euler's formula** (we will derive this very important result later),

$$\boxed{e^{j\theta} = \cos\theta + j\sin\theta}$$

we get

$$i(t) = e^{-3t}(A_1 \cos 4t - jA_1 \sin 4t + A_2 \cos 4t + jA_2 \sin 4t)$$
$$= e^{-3t}[(A_1 + A_2)\cos 4t + j(-A_1 + A_2)\sin 4t]$$
$$= e^{-3t}(B_1 \cos 4t + B_2 \sin 4t)$$

Setting $t = 0$, we get

$$i(0) = e^{-0}(B_1 \cos 0 + B_2 \sin 0) \quad \Rightarrow \quad 1 = B_1$$

Taking the derivative of $i(t)$ results in

$$\frac{di(t)}{dt} = e^{-3t}(4B_2 \cos 4t - 4B_1 \sin 4t) - 3e^{-3t}(B_1 \cos 4t + B_2 \sin 4t)$$

and setting $t = 0$ yields

$$\frac{di(0)}{t} = 4B_2 - 3B_1 = 4B_2 - 3 \quad \Rightarrow \quad B_2 = \frac{1}{4}\left(\frac{di(0)}{dt} + 3\right)$$

For the circuit, though, we have that

$$L \frac{di(t)}{dt} = v(t) \qquad \Rightarrow \qquad \frac{di(t)}{dt} = \frac{1}{L} v(t)$$

so

$$\frac{di(0)}{dt} = 50v(0) = 50(-0.14) = -7$$

Thus,

$$B_2 = \tfrac{1}{4}(-7 + 3) = -1$$

and the expression for the current is

$$i(t) = e^{-3t}(\cos 4t - \sin 4t) \text{ A} \qquad \text{for} \quad t \geq 0$$

Furthermore,

$$v(t) = \frac{1}{50} \frac{d}{dt} \left[e^{-3t}(\cos 4t - \sin 4t) \right]$$

$$= \tfrac{1}{50}\left[e^{-3t}(-4 \sin 4t - 4 \cos 4t) - 3e^{-3t}(\cos 4t - \sin 4t) \right]$$

$$= \tfrac{1}{50} e^{-3t}\left[-7 \cos 4t - \sin 4t \right] \text{ V} \qquad \text{for} \quad t \geq 0$$

DRILL EXERCISE 6.2

For the circuit given in Fig. DE6.1 (p. 280), change the value of the capacitor to $\tfrac{1}{5}$ F and repeat Drill Exercise 6.1.

Answer: $2e^{-4t}(\cos 2t + 2 \sin 2t) \text{ V}; \; -4e^{-4t} \sin 2t \text{ A}$

In the preceding example, we did not attempt to sketch the functions $i(t)$ and $v(t)$ because of their relatively complicated expressions—each is the product of an exponential and the difference of two sinusoids. However, there is an alternative form for underdamped responses. Let us now show how to obtain such an expression.

For the underdamped case, we can write Equation (6.6) as

$$y(t) = A_1 e^{s_1 t} + A_2 e^{s_2 t} = A_1 e^{-\alpha t} e^{-j\omega_d t} + A_2 e^{-\alpha t} e^{j\omega_d t}$$

$$= e^{-\alpha t}(A_1 e^{-j\omega_d t} + A_2 e^{j\omega_d t})$$

where $\omega_d = \sqrt{\omega_n^2 - \alpha^2}$. Using Euler's formula and combining constants, we have just seen an example of the fact that we can rewrite $y(t)$ in the form

$$y(t) = e^{-\alpha t}(B_1 \cos \omega_d t + B_2 \sin \omega_d t) \tag{6.13}$$

Even so, it is possible further to combine the two sinusoids that have **frequency** ω_d into a single sinusoid of frequency ω_d. One possibility is $B \cos(\omega_d t - \phi)$, where we call B the **amplitude** of the sinusoid and ϕ is the **phase angle**.[†] Since the angle of a sinusoid is measured in radians and the unit of time is the second, and unit of ω_d is radians per second (rad/s).

Now we want to determine under what conditions the following equality holds:

$$B_1 \cos \omega_d t + B_2 \sin \omega_d t = B \cos(\omega_d t - \phi) \qquad (6.14)$$

Using the trigonometric identity for the cosine of the difference of two angles, we get

$$B_1 \cos \omega_d t + B_2 \sin \omega_d t = B(\cos \omega_d t \cos \phi + \sin \omega_d t \sin \phi)$$
$$= B \cos \phi \cos \omega_d t + B \sin \phi \sin \omega_d t$$

and equality holds when

$$B_1 = B \cos \phi \quad \text{and} \quad B_2 = B \sin \phi$$

Thus,

$$\frac{B_2}{B_1} = \frac{B \sin \phi}{B \cos \phi} = \tan \phi \quad \Rightarrow \quad \phi = \tan^{-1}\left(\frac{B_2}{B_1}\right)$$

The angle ϕ can be depicted by the right triangle shown in Fig. 6.9. We then have that

$$B_1 = B \cos \phi \quad \Rightarrow \quad B = \frac{B_1}{\cos \phi} = \frac{B_1}{B_1/\sqrt{B_1^2 + B_2^2}} = \sqrt{B_1^2 + B_2^2}$$

In summary, the conditions for which Equation (6.14) holds are

$$B = \sqrt{B_1^2 + B_2^2} \quad \text{and} \quad \phi = \tan^{-1}\left(\frac{B_2}{B_1}\right) \qquad (6.15)$$

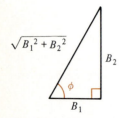

Fig. 6.9   Relationship between B_1, B_2, and ϕ.

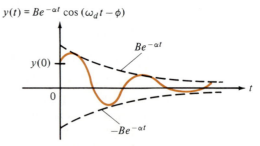

$$y(t) = Be^{-\alpha t} \cos(\omega_d t - \phi)$$

Fig. 6.10   Damped sinusoid.

[†] Among other possibilities are $D \sin(\omega_d t + \theta)$ and $E \cos(\omega_d t + \psi)$.

and the expression given by Equation (6.13) can be rewritten as

$$y(t) = Be^{-\alpha t}\cos(\omega_d t - \phi) \qquad\qquad (6.16)$$

where $\omega_d = \sqrt{\omega_n^2 - \alpha^2}$. A typical sketch of $y(t)$ for $t \geq 0$ is shown in Fig. 6.10. Such a curve is called a **damped sinusoid**.

As a consequence of this discussion, we call α the **damping factor**, since its value determines how fast the sinusoid's amplitude diminishes. We call ω_d the **damped natural frequency**, or **damped frequency** for short. For the case that the damping factor $\alpha = 0$, we have that $\omega_d = \sqrt{\omega_n^2 - \alpha^2} = \omega_n$, and we refer to ω_n as the **undamped natural frequency**, or **undamped frequency**[†] for short.

For Example 6.2, we have that

$$i(t) = e^{-3t}(\cos 4t - \sin 4t) = e^{-3t}(B_1 \cos 4t + B_2 \sin 4t)$$

so

$$B = \sqrt{B_1^2 + B_2^2} = \sqrt{2} \qquad \text{and} \qquad \phi = \tan^{-1}\left(\frac{B_2}{B_1}\right) = \tan^{-1}\left(\frac{-1}{1}\right) = -\frac{\pi}{4}\,\text{rad}$$

Thus, we can also write the current as

$$i(t) = \sqrt{2}e^{-3t}\cos(4t + \pi/4)\,\text{A} \qquad \text{for} \quad t \geq 0$$

The voltage $v(t)$ is

$$v(t) = \frac{1}{50}\frac{d}{dt}\left[e^{-3t}(\cos 4t - \sin 4t)\right]$$

$$= \tfrac{1}{50}\left[e^{-3t}(-4\sin 4t - 4\cos 4t) - 3e^{-3t}(\cos 4t - \sin 4t)\right]$$

$$= \tfrac{1}{50}e^{-3t}\left[-7\cos 4t - \sin 4t\right]\,\text{V}$$

In this case,

$$B = \sqrt{(-7)^2 + (-1)^2} = 5\sqrt{2}$$

and

$$\phi = \tan^{-1}\left(\frac{-1}{-7}\right) = 3.28 = -3.0\,\text{rad}$$

so

$$v(t) = \frac{\sqrt{2}}{10}e^{-3t}\cos(4t + 3.0)\,\text{V} \qquad \text{for} \quad t \geq 0$$

[†] Although some texts refer to ω_n as the "resonance frequency," except for very simple circuits such as the series and parallel *RLC* circuits, the resonance frequency (to be discussed in Chapter 10) of the circuit is generally different from the undamped frequency.

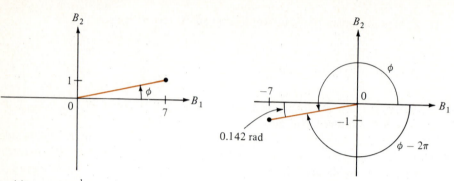

(a) $\phi = \arctan \frac{1}{7} = 0.142$ rad

(b) $\phi = \arctan \frac{-1}{-7} = 3.28$ rad

Fig. 6.11   Determination of arctangent.

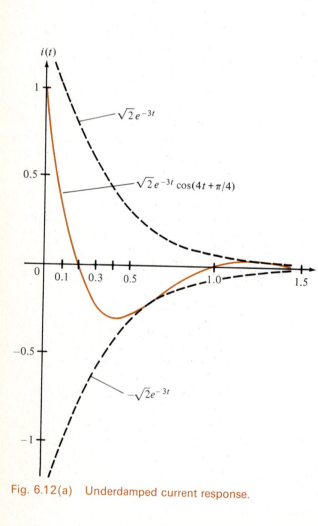

Fig. 6.12(a)   Underdamped current response.

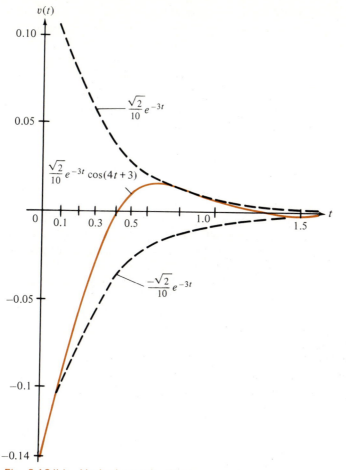

Fig. 6.12(b)   Underdamped voltage response.

What's that? Your calculator says that $\tan^{-1}(-1/-7)$ is equal to 0.142 radian (8 degrees)? If it does, be careful. Your calculator cannot distinguish between $\tan^{-1}(-1/-7)$ and $\tan^{-1}(1/7)$—these are different quantities! And it is the former we require in this case. By inspection of Fig. 6.11, we can see that $\tan^{-1}(1/7) = 0.142$ rad and $\tan^{-1}(-1/-7) = 3.28 = -3.0$ rad.

Plots of $i(t)$ and $v(t)$ for $t \geq 0$ are shown in Fig. 6.12(a) and 6.12(b), respectively.

DRILL EXERCISE 6.3

Express the voltage and current obtained in Drill Exercise 6.2 in the form of Equation (6.16).

Answer: $2\sqrt{5}e^{-4t}\cos(2t - 1.11)$ V; $4e^{-4t}\cos(2t + \pi/2)$ A

What happens in the underdamped case is that the energy that is stored in the inductor and capacitor eventually gets dissipated by the resistor. However, the energy does not simply go from the L and C directly to the R. Instead, it is transferred back and forth between the two energy-storage elements, with the resistance taking its toll during the process. The result of this is a response that is oscillatory (changes sign more than once). In particular, an underdamped response is the product of a real exponential and a sinusoid, that is, a damped sinusoid.

In the example above, although oscillatory, the responses (current and voltage) became negligible before too many oscillations occurred. This is due to the fact that ω_n is not much larger than α (i.e., the circuit is slightly underdamped). By reducing the damping (making α smaller), the circuit becomes more underdamped, and more oscillations occur before the responses get close to zero. A sketch of an underdamped response where α is relatively small is shown in Fig. 6.13. For the parallel RLC circuit when $R = \infty$ or for the series RLC circuit when $R = 0$, we have the underdamped case with no damping ($\alpha = 0$). A consequence of this is a response that will be perfectly sinusoidal, and thus will never decrease in amplitude. Such a situation cannot be physically constructed with ordinary capacitors and inductors. There are, however, electronic ways for producing such a result. A device that accomplishes this is known as an **oscillator**.

Having considered the case of overdamping ($\alpha > \omega_n$) and underdamping ($\omega_n > \alpha$), it is now time to investigate the critical damping condition ($\alpha = \omega_n$). We will do this while we are analyzing a new circuit.

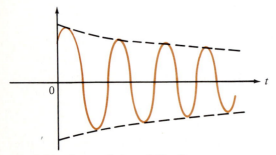

Fig. 6.13 Damped sinusoid having a relatively small damping factor.

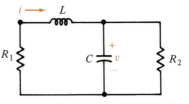

Fig. 6.14 Series-parallel RLC circuit.

6.3 OTHER ZERO-INPUT CIRCUITS

We have seen for the series RLC circuit and the parallel RLC circuit that the undamped frequency in both cases is $\omega_n = 1/\sqrt{LC}$. As a consequence, it is frequently assumed that this is a general result for any circuit containing one inductor and one capacitor. The series-parallel RLC circuit in Fig. 6.14 will show that such an assumption is unwarranted. Applying KVL to the mesh on the left, we get

$$R_1 i + L \frac{di}{dt} + v = 0 \tag{6.17}$$

and applying KCL at the node common to the inductor and the capacitor, we obtain

$$i = C\frac{dv}{dt} + \frac{v}{R_2} \tag{6.18}$$

Substituting Equation (6.18) into Equation (6.17) yields

$$R_1\left(C\frac{dv}{dt} + \frac{v}{R_2}\right) + L\frac{d}{dt}\left(C\frac{dv}{dt} + \frac{v}{R_2}\right) + v = 0$$

from which

$$\frac{d^2v}{dt^2} + \left(\frac{R_1}{L} + \frac{1}{R_2C}\right)\frac{dv}{dt} + \frac{R_1 + R_2}{R_2LC}v = 0 \tag{6.19}$$

Thus, for this circuit,

$$\alpha = \frac{R_1}{2L} + \frac{1}{2R_2C} \qquad \text{and} \qquad \omega_n = \sqrt{\frac{R_1 + R_2}{R_2LC}}$$

Depending on the values of R_1, R_2, L, and C, the circuit can be overdamped ($\alpha > \omega_n$), underdamped ($\alpha < \omega_n$), or critically damped ($\alpha = \omega_n$).

Suppose that the circuit is critically damped. In this case,

$$y(t) = A_1e^{s_1t} + A_2e^{s_2t} = A_1e^{-\alpha t} + A_2e^{-\alpha t} = Ae^{-\alpha t}$$

is not the solution to Equation (6.3). This is so because the two initial conditions $i(0)$ and $v(0)$ cannot be satisfied with the one arbitrary constant A. To determine what the solution is, let us return to Equation (6.3). Using the critically damped condition $\alpha = \omega_n$, Equation (6.3) becomes

$$\frac{d^2y(t)}{dt^2} + 2\alpha\frac{dy(t)}{dt} + \alpha^2y(t) = 0$$

or

$$\frac{d}{dt}\left[\frac{dy(t)}{dt} + \alpha y(t)\right] + \alpha\left[\frac{dy(t)}{dt} + \alpha y(t)\right] = 0 \tag{6.20}$$

If we define the function $f(t)$ by

$$f(t) = \frac{dy(t)}{dt} + \alpha y(t)$$

then Equation (6.20) becomes

$$\frac{df(t)}{dt} + \alpha f(t) = 0$$

which is a first-order differential equation whose solution is $f(t) = A_1e^{-\alpha t}$. Thus,

$$\frac{dy(t)}{dt} + \alpha y(t) = A_1e^{-\alpha t}$$

Multiplying both sides by $e^{\alpha t}$ yields

$$e^{\alpha t}\frac{dy(t)}{dt} + e^{\alpha t}\alpha y(t) = A_1 \qquad \Rightarrow \qquad \frac{d}{dt}[e^{\alpha t}y(t)] = A_1$$

Integrating both sides with respect to t results in

$$\int \frac{d[e^{\alpha t}y(t)]}{dt}\, dt = \int A_1\, dt \qquad \Rightarrow \qquad e^{\alpha t}y(t) = A_1 t + A_2$$

where A_2 is a constant of integration. Multiplying both sides by $e^{-\alpha t}$ gives

$$y(t) = A_1 t e^{-\alpha t} + A_2 e^{-\alpha t} = (A_1 t + A_2)e^{-\alpha t} \tag{6.21}$$

and this is the solution of Equation (6.3) for the case of critical damping.

EXAMPLE 6.3

For the circuit given in Fig. 6.15, let us determine $v(t)$ and $i(t)$.

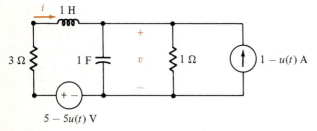

Fig. 6.15 *RLC* circuit for Example 6.3.

For $t < 0$, the equivalent circuit is shown in Fig. 6.16. By KVL,

$$3i + 1(i + 1) - 5 = 0 \qquad \Rightarrow \qquad i = 1\ \text{A}$$

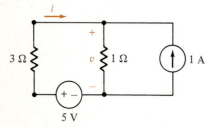

Fig. 6.16 Equivalent circuit for $t < 0$.

Furthermore,

$$v = 1(i + 1) = 2 \text{ V}$$

For $t \geq 0$, the equivalent circuit is given by the circuit in Fig. 6.14, where $i(0) = 1$ A and $v(0) = 2$ V. Thus,

$$\alpha = \frac{R_1}{2L} + \frac{1}{2R_2C} = \frac{3}{2(1)} + \frac{1}{2(1)(1)} = 2 \qquad \omega_n = \sqrt{\frac{R_1 + R_2}{R_2LC}} = \sqrt{\frac{3 + 1}{(1)(1)(1)}} = 2$$

Since $\alpha = \omega_n$, the circuit is critically damped, and the solution to Equation (6.19) is

$$v(t) = A_1 t e^{-2t} + A_2 e^{-2t}$$

Given the initial conditions $i(0) = 1$ A and $v(0) = 2$ V, then setting $t = 0$ yields

$$v(0) = 0 + A_2 = 2 \quad \Rightarrow \quad A_2 = 2$$

Next,

$$\frac{dv(t)}{dt} = -2A_1 t e^{-2t} + A_1 e^{-2t} - 2A_2 e^{-2t}$$

so

$$\frac{dv(0)}{dt} = A_1 - 2A_2 = A_1 - 4$$

From Equation (6.18),

$$\frac{dv(t)}{dt} = -\frac{v(t)}{R_2C} + \frac{i(t)}{C} = -v(t) + i(t)$$

Setting $t = 0$

$$\frac{dv(0)}{dt} = -v(0) + i(0) = -2 + 1 = -1$$

so

$$A_1 - 4 = -1 \quad \Rightarrow \quad A_1 = 3$$

Therefore, the expression for $v(t)$ is

$$v(t) = 3t e^{-2t} + 2e^{-2t} = (3t + 2)e^{-2t} \text{ V} \qquad \text{for} \quad t \geq 0$$

In addition, from Equation (6.18)

$$i(t) = 1\frac{d}{dt}[(3t + 2)e^{-2t}] + (3t + 2)e^{-2t}$$

$$= -2(3t + 2)e^{-2t} + 3e^{-2t} + (3t + 2)e^{-2t}$$

$$= -(3t + 2)e^{-2t} + 3e^{-2t} = (-3t + 1)e^{-2t} \text{ A} \qquad \text{for} \quad t \geq 0$$

Sketches of $v(t)$ and $i(t)$ for $t \geq 0$ are shown in Fig. 6.17.

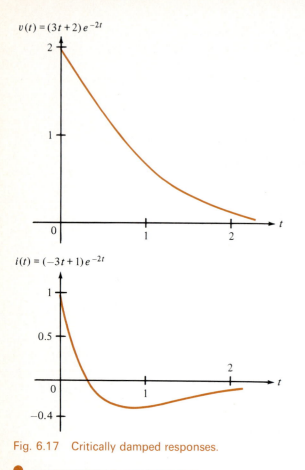

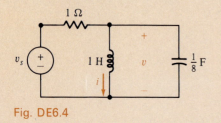

Fig. 6.17   Critically damped responses.

DRILL EXERCISE 6.4

For the *RLC* circuit shown in Fig. DE6.4, suppose that $v_s(t) = 2 - 2u(t)$ V. Find $i(t)$ and $v(t)$ for $t \geq 0$.

Answer: $8te^{-4t} + 2e^{-4t}$ A; $-16te^{-4t}$ V

Fig. DE6.4

It is not necessary for a circuit to contain both an inductor and a capacitor for it to be a second-order circuit—however, at least two energy-storage elements are necessary.

EXAMPLE 6.4

Let us write a second-order differential equation that describes the circuit shown in Fig. 6.18.

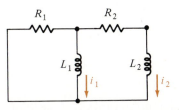

Fig. 6.18   Zero-input circuit with two inductors.

By KVL around the mesh on the left,

$$R_1(i_1 + i_2) + L_1 \frac{di_1}{dt} = 0 \tag{6.22}$$

By KVL around the loop consisting of R_1, R_2, and L_2,

$$R_1(i_1 + i_2) + R_2 i_2 + L_2 \frac{di_2}{dt} = 0 \tag{6.23}$$

From this equation, we can write

$$i_1 = -\frac{L_2}{R_1} \frac{di_2}{dt} - \frac{R_1 + R_2}{R_1} i_2 \tag{6.24}$$

Substituting this expression for i_1 into Equation (6.22) and simplifying, we get

$$\frac{d^2 i_2}{dt^2} + \left(\frac{R_1 + R_2}{L_2} + \frac{R_1}{L_1} \right) \frac{di_2}{dt} + \frac{R_1 R_2}{L_1 L_2} i_2 = 0 \tag{6.25}$$

and we see that

$$\alpha = \frac{R_1 + R_2}{2L_2} + \frac{R_1}{2L_1} \qquad \text{and} \qquad \omega_n = \sqrt{\frac{R_1 R_2}{L_1 L_2}}$$

DRILL EXERCISE 6.5

For the circuit shown in Fig. DE6.5, suppose that $v_s(t) = 12 - 12u(t)$ V. Find $i_2(t)$ for $t \geq 0$.

Answer: $\frac{12}{11}(e^{-3t} - e^{-t/4})$ A

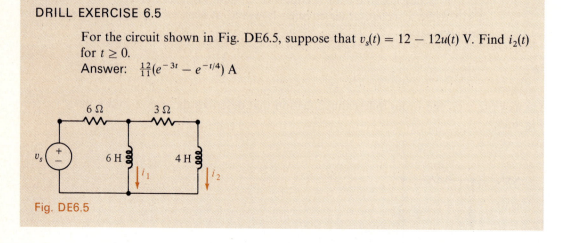

Fig. DE6.5

The circuit given in Fig. 6.18 will always be overdamped regardless of the (positive) values of R_1, R_2, L_1, and L_2. The same statement can be made about the circuit obtained by replacing the inductors with capacitors (see Problem 6.18). However, the addition of an active element such as a dependent source or an operational amplifier can produce a circuit that is critically damped or underdamped.

DRILL EXERCISE 6.6

For the op-amp circuit shown in Fig. DE6.6, suppose that $v_s(t) = 2 - 2u(t)$ V. Find $v_o(t)$ for $t \geq 0$.

Answer: $-4(t + 1)e^{-t}$ V

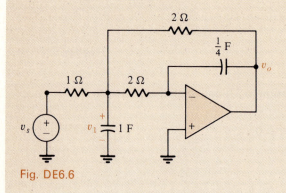

Fig. DE6.6

An important fact may become evident when we look at the results of the previous examples. The natural (zero-input) response of a given circuit has the same form regardless of the variable (voltage or current) that is selected as the output. This result is due to the fact that the voltage and current for a resistor differ by a constant, while inductors and capacitors are elements with differential and integral relationships. Performing such operations as scaling, differentiating, and integrating will not change the form of an expression. Furthermore, applying KVL and KCL (adding such expressions) also does not change the form.

6.4 CIRCUITS WITH NONZERO INPUTS

Having considered some second-order circuits with zero inputs and nonzero initial conditions, let us now look at second-order circuits with nonzero inputs. We shall limit our discussion to forcing functions that are ramps, steps, impulses, or various combinations of these functions. Other types of forcing functions will be dealt with in subsequent chapters when additional concepts are introduced.

Consider the series *RLC* circuit, shown in Fig. 6.19, whose input is a voltage step function. By KVL,

$$V_s u(t) = Ri + L \frac{di}{dt} + v$$

Substituting $i = C \dfrac{dv}{dt}$ into this equation, we obtain

$$\frac{d^2v}{dt^2} + \frac{R}{L}\frac{dv}{dt} + \frac{1}{LC} v = \frac{v_s}{LC} = \frac{V_s}{LC} u(t) \tag{6.26}$$

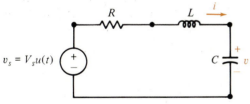

Fig. 6.19   Step of voltage applied to a series *RLC* circuit.

For $t < 0$, the right-hand side of this equation becomes zero, and for zero initial conditions the solution is $v(t) = 0$. However, for $t \geq 0$, Equation (6.26) becomes

$$\frac{d^2v}{dt^2} + \frac{R}{L}\frac{dv}{dt} + \frac{1}{LC} v = \frac{V_s}{LC} \tag{6.27}$$

As in the case of first-order differential equations, the solution $v(t)$ consists of two parts—the force response $v_f(t)$ and the natural response $v_n(t)$, that is, the solution is of the form

$$v(t) = v_f(t) + v_n(t)$$

where $v_n(t)$ is the solution to

$$\frac{d^2v}{dt^2} + 2\alpha\frac{dv}{dt} + \omega_n^2 v = 0$$

where $\alpha = R/2L$ and $\omega_n = 1/\sqrt{LC}$.

In this case, the forcing function is a constant. Thus, the forced response is a constant, say K. If the natural response $v_n(t)$ is substituted into the left side of Equation (6.27), the left side of the equation becomes zero. Thus, the forced response $v_f(t) = K$ must satisfy Equation (6.27), that is,

$$\frac{d^2K}{dt^2} + \frac{R}{L}\frac{dK}{dt} + \frac{1}{LC}K = \frac{V_s}{LC} \quad \Rightarrow \quad \frac{1}{LC}K = \frac{V_s}{LC} \quad \Rightarrow \quad K = V_s$$

Hence, the solution to Equation (6.27) is as follows:
For the overdamped case:

$$v(t) = V_s + A_1 e^{s_1 t} + A_2 e^{s_2 t}$$

For the underdamped case:

$$v(t) = V_s + A_1 e^{-\alpha t}\cos\omega_d t + A_2 e^{-\alpha t}\sin\omega_d t$$

For the critically damped case:

$$v(t) = V_s + A_1 t e^{-\alpha t} + A_2 e^{-\alpha t}$$

where the constants A_1 and A_2 are determined from the circuit topology and the initial conditions $v(0) = 0$ V and $i(0) = 0$ A.

For the circuit in Fig. 6.19, since no energy initially is stored in the inductor and capacitor, when the input voltage is zero, the voltage $v(t)$ and the current $i(t)$ will be zero. At $t = 0$, when the input voltage becomes V_s volts, since the voltage across a capacitor and the current through an inductor cannot change instantaneously, $v(0) = 0$ V and $i(0) = 0$ A. After a long time, the input acts as a constant, the inductor behaves as a short circuit, and the capacitor behaves as an open circuit. Thus, eventually, the voltage across the capacitor will be V_s volts and the current through the inductor will be zero amperes. The shape of the voltage and current waveforms between initial and final values will depend upon whether the circuit is overdamped, underdamped, or critically damped.

EXAMPLE 6.5

For the series RLC circuit given in Fig. 6.19, let us find the zero-state step responses $v(t)$ and $i(t)$. The underdamped case results when $R = 12\ \Omega$, $L = 2$ H, and $C = \frac{1}{50}$ F, since $\alpha = 3$ and $\omega_n = 5$. Also, $\omega_d = 4$. If $V_s = \frac{2}{5}$ V, then the solution of Equation (6.27) is

$$v(t) = \tfrac{2}{5} + A_1 e^{-3t} \cos 4t + A_2 e^{-3t} \sin 4t$$

Setting $t = 0$ yields

$$v(0) = \tfrac{2}{5} + A_1 = 0 \quad \Rightarrow \quad A_1 = -\tfrac{2}{5}$$

Taking the derivative of $v(t)$, we get

$$\frac{dv(t)}{dt} = -3A_1 e^{-3t} \cos 4t - 4A_1 e^{-3t} \sin 4t - 3A_2 e^{-3t} \sin 4t + 4A_2 e^{-3t} \cos 4t$$

so

$$\frac{dv(0)}{dt} = -3A_1 + 4A_2 = \frac{6}{5} + 4A_2$$

Since $i(t) = C\, dv(t)/dt$, then

$$\frac{dv(0)}{dt} = \frac{1}{C} i(0) = 0 = \frac{6}{5} + 4A_2 \quad \Rightarrow \quad A_2 = -\frac{3}{10}$$

Therefore, for $t \geq 0$,

$$v(t) = \tfrac{2}{5} - \tfrac{2}{5} e^{-3t} \cos 4t - \tfrac{3}{10} e^{-3t} \sin 4t$$
$$= \tfrac{2}{5} - \tfrac{1}{10} e^{-3t}(4 \cos 4t + 3 \sin 4t) = \tfrac{2}{5} - \tfrac{1}{2} e^{-3t} \cos(4t - 0.64)$$

Combining this with the fact that $v(t) = 0$ for $t < 0$ results in the voltage step response,

$$v(t) = [\tfrac{2}{5} - \tfrac{1}{2} e^{-3t} \cos(4t - 0.64)]u(t)\ \text{V}$$

The current for $t \geq 0$ is

$$i(t) = C \frac{dv(t)}{dt} = \frac{1}{50} \frac{d}{dt}\left(\frac{2}{5} - \frac{2}{5} e^{-3t} \cos 4t - \frac{3}{10} e^{-3t} \sin 4t\right)$$

$$= \tfrac{1}{50}(\tfrac{6}{5} e^{-3t} \cos 4t + \tfrac{8}{5} e^{-3t} \sin 4t + \tfrac{9}{10} e^{-3t} \sin 4t - \tfrac{12}{10} e^{-3t} \cos 4t)$$

$$= \tfrac{1}{50}(\tfrac{25}{10} e^{-3t} \sin 4t) = \tfrac{1}{20} e^{-3t} \sin 4t$$

Thus, the current step response is

$$i(t) = (\tfrac{1}{20} e^{-3t} \sin 4t)u(t)\ \text{A}$$

Sketches of $v(t)$ and $i(t)$ are shown in Fig. 6.20.

$v(t) = [0.4 - 0.5\,e^{-3t}\cos(4t - 0.64)]\,u(t)$

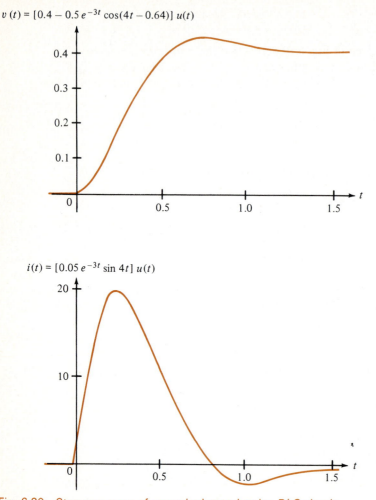

$i(t) = [0.05\,e^{-3t}\sin 4t]\,u(t)$

Fig. 6.20 Step responses of an underdamped series *RLC* circuit.

DRILL EXERCISE 6.7

For the series *RLC* circuit given in Fig. 6.19, find the zero-state step responses $v(t)$ and $i(t)$ for the case that $R = 5\ \Omega$, $L = \frac{1}{2}$ H, $C = \frac{1}{8}$ F, and $v_s(t) = 3u(t)$ V.
Answer: $(3 + e^{-8t} - 4e^{-2t})u(t)$ V; $(e^{-2t} - e^{-8t})u(t)$ A

Suppose that for the circuit given in Fig. 6.19, the input is changed from the step function $V_s u(t)$ to the impulse function $V_s \delta(t)$. Then using the reasoning discussed in the chapter on first-order circuits (Chapter 5), the (zero-state) impulse response is just the derivative of the (zero-state) step response.[†] For the values given in Example 6.5, the resulting voltage across the $\frac{1}{50}$-F capacitor is

$$v_\delta(t) = \frac{dv(t)}{dt} = \left(\frac{5}{2} e^{-3t} \sin 4t\right) u(t) \text{ V}$$

and the zero-state current impulse response is

$$i_\delta(t) = \frac{di(t)}{dt} = \frac{d}{dt}\left[\left(\frac{1}{20} e^{-3t} \sin 4t\right) u(t)\right]$$

$$= \left(\tfrac{1}{20} e^{-3t} \sin 4t\right) \delta(t) + \tfrac{1}{20}(-3e^{-3t} \sin 4t + 4e^{-3t} \cos 4t)u(t)$$

$$= \left[\tfrac{1}{4} e^{-3t} \cos(4t + 0.64)\right]u(t) \text{ A}$$

As a consequence of the fact that R, L, and C have constant values, the resulting differential equation describing the circuit has constant coefficients. As was the case for first-order circuits, this means that the time-invariance property holds for such second-order circuits—and higher-order circuits, too. In other words, if $y(t)$ is the response to the input $x(t)$ subject to the initial condition $y(0)$, then the response to the input $x(t - t_0)$ subject to the boundary condition $y(t_0) = y(0)$ is $y(t - t_0)$. For example, the zero-state current response to the input $\frac{2}{5}u(t - 2)$ V is

$$i(t - 2) = \left[\tfrac{1}{20}e^{-3(t-2)} \sin 4(t - 2)\right]u(t - 2) \text{ A}$$

In addition, since the circuit is linear, scaling the input by the constant K also scales the zero-state response by the same constant K. For example, the current zero-state (unit) step response to the unit step function $u(t) = \left(\frac{5}{2}\right)\left[\left(\frac{2}{5}\right)u(t)\right]$ is

$$i_u(t) = \tfrac{5}{2}i(t) = \left(\tfrac{1}{8} e^{-3t} \sin 4t\right)u(t) \text{ A}$$

DRILL EXERCISE 6.8

For the series RLC circuit described in Drill Exercise 6.7, find the zero-state response $v(t)$ when the input voltage is $v_s(t) = 3r(t)$ V.

Answer: $3r(t) + \tfrac{1}{8}(1 - e^{-8t})u(t) - 2(1 - e^{-2t})u(t)$ V

Nonzero Initial Conditions

Let us now look at a practical series RLC circuit in which not only is the input nonzero, but an initial condition is nonzero as well.

[†] The ramp response is the integral of the step response.

EXAMPLE 6.6

The circuit shown in Fig. 6.21 is in essence an old-fashioned (nonelectronic) automobile ignition system. The input of this circuit is a 12-V automobile battery. The series resistance consists of a ballast resistor, the resistance of the ignition switch, and the series resistance of the inductor (known as the "ignition coil"). The capacitor (called a "condenser" by mechanics) is in parallel with a switch (called the "points") that is closed for $t < 0$ and open for $t \geq 0$. (In actuality, the points open and close periodically—the rate depending on the engine rpm.) It is the voltage produced across the coil that is applied to the spark plugs. This in turn produces a spark that ignites the fuel mixture.

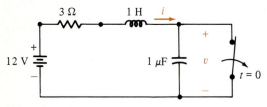

Fig. 6.21   Automobile ignition system.

For the given circuit, for $t < 0$, clearly $v(t) = 0$ V and $i(t) = \frac{12}{3} = 4$ A. Thus, $v(0) = 0$ V and $i(0) = 4$ A. For $t \geq 0$, by KVL,

$$Ri + L\frac{di}{dt} + \frac{1}{C}\int_0^t i\, dt + v(0) = 12 \qquad \Rightarrow \qquad 3i + \frac{di}{dt} + 10^6 \int_0^t i\, dt + 0 = 12$$

and taking the derivative of this equation we get

$$\frac{d^2 i}{dt^2} + 3\frac{di}{dt} + 10^6 i = 0$$

Hence, $\alpha = \frac{3}{2} < \omega_n = 10^3$, and this circuit is (very) underdamped. We then have that

$$\omega_d = \sqrt{\omega_n^2 - \alpha^2} \approx \omega_n = 10^3 \text{ rad/s}$$

and since the forced response is zero, the approximate current has the form

$$i(t) \approx A_1 e^{-3t/2} \cos 10^3 t + A_2 e^{-3t/2} \sin 10^3 t$$

Setting $t = 0$, we have that

$$i(0) = A_1 + 0 \qquad \Rightarrow \qquad A_1 = 4$$

Next

$$\frac{di(t)}{dt} = -\frac{3}{2}(4)e^{-3t/2}\cos 10^3 t - 4(10^3)e^{-3t/2}\sin 10^3 t$$

$$= -\frac{3}{2}A_2 e^{-3t/2}\sin 10^3 t + 10^3 A_2 e^{-3t/2}\cos 10^3 t$$

from which

$$\frac{di(0)}{dt} = -6 - 0 - 0 + 10^3 A_2$$

However, from the circuit (for $t \geq 0$) by KVL

$$12 = 3i + 1\frac{di}{dt} + v \qquad \Rightarrow \qquad \frac{di}{dt} = 12 - 3i - v$$

and

$$\frac{di(0)}{dt} = 12 - 3i(0) - v(0) = 12 - 12 - 0 = 0$$

Thus,

$$-6 + 10^3 A_2 = 0 \qquad \Rightarrow \qquad A_2 = 6 \times 10^{-3}$$

The current expression is then

$$i(t) \approx 4e^{-3t/2}\cos 10^3 t + (6 \times 10^{-3})e^{-3t/2}\sin 10^3 t \text{ A}$$

and the voltage across the inductor is

$$v_L(t) = L\frac{di(t)}{dt} \approx -(4 \times 10^3)e^{-3t/2}\sin 10^3 t \text{ V}$$

Let's evaluate this formula the first time the sine term equals unity—that is, for $t = (\pi/2)$ ms. Then we get

$$v_L\left[\frac{\pi}{2}(10^{-3})\right] \approx -4(10^3)e^{-(3/2)(\pi/2)10^{-3}} \approx -4000 \text{ V}$$

Although the values of L and C given in this example are practical in nature, they were still chosen to yield computational convenience. In a typical automobile, the voltage required to produce a spark across the gap of a spark plug is between 6000 and 10,000 V.

Having analyzed a series RLC circuit prior to this example, we could have used the previously obtained differential equation (6.27) to determine $v(t)$. In that case, the solution would contain a nonzero forced response. However, we instead wrote a differential equation in the variable $i(t)$.

For the parallel RLC circuit shown in Fig. 6.22, by KCL,

$$\frac{v}{R} + i + C\frac{dv}{dt} = i_s$$

Substituting $v = L\,di/dt$ into this equation, we get

$$\frac{d^2 i}{dt^2} + \frac{1}{RC}\frac{di}{dt} + \frac{1}{LC}i = \frac{1}{LC}i_s \tag{6.28}$$

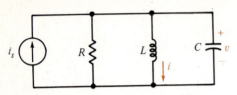

Fig. 6.22   Parallel *RLC* circuit with an applied current.

Again, the solution of this equation has the form

$$i(t) = i_f(t) + i_n(t)$$

where $i_f(t)$ is the forced response and $i_n(t)$ is the natural response. In determining the natural response—whether the circuit is overdamped, underdamped, or critically damped—we use the fact that for a parallel *RLC* circuit

$$\alpha = \frac{1}{2RC} \quad \text{and} \quad \omega_n = \frac{1}{\sqrt{LC}}$$

EXAMPLE 6.7

For the circuit given in Fig. 6.22, suppose that $R = 6\ \Omega$, $L = 7\ \mathrm{H}$, $C = \frac{1}{42}\ \mathrm{F}$, and $i_s(t) = -4 + 10u(t)\ \mathrm{A}$. Let us find the resulting inductor current $i(t)$ for all t.

For $t < 0$, the circuit in Fig. 6.22 is a dc circuit with $i_s(t) = i(t) = -4\ \mathrm{A}$ and $v(t) = 0\ \mathrm{V}$. Thus, $i(0) = -4\ \mathrm{A}$ and $v(0) = 0\ \mathrm{V}$.

For $t \geq 0$, $i_s(t) = -4 + 10 = 6\ \mathrm{A}$ and Equation (6.28) becomes

$$\frac{d^2i}{dt^2} + 7\frac{di}{dt} + 6i = 36 \tag{6.29}$$

and $\alpha = \frac{7}{2} > \omega_n = \sqrt{6}$, so the circuit is overdamped. Since

$$s = -\alpha \pm \sqrt{\alpha^2 - \omega_n^2} = -\tfrac{7}{2} \pm \sqrt{\tfrac{49}{4} - 6} = -\tfrac{7}{2} \pm \tfrac{5}{2}$$

then

$$s_1 = -6 \quad \text{and} \quad s_2 = -1$$

and therefore the natural response has the form

$$i_n(t) = A_1 e^{-6t} + A_2 e^{-t}$$

For $t \geq 0$, the forcing function is a constant, so the forced response is a constant K that can be obtained by substituting K into the differential equation (6.29). Also, from the circuit, for the dc case we have $i_f(t) = 6\ \mathrm{A}$. Hence, the complete response has the form

$$i(t) = 6 + A_1 e^{-6t} + A_2 e^{-t}$$

Setting $t = 0$, we get

$$i(0) = 6 + A_1 + A_2 = -4 \quad \Rightarrow \quad A_1 + A_2 = -10 \tag{6.30}$$

Also,

$$\frac{di(t)}{dt} = -6A_1 e^{-6t} - A_2 e^{-t} \qquad \Rightarrow \qquad \frac{di(0)}{dt} = -6A_1 - A_2$$

But from the circuit,

$$v(t) = L\frac{di(t)}{dt} \qquad \Rightarrow \qquad \frac{di(t)}{dt} = \frac{1}{L} v(t)$$

and

$$\frac{di(0)}{dt} = \frac{1}{7} v(0) = 0 = -6A_1 - A_2 \qquad\qquad (6.31)$$

From Equations (6.30) and (6.31) we get

$$A_1 = 2 \qquad \text{and} \qquad A_2 = -12$$

Therefore, the complete response is

$$i(t) = 6 + 2e^{-6t} - 12e^{-t} \text{ A} \qquad \text{for} \quad t \geq 0$$

Hence, for all t,

$$i(t) = -4 + 4u(t) + (6 + 2e^{-6t} - 12e^{-t})u(t)$$
$$= -4 + 2(5 + e^{-6t} - 6e^{-t})u(t) \text{ A} \qquad\qquad (6.32)$$

DRILL EXERCISE 6.9

For the parallel *RLC* circuit given in Fig. 6.22, suppose that $R = 1\,\Omega$, $L = 2$ H, $C = \frac{1}{2}$ F, and $i_s(t) = u(t)$ V. Find the zero-state step responses $i(t)$ and $v(t)$.
Answer: $(1 - te^{-t} - e^{-t})u(t)$ A; $2te^{-t}u(t)$ V

As was the case for first-order circuits, we can use the property of linearity for purposes of analyzing second-order circuits. For instance, for the situation described in Example 6.7, we can express the input current as $i_s(t) = i_1(t) + i_2(t)$, where $i_1(t) = -4$ A is a dc input and $i_2(t) = 10u(t)$ A is a step input. If $i_a(t)$ is the response to $i_1(t)$ and $i_b(t)$ is the response to $i_2(t)$, then the response to $i_s(t) = i_1(t) + i_2(t)$ is $i(t) = i_a(t) + i_b(t)$. By inspection of Equation (6.32), it should be apparent that $i_a(t) = -4$ A and $i_b(t) = 2(5 + e^{-6t} - 6e^{-t})u(t)$ A.

6.5 OTHER SECOND-ORDER CIRCUITS

Consider the op-amp circuit shown in Fig. 6.23. By KCL at node v_1,

$$\frac{v_1 - v_s}{1} + \frac{v_1 - v_o}{1} + 1\frac{d}{dt}(v_1 - v_o) = 0 \qquad\qquad (6.33)$$

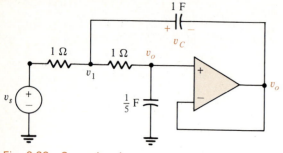

Fig. 6.23   Second-order op-amp circuit.

By KCL at the noninverting input of the operational amplifier,

$$\frac{v_o - v_1}{1} + \frac{1}{5}\frac{dv_o}{dt} = 0$$

from which

$$v_1 = \frac{1}{5}\frac{dv_o}{dt} + v_o \tag{6.34}$$

Substituting this expression into Equation (6.33) and simplifying results in

$$\frac{d^2v_o}{dt^2} + 2\frac{dv_o}{dt} + 5v_o = 5v_s \tag{6.35}$$

Let us find the zero-state (unit) step response $v_o(t)$. First we set $v_s(t) = u(t)$ V. For $t < 0$, we must have that $v_o(t) = 0$ V. For $t \geq 0$, Equation (6.35) becomes

$$\frac{d^2v_o}{dt^2} + 2\frac{dv_o}{dt} + 5v_o = 5 \tag{6.36}$$

Since $2\alpha = 2$ and $\omega_n^2 = 5$, then $\alpha = 1 < \omega_n = \sqrt{5}$, and we have the underdamped case. Thus, the solution takes the form

$$v_o(t) = K + e^{-\alpha t}(A_1 \cos \omega_d t + A_2 \sin \omega_d t)$$

Substituting $v_o(t) = K$ into Equation (6.35) yields $K = 1$. Furthermore,

$$\omega_d = \sqrt{\omega_n^2 - \alpha^2} = \sqrt{5 - 1} = 2 \text{ rad/s}$$

Thus,

$$v_o(t) = 1 + e^{-t}(A_1 \cos 2t + A_2 \sin 2t) \tag{6.37}$$

Since $v_o(t) = v_1(t) = v_C(t) = 0$ V for $t < 0$, then because $v_o(t)$ and $v_C(t)$ are voltages across capacitors, then $v_o(0) = v_C(0) = 0$ V. Thus, $v_1(0) = v_C(0) + v_o(0) = 0$ V. From Equation (6.37), setting $t = 0$, we get

$$v_o(0) = 1 + A_1 = 0 \quad \Rightarrow \quad A_1 = -1$$

Furthermore, from Equation (6.37),

$$\frac{dv_o(t)}{dt} = e^{-t}(-2A_1 \sin 2t + 2A_2 \cos 2t) - e^{-t}(A_1 \cos 2t + A_2 \sin 2t)$$

so

$$\frac{dv_o(0)}{dt} = 2A_2 - A_1$$

But, from Equation (6.34)

$$\frac{dv_o(0)}{dt} = 5[v_1(0) - v_o(0)] = 5[0 - 0] = 0 \text{ V/s}$$

Thus,

$$0 = 2A_2 - A_1 \quad \Rightarrow \quad A_2 = \tfrac{1}{2}A_1 = -\tfrac{1}{2}$$

and therefore,

$$v_o(t) = 1 + e^{-t}(-\cos 2t - \tfrac{1}{2} \sin 2t) \quad \text{for} \quad t \ge 0$$

Hence, the step response is

$$v_o(t) = [1 - e^{-t}(\cos 2t + \tfrac{1}{2} \sin 2t)]u(t) \text{ V}$$

$$= \left[1 - \frac{\sqrt{5}}{2} e^{-t} \cos(2t - 0.464) \right] u(t) \text{ V}$$

$$= \left[1 + \frac{\sqrt{5}}{2} e^{-t} \cos(2t + 2.68) \right] u(t) \text{ V}$$

DRILL EXERCISE 6.10

For the op-amp circuit given in Fig. 6.23, change the value of the $\frac{1}{5}$-F capacitor to $\frac{25}{16}$ F, and find the step response $v_o(t)$ to the input voltage $v_s(t) = 3u(t)$ V.
Answer: $(3 + e^{-8t/5} - 4e^{-2t/5})u(t)$ V

Now consider the series-parallel circuit shown in Fig. 6.24. By KVL,

$$v = R_1 i + L \frac{di}{dt} \tag{6.38}$$

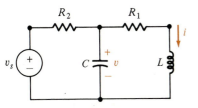

Fig. 6.24 Series-parallel *RLC* circuit.

By KCL,

$$\frac{v - v_s}{R_2} + C\frac{dv}{dt} + i = 0 \tag{6.39}$$

Substituting the expression for v given by Equation (6.38) into Equation (6.39), we get

$$\frac{1}{R_2}\left(R_1 i + L\frac{di}{dt}\right) - \frac{v_s}{R_2} + C\frac{d}{dt}\left(R_1 i + L\frac{di}{dt}\right) + i = 0$$

Simplifying this, we obtain

$$\frac{d^2 i}{dt^2} + \left(\frac{R_1}{L} + \frac{1}{R_2 C}\right)\frac{di}{dt} + \left(\frac{R_1 + R_2}{R_2 LC}\right)i = \frac{v_s}{R_2 LC} \tag{6.40}$$

Thus, for the given series-parallel circuit,

$$\alpha = \frac{R_1}{2L} + \frac{1}{2R_2 C} \quad \text{and} \quad \omega_n = \sqrt{\frac{R_1 + R_2}{R_2 LC}}$$

Let us now work a numerical example of the circuit given in Fig. 6.24. However, since we have been preoccupied with constant (for $t \geq 0$) forcing functions, let us consider an exponential forcing function.

EXAMPLE 6.8

For the series-parallel RLC circuit given in Fig. 6.24, suppose that $R_1 = \frac{7}{2}\,\Omega$, $R_2 = 1\,\Omega$, $L = 1$ H, $C = 1$ F, and $v_s(t) = 3e^{-2t}u(t)$ V. Let us determine the zero-state response $i(t)$.

Using the above values for R_1, R_2, L, C, and $v_s(t)$, Equation (6.40) becomes

$$\frac{d^2 i}{dt^2} + \frac{9}{2}\frac{di}{dt} + \frac{9}{2}i = 3e^{-2t}u(t) \tag{6.41}$$

Since $\alpha = \frac{9}{4} > \omega_n = 3/\sqrt{2}$, then the circuit is overdamped, and

$$s_1 = -\alpha - \sqrt{\alpha^2 - \omega_n^2} = -\frac{9}{4} - \sqrt{\frac{81}{16} - \frac{9}{2}} = -\frac{9}{4} - \frac{3}{4} = -3$$

$$s_2 = -\alpha + \sqrt{\alpha^2 - \omega_n^2} = -\frac{9}{4} + \frac{3}{4} = -\frac{3}{2}$$

For $t < 0$, $i(t) = 0$ A and $v(t) = 0$ V. Thus, $i(0) = 0$ A and $v(0) = 0$ V. For $t \geq 0$, Equation (6.41) becomes

$$\frac{d^2 i}{dt^2} + \frac{9}{2}\frac{di}{dt} + \frac{9}{2}i = 3e^{-2t} \tag{6.42}$$

Since the forcing function is an exponential, the forced response is also an exponential, with the same exponent. Thus, we assume a forced response of the form Ke^{-2t}. Since the forced response satisfies Equation (6.42), we must have that

$$\frac{d^2}{dt^2}(Ke^{-2t}) + \frac{9}{2}\frac{d}{dt}(Ke^{-2t}) + \frac{9}{2}(Ke^{-2t}) = 3e^{-2t}$$

or

$$4Ke^{-2t} - 9Ke^{-2t} + \tfrac{9}{2}Ke^{-2t} = 3e^{-2t}$$

Dividing both sides of this equation by e^{-2t} and solving for K, we find that $K = -6$. Hence, the solution to Equation (6.42) has the form

$$i(t) = -6e^{-2t} + A_1 e^{-3t} + A_2 e^{-3t/2}$$

Setting $t = 0$, we get

$$i(0) = -6 + A_1 + A_2 = 0 \quad \Rightarrow \quad A_1 + A_2 = 6 \qquad (6.43)$$

Since

$$\frac{di(t)}{dt} = 12e^{-2t} - 3A_1 e^{-3t} - \tfrac{3}{2} A_2$$

then

$$\frac{di(0)}{dt} = 12 - 3A_1 - \tfrac{3}{2} A_2 \qquad (6.44)$$

However, from Equation (6.38),

$$L\frac{di(0)}{dt} = v(0) - R_1 i(0) = 0 - 0 = 0 \quad \Rightarrow \quad \frac{di(0)}{dt} = 0 \text{ A/s}$$

Thus, from Equation (6.44),

$$3A_1 + \tfrac{3}{2}A_2 = 12 \qquad (6.45)$$

Solving Equations (6.43) and (6.45), we get $A_1 = 2$ and $A_2 = 4$. Hence,

$$i(t) = -6e^{-2t} + 2e^{-3t} + 4e^{-3t/2} \text{ A} \qquad \text{for} \quad t \geq 0$$

Therefore, the zero-state response is

$$i(t) = 2(e^{-3t} - 3e^{-2t} + 2e^{-3t/2})u(t) \text{ A}$$

DRILL EXERCISE 6.11

For the series-parallel circuit given in Fig. 6.24, suppose that $R_1 = R_2 = 1\,\Omega$, $L = 1$ H, $C = 1$ F, and $v_s(t) = 2e^{-2t}u(t)$ V. Find the zero-state response $i(t)$.
Answer: $[e^{-2t} + \sqrt{2}e^{-t}\cos(t - 3\pi/4)]u(t)$ A

Needless to say, a zero-state second-order circuit with more than one independent source can be analyzed by using the principle of superposition.

In determining differential equation (6.40) as well as the other second-order differential equations in this chapter, we did not proceed by exclusively using either nodal or mesh analysis. Although such an approach is valid, it may not be the easiest algebraically. For the circuit in Fig. 6.24, Equation (6.40) was obtained from Equations (6.38) and (6.39). The latter two equations are known as the "state equations" of the circuit, and this subject is discussed in the next chapter.

● SUMMARY

1. The natural response of a second-order circuit is either overdamped, underdamped, or critically damped.

2. An overdamped response is the sum of two (real) exponentials.

3. An underdamped response is a damped sinusoid.

4. A critically damped response is the sum of an exponential and another exponential (with the same time constant) multiplied by time.

5. As with the case of first-order circuits, the complete response is the sum of two terms—one is the forced response and the other has the form of the natural response.

6. The comments about the linearity and time-invariance properties made for first-order circuits hold for second-order circuits (and higher-order circuits, too). (See items 5 through 8 in the summary for Chapter 5 on p. 266.)

● PROBLEMS FOR CHAPTER 6

6.1 For the *RLC* circuit shown in Fig. P6.1, find $v(t)$ and $i(t)$ for all t.

6.2 For the *RLC* circuit shown in Fig. P6.2, find $v(t)$ and $i(t)$ for all t.

6.3 For the *RLC* circuit given in Fig. P6.2, interchange the 6-Ω resistor and the 1-H inductor such that $i(t)$ is directed down. Find $v(t)$ and $i(t)$ for all t.

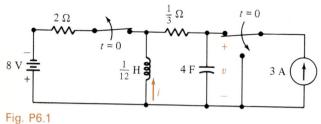
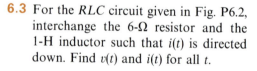

Fig. P6.1

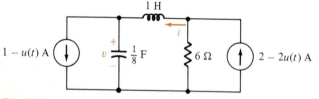

Fig. P6.2

6.4 For the *RLC* circuit given in Fig. 6.19 (p. 295), suppose that $R = 4\,\Omega$, $L = \frac{1}{2}$ H, $C = \frac{1}{6}$ F, and $v_s(t) = 1 - u(t)$ V. Find $v(t)$ and $i(t)$ for all t.

6.5 For the *RLC* circuit given in Fig. 6.19 (p. 295), suppose that $R = 7\,\Omega$, $L = 1$ H, $C = \frac{1}{10}$ F, and $v_s(t) = 1 - u(t)$ V. Find $v(t)$ and $i(t)$ for all t.

6.6 For the *RLC* circuit shown in Fig. P6.6, suppose that $R = 1\,\Omega$, $L = \frac{1}{2}$ H, $C = \frac{1}{4}$ F, and $V_s = 4$ V. Find $i(t)$ and $v(t)$ for all t.

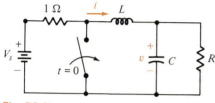

Fig. P6.6

6.7 For the *RLC* circuit shown in Fig. P6.6, suppose that $R = \frac{1}{3}\,\Omega$, $L = \frac{1}{4}$ H, $C = \frac{1}{2}$ F, and $V_s = 4$ V. Find $i(t)$ and $v(t)$ for all t.

6.8 For the *RLC* circuit shown in Fig. P6.8, suppose that $R = 1\,\Omega$, $L = \frac{1}{2}$ H, $C = \frac{1}{4}$ F, and $v_s(t) = 4 - 4u(t)$ V. Find $i(t)$ and $v(t)$ for all t.

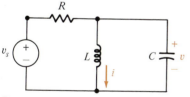

Fig. P6.8

6.9 For the *RLC* circuit given in Fig. P6.8, suppose that $R = \frac{1}{3}\,\Omega$, $L = \frac{1}{4}$ H, $C = \frac{1}{2}$ F, and $v_s(t) = 1 - u(t)$ V. Find $i(t)$ and $v(t)$ for all t.

6.10 Repeat Problem 6.8 for the *RLC* circuit shown in Fig. P6.10.

6.11 Repeat Problem 6.9 for the *RLC* circuit given in Fig. P6.10.

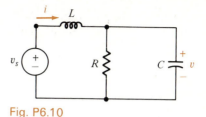

Fig. P6.10

6.12 For the *RLC* circuit shown in Fig. P6.6, suppose that $R = \frac{1}{2}\,\Omega$, $L = 1$ H, $C = 1$ F, and $V_s = 3$ V. Find $i(t)$ and $v(t)$ for all t.

6.13 For the *RLC* circuit given in Fig. 6.24 (p. 305), suppose that $R_1 = R_2 = 1\,\Omega$, $L = 1$ H, $C = 1$ F, and $v_s(t) = 2 - 2u(t)$ V. Find $v(t)$ and $i(t)$ for all t.

6.14 Repeat Problem 6.13 for the case that the inductor and the capacitor are interchanged.

6.15 For the *RLC* circuit shown in Fig. 6.24 (p. 305), suppose that $R_1 = 2\,\Omega$, $R_2 = 1\,\Omega$, $L = \frac{1}{2}$ H, $C = 1$ F, and $v_s(t) = 3 - 3u(t)$ V. Find $v(t)$ and $i(t)$ for all t.

6.16 For the series *RLC* circuit given in Fig. 6.19 (p. 295), suppose that $R = 2\,\Omega$, $L = 1$ H, $C = 1$ F, and $v_s(t) = 2 - 2u(t)$ V. Find $v(t)$ and $i(t)$ for all t.

6.17 For the circuit shown in Fig. P6.17, suppose that $R_1 = \frac{1}{2}\,\Omega$, $R_2 = 1\,\Omega$, $C_1 = \frac{1}{2}$ F, $C_2 = \frac{1}{4}$ F, and $v_s(t) = 1 - u(t)$ V. Find $v_2(t)$ for all t.

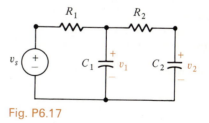

Fig. P6.17

6.18 For the circuit given in Fig. P6.17, suppose that $v_s(t) = 0$ V. Write a second-order differential equation in the variable v_2.

6.19 For the circuit shown in Fig. P6.19, suppose that $v_s(t) = 6 - 6u(t)$ V. Find $v(t)$ and $i(t)$ for all t.

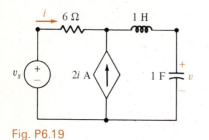

Fig. P6.19

6.20 For the circuit shown in Fig. P6.20, suppose that $v_s(t) = 3 - 3u(t)$ V. Find $v(t)$ for all t.

6.21 For the op-amp circuit given in Fig. 6.23 (p. 304), change the $\frac{1}{5}$-F capacitor to a 1-F capacitor. Suppose that $v_s(t) = 2 - 2u(t)$ V. Find $v_o(t)$ for all t.

6.22 For the op-amp circuit given in Fig. 6.23 (p. 304), change the $\frac{1}{5}$-F capacitor to a $\frac{4}{3}$-F capacitor. Suppose that $v_s(t) = 2 - 2u(t)$ V. Find $v_o(t)$ for all t.

6.23 For the series RLC circuit given in Fig. 6.19 (p. 295), suppose that $R = 16 \, \Omega$, $L = 4$ H, and $C = \frac{1}{16}$ F. Find the zero-state response $v(t)$ for the case that (a) $v_s(t) = u(t)$ V, and (b) $v_s(t) = \delta(t)$ V.

6.24 For the series RLC circuit given in Fig. 6.19 (p. 295), suppose that $R = 5 \, \Omega$, $L = \frac{1}{2}$ H, $C = \frac{1}{8}$ F. Find $v(t)$ and $i(t)$ for the case that $v_s(t) = 3 - 6u(t)$ V.

6.25 For the parallel RLC circuit given in Fig. 6.22 (p. 302), suppose that $R = \frac{1}{2} \, \Omega$,

$L = \frac{1}{5}$ H, and $C = \frac{1}{4}$ F. Find the zero-state response $i(t)$ for the case that (a) $i_s(t) = u(t)$ A and (b) $i_s(t) = \delta(t)$ A.

6.26 For the parallel RLC circuit given in Fig. 6.22 (p. 302), suppose that $R = 1 \, \Omega$, $L = 2$ H, $C = \frac{1}{2}$ F, and $i_s(t) = 1 - 2u(t)$ A. Find $i(t)$ and $v(t)$.

6.27 For the parallel RLC circuit given in Fig. 6.22 (p. 302), suppose that $R = 6 \, \Omega$, $L = 7$ H, and $C = \frac{1}{42}$ F. Find the zero-state response $i(t)$ for the case that $i_s(t) = r(t)$ A.

6.28 For the circuit given in Fig. 6.21 (p. 300), change the values of the battery to 1 V, of the resistor to 2 Ω, and of the capacitor to 1 F. Find $v(t)$ for all t.

6.29 For the circuit shown in Fig. P6.29, find $i(t)$ for all t.

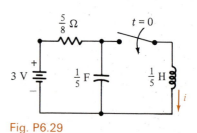

Fig. P6.29

6.30 For the op-amp circuit given in Fig. 6.23 (p. 304), change the $\frac{1}{5}$-F capacitor to a 1-F capacitor and find the zero-state step response $v_o(t)$ when $v_s(t) = u(t)$ V.

6.31 Repeat Problem 6.30 for the case that $v_s(t) = 2e^{-2t}u(t)$ V.

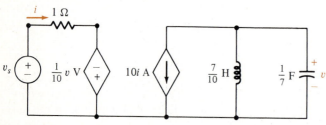

Fig. P6.20

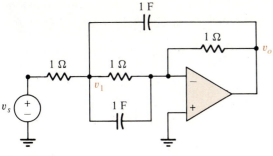

Fig. P6.34

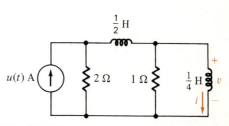

Fig. P6.40

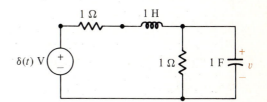

Fig. P6.41

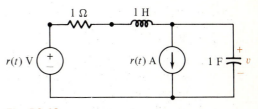

Fig. P6.42

6.32 For the op-amp circuit given in Fig. DE6.6 (p. 294), find the zero-state step response $v_o(t)$ for the case that $v_s(t) = u(t)$ V.

6.33 For the op-amp circuit given in Fig. DE6.6 (p. 294), change the $\frac{1}{4}$-F capacitor to a $\frac{1}{16}$-F capacitor. Find the zero-state step response $v_o(t)$ for the case that $v_s(t) = u(t)$ V.

6.34 For the op-amp circuit shown in Fig. P6.34, find the zero-state step response $v_1(t)$ for the case that $v_s(t) = u(t)$ V.

6.35 Repeat Problem 6.34 for the case that $v_s(t) = 4e^{-3t}u(t)$ V.

6.36 For the circuit given in Fig. P6.17, suppose that $R_1 = \frac{1}{2}\Omega$, $R_2 = 1\,\Omega$, $C_1 = \frac{1}{2}$ F, $C_2 = \frac{1}{4}$ F, and $v_s(t) = 3u(t)$ V. Find the zero-state response $v_2(t)$.

6.37 For the circuit given in Fig. 6.24 (p. 305), suppose that $R_1 = 3\,\Omega$, $R_2 = 1\,\Omega$, $L = 1$ H, $C = 1$ F, and $v_s(t) = u(t)$ V. Find the zero-state step responses $i(t)$ and $v(t)$.

6.38 For the circuit given in Fig. P6.19, suppose that $v_s(t) = u(t)$ V. Find the zero-state step response $v(t)$.

6.39 For the circuit given in Fig. P6.20, suppose that $v_s(t) = 3u(t)$ V. Find the zero-state step response $v(t)$.

6.40 For the circuit shown in Fig. P6.40, find the zero-state step responses $i(t)$ and $v(t)$.

6.41 For the circuit shown in Fig. P6.41, find the zero-state impulse response $v(t)$.

6.42 For the circuit shown in Fig. P6.42, find the zero-state response $v(t)$.

6.43 For the series RLC circuit given in Fig. 6.19 (p. 295), suppose that $R = 5\,\Omega$, $L = \frac{1}{2}$ H, $C = \frac{1}{8}$ F, and $v_s(t) = 3e^{-2t}u(t)$ V. Because the natural response contains an exponential with the same exponent as the forcing function, assume that the forced response has the form Kte^{-2t} and find the zero-state response $v(t)$.

6.44 For the parallel RLC circuit given in Fig. 6.22 (p. 302), suppose that $R = 1\,\Omega$, $L = 2$ H, $C = \frac{1}{2}$ F, and $v_s(t) = e^{-t}u(t)$ V. Because the natural response contains terms $A_1 te^{-t}$ and $A_2 e^{-t}$, assume that the forced response has the form $Kt^2 e^{-t}$ and find the zero-state response $i(t)$.

CHAPTER 7

Computer-Aided Circuit Analysis

We have studied first- and second-order circuits in the two preceding chapters. What is done for a third- or higher-order circuit? Although a higher-order differential equation can be written, we shall not attempt to solve it directly—solving a second-order differential equation is involved enough. Instead, for an nth-order circuit, we shall write a set of n simultaneous first-order differential equations, which by means of a matrix formulation can be expressed as a single first-order matrix differential equation. Although the solution of such a matrix equation is analogous to the case of an ordinary differential equation, we can find a numerical solution instead of the closed-form solutions that we have been obtaining. In order to do this, we will enlist the aid of a computer. The resulting numerical calculations can be done on a mainframe computer, a minicomputer, or even a personal computer.

7.1 ZERO-INPUT CIRCUITS

Let us return to the series RLC circuit shown in Fig. 7.1. Suppose that for this circuit, which has a zero input, the inductor current at time $t = 0$ is $i_L(0)$ and the capacitor voltage at time $t = 0$ is $v_C(0)$. Thus, we can say that the "condition" or "state" of the circuit at time $t = 0$ is specified by the inductor current and the capacitor voltage. For this reason we call the pair of numbers $[i_L(0), v_C(0)]$ the **initial state** of the circuit. Extending this concept, we can refer to the pair $[i_L(t), v_C(t)]$ as the **state** of the circuit at time t. Furthermore, the variables i_L and v_C are called the **state variables** of the circuit—these are the variables that do not change instantaneously.

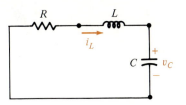

Fig. 7.1   Series *RLC* zero-input circuit.

Applying KVL to this circuit, we obtain

$$L\frac{di_L}{dt} + v_C + Ri_L = 0 \tag{7.1}$$

Furthermore,

$$i_L = C\frac{dv_C}{dt} \tag{7.2}$$

Substituting this equation into Equation (7.1), after division by *LC*, we get

$$\frac{d^2v_C}{dt^2} + \frac{R}{L}\frac{dv_C}{dt} + \frac{1}{LC}v_C = 0$$

This, of course, can be written as

$$\frac{d^2v_C}{dt^2} + 2\alpha\frac{dv_C}{dt} + \omega_n^2 v_C = 0$$

where $\alpha = R/2L$ and $\omega_n = 1/\sqrt{LC}$. We may then proceed, as we have discussed earlier, to solve this differential equation for $v_C(t)$.

In Equations (7.1) and (7.2), the only variables present are state variables. Let us rewrite these equations such that the coefficients of the derivatives are unity, and the derivatives alone are on one side of the equation. In other words, let us write Equations (7.1) and (7.2) in the form

$$\frac{di_L}{dt} = -\frac{R}{L}i_L - \frac{1}{L}v_C \qquad \text{and} \qquad \frac{dv_C}{dt} = \frac{1}{C}i_L$$

We call equations in this form, where all the variables present are state variables, **state equations**.

We may now write the above two state equations as a single matrix state equation as follows:

$$\begin{bmatrix} \dfrac{di_L}{dt} \\[2ex] \dfrac{dv_C}{dt} \end{bmatrix} = \begin{bmatrix} -\dfrac{R}{L} & -\dfrac{1}{L} \\[2ex] \dfrac{1}{C} & 0 \end{bmatrix} \begin{bmatrix} i_L \\[2ex] v_C \end{bmatrix} \tag{7.3}$$

By definition, the derivative of a matrix is

$$\frac{d}{dt}\begin{bmatrix} a_{11} & a_{12} & \cdots & a_{1m} \\ a_{21} & a_{22} & \cdots & a_{2m} \\ \vdots & \vdots & \ddots & \vdots \\ a_{n1} & a_{n2} & \cdots & a_{nm} \end{bmatrix} = \begin{bmatrix} \dfrac{da_{11}}{dt} & \dfrac{da_{12}}{dt} & \cdots & \dfrac{da_{1m}}{dt} \\ \dfrac{da_{21}}{dt} & \dfrac{da_{22}}{dt} & \cdots & \dfrac{da_{2m}}{dt} \\ \vdots & \vdots & \ddots & \vdots \\ \dfrac{da_{n1}}{dt} & \dfrac{da_{n2}}{dt} & \cdots & \dfrac{da_{nm}}{dt} \end{bmatrix}$$

Therefore, we can write the matrix state equation (7.3) as

$$\frac{d}{dt}\begin{bmatrix} i_L \\ v_C \end{bmatrix} = \begin{bmatrix} -\dfrac{R}{L} & -\dfrac{1}{L} \\ \dfrac{1}{C} & 0 \end{bmatrix}\begin{bmatrix} i_L \\ v_C \end{bmatrix}$$

If we define the matrices $\mathbf{X}(t)$ and $\mathbf{A}$ by

$$\mathbf{X}(t) = \begin{bmatrix} i_L \\ v_C \end{bmatrix} \quad \text{and} \quad \mathbf{A} = \begin{bmatrix} -\dfrac{R}{L} & -\dfrac{1}{L} \\ \dfrac{1}{C} & 0 \end{bmatrix}$$

then the matrix state equation can be written as

$$\frac{d\mathbf{X}(t)}{dt} = \mathbf{A}\mathbf{X}(t) \tag{7.4}$$

Since the components of the column matrix $\mathbf{X}(t)$ constitute the state of the circuit, we shall call $\mathbf{X}(t)$ the **state vector**. Consequently, $\mathbf{X}(0)$ will be called the **initial-state vector**. The process of finding the solution to the state equation (7.4) is known as **state-variable analysis**.

We may now ask, "What is the solution to the state equation?" To answer this, consider the first-order ordinary (scalar) differential equation

$$\frac{dx(t)}{dt} = ax(t)$$

This equation can be rewritten as

$$\frac{dx(t)}{dt} - ax(t) = 0$$

We have seen [Equations (5.5) and (5.6)] that the solution to this differential equation is

$$x(t) = x(0)e^{at} \qquad \text{for} \quad t \geq 0$$

In the same vein as this, it can be shown that the solution to the matrix state equation (7.4) is

$$\mathbf{X}(t) = e^{\mathbf{A}t}\mathbf{X}(0) \qquad \text{for} \quad t \geq 0 \tag{7.5}$$

For any specific value of t and any real number a, e^{at} is also a real number. However, since $\mathbf{A}$ is a matrix, $e^{\mathbf{A}t}$ is also a matrix (called the **state-transition matrix**). It is for this reason that we write the solution of the state equation as we do—with $\mathbf{X}(0)$ multiplying $e^{\mathbf{A}t}$ on the right—so that we have the proper ordering of the matrices for matrix multiplication.

One technique for evaluating $e^{\mathbf{A}t}$ is by using a power series expansion. In freshman calculus we learned that the Taylor series expansion of e^{at} is

$$e^{at} = 1 + at + \frac{a^2t^2}{2!} + \frac{a^3t^3}{3!} + \cdots$$

The analogous result for $e^{\mathbf{A}t}$ is

$$e^{\mathbf{A}t} = \mathbf{I} + \mathbf{A}t + \frac{\mathbf{A}^2t^2}{2!} + \frac{\mathbf{A}^3t^3}{3!} + \cdots$$

where $\mathbf{I}$ is the identity matrix.

Calculating the matrix $e^{\mathbf{A}t}$ this way by hand is simply out of the question. The amount of time and effort required is just too much. Writing a computer program, or having one available as a subroutine, that calculates $e^{\mathbf{A}t}$ is one approach for the computer solution of the state equation. However, we shall shortly discuss a simple numerical technique for solving state equations that can be readily implemented with a digital computer. Before we do, though, let us get some practice writing state equations for circuits with zero inputs.

Although the next few examples use inspection to obtain state equations, this process can be used often. However, such a hit-and-miss approach can be cumbersome for some types of circuits. Toward the end of this chapter, after the reader has received some feel for writing state equations, we shall formally present the rules to follow in order to obtain state equations.

In the following examples, the rule of thumb is that we choose the inductor currents and the capacitor voltages as the state variables of a circuit.

EXAMPLE 7.1

Consider the zero-input parallel *RLC* shown in Fig. 7.2. The state variables for this circuit are i_L and v_C. We now wish, therefore, to express di_L/dt in terms of i_L and v_C. We also wish to express dv_C/dt in terms of i_L and v_C. To obtain the former, we use

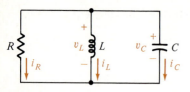

Fig. 7.2   Zero-input parallel *RLC* circuit.

the fact that $L \, di_L/dt = v_C$. Thus,

$$\frac{di_L}{dt} = \frac{1}{L} v_C \tag{7.6}$$

This is the first of the two state equations. To obtain the second, we use the fact that $C \, dv_C/dt = i_C$. However, since i_C is not a state variable, we can apply KCL and write

$$C \frac{dv_C}{dt} = -i_L - i_R$$

Here i_L is a state variable, but i_R is not. But, by Ohm's law, $i_R = v_C/R$. Thus,

$$C \frac{dv_C}{dt} = -i_L - \frac{v_C}{R}$$

whence we get the second state equation

$$\frac{dv_C}{dt} = -\frac{1}{C} i_L - \frac{1}{RC} v_C \tag{7.7}$$

Expressing the two state equations (7.6) and (7.7) as a single matrix state equation, we have

$$\frac{d}{dt}\begin{bmatrix} i_L \\ v_C \end{bmatrix} = \begin{bmatrix} \dfrac{di_L}{dt} \\ \dfrac{dv_C}{dt} \end{bmatrix} = \begin{bmatrix} 0 & \dfrac{1}{L} \\ -\dfrac{1}{C} & -\dfrac{1}{RC} \end{bmatrix} \begin{bmatrix} i_L \\ v_C \end{bmatrix}$$

which has the form of Equation (7.4).

DRILL EXERCISE 7.1

Write the matrix state equation for the zero-input *RLC* circuit shown in Fig. DE 7.1

Answer:

$$\frac{d}{dt}\begin{bmatrix} i_L \\ v_C \end{bmatrix} = \begin{bmatrix} -\frac{5}{2} & \frac{1}{2} \\ -\frac{1}{3} & -\frac{1}{12} \end{bmatrix} \begin{bmatrix} i_L \\ v_C \end{bmatrix}$$

Fig. DE7.1

Having considered some zero-input circuits that do not contain dependent sources, let us now consider the case of writing state equations for zero-input *RLC* circuits which contain dependent sources.

EXAMPLE 7.2

Let us write the matrix state equation for the zero-input *RLC* circuit shown in Fig. 7.3.

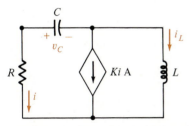

Fig. 7.3   *RLC* circuit with dependent source.

By KCL,

$$i + Ki + i_L = 0 \tag{7.8}$$

Since $-i = C\, dv_C/dt$, then Equation (7.8) becomes

$$(1 + K)\left(-C\frac{dv_C}{dt}\right) + i_L = 0$$

from which

$$\frac{dv_C}{dt} = \frac{1}{(1 + K)C} i_L \tag{7.9}$$

and this is one of the two state equations.

By KVL,

$$v_C + L\frac{di_L}{dt} - Ri = 0 \tag{7.10}$$

Since we have the term di_L/dt in this equation, we do not want to introduce dv_C/dt into it as well. Therefore, we will not substitute $i = -C\,dv_C/dt$ into Equation (7.10). However, from Equation (7.8),

$$i = \frac{-1}{1+K}i_L$$

Substituting this expression in Equation (7.10) and simplifying yields

$$\frac{di_L}{dt} = -\frac{R}{(1+K)L}i_L - \frac{1}{L}v_C \tag{7.11}$$

and this is the other state equation.

Writing Equations (7.9) and (7.11) in matrix form, we have that

$$\frac{d}{dt}\begin{bmatrix} i_L \\ v_C \end{bmatrix} = \begin{bmatrix} -\dfrac{R}{(1+K)L} & -\dfrac{1}{L} \\[2ex] \dfrac{1}{(1+K)C} & 0 \end{bmatrix}\begin{bmatrix} i_L \\ v_C \end{bmatrix}$$

DRILL EXERCISE 7.2

Find the matrix state equation for the circuit shown in Fig. DE7.2.
Answer:

$$\frac{d}{dt}\begin{bmatrix} i_L \\ v_C \end{bmatrix} = \begin{bmatrix} -4 & 2 \\ -8 & -1 \end{bmatrix}\begin{bmatrix} i_L \\ v_C \end{bmatrix}$$

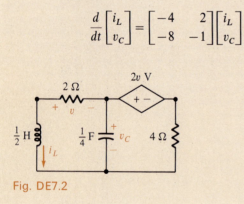

Fig. DE7.2

Let us now write the state equations for a circuit with three state variables.

EXAMPLE 7.3

The zero-input circuit shown in Fig. 7.4 has three state variables: i_L, v_1, and v_2. We may write the first state equation immediately. For the inductor, $4\, di_L/dt = v_2$. Thus,

$$\frac{di_L}{dt} = \frac{1}{4} v_2$$

and this is the first state equation.

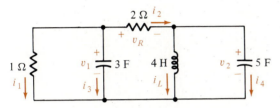

Fig. 7.4 Circuit with three state variables.

Next we have for the 3-F capacitor, by KCL,

$$3 \frac{dv_1}{dt} = i_3 = -i_1 - i_2 = -\frac{v_1}{1} - \frac{v_R}{2} = -v_1 - \frac{(v_1 - v_2)}{2} = -\frac{3}{2} v_1 + \frac{1}{2} v_2$$

and therefore

$$\frac{dv_1}{dt} = -\frac{1}{2} v_1 + \frac{1}{6} v_2$$

which is the second state equation.

Finally, for the 5-F capacitor,

$$5 \frac{dv_2}{dt} = i_4 = -i_L + i_2 = -i_L + \frac{v_R}{2} = -i_L + \frac{v_1 - v_2}{2}$$

and thus the third state equation is

$$\frac{dv_2}{dt} = -\frac{1}{5} i_L + \frac{1}{10} v_1 - \frac{1}{10} v_2$$

Expressing the state equations in the matrix form of Equation (7.4), we have

$$\frac{d}{dt} \begin{bmatrix} i_L \\ v_1 \\ v_2 \end{bmatrix} = \begin{bmatrix} 0 & 0 & \frac{1}{4} \\ 0 & -\frac{1}{2} & \frac{1}{6} \\ -\frac{1}{5} & \frac{1}{10} & -\frac{1}{10} \end{bmatrix} \begin{bmatrix} i_L \\ v_1 \\ v_2 \end{bmatrix}$$

DRILL EXERCISE 7.3

Find the matrix state equation for the circuit shown in Fig. DE7.3.
Answer:

$$\frac{d}{dt}\begin{bmatrix} i_1 \\ i_2 \\ v_C \end{bmatrix} = \begin{bmatrix} -3 & 0 & -1 \\ 0 & -8 & 2 \\ 5 & -5 & -1 \end{bmatrix}\begin{bmatrix} i_1 \\ i_2 \\ v_C \end{bmatrix}$$

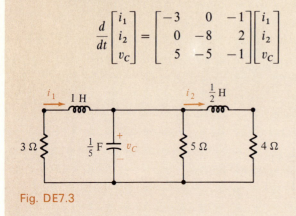

Fig. DE7.3

7.2 NUMERICAL ANALYSIS OF ZERO-INPUT CIRCUITS

As we have mentioned before, the solution of the state equation

$$\frac{d\mathbf{X}(t)}{dt} = \mathbf{A}\mathbf{X}(t) \qquad \text{is} \qquad \mathbf{X}(t) = e^{\mathbf{A}t}\mathbf{X}(0) \qquad \text{for} \quad t \geq 0$$

Clearly, if we have the capability of determining the matrix $e^{\mathbf{A}t}$ for any value of t, then it is merely a matter of multiplication of this matrix by the zero-state vector $\mathbf{X}(0)$ to obtain the corresponding state $\mathbf{X}(t)$.

Alternatively, we shall now present a numerical technique (known as **Euler's method**) that will allow us to determine the state of the circuit at any time, with any degree of accuracy, without having to evaluate the matrix $e^{\mathbf{A}t}$.

We begin by first considering the case of a single state variable $x(t)$ described by the first-order differential state equation

$$\frac{dx(t)}{dt} = Ax(t) \tag{7.12}$$

subject to the initial state $x(0)$. The extension of the procedure to be described to the case of two, three, four, or more variables is immediate and straightforward.

Whether the variable $x(t)$ describes voltage or current (or anything else, for that matter) is immaterial. Suppose that $x(t)$ describes the (one-dimensional) position of a particle. Then $dx(t)/dt$ is the velocity of the particle. In particular, the initial position ($t = 0$) is $x(0)$ and the initial velocity is $dx(0)/dt$. From elementary physics we know that if velocity is constant, then distance is the product of velocity and time. Thus, for the case that the initial velocity is a constant, the position of the particle at time Δt is

$$x(\Delta t) = x(0) + \frac{dx(0)}{dt} \Delta t$$

However, in general, velocity (initial or otherwise) is not a constant. But, if we make the time interval Δt sufficiently small, the velocity during this time interval will be approximately constant.[†] Thus, we can write the approximate formula

$$x(\Delta t) \approx x(0) + \frac{dx(0)}{dt} \Delta t$$

and the smaller the interval Δt, the better the approximation. Substituting the state equation (7.12) into this equation, we get

$$x(\Delta t) \approx x(0) + Ax(0) \Delta t$$

Thus, we see that if we choose Δt sufficiently small, we can approximately determine the position at time $t = \Delta t$ from the initial position $x(0)$, the constant A, and the number Δt.

Once we have determined the approximate position at time $t = \Delta t$, using reasoning as above, we can determine the approximate position at time $t = 2\Delta t$ from

$$x(2\,\Delta t) \approx x(\Delta t) + \frac{dx(\Delta t)}{dt} \Delta t$$

Substituting the state equation (7.12) into this approximation, we obtain

$$x(2\,\Delta t) \approx x(\Delta t) + Ax(\Delta t)\,\Delta t$$

Repeating this process, we get

$$x(3\,\Delta t) \approx x(2\,\Delta t) + Ax(2\,\Delta t)\,\Delta t$$

and so on, and thus a general expression is

$$x([k+1]\,\Delta t) \approx x(k\,\Delta t) + Ax(k\,\Delta t)\,\Delta t = x(k\,\Delta t)[1 + A\,\Delta t]$$

for $k = 0, 1, 2, 3, \ldots$.

EXAMPLE 7.4

For a simple RC zero-input circuit (see Fig. 5.1 on p. 219), we choose the voltage $v(t)$ across the capacitor as the state variable. We have already seen that

$$\frac{dv_C}{dt} + \frac{1}{RC} v_C = 0$$

[†] An exception is when $x(t)$ is discontinuous somewhere in the interval Δt. Fortunately, though, when no impulses are present, the voltage across a capacitor and the current through an inductor do not change instantaneously.

from which we obtain the state equation

$$\frac{dv_C}{dt} = -\frac{1}{RC} v_C = Av_C$$

where $A = -1/RC$. Even though we already know that the solution of this differential equation is $v_C(t) = v_C(0)e^{-t/RC}$ for $t \geq 0$, let us determine the approximate numerical solution as described above for the case that $R = 1\ \Omega$, $C = 1\ F$, and $v_C(0) = 1\ V$. We arbitrarily select $\Delta t = 0.1\ s$. (In the calculations below for comparison purposes, the numbers on the right in the parentheses are the actual values of the voltage obtained from the formula $v_C(t) = e^{-t}$.) We have the following results:

$$v_C(0.1) \approx v_C(0)[1 + A\,\Delta t] = 1[1 + (-1)(0.1)] = 0.9 \quad (0.905)$$

$$v_C(0.2) \approx v_C(0.1)[1 + A\,\Delta t] = 0.9[0.9] = 0.81 \qquad (0.819)$$

$$v_C(0.3) \approx v_C(0.2)[1 + A\,\Delta t] = 0.81[0.9] = 0.729 \qquad (0.741)$$

$$v_C(0.4) \approx v_C(0.3)[1 + A\,\Delta t] = 0.729[0.9] = 0.656 \qquad (0.670)$$

$$v_C(0.5) \approx v_C(0.4)[1 + A\,\Delta t] = 0.656[0.9] = 0.5904 \qquad (0.607)$$

and so on. In this example we see that the choice of $\Delta t = 0.1\ s$ results in values of $v_C(t)$ that are progressively farther from the actual value. This indicates that the choice of Δt is too large, and that the selection of $\Delta t = 0.01\ s$ would be better, and $\Delta t = 0.001\ s$ even better than that. Of course, the choice of a smaller value of Δt requires more calculations for a given interval of time—the price of greater accuracy. However, this is not a problem for a computer. Just remember, though, even if $\Delta t = 0.001\ s$ is used, you can have the computer to print out values of the voltage only every 0.1 s.

● ──

DRILL EXERCISE 7.4

For a simple RL circuit (see Fig. 5.10 on p. 227), suppose that $R = 5\ \Omega$, $L = \frac{1}{10}\ H$, and $i_L(0) = 2\ A$. Use Euler's method with $\Delta t = 0.01\ s$ and your pocket calculator to determine the approximate values of $i_L(0.01)$, $i_L(0.02)$, $i_L(0.03)$, $i_L(0.04)$, and $i_L(0.05)$. Compare these approximate values to the actual values.
Answer: 1 A, 0.5 A, 0.25 A, 0.125 A, 0.0625 A; 1.213 A, 0.736 A, 0.446 A, 0.271 A, 0.164 A

In the above example we were able to conclude that $\Delta t = 0.1\ s$ was too large by comparing the numerical results with the answer! When applying this technique to a situation where we don't yet know the actual answer, we do the following: Arbitrarily pick a value for Δt that seems to be small, and then let the computer print out the results. Next, pick a new value of Δt—say, 10 percent of the original value. Repeat the process (remember, the computer is doing all the work) and compare the results with those of the first run. If the values obtained from the second run do not differ significantly (less than 1 percent) from those calculated previously, then

Δt is small enough. If the difference is significant, again decrease Δt by a factor of 10, and calculate a new set of numbers. Continue this routine until there is an insignificant difference between the latest two runs. At such a time, a small enough value of Δt has been obtained.

This numerical technique—Euler's method—is rather elementary, and consequently, not as preferable as some of the more sophisticated procedures that are available. However, such techniques are beyond the scope of this book and are left for more advanced courses in engineering or mathematics.

Although the discussion above specifically considered the case of a single state variable, a similar approach can be taken for two or more state variables.

Let us investigate the case of two state variables, $x_1(t)$ and $x_2(t)$, given the initial states $x_1(0)$ and $x_2(0)$. The state equations have the form

$$\frac{dx_1(t)}{dt} = a_{11}x_1(t) + a_{12}x_2(t)$$

$$\frac{dx_2(t)}{dt} = a_{21}x_1(t) + a_{22}x_2(t)$$

If we make the time interval Δt sufficiently small, we have the approximations

$$x_1(\Delta t) \approx x_1(0) + \frac{dx_1(0)}{dt}\Delta t$$

$$x_2(\Delta t) \approx x_2(0) + \frac{dx_2(0)}{dt}\Delta t$$

Using the state equations above, we get the approximations

$$x_1(\Delta t) \approx x_1(0) + \left[a_{11}x_1(0) + a_{12}x_2(0)\right]\Delta t$$

$$x_2(\Delta t) \approx x_2(0) + \left[a_{21}x_1(0) + a_{22}x_2(0)\right]\Delta t$$

Once we have determined the approximate states at time $t = \Delta t$, we can determine the approximate states at time $t = 2\Delta t$ and so forth. Assuming that Δt is sufficiently small and using reasoning as above, we eventually obtain the general approximations

$$x_1([k + 1]\Delta t) \approx x_1(k\,\Delta t) + \frac{dx_1(k\,\Delta t)}{dt}\Delta t$$

$$x_2([k + 1]\Delta t) \approx x_2(k\,\Delta t) + \frac{dx_2(k\,\Delta t)}{dt}\Delta t$$

Using the state equations, we get

$$x_1([k + 1]\Delta t) \approx x_1(k\,\Delta t) + \left[a_{11}x_1(k\,\Delta t) + a_{12}x_2(k\,\Delta t)\right]\Delta t$$

$$x_2([k + 1]\Delta t) \approx x_2(k\,\Delta t) + \left[a_{21}x_1(k\,\Delta t) + a_{22}x_2(k\,\Delta t)\right]\Delta t$$

for $k = 0, 1, 2, 3, \ldots$.

Although the discussion above specifically considered the case of two state variables, it should be clear that the same approach is valid for any number of state variables.

● ──

EXAMPLE 7.5

Suppose that for the circuit shown in Fig. 7.1 (p. 313), $R = \frac{1}{3}\,\Omega$, $L = \frac{1}{12}\,H$, $C = 4\,F$, and the initial state is $i_L(0) = 1\,A$, $v_C(0) = 1\,V$. Arbitrarily choosing $\Delta t = 0.1\,s$, let us use Euler's method to calculate approximate values for the states at $t = 0.1\,s$, $t = 0.2\,s$, and $t = 0.3\,s$.

From Equation (7.1) [p. 313],

$$\frac{di_L}{dt} = -4i_L - 12v_C$$

From Equation (7.2) [p. 313],

$$\frac{dv_C}{dt} = \frac{1}{4}i_L$$

From the initial state, we can now calculate the approximate state at time $t = 0.1\,s$. We have the approximations

$$i_L(\Delta t) \approx i_L(0) + \frac{di_L(0)}{dt}\Delta t \qquad \text{and} \qquad v_C(\Delta t) \approx v_C(0) + \frac{dv_C(0)}{dt}\Delta t$$

Using the state equations, these approximations become

$$i_L(\Delta t) \approx i_L(0) + [-4i_L(0) - 12v_C(0)]\Delta t$$
$$i_L(0.1) \approx 1 + [-4 - 12](0.1) = -0.6\,A$$

and

$$v_C(\Delta t) \approx v_C(0) + [\tfrac{1}{4}i_L(0)]\Delta t$$
$$v_C(0.1) \approx 1 + \tfrac{1}{4}(0.1) = 1.025\,V$$

In a similar manner we can determine the approximate state at time $t = 0.2\,s$ by using

$$i_L(2\,\Delta t) \approx i_L(\Delta t) + [-4i_L(\Delta t) - 12v_C(\Delta t)]\Delta t$$
$$i_L(0.2) \approx -0.6 + [-4(-0.6) - 12(1.025)](0.1) = -1.59\,A$$

and

$$v_C(2\,\Delta t) \approx v_C(\Delta t) + [\tfrac{1}{4}i_L(\Delta t)]\Delta t$$
$$v_C(0.2) \approx 1.025 + [\tfrac{1}{4}(-0.6)](0.1) = 1.01\,V$$

Continuing,

$$i_L(3\,\Delta t) \approx i_L(2\,\Delta t) + [-4i_L(2\,\Delta t) - 12v_C(2\,\Delta t)]\Delta t$$
$$i_L(0.3) \approx -1.59 + [-4(-1.59) - 12(1.01)](0.1) = -2.17\,A$$

and

$$v_C(3\,\Delta t) \approx v_C(2\,\Delta t) + \left[\tfrac{1}{4}i_L(2\,\Delta t)\right]\Delta t$$

$$v_C(0.3) \approx 1.01 + \left[\tfrac{1}{4}(-1.59)\right](0.1) = 0.97 \text{ V}$$

DRILL EXERCISE 7.5

For the circuit given in Fig. DE7.1 (p. 317), suppose that $i_L(0) = 0$ A and $v_C(0) =$ 12 V. Use $\Delta t = 0.1$ s to calculate the approximate states at (a) $t = 0.1$ s, (b) $t = 0.2$ s, and (c) $t = 0.3$ s.
Answer: (a) 0.6 A, 11.9 V; (b) 1.045 A, 11.78 V; (c) 1.373 A, 11.65 V

By now you should be convinced that doing Euler's method with a (non-programmable) hand-held calculator is out of the question. Therefore, let us now see an example of how we can program a computer to analyze a circuit numerically.

EXAMPLE 7.6

The zero-input circuit shown in Fig. 7.5 has three state variables. It is a simple matter to obtain the state equations, which are

$$\frac{di_1}{dt} = -i_1 - v \qquad \frac{di_2}{dt} = -i_2 + v \qquad \frac{dv}{dt} = \frac{1}{2}(i_1 - i_2)$$

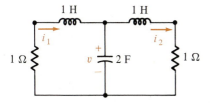

Fig. 7.5   Circuit to be analyzed numerically.

Table 7.1 shows a FORTRAN computer program in which the current $i_2(t)$ is printed out every 0.1 s from $t = 0$ to $t = 10$ s. The initial conditions were chosen arbitrarily to be $i_1(0) = 0$ A, $i_2(0) = 1$ A, and $v(0) = -2$ V. Lines 14, 15, and 16 are the approximations used to obtain the states at time $(k + 1)\,\Delta t$ from the states at time $k\,\Delta t$. The value used for the time increment is $\Delta t = 0.001$ s. (Using $\Delta t = 0.0001$ s yields the same results.) A computer printout and plot of $i_2(t)$ versus t are given in Fig. 7.6. The computer plot was done by a subroutine that is not a part of the program shown.

Table 7.1

```
00001        PROGRAM SVAP(INPUT,OUTPUT,TAPE6=OUTPUT)
00002        REAL I1,I2,I1K,I2K
00003        WRITE(6,30)
00004        30 FORMAT(6X,*TIME*,4X,*CURRENT*)
00005        X=0.
00006        V=-2.
00007        I1=0.
00008        I2=1.
00009        T=0.
00010        DELT=0.001
00011        40 WRITE(6,50) T,I2
00012        50 FORMAT(3X,F7.2,5X,F5.2)
00013        DO 60 J=1,100
00014           VK=V+0.5*(I1-I2)*DELT
00015           I1K=I1+(-I1-V)*DELT
00016           I2K=I2+(-I2-V)*DELT
00017           V=VK
00018           I1=I1K
00019           I2=I2K
00020        60 T=T+DELT
00021        X=X+1.
00022        IF(100.-X)70,40,40
00023        70 CONTINUE
00024        END
```

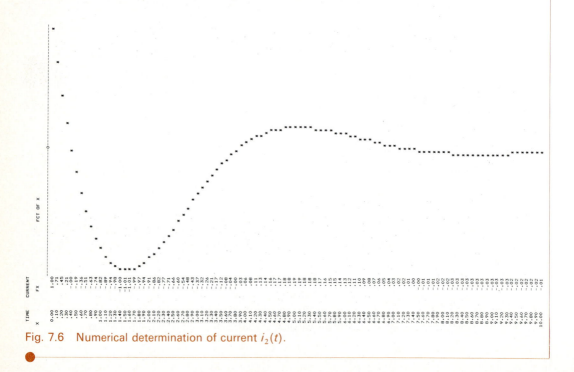

Fig. 7.6   Numerical determination of current $i_2(t)$.

7.3 CIRCUITS WITH NONZERO INPUTS

Having already considered circuits with no input, our next step is to consider circuits having nonzero inputs.

Let us again look at the series RLC circuit which is shown in Fig. 7.7. We have already analyzed this circuit for the case when $v_s(t)$ is a step function by writing a second-order differential equation in the variable v_C and solving it. Now let us see how to extend the ideas of state-variable analysis to deal with circuits of this type—that is, circuits with nonzero inputs.

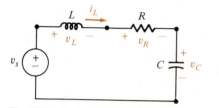

Fig. 7.7   Series RLC circuit with nonzero input.

Again we choose our state variables to be the inductor current i_L and the capacitor voltage v_C. Since, for the inductor, $L\, di_L/dt = v_L$, then, by KVL,

$$L\frac{di_L}{dt} = -v_R - v_C + v_s = -Ri_L - v_C + v_s$$

from which we obtain the first state equation—that being

$$\frac{di_L}{dt} = -\frac{R}{L}i_L - \frac{1}{L}v_C + \frac{1}{L}v_s$$

In this case, we have expressed the derivative of one of the state variables in terms of both state variables and the input. (The input is in general a given time-varying quantity, not a circuit variable.)

We also have that for the capacitor, $C\, dv_C/dt = i_L$, from which we get the second state equation

$$\frac{dv_C}{dt} = \frac{1}{C}i_L$$

We have seen that when $v_s = 0$, we can write state equations in the form

$$\frac{d\mathbf{X}(t)}{dt} = \mathbf{AX}(t)$$

However, since $v_s \neq 0$ in general, in order to write state equations in matrix form, we must include another term in the matrix expression.

For the state equations, given above, we can write

$$\frac{d}{dt}\begin{bmatrix} i_L \\ v_C \end{bmatrix} = \begin{bmatrix} \dfrac{di_L}{dt} \\ \dfrac{dv_C}{dt} \end{bmatrix} = \begin{bmatrix} -\dfrac{R}{L} & -\dfrac{1}{L} \\ \dfrac{1}{C} & 0 \end{bmatrix}\begin{bmatrix} i_L \\ v_C \end{bmatrix} + \begin{bmatrix} \dfrac{1}{L} \\ 0 \end{bmatrix}v_s$$

In this case, we added the product of a matrix (whose entries are scalars) and the input such that the resulting additional terms yield the proper state equations.
The form of the above matrix state equation is

$$\frac{d\mathbf{X}(t)}{dt} = \mathbf{A}\mathbf{X}(t) + \mathbf{B}w(t) \tag{7.13}$$

where $\mathbf{X}(t)$ is the state vector and $w(t)$ results from the input.

EXAMPLE 7.7

Let us write the matrix state equation for the circuit shown in Fig. 7.8.

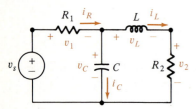

Fig. 7.8   Circuit for Example 7.7.

For this circuit we have that

$$L\frac{di_L}{dt} = v_L = -v_2 + v_C = -R_2 i_L + v_C$$

so that the first state equation is

$$\frac{di_L}{dt} = -\frac{R_2}{L}i_L + \frac{1}{L}v_C$$

Furthermore,

$$C\frac{dv_C}{dt} = i_C = -i_L + i_R = -i_L + \frac{v_1}{R_1} = -i_L + \frac{v_s - v_C}{R_1} = -i_L - \frac{v_C}{R_1} + \frac{v_s}{R_1}$$

from which we get the second state equation—that being

$$\frac{dv_C}{dt} = -\frac{1}{C}i_L - \frac{1}{R_1 C}v_C + \frac{1}{R_1 C}v_s$$

Thus, we can write these state equations in the matrix form of Equation (7.13) as

$$\frac{d}{dt}\begin{bmatrix} i_L \\ v_C \end{bmatrix} = \begin{bmatrix} -\dfrac{R_2}{L} & \dfrac{1}{L} \\ -\dfrac{1}{C} & -\dfrac{1}{R_1 C} \end{bmatrix}\begin{bmatrix} i_L \\ v_C \end{bmatrix} + \begin{bmatrix} 0 \\ \dfrac{1}{R_1 C} \end{bmatrix}v_s$$

DRILL EXERCISE 7.6

Write the matrix state equation for the circuit shown in Fig. DE7.6.
Answer:

$$\frac{d}{dt}\begin{bmatrix} i_L \\ v_C \end{bmatrix} = \begin{bmatrix} -8 & -4 \\ 6 & -2 \end{bmatrix}\begin{bmatrix} i_L \\ v_C \end{bmatrix} + \begin{bmatrix} 4 \\ 0 \end{bmatrix} v_s$$

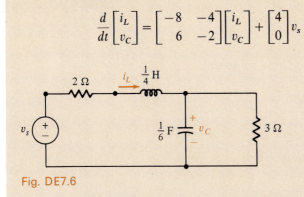

Fig. DE7.6

Next, we do an example of determining the state equations for an op-amp circuit.

EXAMPLE 7.8
Let us write the matrix state equation for the op-amp circuit shown in Fig. 7.9.

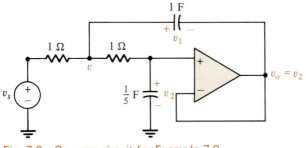

Fig. 7.9 Op-amp circuit for Example 7.8.

The state variables for this circuit are the capacitor voltages v_1 and v_2. However, since $v_o = v_2$, then by KVL, $v = v_1 + v_2$. Thus, by KCL at node v, we have

$$\frac{v_1 + v_2 - v_s}{1} + \frac{v_1 + v_2 - v_2}{1} + 1\frac{dv_1}{dt} = 0$$

from which

$$\frac{dv_1}{dt} = -2v_1 - v_2 + v_s$$

and this is the first state equation.

By KCL at the noninverting input of the op-amp,

$$\frac{v_2 - (v_1 + v_2)}{1} + \frac{1}{5}\frac{dv_2}{dt} = 0$$

and this yields the second state equation

$$\frac{dv_2}{dt} = 5v_1$$

Writing the state equations in matrix form, we have

$$\frac{d}{dt}\begin{bmatrix} v_1 \\ v_2 \end{bmatrix} = \begin{bmatrix} -2 & -1 \\ 5 & 0 \end{bmatrix}\begin{bmatrix} v_1 \\ v_2 \end{bmatrix} + \begin{bmatrix} 1 \\ 0 \end{bmatrix}v_s$$

DRILL EXERCISE 7.7

Write the matrix state equation for the op-amp circuit given in Fig. DE6.6 (p. 294).
Answer:

$$\frac{d}{dt}\begin{bmatrix} v_1 \\ v_o \end{bmatrix} = \begin{bmatrix} -2 & 0.5 \\ -2 & 0 \end{bmatrix}\begin{bmatrix} v_1 \\ v_o \end{bmatrix} + \begin{bmatrix} 1 \\ 0 \end{bmatrix}v_s$$

Now let us look at a circuit with three state variables.

EXAMPLE 7.9

The circuit in Fig. 7.10 has three state variables: i_L, v_1, and v_2. Let us write the matrix state equation for this circuit.

For this circuit we have that

$$L\frac{di_L}{dt} = v_2 \qquad \Rightarrow \qquad \frac{di_L}{dt} = \frac{1}{L}v_2$$

and this is the first state equation.

Since

$$C_1\frac{dv_1}{dt} = i_1 = -\frac{v}{R} = -\frac{1}{R}(v_1 - v_2)$$

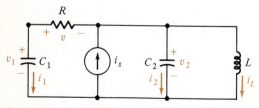

Fig. 7.10   Circuit with three state variables.

then the second state equation is

$$\frac{dv_1}{dt} = -\frac{1}{RC_1} v_1 + \frac{1}{RC_1} v_2$$

Furthermore,

$$C_2 \frac{dv_2}{dt} = i_2 = -i_L - i_1 + i_s = -i_L + \frac{v}{R} + i_s = -i_L + \frac{v_1 - v_2}{R} + i_s$$

and thus the third state equation is

$$\frac{dv_2}{dt} = -\frac{1}{C_2} i_L + \frac{1}{RC_2} v_1 - \frac{1}{RC_2} v_2 + \frac{1}{C_2} i_s$$

Writing the state equations in matrix form, we have

$$\frac{d}{dt} \begin{bmatrix} i_L \\ v_1 \\ v_2 \end{bmatrix} = \begin{bmatrix} 0 & 0 & \dfrac{1}{L} \\ 0 & -\dfrac{1}{RC_1} & \dfrac{1}{RC_1} \\ -\dfrac{1}{C_2} & \dfrac{1}{RC_2} & -\dfrac{1}{RC_2} \end{bmatrix} \begin{bmatrix} i_L \\ v_1 \\ v_2 \end{bmatrix} + \begin{bmatrix} 0 \\ 0 \\ \dfrac{1}{C_2} \end{bmatrix} i_s$$

DRILL EXERCISE 7.8

Write the matrix state equation for the circuit shown in Fig. DE7.8.
Answer:

$$\frac{d}{dt} \begin{bmatrix} i_1 \\ i_2 \\ v_C \end{bmatrix} = \begin{bmatrix} -6 & 0 & -3 \\ 0 & -6 & 2 \\ 4 & -4 & -2 \end{bmatrix} \begin{bmatrix} i_1 \\ i_2 \\ v_C \end{bmatrix} + \begin{bmatrix} 3 \\ 0 \\ 2 \end{bmatrix} v_s$$

Fig. DE7.8

Numerical Analysis

The numerical analysis of circuits with nonzero inputs is accomplished as was the analysis of zero-input circuits.

For the case of two state variables $x_1(t)$, $x_2(t)$, and a single input $w(t)$, the state equations have the form

$$\frac{dx_1(t)}{dt} = a_{11}x_1(t) + a_{12}x_2(t) + b_1w(t)$$

$$\frac{dx_2(t)}{dt} = a_{21}x_1(t) + a_{22}x_2(t) + b_2w(t)$$

Given the initial state $x_1(0)$, $x_2(0)$, the approximate state at time $t = \Delta t$ is given by

$$x_1(\Delta t) \approx x_1(0) + \frac{dx_1(0)}{dt} \Delta t$$

$$x_2(\Delta t) \approx x_2(0) + \frac{dx_2(0)}{dt} \Delta t$$

Using the state equations, these approximations become

$$x_1(\Delta t) \approx x_1(0) + [a_{11}x_1(0) + a_{12}x_2(0) + b_1w(0)] \Delta t$$

$$x_2(\Delta t) \approx x_2(0) + [a_{21}x_1(0) + a_{22}x_2(0) + b_2w(0)] \Delta t$$

Continuing, the state at time $t = 2\Delta t$ is given by the approximations

$$x_1(2\Delta t) \approx x_1(\Delta t) + [a_{11}x_1(\Delta t) + a_{12}x_2(\Delta t) + b_1w(\Delta t)] \Delta t$$

$$x_2(2\Delta t) \approx x_2(\Delta t) + [a_{21}x_1(\Delta t) + a_{22}x_2(\Delta t) + b_2w(\Delta t)]\Delta t$$

In general, we have the approximations,

$$x_1([k+1]\Delta t) \approx x_1(k\Delta t) + [a_{11}x_1(k\Delta t) + a_{12}x_2(k\Delta t) + b_1w(k\Delta t)] \Delta t$$

$$x_2([k+1]\Delta t) \approx x_2(k\Delta t) + [a_{21}x_1(k\Delta t) + a_{22}x_2(k\Delta t) + b_2w(k\Delta t)] \Delta t$$

for $k = 0, 1, 2, 3, \ldots$.

For the case that $w(t) = 0$ but $x_1(0) \neq 0$ and/or $x_2(0) \neq 0$, the result of the above numerical analysis is the zero-input (natural) response. If $x_1(0) = x_2(0) = 0$ and $w(t) \neq 0$, then the zero-state response results. For the case of a step response, $w(t) = u(t) = 1$ for $t \geq 0$.

● ───────────

EXAMPLE 7.10

The circuit shown in Fig. 7.11 has three state variables. Let us determine zero-state responses numerically via Euler's method.

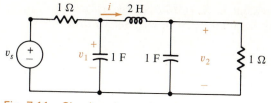

Fig. 7.11 Circuit to be analyzed numerically.

The following state equations can easily be obtained (see Problem 7.28):

$$\frac{di(t)}{dt} = \frac{1}{2}(v_1 - v_2) \qquad \frac{dv_1(t)}{dt} = -i - v_1 + v_s \qquad \frac{dv_2(t)}{dt} = i - v_2$$

A FORTRAN program for the case $v_s(t) = u(t)$ is given in Table 7.2, in which the voltage $v_2(t)$ is printed out every 0.1 s from $t = 0$ to $t = 10$ s. Lines 15, 16, and 17 are the approximations used to obtain the states at time $(k + 1)\Delta t$ from the states

Table 7.2

```
00001      PROGRAM SVAPN(INPUT,OUTPUT,TAPE6=OUTPUT)
00002      REAL I,IK
00003      WRITE(6,30)
00004   30 FORMAT(6X,*TIME*,4X,*VOLTAGE*)
00005      X=0.
00006      I=0.
00007      V1=0.
00008      V2=0.
00009      T=0.
00010      DELT=0.001
00011   40 WRITE(6,50) T,V2
00012   50 FORMAT(3X,F7.2,5X,F5.2)
00013      DO 60 J=1,100
00014         VS=1.
00015         IK=I+0.5*(V1-V2)*DELT
00016         V1K=V1+(VS-I-V1)*DELT
00017         V2K=V2+(I-V2)*DELT
00018         I=IK
00019         V1=V1K
00020         V2=V2K
00021   60 T=T+DELT
00022      X=X+1.
00023      IF(100.-X)70,40,40
00024   70 CONTINUE
00025      END
```

at time $k \Delta t$. The value used for the time increment is $\Delta t = 0.001$ s. (Using $\Delta t = 0.0001$ s yields the same results.) A printout and computer plot of $v_2(t)$ versus t are shown in Fig. 7.12.

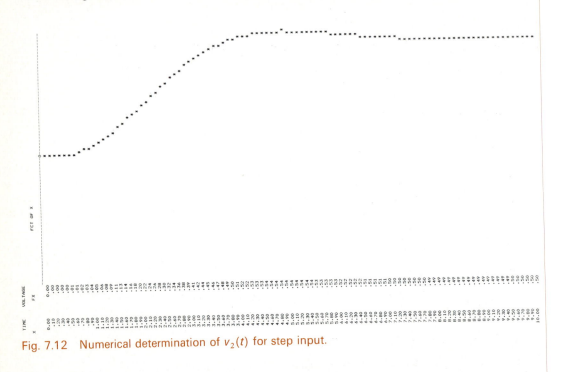

Fig. 7.12 Numerical determination of $v_2(t)$ for step input.

Having numerically determined the step response for the circuit given in Fig. 7.11, let us determine the zero-state response to the input voltage $v_s(t) = |20 \sin 2\pi t| u(t)$ shown in Fig. 7.13. The only modification to the program needed is to change the line corresponding to the input voltage $v_s(t)$ appropriately. However, for aesthetic reasons, the voltage is printed out every 0.15 s from $t = 0$ to $t = 15$ s. The computer printout and plot are given in Fig. 7.14. This circuit configuration is often employed as a "power supply filter," a network whose input is a "rectified" sine wave specified by $v_s(t)$ in Fig. 7.13 and whose output $v_2(t)$ is very nearly a constant.

$v_s(t) = |20 \sin 2\pi t| u(t)$

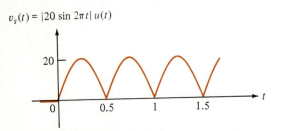

Fig. 7.13 Rectified sine wave.

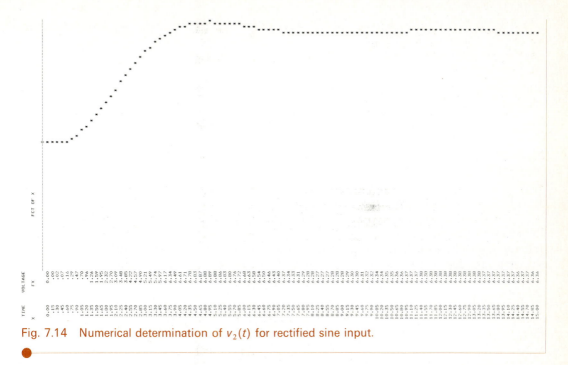

Fig. 7.14   Numerical determination of $v_2(t)$ for rectified sine input.

7.4 RULES FOR WRITING CIRCUIT EQUATIONS

Having seen how state equations were written for numerous examples, we should now have a little feeling for this procedure. However, the judicious choice of circuits was responsible for the relative ease in which the results were obtained. There are some situations, though, that are more subtle. One difficulty arises when we cannot express the voltage across a resistor as a sum of capacitor and independent-source voltages, and we also cannot express the current through that resistor as a sum of inductor and independent-source currents. Thus, it is now time—as was promised earlier—to give a formal set of rules for writing state equations.

Before we do, however, we need to define another graph-theoretical term. Given a connected graph, a set of edges whose removal disconnects some of the nodes is called a **cut-set** provided that no portion of this set (called a **subset**) of edges will also disconnect some of the nodes.

EXAMPLE 7.11

For the connected graph shown in Fig. 7.15, the set of edges $\{e_2, e_3, e_5\}$ is a cut-set since the removal of these edges disconnects node b from the other three nodes, whereas removal of any two of the three edges will not. Moreover, $\{e_1, e_3, e_4, e_5\}$ is also a cut-set since the removal of these edges disconnects nodes a and b from nodes c and d. The set of edges $\{e_1, e_2, e_4, e_5\}$ is not a cut-set since a subset of it, specifically $\{e_1, e_2, e_4\}$, disconnects node a from the other three nodes.

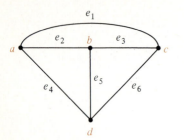

Fig. 7.15   Graph for Example 7.11.

For each cut-set there corresponds a node or a supernode that is obtained by passing a closed curve through the edges forming the cut-set. Shown in Fig. 7.16 are the nodes or supernodes (indicated by shaded regions) associated with the cut-sets $\{e_2, e_3, e_5\}$, $\{e_1, e_3, e_4, e_5\}$, and $\{e_1, e_2, e_4\}$. In the last case, two apparently different situations are depicted. However, as far as KCL is concerned, they are equivalent.

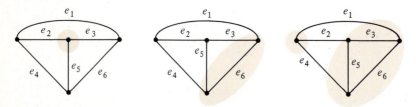

Fig. 7.16   Supernodes associated with cut-sets.

Given a connected graph and a spanning tree, for each branch of the tree there is a unique cut-set consisting of that tree branch and nonbranch edges. Such a cut-set is called a **fundamental cut-set** (with respect to that tree).

For the graph given in Fig. 7.15, let us select the spanning tree indicated by the colored edges in Fig. 7.17. The fundamental cut-set corresponding to branch e_3 is $\{e_1, e_3, e_6\}$. For branch e_4 it is $\{e_1, e_2, e_4\}$, and for branch e_5 it is $\{e_1, e_2, e_5, e_6\}$.

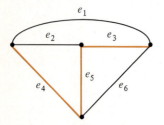

Fig. 7.17   Given graph with tree indicated.

DRILL EXERCISE 7.9

Find the fundamental cut-sets for the graph and indicated tree shown in Fig. DE7.9.

Answer: $\{e_1, e_5, e_6, e_7\}, \{e_2, e_5, e_6, e_7\}, \{e_3, e_5, e_6, e_9\}, \{e_4, e_5, e_8, e_9\}$

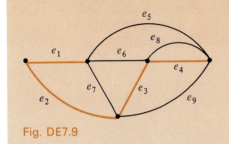

Fig. DE7.9

With these new definitions, it is now possible to give a formal procedure for obtaining state equations:

Step 1. Pick a spanning tree such that voltage sources and capacitors correspond to branches, whereas current sources and inductors correspond to nonbranch edges. Furthermore, if possible, an element whose voltage controls a dependent source should correspond to a branch, and one whose current controls a dependent source should correspond to a nonbranch edge. More than one such tree may exist—or none at all.

Step 2. Arbitrarily assign a voltage to each branch capacitor and a current to each nonbranch inductor; these are the state variables. If possible, express the voltage across each element corresponding to a branch and the current through each element corresponding to a nonbranch edge in terms of voltage sources, current sources, and state variables. If it is not possible, assign a new voltage variable to a resistor corresponding to a branch and new current variable to a resistor corresponding to a nonbranch edge.

Step 3. Apply KVL to the fundamental loop determined by each nonbranch inductor.

Step 4. Apply KCL to the node or supernode corresponding to the fundamental cut-set determined by each branch capacitor.

Step 5. Apply KVL to the fundamental loop determined by each resistor with a new current variable assigned in step 2.

Step 6. Apply KCL to the node or supernode corresponding to the fundamental cut-set determined by each resistor with a new voltage variable assigned in step 2.

Step 7. Solve the simultaneous equations obtained from steps 5 and 6 for the new variables in terms of the voltage sources, current sources, and state variables.

Step 8. Substitute the expressions obtained in step 7 into the equations determined in steps 3 and 4.

●

EXAMPLE 7.12

For the circuit shown in Fig. 7.18, the tree selected is indicated with bold lines. According to step 1, the only option available is to choose between R_1 and R_2 as a tree element. The former choice was made arbitrarily, as was the polarity of the voltage across the capacitor and the direction of the current through the inductor. Since the voltage across R_1 cannot be expressed readily in terms of v_s, v_C, and i, according to step 2, we assign the new variable v_1. Similarly, we assign the current i_2.

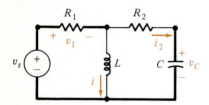

Fig. 7.18   Circuit for Example 7.12.

From step 3,

$$L\frac{di}{dt} = -v_1 + v_s \quad \Rightarrow \quad \frac{di}{dt} = -\frac{1}{L}v_1 + \frac{1}{L}v_s \tag{7.14}$$

and from step 4 we have

$$i_2 = C\frac{dv_C}{dt} \quad \Rightarrow \quad \frac{dv_C}{dt} = \frac{1}{C}i_2 \tag{7.15}$$

From step 5, we have

$$-i_2 R_2 = v_C - v_s + v_1 \tag{7.16}$$

and, from step 6,

$$\frac{v_1}{R_1} = i_2 + i \tag{7.17}$$

Solving Equations (7.16) and (7.17) for v_1 and i_2 in terms of v_s, v_C, and i, we get

$$i_2 = \frac{-R_1}{R_1 + R_2}i - \frac{1}{R_1 + R_2}v_C + \frac{1}{R_1 + R_2}v_s$$

and

$$v_1 = \frac{R_1 R_2}{R_1 + R_2}i - \frac{R_1}{R_1 + R_2}v_C + \frac{R_1}{R_1 + R_2}v_s$$

Substituting these expressions for i_2 and v_1 into Equations (7.14) and (7.15) results in the state equations

$$\frac{di}{dt} = \frac{-R_1 R_2}{L(R_1 + R_2)} i + \frac{R_1}{L(R_1 + R_2)} v_C + \frac{R_2}{L(R_1 + R_2)} v_s$$

$$\frac{dv_C}{dt} = \frac{-R_1}{C(R_1 + R_2)} i - \frac{1}{C(R_1 + R_2)} v_C + \frac{1}{C(R_1 + R_2)} v_s$$

DRILL EXERCISE 7.10

Write the matrix state equation for the circuit shown in Fig. DE7.10.

Answer: $\dfrac{d}{dt}\begin{bmatrix} i \\ v \end{bmatrix} = \begin{bmatrix} -4 & -2 \\ \frac{4}{3} & -1 \end{bmatrix}\begin{bmatrix} i \\ v \end{bmatrix} + \begin{bmatrix} 2 \\ \frac{1}{3} \end{bmatrix} v_s$

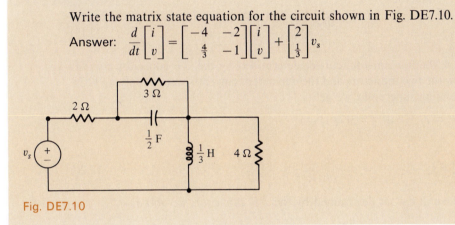

Fig. DE7.10

EXAMPLE 7.13

The circuit shown in Fig. 7.19 contains a current-dependent current source and four state variables: i_1, i_2, v_1, and v_2. Let us find the matrix state equation for this circuit.

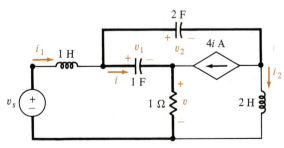

Fig. 7.19   Circuit with four state variables.

According to step 1, the two capacitors and the voltage source correspond to branches, whereas the inductors and current source do not. Consequently, the 1-Ω resistor must correspond to a branch. Thus, it is not possible to have the element (the 1-F capacitor) whose current controls the dependent current source correspond to a nonbranch edge.

According to step 2, we assign capacitor voltages and inductor currents as shown. Since an expression, in terms of the voltage source and the state variables, for the voltage across the 1-Ω resistor may not be immediately recognizable, we assign the new variable, v.

From step 3, for the 1-H inductor,

$$1 \frac{di_1}{dt} = v_s - v - v_1 \tag{7.18}$$

and, for the 2-H inductor,

$$2 \frac{di_2}{dt} = v_1 - v_2 + v \quad \Rightarrow \quad \frac{di_2}{dt} = \frac{1}{2} v_1 - \frac{1}{2} v_2 + \frac{1}{2} v \tag{7.19}$$

For step 4, the fundamental cut-set determined by the 1-F capacitor consists of the capacitor, the two inductors and the dependent current source. Applying KCL to the corresponding supernode, we get

$$i + 4i = i_1 - i_2 \quad \Rightarrow \quad 5i = i_1 - i_2$$

Thus,

$$5 \left(1 \frac{dv_1}{dt} \right) = i_1 - i_2 \quad \Rightarrow \quad \frac{dv_1}{dt} = \frac{1}{5} i_1 - \frac{1}{5} i_2 \tag{7.20}$$

For the fundamental cut-set determined by the 2-F capacitor, we obtain

$$2 \frac{dv_2}{dt} = 4i + i_2 \quad \Rightarrow \quad \frac{dv_2}{dt} = 2i + \frac{1}{2} i_2 \tag{7.21}$$

From step 6, the fundamental cut-set determined by the 1-Ω resistor consists of the resistor and the two inductors. Applying KCL to the correspond supernode, we get

$$\frac{v}{1} = i_1 - i_2$$

Substituting this result into Equations (7.18) and (7.19) yields the state equations

$$\frac{di_1}{dt} = -i_1 + i_2 - v_1 + v_s$$

and

$$\frac{di_2}{dt} = \frac{1}{2} i_1 - \frac{1}{2} i_2 + \frac{1}{2} v_1 - \frac{1}{2} v_2$$

Equation (7.20) is already a state equation. To convert Equation (7.21) into a state equation, we use the fact that, by KCL,

$$i + 4i = \frac{v}{1} \quad \Rightarrow \quad 5i = v \quad \Rightarrow \quad i = \frac{1}{5} v = \frac{1}{5} i_1 - \frac{1}{5} i_2$$

Substituting this into Equation (7.21), we get the final state equation

$$\frac{dv_2}{dt} = \frac{2}{5}i_1 + \frac{1}{10}i_2$$

Therefore, the matrix state equation is

$$\frac{d}{dt}\begin{bmatrix} i_1 \\ i_2 \\ v_1 \\ v_2 \end{bmatrix} = \begin{bmatrix} -1 & 1 & -1 & 0 \\ \frac{1}{2} & -\frac{1}{2} & \frac{1}{2} & -\frac{1}{2} \\ \frac{1}{5} & -\frac{1}{5} & 0 & 0 \\ \frac{2}{5} & \frac{1}{10} & 0 & 0 \end{bmatrix}\begin{bmatrix} i_1 \\ i_2 \\ v_1 \\ v_2 \end{bmatrix} + \begin{bmatrix} 1 \\ 0 \\ 0 \\ 0 \end{bmatrix}v_s$$

DRILL EXERCISE 7.11

Write the matrix state equation for the circuit shown in Fig. DE.7.11.
Answer:

$$\frac{d}{dt}\begin{bmatrix} i_1 \\ i_2 \\ v_C \end{bmatrix} = \begin{bmatrix} 0 & 0 & \frac{4}{7} \\ 0 & 0 & -3 \\ -4 & 4 & -\frac{4}{7} \end{bmatrix}\begin{bmatrix} i_1 \\ i_2 \\ v_C \end{bmatrix} + \begin{bmatrix} \frac{10}{7} \\ 3 \\ \frac{4}{7} \end{bmatrix}v_s$$

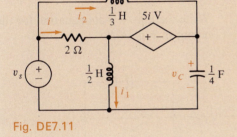

Fig. DE7.11

● SUMMARY

1. The currents through the inductors and the voltages across the capacitors describe the state of a circuit. These voltages and currents are the state variables.

2. An nth-order circuit can be described by a set of n first-order differential equations whose variables are the state variables.

3. These simultaneous equations can be written as a single matrix state equation.

4. The zero-input or zero-state responses of a circuit can be determined by numerical techniques.

5. The numerical-solution approach allows for the analysis of circuits with nonzero inputs and initial conditions as well.

● PROBLEMS FOR CHAPTER 7

7.1 Write the state equation for the zero-input circuit shown in Fig. P7.1.

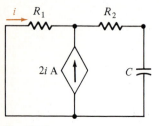

Fig. P7.1

7.2 Write the matrix state equation for the zero-input circuit in Fig. P7.2.

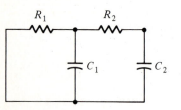

Fig. P7.2

7.3 For the circuit given in Fig. P7.2, replace the capacitors with inductors and repeat Problem 7.2.

7.4 For the circuit given in Fig. P7.1, replace R_2 with an inductor and write the resulting matrix state equation.

7.5 Write the matrix state equation for the circuit in Fig. P7.5.

7.6 Write the matrix state equation for the circuit in Fig. P7.6.

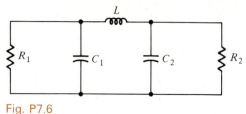

Fig. P7.6

7.7 Write the matrix state equation for the circuit in Fig. P7.7.

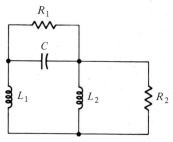

Fig. P7.7

7.8 Write the matrix state equation for the circuit in Fig. P7.8.

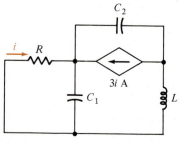

Fig. P7.8

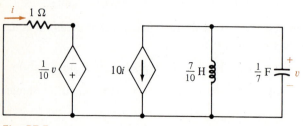

Fig. P7.5

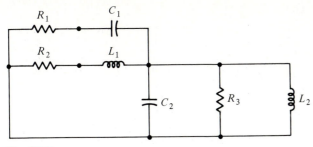

Fig. P7.9

7.9 Write the matrix state equation for the circuit in Fig. P7.9.

7.10 Write the matrix state equation for the circuit in Fig. P7.10.

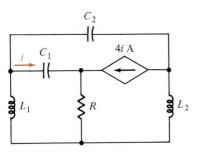

Fig. P7.10

7.11 For the simple *RC* circuit shown in Fig. P7.11, use Euler's method, with $\Delta t = 0.001$ s, to determine a sufficient number of values to plot $v(t)$ in the interval
  (a) 0–1 s, given that $R = 4\,\Omega$ and $v(0) = 8$ V.
  (b) 1–3 s, given that $R = 2.4\,\Omega$ and $v(1) = 2.943$ V.

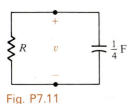

Fig. P7.11

7.12 For the series *RLC* circuit in Fig. P7.12 given the initial conditions $i(0) = 1$ A

and $v(0) = 2$ V, use Euler's method, with $\Delta t = 0.001$ s, to plot $i(t)$ and $v(t)$ in the interval 0–2 s.

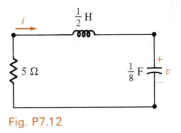

Fig. P7.12

7.13 Repeat Problem 7.12 for the parallel *RLC* circuit in Fig. P7.13 subject to the initial conditions $i(0) = 1$ A and $v(0) = -0.14$ V.

7.14 For the series-parallel *RLC* circuit in Fig. P7.14, given the initial conditions

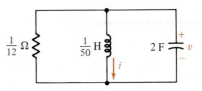

Fig. P7.13

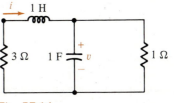

Fig. P7.14

$i(0) = 1$ A and $v(0) = 2$ V, use Euler's method, with $\Delta t = 0.001$ s, to plot $i(t)$ and $v(t)$ in the interval 0–2.5 s.

7.15 For the circuit shown in Fig. P7.15, repeat Problem 7.14 for the interval 0–4 s, and subject to the initial conditions $i(0) = 1$ A and $v(0) = 1$ V.

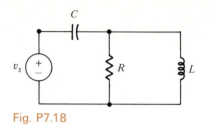

Fig. P7.18

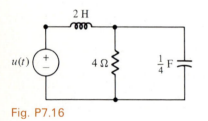

Fig. P7.15

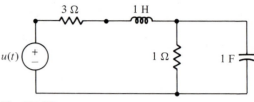

Fig. P7.19

7.16 Write the matrix state equation for the circuit shown in Fig. P7.16.

7.20 Write the matrix state equation for the circuit in Fig. P7.20.

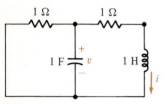

Fig. P7.16

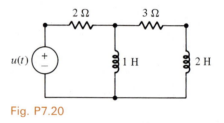

Fig. P7.20

7.17 Write the matrix state equation for the circuit shown in Fig. P7.17.

7.21 Write the matrix state equation for the circuit shown in Fig. P7.21.

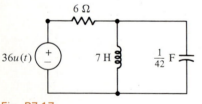

Fig. P7.17

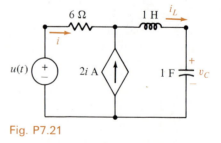

Fig. P7.21

7.18 Write the matrix state equation for the circuit shown in Fig. P7.18.

7.19 For the circuit in Fig. P7.19, write the matrix state equation.

7.22 For the circuit in Fig. P7.22, write the matrix state equation.

7.23 Write the matrix state equation for the circuit in Fig. P6.40 (p. 311).

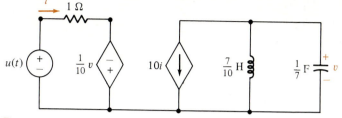

Fig. P7.22

7.24 For the circuit given in Fig. P6.40 (p. 311), replace the $\frac{1}{4}$-H inductor with a 1-F capacitor, and write the matrix state equation for the resulting circuit.

7.25 Write the matrix state equation for the op-amp circuit shown in Fig. P7.25.

7.26 Write the matrix state equation for the op-amp circuit shown in Fig. P7.26.

7.27 Write the matrix state equation for the op-amp circuit shown in Fig. P7.27.

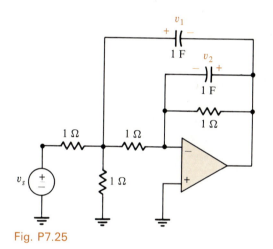

Fig. P7.25

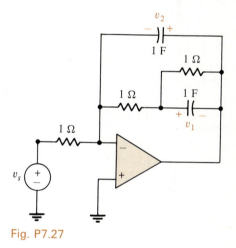

Fig. P7.27

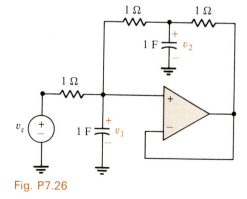

Fig. P7.26

7.28 Write the matrix state equation for the circuit shown in Fig. 7.11 (p. 333).

7.29 Use Euler's method to find the zero-state response of a series RLC circuit ($R = 12\ \Omega$, $L = 2$ H, $C = \frac{1}{50}$ F) whose input voltage is $0.4u(t)$ V. Use $\Delta t = 0.001$ s and plot $i_L(t)$ and $v_C(t)$ up to $t = 2$ s.

7.30 For the circuit given in Fig. P7.16, find the zero-state step responses $i_L(t)$ and $v_C(t)$ using Euler's method. Use $\Delta t = 0.001$ s and plot $i_L(t)$ and $v_C(t)$ up to $t = 10$ s.

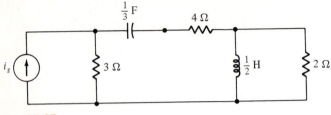

Fig. P7.37

7.31 For the circuit given in Fig. P7.17, use Euler's method to find the inductor current $i_L(t)$ (directed downward) and the capacitor voltage $v(t)$ (plus on the top plate) given that $i_L(0) = -4$ A and $v(0) = 0$ V. Use $\Delta t = 0.001$ s and plot $i_L(t)$ and $v_C(t)$ up to $t = 5$ s.

7.32 Use Euler's method to find the zero-state step responses $i_L(t)$ and $v_C(t)$ for the circuit given in Fig. 7.8 (p. 328), where $R_1 = R_2 = 1\,\Omega$, $L = 1$ H, and $C = 1$ F. Use $\Delta t = 0.001$ s and plot $i_L(t)$ and $v_C(t)$ up to $t = 4$ s.

7.33 Repeat Problem 7.32 for the circuit given in Fig. P7.21.

7.34 For the circuit given in Fig. P7.22, find the zero-state step response $v(t)$ using Euler's method.

7.35 Repeat Problem 7.34 given that the input voltage is $|10 \sin 2\pi t| u(t)$ V.

7.36 For the circuit given in Fig. DE7.10 (p. 339) change the $\frac{1}{2}$-F capacitor to a $\frac{1}{2}$-H inductor, and write the matrix state equation for the resulting circuit.

7.37 For the circuit in Fig. P7.37, write the matrix state equation.

7.38 For the circuit in Fig. P7.38, write the matrix state equation.

7.39 Write the matrix state equation for the circuit in Fig. P7.39.

7.40 For the circuit in Fig. P7.40, write the matrix state equation.

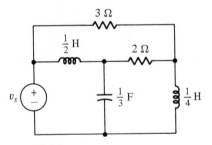

Fig. P7.39

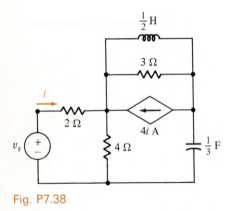

Fig. P7.38

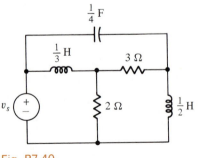

Fig. P7.40

Sinusoidal Analysis

● INTRODUCTION

Step and impulse functions are useful in determining the responses of circuits when they are first turned on or when sudden or irregular changes occur in the input; this is called **transient analysis**. However, to see how a circuit responds to a regular or repetitive input—the **steady-state analysis**—the function that is by far the most useful is the sinusoid.

The sinusoid is an extremely important and ubiquitous function. To begin with, the shape of ordinary household voltage is sinusoidal. Consumer radio transmissions are either amplitude modulation (AM), in which the amplitude of a sinusoid is changed or modulated according to some information signal, or frequency modulation (FM), in which the frequency of a sinusoid is modulated. Consumer television uses AM for the picture (video) and FM for the sound (audio). Sinusoids even occur in subtle ways, for as we shall see in Chapter 13 (Fourier series), a nonsinusoidal waveform (like a sawtooth or a pulse train) is in essence just a sum of sinusoids! For these reasons and more, sinusoidal analysis is a fundamental topic in the study of electric circuits.

In this chapter we shall see that although we can analyze sinusoidal circuits with the techniques discussed previously, by generalizing the sinusoid we can perform analysis in a more simplified manner that avoids the direct solution of differential equations.

8.1 TIME-DOMAIN ANALYSIS

Of all the functions encountered in electrical engineering, perhaps the most important is the sinusoid.

From trigonometry, recall the plot of $\cos x$ versus the angle x (whose units are radians) shown in Fig. 8.1(a). By changing the angle from x to ωt, we get the plot shown in Fig. 8.1(b), where t is time in seconds, so that ω must be in radians per second (rad/s). We say that ω is the **radian** or **angular frequency** of $\cos \omega t$. To plot $\cos \omega t$ versus time t, divide the numbers on the horizontal axis (abscissa) by ω. The result is shown in Fig. 8.1(c). From this plot, it is easy to see that this function goes through a complete cycle in $2\pi/\omega$ seconds. We call the time to complete one cycle the **period** of the sinusoid and denote it by T, that is, the number of seconds per cycle is

$$T = \frac{2\pi}{\omega} \quad \text{seconds}$$

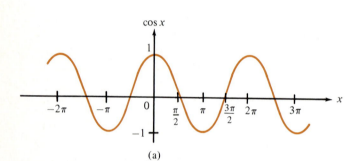

(a)

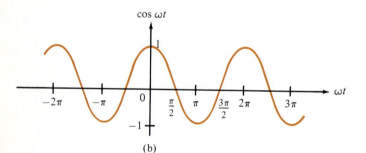

(b)

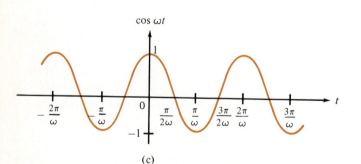

(c)

Fig. 8.1   Cosine function versus angle [(a) and (b)] and versus time (c).

The inverse of this quantity is the number of cycles that occur in one second. That is, the number of cycles per second is

$$\frac{1}{T} = \frac{\omega}{2\pi} \qquad \frac{1}{\text{seconds}}$$

The number of cycles per second is designated by f and is called the **cyclical** or **ordinary frequency** of the sinusoid. The term "cycles per second" has been replaced by "hertz" (Hz).[†] Thus, the relationships between cyclical and radian frequencies are

$$f = \frac{\omega}{2\pi} \quad \text{Hz} \qquad \text{and} \qquad \omega = 2\pi f \quad \text{rad/s}$$

To obtain a plot of the general sinusoid $\cos(\omega t + \phi)$ versus t, reconsider the plot of $\cos \omega t$ versus ωt. Replacing ωt by $\omega t + \phi$, where ϕ is a positive quantity, corresponds to translating (or shifting) the sinusoid to the left by the amount ϕ; that is, we obtain the plot shown in Fig. 8.2. Then in dividing by ω, we get the plot shown in Fig. 8.3. Of course, if ϕ is a negative quantity, the shift is to the right. We call ϕ the **phase angle** or simply **angle** of the sinusoid. Note that when $\phi = -\pi/2$ radians (-90 degrees),

$$\cos\left(\omega t - \frac{\pi}{2}\right) = \sin \omega t$$

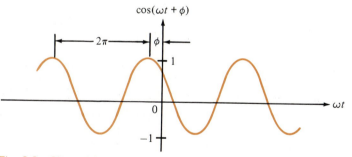

Fig. 8.2   Sinusoid versus angle.

Similarly,

$$\sin\left(\omega t + \frac{\pi}{2}\right) = \cos \omega t$$

Consider a circuit with a sinusoidal input. In general, the response consists of the natural response and the forced response. In particular, let us concentrate on the

---

[†] Named for the German physicist Heinrich Hertz (1857–1894).

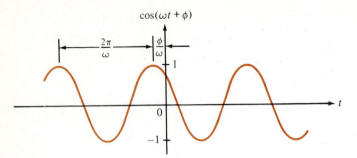

Fig. 8.3   Sinusoid versus time.

forced or steady-state response. We know that the integral or derivative of a sinusoid that has a given frequency is again a sinusoid of that frequency. For a resistor, the voltage and the current differ by a constant, while for an inductor and a capacitor, the relationships between voltage and current are given in terms of integrals and derivatives. Thus, for each of these elements, a sinusoidal excitation produces a sinusoidal response. Since adding sinusoids of frequency ω results in a single sinusoid of frequency ω [for example, see Equation (6.14) on p. 284], we can deduce that the forced response of an *RLC* circuit whose input is a sinusoid of frequency ω is also a sinusoid of frequency ω.

EXAMPLE 8.1
Consider the sinusoidal circuit shown in Fig. 8.4(a). Since

$$v_s = 1i + v_o \quad \text{and} \quad i = \frac{1}{2}\frac{dv_o}{dt}$$

then

$$\frac{dv_o}{dt} + 2v_o = 2v_s = 12\sin 2t \qquad (8.1)$$

Since the forced response is a sinusoid of frequency $\omega = 2$ rad/s, it has the general form $A\cos(2t + \phi)$. However, to avoid using the trigonometric identity for the cosine of the sum of two angles, let us use the alternative form [see Equation (6.14) on p. 284]:

$$v_o(t) = A_1\cos 2t + A_2\sin 2t$$

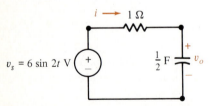

Fig. 8.4(a)   Simple sinusoidal circuit.

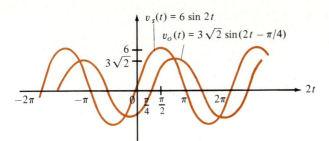

Fig. 8.4(b)   Output voltage $v_o(t)$ lags input voltage $v_s(t)$ by 45°.

Substituting this into Equation (8.1) results in

$$(-2A_1 + 2A_2)\sin 2t + (2A_1 + 2A_2)\cos 2t = 12 \sin 2t$$

Equating coefficients yields the simultaneous equations

$$-2A_1 + 2A_2 = 12 \quad \text{and} \quad 2A_1 + 2A_2 = 0$$

the solution of which is $A_1 = -3$ and $A_2 = 3$. Hence, the forced response is

$$v_o(t) = -3\cos 2t + 3\sin 2t$$

By Equation (6.14),

$$v_o(t) = 3\sqrt{2}\cos\left(2t - \frac{3\pi}{4}\right) \text{ V}$$

Also,

$$v_o(t) = 3\sqrt{2}\cos\left(2t - \frac{\pi}{2} - \frac{\pi}{4}\right) = 3\sqrt{2}\sin\left(2t - \frac{\pi}{4}\right) \text{ V}$$

A plot of the functions $v_s(t)$ and $v_o(t)$ versus ωt is shown in Fig. 8.4(b). Since $v_s(t)$ reaches its peak before $v_o(t)$, we can say that $v_s(t)$ **leads** $v_o(t)$ by $\pi/4$ radians (45°) or that $v_o(t)$ **lags** $v_s(t)$ by $\pi/4$ radians. Since the output of the circuit lags the input, the given circuit is an example of what is called a **lag network**.

The current in this circuit is

$$i(t) = C\frac{dv_o(t)}{dt} = \frac{1}{2}\frac{dv_o(t)}{dt} = \frac{1}{2}(6\sin 2t + 6\cos 2t)$$

$$= 3\cos 2t + 3\sin 2t = 3\sqrt{2}\cos\left(2t - \frac{\pi}{4}\right) \text{ A}$$

$$= 3\sqrt{2}\cos\left(2t - \frac{\pi}{2} + \frac{\pi}{4}\right) = 3\sqrt{2}\sin\left(2t + \frac{\pi}{4}\right) \text{ A}$$

Thus, the current $i(t)$ leads the voltage $v_s(t)$ by 45°, and $i(t)$ leads the voltage $v_o(t)$ by 90°.

DRILL EXERCISE 8.1

Find $i(t)$ and $v(t)$ for the circuit shown in Fig. DE8.1.
Answer: $2 \cos 2t$ A; $-8 \sin 2t$ V

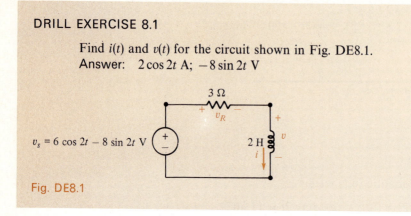

Fig. DE8.1

Having analyzed a first-order sinusoidal circuit, let us now look at an example of a second-order sinusoidal circuit.

EXAMPLE 8.2

For the series *RLC* shown in Fig. 8.5, we have already seen [Equation (6.26) on p. 295] that

$$\frac{d^2 v_C}{dt^2} + \frac{R}{L}\frac{dv_C}{dt} + \frac{1}{LC}v_C = \frac{v_s}{LC}$$

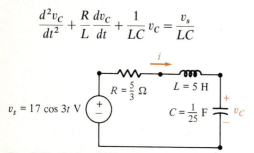

Fig. 8.5   Series *RLC* sinusoidal circuit.

Thus,

$$\frac{d^2 v_C}{dt^2} + \frac{1}{3}\frac{dv_C}{dt} + 5v_C = 85 \cos 3t$$

and the forced response has the form

$$v_C(t) = A_1 \cos 3t + A_2 \sin 3t$$

Substituting this into the differential equation and collecting terms, we get

$$(-4A_1 + A_2)\cos 3t + (-A_1 - 4A_2)\sin 3t = 85 \cos 3t$$

Equating coefficients yields the pair of simultaneous equations

$$-4A_1 + A_2 = 85 \quad \text{and} \quad -A_1 - 4A_2 = 0$$

the solution of which is $A_1 = -20$ and $A_2 = 5$. Thus,

$$v_C(t) = -20 \cos 3t + 5 \sin 3t = 5\sqrt{17} \cos(3t - 2.9 \text{ rad})$$
$$= 5\sqrt{17} \cos(3t - 166°) = 20.6 \cos(3t - 166°) \text{ V}$$

and since the angle of $v_C(t)$ is less than the angle of $v_s(t)$, $v_C(t)$ lags $v_s(t)$ by 166°.

The current is

$$i(t) = C\frac{dv_C}{dt} = \frac{1}{25}\frac{dv_C}{dt} = \frac{1}{25}\frac{d}{dt}(-20\cos 3t + 5\sin 3t)$$

$$= \frac{1}{25}(60\sin 3t + 15\cos 3t) = \frac{3\sqrt{17}}{5}\cos(3t - 1.33 \text{ rad})$$

$$= \frac{3\sqrt{17}}{5}\cos(3t - 76°) = 2.47\cos(3t - 76°) \text{ A}$$

Thus, we see that $i(t)$ lags $v_s(t)$ by 76°.

DRILL EXERCISE 8.2

Find $i_L(t)$ and $v(t)$ for the circuit shown in Fig. DE8.2.
Answer: $30 \sin 4t$ A; $15 \cos 4t$ V

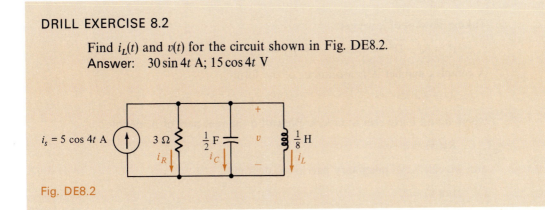

Fig. DE8.2

If two sinusoids having the same frequency reach their peak (or maximum) values at exactly the same time, we say that they are **in phase**. For example, $3 \sin 2\pi t$ and $5 \sin 2\pi t$ are in phase. So are $12 \cos(3t - \pi/12)$ and $8 \cos(3t - \pi/12)$. Even $4 \cos(\omega t - \pi/3)$ and $7 \sin(\omega t + \pi/6)$ are in phase! That's because $\sin(\omega t + \pi/2) = \cos \omega t$ means that $4 \cos(\omega t - \pi/3) = 4 \sin(\omega t + \pi/2 - \pi/3) = 4 \sin(\omega t + \pi/6)$.

For the case that one sinusoid reaches its maximum value at the exact time when a second sinusoid (of the same frequency) reaches its minimum value, we say that they are **180° out of phase**. For instance, $3 \cos \omega t$ and $-4 \cos \omega t = 4 \cos(\omega t - \pi) = 4 \cos(\omega t + \pi)$ are 180° out of phase. In general, $A \cos(\omega t + \phi)$ and $-A \cos(\omega t + \phi)$ are 180° out of phase.

When referring to two sinusoids of the same frequency, if they are not in phase or 180° out of phase, we shall say that one leads or lags the other by an amount between 0° and 180°. For example, given that $v_1(t) = 3 \cos(\omega t + 70°)$ and $v_2(t) =$

$\cos(\omega t - 150°)$, instead of saying that $v_1(t)$ leads $v_2(t)$ by 220°, we shall say that $v_1(t)$ lags $v_2(t)$ by 140° (or, equivalently, $v_2(t)$ leads $v_1(t)$ by 140°).

In general, given sinusoids $A\cos(\omega t + \theta)$ and $B\cos(\omega t + \phi)$, if $\theta > \phi$ and $0 < \theta - \phi < 180°$, then $A\cos(\omega t + \theta)$ leads $B\cos(\omega t + \phi)$ by $\theta - \phi$ [or $B\cos(\omega t + \phi)$ lags $A\cos(\omega t + \theta)$ by $\theta - \phi$].

As indicated by the preceding examples, sinusoidal analysis is straightforward. However, the amount of arithmetic required can be extremely tedious. A lot of drudgery involved in analyzing sinusoidal circuits can be eliminated if we utilize the concept of a complex sinusoid and the property of linearity. Such an approach not only will be numerically advantageous, but will give rise to concepts that will prove invaluable in the future. To proceed, though, it will be necessary to study complex numbers.

8.2 COMPLEX NUMBERS

As mentioned previously, we designate the constant $\sqrt{-1}$ by j, that is,

$$j = \sqrt{-1}$$

Taking powers of j, we get

$$j^2 = (\sqrt{-1})^2 = -1 \qquad j^3 = j^2 j = -j \qquad \cdots$$

A **complex number** $\mathbf{A}$ is a number of the form

$$\mathbf{A} = a + jb$$

where a and b are real numbers. We call a the **real part** of $\mathbf{A}$, denoted

$$\text{Re}(\mathbf{A}) = a$$

and we call b the **imaginary part** of $\mathbf{A}$, denoted

$$\text{Im}(\mathbf{A}) = b$$

If $a = 0$, we say that $\mathbf{A}$ is **purely imaginary**, and if $b = 0$, we say that $\mathbf{A}$ is **purely real**. Two complex numbers $\mathbf{A}_1 = a_1 + jb_1$ and $\mathbf{A}_2 = a_2 + jb_2$ are **equal** if both

$$a_1 = a_2 \qquad \text{and} \qquad b_1 = b_2$$

The **sum** of two complex numbers is

$$\mathbf{A}_1 + \mathbf{A}_2 = (a_1 + jb_1) + (a_2 + jb_2) = (a_1 + a_2) + j(b_1 + b_2)$$

and the **difference** is

$$\mathbf{A}_1 - \mathbf{A}_2 = (a_1 + jb_1) - (a_2 + jb_2) = (a_1 - a_2) + j(b_1 - b_2)$$

The **complex conjugate** of $\mathbf{A} = a + jb$ is denoted by $\mathbf{A}^*$ and is defined as

$$\mathbf{A}^* = a - jb$$

The **product** of two complex numbers is

$$\mathbf{A}_1\mathbf{A}_2 = (a_1 + jb_1)(a_2 + jb_2) = a_1a_2 + ja_1b_2 + ja_2b_1 + j^2b_1b_2$$
$$= (a_1a_2 - b_1b_2) + j(a_1b_2 + a_2b_1)$$

and the **quotient** is

$$\frac{\mathbf{A}_1}{\mathbf{A}_2} = \frac{a_1 + jb_1}{a_2 + jb_2} = \frac{(a_1 + jb_1)(a_2 - jb_2)}{(a_2 + jb_2)(a_2 - jb_2)} = \frac{a_1a_2 + b_1b_2}{a_2^2 + b_2^2} + j\frac{b_1a_2 - a_1b_2}{a_2^2 + b_2^2}$$

Although addition and subtraction of complex numbers are simple operations, multiplication and division are a little more complicated. This is a consequence of the form of a complex number, that is, a complex number $\mathbf{A}$ can be written as $\mathbf{A} = a + jb$. We call this the **rectangular form** of the complex number $\mathbf{A}$. Fortunately, there is an alternative form for a complex number that lends itself very nicely to multiplication and division, although not to addition and subtraction. To develop this form, we first derive Euler's[†] formula, which was mentioned earlier on p. 282.

Let θ be a real variable. Define the function $f(\theta)$ by

$$f(\theta) = \cos\theta + j\sin\theta$$

Taking the derivative with respect to θ yields

$$\frac{df(\theta)}{d\theta} = -\sin\theta + j\cos\theta = j^2\sin\theta + j\cos\theta = j(\cos\theta + j\sin\theta) = jf(\theta)$$

from which

$$j = \frac{1}{f(\theta)}\frac{df(\theta)}{d\theta}$$

Integrating both sides with respect to θ results in

$$\int j\,d\theta = \int \frac{1}{f(\theta)}\frac{df(\theta)}{d\theta}\,d\theta = \int \frac{df(\theta)}{f(\theta)}$$

Integrating yields

$$j\theta' + K = \ln f(\theta) = \ln(\cos\theta + j\sin\theta)$$

where K is a constant of integration. Setting $\theta = 0$ gives

$$K = \ln 1 = 0$$

so

$$j\theta = \ln(\cos\theta + j\sin\theta)$$

[†] Named for the Swiss mathematician Leonhard Euler (1707–1783).

Taking powers of e, we get

$$e^{j\theta} = \cos\theta + j\sin\theta \qquad (8.2)$$

and this result is know as **Euler's formula**. Replacing θ by $-\theta$, we obtain another version:

$$e^{-j\theta} = \cos\theta - j\sin\theta \qquad (8.3)$$

Thus, we see that $e^{j\theta}$ is a complex number such that

$$\text{Re}(e^{j\theta}) = \cos\theta \qquad \text{and} \qquad \text{Im}(e^{j\theta}) = \sin\theta$$

By adding and subtracting Equations (8.2) and (8.3), we can get, respectively,

$$\cos\theta = \frac{1}{2}(e^{j\theta} + e^{-j\theta}) \qquad \text{and} \qquad \sin\theta = \frac{1}{2j}(e^{j\theta} - e^{-j\theta}) \qquad (8.4)$$

If M is a constant, then

$$Me^{j\theta} = M(\cos\theta + j\sin\theta) = M\cos\theta + jM\sin\theta$$

is a complex number where

$$\text{Re}(Me^{j\theta}) = M\cos\theta \qquad \text{and} \qquad \text{Im}(Me^{j\theta}) = M\sin\theta$$

Given a (nonzero) complex number $\mathbf{A} = a + jb$, is there a complex number of the form $Me^{j\theta}$ (where $M > 0$) that equals $\mathbf{A}$? If there is, then

$$a + jb = M\cos\theta + jM\sin\theta$$

or

$$a = M\cos\theta \qquad \text{and} \qquad b = M\sin\theta$$

so

$$\cos\theta = a/M \qquad \text{and} \qquad \sin\theta = b/M$$

from which

$$\tan\theta = \frac{\sin\theta}{\cos\theta} = \frac{b/M}{a/M} = \frac{b}{a} \qquad \Rightarrow \qquad \theta = \tan^{-1}\left(\frac{b}{a}\right)$$

Pictorially, we have the right triangle shown in Fig. 8.6. Thus,

$$a = M\cos\theta \qquad \Rightarrow \qquad M = \frac{a}{\cos\theta} = \frac{a}{a/\sqrt{a^2 + b^2}} = \sqrt{a^2 + b^2}$$

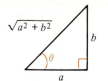

Fig. 8.6   Right triangle describing angle θ.

In summary,

$$a + jb = Me^{j\theta}$$

when

$$M = \sqrt{a^2 + b^2}$$
$$\theta = \tan^{-1}\left(\frac{b}{a}\right)$$

or

$$a = M \cos \theta$$
$$b = M \sin \theta$$

We say that $Me^{j\theta}$ is the **exponential** (or **polar**) **form** of a (nonzero) complex number, where the positive number M is called the **magnitude** and θ is called the **angle** (or **argument**) of the complex number. We denote the magnitude of **A** by $|\mathbf{A}|$ and the angle of **A** by ang(**A**).

Note that by using the exponential forms of the complex numbers $\mathbf{A}_1 = M_1 e^{j\theta_1}$ and $\mathbf{A}_2 = M_2 e^{j\theta_2}$, the product is

$$\mathbf{A}_1 \mathbf{A}_2 = (M_1 e^{j\theta_1})(M_2 e^{j\theta_2}) = M_1 M_2 e^{j(\theta_1 + \theta_2)}$$

Thus,

$$|\mathbf{A}_1 \mathbf{A}_2| = M_1 M_2 = |\mathbf{A}_1||\mathbf{A}_2| \qquad \text{ang}(\mathbf{A}_1 \mathbf{A}_2) = \theta_1 + \theta_2 = \text{ang}(\mathbf{A}_1) + \text{ang}(\mathbf{A}_2)$$

The quotient is

$$\frac{\mathbf{A}_1}{\mathbf{A}_2} = \frac{M_1 e^{j\theta_1}}{M_2 e^{j\theta_2}} = \frac{M_1}{M_2} e^{j(\theta_1 - \theta_2)}$$

Thus,

$$\left|\frac{\mathbf{A}_1}{\mathbf{A}_2}\right| = \frac{M_1}{M_2} = \frac{|\mathbf{A}_1|}{|\mathbf{A}_2|} \qquad \text{ang}\left(\frac{\mathbf{A}_1}{\mathbf{A}_2}\right) = \theta_1 - \theta_2 = \text{ang}(\mathbf{A}_1) - \text{ang}(\mathbf{A}_2)$$

Note that

$$(Me^{j\theta})^* = (M \cos \theta + jM \sin \theta)^* = M \cos \theta - jM \sin \theta = Me^{-j\theta}$$

Furthermore, if $\mathbf{A}_1 = \mathbf{A}_2$, then $M_1 = M_2$ and $\theta_1 = \theta_2$.

EXAMPLE 8.3

If

$$\mathbf{A}_1 = -3 + j4 = M_1 e^{j\theta_1} \quad \text{and} \quad \mathbf{A}_2 = -5 - j12 = M_2 e^{j\theta_2}$$

then

$$|\mathbf{A}_1| = M_1 = \sqrt{(-3)^2 + (4)^2} = 5 \quad \text{and} \quad |\mathbf{A}_2| = M_2 = \sqrt{(-5)^2 + (-12)^2} = 13$$

Also,

$$\theta_1 = \tan^{-1}\left(\frac{4}{-3}\right) = 2.21 \text{ rad} = 126.9°$$

and

$$\theta_2 = \tan^{-1}\left(\frac{-12}{-5}\right) = -1.97 \text{ rad} = -112.6°$$

Thus,

$$\mathbf{A}_1\mathbf{A}_2 = 5e^{j126.9°}13e^{-j112.6°} = 5(13)e^{j(126.9°-112.6°)} = 65e^{j14.3°}$$

Also,

$$\mathbf{A}_1\mathbf{A}_2 = 65\cos(14.3°) + j65\sin(14.3°) = 63.0 + j16.1$$

DRILL EXERCISE 8.3

Given $\mathbf{A}_1 = 10e^{j36.87°}$ and $\mathbf{A}_2 = 13e^{-j67.38°}$, find $\mathbf{A}_1 + \mathbf{A}_2$ in (a) rectangular form and (b) exponential form.
Answer: (a) $13.0 - j6.0$; (b) $14.32e^{-j24.78°}$

8.3 FREQUENCY-DOMAIN ANALYSIS

Given a linear circuit whose input is the sinusoid $A\cos(\omega t + \theta)$, the forced response is a sinusoid of frequency ω, say $B\cos(\omega t + \phi)$. If the input is delayed by 90°, that is, if the input is $A\sin(\omega t + \theta)$, then by the time-invariance property, the corresponding response is $B\sin(\omega t + \phi)$. Furthermore, if the input is scaled by a constant K, then by the property of linearity, so will be the response; that is, the response to $KA\sin(\omega t + \theta)$ is $KB\sin(\omega t + \phi)$. Again, by linearity, the response to

$$A\cos(\omega t + \theta) + KA\sin(\omega t + \theta)$$

is

$$B\cos(\omega t + \phi) + KB\sin(\omega t + \phi)$$

These situations are summarized symbolically by Fig. 8.7.

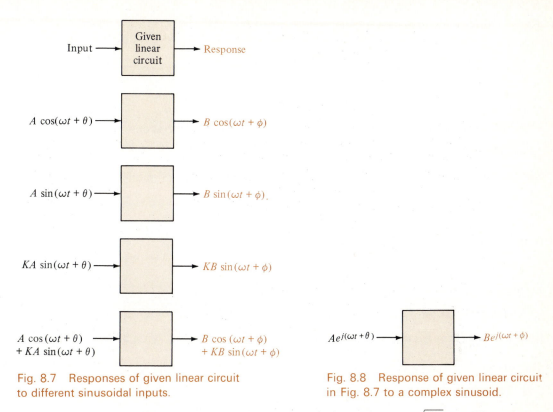

Fig. 8.7   Responses of given linear circuit to different sinusoidal inputs.

Fig. 8.8   Response of given linear circuit in Fig. 8.7 to a complex sinusoid.

Consider now the special case that the constant $K = \sqrt{-1} = j$. Thus, the response to

$$A \cos(\omega t + \theta) + jA \sin(\omega t + \theta) = Ae^{j(\omega t + \theta)}$$

is

$$B \cos(\omega t + \phi) + jB \sin(\omega t + \phi) = Be^{j(\omega t + \phi)}$$

This situation is depicted in Fig. 8.8.

We therefore see that whether we wish to find the response to $A \cos(\omega t + \theta)$ or the response to $Ae^{j(\omega t + \theta)}$, we must determine the same two constants B and ϕ. We have seen examples of what it is like to find a response when the input is the sinusoid $A \cos(\omega t + \theta)$. Now let us look at an example of finding the response to the **complex sinusoid** $Ae^{j(\omega t + \theta)}$.

EXAMPLE 8.4

Reconsider the RC circuit shown in Fig. 8.4(a) on p. 350. We have already seen [Equation (8.1) on p. 350] that

$$\frac{dv_o}{dt} + 2v_o = 2v_s$$

The forced response to

$$v_s(t) = 6 \sin 2t = 6 \cos\left(2t - \frac{\pi}{2}\right) = A \cos(\omega t + \theta)$$

is

$$v_o(t) = B \cos(2t + \phi)$$

Instead of solving directly for B and ϕ, let us use the fact that the response to

$$v_s(t) = A e^{j(\omega t + \theta)} = 6 e^{j(2t - \pi/2)} \qquad \text{is} \qquad v_o(t) = B e^{j(2t + \phi)}$$

Substituting this into the above differential equation yields

$$\frac{d}{dt}(Be^{j(2t + \phi)}) + 2(Be^{j(2t + \phi)}) = 12 e^{j(2t - \pi/2)}$$

from which

$$2jBe^{j2t}e^{j\phi} + 2Be^{j2t}e^{j\phi} = 12 e^{j2t}e^{-j\pi/2}$$

Dividing both sides by $2e^{j2t}$ gives

$$(j + 1)Be^{j\phi} = 6e^{-j\pi/2}$$

from which

$$Be^{j\phi} = \frac{6}{1 + j}e^{-j\pi/2} = \frac{6(1 - j)}{(1 + j)(1 - j)}e^{-j\pi/2} = \frac{6(1 - j)}{1 + j - j - j^2}e^{-j\pi/2}$$

$$= 3(1 - j)e^{-j\pi/2} = 3(\sqrt{2}e^{-j\pi/4})e^{-j\pi/2} = 3\sqrt{2}e^{-j3\pi/4}$$

Thus $B = 3\sqrt{2}$ and $\phi = -3\pi/4$. We conclude therefore that the response to

$$v_s(t) = 6e^{j(2t - \pi/2)} \text{ V} \qquad \text{is} \qquad v_o(t) = 3\sqrt{2}e^{j(2t - 3\pi/4)} \text{ V}$$

and using the same values for B and ϕ, therefore, the response to

$$v_s(t) = 6 \sin 2t = 6 \cos\left(2t - \frac{\pi}{2}\right) = A \cos(\omega t + \theta)$$

is

$$v_o(t) = B \cos(\omega t + \phi) = 3\sqrt{2}\cos\left(2t - \frac{3\pi}{4}\right) = 3\sqrt{2}\sin\left(2t - \frac{\pi}{4}\right) \text{ V}$$

DRILL EXERCISE 8.4

For the circuit given in Fig. DE8.1, suppose that $v_s(t) = 6e^{j2t}$ V. Find $i(t)$. What is $i(t)$ when $v_s(t) = 6 \cos 2t$ V?
Answer: $1.2e^{j(2t - 53.13°)}$ A; $1.2 \cos(2t - 53.13°)$ A

Although it may be somewhat easier computationally to find the response to a (real) sinusoid by considering the corresponding complex sinusoidal case instead, the determination of the appropriate differential equation is still required. By intro-ducing certain important concepts, however, we will be able to eliminate this require-ment, and the result will be the simplification of sinusoidal analysis.

Phasors

Just as the sinusoid $A\cos(\omega t + \theta)$ has frequency ω, amplitude A, and phase angle θ, we can say that the complex sinusoid

$$Ae^{j(\omega t + \theta)} = Ae^{j\theta}e^{j\omega t}$$

also has frequency ω, amplitude A, and phase angle θ. Let us denote the complex number

$$\mathbf{A} = Ae^{j\theta}$$

by

$$\mathbf{A} = A\underline{/\theta}$$

which is known as the **phasor** representation of the (real or complex) sinusoid.

Why do we do this? We begin to answer this question by considering a resistor. If the current is a complex sinusoid, say, $i = Ie^{j(\omega t + \theta)}$, then so is the voltage, say, $v = Ve^{j(\omega t + \phi)}$. Thus, by Ohm's law,

$$v = Ri$$

$$Ve^{j(\omega t + \phi)} = RIe^{j(\omega t + \theta)}$$

$$Ve^{j\omega t}e^{j\phi} = RIe^{j\omega t}e^{j\theta}$$

and dividing by $e^{j\omega t}$ yields

$$Ve^{j\phi} = RIe^{j\theta}$$

From this equation, we deduce that $V = RI$ and $\phi = \theta$. Using the phasor forms of the voltage and current, we can write

$$V\underline{/\phi} = RI\underline{/\theta}$$

Thus, we have the phasor equation

$$\boxed{\mathbf{V} = R\mathbf{I}}$$

where $\mathbf{V} = V\underline{/\phi}$ and $\mathbf{I} = I\underline{/\theta}$. Since $\phi = \theta$, the voltage and the current are in phase for a resistor.

For an inductor, if $i = Ie^{j(\omega t + \theta)}$ and $v = Ve^{j(\omega t + \phi)}$, then

$$v = L\frac{di}{dt}$$

$$Ve^{j(\omega t + \phi)} = L\frac{d}{dt}\left(Ie^{j(\omega t + \theta)}\right)$$

$$Ve^{j\omega t}e^{j\phi} = j\omega LIe^{j\omega t}e^{j\theta} \qquad \Rightarrow \qquad Ve^{j\phi} = j\omega LIe^{j\theta}$$

and using the phasor forms of voltage and current

$$V\underline{/\phi} = j\omega LI\underline{/\theta}$$

Therefore,

$$\boxed{\mathbf{V} = j\omega L\mathbf{I}}$$

where $\mathbf{V} = V\underline{/\phi}$ and $\mathbf{I} = I\underline{/\theta}$. Note that since

$$\text{ang}(\mathbf{V}) = \text{ang}(j\omega L\mathbf{I}) = \text{ang}(j\omega L) + \text{ang}(\mathbf{I})$$

then

$$\phi = 90° + \theta \quad\Rightarrow\quad \theta = \phi - 90°$$

Thus, we see that for an inductor, the current lags the voltage by 90°.

For a capacitor, if $i = Ie^{j(\omega t + \theta)}$ and $v = Ve^{j(\omega t + \phi)}$, then

$$i = C\frac{dv}{dt}$$

$$Ie^{j(\omega t + \theta)} = C\frac{d}{dt}(Ve^{j(\omega t + \phi)})$$

$$Ie^{j\omega t}e^{j\theta} = j\omega CVe^{j\omega t}e^{j\phi} \quad\Rightarrow\quad Ie^{j\theta} = j\omega CVe^{j\phi}$$

and

$$I\underline{/\theta} = j\omega CV\underline{/\phi} \quad\Rightarrow\quad \mathbf{I} = j\omega C\mathbf{V}$$

from which

$$\boxed{\mathbf{V} = \frac{1}{j\omega C}\mathbf{I}}$$

Using reasoning as was used for the inductor, we deduce that for a capacitor, the current leads the voltage by 90°. Specifically,

$$\theta = \phi + 90°$$

(If you would like an easy way to remember whether current leads or lags voltage for a capacitor or an inductor, just think of the word "capacitor" as the key. Let the first three letters stand for "**c**urrent **a**nd **p**otential," thus indicating that current comes before (leads) voltage for a cacpacitor. This, of course, implies that current lags voltage for an inductor.)

Since a phasor is a complex number, we can represent it as a point in the complex-number plane, and therefore, specify it by an arrow directed from the origin to the point. For example, for a resistor R having a voltage phasor $\mathbf{V} = V\underline{/\phi}$ and a current phasor $\mathbf{I} = I\underline{/\theta}$, a diagram characterizing the relationship between these two phasors is as shown in Fig. 8.9(a). We refer to this as a **phasor diagram**. Note that because $\phi = \theta$ for a resistor, the voltage and current phasors are collinear.

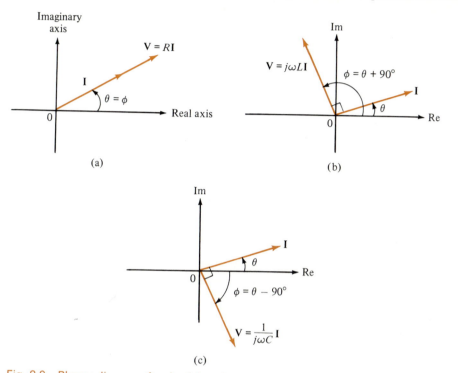

Fig. 8.9   Phasor diagrams for the (a) resistor, (b) inductor, and (c) capacitor.

The phasor diagram for an L-henry inductor is shown in Fig. 8.9(b). Given the voltage phasor $\mathbf{V} = V\underline{/\phi}$ and the current phasor $\mathbf{I} = I\underline{/\theta}$, the phasor diagram displays the fact that the current lags the voltage by 90°—this is indicated by the voltage phasor having an angle that is 90° greater than the current phasor.

Figure 8.9(c) shows the phasor diagram for a C-farad capacitor whose voltage phasor is $\mathbf{V} = V\underline{/\phi}$ and whose current phasor is $\mathbf{I} = I\underline{/\theta}$. In this case, the current angle is 90° greater than the voltage angle (i.e., $\theta = 90° + \phi$), so the current leads the voltage by 90°.

Impedance and Admittance

We have seen that for the resistor, inductor, and capacitor, we get a phasor equation of the form

$$\mathbf{V} = \mathbf{ZI}$$

and we call the quantity **Z** the **impedance** of the element. In other words, the impedance of an R-ohm resistor, L-henry inductor, and C-farad capacitor are, respectively,

$$\mathbf{Z}_R = R \qquad \mathbf{Z}_L = j\omega L \qquad \mathbf{Z}_C = \frac{1}{j\omega C}$$

The equation $\mathbf{V} = \mathbf{ZI}$ is the phasor version of Ohm's law. From this equation, we have that impedance is the ratio of voltage phasor to current phasor, that is,

$$\mathbf{Z} = \frac{\mathbf{V}}{\mathbf{I}}$$

Furthermore, $\mathbf{I} = \mathbf{V}/\mathbf{Z}$. In this expression, the reciprocal of impedance appears. As this can occur frequently, it is useful to give it a name. We call the ratio of current phasor to voltage phasor **admittance** and denote it by the symbol **Y**, that is,

$$\mathbf{Y} = \frac{\mathbf{I}}{\mathbf{V}} \qquad \Rightarrow \qquad \mathbf{Y}_R = \frac{1}{R} \qquad \mathbf{Y}_L = \frac{1}{j\omega L} \qquad \mathbf{Y}_C = j\omega C$$

Thus, $\mathbf{I} = \mathbf{YV}$ and $\mathbf{V} = \mathbf{I}/\mathbf{Y}$. As for the resistive case, the units of impedance are ohms (Ω) and those of admittance are siemens (S), although mhos ($\mho$) are used frequently for admittance.

EXAMPLE 8.5

Given a sinusoid whose frequency is $\omega = 100$ rad/s, for a 25-Ω resistor

$$\mathbf{Z}_R = 25 \, \Omega, \qquad \mathbf{Y}_R = \tfrac{1}{25} = 0.04 \, \text{S}$$

for a $\frac{1}{20}$-H inductor

$$\mathbf{Z}_L = j5 \, \Omega, \qquad \mathbf{Y}_L = \frac{1}{j5} = -j(0.2) \, \text{S}$$

and for a $\frac{1}{50}$-F capacitor

$$\mathbf{Z}_C = \frac{1}{j2} = -j(0.5) \, \Omega, \qquad \mathbf{Y}_C = j2 \, \text{S}$$

DRILL EXERCISE 8.5

The frequency of a sinusoidal circuit is 60 Hz. Find the impedance and admittance of (a) a 100-Ω resistor, (b) a 50-mH inductor, and (c) a 100-μF capacitor.
Answer: (a) 100 Ω, 0.01 S; (b) $j(0.189)$ Ω, $-j(0.053)$ S; (c) $-j26.5$ Ω, $j(0.0377)$ S

In general, given a circuit consisting of a connection of elements such as resistors, inductors, capacitors, dependent sources, and op amps—but no independent sources—let us identify a pair of terminals as depicted in Fig. 8.10(a). Suppose that such a circuit is excited sinusoidally at frequency ω. What results are a sinusoidal voltage $v(t)$ and a sinusoidal current $i(t)$ having frequency ω. Suppose that the voltage across the terminals is $v(t) = V \cos(\omega t + \phi)$ and the current going into the circuit is $i(t) = I \cos(\omega t + \theta)$ as indicated in Fig. 8.10(a). Then the corresponding phasor representation is as shown in Fig. 8.10(b). We define the impedance $\mathbf{Z}$ of the circuit (between the two terminals) to be the ratio of the voltage phasor to the current phasor. That is,

$$\mathbf{Z} = \frac{\mathbf{V}}{\mathbf{I}} = \frac{V\underline{/\phi}}{I\underline{/\theta}} = \frac{V}{I}\underline{/\phi - \theta} \qquad (8.5)$$

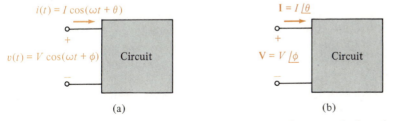

$i(t) = I \cos(\omega t + \theta)$

$v(t) = V \cos(\omega t + \phi)$ | Circuit

(a)

$\mathbf{I} = I\underline{/\theta}$

$\mathbf{V} = V\underline{/\phi}$ | Circuit

(b)

Fig. 8.10 Arbitrary circuit with sinusoidal voltage and current designations as (a) functions of time, (b) phasors.

Furthermore, the admittance of the circuit is

$$\mathbf{Y} = \frac{1}{\mathbf{Z}} = \frac{\mathbf{I}}{\mathbf{V}} = \frac{I\underline{/\theta}}{V\underline{/\phi}} = \frac{I}{V}\underline{/\theta - \phi}$$

Although the resistance of a resistive circuit (with respect to a pair of terminals) is defined to be the ratio of time functions $v(t)$ and $i(t)$, for the case of sinusoids, the impedance of a circuit (with no independent sources) is defined to be the ratio of phasors $\mathbf{V}$ and $\mathbf{I}$. Hence, in general, impedance is a complex quantity which can be expressed either in polar or rectangular form.

For the impedance $\mathbf{Z} = a + jb$, we call the real part a the **resistance** and the imaginary part b the **reactance**. For the case that b is negative, we say that the reactance is **capacitive** and denote it by X_C. If b is positive, we say that the reactance is **inductive** and denote it by X_L. In other words, an impedance has the form $\mathbf{Z} = R + jX$.

For an impedance with an inductive reactance, we can write

$$\mathbf{Z} = R + jX_L = \sqrt{R^2 + X_L^2} \left/ \tan^{-1}\left(\frac{X_L}{R}\right)\right.$$

where $X_L > 0$. Comparing this with Equation (8.5), we have that

$$\phi - \theta = \tan^{-1}\left(\frac{X_L}{R}\right) \quad \Rightarrow \quad \phi = \theta + \tan^{-1}\left(\frac{X_L}{R}\right)$$

where $\phi = \text{ang}\,\mathbf{V}$, $\theta = \text{ang}\,\mathbf{I}$, and $0 < \tan^{-1}(X_L/R) < 90°$ for $R > 0$. Thus, for an impedance with an inductive reactance (and $R > 0$), the current lags the voltage by $\tan^{-1}(X_L/R)$, which is between 0 and 90°. If $R = 0$, then the impedance is purely inductive, and the current lags the voltage by 90°—as we have already seen.

For an impedance with a capacitive reactance, we can write

$$\mathbf{Z} = R + jX_C = \sqrt{R^2 + X_C^2} \left/ \tan^{-1}\left(\frac{X_C}{R}\right)\right.$$

where $X_C < 0$. Comparing this with Equation (8.5), we have that

$$\phi - \theta = \tan^{-1}\left(\frac{X_C}{R}\right) = -\tan^{-1}\left(\frac{-X_C}{R}\right) \quad \Rightarrow \quad \theta = \phi + \tan^{-1}\left(\frac{-X_C}{R}\right)$$

where $0 < \tan^{-1}(-X_C/R) < 90°$ for $R > 0$. Thus, for an impedance with a capacitive reactance (and $R > 0$), the current leads the voltage by $\tan^{-1}(-X_C/R)$, which is between 0 and 90°. If $R = 0$, then the impedance is purely capacitive, and the current leads the voltage by 90°—as we have already seen.

But what happens if the circuit in Fig. 8.10 contains an independent source? In such a case, the circuit cannot be characterized (with respect to the two terminals) simply by either its impedance or its admittance. Instead, the circuit can be characterized by its Thévenin- or Norton-equivalent circuit. This subject will be discussed in more detail shortly.

Sinusoidal Analysis Using Phasors

Suppose that for a sinusoidal circuit, writing KVL around a loop results in the equation

$$v_1(t) + v_2(t) + v_3(t) + \cdots + v_n(t) = 0$$

For the case of a real sinusoid, this equation takes the form

$$V_1 \cos(\omega t + \theta_1) + V_2 \cos(\omega t + \theta_2) + \cdots + V_n \cos(\omega t + \theta_n) = 0$$

while for the case of a complex sinusoid,

$$V_1 e^{j(\omega t + \theta_1)} + V_2 e^{j(\omega t + \theta_2)} + \cdots + V_n e^{j(\omega t + \theta_n)} = 0$$

Dividing both sides of the preceding equation by $e^{j\omega t}$ yields

$$V_1 e^{j\theta_1} + V_2 e^{j\theta_2} + \cdots + V_n e^{j\theta_n} = 0$$

or using phasor notation

$$V_1/\underline{\theta_1} + V_2/\underline{\theta_2} + \cdots + V_n/\underline{\theta_n} = 0 \qquad \Rightarrow \qquad \mathbf{V}_1 + \mathbf{V}_2 + \cdots + \mathbf{V}_n = 0$$

where $\mathbf{V}_i = V_i/\underline{\theta_i}$. Thus, we see that in addition to voltage functions of time, KVL holds for voltage phasors. We similarly can draw the conclusion that KCL holds for current phasors as well as for time functions. However, complex-number arithmetic must be used when adding phasors.

For inductors and capacitors, as well as resistors, the phasor relationships between voltage, current, and impedance are

$$\mathbf{V} = \mathbf{Z}\mathbf{I} \qquad \mathbf{I} = \frac{\mathbf{V}}{\mathbf{Z}} \qquad \mathbf{Z} = \frac{\mathbf{V}}{\mathbf{I}}$$

That is, these are the phasor versions of Ohm's law. By using KVL and KCL, we can analyze a sinusoidal circuit without resorting to differential equations—we simply look at the circuit from the phasor point of view and then proceed as was done for resistive circuits using nodal, mesh, or loop analysis. For resistive circuits, we have to manipulate real numbers; for sinusoidal circuits, complex-number arithmetic is required.

If we analyze a circuit by using time functions and the various differential and integral relationships between voltage and current—and, hence, are required to solve differential equations—we say that we are working in the **time domain**. However, if we have a sinusoidal circuit, we can use the phasor representations of the time functions and the impedances (or admittances) of the various (nonsource) elements or combinations of elements. This is said to be the **frequency-domain** approach.

Making the transformation from the time domain to the frequency domain is a simple matter. Just express a function of time by its phasor representation and resistors, inductors, and capacitors (or combinations of them) by their impedances or admittances. Proceed as for resistive circuits to find the phasor representations of the desired responses. The transformation back to the time domain then is done by inspection.

EXAMPLE 8.6

For the circuit given in Fig. 8.4(a) on p. 350, let us find $v_o(t)$ and $i(t)$ via frequency-domain analysis. Let us also determine the impedance seen by the voltage source.

The given circuit is shown in the frequency domain in Fig. 8.11(a) [note that $6\cos(2t - 90°) = 6\sin 2t$]. By KVL,

$$\mathbf{V}_S = 1\mathbf{I} - j\mathbf{I} \qquad \Rightarrow \qquad 6/\underline{-90°} = (1 - j)\mathbf{I} = \sqrt{2}/\underline{-45°}\,\mathbf{I}$$

from which

$$\mathbf{I} = \frac{6/\underline{-90°}}{\sqrt{2}/\underline{-45°}} = 3\sqrt{2}/\underline{-45°}\ \text{A}$$

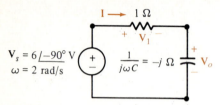

Fig. 8.11(a)   Frequency-domain
representation of circuit in Fig. 8.4(a).

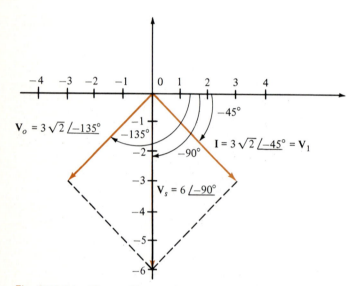

Fig. 8.11(b)   Phasor diagram for given circuit.

Also,

$$\mathbf{V}_o = -j\mathbf{I} = (1\underline{/-90°})(3\sqrt{2}\underline{/-45°}) = 3\sqrt{2}\underline{/-135°} \text{ V}$$

The phasor diagram for this circuit is shown in Fig. 8.11(b). From this diagram, we note that the capacitor voltage lags the applied voltage by 45°. Therefore, if the capacitor voltage is considered to be the output voltage, then the circuit is a lag network. Note, however, that the current leads the applied voltage by 45°. Since $\mathbf{V}_1 = 1\mathbf{I}$, then the voltage across the resistor leads the applied voltage by 45°. Consequently, if the voltage across the resistor is considered to be the output, then the given circuit is a **lead network**.

For this circuit, by KVL,

$$\mathbf{V}_s = \mathbf{V}_1 + \mathbf{V}_o$$

The phasor diagram shows that, indeed, $\mathbf{V}_s$ is the (complex-number) sum of $\mathbf{V}_o$ and $\mathbf{V}_1$. (Phasors can be added graphically just as can two-dimensional vectors.)

Having found the voltage phasor $\mathbf{V}_o$ and the current phasor $\mathbf{I}$, we can write the corresponding time functions, respectively,

$$v_o(t) = 3\sqrt{2}\cos(2t - 135°)\text{ V} \qquad \text{and} \qquad i(t) = 3\sqrt{2}\cos(2t - 45°)\text{ A}$$

The impedance seen by the voltage source is

$$\mathbf{Z} = \frac{\mathbf{V}_s}{\mathbf{I}} = \frac{6\underline{/-90°}}{3\sqrt{2}\underline{/-45°}} = \sqrt{2}\underline{/-45°} = 1 - j\,\Omega$$

As will be seen shortly, this result indicates that impedances in series can be combined as resistances connected in series can be combined.

DRILL EXERCISE 8.6

For the circuit given in Fig. DE8.1 (p. 352), determine the phasors $\mathbf{V}_s$, $\mathbf{I}$, $\mathbf{V}$, and $\mathbf{V}_R$. Sketch the corresponding phasor diagram.
Answer: $10\underline{/53.13°}$ V; $2\underline{/0°}$ A; $8\underline{/90°}$ V; $6\underline{/0°}$ V

Having analyzed a first-order sinusoidal circuit using phasors (i.e., in the frequency domain), let us now look at an example of the frequency-domain analysis of a second-order circuit.

EXAMPLE 8.7
The frequency-domain representation of the series RLC circuit given in Fig. 8.5 on p. 352 is shown in Fig. 8.12. Let us find the phasors indicated and the corresponding functions of time.

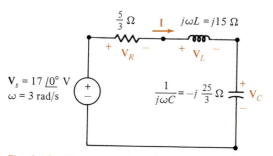

Fig. 8.12 Frequency-domain representation of circuit in Fig. 8.5.

By KVL,

$$\mathbf{V}_s = \mathbf{V}_R + \mathbf{V}_L + \mathbf{V}_C = R\mathbf{I} + j\omega L\mathbf{I} + \frac{1}{j\omega C}\mathbf{I}$$

Therefore,

$$17\underline{/0°} = \frac{5}{3}I + j15I + \frac{25}{j3}I = \frac{5}{3}(1+j4)I$$

from which

$$I = \frac{3}{5}\frac{17\underline{/0°}}{1+j4} = \frac{3}{5}\frac{17\underline{/0°}}{\sqrt{17}\underline{/76°}} = \frac{3}{5}\sqrt{17}\underline{/-76°} = 2.47\underline{/-76°}\ A$$

so the corresponding sinusoidal time function is

$$i(t) = \frac{3}{5}\sqrt{17}\cos(3t - 76°) = 2.47\cos(3t - 76°)\ A$$

The impedance seen by the voltage source is

$$Z = \frac{V_s}{I} = \frac{17\underline{/0°}}{\frac{3}{5}\sqrt{17}\underline{/-76°}} = \frac{5\sqrt{17}}{3}\underline{/76°} = 6.87\underline{/76°} = 1.66 + j6.67\ \Omega$$

Since $V_C = (1/j\omega C)I$, then

$$V_C = \frac{25}{j3}\left(\frac{3}{5}\sqrt{17}\underline{/-76°}\right) = \frac{5\sqrt{17}\underline{/-76°}}{1\underline{/90°}} = 5\sqrt{17}\underline{/-166°} = 20.6\underline{/-166°}\ V$$

and the corresponding sinusoidal time function is

$$v_C(t) = 5\sqrt{17}\cos(3t - 166°) = 20.6\cos(3t - 166°)\ V$$

Since $V_L = j\omega LI$, then

$$V_L = j15(\tfrac{3}{5}\sqrt{17}\underline{/-76°}) = (15\underline{/90°})(\tfrac{3}{5}\sqrt{17}\underline{/-76°}) = 9\sqrt{17}\underline{/14°} = 37.1\underline{/14°}\ V$$

and

$$v_L(t) = 9\sqrt{17}\cos(3t + 14°) = 37.1\cos(3t + 14°)\ V$$

Note that since $V_C = 20.6\underline{/-166°} = (-1)(-20.6\underline{/-166°}) = (1\underline{/180°})(-20.6\underline{/-166°}) = -20.6\underline{/14°}$, then

$$V_L + V_C = 37.1\underline{/14°} - 20.6\underline{/14°} = 16.5\underline{/14°}\ V$$

Finally,

$$V_R = RI = \tfrac{5}{3}(\tfrac{3}{5}\sqrt{17}\underline{/-76°}) = \sqrt{17}\underline{/-76°} = 4.12\underline{/-76°}\ V$$

and

$$v_R(t) = \sqrt{17}\cos(3t - 76°) = 4.12\cos(3t - 76°)\ V$$

A phasor diagram for the indicated voltages in the given circuit is shown in Fig. 8.13. The current phasor $I = 2.47\underline{/-76°}$ (not shown) is collinear with V_R.

From the phasor diagram, we see immediately that $v_L(t)$ leads $v_s(t)$ by 14°, while $v_R(t)$ lags $v_s(t)$ by 76° and $v_C(t)$ lags $v_s(t)$ by 166°. Furthermore, $v_C(t)$ and $v_L(t)$ are 180°

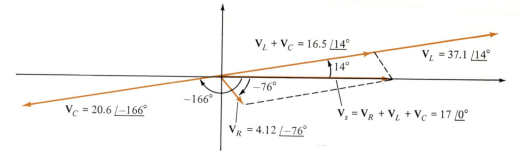

Fig. 8.13   Phasor diagram for circuit in Fig. 8.12.

out of phase—and this is always true for a series LC combination. For suppose that $\mathbf{I} = I\underline{/\theta}$ is the current through a series LC connection. Then

$$\mathbf{V}_L = j\omega L\mathbf{I} = (\omega L\underline{/90°})(I\underline{/\theta}) = \omega LI\underline{/\theta + 90°}$$

and

$$\mathbf{V}_C = \frac{1}{j\omega C}\mathbf{I} = \frac{1}{\omega C\underline{/90°}}(I\underline{/\theta}) = \frac{I}{\omega C}\underline{/\theta - 90°}$$

Therefore, the phase difference between $v_L(t)$ and $v_C(t)$ is

$$(\theta + 90°) - (\theta - 90°) = 180°$$

But, what happens when $|\mathbf{V}_L| = |\mathbf{V}_C|$? This important case will be discussed in Chapter 10.

DRILL EXERCISE 8.7

For the parallel RLC circuit given in Fig. DE8.2 (p. 353), change the value of the capacitor to $\frac{1}{6}$ F, the value of the inductor to $\frac{1}{4}$ H, and then find $v(t)$, $i_L(t)$, $i_C(t)$, and $i_R(t)$. Draw the phasor diagram for the circuit.
Answer: $10.6\cos(4t + 45°)$ V; $10.6\cos(4t - 45°)$ A; $7.07\cos(4t + 135°)$ A; $3.53\cos(4t + 45°)$ A

8.4 FREQUENCY-DOMAIN CIRCUIT CONCEPTS

Just as we can employ voltage division to two resistors in series, so too we can use the phasor version of voltage division when we have two impedances connected in series. Specifically, consider the situation depicted in Fig. 8.14. By KVL,

$$\mathbf{V} = \mathbf{Z}_1\mathbf{I} + \mathbf{Z}_2\mathbf{I} = (\mathbf{Z}_1 + \mathbf{Z}_2)\mathbf{I}$$

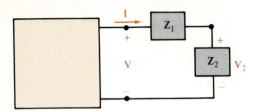

Fig. 8.14   Voltage division.

from which

$$I = \frac{V}{Z_1 + Z_2} \tag{8.6}$$

and since $V_2 = Z_2 I$, then

$$\boxed{V_2 = \frac{Z_2}{Z_1 + Z_2} V}$$

Note also that the current through the series connection of Z_1 and Z_2 is given by Equation (8.6). That is, the series combination behaves as a single impedance Z, where $Z = Z_1 + Z_2$. This is shown in Fig. 8.15.

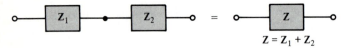

Fig. 8.15   Combining impedances in series.

EXAMPLE 8.8

For the circuit given in Fig. 8.12 (p. 369), let us determine V_C by using voltage division.

Since the series connection of the resistor and the inductor has an impedance of Z_{RL}, where

$$Z_{RL} = Z_R + Z_L = \tfrac{5}{3} + j15 \ \Omega$$

then by voltage division,

$$V_C = \frac{Z_C}{Z_{RL} + Z_C} V_s = \frac{-j\frac{25}{3}}{\frac{5}{3} + j15 - j\frac{25}{3}}(17 \underline{/0^\circ}) = \frac{-j25}{5 + j20}(17)$$

$$= \frac{-j85}{1 + j4} = \frac{85\underline{/-90^\circ}}{\sqrt{17}\underline{/76^\circ}} = 5\sqrt{17}\underline{/-166^\circ} = 20.6\underline{/-166^\circ} \ V$$

as was obtained in Example 8.7.

DRILL EXERCISE 8.8

For the circuit given in Fig. 8.12 (p. 369), determine $\mathbf{V}_R$ and $\mathbf{V}_L$ by using voltage division.
Answer: $4.12\underline{/-76°}$ V; $37.1\underline{/14°}$ V

Consider now the case of current division depicted in Fig. 8.16. Since

$$\mathbf{I} = \frac{\mathbf{V}}{\mathbf{Z}_1} + \frac{\mathbf{V}}{\mathbf{Z}_2} = \left(\frac{1}{\mathbf{Z}_1} + \frac{1}{\mathbf{Z}_2}\right)\mathbf{V}$$

then

$$\mathbf{V} = \frac{\mathbf{I}}{(1/\mathbf{Z}_1) + (1/\mathbf{Z}_2)} = \frac{\mathbf{Z}_1\mathbf{Z}_2\mathbf{I}}{\mathbf{Z}_1 + \mathbf{Z}_2} \tag{8.7}$$

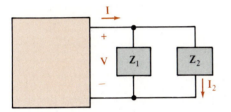

Fig. 8.16   Current division.

But $\mathbf{I}_2 = \mathbf{V}/\mathbf{Z}_2$, so

$$\mathbf{I}_2 = \frac{\mathbf{Z}_1}{\mathbf{Z}_1 + \mathbf{Z}_2}\,\mathbf{I}$$

is the current-division formula. From Equation (8.7), we have that the impedance of the parallel connection of $\mathbf{Z}_1$ and $\mathbf{Z}_2$ is

$$\mathbf{Z} = \frac{\mathbf{V}}{\mathbf{I}} = \frac{1}{(1/\mathbf{Z}_1) + (1/\mathbf{Z}_2)} = \frac{\mathbf{Z}_1\mathbf{Z}_2}{\mathbf{Z}_1 + \mathbf{Z}_2}$$

Thus, two impedances connected in parallel behave as a single impedance $\mathbf{Z}$, where $1/\mathbf{Z} = 1/\mathbf{Z}_1 + 1/\mathbf{Z}_2$. This is shown pictorially in Fig. 8.17. We now conclude that impedances in series and parallel combine as resistances do. Using dual arguments, we deduce that admittances in parallel and series combine as conductances do. This is demonstrated in Fig. 8.18.

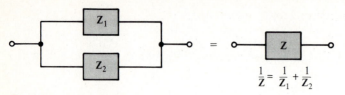

Fig. 8.17 Combining impedances in parallel.

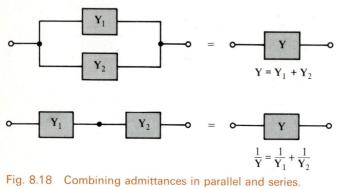

Fig. 8.18 Combining admittances in parallel and series.

For the situation depicted in Fig. 8.16, using admittances the current-division formula is

$$\mathbf{I}_2 = \frac{\mathbf{Y}_2}{\mathbf{Y}_1 + \mathbf{Y}_2}\mathbf{I}$$

where $\mathbf{Y}_1 = 1/\mathbf{Z}_1$ and $\mathbf{Y}_2 = 1/\mathbf{Z}_2$.

EXAMPLE 8.9

For the parallel *RLC* circuit shown in Fig. 8.19, let us find $i_L(t)$ by using current division.

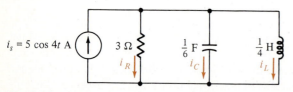

Fig. 8.19 Application of current division.

For the given circuit, which is represented in the time domain, we have the following frequency-domain quantities:

$$\mathbf{I}_s = 5\underline{/0°} \text{ A} \qquad (\omega = 4 \text{ rad/s}) \qquad \mathbf{Z}_R = 3 \text{ }\Omega$$

$$\mathbf{Z}_C = \frac{1}{j\omega C} = -j\frac{1}{4(1/6)} = -j\frac{3}{2}\text{ }\Omega \qquad \mathbf{Z}_L = j\omega L = j(4)(1/4) = j1 \text{ }\Omega$$

Thus, the frequency-domain representation of the given circuit is shown in Fig. 8.20.

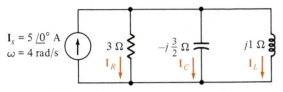

Fig. 8.20   Frequency-domain representation.

The parallel connection of the resistor and the capacitor have an impedance of $\mathbf{Z}_{RC}$, where

$$\mathbf{Z}_{RC} = \frac{\mathbf{Z}_R \mathbf{Z}_C}{\mathbf{Z}_R + \mathbf{Z}_C} = \frac{(3)(-j3/2)}{3 - j3/2} = \frac{-j9}{6 - j3} = \frac{-j3}{2 - j}\text{ }\Omega$$

Thus, by current division,

$$\mathbf{I}_L = \frac{\mathbf{Z}_{RC}}{\mathbf{Z}_{RC} + \mathbf{Z}_L}\mathbf{I}_s = \frac{-j3/(2 - j)}{-j3/(2 - j) + j1}(5\underline{/0°}) = \frac{-j3}{-j3 + j(2 - j)} \quad (5)$$

$$= \frac{-j15}{1 - j} = \frac{15\underline{/-90°}}{\sqrt{2}\underline{/-45°}} = \frac{15}{\sqrt{2}}\underline{/-45°} = 10.6\underline{/-45°} \text{ A}$$

Hence,

$$i_L(t) = 10.6\cos(4t - 45°) \text{ A}$$

DRILL EXERCISE 8.9

For the circuit given in Fig. 8.19, determine $i_R(t)$ and $i_C(t)$ by using current division.
Answer: $3.54\cos(4t + 45°)$ A; $7.07\cos(4t + 135°)$ A

Thévenin's and Norton's Theorems

Other resistive network concepts apply equally well to sinusoidal circuits if such networks are described in the frequency domain—that is, in terms of phasors and impedances (or admittances). One very important example is Thévenin's theorem, which says in essence that (with a few exceptions, of course) a circuit is equivalent to an appropriate voltage source in series with an appropriate impedance. This situation is depicted in Fig. 8.21.

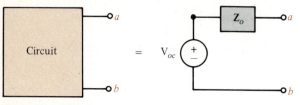

Fig. 8.21   Thévenin's theorem.

EXAMPLE 8.10

For the circuit shown in Fig. 8.22, we can determine the effect of the circuit on the load impedance $\mathbf{Z}_L$ by employing Thévenin's theorem. Let us find the Thévenin equivalent of the circuit to the left of the load.

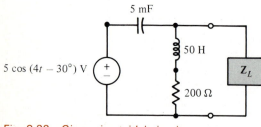

Fig. 8.22   Given sinusoidal circuit.

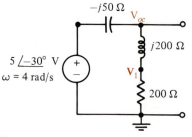

Fig. 8.23   Determination of open-circuit voltage.

We first determine $\mathbf{V}_{oc}$ from Fig. 8.23. By KCL at the node labeled $\mathbf{V}_{oc}$,

$$\frac{\mathbf{V}_{oc} - 5\underline{/-30°}}{-j50} + \frac{\mathbf{V}_{oc} - \mathbf{V}_1}{j200} = 0$$

from which

$$3\mathbf{V}_{oc} + \mathbf{V}_1 = 20\underline{/-30°} \tag{8.8}$$

At the node labeled $\mathbf{V}_1$, by KCL

$$\frac{\mathbf{V}_1 - \mathbf{V}_{oc}}{j200} + \frac{\mathbf{V}_1}{200} = 0$$

from which

$$\mathbf{V}_{oc} = \mathbf{V}_1 + j\mathbf{V}_1 = (1 + j)\mathbf{V}_1 \quad \Rightarrow \quad \mathbf{V}_1 = \frac{1}{1+j}\mathbf{V}_{oc}$$

Substituting this result into Equation (8.8) yields

$$3\mathbf{V}_{oc} + \frac{1}{1+j}\mathbf{V}_{oc} = 20\underline{/-30°} = \frac{4+j3}{1+j}\mathbf{V}_{oc}$$

from which[†]

$$\mathbf{V}_{oc} = \frac{1+j}{4+j3}(20\underline{/-30°}) = \frac{\sqrt{2}\underline{/45°}}{5\underline{/36.9°}}(20\underline{/-30°}) = 4\sqrt{2}\underline{/-21.9°} \text{ V}$$

Thus,

$$v_{oc}(t) = 4\sqrt{2}\cos(4t - 21.9°) \text{ V}$$

To find Thévenin-equivalent (output) impedance $\mathbf{Z}_o$, set the independent source to zero. The resulting circuit is shown in Fig. 8.24. We can find $\mathbf{Z}_o$ by combining impedances in series and parallel. In particular (the symbol ‖ means "in parallel with"),

$$\mathbf{Z}_o = (\mathbf{Z}_L + \mathbf{Z}_R)\|\mathbf{Z}_C$$

$$= \frac{(j200 + 200)(-j50)}{j200 + 200 - j50} = \frac{200(1-j)}{(4+j3)} = 8 - j56 = 40\sqrt{2}\underline{/-81.9°} \text{ }\Omega$$

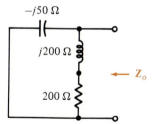

Fig. 8.24 Determination of Thévenin-equivalent (output) impedance.

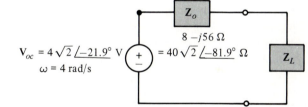

Fig. 8.25 Thévenin-equivalent circuit in the frequency domain.

In the frequency domain, we have, therefore, the Thévenin-equivalent circuit shown in Fig. 8.25. In representing this circuit in the time domain, we can use the *RLC* combination from which we determined $\mathbf{Z}_o$, thus yielding the circuit in Fig. 8.26(a).

[†] Verify this result by combining the impedances of the inductor and the resistor, and then using the formula for voltage division.

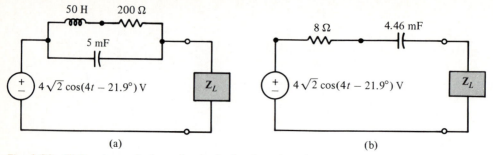

Fig. 8.26 Thévenin-equivalent circuits in the time domain.

Alternatively, we can use the fact that $\mathbf{Z}_o = 8 - j56 \ \Omega$ has the form of a resistor in series with a capacitor, that is,

$$\mathbf{Z}_o = R + \frac{1}{j\omega C} = R - \frac{j}{\omega C}$$

Thus,

$$R = 8 \ \Omega \quad \text{and} \quad \frac{1}{\omega C} = 56 \quad \Rightarrow \quad C = \frac{1}{224} = 4.46 \text{ mF}$$

and an alternative equivalent circuit is as shown in Fig. 8.26(b).

DRILL EXERCISE 8.10

For the circuit given in Fig. 8.19 (p. 374), consider the inductor to be the load. Find the Thévenin equivalent of the circuit to the left of the load, and use this Thévenin-equivalent circuit to find the voltage $v_L(t)$ across the inductor.
Answer: $6.71\underline{/-63.43°}$ V; $0.6 - j1.2 \ \Omega$; $10.6 \cos(4t + 45°)$ V

Just as we have Thévenin's theorem for sinusoidal circuits, so too do we have Norton's theorem. Specifically, with respect to a pair of terminals a and b, an arbitrary circuit behaves as an independent current source $\mathbf{I}_{sc}$ in parallel with an impedance $\mathbf{Z}_o$ (the Thévenin-equivalent or output impedance). This situation is depicted in Fig. 8.27.

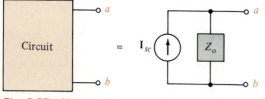

Fig. 8.27 Norton's theorem.

EXAMPLE 8.11

Let us find the Norton equivalent of the circuit to the left of load in Fig. 8.22 (p. 376).

To find $\mathbf{I}_{sc}$, we replace the load with a short circuit. The resulting circuit, in the frequency domain, is shown in Fig. 8.28. Since the short circuit constrains the voltage across the series RL connection to be 0 V, then the current through this combination is

$$\mathbf{I}_{RL} = \frac{\mathbf{V}_{RL}}{\mathbf{Z}_{RL}} = \frac{0}{200 + j200} = 0 \text{ A}$$

Thus,

$$\mathbf{I}_{sc} = \mathbf{I}_C = \frac{5\,\underline{/-30°}}{50\,\underline{/-90°}} = 0.1\,\underline{/60°} \text{ A}$$

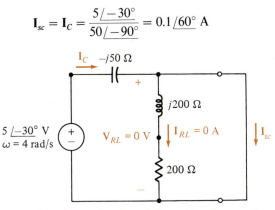

Fig. 8.28   Determination of short-circuit current.

The Norton- (or Thévenin-) equivalent impedance $\mathbf{Z}_o$ can be determined from Fig. 8.24 on p. 377. As was done in Example 8.10, we get

$$\mathbf{Z}_o = 8 - j56 \ \Omega$$

Hence, the Norton equivalent, in the frequency domain, of the circuit to the left of the load in Fig. 8.22 is shown in Fig. 8.29(a). Using the time-domain realization of $\mathbf{Z}_o$ described in Example 8.10, we get the time-domain Norton-equivalent circuit shown in Fig. 8.29(b).

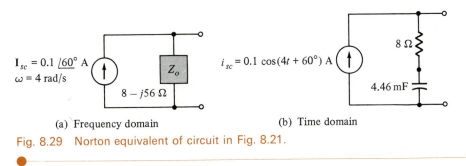

(a) Frequency domain   (b) Time domain

Fig. 8.29   Norton equivalent of circuit in Fig. 8.21.

DRILL EXERCISE 8.11

For the circuit given in Fig. 8.5 (p. 352), consider the capacitor to be the load. Find the Norton equivalent of the circuit to the left of the load, and use this Norton-equivalent circuit to find the voltage $v_C(t)$.

Answer: $1.127\underline{/-83.7°}$ A; $\frac{5}{3} + j15$ Ω; $20.6\cos(3t - 166°)$ V

Another useful concept is that of a source transformation. Figure 8.30(a) depicts a voltage-to-current source transformation, whereas Fig. 8.30(b) illustrates a current-to-voltage source transformation. In a similar manner, source transformations can be performed on dependent sources as well as independent sources.

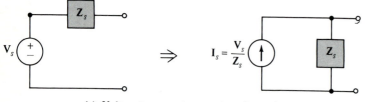

(a) Voltage-to-current source transformation

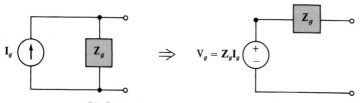

(b) Current-to-voltage source transformation

Fig. 8.30   Source transformations.

As an example, let us perform a current-to-voltage source transformation on the (Norton-equivalent) circuit given in Fig. 8.29(a). The resulting voltage source has a phasor value of

$$(0.1\underline{/60°})(8 - j56) = (0.1\underline{/60°})(40\sqrt{2}\underline{/-81.9°}) = 4\sqrt{2}\underline{/-21.9°}\text{ V}$$

and this voltage source is in series with $\mathbf{Z}_o = 8 - j56$ Ω.

The circuit in Fig. 8.29(a) is the Norton equivalent of the circuit in Fig. 8.22. However, performing a source transformation on the Norton-equivalent circuit yields the Thévenin-equivalent circuit (see Fig. 8.25). In general, when $|\mathbf{Z}_o|$ is neither zero nor infinity, the Thévenin-equivalent circuit can be obtained from the Norton-equivalent circuit, or vice versa, by a source transformation; and the following relationships hold:

$$\mathbf{V}_{oc} = \mathbf{Z}_o\mathbf{I}_{sc} \qquad \mathbf{I}_{sc} = \frac{\mathbf{V}_{oc}}{\mathbf{Z}_o} \qquad \mathbf{Z}_o = \frac{\mathbf{V}_{oc}}{\mathbf{I}_{sc}}$$

8.5 ADDITIONAL SINUSOIDAL CIRCUITS

Having analyzed some *RLC* sinusoidal circuits, let us now turn our attention to the analysis of sinusoidal circuits containing active elements such as dependent sources or op amps. In the process, we will see how Cramer's rule can be used for frequency-domain analysis.

EXAMPLE 8.12
Let us find the mesh currents $i_1(t)$ and $i_2(t)$ for the circuit shown in Fig. 8.31(a).

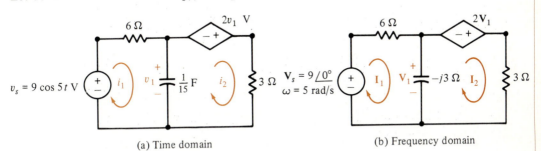

(a) Time domain   (b) Frequency domain

Fig. 8.31   Example of mesh analysis.

Figure 8.31(b) shows the given circuit in the frequency domain. By KVL, for mesh $\mathbf{I}_1$, we have that

$$6\mathbf{I}_1 - j3(\mathbf{I}_1 - \mathbf{I}_2) - 9 = 0 \qquad \Rightarrow \qquad (2 - j)\mathbf{I}_1 + j\mathbf{I}_2 = 3 \qquad (8.9)$$

For mesh $\mathbf{I}_2$, by KVL,

$$-\mathbf{V}_1 - 2\mathbf{V}_1 + 3\mathbf{I}_2 = 0 \qquad \Rightarrow \qquad -\mathbf{V}_1 + \mathbf{I}_2 = 0$$

and since $\mathbf{V}_1 = -j3(\mathbf{I}_1 - \mathbf{I}_2)$, we get

$$j3(\mathbf{I}_1 - \mathbf{I}_2) + \mathbf{I}_2 = 0 \qquad \Rightarrow \qquad j3\mathbf{I}_1 + (1 - j3)\mathbf{I}_2 = 0 \qquad (8.10)$$

Calculating determinants for Equations (8.9) and (8.10) yields

$$\Delta = \begin{vmatrix} 2 - j & j \\ j3 & 1 - j3 \end{vmatrix} = (2 - j)(1 - j3) - (j3)(j) = 2 - j7$$

$$\Delta_1 = \begin{vmatrix} 3 & j \\ 0 & 1 - j3 \end{vmatrix} = 3(1 - j3) \qquad \Delta_2 = \begin{vmatrix} 2 - j & 3 \\ j3 & 0 \end{vmatrix} = -j9$$

By Cramer's rule,

$$\mathbf{I}_1 = \frac{\Delta_1}{\Delta} = \frac{3(1 - j3)}{2 - j7} = \frac{3(23 + j)}{53} = 1.30\underline{/2.49°}\ \text{A}$$

$$\mathbf{I}_2 = \frac{\Delta_2}{\Delta} = \frac{-j9}{2 - j7} = \frac{-j9(2 + j7)}{(2 - j7)(2 + j7)} = \frac{9(7 - j2)}{53} = 1.24\underline{/-15.95°}\ \text{A}$$

Therefore,

$$i_1(t) = 1.30\cos(5t + 2.49°)\ \text{A} \qquad \text{and} \qquad i_2(t) = 1.24\cos(5t - 15.95°)\ \text{A}$$

DRILL EXERCISE 8.12

Find the mesh currents $i_1(t)$, $i_2(t)$, and $i_3(t)$ for the circuit shown in Fig. DE8.12.
Answer: $3.91 \cos(4t + 21.16°)$ A; $1.27 \cos(4t + 77.47°)$ A; $9.20 \cos(4t + 32.47°)$ A

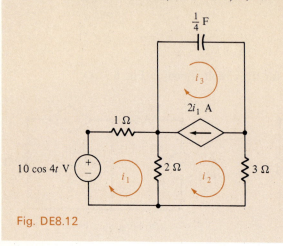

Fig. DE8.12

Let us now analyze a sinusoidal op-amp circuit via nodal analysis.

EXAMPLE 8.13

Let us find the output voltage $v_o(t)$ for the op-amp circuit shown in Fig. 8.32(a).

Figure 8.32(b) shows the frequency-domain representation of the given op-amp circuit. By KCL at node **V**,

$$\frac{\mathbf{V} - 8\underline{/0°}}{3} + \frac{\mathbf{V}}{1} + \frac{\mathbf{V} - \mathbf{V}_o}{-j3/2} = 0$$

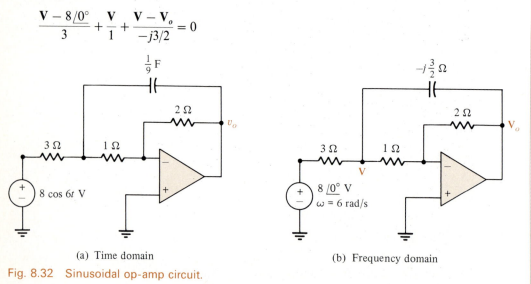

(a) Time domain

(b) Frequency domain

Fig. 8.32 Sinusoidal op-amp circuit.

from which

$$(2 + j)\mathbf{V} - j\mathbf{V}_o = 4$$

By KCL at the inverting input of the op-amp,

$$\frac{\mathbf{V}}{1} + \frac{\mathbf{V}_o}{2} = 0 \qquad \Rightarrow \qquad \mathbf{V} = -\frac{\mathbf{V}_o}{2}$$

Substituting this into the equation immediately above yields

$$(2 + j)\left(-\frac{\mathbf{V}_o}{2} \right) - j\mathbf{V}_o = 4$$

and solving this equation we get

$$\mathbf{V}_o = \frac{-8}{2 + j3} = \frac{8\underline{/180°}}{\sqrt{13}\underline{/56.3°}} = 2.22\underline{/123.7°} \text{ V}$$

Therefore,

$$v_o(t) = 2.22\cos(6t + 123.7°) \text{ V}$$

DRILL EXERCISE 8.13

Find $v_o(t)$ and $i_o(t)$ for the op-amp circuit shown in Fig. DE8.13.
Answer: $10.6\cos(2t + 135°)$ V; $\cos 2t$ A

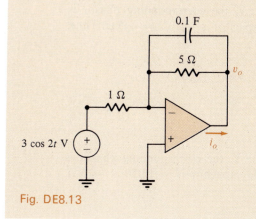

Fig. DE8.13

Linearity

For a linear circuit with more than one input, regardless of whether or not the inputs are sinusoidal, we can apply the principle of superposition if we so desire.

Of course for a linear circuit we can employ the linearity property which can be stated as follows: If a given excitation can be expressed as a sum of excitations, then the response to the given excitation is equal to the sum of the responses to the individual components of the excitation.

EXAMPLE 8.14

Let us find $v_o(t)$ for the series RC circuit shown in Fig. 8.33(a), given that $v_s(t) = 10 \cos 2t + 10 \cos 50t$ V.

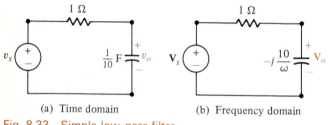

(a) Time domain   (b) Frequency domain

Fig. 8.33 Simple low-pass filter.

The frequency-domain representation of the given circuit is shown in Fig. 8.33(b). Note that the impedance of the capacitor is labeled $1/j\omega C = -j10/\omega$. This is because the excitation $v_s(t)$ is not a single sinusoid, but is the sum of two sinusoids having different frequencies. Therefore, the impedance of the capacitor is different for the two components of the excitation.

Let us find the response to $v_s(t)$ by finding the response to $10 \cos 2t$ V and the response to $10 \cos 50t$ V, and then taking the sum of these responses.

For the case that the excitation is $10 \cos 2t$ V, the corresponding phasor is $10/\underline{0°}$ V ($\omega = 2$ rad/s), and the impedance of the capacitor is $-j10/2 = -j5\ \Omega$. Thus, by voltage divison, the resulting output is

$$\mathbf{V}_{o1} = \frac{-j5}{1 - j5}(10/\underline{0°}) = \frac{5/\underline{-90°}}{\sqrt{26}/\underline{-78.7°}}(10/\underline{0°}) = 9.81/\underline{-11.3°}\ \text{V}$$

Therefore, the response to $10 \cos 2t$ V is

$$v_{o1}(t) = 9.81 \cos(2t - 11.3°)\ \text{V}$$

For the case that the excitation is $10 \cos 50t$ V, the corresponding phasor is $10/\underline{0°}$ V ($\omega = 50$ rad/s), and the impedance of the capacitor is $-j10/50 = -j/5\ \Omega$. Thus, by voltage division, the resulting output is

$$\mathbf{V}_{o2} = \frac{-j/5}{1 - j/5}(10/\underline{0°}) = \frac{0.2/\underline{-90°}}{\sqrt{1.04}/\underline{-11.3°}}(10/\underline{0°}) = 1.96/\underline{-78.7°}\ \text{V}$$

Therefore, the response to $10 \cos 50t$ V is

$$v_{o2}(t) = 1.96 \cos(50t - 78.7°)\ \text{V}$$

Hence, the response to $v_s(t) = 10 \cos 2t + 10 \cos 50t$ V is

$$v_o(t) = v_{o1}(t) + v_{o2}(t) = 9.81 \cos(2t - 11.3°) + 1.96 \cos(50t - 78.7°) \text{ V}$$

For the given circuit, the input voltage $v_s(t)$ has two components: a lower frequency sinusoid ($10 \cos 2t$ V) and a higher frequency sinusoid ($10 \cos 50t$ V)—both have an amplitude of 10 V. The response to the low-frequency sinusoid has an amplitude of 9.81 V, while the response to the high-frequency sinusoid has an amplitude of only 1.96 V. These facts demonstrate that the given series RC circuit tends to "pass" lower frequency sinusoids and "stop" (not pass) higher frequency sinusoids. The given circuit is an example of a simple **low-pass filter**. (More will be said on the subject of "filters" in Chapter 10.)

DRILL EXERCISE 8.14

For the circuit given in Fig. 8.33(a), replace the capacitor with a $\frac{1}{10}$-H inductor. For the resulting simple **high-pass filter**, find $v_o(t)$ for the case that $v_s(t) = 10 \cos 2t + 10 \cos 50t$ V.
Answer: $1.96 \cos(2t + 78.7°) + 9.81 \cos(50t + 11.3°)$ V

● SUMMARY

1. If the input of a linear, time-invariant circuit is a sinusoid, then the response is a sinusoid of the same frequency.

2. A complex number $\mathbf{c}$ can be written in rectangular form as $\mathbf{c} = a + jb$, where a is the real part of $\mathbf{c}$ and b is the imaginary part of $\mathbf{c}$. It can also be written in exponential form as $\mathbf{c} = Me^{j\theta}$, where M, the magnitude of $\mathbf{c}$ (also denoted $|\mathbf{c}|$), is a positive number and θ is the angle of $\mathbf{c}$.

3. Finding the magnitude and phase angle of a sinusoidal steady-state response can be accomplished with either real or complex sinusoids.

4. If the output of a sinusoidal circuit reaches its peak before the input, the circuit is a lead network. Conversely, it is a lag network.

5. Using the concepts of phasors and impedance (or admittance), sinusoidal circuits can be analyzed in the frequency domain in a manner analogous to resistive circuits by using the phasor versions of KCL, KVL, nodal analysis, mesh analysis, and loop analysis.

6. Such important circuit concepts as the principle of superposition and Thévenin's theorem are also applicable in the frequency domain.

● PROBLEMS FOR CHAPTER 8

8.1 For the circuit shown in Fig. P8.1, suppose that $v_s(t) = 12 \cos 2t + 5 \sin 2t$ V. Find $i(t)$ and $v_o(t)$ using time-domain analysis, and determine by how much $v_o(t)$ either leads or lags $v_s(t)$.

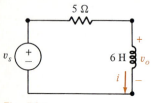

Fig. P8.1

8.2 For the circuit shown in Fig. P8.2, suppose that $i_s(t) = 8 \sin \sqrt{3}t$ A. Find $v_o(t)$ using time-domain analysis, and determine by how much $v_o(t)$ either leads or lags $v_s(t)$.

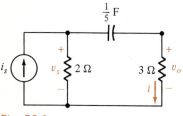

Fig. P8.2

8.3 For the circuit given in Fig. P8.1, place an additional 5-Ω resistor in parallel with the inductor and repeat Problem 8.1.

8.4 For the simple series RC circuit given in Fig. 8.4(a) (p. 350), place an additional 1-Ω resistor in parallel with the capacitor. Find $v_o(t)$ and $i(t)$ using time-domain analysis for the resulting circuit, and determine by how much $v_o(t)$ either leads or lags $v_s(t)$.

8.5 For the series RLC circuit given in Fig. 8.5 (p. 352) suppose that $R = \frac{5}{4}\Omega$, $L = \frac{1}{4}$ H, $C = 1$ F, and $v_s(t) = 4 \cos 2t$ V. Find $v_C(t)$ using time-domain analysis,

and determine by how much $v_C(t)$ either leads or lags $v_s(t)$.

8.6 For the RLC circuit shown in Fig. P8.6, suppose that $v_s(t) = 3 \cos t$ V. Find $v_C(t)$ using time-domain analysis, and determine by how much $v_C(t)$ either leads or lags $v_s(t)$.

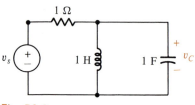

Fig. P8.6

8.7 For the RC circuit given in Fig. 8.4(a) (p. 350), find the zero-state response $v_o(t)$ for the case that the input voltage is $v_s(t) = 6 \sin 2t \, u(t)$ V. (*Note:* The zero-state response includes both the forced and the natural responses.)

8.8 For the series RLC circuit given in Fig. 8.5 (p. 352), suppose that $R = \frac{5}{4}\Omega$, $L = \frac{1}{4}$ H, and $C = 1$ F. Find the zero-state response $v_C(t)$ for the case that the input voltage is $v_s(t) = 4 \cos 2t \, u(t)$ V.

8.9 For the circuit given in Fig. P8.6, find the zero-state response $v_C(t)$ for the case that the input voltage is $v_s(t) = 3 \cos t \, u(t)$ V.

8.10 Repeat Problem 8.9 for the case that the value of the resistor is changed to 0.5 Ω.

8.11 Find the exponential form of the following complex numbers given in rectangular form:
  (a) $4 + j7$ (e) 4
  (b) $3 - j5$ (f) -5
  (c) $-2 + j3$ (g) $j7$
  (d) $-1 - j6$ (h) $-j2$

8.12 Find the rectangular form of the following complex numbers given in exponential form:

(a) $3e^{j70°}$

(b) $2e^{j120°}$

(c) $5e^{-j60°}$

(d) $4e^{-j150°}$

(e) $6e^{j90°}$

(f) $e^{-j90°}$

(g) $2e^{j180°}$

(h) $2e^{-j180°}$

8.13 Find the rectangular form of the sum $\mathbf{A}_1 + \mathbf{A}_2$ given that

(a) $\mathbf{A}_1 = 3e^{j30°}$; $\mathbf{A}_2 = 4e^{j60°}$

(b) $\mathbf{A}_1 = 3e^{j30°}$; $\mathbf{A}_2 = 4e^{-j30°}$

(c) $\mathbf{A}_1 = 5e^{-j60°}$; $\mathbf{A}_2 = 2e^{j120°}$

(d) $\mathbf{A}_1 = 4e^{j45°}$; $\mathbf{A}_2 = 2e^{-j90°}$

8.14 Express the following sums as a single sinusoid of the form $A\cos(\omega t + \theta)$:

(a) $3\cos(\omega t + 30°) + 4\cos(\omega t + 60°)$

(b) $3\cos(\omega t + 30°) + 4\cos(\omega t - 60°)$

(c) $5\cos(\omega t - 60°) + 2\cos(\omega t + 120°)$

(d) $4\cos(\omega t + 45°) + 2\sin\omega t$

8.15 For the complex numbers given in Problem 8.13, find the rectangular form of the product $\mathbf{A}_1\mathbf{A}_2$.

8.16 Verify the following identities:

(a) $Me^{j90°} = jM$

(b) $Me^{-j90°} = -jM$

(c) $Me^{j180°} = -M$

(d) $Me^{-j180°} = -M$

(e) $Me^{j0°} = M$

(f) $-Me^{j\theta} = Me^{j(\theta \pm 180°)}$

8.17 Express the following as a single complex number in exponential form:

(a) $\dfrac{-j6}{1+j}$

(b) $\dfrac{-8}{2+j3}$

(c) $\dfrac{j3}{-2+j}$

(d) $\dfrac{85}{-1-j4}$

(e) $\dfrac{200(1-j)}{4+j3}$

(f) $\dfrac{20(1+j)}{4+j3}e^{-j30°}$

(g) $37.1e^{j14°} + 20.6e^{-j166°}$

(h) $16.5e^{j14°} + 4.12e^{-j76°}$

8.18 Express each part of Problem 8.17 as a single complex number in rectangular form.

8.19 Express each of the following as a single complex number:

(a) $2 + 2e^{j120°} + 2e^{-j120°}$

(b) $2e^{j60°} + 2e^{j180°} + 2e^{-j60°}$

(c) $2e^{j45°} + 2e^{j165°} + 2e^{-j75°}$

8.20 Repeat Problem 8.1 using frequency-domain analysis. Draw the corresponding phasor diagram.

8.21 Repeat Problem 8.2 using frequency-domain analysis. Draw the corresponding phasor diagram.

8.22 Repeat Problem 8.3 using frequency-domain analysis. Draw the corresponding phasor diagram.

8.23 Repeat Problem 8.4 using frequency-domain analysis. Draw the corresponding phasor diagram.

8.24 Repeat Problem 8.5 using frequency-domain analysis. Draw the corresponding phasor diagram.

8.25 Repeat Problem 8.6 using frequency-domain analysis. Draw the corresponding phasor diagram.

8.26 For the series RLC circuit given in Fig. 8.5 (p. 352), suppose that $R = 4\,\Omega$, $L = 2$ H, and $v_s(t) = A\cos(3t + \theta)$ V. Determine by how much $v_C(t)$ either leads or lags $v_s(t)$ when C is (a) $\frac{1}{8}$ F, (b) $\frac{1}{18}$ F, and (c) $\frac{1}{32}$ F.

8.27 For the circuit shown in Fig. P8.27, (a) use mesh analysis to find $v_o(t)$, and

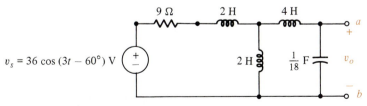

Fig. P8.27

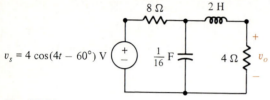

Fig. P8.28

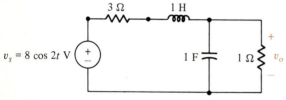

Fig. P8.29

(b) find the impedance seen by the voltage source.

8.28 For the circuit shown in Fig. P8.28, (a) use nodal analysis to find $v_o(t)$, and (b) find the impedance seen by the voltage source.

8.29 For the circuit shown in Fig. P8.29, (a) use nodal analysis to find $v_o(t)$, and (b) find the impedance seen by the voltage source.

8.30 For the circuit given in Fig. P8.29, change the value of the inductor to $\frac{1}{5}$ H, and repeat Problem 8.29.

8.31 For the *RLC* connection shown in Fig. P8.31, find the impedance **Z** when (a) $\omega = 1$ rad/s, (b) $\omega = 4$ rad/s, and (c) $\omega = 8$ rad/s.

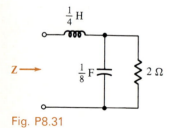

Fig. P8.31

8.32 For the *RLC* connection shown in Fig. P8.32, find the admittance **Y** when

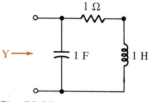

Fig. P8.32

(a) $\omega = 1$ rad/s, (b) $\omega = \frac{1}{2}$ rad/s, and (c) $\omega = \frac{1}{4}$ rad/s.

8.33 Consider the circuit given in Fig. P8.1. (a) Find $v_o(t)$ by using voltage division. (b) Place an additional 5-Ω resistor in parallel with the inductor, and find $v_o(t)$ for the resulting circuit by using voltage division.

8.34 For the circuit given in Fig. P8.2, find $i(t)$ by using current division.

8.35 For the circuit given in Fig. P8.27, find the Thévenin-equivalent circuit with respect to terminals a and b.

8.36 For the circuit given in Fig. P8.28, find $v_o(t)$ by first replacing the portion of the circuit to the left of the 4-Ω resistor with its Thévenin equivalent.

8.37 For the circuit given in Fig. P8.29, find $v_o(t)$ by first replacing the portion of the circuit to the left of the 1-Ω resistor with its Norton equivalent.

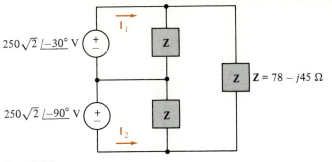

$250\sqrt{2}\,\underline{/-30°}$ V

$250\sqrt{2}\,\underline{/-90°}$ V

$\mathbf{Z} = 78 - j45\ \Omega$

Fig P8.39

8.38 For the circuit given in Fig. P8.29, change the value of the inductor to $\frac{1}{5}$ H. Find $v_o(t)$ by first replacing the portion of the circuit to the left of the 1-Ω resistor with its Thévenin equivalent.

8.39 For the circuit shown in Fig. P8.39, find the (phasor) currents $\mathbf{I}_1$ and $\mathbf{I}_2$.

8.40 For the circuit shown in Fig. P8.40, find the (phasor) currents $\mathbf{I}_1$ and $\mathbf{I}_2$.

8.41 For the circuit shown in Fig. P8.41, find

(a) $v_o(t)$, and (b) the impedance seen by the current source.

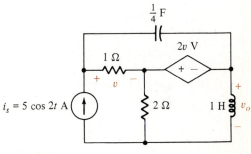

$i_s = 5 \cos 2t$ A

Fig. P8.41

8.42 For the circuit shown in Fig. P8.42, find (a) $v(t)$, and (b) the impedance seen by the voltage source.

8.43 Find the impedance seen by the independent voltage source for the circuit given in (a) Fig. 8.31 (p. 381), (b) Fig. DE8.12 (p. 382), (c) Fig. 8.32 (p. 382), and (d) Fig. DE8.13 (p. 383).

8.44 For the op-amp circuit shown in Fig. P8.44, find $v_o(t)$.

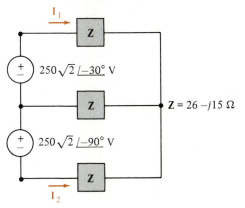

$250\sqrt{2}\,\underline{/-30°}$ V

$250\sqrt{2}\,\underline{/-90°}$ V

$\mathbf{Z} = 26 - j15\ \Omega$

Fig. P8.40

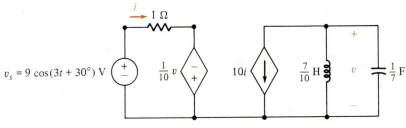

$v_s = 9 \cos(3t + 30°)$ V

Fig. P8.42

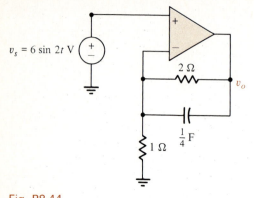

Fig. P8.44

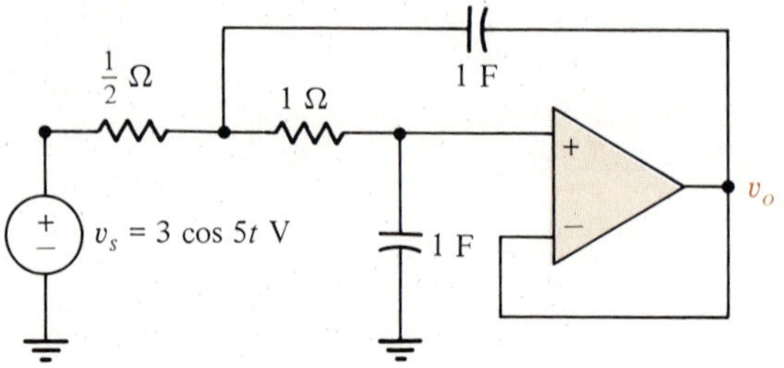

Fig. P8.45

8.45 For the op-amp circuit shown in Fig. P8.45, find (a) $v_o(t)$, and (b) the impedance seen by the voltage source.

8.46 Repeat Problem 8.45 for the op-amp circuit shown in Fig. P8.46.

8.47 For the op-amp circuit shown in Fig. P8.47, find $v_o(t)$.

8.48 For the series RC circuit shown in Fig. 8.33(a) [p. 384], change the value of the capacitor to 1 F and find $v_o(t)$ for the case that

$$v_s(t) = \frac{1}{\pi} + \frac{1}{2}\sin \pi t - \frac{2}{3\pi}\cos 2\pi t \text{ V}$$

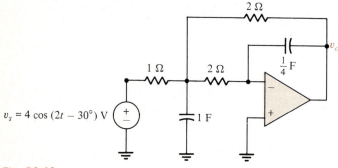

Fig. P8.46

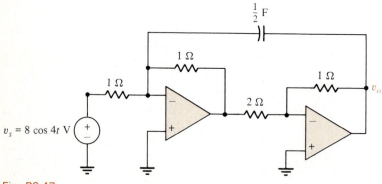

Fig. P8.47

CHAPTER 9

Power

● INTRODUCTION

In our previous analyses our major concern has been with determining voltages and currents. In many applications (e.g., electric utilities), energy or power supplied and absorbed are extremely important parameters. Knowing the instantaneous power is useful, since many electrical and electronic devices have maximum instantaneous or "peak" power ratings that, for satisfactory operation, should not be exceeded. By averaging instantaneous power we get "average power," which is the average rate at which energy is supplied or absorbed. Power usages vary from a fraction of a watt for small electronic circuits to millions of watts for large electric utilities.

We have previously defined power to be the product of voltage and current. For the case that voltage and current are constants (the dc case), the instantaneous power is equal to the average value of the power. This result is a consequence of the fact that the instantaneous and average values of a constant are equal. A sinusoid, however, has an average value of zero. This does not mean that power due to a sinusoid is zero. We shall see what effect sinusoids have in terms of power.

Just as we were able to determine under what condition maximum power transfer occurred for resistive circuits, in this chapter we deal with *RLC* sinusoidal circuits.

Although our prime interest in this chapter will be with the sinusoid, we shall also be able to discuss average power for the case of repetitive or periodic nonsinusoidal waveforms by using the notion of effective values. Yet it is the sinusoid that gets the greatest attention, since it is in this form that electric power is produced and distributed.

9.1 AVERAGE POWER

Recall that for the arbitrary element shown in Fig. 9.1, the instantaneous power absorbed by the element is $p(t) = v(t)i(t)$. For the case that the voltage is a sinusoid, say $v(t) = V \cos(\omega t + \phi_1)$, the current will also be sinusoidal, say $i(t) = I \cos(\omega t + \phi_2)$. Then the instantaneous power absorbed by the element is

$$p(t) = [V \cos(\omega t + \phi_1)][I \cos(\omega t + \phi_2)]$$

Using the trigonometric identity $(\cos \alpha)(\cos \beta) = \frac{1}{2}\cos(\alpha - \beta) + \frac{1}{2}\cos(\alpha + \beta)$, we get

$$p(t) = VI\left[\frac{1}{2}\cos(\phi_1 - \phi_2) + \frac{1}{2}\cos(2\omega t + \phi_1 + \phi_2)\right]$$

$$= \frac{VI}{2}\cos(\phi_1 - \phi_2) + \frac{VI}{2}\cos(2\omega t + \phi_1 + \phi_2)$$

If this is the instantaneous power, what is the average power P? The second term on the right in the last equation is a sinusoid of radian frequency 2ω. We know that the average value of a sinusoid is zero—this can be verified with calculus. Thus, the **average power** absorbed is

$$P = \tfrac{1}{2}VI\cos(\phi_1 - \phi_2) = \tfrac{1}{2}VI\cos\theta$$

where $\theta = \phi_1 - \phi_2$ is the difference in phase angles between voltage and current.

For the special case of a resistor, since the voltage and current are in phase, then the average power absorbed by the resistor is

$$P_R = \tfrac{1}{2}VI\cos 0 = \tfrac{1}{2}VI$$

From the fact that $V = RI$, we get

$$P_R = \tfrac{1}{2}VI = \tfrac{1}{2}RI^2 = \tfrac{1}{2}V^2/R$$

For an impedance that is purely imaginary (reactive), that is, $\mathbf{Z} = jX$, where X is a positive or a negative number, as depicted in Fig. 9.2, let us find the average power absorbed by such an element. Since

$$\mathbf{Z} = \frac{\mathbf{V}}{\mathbf{I}} = \frac{V\,\underline{/\phi_1}}{I\,\underline{/\phi_2}} = \frac{V}{I}\,\underline{/(\phi_1 - \phi_2)}$$

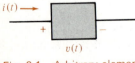

$i(t) \longrightarrow$

$v(t)$

Fig. 9.1 Arbitrary element.

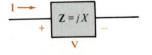

$I \longrightarrow$ $\mathbf{Z} = jX$

V

Fig. 9.2 Arbitrary reactance.

then for positive X, we have $jX = X\underline{/90°}$; while for negative X, we have $jX = -j(-X) = -X\underline{/-90°}$. Thus,

$$\mathbf{Z} = |X|\underline{/\pm 90°} = \frac{V}{I}\underline{/(\phi_1 - \phi_2)}$$

and the average power P_X absorbed by the reactance is

$$P_X = \tfrac{1}{2}VI\cos(\phi_1 - \phi_2) = \tfrac{1}{2}VI\cos(\pm 90°) = 0 \text{ W}$$

In other words, purely reactive impedances, such as (ideal) inductors and capacitors or combinations of the two, absorb zero average power, and are referred to as **lossless elements**.

EXAMPLE 9.1

For the RC circuit shown in Fig. 9.3(a), the corresponding frequency-domain representation is shown in Fig. 9.3(b). Since

$$\mathbf{I} = \frac{\mathbf{V}_s}{\mathbf{Z}} = \frac{6\underline{/-90°}}{1-j} = \frac{6\underline{/-90°}}{\sqrt{2}\underline{/-45°}} = 3\sqrt{2}\underline{/-45°}$$

then the average power absorbed by the series RC impedance (supplied by the voltage source) is

$$P = \tfrac{1}{2}VI\cos\theta = \tfrac{1}{2}(6)(3\sqrt{2})\cos(-90° + 45°) = 9\sqrt{2}\cos(-45°) = 9 \text{ W}$$

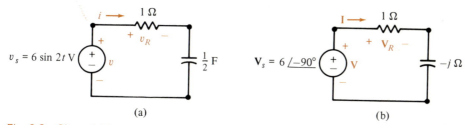

(a)   (b)

Fig. 9.3 Sinusoidal circuit in (a) the time domain and (b) the frequency domain.

By voltage division, the voltage across the resistor is

$$\mathbf{V}_R = \frac{\mathbf{Z}_R}{\mathbf{Z}_R + \mathbf{Z}_C}\mathbf{V}_s = \frac{1}{1-j}(6\underline{/-90°}) = \frac{6\underline{/-90°}}{\sqrt{2}\underline{/-45°}} = \frac{6}{\sqrt{2}}\underline{/-45°} = V_R\underline{/\phi_R}$$

and the power absorbed by the resistor is

$$P_R = \frac{1}{2}\frac{V_R^2}{R} = \frac{1}{2}\left(\frac{18}{1}\right) = 9 \text{ W}$$

Of course, this conclusion could have been obtained using the fact that the impedance of a capacitor is purely imaginary, so the power absorbed by the capacitor is $P_C = 0$, and all of the power supplied by the source, therefore, must be absorbed by the resistor.

DRILL EXERCISE 9.1

For the circuit given in Fig. 8.31 (p. 381), find the average power absorbed by the (a) 3-Ω resistor, (b) 6-Ω resistor, (c) capacitor, (d) dependent voltage source, and (e) independent voltage source.

Answer: (a) 2.31 W; (b) 5.07 W; (c) 0 W; (d) −1.54 W; (e) −5.84 W

Maximum Power Transfer

In the preceding example, we specifically considered a resistor connected in series with a capacitor. However, since an arbitrary load $\mathbf{Z}_L$ generally has a real and an imaginary part, i.e., $\mathbf{Z}_L = R_L + jX_L$, we can model $\mathbf{Z}_L$ as a resistance R_L connected in series with a reactance X_L (remember, X_L can be either positive or negative) as shown in Fig. 9.4. Since a pure reactance absorbs zero average power, if the current through $\mathbf{Z}_L$ is $\mathbf{I}_L$, then the average power absorbed by $\mathbf{Z}_L$ is

$$P = \tfrac{1}{2}|\mathbf{I}_L|^2 R_L$$

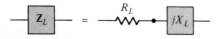

Fig. 9.4   Arbitrary load impedance modeled by a resistance in series with a reactance.

Given a circuit having a load impedance $\mathbf{Z}_L = R_L + jX_L$, as shown in Fig. 9.5(a), what impedance $\mathbf{Z}_L$ will result in the maximum average power being absorbed by the load?

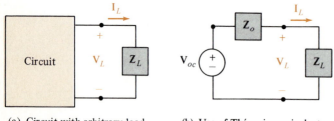

(a) Circuit with arbitrary load   (b) Use of Thévenin equivalent

Fig. 9.5   Determination of maximum power transfer.

The effect on the load is the same if the circuit is replaced by its Thévenin equivalent, as shown in Fig. 9.5(b), where $\mathbf{Z}_o = R_o + jX_o$. We have already seen that if $\mathbf{Z}_o = R_o$ and $\mathbf{Z}_L = R_L$, then the maximum power is absorbed by the load (i.e., maximum power is transferred to the load) when $R_L = R_o$. However, for the general case, we have

$$\mathbf{I}_L = \frac{\mathbf{V}_{oc}}{\mathbf{Z}_L + \mathbf{Z}_o} \quad \Rightarrow \quad |\mathbf{I}_L| = \frac{|\mathbf{V}_{oc}|}{|\mathbf{Z}_L + \mathbf{Z}_o|}$$

Let $\mathbf{V}_{oc} = V_{oc}/\underline{\phi_{oc}}$. Since $\mathbf{Z}_L + \mathbf{Z}_o = R_L + jX_L + R_o + jX_o = (R_L + R_o) + j(X_L + X_o)$, then

$$|\mathbf{I}_L| = \frac{V_{oc}}{\sqrt{(R_L + R_o)^2 + (X_L + X_o)^2}}$$

and the average power absorbed by the load is

$$P_L = \frac{1}{2}|\mathbf{I}_L|^2 R_L = \frac{1}{2}\frac{V_{oc}^2 R_L}{(R_L + R_o)^2 + (X_L + X_o)^2}$$

The quantity V_{oc} is a constant which depends upon the given circuit. Once the values of R_o and R_L have been selected, the term $(X_L + X_o)^2$ tends only to reduce P_L. To make P_L as large as possible, make $(X_L + X_o)^2$ zero by choosing $X_L = -X_o$. Then

$$P_L = \frac{1}{2}\frac{R_L V_{oc}^2}{(R_L + R_o)^2}$$

and just as in the case of maximum power transfer when $\mathbf{Z}_o = R_o$ and $\mathbf{Z}_L = R_L$, then the quantity P_L is maximum when $R_L = R_o$. Thus, in order to get maximum power to $\mathbf{Z}_L$, we select

$$\boxed{\mathbf{Z}_L = R_L + jX_L = R_o - jX_o = \mathbf{Z}_o^*}$$

Under this condition, the power absorbed by $\mathbf{Z}_L$ is

$$P_{L(max)} = \frac{1}{2}\frac{R_o V_{oc}^2}{(R_o + R_o)^2} = \frac{V_{oc}^2}{8R_o}$$

Suppose now that $\mathbf{Z}_L$ is restricted to be purely real (resistive). What value of R_L would result in maximum power transfer to the load? For the circuit in Fig. 9.6,

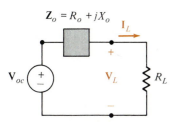

Fig. 9.6   Arbitrary circuit with resistive load.

we have that

$$\mathbf{I}_L = \frac{\mathbf{V}_{oc}}{R_L + \mathbf{Z}_o} \quad \Rightarrow \quad |\mathbf{I}_L| = \frac{V_{oc}}{\sqrt{(R_L + R_o)^2 + X_o^2}}$$

Then

$$P_L = \frac{1}{2}|\mathbf{I}_L|^2 R_L = \frac{1}{2}\frac{V_{oc}^2 R_L}{(R_L + R_o)^2 + X_o^2}$$

To determine for what value of R_L this is maximum, set $dP_L/dR_L = 0$. Thus,

$$\frac{dP_L}{dR_L} = \frac{1}{2}\left(\frac{[(R_L + R_o)^2 + X_o^2]V_{oc}^2 - 2(R_L + R_o)V_{oc}^2 R_L}{[(R_L + R_o)^2 + X_o^2]^2}\right) = 0$$

and equality holds when

$$[(R_L + R_o)^2 + X_o^2]V_{oc}^2 = 2(R_L + R_o)V_{oc}^2 R_L$$

From this expression,

$$R_L^2 = R_o^2 + X_o^2$$

Hence,

$$\boxed{R_L = \sqrt{R_o^2 + X_o^2} = |\mathbf{Z}_o|}$$

and this is the condition for either maximum P_L or minimum P_L. Since it is obvious that minimum load power occurs when $R_L = 0$, this is the condition for maximum power transfer to a purely resistive load R_L.

EXAMPLE 9.2

For the circuit shown in the colored box in Fig. 9.7, we leave it to the reader to verify that

$$\mathbf{V}_{oc} = \frac{189}{53} - j\frac{54}{53} = 3.71\underline{/-16^\circ}\ \text{V} \quad \text{and} \quad \mathbf{Z}_o = \frac{126}{53} - j\frac{36}{53} = 2.47\underline{/-16^\circ}\ \Omega$$

Thus maximum power is delivered to the load $\mathbf{Z}_L$ when

$$\mathbf{Z}_L = \mathbf{Z}_o^* = \frac{126}{53} + j\frac{36}{53} = 2.47\underline{/16^\circ}\ \Omega$$

Since $\mathbf{Z}_L$ has the form $\mathbf{Z}_L = R_L + j\omega L$, we have that

$$R_L = \frac{126}{53} = 2.38\ \Omega \quad \text{and} \quad \omega L = \frac{36}{53} \quad \Rightarrow \quad L = \frac{36}{53\omega} = \frac{36}{265} = 0.136\ \text{H}$$

Thus, $\mathbf{Z}_L$ is given in Fig. 9.8, and the power absorbed by $\mathbf{Z}_L$ is

$$P_{L(max)} = \frac{V_{oc}^2}{8R_o} = \frac{(3.71)^2}{8(2.38)} = 0.723\ \text{W}$$

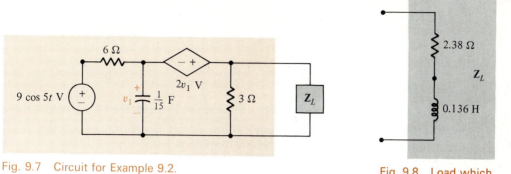

Fig. 9.7   Circuit for Example 9.2.

Fig. 9.8   Load which absorbs maximum power.

The load R_L that absorbs the maximum amount of power when R_L is constrained to be a resistance is

$$R_L = \sqrt{R_o^2 + X_o^2} = \sqrt{\left(\frac{126}{53}\right)^2 + \left(\frac{36}{53}\right)^2} = \frac{131}{53} = 2.47 \, \Omega$$

and the power delivered to R_L is

$$P_L = \frac{1}{2}\frac{V_{oc}^2 R_L}{(R_L + R_o)^2 + X_o^2} = \frac{1}{2}\frac{(3.71)^2(2.47)}{(2.47 + 2.38)^2 + (0.68)^2} = 0.709 \, W$$

DRILL EXERCISE 9.2

For the circuit given in Fig. 8.22 (p. 376), (a) find the impedance Z_L which absorbs maximum power, and calculate this power; (b) given that Z_L is constrained to be a resistance, find the resistance R_L which absorbs maximum power, and calculate this power.
Answer: (a) $8 + j56 \, \Omega$ (8 Ω, 14 H), 0.5 W; (b) 56.57 Ω, 0.124 W

9.2 EFFECTIVE VALUES

We have seen that for a resistor with a sinusoidal current through it, say $i(t) = I\cos(\omega t + \phi)$, the average power dissipated by R is $\frac{1}{2}RI^2$. What direct (constant) current I_e would yield the same power absorption by R? Since the power absorbed by R due to a direct (constant) current I_e is RI_e^2, we get the equality

$$RI_e^2 = \tfrac{1}{2}RI^2$$

from which

$$I_e = \frac{I}{\sqrt{2}} \approx 0.707\ I$$

Thus, the constant current $I_e = I/\sqrt{2}$ and the sinusoidal current $i(t) = I\cos(\omega t + \phi)$ result in the same average power absorption by R. For this reason, we say that $I/\sqrt{2}$ is the **effective value** of the sinusoid whose amplitude is I.

Since the voltage across R is

$$v(t) = Ri(t) = RI\cos(\omega t + \phi) = V\cos(\omega t + \phi)$$

then the effective value of $v(t)$ is $V_e = V/\sqrt{2}$. Furthermore, the average power absorbed by R is

$$P_R = \frac{VI}{2} = \frac{V}{\sqrt{2}}\frac{I}{\sqrt{2}} = V_e I_e$$

Alternatively, since $V = RI$, then

$$P_R = \frac{RI^2}{2} = R\frac{I}{\sqrt{2}}\frac{I}{\sqrt{2}} = RI_e^2$$

and since $I = V/R$, we also have that

$$P_R = \frac{V^2}{2R} = \frac{1}{R}\frac{V}{\sqrt{2}}\frac{V}{\sqrt{2}} = \frac{V_e^2}{R}$$

In summary, given a resistor R having current $i(t) = I\cos(\omega t + \phi)$ through it and voltage $v(t) = V\cos(\omega t + \phi)$ across it, then the average power absorbed by the resistor is

$$P_R = V_e I_e = RI_e^2 = \frac{V_e^2}{R}$$

where $V_e = V/\sqrt{2}$ and $I_e = I/\sqrt{2}$ are the effective values of the voltage and the current, respectively.

For an arbitrary element

$$P = \tfrac{1}{2}VI\cos\theta = V_e I_e \cos\theta \qquad (9.1)$$

where θ is the difference in phase between the voltage and the current.

EXAMPLE 9.3

Ordinary household voltage is designated typically as 115 V ac, 60 Hz. The term "ac," which stands for **alternating current**, indicates a sinusoid, and 60 Hz is the frequency of the sinusoid. However, the 115 V does not refer to the amplitude of the sinusoid, but rather to its effective value. Thus, the amplitude of the sinusoid is $115\sqrt{2} \approx 163$ V.

RMS Values

Again, for a resistor R whose current is $i(t)$ and whose voltage is $v(t)$, consider the case that the current (or the voltage) is nonsinusoidal. Since the instantaneous power absorbed by the resistor is $p(t) = v(t)i(t)$, then by Ohm's law, we get

$$p(t) = Ri^2(t)$$

Summing the instantaneous power from time t_1 to t_2 and dividing by the width of the interval $t_2 - t_1$ yields the average power absorbed in the interval, that is,

$$P = \frac{1}{t_2 - t_1} \int_{t_1}^{t_2} p(t)\,dt = \frac{1}{t_2 - t_1} \int_{t_1}^{t_2} Ri^2(t)\,dt$$

Suppose that the current (and hence the voltage) is "repetitive" or "periodic," and the period is T. Then the average power absorbed in one period is

$$P = \frac{1}{T} \int_{t_o}^{t_o+T} p(t)\,dt = \frac{1}{T} \int_{t_o}^{t_o+T} Ri^2(t)\,dt$$

where t_o is an arbitrary value. Again, let I_e be the constant current that results in the same amount of average power absorption. Thus,

$$RI_e^2 = \frac{1}{T} \int_{t_o}^{t_o+T} Ri^2(t)\,dt$$

from which the expression for I_e, the effective value of $i(t)$, is

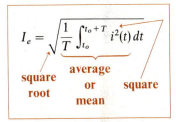

$$I_e = \sqrt{\frac{1}{T} \int_{t_o}^{t_o+T} i^2(t)\,dt}$$

square root — **average or mean** — **square**

and for this reason the effective value is also known as the **root-mean-square** or **rms** value. Similarly, the effective or rms value of $v(t)$ is

$$V_e = \sqrt{\frac{1}{T} \int_{t_o}^{t_o+T} v^2(t)\,dt}$$

It is a routine exercise in integral calculus to confirm that the rms value of the sinusoid $A \cos(\omega t + \phi)$, whose period is $T = 2\pi/\omega$, is $A/\sqrt{2}$.

EXAMPLE 9.4

The function $f(t)$ shown in Fig. 9.9 is periodic, where the period is $T = 4$ s. Although the average or mean value of this function is zero (why?), the rms value of $f(t)$ is

$$\sqrt{\frac{1}{T} \int_{-2}^{2} f^2(t) \, dt} = \sqrt{\frac{1}{4} \left[\int_{-2}^{-1} 1^2 \, dt + \int_{-1}^{1} (-t)^2 \, dt + \int_{1}^{2} (-1)^2 \, dt \right]}$$

$$= \sqrt{\frac{1}{4} \left[t \Big|_{-2}^{-1} + \frac{t^3}{3} \Big|_{-1}^{1} + t \Big|_{1}^{2} \right]} = \sqrt{\frac{1}{4} \left(1 + \frac{2}{3} + 1\right)} = \sqrt{\frac{2}{3}}$$

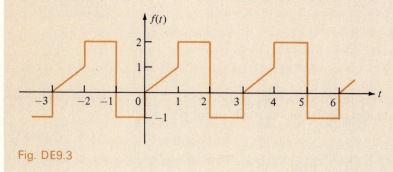

Fig. 9.9   Nonsinusoidal, periodic waveform.

In other words, if the current through a resistor R is $i(t) = f(t)$, then the average power absorbed by R is

$$P = RI_e^2 = R\left(\sqrt{\frac{2}{3}}\right)^2 = \frac{2R}{3} \text{ W}$$

DRILL EXERCISE 9.3

Find the rms value of the function shown in Fig. DE9.3.
Answer: $\frac{4}{3}$

Fig. DE9.3

There are times when a sinusoidal current or voltage is referred to by its rms value alone. For such a circumstance, it is a simple matter to deduce the value of the amplitude of the sinusoid—but not the angle of the sinusoid. Yet, knowledge of rms values and other quantities, such as power absorbed, may provide enough information for a complete circuit analysis.

● ───

EXAMPLE 9.5

For the series RC circuit shown in Fig. 9.10(a), suppose that the capacitor voltage is 6 V rms and the power absorbed by the resistor is 18 W. Let us determine the values of R and C.

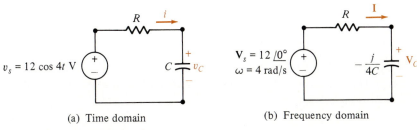

          (a) Time domain   (b) Frequency domain

Fig. 9.10   Series RC circuit.

The frequency-domain representation of the circuit is shown in Fig. 9.10(b). By voltage division,

$$\mathbf{V}_C = \frac{-j/4C}{R - j/4C}\,\mathbf{V}_s = \frac{-j}{4RC - j}\,(12\underline{/0^\circ}) \tag{9.2}$$

Since the rms value of the capacitor voltage is 6 V, then $|\mathbf{V}_C| = 6\sqrt{2}$ V. Thus, from Equation (9.2),

$$|\mathbf{V}_C| = \left|\frac{-j12}{4RC - j}\right| = \frac{|-j12|}{|4RC - j|}$$

or

$$6\sqrt{2} = \frac{12}{\sqrt{16R^2C^2 + 1}} \quad\Rightarrow\quad RC = \frac{1}{4}$$

For the circuit in Fig. 9.10(b), we also have that

$$\mathbf{I} = \frac{\mathbf{V}_s}{R - j/4C} = \frac{4C\mathbf{V}_s}{4RC - j} = \frac{48C}{4RC - j}$$

Since the power absorbed by the resistor is 18 W, then

$$P = \frac{1}{2}R|\mathbf{I}|^2 = \frac{1}{2}R\left|\frac{48C}{4RC - j}\right|^2 = \frac{1}{2}R\frac{|48C|^2}{|4RC - j|^2}$$

or

$$18 = \frac{1}{2} R \frac{48^2 C^2}{16R^2C^2 + 1} \tag{9.3}$$

Substituting $RC = \frac{1}{4}$ into Equation (9.3) and simplifying yields

$$C = \frac{1}{8} \text{ F} \quad \Rightarrow \quad R = \frac{1}{4C} = \frac{1}{4(1/8)} = 2\ \Omega$$

It is now a routine matter to determine the angle of the voltage across the capacitor and the magnitude and the angle of the current (and hence the voltage across the resistor) for the given circuit. We leave this as an exercise for the reader.

DRILL EXERCISE 9.4

For the circuit given in Fig. 9.10(a), replace the C-farad capacitor with an L-henry inductor. Find R and L for the case that the inductor voltage is 6 V rms and the power absorbed by the resistor is 18 W.
Answer: $2\ \Omega, 0.5$ H

9.3 IMPORTANT POWER CONCEPTS

Consider the arbitrary load, as depicted in Fig. 9.11, where $v(t) = V\cos(\omega t + \phi_1)$ and $i(t) = I\cos(\omega t + \phi_2)$. Then the average power absorbed by the load is, repeating Equation (9.1),

$$P = \tfrac{1}{2}VI\cos\theta = V_e I_e \cos\theta \tag{9.1}$$

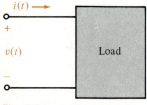

Fig. 9.11 Arbitrary load.

where $\theta = \phi_1 - \phi_2$. If the load is purely resistive, then the average power it absorbs is $P_R = V_e I_e$. However, if the load is not purely resistive, even though it might "appear" at first glance that the average power absorbed is $V_e I_e$, the average power absorbed is given by Equation (9.1). We call $V_e I_e$ the **apparent power** and use the unit **voltampere** (VA) to distinguish this quantity from the actual power (the average power) that is absorbed by the load. The quantity $\cos\theta$, called the **power factor** and abbreviated pf, is the ratio of average power to apparent power, that is,

$$\text{pf} = \frac{\text{average power}}{\text{apparent power}} = \cos \theta = \frac{P}{V_e I_e}$$

The angle θ is referred to as the **power-factor angle**.

The impedance of the load is

$$\mathbf{Z} = \frac{\mathbf{V}}{\mathbf{I}} = \frac{V \underline{/\phi_1}}{I \underline{/\phi_2}} = \frac{V}{I} \underline{/(\phi_1 - \phi_2)} = \frac{V}{I} \underline{/\theta}$$

so that the angle of the load is the pf angle. The general form of a load impedance is $\mathbf{Z} = R + jX$. If $X > 0$, we say that the load is **inductive**; if $X < 0$, we say it is **capacitive**. Assuming a positive resistance R, then for an inductive load

$$\theta = \text{ang } \mathbf{Z} = \tan^{-1} \frac{X}{R} > 0$$

that is, the pf angle is positive; while for a capacitive load

$$\theta = \text{ang } \mathbf{Z} = \tan^{-1} \frac{X}{R} < 0$$

that is, the pf angle is negative. The former case ($\phi_1 > \phi_2$) implies that the current lags the voltage, whereas the latter case ($\phi_1 < \phi_2$) implies that the current leads the voltage. In the vernacular of the power industry, we refer to the pf as being **lagging** or **leading**, respectively. In other words, if the current lags the voltage for a load (the inductive case), the result is a lagging pf; if the current leads the voltage (the capacitive case), the result is a leading pf.

You may ask, "Why talk about lagging and leading pf at all? Why not just talk about the impedance of the load?" One reason is that, in some applications (e.g., power systems), a load may not consist simply of ordinary inductors, capacitors, and resistors. In the following example, the load is an electric motor.

EXAMPLE 9.6

A 1000-W electric motor is connected to a 200-V rms ac, 60-Hz source, and the result is a lagging pf of 0.8. Since the pf is lagging, the angle of the current is less than the voltage angle by $\cos^{-1}(0.8) = 36.9°$. Arbitrarily selecting the voltage angle to be zero, we can depict the given situation as shown in Fig. 9.12. From Equation (9.1), we

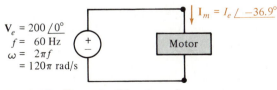

$V_e = 200 \underline{/0°}$
$f = 60$ Hz
$\omega = 2\pi f$
$\quad = 120\pi$ rad/s

$\mathbf{I}_m = I_e \underline{/-36.9°}$

Motor

Fig. 9.12 Example of lagging pf.

have

$$I_e = \frac{P}{V_e \cos \theta} = \frac{1000}{200(0.8)} = \frac{25}{4} = 6.25 \text{ A (rms)}$$

so that

$$\mathbf{I}_m = 6.25 \underline{/-36.9°} = 5 - j3.75 \text{ A}$$

Of course, since the motor absorbs 1000 W of average power, then the source supplies this power. But suppose that a 28-μF capacitor is placed in parallel with the motor. Since the current through the motor does not change, we have the situation shown in Fig. 9.13(a). Then

$$\mathbf{I}_C = \frac{\mathbf{V}_e}{\mathbf{Z}_C} = j\omega C \mathbf{V}_e = (1 \underline{/90°})(120\pi)(28 \times 10^{-6})(200 \underline{/0°}) = 2.11 \underline{/90°} = j2.11 \text{ A}$$

and

$$\mathbf{I} = \mathbf{I}_m + \mathbf{I}_C = 5 - j1.64 = 5.26 \underline{/-18.1°} \text{ A}$$

and the pf for the new load (the motor in parallel with the capacitor) is $\cos(18.1°) = 0.95$, and since the angle of **I** is negative, the pf is lagging. These results are summarized by the phasor diagram shown in Fig. 9.13(b).

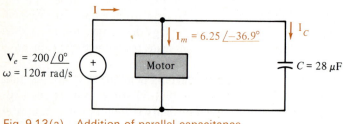

Fig. 9.13(a)   Addition of parallel capacitance.

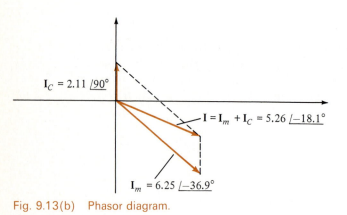

Fig. 9.13(b)   Phasor diagram.

We now see that placing a capacitor in parallel with the motor increases the lagging pf from 0.8 to 0.95. Since capacitors absorb zero average power, and since the motor absorbs 1000 W in either case, the voltage source supplies 1000 W in both cases. Note, however, that originally 6.25 A of rms current is drawn from the voltage source, while after the capacitor is connected in parallel, the rms current is 5.26 A—a decrease of about 16 percent.

DRILL EXERCISE 9.5

A 1200-W electric motor, which operates at 200 V rms, 60 Hz, has a lagging pf of 0.5. Determine the value of the capacitor C, which when placed in parallel with the motor, will result in a pf of unity (i.e., $\cos \theta = 1$) for the parallel combination. Draw the corresponding phasor diagram.
Answer: 137.8 μF

There are situations in which current changes, such as the one in Example 9.6, have significant implications. One important case is when the voltage source is an electric utility-company generator and the load is some demand by a consumer. Between the two is the power transmission line, which is not ideal and has some associated nonzero resistance.

EXAMPLE 9.7
Suppose that a large consumer of electricity requires 10 kW of power by using 230 V rms at a pf angle of 60° lagging, that is, a pf of 0.5 lagging. We conclude that the current drawn by the load has an effective value of

$$I_e = \frac{P}{V_e \cos \theta} = \frac{10,000}{230(0.5)} \approx 87 \text{ A (rms)}$$

If the transmission-line resistance is $R = 0.1 \ \Omega$, then, as indicated in Fig. 9.14,

$$\mathbf{V}_e = 0.1\mathbf{I}_L + \mathbf{V}_L \approx (8.7\underline{/-60°}) + (230\underline{/0°}) = 234.5\underline{/-1.8°} \text{ V}$$

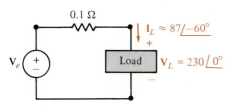

Fig. 9.14   Inclusion of transmission-line resistance.

Thus, the voltage that must be generated by the power company must have an effective value of $V_e \approx 234.5$ V. Also, the line loss is $RI_e^2 = 756$ W. Although the utility gets paid for 10 kW of power, it has to produce 10,756 W.

If the consumer can change the pf from 0.5 to 0.9 lagging, the load current will become $I_e \approx 48$ A rms, so the line loss will be approximately 233 W—which is about 30 percent of the loss at the lower pf. It is for this reason that an electric utility takes pf into consideration when dealing with large consumers. The process of increasing a lagging pf is an example of **power-factor correction**.

An average household uses relatively small amounts of power and typically has a reasonably high pf. Thus, pf is not a consideration in home electricity usage.

Complex Power

Previously, we found it computationally convenient to introduce the abstract concept of a complex sinusoid—a real sinusoid is just a special case. So, too, we now discuss and apply the notion of "complex power."

Again consider the arbitrary load depicted in Fig. 9.15, where $\mathbf{V} = V\underline{/\phi_1}$, $\mathbf{I} = I\underline{/\phi_2}$, $V_e = V/\sqrt{2}$, $I_e = I/\sqrt{2}$. Since $P = V_e I_e \cos\theta$, and $\cos\theta = \text{Re}[e^{j\theta}]$, then

$$P = V_e I_e(\text{Re}[e^{j\theta}]) = V_e I_e(\text{Re}[e^{j(\phi_1 - \phi_2)}]) = V_e I_e(\text{Re}[e^{j\phi_1}e^{-j\phi_2}])$$

$$= \text{Re}[V_e I_e e^{j\phi_1}e^{-j\phi_2}] = \text{Re}[(V_e e^{j\phi_1})(I_e e^{-j\phi_2})]$$

$$= \text{Re}[(V_e e^{j\phi_1})(I_e e^{j\phi_2})^*]$$

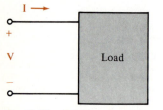

Fig. 9.15 Arbitrary load.

That is, the average power absorbed by the load is equal to the real part of some complex quantity. Defining $\mathbf{V}_{rms}$ and $\mathbf{I}_{rms}$, respectively, by

$$\mathbf{V}_{rms} = V_e e^{j\phi_1} \quad \text{and} \quad \mathbf{I}_{rms} = I_e e^{j\phi_2}$$

then

$$P = \text{Re}[\mathbf{V}_{rms}\mathbf{I}_{rms}^*]$$

That is, the average power absorbed is the real part of the quantity

$$\boxed{\mathbf{S} = \mathbf{V}_{rms}\mathbf{I}_{rms}^*}$$

which is called the **complex power** absorbed by the load. That is,

$$\mathbf{S} = (V_e e^{j\phi_1})(I_e e^{-j\phi_2}) = V_e I_e e^{j(\phi_1 - \phi_2)} = V_e I_e e^{j\theta}$$

Thus, we see that the magnitude of the complex power is the apparent power $|\mathbf{S}| = V_e I_e$, and the angle of the complex power is the pf angle. By Euler's formula, we can write the complex power in rectangular form as follows:

$$\mathbf{S} = V_e I_e(\cos\theta + j\sin\theta) = V_e I_e \cos\theta + jV_e I_e \sin\theta = P + jQ$$

where $P = V_e I_e \cos\theta$ is the average power absorbed by the load—also called the **real power**—and $Q = V_e I_e \sin\theta$ is called the **reactive power**. As mentioned before, the unit of P is the watt (W). The unit of Q is the **var**—short for voltampere reactive. The unit of complex power $\mathbf{S}$, like its magnitude $|\mathbf{S}|$ (apparent power), is the voltampere (VA). Thus, we have

$$V_e I_e = |\mathbf{S}| = \sqrt{P^2 + Q^2}$$

and the angle of $\mathbf{S}$ is the pf angle θ, so

$$\theta = \tan^{-1}\left(\frac{Q}{P}\right)$$

From the triangle—called a **power triangle**—shown in Fig. 9.16, we deduce that the pf is

$$\cos\theta = \frac{P}{\sqrt{P^2 + Q^2}} = \frac{P}{|\mathbf{S}|}$$

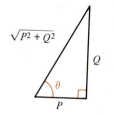

Fig. 9.16   Power triangle.

EXAMPLE 9.8

For the circuit shown in Fig. 9.17, the source is given in terms of the ordinary (non-rms) phasor representation. The impedance loading the voltage source is

$$\mathbf{Z}_1 = \frac{\mathbf{V}}{\mathbf{I}} = \frac{R[(1/j\omega C) + j\omega L]}{R + (1/j\omega C) + j\omega L} = \frac{R(1 - \omega^2 LC)}{1 - \omega^2 LC + j\omega RC}$$

$$= \frac{40(1 - 4)}{(1 - 4) + j4} = \frac{-120}{-3 + j4} = \frac{120}{3 - j4} = \frac{120}{5\,\underline{/-53°}} = 24\,\underline{/53°}\ \Omega$$

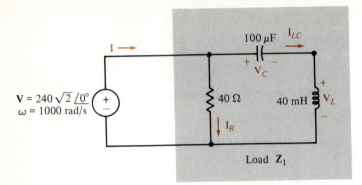

Fig. 9.17   Voltage source and its associated load.

Thus,

$$\mathbf{I} = \frac{\mathbf{V}}{\mathbf{Z}_1} = \frac{240\sqrt{2}\underline{/0^\circ}}{24\underline{/53^\circ}} = 10\sqrt{2}\underline{/-53^\circ} \text{ A}$$

so that the complex power *supplied* by the source is

$$\mathbf{S} = \mathbf{V}_{rms}\mathbf{I}^*_{rms} = (240\underline{/0^\circ})(10\underline{/53^\circ}) = 2400\underline{/53^\circ} = 1440 + j1920 \text{ VA}$$

Hence, the apparent power is $|\mathbf{S}| = 2400$ VA, the pf angle is $\text{ang}(\mathbf{S}) = 53^\circ$, and thus the pf is $\cos 53^\circ = 0.6$ lagging. The real power is $P = 1440$ W and the reactive power is $Q = 1920$ var.

Since a pf that is too small may cost money, let us try to increase the pf. As $\text{pf} = \cos\theta = P/|\mathbf{S}|$, one way to increase the pf is to increase the real power P. But real power is costly. Instead, let us place another load in parallel with the given one. This will not affect the voltage and current of the original load, but it will have an effect on the current through the voltage source. The resulting situation is depicted in Fig. 9.18, where $\mathbf{Z}_1 = 24\underline{/53^\circ}$, $\mathbf{I}_1 = 10\sqrt{2}\underline{/-53^\circ}$, and $\mathbf{S}_1 = 2400\underline{/53^\circ} = 1440 + j1920$. Suppose we wish to raise the lagging pf to 0.9. Since $\cos^{-1}(0.9) = 25.84^\circ$, let us call the current drain on the source $\mathbf{I} = \sqrt{2}I\underline{/-25.84^\circ}$. The resulting complex power supplied by the source is

$$\mathbf{S} = \mathbf{V}_{rms}\mathbf{I}^*_{rms} = (240\underline{/0^\circ})(I\underline{/25.84^\circ}) = 240I\underline{/25.84^\circ} \text{ VA}$$

As we wish the real power to remain the same as before, we have

$$P = |\mathbf{S}|\cos\theta = (240I)(0.9) = 1440 \text{ W}$$

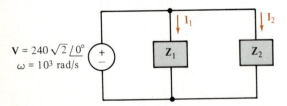

Fig. 9.18   Power-factor correction for $\mathbf{Z}_1$.

from which

$$I = \frac{1440}{(240)(0.9)} = 6.67 \quad \Rightarrow \quad \mathbf{I} = 6.67\sqrt{2}\underline{/-25.84°} \text{ A}$$

By KCL,

$$\mathbf{I}_2 = \mathbf{I} - \mathbf{I}_1 = (6.67\sqrt{2}\underline{/-25.84°}) - (10\sqrt{2}\underline{/-53°}) = 5.1\sqrt{2}\underline{/90°} \text{ A}$$

Thus,

$$\mathbf{Z}_2 = \frac{\mathbf{V}}{\mathbf{I}_2} = \frac{240\underline{/0°}}{5.1\underline{/90°}} = 47\underline{/-90°} = -j47 \ \Omega$$

This is purely reactive, which might have been expected because of the constraint that there be no additional real power supplied by the source. This impedance can be realized with a capacitor as follows:

$$\frac{1}{j\omega C} = \frac{-j}{\omega C} = -j47 \quad \Rightarrow \quad C = \frac{1}{47\omega} = \frac{1}{47(10^3)} = 21.3 \ \mu\text{F}$$

Return now to the original circuit given in Fig. 9.17. The current through the resistor is

$$\mathbf{I}_R = \frac{\mathbf{V}}{40} = 6\sqrt{2}\underline{/0°} = 6\sqrt{2} \text{ A}$$

and the complex power absorbed by the resistor is

$$\mathbf{S}_R = (240\underline{/0°})(6\underline{/0°}) = 1440 \text{ W}$$

which, of course, is real. The current through the series LC combination is

$$\mathbf{I}_{LC} = \frac{1}{(1/j\omega C) + j\omega L} = \frac{240\sqrt{2}\underline{/0°}}{(10/j) + j40} = -j8\sqrt{2} = 8\sqrt{2}\underline{/-90°} \text{ A}$$

The voltage across the capacitor is

$$\mathbf{V}_C = \frac{1}{j\omega C}\mathbf{I}_{LC} = \frac{-j8\sqrt{2}}{j10^{-1}} = -80\sqrt{2} = 80\sqrt{2}\underline{/180°} \text{ V}$$

and the voltage across the inductor is

$$\mathbf{V}_L = j\omega L\mathbf{I}_{LC} = j40(-j8\sqrt{2}) = 320\sqrt{2} \text{ V}$$

The complex power[†] absorbed by the capacitor is

$$\mathbf{S}_C = \tfrac{1}{2}\mathbf{V}_C\mathbf{I}_{LC}^* = (80\underline{/180°})(8\underline{/90°}) = 640\underline{/-90°} = -j640 \text{ VA}$$

and the complex power absorbed by the inductor is

$$\mathbf{S}_L = \tfrac{1}{2}\mathbf{V}_L\mathbf{I}_{LC}^* = (320\underline{/0°})(8\underline{/90°}) = 2560\underline{/90°} = j2560 \text{ VA}$$

[†] In terms of ordinary non-rms phasors $\mathbf{V}$ and $\mathbf{I}$, the formula for complex power is $\mathbf{S} = \tfrac{1}{2}\mathbf{VI}^*$.

The sum of the complex powers absorbed by the resistor, capacitor, and inductor is

$$\mathbf{S}_R + \mathbf{S}_C + \mathbf{S}_L = 1440 - j640 + j2560 = 1440 + j1920 \text{ VA}$$

and this is exactly the complex power supplied by the source. This result is a consequence of the fact that, as with the case of real power, complex power is conserved. The implication is, therefore, that reactive power is also conserved.

DRILL EXERCISE 9.6

For the circuit shown in Fig. DE9.6, $\mathbf{Z}_1 = 3 + j4 \ \Omega$ is the impedance of a transmission line and $\mathbf{Z}_L = 27 + j36 \ \Omega$ is the impedance of a load. Use the concept of complex power to determine the real power and reactive power absorbed by (a) the line, (b) the load, and (c) the voltage source.
Answer: (a) 69.12 W, 92.16 var; (b) 622.08 W, 829.44 var; (c) −691.2 W, −921.6 var

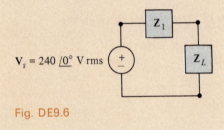

$\mathbf{V}_s = 240 \ \underline{/0°}$ V rms

Fig. DE9.6

Single-Phase, Three-Wire Circuits

Previously, we mentioned that ordinary household voltage is sinusoidal, having an approximate rms value of 115 V and a frequency of 60 Hz. Let us discuss the subject further.

Coming from a power line into a home's service panel or fuse box are three wires. One wire is bare; it has no insulation. This is the **neutral** or **ground wire**, so called since it must be connected to a water pipe or a rod (or both) that goes into the ground. (The earth is the reference potential of zero volts.) Typically, another wire is red and a third is black. The voltage between the red and neutral wires (plus sign at the red wire) is $v_{rn}(t) = 115\sqrt{2}\cos(120\pi t + \phi)$—that is, 115 V (rms) ac, 60 Hz. The voltage $v_{bn}(t)$ between the black and the neutral wires (plus at the black wire) is $v_{bn}(t) = -v_{rn}(t)$. This means that the voltage between the neutral and black wires (with the plus at the neutral wire is $v_{nb}(t) = -v_{bn}(t) = v_{rn}(t)$, and, therefore, the two voltages have the same phase angle. As these voltages remain fairly constant for a wide variety of practical loads (applicances), we can reasonably approximate the **single-phase, three-wire source** just described as shown in Fig. 9.19(a), where $v_{rn}(t) = v_{nb}(t) = v_s(t) = 115\sqrt{2}\cos(120\pi t + \phi)$. By KVL, we have that $v_{rb}(t) = 230\sqrt{2}\cos(120\pi t + \phi)$. Thus, in addition to two 115-V ac, 60-Hz sources, there is a supply of 230 V (rms) ac, 60 Hz.

This higher voltage is useful for higher power appliances, since for a given higher power requirement, a higher voltage uses less current than a lower voltage. The result is a lower line loss.

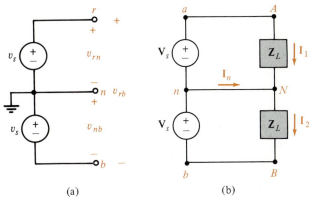

(a)   (b)

Fig. 9.19   (a) Single-phase, three-wire source. (b) Single-phase, three-wire circuit.

The single-phase, three-wire circuit of Fig. 9.19(b), (which is represented in the frequency domain), consists of a single-phase, three-wire source and two identical loads. By Ohm's law,

$$I_1 = \frac{V_s}{Z_L} = I_2 \quad \Rightarrow \quad I_n = I_2 - I_1 = 0$$

and we see that there is no current in the "neutral wire" (the short circuit between nodes n and N). If this wire is removed (replaced by an open circuit), the voltage across each load Z_L is still V_s and the currents I_1 and I_2 remain V_s/Z_L.

The short circuits between nodes a and A and between nodes b and B are the **lines** of the circuit. Suppose that they both have the same impedance Z_g. Since each such impedance is in series with an impedance Z_L, we can treat the resulting circuit as the simple system in Fig. 9.19(b), where the loads are $Z_L + Z_g$. We can then deduce that again $I_n = 0$, and the neutral wire can be removed without affecting the voltages and currents. But what if the neutral wire has a nonzero impedance? (This also corresponds to a line impedance.) Furthermore, what happens if another load Z is connected between nodes A and B? To answer these questions, consider the circuit shown in Fig. 9.20.

By KVL, for mesh I_1,

$$V_s = (Z_g + Z_L + Z_n)I_1 - Z_nI_2 - Z_LI_3 \tag{9.4}$$

and, for mesh I_2,

$$V_s = -Z_nI_1 + (Z_g + Z_L + Z_n)I_2 - Z_LI_3 \tag{9.5}$$

Subtracting Equation (9.5) from Equation (9.4) we obtain

$$0 = (Z_g + Z_L + Z_n)(I_1 - I_2) + Z_n(I_1 - I_2)$$

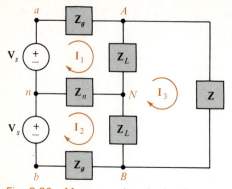

Fig. 9.20   More complex single-phase, three-wire circuit.

from which

$$0 = (\mathbf{Z}_g + \mathbf{Z}_L + 2\mathbf{Z}_n)(\mathbf{I}_1 - \mathbf{I}_2) \qquad \Rightarrow \qquad \mathbf{I}_1 = \mathbf{I}_2$$

Thus,

$$\mathbf{I}_n = \mathbf{I}_2 - \mathbf{I}_1 = 0$$

as before. Note that this result was obtained without writing the equation for mesh $\mathbf{I}_3$; that is, the value for $\mathbf{Z}$ does not influence this outcome. Specifically, for the special case that $\mathbf{Z}$ is infinite (an open circuit), then $\mathbf{I}_3 = 0$, and again subtracting Equation (9.5) from Equation (9.4) yields $\mathbf{I}_n = 0$.

The circuit in Fig. 9.20 has a symmetry with respect to the neutral connection between nodes n and N, and this symmetry (we call the load consisting of both impedances labeled $\mathbf{Z}_L$ and $\mathbf{Z}$ **symmetrical** or **balanced**) results in a zero neutral current regardless of the neutral impedance $\mathbf{Z}_n$.

EXAMPLE 9.9

The load for a single-phase three-wire circuit is generally not balanced. For the circuit in Fig. 9.20, suppose that $\mathbf{Z}_g = 0.1\ \Omega$, $\mathbf{Z}_n = 2\ \Omega$, the load impedance between nodes A and N is $60\ \Omega$, the load impedance between nodes N and B is $80\ \Omega$, and $\mathbf{Z} = 10 + j15\ \Omega$. Suppose that the rms phasor for the sources is $\mathbf{V}_s = 115\underline{/0°}$. Then for mesh $\mathbf{I}_1$ we get

$$115 = 62.1\mathbf{I}_1 - 2\mathbf{I}_2 - 60\mathbf{I}_3 \tag{9.6}$$

and, for mesh $\mathbf{I}_2$,

$$115 = -2\mathbf{I}_1 + 82.1\mathbf{I}_2 - 80\mathbf{I}_3 \tag{9.7}$$

Finally, for mesh $\mathbf{I}_3$,

$$-60\mathbf{I}_1 - 80\mathbf{I}_2 + (150 + j15)\mathbf{I}_3 = 0 \tag{9.8}$$

Solving these equations, we get the mesh currents

$$\mathbf{I}_1 = 13.8\underline{/-49.26°} \text{ A rms}$$

$$\mathbf{I}_2 = 13.51\underline{/-50.71°} \text{ A rms}$$

$$\mathbf{I}_3 = 12.66\underline{/-55.8°} \text{ A rms}$$

Thus, the power delivered to the loads is $P_{AN} + P_{NB} + P_{AB}$, where

$$P_{AN} = |\mathbf{I}_1 - \mathbf{I}_3|^2(60) = (1.88)^2(60) = 212 \text{ W}$$

$$P_{NB} = |\mathbf{I}_2 - \mathbf{I}_3|^2(80) = (1.44)^2(80) = 165 \text{ W}$$

$$P_{AB} = |\mathbf{I}_3|^2(10) = (12.66)^2(10) = 1603 \text{ W}$$

and

$$P_{AN} + P_{NB} + P_{AB} = 1980 \text{ W}$$

The line loss is $P_{aA} + P_{bB} + P_{nN}$, where

$$P_{aA} = |\mathbf{I}_1|^2(0.1) = (13.8)^2(0.1) = 19 \text{ W}$$

$$P_{bB} = |\mathbf{I}_2|^2(0.1) = (13.51)^2(0.1) = 18.3 \text{ W}$$

$$P_{nN} = |\mathbf{I}_1 - \mathbf{I}_2|^2(2) = (0.44)^2(2) = 0.4 \text{ W}$$

so

$$P_{aA} + P_{bB} + P_{nN} = 37.7 \text{ W}$$

and the total power supplied by the sources must be

$$P = 1980 + 37.7 \approx 2018 \text{ W}$$

As a check, the power supplied by the upper source is

$$|\mathbf{V}_s||\mathbf{I}_1|\cos\theta_1 = (115)(13.8)\cos 49.26° = 1035 \text{ W}$$

and the power supplied by the lower source is

$$|\mathbf{V}_s||\mathbf{I}_2|\cos\theta_2 = (115)(13.51)\cos 50.71° = 984 \text{ W}$$

for a total of $1035 + 984 = 2019$ W. The apparent discrepancy in power absorbed and power supplied is due to roundoff error (after all, 1 out of 2018 is an error of only about 0.05 percent).

DRILL EXERCISE 9.7

For the single-phase, three-wire circuit given in Fig. 9.20, suppose that $\mathbf{Z}_g = \mathbf{Z}_n = 0$ Ω, the load between nodes A and N is 60 Ω, the load between nodes B and N is 80 Ω, and $\mathbf{Z} = 10 + j15$ Ω. For the case that $\mathbf{V}_s = 115\underline{/0°}$ V rms, find the power absorbed by each impedance, and the power supplied by each voltage source.
Answer: 220.4 W; 165.3 W; 1627.7 W; 1034.3 W; 979.2 W

9.4 THREE-PHASE CIRCUITS

A single-phase, three-wire circuit contains a source that produces two sinusoidal voltages that have the same amplitude and the same phase angle. A circuit that contains a source that produces (sinusoidal) voltages with different phases is called a **polyphase system**. The importance of this concept lies in the fact that most of the generation and distribution of electric power in the United States is accomplished with polyphase systems. The most common polyphase system is the balanced three-phase system, which has the property that it supplies constant instantaneous power. This results in less vibration of the rotating machinery used to generate electric power.

A **Y(wye)-connected three-phase source** in the frequency domain is shown in Fig. 9.21. Terminals *a*, *b*, and *c* are called the **line terminals** and *n* is called the **neutral terminal**. The source is said to be **balanced** if the voltages $\mathbf{V}_{an}$, $\mathbf{V}_{bn}$, and $\mathbf{V}_{cn}$, called **phase voltages**, have the same amplitude and sum to zero, that is, if

$$|\mathbf{V}_{an}| = |\mathbf{V}_{bn}| = |\mathbf{V}_{cn}| \quad \text{and} \quad \mathbf{V}_{an} + \mathbf{V}_{bn} + \mathbf{V}_{cn} = 0$$

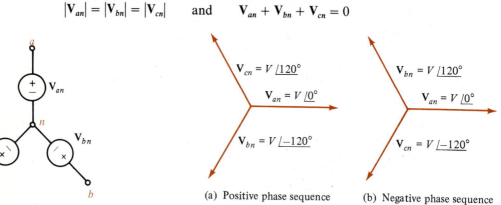

Fig. 9.21   A Y-connected three-phase source.

Fig. 9.22   Phasor diagrams.

Suppose that the amplitude of the sinusoids is *V*. If we arbitrarily select the angle of $\mathbf{V}_{an}$ to be zero, that is, if $\mathbf{V}_{an} = V\underline{/0°}$, then the two situations that result in a balanced source are as follows:

Case I	*Case II*
$\mathbf{V}_{an} = V\underline{/0°}$	$\mathbf{V}_{an} = V\underline{/0°}$
$\mathbf{V}_{bn} = V\underline{/-120°}$	$\mathbf{V}_{bn} = V\underline{/120°} = V\underline{/-240°}$
$\mathbf{V}_{cn} = V\underline{/-240°} = V\underline{/120°}$	$\mathbf{V}_{cn} = V\underline{/240°} = V\underline{/-120°}$

For Case I, $v_{an}(t)$ leads $v_{bn}(t)$ by 120°, and $v_{bn}(t)$ leads $v_{cn}(t)$ by 120°. It is, therefore, called a **positive** or **abc phase sequence**. Similarly, Case II is called a **negative** or **acb phase sequence**. Phasor diagrams for the positive and negative phase sequences are shown in Fig. 9.22. Clearly, a negative phase sequence can be converted to a positive phase sequence simply by relabeling the terminals. Thus, we need only consider positive phase sequences.

It is a simple matter to determine the voltages between the line terminals—called **line voltages**. By KVL,

$$\mathbf{V}_{ab} = \mathbf{V}_{an} - \mathbf{V}_{bn} = V\underline{/0°} - V\underline{/-120°} = \sqrt{3}V\underline{/30°}$$

Similarly,

$$\mathbf{V}_{bc} = \sqrt{3}V\underline{/-90°} \quad \text{and} \quad \mathbf{V}_{ca} = \sqrt{3}V\underline{/-210°} = \sqrt{3}V\underline{/150°}$$

A phasor diagram showing the relationships between the phase voltages and the line voltages is given in Fig. 9.23.

Let us now connect our balanced source to a **balanced Y-connected three-phase load** as shown in Fig. 9.24. The short circuits between nodes *a* and *A*, between nodes

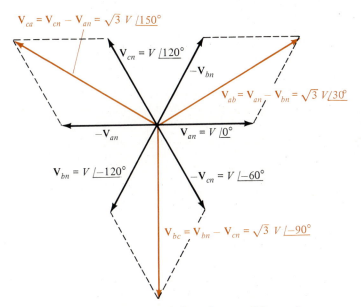

Fig. 9.23   Phasor diagram relating phase and line voltages.

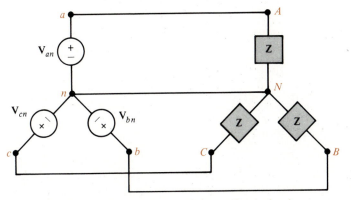

Fig. 9.24   Balanced Y-Y-connected three-phase circuit.

b and B, and between nodes c and C are the **lines** of the system. If we denote the current through $\mathbf{Z}$ from terminal x to terminal y by $\mathbf{I}_{xy}$, then the line currents are

$$\mathbf{I}_{AN} = \frac{\mathbf{V}_{an}}{\mathbf{Z}} = \frac{V\underline{/0°}}{\mathbf{Z}} = \frac{V}{\mathbf{Z}}$$

$$\mathbf{I}_{BN} = \frac{\mathbf{V}_{bn}}{\mathbf{Z}} = \frac{V\underline{/-120°}}{\mathbf{Z}} = \frac{V}{\mathbf{Z}}(1\underline{/-120°}) = \mathbf{I}_{AN}(1\underline{/-120°})$$

$$\mathbf{I}_{CN} = \frac{\mathbf{V}_{cn}}{\mathbf{Z}} = \frac{V\underline{/-240°}}{\mathbf{Z}} = \frac{V}{\mathbf{Z}}(1\underline{/-240°}) = \mathbf{I}_{AN}(1\underline{/120°})$$

By KCL,

$$\mathbf{I}_{Nn} = \mathbf{I}_{AN} + \mathbf{I}_{BN} + \mathbf{I}_{CN} = \mathbf{I}_{AN} + \mathbf{I}_{AN}(1\underline{/-120°}) + \mathbf{I}_{AN}(1\underline{/120°}) = 0$$

so we see that there is no current in the "neutral wire" (the short circuit between terminals n and N). We deduce that the neutral wire can be removed without affecting the voltages and currents of the circuit.

If the lines all have the same impedance, the effective load is still balanced and so the neutral current is zero, and the neutral wire can again be removed. For the case of a balanced source, balanced load, and balanced (equal) line impedances (called a **balanced system**), whether or not there is a neutral wire connecting terminals n and N, it is convenient to think of these two points as being connected by a short circuit. In this way, we can analyze the system on a "per-phase" basis, that is, as three separate single-phase problems. This can greatly simplify the analysis of the circuit.

EXAMPLE 9.10

For the balanced three-phase circuit given in Fig. 9.24, suppose that $\mathbf{V}_{an} = 120\underline{/0°}$ is an rms phasor. Assuming a positive phase sequence, then $\mathbf{V}_{bn} = 120\underline{/-120°}$ and $\mathbf{V}_{cn} = 120\underline{/120°}$. Thus, the rms line voltage phasors are

$$\mathbf{V}_{ab} = 120\sqrt{3}\underline{/30°} \qquad \mathbf{V}_{bc} = 120\sqrt{3}\underline{/-90°} \qquad \mathbf{V}_{ca} = 120\sqrt{3}\underline{/150°}$$

and the line voltage is $120\sqrt{3} = 208$ V rms.

If $\mathbf{Z} = 30 + j40 = 50\underline{/53°}\ \Omega$, then the line current $\mathbf{I}_{aA} = \mathbf{I}_{AN}$ is

$$\mathbf{I}_{aA} = \frac{\mathbf{V}_{an}}{\mathbf{Z}} = \frac{120\underline{/0°}}{50\underline{/53°}} = 2.4\underline{/-53°}\ \text{A rms}$$

The other line currents are

$$\mathbf{I}_{bB} = \frac{\mathbf{V}_{bn}}{\mathbf{Z}} = \frac{120\underline{/-120°}}{50\underline{/53°}} = 2.4\underline{/-173°}\ \text{A rms}$$

$$\mathbf{I}_{cC} = \frac{\mathbf{V}_{cn}}{\mathbf{Z}} = \frac{120\underline{/120°}}{50\underline{/53°}} = 2.4\underline{/67°}\ \text{A rms}$$

The phasor diagram depicting the phase voltages, the line voltages, and the line currents is shown in Fig. 9.25.

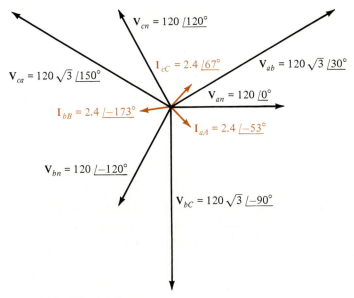

Fig. 9.25   Phasor diagram.

The power absorbed by the single load **Z** between terminals A and N is

$$P_{AN} = |\mathbf{V}_{an}|\,|\mathbf{I}_{AN}|\cos 53° = 120(2.4)(0.6) = 172.8 \text{ W}$$

so that the total power absorbed by the three-phase load is $3(172.8) = 518.4$ W.

The powers mentioned above are average powers. How does this compare with the instantaneous power? For the single load between A and N, the instantaneous power absorbed is

$$p_{AN}(t) = v_{an}(t)i_{AN}(t) = [120\sqrt{2}\cos \omega t][2.4\sqrt{2}\cos(\omega t - 53°)]$$
$$= 576\cos \omega t \cos(\omega t - 53°)$$

which is a time-varying quantity. However, the total instantaneous power absorbed by the three-phase load is

$$p(t) = p_{AN}(t) + p_{BN}(t) + p_{CN}(t)$$

where

$$p_{BN}(t) = v_{bn}(t)i_{BN}(t) = [120\sqrt{2}\cos(\omega t - 120°)][2.4\sqrt{2}\cos(\omega t - 53° - 120°)]$$
$$p_{CN}(t) = v_{cn}(t)i_{CN}(t) = [120\sqrt{2}\cos(\omega t - 240°)][2.4\sqrt{2}\cos(\omega t - 53° - 240°)]$$

Using the trigonometric identity $\cos \alpha \cos \beta = \frac{1}{2}\cos(\alpha + \beta) + \frac{1}{2}\cos(\alpha - \beta)$, we get

$$p(t) = 288[\cos(2\omega t - 53°) + \cos 53°] + 288[\cos(2\omega t - 53° - 240°) + \cos 53°]$$
$$+ 288[\cos(2\omega t - 53° - 120°) + \cos 53°]$$

It is a routine matter to show that since the above three sinusoids are spaced 120° apart, they sum to zero. Thus,

$$p(t) = 288[3\cos 53°] = 518.4 \text{ W}$$

so we see that the instantaneous power absorbed by the load (supplied by the source) is constant! This result holds for any balanced Y-Y-connected three-phase circuit, which is one reason for its importance.

DRILL EXERCISE 9.8

For the balanced three-phase circuit given in Fig. 9.24 (p. 415), the 60-Hz line current is 2 A rms. Each impedance $\mathbf{Z}$ consists of a 30-Ω resistance connected in series with a 106-mH inductance. Find the power absorbed by the three-phase load.
Answer: 360 W

EXAMPLE 9.11

Suppose now that the balanced three-phase circuit given in Fig. 9.24 has a line voltage of 250 V rms and the total power absorbed by the load is 600 W at a leading pf angle of 30°. Thus, the per-phase voltage—for example, $\mathbf{V}_{an}$—has the rms magnitude $|\mathbf{V}_{an}| = |\mathbf{V}_{ab}|/\sqrt{3} = 250/\sqrt{3}$. Since the per-phase power absorbed is 200 W, from the fact that $P_{AN} = |\mathbf{V}_{an}||\mathbf{I}_{AN}|\cos \theta$, we have that the rms line current has the magnitude

$$|\mathbf{I}_{AN}| = \frac{P_{AN}}{|\mathbf{V}_{an}|\cos \theta} = \frac{200}{(250/\sqrt{3})(\sqrt{3}/2)} = 1.6 \text{ A}$$

The per-phase impedance has magnitude

$$\mathbf{Z} = \frac{|\mathbf{V}_{an}|}{|\mathbf{I}_{AN}|} = \frac{250/\sqrt{3}}{1.6} = 90 \ \Omega$$

and since the pf is leading, the current leads the voltage so

$$\mathbf{Z} = 90\underline{/-30°} = 78 - j45 \ \Omega$$

DRILL EXERCISE 9.9

For the balanced three-phase circuit given in Fig. 9.24 (p. 415), the 60-Hz line voltage is 200 V rms and the line current is 2 A rms. Each impedance **Z** consists of a resistance R connected in series with an inductance L. Given that the three-phase load absorbs 600 W, determine R and L.
Answer: 50 Ω, 76.7 mH

9.5 DELTA CONNECTIONS

More common than a balanced Y-connected three-phase load is a Δ **(delta)-connected** load. A Y-connected source with a balanced Δ-connected load is shown in Fig. 9.26. We see that the individual loads are connected directly across the lines, and, consequently, it is relatively easier to add or remove one of the components of a Δ-connected load than with a Y-connected load. As a matter of fact, it may not even be possible to do so for a Y-connected load, since the neutral terminal may not be accessible.

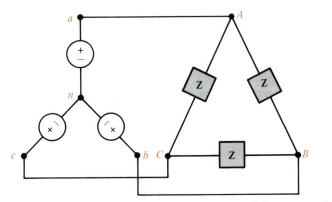

Fig. 9.26   Three-phase circuit with a balanced Δ-connected load.

Suppose that the voltage between terminals x and y (plus at x) is denoted by $\mathbf{V}_{xy}$. For a balanced source

$$\mathbf{V}_{an} = V \underline{/0^\circ} \qquad \mathbf{V}_{bn} = V \underline{/-120^\circ} \qquad \mathbf{V}_{cn} = V \underline{/-240^\circ}$$

and as was shown previously, the line voltages are

$$\mathbf{V}_{ab} = \sqrt{3} V \underline{/30^\circ} \qquad \mathbf{V}_{bc} = \sqrt{3} V \underline{/-90^\circ} \qquad \mathbf{V}_{ca} = \sqrt{3} V \underline{/-210^\circ}$$

which are the phase voltages for a Δ-connected load. The phase currents are

$$\mathbf{I}_{AB} = \frac{\mathbf{V}_{ab}}{\mathbf{Z}} \qquad \mathbf{I}_{BC} = \frac{\mathbf{V}_{bc}}{\mathbf{Z}} \qquad \mathbf{I}_{CA} = \frac{\mathbf{V}_{ca}}{\mathbf{Z}}$$

Thus, by KCL, the line current $\mathbf{I}_{aA}$ is

$$\mathbf{I}_{aA} = \mathbf{I}_{AB} - \mathbf{I}_{CA} = \frac{\mathbf{V}_{ab}}{\mathbf{Z}} - \frac{\mathbf{V}_{ca}}{\mathbf{Z}} = \frac{1}{\mathbf{Z}}(\mathbf{V}_{ab} - \mathbf{V}_{ca})$$

$$= \frac{1}{\mathbf{Z}}(\sqrt{3}V\underline{/30°} - \sqrt{3}V\underline{/-210°}) = \frac{3V\underline{/0°}}{\mathbf{Z}}$$

Similarly, in a balanced system,

$$\mathbf{I}_{bB} = \frac{3V\underline{/-120°}}{\mathbf{Z}} \qquad \mathbf{I}_{cC} = \frac{3V\underline{/-240°}}{\mathbf{Z}}$$

Since the magnitude of a phase current—for example $\mathbf{I}_{AB}$—is $|\mathbf{I}_{AB}| = |\mathbf{V}_{ab}|/|\mathbf{Z}| = \sqrt{3}V/|\mathbf{Z}|$, and the magnitude of a line current—for example, $\mathbf{I}_{aA}$—is $|\mathbf{I}_{aA}| = 3V/|\mathbf{Z}|$, then

$$|\mathbf{I}_{aA}| = \sqrt{3}|\mathbf{I}_{AB}|$$

That is, a line current is $\sqrt{3}$ times as great as a phase current. Furthermore, since the phase currents are 120° apart, they are a balanced set, as are the line currents.

A phasor diagram showing the relationship between the line currents ($\mathbf{I}_{aA}, \mathbf{I}_{bB}, \mathbf{I}_{cC}$) and the phase currents ($\mathbf{I}_{AB}, \mathbf{I}_{BC}, \mathbf{I}_{CA}$) for the case that ang $\mathbf{Z} = \theta$ ($0 < \theta < 30°$) is given in Fig. 9.27.

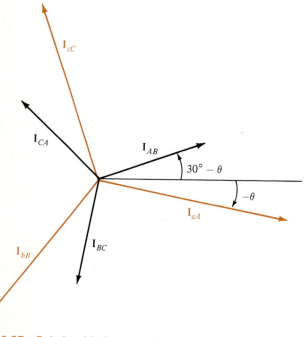

Fig. 9.27 Relationship between line and phase currents.

EXAMPLE 9.12

Suppose that, for the balanced three-phase circuit given in Fig. 9.26, the line voltage is 250 V rms and the total power absorbed is 600 W at a leading pf angle of 30°. Since the per-phase power absorbed is 200 W, from the fact that $P_{AB} = |\mathbf{V}_{ab}||\mathbf{I}_{AB}| \cos \theta$, we have that the rms phase current—for example, $\mathbf{I}_{AB}$—has magnitude

$$|\mathbf{I}_{AB}| = \frac{P_{AB}}{|\mathbf{V}_{ab}| \cos \theta} = \frac{200}{250(\sqrt{3}/2)} = 0.92 \text{ A}$$

while the rms line current—for example, $\mathbf{I}_{aA}$—has magnitude

$$|\mathbf{I}_{aA}| = \sqrt{3}|\mathbf{I}_{AB}| = 1.6 \text{ A}$$

The per-phase impedance has magnitude

$$|\mathbf{Z}| = \frac{|\mathbf{V}_{ab}|}{|\mathbf{I}_{AB}|} = \frac{250}{0.92} = 271 \ \Omega$$

and since the pf is leading, the current leads the voltage, so

$$\mathbf{Z} = 271\underline{/-30^\circ} = 234 - j135 \ \Omega$$

DRILL EXERCISE 9.10

For the balanced three-phase circuit given in Fig. 9.26, the 60-Hz line current is 8.3 A rms. Given that each impedance consists of a 30-Ω resistance connected in series with a 106-mH inductance, determine the power absorbed by the three-phase load.

Answer: 2068.2 W

Suppose now that a balanced three-phase load is Y-connected, the magnitude of the line voltage is V_L volts rms, and the line current is I_L amperes rms. If the power P_1 absorbed per phase is due to an rms voltage V and an rms current I with pf angle θ, then

$$P_1 = VI \cos \theta = \frac{V_L}{\sqrt{3}} I_L \cos \theta$$

and, therefore, the total power absorbed is

$$P = 3P_1 = \sqrt{3} V_L I_L \cos \theta$$

For the case of a balanced Δ-connected load,

$$P_1 = VI \cos \theta = V_L \left(\frac{I_L}{\sqrt{3}}\right) \cos \theta$$

and again

$$P = 3P_1 = \sqrt{3}V_L I_L \cos\theta$$

Thus, we see that regardless of whether a balanced load is Y-connected or Δ-connected, in terms of the line voltage, line current, and load impedance phase angle, we can use the same formula for the total power absorbed by the load:

$$P = \sqrt{3}V_L I_L \cos\theta$$

Δ-Y and Y-Δ Transformations

In our discussions, we have assumed that the source is balanced and Y-connected. Although the same conclusions can be obtained for a balanced Δ-connected source, for practical reasons, such sources are uncommon. If a Δ-connected source is not balanced exactly, a large current can circulate around the loop formed by the elements comprising the delta. The result is the reduction of the source's current-delivering capacity and an increase in the system's losses.

One might feel that a Y connection is equivalent to a Δ connection, and vice versa. But under what conditions is equivalence obtained? To answer this question, consider the Δ and Y connections shown in Fig. 9.28. For the Δ connection, the mesh equations are

$$\mathbf{V}_1 = \mathbf{Z}_{AC}\mathbf{I}_1 - \mathbf{Z}_{AC}\mathbf{I}_3 \tag{9.9}$$

$$\mathbf{V}_2 = \mathbf{Z}_{BC}\mathbf{I}_2 - \mathbf{Z}_{BC}\mathbf{I}_3 \tag{9.10}$$

$$0 = -\mathbf{Z}_{AC}\mathbf{I}_1 - \mathbf{Z}_{BC}\mathbf{I}_2 + (\mathbf{Z}_{AB} + \mathbf{Z}_{BC} + \mathbf{Z}_{AC})\mathbf{I}_3 \tag{9.11}$$

From Equation (9.11),

$$\mathbf{I}_3 = \frac{\mathbf{Z}_{AC}\mathbf{I}_1}{\mathbf{Z}_{AB} + \mathbf{Z}_{BC} + \mathbf{Z}_{AC}} + \frac{\mathbf{Z}_{BC}\mathbf{I}_2}{\mathbf{Z}_{AB} + \mathbf{Z}_{BC} + \mathbf{Z}_{AC}}$$

and by substituting this expression for $\mathbf{I}_3$ into Equations (9.9) and (9.10), we get, respectively,

$$\mathbf{V}_1 = \frac{\mathbf{Z}_{AB}\mathbf{Z}_{AC} + \mathbf{Z}_{AC}\mathbf{Z}_{BC}}{\mathbf{Z}_{AB} + \mathbf{Z}_{BC} + \mathbf{Z}_{AC}}\mathbf{I}_1 - \frac{\mathbf{Z}_{AC}\mathbf{Z}_{BC}}{\mathbf{Z}_{AB} + \mathbf{Z}_{BC} + \mathbf{Z}_{AC}}\mathbf{I}_2$$

and

$$\mathbf{V}_2 = \frac{-\mathbf{Z}_{AC}\mathbf{Z}_{BC}}{\mathbf{Z}_{AB} + \mathbf{Z}_{BC} + \mathbf{Z}_{AC}}\mathbf{I}_1 - \frac{\mathbf{Z}_{AB}\mathbf{Z}_{BC} + \mathbf{Z}_{AC}\mathbf{Z}_{BC}}{\mathbf{Z}_{AB} + \mathbf{Z}_{BC} + \mathbf{Z}_{AC}}\mathbf{I}_2$$

The mesh equations for the Y connection are

$$\mathbf{V}_1 = (\mathbf{Z}_A + \mathbf{Z}_C)\mathbf{I}_1 - \mathbf{Z}_C\mathbf{I}_2$$

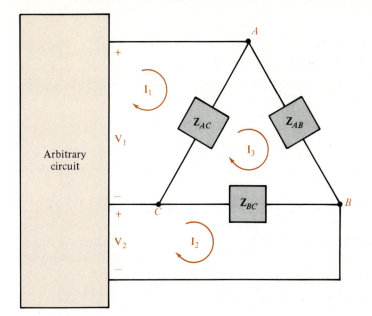

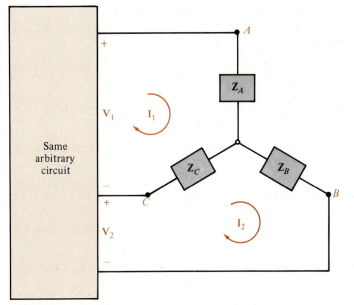

Fig. 9.28 Equivalence of Δ and Y connections.

and

$$\mathbf{V}_2 = -\mathbf{Z}_C\mathbf{I}_1 + (\mathbf{Z}_B + \mathbf{Z}_C)\mathbf{I}_2$$

Since the two connections are equivalent when the values of $\mathbf{V}_1$ and $\mathbf{V}_2$ and $\mathbf{I}_1$ and $\mathbf{I}_2$ are the same for both cases, by equating coefficients we get

$$\mathbf{Z}_A = \frac{\mathbf{Z}_{AB}\mathbf{Z}_{AC}}{\mathbf{Z}_{AB} + \mathbf{Z}_{BC} + \mathbf{Z}_{AC}} \qquad \mathbf{Z}_B = \frac{\mathbf{Z}_{AB}\mathbf{Z}_{BC}}{\mathbf{Z}_{AB} + \mathbf{Z}_{BC} + \mathbf{Z}_{AC}}$$

$$\mathbf{Z}_C = \frac{\mathbf{Z}_{AC}\mathbf{Z}_{BC}}{\mathbf{Z}_{AB} + \mathbf{Z}_{BC} + \mathbf{Z}_{AC}}$$

and these are the conditions for finding the equivalent Y connection given a Δ connection. By using dual arguments, we can derive the conditions for finding the equivalent Δ connection given a Y connection. (In this case, we can use admittances instead of impedances.) They are

$$\mathbf{Y}_{AB} = \frac{\mathbf{Y}_A\mathbf{Y}_B}{\mathbf{Y}_A + \mathbf{Y}_B + \mathbf{Y}_C} \qquad \mathbf{Y}_{BC} = \frac{\mathbf{Y}_B\mathbf{Y}_C}{\mathbf{Y}_A + \mathbf{Y}_B + \mathbf{Y}_C} \qquad \mathbf{Y}_{AC} = \frac{\mathbf{Y}_A\mathbf{Y}_C}{\mathbf{Y}_A + \mathbf{Y}_B + \mathbf{Y}_C}$$

Alternatively, it is a simple matter to express these conditions in terms of impedances as follows:

$$\mathbf{Z}_{AB} = \frac{\mathbf{Z}_A\mathbf{Z}_B + \mathbf{Z}_B\mathbf{Z}_C + \mathbf{Z}_A\mathbf{Z}_C}{\mathbf{Z}_C} \qquad \mathbf{Z}_{BC} = \frac{\mathbf{Z}_A\mathbf{Z}_B + \mathbf{Z}_B\mathbf{Z}_C + \mathbf{Z}_A\mathbf{Z}_C}{\mathbf{Z}_A}$$

$$\mathbf{Z}_{AC} = \frac{\mathbf{Z}_A\mathbf{Z}_B + \mathbf{Z}_B\mathbf{Z}_C + \mathbf{Z}_A\mathbf{Z}_C}{\mathbf{Z}_B}$$

Going from a Y connection to its equivalent Δ connection, or vice versa, is called a **Y-Δ (wye–delta) transformation** or **Δ-Y (delta–wye) transformation** respectively. Since the equivalence is with respect to the three terminals A, B, and C, the equivalence holds for any pair of them also.

For the special case that a Δ-connected load is balanced, that is, $\mathbf{Z}_{AB} = \mathbf{Z}_{AC} = \mathbf{Z}_{BC} = \mathbf{Z}_\Delta$, then by performing a Δ-Y transformation, we get a balanced Y-connected load with

$$\mathbf{Z}_A = \mathbf{Z}_B = \mathbf{Z}_C = \mathbf{Z}_\Delta/3$$

Conversely, for a balanced Y-connected load with $\mathbf{Z}_A = \mathbf{Z}_B = \mathbf{Z}_C = \mathbf{Z}_Y$, by performing a Y-$\Delta$ transformation we get a balanced Δ-connected load with

$$\mathbf{Z}_{AB} = \mathbf{Z}_{AC} = \mathbf{Z}_{BC} = 3\mathbf{Z}_Y$$

EXAMPLE 9.13

Suppose that for the balanced three-phase load shown in Fig. 9.29, $\mathbf{Z}_Y = 20 - j20 \ \Omega$ and $\mathbf{Z}_\Delta = 40 + j40 \ \Omega$. Let us find the power absorbed by this load when it is connected to a balanced, Y-connected three-phase source having a per-phase voltage of 130 V rms.

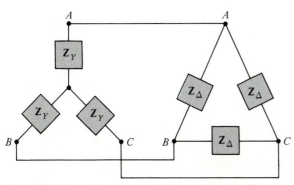

Fig. 9.29   Parallel-connected three-phase load.

Performing a Y-Δ transformation on the Y-connected portion of the load, we obtain a Δ-connection having impedances

$$\mathbf{Z}'_\Delta = 3\mathbf{Z}_Y = 60 - j60 \ \Omega$$

Since each impedance $\mathbf{Z}'_\Delta$ is connected in parallel with an impedance $\mathbf{Z}_\Delta$, the impedance of the parallel combination is

$$\mathbf{Z}_P = \mathbf{Z}'_\Delta \| \mathbf{Z}_\Delta = \frac{\mathbf{Z}'_\Delta \mathbf{Z}_\Delta}{\mathbf{Z}'_\Delta + \mathbf{Z}_\Delta} = \frac{(60 - j60)(40 + j40)}{(60 - j60) + (40 + j40)} = \frac{600}{13} + j\frac{120}{13} \ \Omega$$

and we have the equivalent Δ-connected load shown in Fig. 9.30(a). Performing a Δ-Y transformation on this load, we obtain the Y-connected load shown in Fig. 9.30(b),

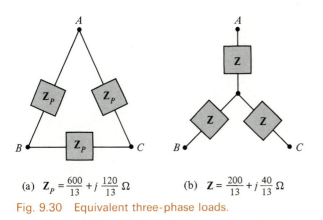

(a) $\mathbf{Z}_P = \frac{600}{13} + j\frac{120}{13} \ \Omega$ (b) $\mathbf{Z} = \frac{200}{13} + j\frac{40}{13} \ \Omega$

Fig. 9.30   Equivalent three-phase loads.

where

$$\mathbf{Z} = \frac{\mathbf{Z}_P}{3} = \frac{200}{13} + j\frac{40}{13} = 15.69\underline{/11.31°}\ \Omega$$

Since the per-phase voltage for this load is 130 V rms, then for $\mathbf{V}_{an} = 130\underline{/0°}$, we get

$$\mathbf{I}_{aA} = \frac{\mathbf{V}_{an}}{\mathbf{Z}} = \frac{130\underline{/0°}}{15.69\underline{/11.31°}} = 8.29\underline{/-11.31°}\ A$$

and the power absorbed per phase is

$$|\mathbf{V}_{an}||\mathbf{I}_{aA}|\cos\theta = (130)(8.29)\cos(11.31°) = 1056.8\ W$$

Therefore, the power absorbed by the load is

$$P = 3(1056.8) = 3170.4\ W$$

DRILL EXERCISE 9.11

Find the power absorbed by the load for the balanced three-phase circuit described in Example 9.13 given that the impedance of each line is 1 Ω.
Answer: 2808.0 W

9.6 POWER MEASUREMENTS

The **wattmeter** is a device that measures the average power absorbed by a two-terminal load. Such a device is depicted in Fig. 9.31. The wattmeter, which is used typically at frequencies between a few hertz and a few hundred hertz, has two coils. One, the current coil, has a very low impedance (ideally zero), and the other, the voltage coil, has a very high impedance (ideally infinite). The current coil is connected

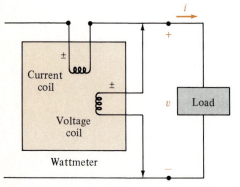

Fig. 9.31   Wattmeter connected to a load.

in series with the load and the voltage coil is connected in parallel with the load. When the current and the voltage shown for the load are both positive valued, the wattmeter has an upscale deflection and indicates the average power absorbed by the load. The same result occurs when both the current and voltage are negative valued.

Specifically, for the configuration shown in Fig. 9.31, if $v(t) = V \cos(\omega t + \phi_1)$ and $i(t) = I \cos(\omega t + \phi_2)$, then the corresponding rms phasors are

$$\mathbf{V} = \frac{V}{\sqrt{2}} \underline{/\phi_1} \qquad \text{and} \qquad \mathbf{I} = \frac{I}{\sqrt{2}} \underline{/\phi_2}$$

and the wattmeter indicates the power absorbed by the load, which is

$$P = |\mathbf{V}||\mathbf{I}| \cos \theta = \tfrac{1}{2} VI \cos(\phi_1 - \phi_2)$$

EXAMPLE 9.14

For the connection shown in Fig. 9.31, suppose that the load has an impedance of $\mathbf{Z} = 40 + j30 \ \Omega$, and the wattmeter indicates 1000 W. Let us find the rms voltage and current for the load.

We have that

$$\mathbf{Z} = 40 + j30 = 50 \underline{/36.87°} \ \Omega = |\mathbf{Z}| \underline{/\theta}$$

Since $P = |\mathbf{V}||\mathbf{I}| \cos \theta$, then

$$|\mathbf{V}||\mathbf{I}| = \frac{P}{\cos \theta} = \frac{1000}{\cos 36.87°} = 1250 \qquad\qquad (9.12)$$

Also,

$$|\mathbf{Z}| = \frac{|\mathbf{V}|}{|\mathbf{I}|} = 50 \qquad \Rightarrow \qquad |\mathbf{V}| = 50|\mathbf{I}|$$

Substituting this into Equation (9.12) yields

$$50|\mathbf{I}||\mathbf{I}| = 1250 \qquad \Rightarrow \qquad |\mathbf{I}| = 5 \text{ A rms}$$

and

$$|\mathbf{V}| = 50|\mathbf{I}| = 50(5) = 250 \text{ V rms}$$

DRILL EXERCISE 9.12

For the connection shown in Fig. 9.31, the wattmeter indicates 500 W when the voltage across the load is 200 V rms, 60 Hz and the current through the load is 5 A rms. Given that the load is a resistance R connected in series with an inductance L, find R and L.
Answer: $20 \ \Omega$; 91.9 mH

Now that we have determined how to measure the power absorbed by a single load, how can the wattmeter be used to measure the power absorbed by a three-phase load? For a balanced load, if we can connect a wattmeter to one phase of the load as shown in Fig. 9.31, then the total power absorbed is three times the reading. For an unbalanced load, if three separate wattmeters can be connected, then the total power absorbed is the sum of the three readings. However, a Y-connected load may not have its neutral terminal accessible. In such a case, although the current coil can be connected properly, the voltage coil cannot. On the other hand, for a Δ-connected load like a three-phase rotating machine, only the three terminals of the load are accessible. This means that the voltage coil can be connected appropriately, but the current coil cannot. Don't give up, however; there is a way to measure the power absorbed by a three-phase load, whether balanced or unbalanced, with the use of wattmeters. To see how, consider three wattmeters and a Δ-connected load, as shown in Fig. 9.32. In this situation, the current coils of the wattmeters are connected in series with the lines aA, bB, and cC. The voltage coils are connected between a line and some arbitrary point m. The average power indicated on wattmeter A is

$$P_A = \frac{1}{T} \int_0^T v_{am} i_{aA} \, dt$$

and similar expressions are obtained for wattmeters B and C. Summing these average powers, we get

$$P = P_A + P_B + P_C = \frac{1}{T} \int_0^T v_{am} i_{aA} \, dt + \frac{1}{T} \int_0^T v_{bm} i_{bB} \, dt + \frac{1}{T} \int_0^T v_{cm} i_{cC} \, dt$$

$$= \frac{1}{T} \int_0^T (v_{am} i_{aA} + v_{bm} i_{bB} + v_{cm} i_{cC}) \, dt$$

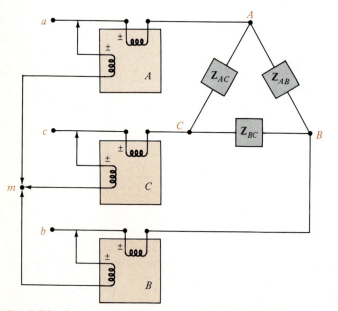

Fig. 9.32   Power measurement for a three-phase load.

But, by KCL,

$$i_{aA} = i_{AB} + i_{AC} \qquad i_{bB} = -i_{AB} + i_{BC} \qquad i_{cC} = -i_{AC} - i_{BC}$$

Substituting these expressions for the line currents into the preceding integral, we obtain

$$P = \frac{1}{T} \int_0^T \left[(v_{am} - v_{bm})i_{AB} + (v_{bm} - v_{cm})i_{BC} + (v_{am} - v_{cm})i_{AC} \right] dt$$

and, by KVL,

$$P = \frac{1}{T} \int_0^T (v_{ab}i_{AB} + v_{bc}i_{BC} + v_{ac}i_{AC}) \, dt$$

$$= \frac{1}{T} \int_0^T v_{ab}i_{AB} \, dt + \frac{1}{T} \int_0^T v_{bc}i_{BC} \, dt + \frac{1}{T} \int_0^T v_{ac}i_{AC} \, dt$$

which is the total power absorbed by the three-phase load.

Since the point m was chosen arbitrarily, we can place it anywhere without it affecting the end result: The sum of the three wattmeter readings is the power absorbed by the load. The judicious choice of point m to be on the line cC means that wattmeter C will have zero volts across its voltage coil, and hence will indicate 0 W. For such a case, wattmeter C is superfluous and is not needed. The resulting configuration, shown in Fig. 9.33, is an example of what is known as the **two-wattmeter method** for measuring power. It can also be applied when a three-phase load is Y-connected, and, as for the case of a Δ connection, the load can be unbalanced as well as balanced. Furthermore, it is immaterial whether or not the source is balanced—the variables utilized are line voltages and line currents.

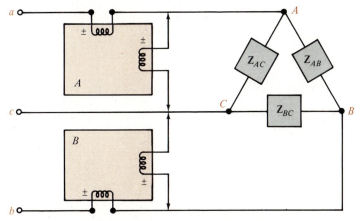

Fig. 9.33 Two-wattmeter method for measuring power.

EXAMPLE 9.15

For the Δ-connected three-phase load given in Fig. 9.33, suppose that $\mathbf{Z}_{AB} = \mathbf{Z}_{BC} = \mathbf{Z}_{AC} = 30 + j40 \ \Omega$. Let us find the wattmeter readings—and hence, the power absorbed by the load—given that the line voltage is 240 V rms.

Since the line voltage is 240 V rms, we have that

$$\mathbf{V}_{ab} = 240\underline{/30^\circ} \qquad \mathbf{V}_{bc} = 240\underline{/-90^\circ} \qquad \mathbf{V}_{ca} = 240\underline{/-210^\circ}$$

Thus,

$$\mathbf{I}_{aA} = \frac{\mathbf{V}_{ab}}{\mathbf{Z}} - \frac{\mathbf{V}_{ca}}{\mathbf{Z}} = \frac{\mathbf{V}_{ab} - \mathbf{V}_{ca}}{\mathbf{Z}} = \frac{240\underline{/30^\circ} - 240\underline{/-210^\circ}}{30 + j40}$$

$$= \frac{240\underline{/30^\circ} + 240\underline{/-30^\circ}}{30 + j40} = \frac{240(\sqrt{3}/2 + j1/2) + 240(\sqrt{3}/2 - j1/2)}{30 + j40}$$

$$= \frac{240\sqrt{3}}{50\underline{/53.13^\circ}} = 4.8\sqrt{3}\underline{/-53.13^\circ} = 8.314\underline{/-53.13^\circ} \text{ A rms}$$

Since $\mathbf{V}_{ac} = -\mathbf{V}_{ca} = -240\underline{/-210^\circ} = (1\underline{/180^\circ})(240\underline{/-210^\circ}) = 240\underline{/-30^\circ}$, then watt-meter A indicates

$$P_A = |\mathbf{V}_{ac}||\mathbf{I}_{aA}|\cos(-30^\circ - [-53.13^\circ]) = (240)(8.314)\cos 23.13^\circ = 1835.0 \text{ W}$$

Furthermore,

$$\mathbf{I}_{bB} = \frac{\mathbf{V}_{bc}}{\mathbf{Z}} - \frac{\mathbf{V}_{ab}}{\mathbf{Z}} = \frac{\mathbf{V}_{bc} - \mathbf{V}_{ab}}{\mathbf{Z}} = \frac{240\underline{/-90^\circ} - 240\underline{/30^\circ}}{30 + j40}$$

$$= \frac{-j240 - (240\cos 30^\circ + j240\sin 30^\circ)}{30 + j40} = \frac{-j240 - 240(\sqrt{3}/2) - j240(1/2)}{30 + j40}$$

$$= \frac{-120\sqrt{3} - j360}{30 + j40} = \frac{-120\sqrt{3}(1 + j\sqrt{3})}{30 + j40}$$

$$= \frac{(120\sqrt{3}\underline{/-180^\circ})(2\underline{/60^\circ})}{50\underline{/53.13^\circ}} = 4.8\sqrt{3}\underline{/-173.13^\circ} = 8.314\underline{/-173.13^\circ} \text{ A rms}$$

Therefore, wattmeter B indicates

$$P_B = |\mathbf{V}_{bc}||\mathbf{I}_{bB}|\cos(-90^\circ - [-173.13^\circ]) = (240)(8.314)\cos 83.13^\circ = 238.7 \text{ W}$$

Hence, the power absorbed by the three-phase load is

$$P = P_A + P_B = 1835.0 + 238.7 = 2073.7 \text{ W}$$

DRILL EXERCISE 9.13

For the configuration given in Fig. 9.33, suppose that $\mathbf{Z}_{AB} = 25\sqrt{3} + j25 \; \Omega$, $\mathbf{Z}_{BC} = 50 \; \Omega$, and $\mathbf{Z}_{AC} = 25 + j25\sqrt{3} \; \Omega$. Find the wattmeter readings given that the line voltage is 250 V rms.
Answer: 1707.5 W; 1250 W

For the case that a load is balanced, it is also possible to determine the pf angle with the two-wattmeter method. Consider the Δ-connected load shown in Fig. 9.33, where $\mathbf{Z}_{AB} = \mathbf{Z}_{BC} = \mathbf{Z}_{AC} = \mathbf{Z} = |\mathbf{Z}|\underline{/\theta}$—that is, a balanced Δ-connected load. For the balanced source,

$$\mathbf{V}_{an} = V\underline{/0^\circ} \qquad \mathbf{V}_{bn} = V\underline{/-120^\circ} \qquad \mathbf{V}_{cn} = V\underline{/-240^\circ}$$

We have seen previously that

$$\mathbf{V}_{ab} = \sqrt{3}V\underline{/30^\circ} \qquad \mathbf{V}_{bc} = \sqrt{3}V\underline{/-90^\circ} \qquad \mathbf{V}_{ca} = \sqrt{3}V\underline{/150^\circ}$$

$$\mathbf{I}_{aA} = \frac{3V\underline{/0^\circ}}{\mathbf{Z}} \qquad \mathbf{I}_{bB} = \frac{3V\underline{/-120^\circ}}{\mathbf{Z}} \qquad \mathbf{I}_{cC} = \frac{3V\underline{/-240^\circ}}{\mathbf{Z}}$$

Since

$$P_A = |\mathbf{V}_{AC}||\mathbf{I}_{aA}|\cos(\text{ang}\,\mathbf{V}_{AC} - \text{ang}\,\mathbf{I}_{aA})$$
$$= V_L I_L \cos(-30^\circ + \theta) = V_L I_L \cos(30^\circ - \theta)$$

and

$$P_B = |\mathbf{V}_{BC}||\mathbf{I}_{bB}|\cos(\text{ang}\,\mathbf{V}_{BC} - \text{ang}\,\mathbf{I}_{bB})$$
$$= V_L I_L \cos(-90^\circ - [-120^\circ - \theta]) = V_L I_L \cos(30^\circ + \theta)$$

taking the ratio of P_A to P_B we get

$$\frac{P_A}{P_B} = \frac{\cos(30^\circ - \theta)}{\cos(30^\circ + \theta)}$$

and by the trigonometric identity $\cos(\alpha + \beta) = \cos\alpha\cos\beta - \sin\alpha\sin\beta$, this ratio becomes

$$\frac{P_A}{P_B} = \frac{\cos 30^\circ \cos\theta + \sin 30^\circ \sin\theta}{\cos 30^\circ \cos\theta - \sin 30^\circ \sin\theta} = \frac{(\sqrt{3}/2)\cos\theta + (1/2)\sin\theta}{(\sqrt{3}/2)\cos\theta - (1/2)\sin\theta}$$

from which

$$\sqrt{3}(P_A - P_B)\cos\theta = (P_A + P_B)\sin\theta \qquad \Rightarrow \qquad \frac{\sin\theta}{\cos\theta} = \frac{\sqrt{3}(P_A - P_B)}{P_A + P_B} = \tan\theta$$

Thus, the pf angle θ is

$$\theta = \tan^{-1}\frac{\sqrt{3}(P_A - P_B)}{P_A + P_B}$$

EXAMPLE 9.16

Suppose that a balanced Δ-connected load as shown in Fig. 9.33 has a line voltage of 240 V rms and wattmeter readings $P_A = 1000$ W and $P_B = 300$ W. Thus, the pf angle is

$$\theta = \tan^{-1}\frac{\sqrt{3}(1000 - 300)}{1000 + 300} = \tan^{-1}(0.93) = 43^\circ$$

Since the total power absorbed by the load is $1000 + 300 = 1300$ W, the per-phase power absorbed is $(1300/3)$ W. Since

$$P_{AB} = |\mathbf{V}_{ab}||\mathbf{I}_{AB}| \cos \theta \quad \Rightarrow \quad |\mathbf{I}_{AB}| = \frac{P_{AB}}{|\mathbf{V}_{ab}| \cos \theta}$$

Then

$$|\mathbf{Z}| = \frac{|\mathbf{V}_{ab}|}{|\mathbf{I}_{AB}|} = \frac{|\mathbf{V}_{ab}|^2 \cos \theta}{P_{AB}} = \frac{(240)^2 \cos 43°}{1300/3} = 97.2$$

Thus,

$$\mathbf{Z} = 97.2\underline{/43°} = 71.1 + j66.3 \ \Omega$$

DRILL EXERCISE 9.14

Suppose that a balanced Δ-connected load as shown in Fig. 9.33 has $\mathbf{Z}_{AB} = \mathbf{Z}_{BC} = \mathbf{Z}_{AC} = 12 + j12 \ \Omega$. Given that wattmeter A indicates 1666 W, find the reading of wattmeter B, the line voltage, and the line current.
Answer: 446.4 W; 130 V rms; 13.27 A rms

● SUMMARY

1. The instantaneous power absorbed by an element is equal to the product of the voltage across it and the current through it.

2. The average power absorbed by a resistance R having a sinusoidal current of amplitude I and voltage of amplitude V is $P_R = VI/2 = RI^2/2 = V^2/2R$.

3. The average power absorbed by a capacitance or an inductance is zero.

4. A nonideal source whose internal impedance is $\mathbf{Z}_o$ or a circuit whose Thévenin-equivalent (output) impedance is $\mathbf{Z}_o$ transfers maximum power to a load $\mathbf{Z}_L$ when $\mathbf{Z}_L$ is equal to the complex conjugate of $\mathbf{Z}_o$.

5. For the case that $\mathbf{Z}_L$ is restricted to being purely resistive, maximum power is transferred when $\mathbf{Z}_L$ equals the magnitude of $\mathbf{Z}_o$.

6. The effective or rms value of a sinusoid of amplitude A is $A/\sqrt{2}$.

7. The average power absorbed by a resistance R having a current whose effective value is I_e and a voltage whose effective value is V_e is $P_R = V_e I_e = RI_e^2 = V_e^2/R$.

8. The power factor (pf) is the ratio of average power to apparent power.

9. If current lags voltage, the pf is lagging. If current leads voltage, the pf is leading.

10. Average or real power can be generalized with the notion of complex power.

11. The ordinary household uses a single-phase, three-wire electric system.

12. The most common polyphase electric system is the balanced three-phase system.

13. Three-phase sources are generally Y-connected, and three-phase loads are generally Δ-connected.

14. The device commonly used to measure power is the wattmeter.

15. Three-phase load power measurements can be taken with the two-wattmeter method.

● *PROBLEMS FOR CHAPTER 9*

9.1 For the *RLC* circuit shown in Fig. P9.1, find the average power absorbed by the 4-Ω load resistor for the case that (a) $C = \frac{1}{6}$ F, (b) $C = \frac{1}{18}$ F, and (c) $C = \frac{1}{30}$ F.

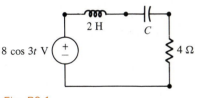

Fig. P9.1

9.2 For the circuit shown in Fig. P9.2, find the average power absorbed by each element for the case that $\mathbf{Z}_L = 4$ Ω.

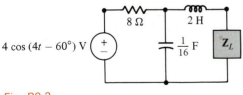

Fig. P9.2

9.3 For the circuit given in Fig. P9.2, (a) determine the load $\mathbf{Z}_L$ which absorbs maximum power, and find this power; and (b) determine the load R_L which absorbs maximum power for resistive loads, and find this power.

9.4 For the circuit shown in Fig. P9.4, find the average power absorbed by each element for the case that $\mathbf{Z}_L = 1$ Ω.

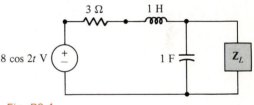

Fig. P9.4

9.5 Repeat Problem 9.3 for the circuit given in Fig. P9.4.

9.6 Find the average power absorbed by each element in the op-amp circuit given in Fig. P8.44 (p. 390).

9.7 Find the average power absorbed by each element in the op-amp circuit given in Fig. P8.45 (p. 390).

9.8 Find the average power absorbed by each element in the op-amp circuit given in Fig. P8.46 (p. 390).

9.9 For the circuit given in Fig. P8.39 (p. 389), (a) find the average power absorbed by each impedance and (b) find the average power supplied by each source.

9.10 For the circuit given in Fig. P8.40 (p. 389), (a) find the average power absorbed by each impedance and (b) find the average power supplied by each source.

9.11 For the op-amp circuit shown in Fig. P9.11, the rms value of $v_s(t)$ is 1 V. Find the average power absorbed by each resistor.

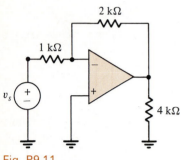

Fig. P9.11

9.12 For the op-amp circuit shown in Fig. P9.12, the rms value of $v_s(t)$ is 1 V. Find the average power absorbed by each resistor.

9.13 For the op-amp circuit given in Fig. P9.11, find the average power absorbed by each resistor when the input voltage $v_s(t)$ is as shown in Fig. P9.13.

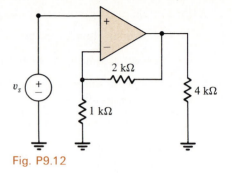

Fig. P9.12

9.14 For the op-amp circuit given in Fig. P9.12, find the average power absorbed by each resistor when the input voltage $v_s(t)$ is as shown in Fig. P9.13.

9.15 Find the rms values of the functions shown in Fig. P9.15.

9.16 Find the rms values of the "rectified" sine waves shown in Fig. P9.16. [*Hint:* $\sin^2 x = \frac{1}{2}(1 - \cos 2x)$.]

9.17 Figure P9.17(a) shows a BJT (common-emitter) amplifier. Suppose that the applied voltage $v_s(t)$ is described by Fig. P9.17(b). Find the average power absorbed by each resistor.

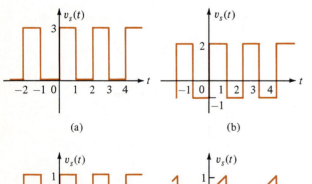

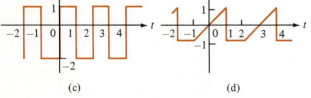

Fig. P9.13

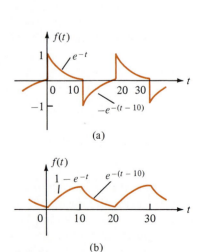

Fig. P9.15

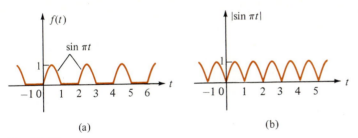

(a)   (b)

Fig. P9.16

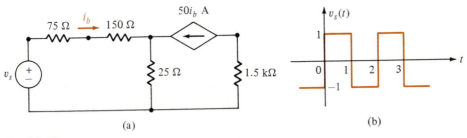

(a)   (b)

Fig. P9.17

9.18 Figure P9.18 shows a BJT (common-base) amplifier. Suppose that the applied voltage $v_s(t)$ is described by Fig. P9.17(b). Find the average power absorbed by each resistor.

9.19 A voltage source $v_s(t) = 6\cos(2t - 90°)$ V, a resistor R, and a capacitor C are all connected in series. Given that the voltage across the resistor is 3 V rms and the resistor absorbs 9 W, find R and C.

9.20 A voltage source $v_s(t) = 4\cos 2t$ V, a $\frac{1}{4}$-F capacitor, an inductor L, and a resistor R are all connected in series. Given that the voltage across the resistor is 2 V rms and the resistor absorbs 1 W, find R and L.

9.21 For the sinusoidal circuit shown in Fig. P9.21, the voltage between terminals a and b is 13 V rms. When a 3-Ω resistor is placed between terminals a and b, the voltage across it is 3 V rms. When a 14-Ω resistor is placed between terminals a and b, the voltage across it is 9.1 V rms. The given circuit has an output impedance of $\mathbf{Z}_o = R_o + jX_o$. Find R_o and $|X_o|$.

9.22 The load shown in Fig. P9.22 operates at 60 Hz.
(a) What are the pf and the pf angle of this load?
(b) Is the pf leading or lagging?

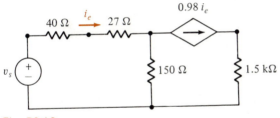

Fig. P9.18

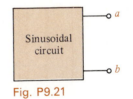

Fig. P9.21

(c) To what value should the capacitor be changed to get a lagging pf of 0.8?

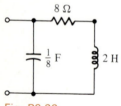

Fig. P9.22

9.23 A 115-V rms, 60-Hz electric hair dryer absorbs 500 W at a lagging pf of 0.95. What rms-valued current is drawn by this dryer?

9.24 Two loads, which are connected in parallel, operate at 230 V rms. One load absorbs 500 W at a pf of 0.8 lagging, and the other absorbs 1000 W at a pf of 0.9 lagging.
   (a) What is the current drawn by the combined load?
   (b) Find the pf of the combined load.
   (c) Is this pf leading or lagging?

9.25 The combined load given in Problem 9.24 is connected to a series combination of a voltage source and a resistance of 1 Ω. What is the rms value of the source?

9.26 For the combined load given in Problem 9.24, a third load, which operates at 1500 W with a pf of 0.9 leading, is connected in parallel.
   (a) What is the current drawn by the resulting composite load?

   (b) Find the pf of the composite load.
   (c) Is this pf leading or lagging?

9.27 The parallel connection of two 115-V rms, 60-Hz loads operates at 2000 W with a lagging pf of 0.95. If one load absorbs 1200 W at a pf of 0.8 lagging:
   (a) What are the power absorbed and the pf angle of the other load?
   (b) What reactive element should be placed in parallel with the load to result in an overall unity pf?

9.28 For the circuit shown in Fig. P9.28:
   (a) Find the complex power supplied by the source.
   (b) Find the apparent power supplied by the source.
   (c) Find the power factor and determine whether it is leading or lagging.

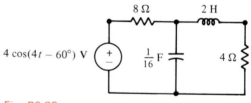

Fig. P9.28

9.29 For the circuit given in Fig. P9.29, the mesh currents shown are $I_1 = 2\sqrt{2}\angle{-105°}$ A and $I_2 = \sqrt{2}\angle{-105°}$ A.
   (a) What is the complex power absorbed by the capacitor?
   (b) What is the real power absorbed by the capacitor?

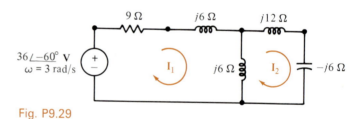

Fig. P9.29

(c) What is the complex power absorbed by the resistor?

(d) What is the real power absorbed by the resistor?

9.30 For the circuit given in Fig. P9.29:

(a) Find the complex power absorbed by each inductor, the capacitor, and the resistor.

(b) Find the complex power supplied by the source.

(c) Is the complex power absorbed equal to the complex power supplied (is complex power conserved)?

9.31 For the circuit given in Fig. P9.29:

(a) Find the apparent power supplied by the source.

(b) Find the apparent power absorbed by each of the remaining elements.

(c) Is the apparent power absorbed equal to the apparent power supplied (is apparent power conserved)?

9.32 A load, which operates at 440 V rms, draws 5 A rms at a leading pf of 0.95. Determine:

(a) the complex power absorbed by the load,

(b) the apparent power absorbed by the load,

(c) the impedance of the load.

9.33 For the single-phase, three-wire circuit shown in Fig. P9.33, find the power supplied by each source if $Z_1 = 60 \, \Omega$, $Z_2 = 80 \, \Omega$, $Z_3 = 40 \, \Omega$, and (a) $R_g = R_n = 0 \, \Omega$; (b) $R_g = 1 \, \Omega$, $R_n = 2 \, \Omega$.

9.34 For the single-phase, three-wire circuit given in Fig. P9.33, suppose $R_g = R_n = 0 \, \Omega$. Assuming Z_1 absorbs 500 W at a lagging pf of 0.8, Z_2 absorbs 1000 W at a lagging pf of 0.9, and Z_3 absorbs 1500 W at a leading pf of 0.95, find the currents through the sources.

9.35 A balanced Y-Y three-phase circuit has 130-V rms phase voltages and per-phase impedance of $Z = 12 + j12 \, \Omega$.

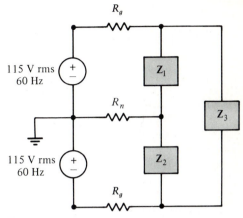

Fig. P9.33

Given that the line impedance is zero, find the line currents and the total power absorbed by the load.

9.36 Repeat Problem 9.35 for the case that the line impedances are 1 Ω.

9.37 A balanced Y-Y three-phase circuit has 210-V rms, 60-Hz line voltages. If the total load absorbs 3 kW of power at a lagging pf of 0.85:

(a) Find the per-phase impedance.

(b) What value capacitors should be placed in parallel with the per-phase impedances to result in a 0.95 lagging pf?

9.38 A balanced, three-phase Y-connected source, whose phase voltages are 115 V rms, has an unbalanced Y-connected load. Given $Z_{AN} = 3 + j4 \, \Omega$, $Z_{BN} = 10 \, \Omega$, and $Z_{CN} = 5 + j12 \, \Omega$, for the case that the lines and the neutral wire have zero impedances, find the line currents and the total power absorbed by the load.

9.39 Repeat Problem 9.38 for the case that there is no neutral wire.

9.40 A balanced Y-Δ three-phase circuit has $V_{an} = 130\underline{/0°}$ V rms and $Z = 4\sqrt{2}\underline{/45°} \, \Omega$. Given that the line impedance is zero, find the line currents and the total power absorbed by the load.

9.41 Repeat Problem 9.40 for the case that the line impedances are 1 Ω.

9.42 A balanced, three-phase Y-connected source with 230-V rms line voltages has an unbalanced Δ-connected load. The load impedances are $\mathbf{Z}_{AB} = 8\ \Omega$, $\mathbf{Z}_{BC} = 4 + j3\ \Omega$, and $\mathbf{Z}_{AC} = 12 - j5\ \Omega$. For the case that the lines have zero impedances, find the line currents and the total power absorbed by the load.

9.43 Repeat Problem 9.37 for a balanced Y-Δ three-phase circuit.

9.44 A balanced, three-phase Y-connected source with 120-V rms line voltages is loaded with a balanced Y-connection having $3 + j4\ \Omega$ per phase and a balanced Δ connection having $5 - j12\ \Omega$ per phase. Find the total power absorbed by the load and the pf.

9.45 A balanced, three-phase Δ-connected load has a per-phase impedance of $\mathbf{Z} = 36 + j36\ \Omega$. For the two-wattmeter connection given in Fig. 9.33, find the two readings for the case of line voltages of $130\sqrt{3}$ V rms produced by a balanced Y-connected source.

9.46 For the circuit given in Fig. P9.46, find the wattmeter readings P_A and P_B.

9.47 Find the wattmeter readings P_A and P_B for the circuit shown in Fig. P9.47.

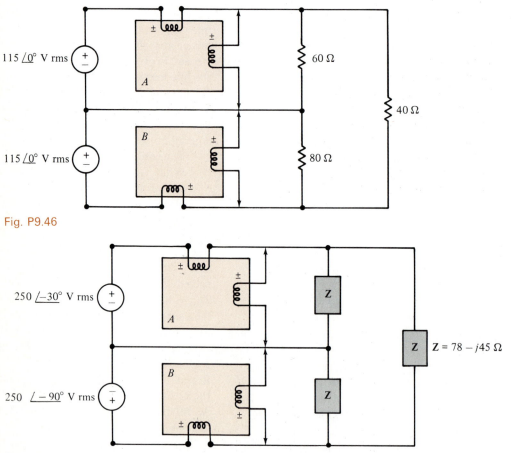

Fig. P9.46

Fig. P9.47

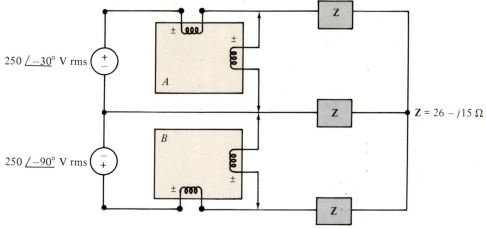

Fig. P9.48

9.48 Find the wattmeter readings P_A and P_B for the circuit given in Fig. P9.48.

9.49 The Y-Δ three-phase circuit given in Problem 9.42 has two wattmeters connected as shown in Fig. 9.33. Find the readings of these wattmeters.

9.50 For the Y-connected three-phase load shown in Fig. P9.50, find the wattmeter readings P_A and P_B when $\mathbf{Z}_{AN} = \mathbf{Z}_{BN} =$

$\mathbf{Z}_{CN} = 12 + j12 \ \Omega$ and the line voltage produced by a balanced three-phase Y-connected source is $130\sqrt{3}$ V rms.

9.51 Repeat Problem 9.50 for the case that $\mathbf{Z}_{AN} = 3 + j4 \ \Omega$, $\mathbf{Z}_{BN} = 10 \ \Omega$, and $\mathbf{Z}_{CN} = 5 + j12 \ \Omega$, and the line voltage produced by a balanced three-phase Y-connected source is $115\sqrt{3}$ V rms.

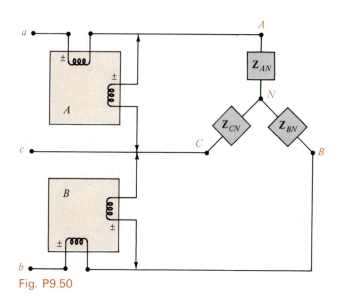

Fig. P9.50

CHAPTER 10

Important AC Concepts

● INTRODUCTION

Since the impedance of capacitors and inductors is frequency-dependent, so is the impedance of an arbitrary *RLC* circuit. This dependence, which can be depicted graphically by plots of magnitude and phase angle versus frequency, constitute the "frequency response" of the impedance. Impedance, which is the ratio of voltage to current (phasors), is only one network function whose frequency response can be displayed. It is the frequency response of a network that describes the network's behavior to all sinusoidal forcing functions and nonsinusoidal forcing functions that are composed of sinusoids.

An important circuit concept deals with that frequency for which a network function reaches a maximum value. In certain simple circuits, this occurs when an impedance or admittance is purely real—a condition known as "resonance." In such a situation we can quantitatively describe the "frequency selectivity" of the network with a figure of merit known as the "quality factor." We can also talk about the notion of "bandwidth."

In this chapter we shall also see how we can easily convert a circuit that consists of elements whose values are computationally convenient but impractical to one with practical values. This process is known as "scaling."

Just as the concept of complex sinusoids allowed us to treat sinusoidal circuits in a simple manner, the concept of complex frequency does a similar job for damped-sinusoidal circuits. This generalization not only allows for the easy determination of forced responses to sinusoidal and damped-sinusoidal forcing functions, but indicates the form of the natural response as well.

10.1 FREQUENCY RESPONSE

For the parallel connection of a resistor R and capacitor C shown in Fig. 10.1, the impedance $\mathbf{Z}$ of the combination is given by

$$\mathbf{Z} = \frac{\mathbf{Z}_R\mathbf{Z}_C}{\mathbf{Z}_R + \mathbf{Z}_C} = \frac{R(1/j\omega C)}{R + (1/j\omega C)} = \frac{R}{1 + j\omega RC}$$

$$= \frac{R}{\sqrt{1 + (\omega RC)^2}} \; \underline{/-\tan^{-1}\omega RC} = |\mathbf{Z}|\underline{/\theta}$$

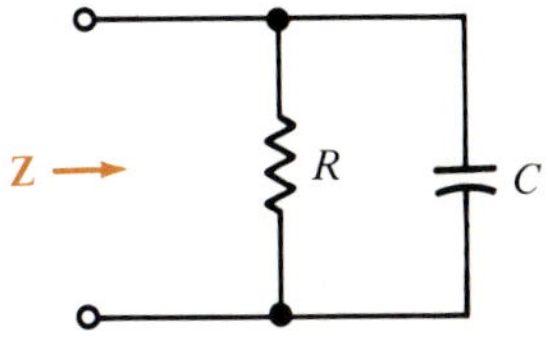

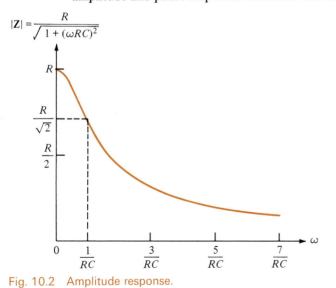

Fig. 10.1 Parallel *RC* impedance.

Since $\mathbf{Z}$ is a complex function—the notation $\mathbf{Z}(j\omega)$ is often used—it can be expressed in terms of a magnitude and an angle as $\mathbf{Z} = |\mathbf{Z}|\underline{/\theta}$. Both the magnitude $|\mathbf{Z}|$ and the angle θ are functions of ω. We therefore may plot $|\mathbf{Z}|$ versus ω and θ versus ω. In obtaining the former, note that when $\omega = 0$, the magnitude is $|\mathbf{Z}| = R$; when $\omega = 1/RC$, then $|\mathbf{Z}| = R/\sqrt{2} \approx 0.707R$. Also, when $\omega \to \infty$, then $|\mathbf{Z}| \to 0$. Thus, we have the plot shown in Fig. 10.2, which we call the **amplitude response** of $\mathbf{Z}$. The plot of θ versus ω is known as the **phase response** of $\mathbf{Z}$, and for this example, it is shown in Fig. 10.3. In this plot, we see that when $\omega = 0$, then $\theta = -\tan^{-1}\omega RC = 0$, and when $\omega = 1/RC$, then $\theta = -\tan^{-1}\omega RC = -45°$. Furthermore, when $\omega \to \infty$, then $\theta \to -90°$. The amplitude and phase responses constitute the **frequency response** of the impedance $\mathbf{Z}$.

$$|\mathbf{Z}| = \frac{R}{\sqrt{1 + (\omega RC)^2}}$$

Fig. 10.2 Amplitude response.

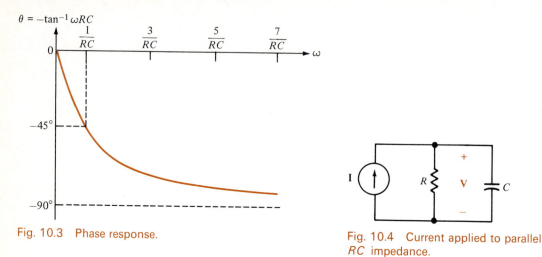

Fig. 10.3   Phase response.

Fig. 10.4   Current applied to parallel *RC* impedance.

Although a frequency response consists of both an amplitude response and a phase response, quite often the amplitude response alone is referred to as the frequency response.

For the circuit shown in Fig. 10.4, $\mathbf{V} = \mathbf{ZI}$ where $\mathbf{Z}$ is the impedance of the parallel *RC* combination. From complex-number arithmetic,

$$|\mathbf{V}| = |\mathbf{ZI}| = |\mathbf{Z}|\,|\mathbf{I}|$$

Given the current $\mathbf{I}$, then $|\mathbf{V}|$ is maximum when $|\mathbf{Z}|$ is maximum. This occurs when $\omega = 0$ where $|\mathbf{Z}| = R$, and the average power absorbed by the resistor is

$$P_0 = \frac{1}{2}\frac{|\mathbf{V}|^2}{R} = \frac{1}{2}\frac{R^2|\mathbf{I}|^2}{R} = \frac{1}{2}R|\mathbf{I}|^2$$

However, when $\omega = 1/RC = \omega_c$, then $|\mathbf{Z}| = R/\sqrt{2}$, so the power absorbed is

$$P_1 = \frac{1}{2}\frac{(R/\sqrt{2})^2|\mathbf{I}|^2}{R} = \frac{1}{2}\left(\frac{R|\mathbf{I}|^2}{2}\right) = \frac{1}{2}P_0$$

That is, P_1 is half of the power P_0. For this reason, we say that $\omega_c = 1/RC$ is the **half-power frequency** or **cutoff frequency**. In general, given an amplitude response whose maximum value is M, the half-power frequencies are those frequencies for which the magnitude is $M/\sqrt{2}$.

EXAMPLE 10.1

For the circuit shown in Fig. 10.5, the input voltage (phasor) is $\mathbf{V}_1$ and the output voltage is $\mathbf{V}_2$. By voltage division,

$$\mathbf{V}_2 = \frac{R}{R + (1/j\omega C)}\mathbf{V}_1 \qquad \Rightarrow \qquad \frac{\mathbf{V}_2}{\mathbf{V}_1} = \frac{j\omega RC}{1 + j\omega RC}$$

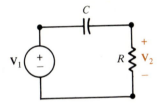

Fig. 10.5   Simple high-pass filter.

Denoting the ratio of output voltage to input voltage by $\mathbf{H}(j\omega)$, that is, $\mathbf{H}(j\omega) = \mathbf{V}_2/\mathbf{V}_1$, then

$$\left|\mathbf{H}(j\omega)\right| = \left|\frac{\mathbf{V}_2}{\mathbf{V}_1}\right| = \frac{|\mathbf{V}_2|}{|\mathbf{V}_1|} = \frac{\omega RC}{\sqrt{1 + (\omega RC)^2}}$$

For $\omega = 0$, we have that $\left|\mathbf{H}(j\omega)\right| = 0$. To determine the value of $\left|\mathbf{H}(j\omega)\right|$ as $\omega \to \infty$, note that

$$\left|\mathbf{H}(j\omega)\right| = \sqrt{\frac{(\omega RC)^2}{1 + (\omega RC)^2}} = \frac{1}{\sqrt{1 + 1/(\omega RC)^2}}$$

Thus, $\left|\mathbf{H}(j\omega)\right| \to 1$ as $\omega \to \infty$. Also, note that for $\omega = 1/RC$, $\left|\mathbf{H}(j\omega)\right| = 1/\sqrt{2}$. The amplitude response of the function $\mathbf{H}(j\omega)$—called a **system function** or a **transfer function**—is shown in Fig. 10.6(a). Clearly, $\omega_c = 1/RC$ is the half-power frequency.

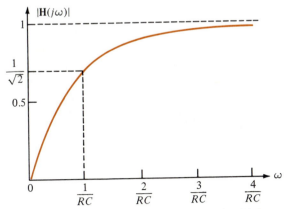

Fig. 10.6(a)   Amplitude response of simple high-pass filter.

Since

$$\mathbf{H}(j\omega) = \frac{j\omega RC}{1 + j\omega RC} = \frac{\omega RC \underline{/90°}}{\sqrt{1 + (\omega RC)^2} \underline{/\tan^{-1}\omega RC}}$$

then

$$\text{ang } \mathbf{H}(j\omega) = 90° - \tan^{-1} \omega RC$$

For $\omega = 0$, ang $\mathbf{H}(j\omega) = 90°$. For the half-power frequency, $\omega_c = 1/RC$, we have

$$\text{ang } \mathbf{H}(j\omega) = \text{ang } \mathbf{H}(j\omega_c) = 90° - \tan^{-1} \omega_c RC = 90° - \tan^{-1} 1 = 45°$$

When $\omega \rightarrow \infty$, then ang $\mathbf{H}(j\omega) \rightarrow 90° - 90° = 0°$. A sketch of the phase response is shown in Fig. 10.6(b).

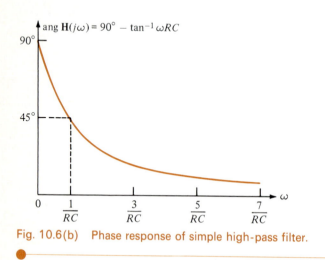

Fig. 10.6(b)   Phase response of simple high-pass filter.

It is possible to obtain a rough sketch of the amplitude response for the circuit in Fig. 10.5 without writing an analytical expression for the transfer function $\mathbf{H}(j\omega)$. For $\omega = 0$—the dc case—the capacitor is an open circuit, so $\mathbf{V}_2$, and consequently $|\mathbf{H}(j\omega)| = 0$. For small values of ω, the impedance of the capacitor is still large relative to R, so by voltage division $\mathbf{V}_2$ is relatively small, as is $|\mathbf{H}(j\omega)|$. However, as frequency (ω) increases, the impedance of the capacitor decreases, so that the values of $\mathbf{V}_2$ and $|\mathbf{H}(j\omega)|$ increase. In the limit, as frequency becomes infinite, the impedance of the capacitor becomes zero, so $\mathbf{V}_2 \rightarrow \mathbf{V}_1 \Rightarrow |\mathbf{H}(j\omega)| \rightarrow 1$.

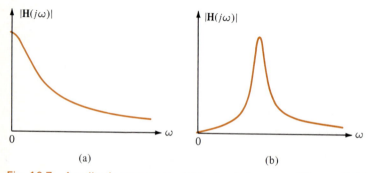

Fig. 10.7   Amplitude responses of (a) simple low-pass filter, and (b) simple bandpass filter.

From the amplitude response of $\mathbf{H}(j\omega)$, we see that if the input voltage is a sinusoid, then the amplitude of the output sinusoid will be relatively small for low frequencies (i.e., frequencies below ω_c). Conversely, for high frequencies (i.e., frequencies above ω_c), the amplitude of the output sinusoid approximately equals the amplitude of the input sinusoid. In other words, the high frequencies are "passed" by the *RC* circuit, while the low frequencies are "stopped." For this reason, we say that the circuit is an example of a simple **high-pass filter**. The amplitude response shown in Fig. 10.7(a) is indicative of a simple **low-pass filter**, and the one depicted in Fig. 10.7(b) describes a simple **bandpass filter**.

DRILL EXERCISE 10.1

For the series *RL* circuit shown in Fig. DE10.1, sketch the amplitude and phase responses for the transfer function $\mathbf{H}(j\omega) = \mathbf{V}_2/\mathbf{V}_1$, indicating the half-power frequency. What type of filter is this circuit?

Answer: $\omega_c = R/L$, high-pass filter.

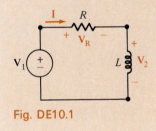

Fig. DE10.1

10.2 BODE PLOTS

The magnitude of a voltage transfer function, that is, $|\mathbf{H}(j\omega)| = |\mathbf{V}_2/\mathbf{V}_1|$, which, in general, is a function of frequency, is also referred to as **voltage gain**. Although we can, as discussed above, directly plot gain versus frequency to obtain the amplitude response, in practice logarithmic scales are used for both the gain and frequency axes rather than linear scales. As a consequence of this, it is often possible to obtain an approximate frequency response without having to perform many calculations. (If more accurate results are required, then a programmable hand calculator or a computer can be employed.)

Suppose that P_1 and P_2 are the input and output (load) powers, respectively, of a circuit or system. We define the power gain to be $\log_{10} P_2/P_1$, where the unit is the **bel** (B), named for Alexander Graham Bell (1847–1922). Since gain in bels is often a relatively small number in practice, the accepted convention is to multiply the value by 10 and express the gain in **decibels** (dB). In other words,

$$\text{gain} = 10 \log_{10} \frac{P_2}{P_1} \quad \text{dB}$$

If the input resistance is R_1 and the load resistance is R_2, then $P_1 = \frac{1}{2}V_1^2/R_1$ and $P_2 = \frac{1}{2}V_2^2/R_2$, where V_1 and V_2 are, respectively, the input and output voltage magnitudes. For the case that $R_1 = R_2$, we have that

$$\text{gain} = 10\log_{10}\frac{V_2^2}{V_1^2} = 20\log_{10}\frac{V_2}{V_1} \quad \text{dB}$$

A plot of gain in decibels on a linear scale versus frequency on a logarithmic scale, and a plot of angle on a linear scale versus frequency, again on a logarithmic scale, constitute a **Bode plot** or **diagram**.[†]

Consider the transfer function

$$\mathbf{H}(j\omega) = \frac{\mathbf{V}_2}{\mathbf{V}_1} = \frac{a}{a + j\omega} = \frac{1}{1 + j\omega/a} \quad (10.1)$$

where $a > 0$. Then

$$\left|\mathbf{H}(j\omega)\right| = \frac{a}{\sqrt{a^2 + \omega^2}} \quad \text{and} \quad \text{ang}\,\mathbf{H}(j\omega) = -\tan^{-1}\frac{\omega}{a}$$

For low frequencies ($\omega \ll a$), $\left|\mathbf{H}(j\omega)\right| \approx 1$. Thus,

$$20\log_{10}\left|\mathbf{H}(j\omega)\right| \approx 20\log_{10} 1 = 0 \quad \text{for} \quad \omega \ll a$$

For high frequencies ($\omega \gg a$), $\left|\mathbf{H}(j\omega)\right| \approx a/\omega$. Thus,

$$20\log_{10}\left|\mathbf{H}(j\omega)\right| \approx 20\log_{10}\frac{a}{\omega} = -20\log_{10}\frac{\omega}{a} \quad \text{for} \quad \omega \gg a$$

The two straight lines 0 and $-20\log_{10}\omega/a$ are called **asymptotes**—the former is the low-frequency asymptote, and the latter is the high-frequency asymptote—of the amplitude response. These asymptotes are depicted in Fig. 10.8.

The frequency for which the asymptotes intersect is called the **corner frequency** or **break frequency**. In this case,

$$-20\log_{10}\frac{\omega}{a} = 0 \quad \Rightarrow \quad \omega = a \text{ rad/s}$$

and this is the corner frequency.

As indicated by Fig. 10.8, a plot of $-20\log_{10}\omega/a$ versus ω on a logarithmic scale is a straight line. For $\omega = a$, $-20\log_{10}\omega/a = 0$; while for $\omega = 10a$, $-20\log_{10}\omega/a = -20\log_{10} 10 = -20$ dB. Since a change in frequency by a factor of 10 is referred to as a **decade**, the straight line $-20\log_{10}\omega/a$ has a slope of -20 dB/decade. Alternatively, for $\omega = 2a$, $-20\log_{10}\omega/a = -20\log_{10} 2 = -6.02 \approx -6$ dB.

[†] Named for the American electrical engineer Hendrick Bode.

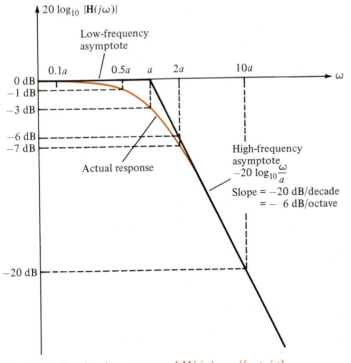

Fig. 10.8   Amplitude response of $\mathbf{H}(j\omega) = a/(a + j\omega)$.

Since a change in frequency by a factor of 2 is referred to as an **octave**, we can also say that the straight line $-20\log_{10} \omega/a$ has a slope of -6 dB/octave.

The low-frequency and high-frequency asymptotes are good approximations for the amplitude response, $|\mathbf{H}(j\omega)|$ versus ω, for low frequencies ($\omega \ll a$) and high frequencies ($\omega \gg a$), respectively. However, at the corner frequency, $\omega = a$,

$$20\log_{10}|\mathbf{H}(j\omega)| = 20\log_{10} \frac{a}{\sqrt{a^2 + a^2}} = 20\log_{10} \frac{1}{\sqrt{2}} = -3.01 \approx -3 \text{ dB}$$

Thus, the actual amplitude response is 3 dB down from the intersection of the asymptotes. At $\omega = 0.5a$, that is, at one octave below the corner frequency,

$$20\log_{10}|\mathbf{H}(j\omega)| = 20\log_{10} \frac{a}{\sqrt{a^2 + (0.5a)^2}} = -0.969 \approx -1.0 \text{ dB}$$

while one octave above the corner frequency at $\omega = 2a$,

$$20\log_{10}|\mathbf{H}(j\omega)| = 20\log_{10} \frac{a}{\sqrt{a^2 + (2a)^2}} = -6.990 \approx -7.0 \text{ dB}$$

Therefore, one octave below and above the corner frequency, the actual amplitude response is 1.0 dB below the approximate amplitude response formed by the asymptotes. One decade below and above the corner frequency, the actual amplitude response is only 0.043 dB below the asymptotes. (Verify this fact.)

For the given transfer function, note that for the corner frequency $\omega = a$, we have

$$|\mathbf{H}(j\omega)| = \frac{a}{\sqrt{a^2 + a^2}} = \frac{1}{\sqrt{2}}$$

Since the maximum value of $|\mathbf{H}(j\omega)|$ occurs when $\omega = 0$ and is $|\mathbf{H}(j0)| = 1$, we see that the corner frequency $\omega = a$ is also the half-power frequency.

Since $\text{ang }\mathbf{H}(j\omega) = -\tan^{-1} \omega/a$, for $\omega \ll a$, $\text{ang }\mathbf{H}(j\omega) \approx 0°$. Furthermore, for $\omega \gg a$, $\text{ang }\mathbf{H}(j\omega) \approx -90°$. In addition, for $\omega = a$, $\text{ang }\mathbf{H}(j\omega) = -\tan^{-1} 1 = -45°$. Therefore, let us approximate the phase response of $\mathbf{H}(j\omega)$ by using three straight-line segments as shown in Fig. 10.9.

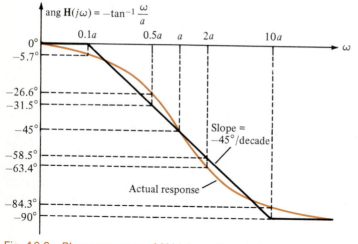

Fig. 10.9   Phase response of $\mathbf{H}(j\omega) = a/(a + j\omega)$.

The actual phase response is also indicated in Fig. 10.9. In this case, at the corner frequency, the approximation gives the actual value of the phase ($-45°$). However, one decade below the corner frequency at $\omega = 0.1a$, the actual phase response is

$$\text{ang }\mathbf{H}(j\omega) = -\tan^{-1} \frac{0.1a}{a} = -5.7°$$

while one decade above the corner frequency at $\omega = 10a$, the actual phase response is

$$\text{ang }\mathbf{H}(j\omega) = -\tan^{-1} \frac{10a}{a} = -84.3°$$

DRILL EXERCISE 10.2

Sketch the Bode plot for the series *RC* circuit shown in Fig. DE10.2.

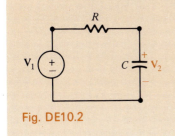

Fig. DE10.2

Other Transfer Functions

Now consider a transfer function of the form

$$\mathbf{H}(j\omega) = \frac{a + j\omega}{a} = 1 + \frac{j\omega}{a} \tag{10.2}$$

For $\omega \ll a$, $|\mathbf{H}(j\omega)| \approx 1$ and

$$20 \log_{10} |\mathbf{H}(j\omega)| \approx 0$$

while for $\omega \gg a$, $|\mathbf{H}(j\omega)| \approx \omega/a$ and

$$20 \log_{10} |\mathbf{H}(j\omega)| \approx 20 \log_{10} \frac{\omega}{a}$$

The corresponding asymptotes, which give an approximate amplitude response of $\mathbf{H}(j\omega)$, along with the actual amplitude-response curve, are shown in Fig. 10.10(a). The approximate and actual phase-response curves are shown in Fig. 10.10(b). As was the case for the simple low-pass filter transfer function given by Equation (10.1), the transfer function given by Equation (10.2) has a corner frequency of $\omega = a$ rad/s.

Suppose that we can express a transfer function $\mathbf{H}(j\omega)$ as the product of two transfer functions $\mathbf{H}_1(j\omega)$ and $\mathbf{H}_2(j\omega)$. In other words, suppose that

$$\mathbf{H}(j\omega) = \mathbf{H}_1(j\omega)\mathbf{H}_2(j\omega)$$

Since

$$|\mathbf{H}(j\omega)| = |\mathbf{H}_1(j\omega)\mathbf{H}_2(j\omega)| = |\mathbf{H}_1(j\omega)||\mathbf{H}_2(j\omega)|$$

then

$$20 \log_{10} |\mathbf{H}(j\omega)| = 20 \log_{10} |\mathbf{H}_1(j\omega)| + 20 \log_{10} |\mathbf{H}_2(j\omega)|$$

Therefore, addition of the amplitude-response curves for $\mathbf{H}_1(j\omega)$ and $\mathbf{H}_2(j\omega)$ results in the amplitude-response curve for $\mathbf{H}(j\omega)$. Furthermore, since

$$\operatorname{ang} \mathbf{H}(j\omega) = \operatorname{ang}[\mathbf{H}_1(j\omega)\mathbf{H}_2(j\omega)] = \operatorname{ang} \mathbf{H}_1(j\omega) + \operatorname{ang} \mathbf{H}_2(j\omega)$$

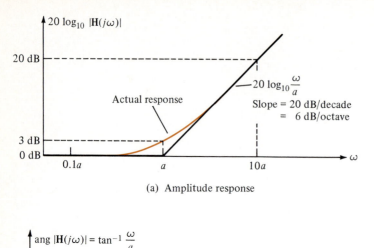

(a) Amplitude response

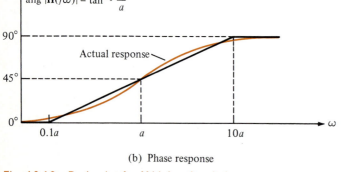

(b) Phase response

Fig. 10.10   Bode plot for $H(j\omega) = 1 + j\omega/a$.

then the addition of the phase-response curves for $H_1(j\omega)$ and $H_2(j\omega)$ yields the phase-response curve for $H(j\omega)$.

EXAMPLE 10.2

Let us sketch the Bode plot for the simple high-pass filter given in Fig. 10.5 on p. 443. We have already seen (Example 10.1) that

$$H(j\omega) = \frac{V_2}{V_1} = \frac{j\omega RC}{1 + j\omega RC}$$

Let us express this transfer function as the product

$$H(j\omega) = H_1(j\omega)H_2(j\omega)$$

where $H_1(j\omega) = j\omega RC$ and $H_2(j\omega) = 1/(1 + j\omega RC)$. The amplitude response for $H_1(j\omega)$ is shown in Fig. 10.11(a)—and this is the actual response curve for $H_1(j\omega)$. On the other hand, Fig. 10.11(b) shows the approximate amplitude response for $H_2(j\omega)$. By adding these two response curves, we obtain the amplitude response for $H(j\omega)$ as shown in Fig. 10.11(c).

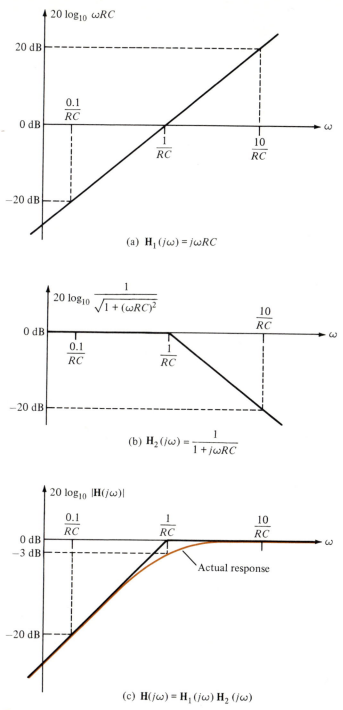

(a) $\mathbf{H}_1(j\omega) = j\omega RC$

(b) $\mathbf{H}_2(j\omega) = \dfrac{1}{1 + j\omega RC}$

(c) $\mathbf{H}(j\omega) = \mathbf{H}_1(j\omega)\,\mathbf{H}_2(j\omega)$

Fig. 10.11   Amplitude responses.

The phase response for $H_1(j\omega) = j\omega RC$ is just the constant $90°$. On the other hand, the phase response for $H_2(j\omega) = 1/(1 + j\omega RC)$ is given by Fig. 10.9 (p. 448), where $a = 1/RC$. Adding the phase responses for $H_1(j\omega)$ and $H_2(j\omega)$, we get the phase response for $H(j\omega) = H_1(j\omega)H_2(j\omega)$ shown in Fig. 10.12.

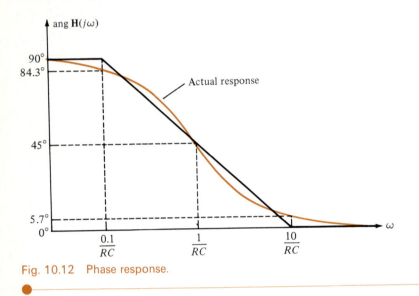

Fig. 10.12 Phase response.

DRILL EXERCISE 10.3

Sketch the Bode plot for

$$H(j\omega) = \frac{1 + j\omega}{1 + j\omega 10}$$

In general, given the transfer function

$$H(j\omega) = H_1(j\omega)H_2(j\omega)H_3(j\omega) \cdots H_n(j\omega)$$

since the logarithm of a product is equal to the sum of the logarithms of each term in the product, then the amplitude response of $H(j\omega)$ can be obtained by adding the amplitude-response curves for $H_1(j\omega)$, $H_2(j\omega)$, $H_3(j\omega)$, ..., and $H_n(j\omega)$. Similarly, the phase response of $H(j\omega)$ can be obtained by adding the phase-response curves for $H_1(j\omega)$, $H_2(j\omega)$, $H_3(j\omega)$, ..., and $H_n(j\omega)$.

A Second-Order Circuit

For the series *RLC* circuit shown in Fig. 10.13, we have that

$$H(j\omega) = \frac{V_2}{V_1} = \frac{1/j\omega C}{1/j\omega C + R + j\omega L} = \frac{1/LC}{1/LC + j\omega R/L + (j\omega)^2}$$

Consider the case that $R = 11\ \Omega$, $L = 1$ H, and $C = \frac{1}{10}$ F. Then

$$\mathbf{H}(j\omega) = \frac{10}{10 + j\omega 11 + (j\omega)^2} = \frac{10}{(1 + j\omega)(10 + j\omega)}$$

Thus, we can express the transfer function as the product

$$\mathbf{H}(j\omega) = \left(\frac{1}{1 + j\omega}\right)\left(\frac{10}{10 + j\omega}\right) = \mathbf{H}_1(j\omega)\mathbf{H}_2(j\omega)$$

The straight-line approximations of the amplitude responses for $\mathbf{H}_1(j\omega)$ and $\mathbf{H}_2(j\omega)$ are shown in Fig. 10.14(a) and (b), respectively. Adding these two response

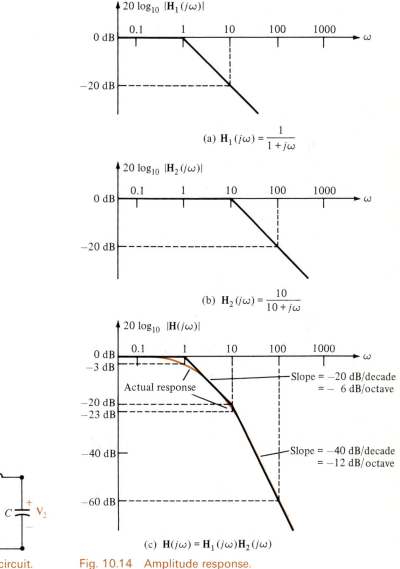

(a) $\mathbf{H}_1(j\omega) = \dfrac{1}{1 + j\omega}$

(b) $\mathbf{H}_2(j\omega) = \dfrac{10}{10 + j\omega}$

(c) $\mathbf{H}(j\omega) = \mathbf{H}_1(j\omega)\mathbf{H}_2(j\omega)$

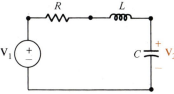

Fig. 10.13 Series *RLC* circuit.

Fig. 10.14 Amplitude response.

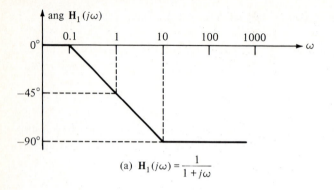

(a) $H_1(j\omega) = \dfrac{1}{1 + j\omega}$

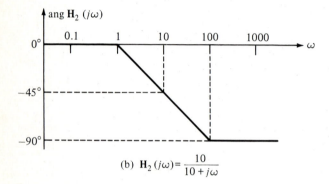

(b) $H_2(j\omega) = \dfrac{10}{10 + j\omega}$

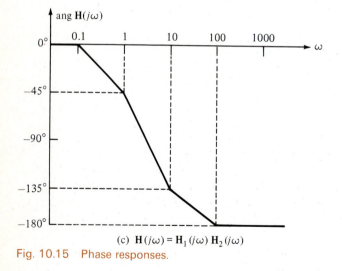

(c) $H(j\omega) = H_1(j\omega)\, H_2(j\omega)$

Fig. 10.15   Phase responses.

curves, we get the amplitude response for $\mathbf{H}(j\omega)$ shown in Fig. 10.14(c). Note that for the transfer function $\mathbf{H}(j\omega)$ there are two break frequencies—one at $\omega = 1$ rad/s and one at $\omega = 10$ rad/s. Since these break frequencies are a decade apart, the actual amplitude response is just 3 dB down from the straight-line approximation at the break frequencies.

If the break frequencies were closer together (due to different values of R, L, and/or C), then the actual amplitude response would be more than 3 dB down from the straight-line approximation at the break frequencies.

The straight-line approximations of the phase responses for $\mathbf{H}_1(j\omega)$ and $\mathbf{H}_2(j\omega)$ are shown in Fig. 10.15(a) and (b), respectively. Adding these two responses, we get the straight-line approximation of the phase response for $\mathbf{H}(j\omega)$ shown in Fig. 10.15(c).

DRILL EXERCISE 10.4

For the second-order circuit given in Fig. 10.13, suppose that $R = 2\,\Omega$, $L = 1$ H, and $C = 1$ F. Sketch the Bode plot for $\mathbf{H}(j\omega) = \mathbf{V}_2/\mathbf{V}_1$.

Note that the transfer function $\mathbf{H}(j\omega) = \mathbf{V}_2/\mathbf{V}_1$ for the second-order circuit given in Fig. 10.13 has the form

$$\mathbf{H}(j\omega) = \frac{\omega_n^2}{\omega_n^2 + 2\alpha j\omega + (j\omega)^2} = \frac{\omega_n^2}{(-s_1 + j\omega)(-s_2 + j\omega)} \tag{10.3}$$

where $\alpha = R/2L$, $\omega_n = 1/\sqrt{LC}$, $s_1 = -\alpha - \sqrt{\alpha^2 - \omega_n^2}$, and $s_2 = -\alpha + \sqrt{\alpha^2 - \omega_n^2}$.

For the case that $\alpha > \omega_n$ (the overdamped case), s_1 and s_2 are distinct, negative real numbers. Therefore, the corresponding amplitude response has two distinct break frequencies ($-s_1$ and $-s_2$).

For the case that $\alpha = \omega_n$ (the critically damped case), $s_1 = s_2 = -\alpha = -\omega_n$, so the resulting straight-line approximation of the amplitude response consists of a horizontal line (0 dB) which intersects with a straight line of slope -40 dB/decade (-12 dB/octave) at the frequency $\omega = \omega_n$ rad/s. Under this circumstance, the actual amplitude response is $3 + 3 = 6$ dB down from the straight-line approximation at $\omega = \omega_n$ rad/s.

For the case that $\alpha < \omega_n$ (the underdamped case), s_1 and s_2 are complex numbers with negative real parts. Under this circumstance, the low-frequency asymptote is the horizontal line 0 dB, while the high-frequency asymptote is a straight line of slope -40 dB/decade which intersects the low-frequency asymptote at $\omega = \omega_n$ rad/s. However, for middle frequencies, the gain can be greater than 0 dB. For example, if $\alpha = 0.05\omega_n$, then for $\omega = \omega_n$, the gain is

$$20\log_{10}|\mathbf{H}(j\omega)| = 20\log_{10}\left|\frac{\omega_n^2}{\omega_n^2 + 2(0.05\omega_n)j\omega_n + (j\omega_n)^2}\right| = 20\log_{10} 10 = 20 \text{ dB}$$

Figure 10.16 shows Bode plots for the transfer function given by Equation (10.3) for selected values of $\alpha < \omega_n$ and for $\alpha = \omega_n$.

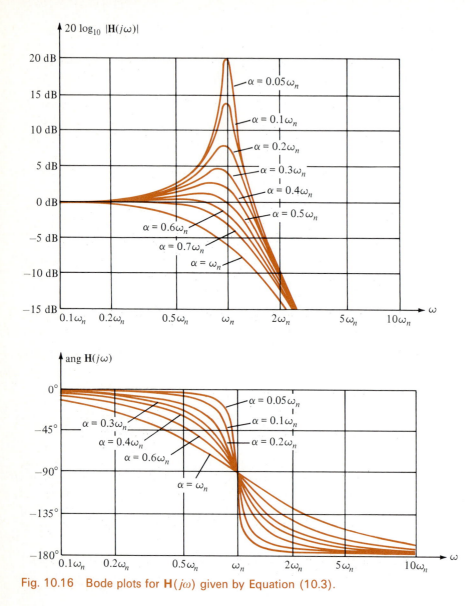

Fig. 10.16   Bode plots for $H(j\omega)$ given by Equation (10.3).

10.3 RESONANCE

For the parallel RLC circuit shown in Fig. 10.17, the admittance seen by the current source is $Y = I/V$, where

$$Y = Y_R + Y_L + Y_C = \frac{1}{R} + \frac{1}{j\omega L} + j\omega C = \frac{1}{R} + j\left(\omega C - \frac{1}{\omega L}\right)$$

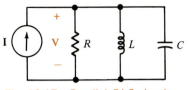

Fig. 10.17 Parallel *RLC* circuit.

From this expression, we can see that there is some frequency ω_r for which the imaginary part of **Y** will be zero, that is,

$$\omega_r C - \frac{1}{\omega_r L} = 0 \quad \Rightarrow \quad \omega_r C = \frac{1}{\omega_r L} \quad \Rightarrow \quad \omega_r = \frac{1}{\sqrt{LC}}$$

We say that a circuit with at least one capacitor and one inductor is in **resonance** or is **resonant** when the imaginary part of its admittance (or impedance) is equal to zero. The circuit given in Fig. 10.17 is in resonance when $\omega = \omega_r = 1/\sqrt{LC}$, and ω_r is called the **resonance frequency**.

DRILL EXERCISE 10.5

Find an expression for the (nonzero) resonance frequency for the impedance shown in Fig. DE10.5.
Answer: $1/\sqrt{LC - R^2 C^2}$

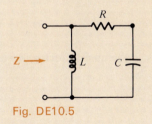

Fig. DE10.5

For the circuit given in Fig. 10.17, since

$$|\mathbf{V}| = \left| \frac{\mathbf{I}}{\mathbf{Y}} \right| = \frac{|\mathbf{I}|}{|\mathbf{Y}|}$$

from the fact that $|\mathbf{Y}|$ is minimum at resonance for this circuit, we conclude that $|\mathbf{V}|$ is maximum at the resonance frequency $\omega_r = 1/\sqrt{LC}$ and is given by

$$|\mathbf{V}| = \frac{|\mathbf{I}|}{1/R} = R|\mathbf{I}|$$

Since, at resonance, the parallel *RLC* combination acts simply as the resistance *R*, the parallel *LC* combination—known as a **tank circuit**—behaves as an open circuit.

For $\omega = 0$, the impedance of the inductor is zero; thus, so is the voltage **V**. As $\omega \to \infty$, the impedance of the capacitor $1/j\omega C \to 0$, and thus $\mathbf{V} \to 0$. A sketch of $|\mathbf{V}|$ versus ω is shown in Fig. 10.18, where ω_1 and ω_2 are the "lower" and "upper" half-power frequencies, respectively.

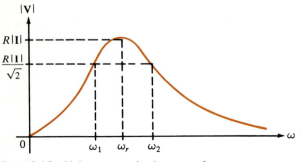

Fig. 10.18   Voltage magnitude versus frequency.

We define the **bandwidth** *BW* of the resonant circuit in terms of the half-power frequencies by

$$BW = \omega_2 - \omega_1$$

Note that the smaller the bandwidth *BW* is, the "sharper" or "narrower" is the amplitude response.

Quality Factor

Another conventional quantity that describes sharpness is the **quality factor**, designated *Q*, which is defined at the resonance frequency to be

$$Q = 2\pi \left(\frac{\text{maximum energy stored}}{\text{total energy lost in a period}} \right)$$

Since energy is stored in capacitors and inductors, the maximum energy stored is designated $[w_C(t) + w_L(t)]_{max}$. Since energy is dissipated by resistors, the energy lost in a period T is $P_R T$, where P_R is the resistive power. Thus,

$$Q = \frac{2\pi [w_C(t) + w_L(t)]_{max}}{P_R T}$$

Now let us determine the quality factor for the parallel *RLC* circuit given in Fig. 10.17. Assume that the current source is given by $i(t) = I \cos \omega_r t$, where $\omega_r = 1/\sqrt{LC}$. At resonance, $\mathbf{Y} = 1/R$, so

$$v(t) = Ri(t) = RI \cos \omega_r t$$

Then the energy stored in the capacitor is

$$w_C(t) = \tfrac{1}{2}Cv^2(t) = \tfrac{1}{2}C(RI\cos\omega_r t)^2 = \tfrac{1}{2}CR^2 I^2 \cos^2\omega_r t$$

Furthermore, since the inductor current $\mathbf{I}_L$ (going down) is $\mathbf{I}_L = \mathbf{V}/j\omega L$, then at resonance, since $v(t) = RI\cos\omega_r t$,

$$\mathbf{I}_L = \frac{RI\underline{/0°}}{\omega_r L\underline{/90°}} = \frac{RI}{\omega_r L}\underline{/-90°} \quad\Rightarrow\quad i_L(t) = \frac{RI}{\omega_r L}\cos(\omega_r t - 90°) = \frac{RI}{\omega_r L}\sin\omega_r t$$

at resonance. The fact that the LC tank portion of the circuit behaves as an open circuit at resonance does not mean that there are no currents in the inductor and capacitor. As a matter of fact, the current, given above, circulates around the loop formed by the inductor and capacitor.

At resonance, the energy stored in the inductor is

$$w_L(t) = \frac{1}{2}Li_L^2(t) = \frac{1}{2}\frac{R^2 I^2}{\omega_r^2 L}\sin^2\omega_r t = \frac{1}{2}CR^2 I^2\sin^2\omega_r t$$

since $\omega_r^2 = 1/LC$. Therefore, the total energy stored is

$$w_C(t) + w_L(t) = \tfrac{1}{2}CR^2 I^2(\cos^2\omega_r t + \sin^2\omega_r t) = \tfrac{1}{2}CR^2 I^2$$

which is a constant. Since the power absorbed by a resistor is $P_R = I^2 R/2$, then the energy lost in a period is

$$P_R T = \frac{1}{2}I^2 RT = \frac{1}{2}I^2 R\left(\frac{2\pi}{\omega_r}\right) = \frac{\pi I^2 R}{\omega_r}$$

Thus, the quality factor of the given parallel RLC circuit is

$$Q = \frac{2\pi(\tfrac{1}{2}CR^2 I^2)}{\pi I^2 R/\omega_r} = \omega_r RC$$

Since $\omega_r C = 1/\omega_r L$, alternatively, we can write

$$Q = \omega_r RC = \frac{R}{\omega_r L} = R\sqrt{\frac{C}{L}}$$

Again considering the expression for the admittance of the circuit in Fig. 10.17, we have that

$$\mathbf{Y} = \frac{1}{R} + j\left(\omega C - \frac{1}{\omega L}\right) = \frac{1}{R} + j\left(\frac{\omega C\omega_r R}{\omega_r R} - \frac{\omega_r R}{\omega L\omega_r R}\right)$$

$$= \frac{1}{R} + j\frac{1}{R}\left(\frac{\omega}{\omega_r}Q - \frac{\omega_r}{\omega}Q\right) = \frac{1}{R}\left[1 + jQ\left(\frac{\omega}{\omega_r} - \frac{\omega_r}{\omega}\right)\right]$$

At the half-power frequencies ω_1 and ω_2,

$$|\mathbf{V}| = \frac{R|\mathbf{I}|}{\sqrt{2}} = \frac{|\mathbf{I}|}{|\mathbf{Y}|} \quad\Rightarrow\quad |\mathbf{Y}| = \frac{\sqrt{2}}{R}$$

This condition occurs when

$$Q\left(\frac{\omega}{\omega_r} - \frac{\omega_r}{\omega}\right) = \pm 1 \qquad (10.4)$$

For the case that the right-hand side of Equation (10.4) is $+1$, then

$$Q\left(\frac{\omega^2 - \omega_r^2}{\omega_r\omega}\right) = 1 \quad\Rightarrow\quad Q\omega^2 - \omega_r\omega - Q\omega_r^2 = 0$$

By the quadratic formula, we get a positive value and a negative value of ω that satisfy this equation. Since the half-power frequencies are positive quantities, we select the positive value. Thus, one of the half-power frequencies is

$$\frac{\omega_r}{2Q} + \omega_r\sqrt{\left(\frac{1}{2Q}\right)^2 + 1}$$

For the case that the right-hand side of Equation (10.4) is -1, as above we can show that the resulting half-power frequency is

$$-\frac{\omega_r}{2Q} + \omega_r\sqrt{\left(\frac{1}{2Q}\right)^2 + 1}$$

Thus, we see that the latter half-power frequency is ω_1, while the former is ω_2; consequently, the bandwidth for the parallel RLC circuit is

$$BW = \omega_2 - \omega_1 = \frac{\omega_r}{Q} \qquad (10.5)$$

We also have that

$$BW = \frac{\omega_r}{\omega_r RC} = \frac{1}{RC}$$

Thus, we see that when the Q of the circuit is relatively small, the bandwidth BW is relatively large; whereas if the Q is relatively large, then the BW is relatively small. The latter case indicates a sharper, or more frequency-selective, amplitude response.

From Equation (10.5), we have that $Q = \omega_r/BW$ for the parallel RLC circuit. This ratio of resonance frequency to bandwidth is sometimes defined to be the **selectivity** of a circuit. For a parallel RLC circuit, we see that the circuit's quality factor and selectivity are equal. In general, though, the selectivity and the quality factor of a circuit will not be the same.

Series Resonance

Let us now consider the case of a series RLC circuit as shown in Fig. 10.19. The impedance $\mathbf{Z} = \mathbf{V}/\mathbf{I}$ is given by

$$\mathbf{Z} = R + j\omega L + \frac{1}{j\omega C} = R + j\left(\omega L - \frac{1}{\omega C}\right)$$

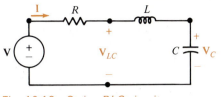

Fig. 10.19   Series *RLC* circuit.

so the resonance frequency ω_r is that frequency for which $\omega_r L - 1/\omega_r C = 0$. Thus,

$$\omega_r = \frac{1}{\sqrt{LC}}$$

as was the case for the parallel *RLC* circuit.

By duality, we have that the quality factor of the series *RLC* circuit is

$$Q = \frac{\omega_r L}{R}$$

and since $\omega_r L = 1/\omega_r C$, then also

$$Q = \frac{1}{\omega_r RC} = \frac{\sqrt{L/C}}{R}$$

In a process similar to that for the parallel *RLC* circuit, it can be shown that the bandwidth for the series *RLC* circuit is again

$$BW = \frac{\omega_r}{Q} = \frac{R}{L}$$

so that the selectivity and the quality factor are equal.

EXAMPLE 10.3

For the series *RLC* circuit shown in Fig. 10.19, where $R = \frac{5}{3}\,\Omega$, $L = 5$ H, and $C = \frac{1}{25}$ F, it can be shown (see Example 8.7 on p. 369) that when $v(t) = 17\cos 3t$ V, then $v_C(t) = 5\sqrt{17}\cos(3t - 166°)$ V. For this circuit, the resonance frequency is $\omega_r = 1/\sqrt{LC} = \sqrt{5}$ rad/s. Thus, the quality factor and bandwidth are, respectively,

$$Q = \frac{\omega_r L}{R} = \frac{5\sqrt{5}}{5/3} = 3\sqrt{5} \qquad BW = \frac{R}{L} = \frac{5/3}{5} = \frac{1}{3}\text{ rad/s}$$

A derivation of the formulas for the half-power frequencies for the series *RLC* circuit can be accomplished as was done for the parallel *RLC* circuit. What result are the same expressions. Thus, the lower half-power frequency is

$$\omega_1 = -\frac{\omega_r}{2Q} + \omega_r \sqrt{\left(\frac{1}{2Q}\right)^2 + 1} = 2.082\text{ rad/s}$$

and the upper half-power frequency is

$$\omega_2 = \frac{\omega_r}{2Q} + \omega_r \sqrt{\left(\frac{1}{2Q}\right)^2 + 1} = 2.415 \text{ rad/s}$$

And as a check on the above result, the bandwidth is

$$BW = \omega_2 - \omega_1 = 0.333 \text{ rad/s}$$

Suppose now that the frequency of the voltage source equals the circuit's resonance frequency, say $v(t) = 17 \cos \sqrt{5}t$ V. Since $|\mathbf{I}| = |\mathbf{V}|/|\mathbf{Z}|$, at resonance

$$|\mathbf{I}| = \frac{|\mathbf{V}|}{5/3} = \frac{3}{5}(17) = \frac{51}{5} \text{ A}$$

Then

$$|\mathbf{V}_C| = |\mathbf{Z}_C||\mathbf{I}| = \frac{1}{\omega C}|\mathbf{I}| = \frac{25}{\sqrt{5}}\left(\frac{51}{5}\right) = 51\sqrt{5} \text{ V}$$

Note that although the amplitude of the input sinusoid is $|\mathbf{V}| = 17$ V, the amplitude of the output voltage is $|\mathbf{V}_C| = 51\sqrt{5}$ V. That is, the output voltage magnitude is $Q = 3\sqrt{5}$ times larger than the input. Furthermore, since

$$\mathbf{V}_{LC} = (\mathbf{Z}_L + \mathbf{Z}_C)\mathbf{I} = \left(j\omega L + \frac{1}{j\omega C}\right)\mathbf{I} = \left(j5\sqrt{5} - \frac{j}{\sqrt{5/25}}\right)\mathbf{I} = 0$$

then the series combination of the inductor and capacitor acts as a short circuit, although the voltage across each element is nonzero.

●───────

DRILL EXERCISE 10.6

For the series RLC circuit given in Fig. 10.19, $\alpha = R/2L$ and $\omega_n = 1/\sqrt{LC}$. Find the bandwidth in terms of ω_n for the case that (a) $\alpha = 0.05\omega_n$, (b) $\alpha = 0.1\omega_n$, (c) $\alpha = 0.5\omega_n$, (d) $\alpha = \omega_n$, and (e) $\alpha = 10\omega_n$.
Answer: (a) $0.1\omega_n$; (b) $0.2\omega_n$; (c) ω_n; (d) $2\omega_n$; (e) $20\omega_n$

Additional Resonant Circuits

Consider the series-parallel RLC circuit shown in Fig. 10.20. We have

$$\mathbf{Y} = \frac{\mathbf{I}}{\mathbf{V}} = \frac{1}{R} + j\omega C + \frac{1}{R_L + j\omega L} = \frac{1}{R} + j\omega C + \frac{R_L - j\omega L}{R_L^2 + \omega^2 L^2}$$

$$= \frac{1}{R} + \frac{R_L}{R_L^2 + \omega^2 L^2} + j\left(\omega C - \frac{\omega L}{R_L^2 + \omega^2 L^2}\right)$$

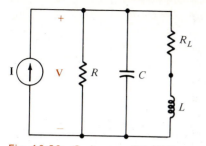

Fig. 10.20   Series-parallel *RLC* circuit.

and thus the imaginary part equals zero[†] when $\omega = \omega_r$, where

$$\omega_r C - \frac{\omega_r L}{R_L^2 + \omega_r^2 L^2} = 0$$

from which we get

$$\omega_r = \sqrt{\frac{1}{LC} - \frac{R_L^2}{L^2}} \qquad\qquad (10.6)$$

Suppose that $R = R_L = 2\,\Omega$, $L = 2$ H, and $C = \frac{1}{20}$ F. Then the resonance frequency is

$$\omega_r = \sqrt{10 - 1} = 3 \text{ rad/s}$$

and the admittance at this frequency is

$$\mathbf{Y}(j3) = \frac{1}{2} + \frac{2}{2^2 + 3^2 2^2} = \frac{11}{20} = 0.55 \text{ S}$$

For the parallel *RLC* circuit shown in Fig. 10.17 (p. 457), the magnitude of the admittance is minimum at resonance. (For the series *RLC* circuit in Fig. 10.19 (p. 461), the magnitude of the impedance is minimum at resonance.) However, for the circuit under consideration, the magnitude of the admittance is not minimum at resonance. It can be shown that the magnitude of the admittance is minimum when $\omega = 3.155$ rad/s, and its value is $|\mathbf{Y}(j3.155)| = 0.5458$ S. This fact can be confirmed with a hand calculator or with computer calculations.

For a series or parallel *RLC* circuit, we have seen that the resonance frequency is $\omega_r = 1/\sqrt{LC}$. Thus, for any positive values for L and C, we can easily determine ω_r. However, from Equation (10.6), for the circuit in Fig. 10.20, when R, L, C, and R_L are positive numbers, we see that if

$$\frac{R_L^2}{L^2} > \frac{1}{LC} \quad \Rightarrow \quad R_L > \sqrt{\frac{L}{C}}$$

[†] The imaginary part also equals zero when $\omega = 0$ rad/s—but this is the trivial case.

then there is no real-valued (nonzero) resonance frequency ω_r. Under this circumstance, the circuit never becomes resonant.

The term $1/\sqrt{LC}$ may seem familiar; it is the undamped frequency ω_n for series and parallel RLC circuits, as well as the resonance frequency. However, in general, the resonance frequency and the undamped frequency are not the same for an arbitrary RLC circuit.

EXAMPLE 10.4

Consider the RLC circuit shown in Fig. 10.21. Let us determine the undamped frequency, the resonance frequency, and the quality factor for this circuit.

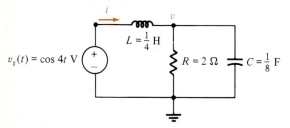

Fig. 10.21 *RLC* circuit.

By KVL, for the mesh on the left,

$$L\frac{di}{dt} + v - v_s = 0 \qquad \Rightarrow \qquad v = v_s - L\frac{di}{dt}$$

while, by KCL at node v

$$-i + C\frac{dv}{dt} + \frac{v}{R} = 0 \tag{10.7}$$

Substituting the above expression for v into Equation (10.7), we get

$$LC\frac{d^2i}{dt^2} + \frac{L}{R}\frac{di}{dt} + i = C\frac{dv_s}{dt} + \frac{v_s}{R}$$

from which

$$\frac{d^2i}{dt^2} + \frac{1}{RC}\frac{di}{dt} + \frac{1}{LC}i = \frac{1}{L}\frac{dv_s}{dt} + \frac{1}{RLC}v_s$$

Thus, we see that the undamped frequency is

$$\omega_n = \frac{1}{\sqrt{LC}} = \frac{1}{\sqrt{\left(\frac{1}{4}\right)\left(\frac{1}{8}\right)}} = \sqrt{32} = 4\sqrt{2} \text{ rad/s}$$

However, the impedance seen by the source is

$$\mathbf{Z} = \frac{j\omega}{4} + \frac{2(8/j\omega)}{2 + (8/j\omega)} = \frac{j\omega}{4} + \frac{16}{8 + j2\omega} = \frac{j\omega}{4} + \frac{8}{4 + j\omega}$$

$$= \frac{j\omega}{4} + \frac{8(4 - j\omega)}{16 + \omega^2} = \frac{32}{16 + \omega^2} + j\omega\left(\frac{1}{4} - \frac{8}{16 + \omega^2}\right)$$

$$= \frac{32}{16 + \omega^2} + \frac{j\omega}{4}\left(\frac{\omega^2 - 16}{16 + \omega^2}\right)$$

Since the imaginary part of $\mathbf{Z}$ vanishes when $\omega^2 - 16 = 0$, we conclude that the (nontrivial) resonance frequency is $\omega_r = 4$ rad/s $\neq \omega_n$.

Since the frequency of the source is $\omega = 4$ rad/s, the circuit given in Fig. 10.21 is in resonance. This circuit is shown in Fig. 10.22 in the frequency domain. By KCL at node $\mathbf{V}$,

$$\frac{\mathbf{V} - 1}{j} + \frac{\mathbf{V}}{2} + \frac{\mathbf{V}}{-j2} = 0 \quad \Rightarrow \quad \mathbf{V} = \sqrt{2}\underline{/-45°}$$

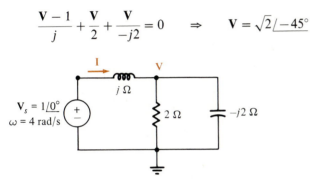

Fig. 10.22 Frequency-domain representation.

Also,

$$\mathbf{I} = \frac{1 - \mathbf{V}}{j} = \frac{1 - 2/(1 + j)}{j} = \frac{(-1 + j)/(1 + j)}{j} = \frac{-1 + j}{-1 + j} = 1\underline{/0°}$$

Thus,

$$v(t) = \sqrt{2}\cos(4t - 45°)\text{ V} \quad\text{and}\quad i(t) = \cos 4t\text{ A}$$

The energies stored in the inductor and capacitor, respectively, are

$$w_L(t) = \tfrac{1}{2}Li^2(t) = \tfrac{1}{8}\cos^2 4t \quad\text{and}\quad w_C(t) = \tfrac{1}{2}Cv^2(t) = \tfrac{1}{8}\cos^2(4t - 45°)$$

Using the trigonometric identity $\cos^2 x = \tfrac{1}{2}(1 + \cos 2x)$, the total energy stored is

$$w_L(t) + w_C(t) = \tfrac{1}{16}[1 + \cos 8t] + \tfrac{1}{16}[1 + \cos(8t - 90°)]$$

$$= \tfrac{1}{16}[2 + \cos 8t + \sin 8t] = \tfrac{1}{16}[2 + \sqrt{2}\cos(8t - 45°)]$$

and this has a maximum value of

$$[w_L(t) + w_C(t)]_{max} = \tfrac{1}{16}[2 + \sqrt{2}]\text{ J}$$

The power dissipated by the resistor and the energy lost in a period are

$$P_R = \frac{1}{2}\frac{|V|^2}{R} = \frac{1}{2}\left(\frac{2}{2}\right) = \frac{1}{2}\,W \qquad P_R T = P_R\left(\frac{2\pi}{\omega_r}\right) = \frac{1}{2}\left(\frac{2\pi}{4}\right) = \frac{\pi}{4}\,J$$

Thus, the Q of the circuit is

$$Q = 2\pi\frac{(1/16)(2 + \sqrt{2})}{\pi/4} = 1 + \frac{1}{\sqrt{2}} = 1.707$$

DRILL EXERCISE 10.7

Find the quality factor of the impedance given in Fig. DE10.5 (p. 457) for the case that $R = 0.5\ \Omega$, $L = 0.5$ H, and $C = 1$ F.
Answer: 1.707

Series and Parallel Reactances

Just as we defined the quality factor Q for a circuit, we can define it for a reactance in series or parallel with a resistance. To demonstrate this fact, first consider the series case for an inductor L as shown in Fig. 10.23. Let us assume that $\mathbf{I} = I\underline{/0^\circ}$. Then the energy stored is given by

$$w(t) = \tfrac{1}{2}Li^2(t) = \tfrac{1}{2}LI^2\cos^2\omega t$$

which has the maximum value

$$w_m = \tfrac{1}{2}LI^2$$

and since $X_s = \omega L \Rightarrow L = X_s/\omega$, then

$$w_m = \frac{X_s}{2\omega}I^2$$

The energy lost per period is

$$P_s T = \frac{1}{2}I^2 R_s\left(\frac{2\pi}{\omega}\right) = \frac{\pi I^2 R_s}{\omega}$$

Therefore, the quality factor is

$$Q = \frac{2\pi(X_s I^2/2\omega)}{\pi I^2 R_s/\omega} = \frac{X_s}{R_s}$$

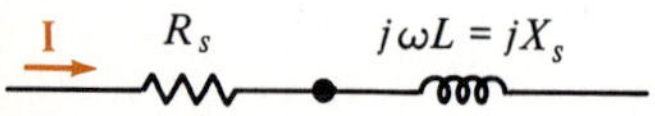

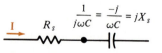

Fig. 10.23 Series inductive reactance.

Fig. 10.24 Series capacitive reactance.

For the case of a resistor in series with a capacitor C, as shown in Fig. 10.24, proceeding as above, we may obtain the fact that $Q = |X_s|/R_s$. Hence, in general, for a resistance in series with a reactance X_s, the quality factor is

$$Q = \frac{|X_s|}{R_s}$$

For the case of a resistance in parallel with a reactance X_p as shown in Fig. 10.25, it can be shown that the quality factor is

$$Q = \frac{R_p}{|X_p|}$$

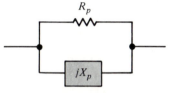

Fig. 10.25   Parallel reactance.

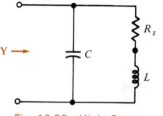

Fig. 10.26   High-Q resonant circuit.

Consider the resonant circuit shown in Fig. 10.26, where the admittance is

$$\mathbf{Y} = j\omega C + \frac{1}{R_s + j\omega L}$$

Suppose that the series reactance, consisting of the inductor L and resistor R_s, has a large (at least 20) quality factor (called a "high-Q coil"). Then

$$\frac{X_L}{R_s} \gg 1 \quad \Rightarrow \quad \frac{\omega L}{R_s} \gg 1 \quad \Rightarrow \quad \omega L \gg R_s$$

Then the admittance is approximated by

$$\mathbf{Y} \approx j\omega C + \frac{1}{j\omega L}$$

Thus, the resonance frequency is approximated by $\omega_r \approx 1\sqrt{LC}$. The impedance is

$$\mathbf{Z} = \frac{(R_s + j\omega L)(1/j\omega C)}{R_s + j\omega L + 1/j\omega C} \approx \frac{(j\omega L)(1/j\omega C)}{R_s + j\omega L + 1/j\omega C}$$

for a high-Q series reactance. Thus, the admittance is approximated by

$$\mathbf{Y} \approx \frac{C}{L}\left(R_s + j\omega L + \frac{1}{j\omega C}\right) = \frac{R_s C}{L} + j\omega C + \frac{1}{j\omega L}$$

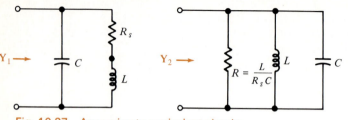

Fig. 10.27   Approximate equivalent circuits.

which is the expression for a parallel RLC circuit, where $R = L/R_sC$. Hence, for a high-Q coil, the two admittances shown in Fig. 10.27 are approximately equal.

EXAMPLE 10.5

The practical tank circuit shown in Fig. 10.28 is to be in resonance at 1 MHz, that is, $\omega_r = 2\pi \times 10^6$ rad/s. Assuming a high-Q coil, $\omega_r \approx 1/\sqrt{LC}$, from which

$$L \approx \frac{1}{\omega_r^2 C} = \frac{1}{(4\pi^2 \times 10^{12})(500 \times 10^{-12})} = 50.7 \ \mu H$$

The quality factor of the series reactance at the resonance frequency is

$$\frac{X_s}{10} = \frac{\omega_r L}{10} = \frac{318}{10} = 31.8$$

which is much greater than 1, as was assumed. Since

$$\frac{L}{R_s C} = 10{,}132 \approx 10{,}000$$

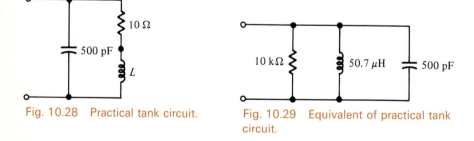

Fig. 10.28   Practical tank circuit.

Fig. 10.29   Equivalent of practical tank circuit.

then the tank circuit given in Fig. 10.28 can be approximated by the parallel RLC circuit shown in Fig. 10.29. The quality factor of this parallel RLC circuit is

$$Q = \omega_r RC = (2\pi \times 10^6)(10 \times 10^3)(500 \times 10^{-12}) = 31.4$$

Scaling

In the last example discussed, the element values given were practical in nature. This, however, has not been the trend previously, nor for the most part will it be in the remainder of this text. The reason for this is the simplification of computations. However, by a process known as "scaling," results obtained for circuits having simplified, nonrealistic element values can be extended easily to practical situations.

There are two ways to scale a circuit—**magnitude** or **impedance scaling** and **frequency scaling**. To magnitude-scale by the factor K_m, just multiply the impedance of each element by the real, positive number K_m. A resistor of R ohms is scaled to a resistor of $R' = K_m R$ ohms. An L-henry inductor of impedance $j\omega L$ ohms is scaled to an impedance of $j\omega K_m L$ ohms—that is, an $L' = K_m L$-henry inductor. A C-farad capacitor of impedance $1/j\omega C$ ohms is scaled to an impedance of $K_m/j\omega C = 1/j\omega(C/K_m)$ ohms—that is, a $C' = C/K_m$-farad capacitor. In summary, to scale an impedance by the factor K_m, scale R, L, and C as follows:

$$R \rightarrow K_m R \qquad L \rightarrow K_m L \qquad C \rightarrow \frac{C}{K_m}$$

EXAMPLE 10.6

The parallel *RLC* circuit shown in Fig. 10.30 has the admittance

$$\mathbf{Y} = \frac{1}{\mathbf{Z}} = \frac{1}{R} + \frac{1}{j\omega L} + j\omega C = \frac{1}{2} + \frac{1}{j\omega} + \frac{j\omega}{25}$$

and the resonance frequency

$$\omega_r = \frac{1}{\sqrt{LC}} = 5 \text{ rad/s}$$

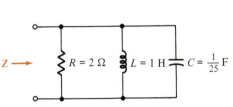

Fig. 10.30   Parallel *RLC* impedance.

Scaling this circuit by $K_m = 5000$, we get $R' = 2K_m = 10 \text{ k}\Omega$, $L' = 1K_m = 5 \text{ kH}$, $C' = 1/25K_m = (1/125{,}000) \text{ F} = 8 \ \mu\text{F}$ and an admittance $\mathbf{Y}'$ given by

$$\mathbf{Y}' = \frac{1}{K_m R} + \frac{1}{j\omega K_m L} + \frac{j\omega C}{K_m} = \frac{1}{10{,}000} + \frac{1}{j\omega 5000} + \frac{j\omega}{125{,}000}$$

and the resulting resonance frequency is

$$\omega_r' = \frac{1}{\sqrt{K_m L(C/K_m)}} = \frac{1}{\sqrt{LC}} = 5 \text{ rad/s}$$

That is, the resonance frequency is not affected by magnitude scaling. In actuality, the shape and the frequency axis of the amplitude response of an impedance are not affected by magnitude scaling, but values on the vertical axis are multiplied by K_m.

To frequency-scale by the factor K_f, since the impedance of a resistor is not frequency dependent, a resistor of R ohms is left as is. However, for an L-henry inductor of impedance $j\omega L$, at frequency $\omega = \omega_0$ the impedance is $j\omega_0 L$. What inductor L'' will have such an impedance at the scaled frequency $K_f\omega_0$? Since

$$j\omega_0 L = j(K_f\omega_0)L'' \quad \Rightarrow \quad L'' = \frac{L}{K_f}$$

to frequency-scale an inductor L by K_f, divide L by K_f.

For a C-farad capacitor of impedance $1/j\omega C$, at frequency $\omega = \omega_0$ the impedance is $1/j\omega_0 C$. The capacitor C'' that has such an impedance at the scaled frequency $K_f\omega_0$ is determined from

$$\frac{1}{j\omega_0 C} = \frac{1}{j(K_f\omega_0)C''} \quad \Rightarrow \quad C'' = \frac{C}{K_f}$$

That is, to frequency-scale a capacitor C by K_f, divide C by K_f. In summary, to frequency-scale by the factor K_f, scale R, L, and C as follows:

$$\boxed{R \rightarrow R \qquad L \rightarrow \frac{L}{K_f} \qquad C \rightarrow \frac{C}{K_f}}$$

EXAMPLE 10.7

To frequency-scale, by $K_f = 10^5$, the previously magnitude-scaled parallel RLC circuit given in the preceding example, we get $R'' = R' = 10 \text{ k}\Omega$, $L'' = L'/K_f = 5000/100,000 = 50 \text{ mH}$, $C'' = C'/K_f = 1/(125,000)(100,000) = 80 \text{ pF}$ and admittance $\mathbf{Y}''$ given by

$$\mathbf{Y}'' = \frac{1}{10^4} + \frac{1}{j\omega 50(10^{-3})} + j\omega 80(10^{-12})$$

and a resonance frequency

$$\omega_r'' = \frac{1}{\sqrt{(50)(10^{-3})(80)(10^{-12})}} = 5(10^5) \text{ rad/s} = 10^5\omega_r = K_f\omega_r$$

That is, the resonance frequency is scaled by the factor $K_f = 10^5$. The vertical axis of the amplitude response of an impedance is not affected by frequency scaling, but values on the horizontal (frequency) axis are multiplied by K_f.

For the unscaled parallel *RLC* circuit in Fig. 10.30, the bandwidth is

$$BW = \frac{1}{RC} = \frac{1}{2(1/25)} = 12.5 \text{ rad/s}$$

For the magnitude-scaled parallel *RLC* circuit in Example 10.6, the bandwidth is

$$BW' = \frac{1}{R'C'} = \frac{1}{(10,000)(1/125,000)} = 12.5 \text{ rad/s} = BW$$

However, after the circuit is frequency-scaled in Example 10.7, the bandwidth is

$$BW'' = \frac{1}{R''C''} = \frac{1}{(10^4)(80)(10^{-12})} = 1.25 \text{ Mrad/s} = 10^5 BW = K_f BW$$

Not only can elements such as resistors, inductors, and capacitors be magnitude-scaled, so can dependent sources. If a dependent source has a value whose units are ohms (i.e., a current-dependent voltage source), then to magnitude-scale we multiply the value by K_m; if the units are siemens (i.e., a voltage-dependent current source), we divide by K_m. Finally, a dependent source whose value is dimensionless (i.e., a voltage-dependent voltage source or a current-dependent current source) is left as is. Dependent sources of the type previously encountered are not affected by frequency scaling.

10.4 COMPLEX FREQUENCY

In the previous two and one-half chapters, our major preoccupation has been with the sinusoid. By generalizing real sinusoids to complex sinusoids we developed the notion of phasors, with which we were able to find forced responses of sinusoidal circuits without having to deal with differential equations. As a consequence, we were able to perform analyses in the frequency domain much more easily than in the time domain.

We are now in a position to go one step further. By extending the above-mentioned concepts, we can employ frequency-domain analysis for damped sinusoidal circuits, that is, circuits having forcing functions of the form $Ae^{\sigma t}\cos(\omega t + \theta)$.

For the damped sinusoidal function $Ae^{\sigma t}\cos(\omega t + \theta)$, we know that the frequency ω has radians per second as its units. Since the power of the natural logarithm base e is to be dimensionless, the units of the (usually nonpositive) damping factor σ have been designated **nepers per second**, where the **neper**[†] (Np) is a dimensionless unit. For this reason σ is referred to as the **neper frequency**.

Now suppose that the input to an *RLC* circuit has the form $Ae^{\sigma t}\cos(\omega t + \theta)$. Using an argument similar to that discussed for the real sinusoidal case, the forced

---

[†] Named for the Scottish mathematician John Napier (1550–1617).

response will have the form $Be^{\sigma t}\cos(\omega t + \phi)$. Thus, by the property of linearity the response to

$$Ae^{\sigma t}\cos(\omega t + \theta) + jAe^{\sigma t}\sin(\omega t + \theta) = Ae^{\sigma t}e^{j(\omega t + \theta)}$$
$$= Ae^{j\theta}e^{(\sigma + j\omega)t}$$
$$= Ae^{j\theta}e^{st}$$
$$= \mathbf{V}_{in}e^{st}$$

where $\mathbf{V}_{in} = Ae^{j\theta}$ and $s = \sigma + j\omega$, which is called **complex frequency**, has the form

$$Be^{\sigma t}\cos(\omega t + \phi) + jBe^{\sigma t}\sin(\omega t + \phi) = Be^{\sigma t}e^{j(\omega t + \phi)}$$
$$= Be^{j\phi}e^{(\sigma + j\omega)t}$$
$$= Be^{j\phi}e^{st}$$
$$= \mathbf{V}_o e^{st}$$

where $\mathbf{V}_o = Be^{j\phi}$. Hence, knowing the response to $Ae^{j\theta}e^{st}$ is tantamount to knowing the response to $Ae^{\sigma t}\cos(\omega t + \theta)$. That is, we can determine B and ϕ by finding the response either to $Ae^{j\theta}e^{st}$ or to $Ae^{\sigma t}\cos(\omega t + \theta)$.

●

EXAMPLE 10.8

To find the voltage $v_C(t)$ across the capacitor in the circuit shown in Fig. 10.31, note that

$$i = i_R + i_C = \frac{v_C}{4} + \frac{1}{4}\frac{dv_C}{dt} \tag{10.8}$$

and

$$v_L = v - v_C = 2\frac{di}{dt} \tag{10.9}$$

Substituting Equation (10.8) into (10.9) yields

$$\frac{d^2v_C}{dt^2} + \frac{dv_C}{dt} + 2v_C = 2v \tag{10.10}$$

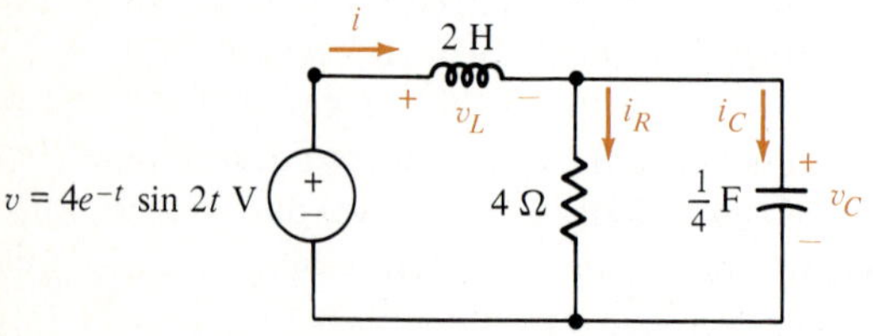

Fig. 10.31 Damped-sinusoidal circuit.

We are given that $v(t) = 4e^{-t}\sin 2t = 4e^{-t}\cos(2t - \pi/2)$ V. Thus, we recognize that we can find $v_C(t)$, which has the form

$$v_C(t) = Be^{\sigma t}\cos(\omega t + \phi) = Be^{-t}\cos(2t + \phi)$$

by finding the response, instead, to

$$v_x(t) = Ae^{j\theta}e^{st} \qquad \text{which is} \qquad v_y(t) = Be^{j\phi}e^{st}$$

Substituting this into Equation (10.10) results in

$$\frac{d^2}{dt^2}[Be^{j\phi}e^{st}] + \frac{d}{dt}[Be^{j\phi}e^{st}] + 2[Be^{j\phi}e^{st}] = 2Ae^{j\theta}e^{st}$$

from which we get

$$Be^{j\phi}s^2e^{st} + Be^{j\phi}se^{st} + 2Be^{j\phi}e^{st} = 2Ae^{j\theta}e^{st}$$

Dividing both sides of this equation by e^{st} yields

$$Be^{j\phi}(s^2 + s + 2) = 2Ae^{j\theta} \qquad \Rightarrow \qquad Be^{j\phi} = \frac{2Ae^{j\theta}}{s^2 + s + 2}$$

Since $A = 4$, $s = \sigma + j\omega = -1 + j2$, and $\theta = -\pi/2$, then

$$Be^{j\phi} = \frac{2(4)e^{-j\pi/2}}{(-1+j2)^2 + (-1+j2) + 2} = \frac{4e^{-j\pi/2}}{-1-j} = \frac{4e^{-j\pi/2}}{\sqrt{2}e^{-3j\pi/4}} = 2\sqrt{2}e^{j\pi/4}$$

In other words, $B = 2\sqrt{2}$ and $\phi = \pi/4$. Thus, the desired forced response is

$$v_C(t) = 2\sqrt{2}e^{-t}\cos\left(2t + \frac{\pi}{4}\right) \text{ V}$$

Just as we associated the real sinusoid $A\cos(\omega t + \theta)$ or the complex sinusoid $Ae^{j(\omega t + \theta)}$ with the phasor $\mathbf{A} = Ae^{j\theta}$, so we can associate the damped sinusoid $Ae^{\sigma t}\cos(\omega t + \theta)$ or the **damped complex sinusoid**

$$Ae^{\sigma t}e^{j(\omega t + \theta)} = Ae^{j\theta}e^{st}$$

with the phasor $\mathbf{A} = Ae^{j\theta}$ also. However, for the latter case, $s = \sigma + j\omega$ must be implicit, whereas only ω need be for the former.

Impedance and Admittance

For a resistor R having voltage v across it and current i through it, if the current is a damped complex sinusoid, say

$$i = Ie^{\sigma t}e^{j(\omega t + \theta)} = Ie^{j\theta}e^{st}$$

then the voltage is also a damped complex sinusoid, say

$$v = Ve^{\sigma t}e^{j(\omega t + \phi)} = Ve^{j\phi}e^{st}$$

Since $v = Ri$, then

$$Ve^{j\phi}e^{st} = RIe^{j\theta}e^{st}$$

and dividing by e^{st} yields

$$Ve^{j\phi} = RIe^{j\theta}$$

from which we make the identities $V = RI$ and $\phi = \theta$. Using phasor notation,

$$V\underline{/\phi} = RI\underline{/\theta} \quad \Rightarrow \quad \mathbf{V} = R\mathbf{I}$$

where $\mathbf{V} = V\underline{/\phi}$ and $\mathbf{I} = I\underline{/\theta}$. Defining the **impedance** $\mathbf{Z}_R$ of the resistance as the ratio of voltage phasor to current phasor, we have

$$\boxed{\mathbf{Z}_R = \frac{\mathbf{V}}{\mathbf{I}} = R}$$

For an inductor L, if $i = Ie^{j\theta}e^{st}$ and $v = Ve^{j\phi}e^{st}$, since $v = L\,di/dt$, then

$$Ve^{j\phi}e^{st} = L\frac{d}{dt}(Ie^{j\theta}e^{st}) = LsIe^{j\theta}e^{st}$$

Dividing by e^{st} gives

$$Ve^{j\phi} = LsIe^{j\theta} \quad \Rightarrow \quad V\underline{/\phi} = LsI\underline{/\theta} \quad \Rightarrow \quad \mathbf{V} = Ls\mathbf{I}$$

Thus, the impedance $\mathbf{Z}_L$ of an inductor is

$$\boxed{\mathbf{Z}_L = \frac{\mathbf{V}}{\mathbf{I}} = Ls}$$

For a capacitor C, since $i = C\,dv/dt$, then

$$Ie^{j\theta}e^{st} = C\frac{d}{dt}(Ve^{j\phi}e^{st}) = CsVe^{j\phi}e^{st}$$

from which

$$Ie^{j\theta} = CsVe^{j\phi} \quad \Rightarrow \quad I\underline{/\theta} = CsV\underline{/\phi} \quad \Rightarrow \quad \mathbf{I} = Cs\mathbf{V}$$

The impedance of a capacitor is, therefore,

$$\boxed{\mathbf{Z}_C = \frac{\mathbf{V}}{\mathbf{I}} = \frac{1}{Cs}}$$

From the definition of impedance, we see that we have the equations

$$\mathbf{V} = \mathbf{Z}\mathbf{I} \quad \text{and} \quad \mathbf{I} = \frac{\mathbf{V}}{\mathbf{Z}}$$

This latter equation suggests the usefulness of the reciprocal of impedance. We, therefore, define the ratio of current phasor to voltage phasor as **admittance**, denoted

Y. Thus, we have the element admittances

$$\mathbf{Y}_R = \frac{1}{R} \qquad \mathbf{Y}_L = \frac{1}{Ls} \qquad \mathbf{Y}_C = Cs$$

and the alternative forms of Ohm's law:

$$\mathbf{Y} = \frac{\mathbf{I}}{\mathbf{V}} \qquad \mathbf{I} = \mathbf{Y}\mathbf{V} \qquad \mathbf{V} = \frac{\mathbf{I}}{\mathbf{Y}}$$

Just as we analyzed sinusoidal circuits with the use of (sinusoidal) phasors and impedance, so can we analyze damped-sinusoidal circuits. For the former case, impedance is a function of ω—denoted $\mathbf{Z}(j\omega)$, and for the latter, it is a function of σ and ω—denoted $\mathbf{Z}(s)$.

EXAMPLE 10.9

For the circuit given in Fig. 10.31 on p. 472, using phasor and impedance notation, we get the circuit shown in Fig. 10.32. By KCL,

$$\frac{\mathbf{V}_C - \mathbf{V}}{2s} + \frac{\mathbf{V}_C}{4} + \frac{\mathbf{V}_C}{4/s} = 0 \qquad \Rightarrow \qquad (s^2 + s + 2)\mathbf{V}_C = 2\mathbf{V}$$

Thus,

$$\mathbf{V}_C = \frac{2\mathbf{V}}{s^2 + s + 2}$$

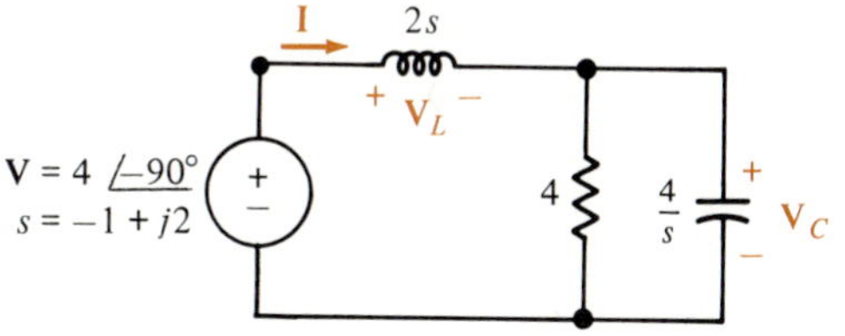

Fig. 10.32   Circuit in the frequency domain.

Alternatively, we can find $\mathbf{V}_C$ as follows: The parallel RC combination has the impedance

$$\mathbf{Z}_{RC} = \frac{4(4/s)}{4 + 4/s} = \frac{4}{s + 1}$$

By voltage division, we have that

$$\mathbf{V}_C = \frac{\mathbf{Z}_{RC}}{\mathbf{Z}_{RC} + \mathbf{Z}_L} \mathbf{V} = \frac{4/(s + 1)}{4/(s + 1) + 2s} \mathbf{V} = \frac{2\mathbf{V}}{s^2 + s + 2}$$

From the fact that $\mathbf{V} = 4\underline{/-90°}$ and $s = -1 + j2$, we get

$$\mathbf{V}_C = \frac{2(4\underline{/-90°})}{(-1 + j2)^2 + (-1 + j2) + 2} = 2\sqrt{2}\underline{/45°}$$

Thus, the forced response is

$$v_C(t) = 2\sqrt{2}e^{-t}\cos(2t + 45°) \text{ V}$$

By removing the capacitor and applying Thévenin's theorem, we obtain the circuits shown in Fig. 10.33(a) and (b). By voltage division

$$\mathbf{V}_{oc} = \frac{4\mathbf{V}}{4 + 2s} = \frac{2\mathbf{V}}{s + 2}$$

and combining the resistor and inductor in parallel,

$$\mathbf{Z}_o = \frac{2s(4)}{2s + 4} = \frac{4s}{s + 2}$$

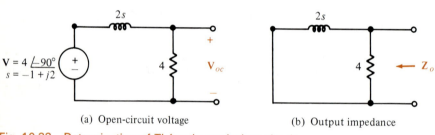

(a) Open-circuit voltage   (b) Output impedance

Fig. 10.33   Determination of Thévenin-equivalent circuit.

Hence, we get the Thévenin-equivalent circuit shown in Fig. 10.34. Again, by voltage division

$$\mathbf{V}_C = \frac{(4/s)\mathbf{V}_{oc}}{4/s + 4s/(s + 2)} = \frac{(s + 2)\mathbf{V}_{oc}}{(s + 2) + s^2} = \frac{2\mathbf{V}}{s^2 + s + 2}$$

as was obtained previously.

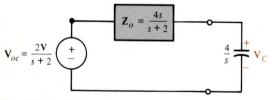

Fig. 10.34   Thévenin-equivalent circuit.

DRILL EXERCISE 10.8

For the op-amp circuit shown in Fig. DE10.8, find $v_2(t)$ for the case that $R_1 = R_2 = 1\ \Omega$, $C = 1$ F, and $v_1(t) = 10e^{-3t}\cos 3t$ V.

Answer: $2e^{-3t}\cos(3t + 143.13°)$ V

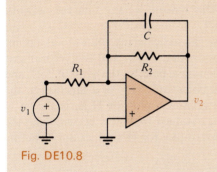

Fig. DE10.8

10.5 POLES AND ZEROS

If we define the voltage transfer function $\mathbf{H}_C(s)$ to be the ratio of $\mathbf{V}_C$ to $\mathbf{V}$, we then have that for the circuit given in Fig. 10.32 on p. 475:

$$\mathbf{H}_C(s) = \frac{\mathbf{V}_C}{\mathbf{V}} = \frac{2}{s^2 + s + 2}$$

Factoring the denominator, we can rewrite $\mathbf{H}_C(s)$ as

$$\mathbf{H}_C(s) = \frac{2}{(s + 1/2 - j\sqrt{7}/2)(s + 1/2 + j\sqrt{7}/2)}$$

Thus, we see for the special case that

$$s = -\frac{1}{2} + j\frac{\sqrt{7}}{2} \qquad \text{or} \qquad s = -\frac{1}{2} - j\frac{\sqrt{7}}{2}$$

the transfer function becomes infinite—which implies that the forced response is infinite.[†] We say that the function $\mathbf{H}_C(s)$ has a **pole** at each of these two complex frequencies.

[†] Even so, as will be indicated in the next chapter, in general the complete response will not be infinite when $\sigma < 0$.

To find the voltage transfer function $\mathbf{H}_L(s) = \mathbf{V}_L/\mathbf{V}$ for the circuit in Fig. 10.32, we can again use voltage division as follows:

$$\mathbf{V}_L = \frac{2s\mathbf{V}}{2s + 4/(s + 1)} = \frac{2s(s + 1)\mathbf{V}}{2s(s + 1) + 4} \quad \Rightarrow \quad \mathbf{H}_L(s) = \frac{\mathbf{V}_L}{\mathbf{V}} = \frac{s(s + 1)}{s^2 + s + 2}$$

Therefore, $\mathbf{H}_L(s)$ has the same poles as $\mathbf{H}_C(s)$. However, there are two frequencies, $s = 0$ and $s = -1$, for which $\mathbf{H}_L(s) = 0$. For this reason, we say that the network function $\mathbf{H}_L(s)$ has **zeros** at $s = 0$ and at $s = -1$.

Since $s = \sigma + j\omega$ is a complex quantity, we can indicate any value of s as a point in a complex-number plane. If we label the horizontal axis σ and the vertical axis $j\omega$, the result is known as the **s-plane**. If we denote a pole by the symbol "$\times$" and a zero by the symbol "$\bigcirc$," then depicting the poles and zeros of a function in the s-plane is referred to as a **pole-zero plot**. The pole-zero plot for $\mathbf{H}_L(s)$ is shown in Fig. 10.35. The pole-zero plot for $\mathbf{H}_C(s)$ can be obtained from this by removing the two zeros on the σ (real) axis, that is, the pole-zero plot for $\mathbf{H}_C(s)$ does not have any (finite) zeros.

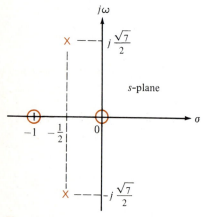

Fig. 10.35   Pole-zero plot.

Analysis of the circuit in Fig. 10.31 on p. 472 results in the differential equation

$$\frac{d^2 v_C(t)}{dt^2} + \frac{dv_C(t)}{dt} + 2v_C(t) = 2v(t)$$

The solution to this equation when $v(t) = 0$ is the natural response. As was done previously, we get the natural response by assuming a solution of the form Ae^{st}. Doing so, we obtain two values for s that satisfy the equation

$$s^2 + s + 2 = 0$$

Using the quadratic formula, we get

$$s = \frac{-1 \pm \sqrt{1 - 8}}{2} = -\frac{1}{2} \pm j\frac{\sqrt{7}}{2}$$

In other words, the natural response $v_n(t)$ has the form

$$v_n(t) = A_1 e^{s_1 t} + A_2 e^{s_2 t}$$

where

$$s_1 = -\frac{1}{2} + j\frac{\sqrt{7}}{2} \qquad \text{and} \qquad s_2 = -\frac{1}{2} - j\frac{\sqrt{7}}{2}$$

But note, these are precisely the poles of the voltage transfer function $\mathbf{H}_C(s) = \mathbf{V}_C/\mathbf{V}$. Thus, and this is true in general, the poles of the transfer function specify the form of the natural response—provided that there was no cancellation of a common pole and zero. In this example, the complex values for s_1 and s_2, that is, the complex poles, indicate that this second-order circuit is underdamped. Thus, the natural response has the more common alternative forms

$$v_n(t) = B_1 e^{-\alpha t} \cos \omega_d t + B_2 e^{-\alpha t} \sin \omega_d t = B e^{-\alpha t} \cos(\omega_d t - \phi)$$

and from the above differential equation, $\alpha = \frac{1}{2}$, $\omega_n = \sqrt{2}$, and

$$\omega_d = \sqrt{\omega_n^2 - \alpha^2} = \sqrt{2 - 1/4} = \sqrt{7}/2$$

Hence, for an input of

$$v(t) = 4e^{-t} \sin 2t\, u(t) \text{ V}$$

the complete response has the form (see Example 10.9 for the forced response)

$$v_C(t) = B e^{-t/2} \cos\left(\frac{\sqrt{7}}{2} t - \phi\right) + 2\sqrt{2} e^{-t} \cos(2t + \pi/4) \text{ V}$$

The constants B and ϕ (or B_1 and B_2) can be determined from the initial conditions $i(0)$ and $v_C(0)$. However, this requires the cumbersome approach discussed in Chapter 6. Therefore, we shall postpone the topic of obtaining the complete response until the next chapter (on the Laplace transform), where we will take a computationally simplified approach.

If in the above discussion, the poles of $\mathbf{H}_C(s)$ were real, say $s_1 = -a_1$ and $s_2 = -a_2$, instead of complex, then the form of the natural response would be that of the overdamped case, that is,

$$v_n(t) = A_1 e^{-a_1 t} + A_2 e^{-a_2 t}$$

Finally, if the two poles of $\mathbf{H}_C(s)$ were real and equal (called a **double pole**), say $s_1 = s_2 = -\alpha$, then the form of the natural response would be that of the critically damped case, that is,

$$v_n(t) = A_1 e^{-\alpha t} + A_2 t e^{-\alpha t}$$

Again let return to the circuit given in Fig. 10.32 on p. 475, and consider yet another network function with respect to the same input variable. This time, suppose that the output variable is the inductor current **I**. Since the impedance seen by the voltage source is

$$\mathbf{Z} = \mathbf{Z}_L + \mathbf{Z}_{RC} = 2s + \frac{4}{s+1} = \frac{2(s^2 + s + 2)}{s+1}$$

and since $\mathbf{Z} = \mathbf{V}/\mathbf{I}$, then the transfer function of interest $\mathbf{I}/\mathbf{V}$ is just the admittance $\mathbf{Y}(s)$ seen by the source, that is,

$$\mathbf{Y}(s) = \frac{\mathbf{I}}{\mathbf{V}} = \frac{\frac{1}{2}(s+1)}{s^2 + s + 2}$$

and again the poles of $\mathbf{Y}(s)$ are the same as the poles of $\mathbf{H}_C(s)$ and $\mathbf{H}_L(s)$. The pole-zero plot for $\mathbf{Y}(s)$ can be obtained from the pole-zero plot for $\mathbf{H}_L(s)$ by removing the zero at the origin of the *s*-plane.

It is not just coincidence that the poles for the network functions $\mathbf{V}_C/\mathbf{V}$, $\mathbf{V}_L/\mathbf{V}$, and $\mathbf{I}/\mathbf{V}$ determined above are the same. Provided that one portion of a circuit is not physically separated from the rest, each transfer function (defined as the ratio of an output to a given input) will have the same poles regardless of which voltage or current is chosen as the output variable. This should not be surprising though, for the poles are those values of *s*, called **natural frequencies**, that determine the natural response. And since the form of the natural response is the same throughout a (nonseparated) circuit, the poles of any transfer function (with respect to a given input variable) will be the same.

EXAMPLE 10.10

A circuit which contains two dependent sources is shown in Fig. 10.36 and again in the frequency domain in Fig. 10.37. Let us determine the poles and zeros for the voltage transfer function $\mathbf{H}(s) = \mathbf{V}_2/\mathbf{V}_1$ and the admittance $\mathbf{Y}(s) = \mathbf{I}_1/\mathbf{V}_1$.

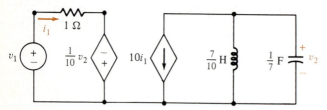

Fig. 10.36   Time-domain circuit.

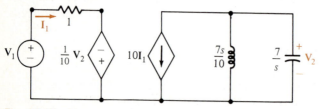

Fig. 10.37   Frequency-domain circuit.

By KCL,

$$10\mathbf{I}_1 + \frac{\mathbf{V}_2}{7s/10} + \frac{\mathbf{V}_2}{7/s} = 0 \quad \text{and} \quad \mathbf{I}_1 = \frac{\mathbf{V}_1 + \frac{1}{10}\mathbf{V}_2}{1}$$

Combining these two equations, we get

$$10\mathbf{V}_1 + \mathbf{V}_2 + \frac{10}{7s}\mathbf{V}_2 + \frac{s}{7}\mathbf{V}_2 = 0$$

from which the voltage transfer function $\mathbf{H}(s) = \mathbf{V}_2/\mathbf{V}_1$ is

$$\mathbf{H}(s) = \frac{\mathbf{V}_2}{\mathbf{V}_1} = \frac{-70s}{s^2 + 7s + 10} = \frac{-70s}{(s+2)(s+5)}$$

In this case, all the poles and zeros are on the nonpositive real axis of the s-plane. There is a zero at the origin and poles at $s = -2$ and $s = -5$.

Solving for $\mathbf{I}_1$ in terms of $\mathbf{V}_1$, we get

$$\mathbf{I}_1 = \mathbf{V}_1 + \frac{1}{10}\mathbf{V}_2 = \mathbf{V}_1 + \frac{1}{10}\left(\frac{-70s\mathbf{V}_1}{s^2 + 7s + 10}\right) = \frac{s^2 + 10}{s^2 + 7s + 10}\mathbf{V}_1$$

from which the admittance $\mathbf{Y}(s)$ is

$$\mathbf{Y}(s) = \frac{\mathbf{I}_1}{\mathbf{V}_1} = \frac{s^2 + 10}{s^2 + 7s + 10} = \frac{(s - j\sqrt{10})(s + j\sqrt{10})}{(s+2)(s+5)}$$

and although the poles are the same as for $\mathbf{H}(s)$, there is a pair of purely imaginary complex conjugate zeros (i.e., zeros on the $j\omega$ axis) as shown in Fig. 10.38—the pole-zero plot for the admittance $\mathbf{Y}(s)$.

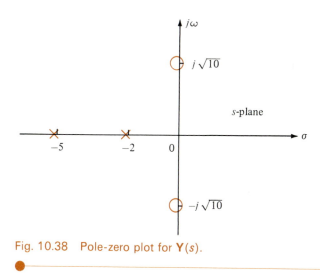

Fig. 10.38   Pole-zero plot for $\mathbf{Y}(s)$.

DRILL EXERCISE 10.9

For the op-amp circuit shown in Fig. DE10.9, suppose that $C = \frac{1}{16}$ F. Find the poles and zeros for $\mathbf{H}(s) = \mathbf{V}_2/\mathbf{V}_1$. Sketch the pole-zero plot.

Answer: $-1 - j\sqrt{3}; -1 + j\sqrt{3}$ (poles)

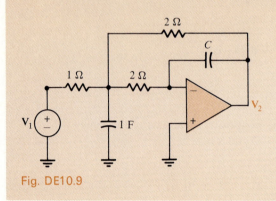

Fig. DE10.9

Pole Locations

As indicated above, the form of the natural response of a circuit depends upon where in the s-plane the corresponding poles are located. Let us demonstrate this fact by specifically considering the series *RLC* circuit shown in Fig. 10.39.

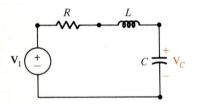

Fig. 10.39   Series *RLC* circuit.

By using voltage division, we can write that the voltage transfer function $\mathbf{H}(s) = \mathbf{V}_C/\mathbf{V}_1$ is given by

$$\mathbf{H}(s) = \frac{\mathbf{V}_C}{\mathbf{V}_1} = \frac{1/Cs}{R + Ls + 1/Cs} = \frac{1/LC}{s^2 + (R/L)s + 1/LC} = \frac{\omega_n^2}{s^2 + 2\alpha s + \omega_n^2} \quad (10.11)$$

where $\alpha = R/2L$ and $\omega_n = 1/\sqrt{LC}$. We can factor the denominator of $\mathbf{H}(s)$ so as to write

$$\mathbf{H}(s) = \frac{\omega_n^2}{(s - s_1)(s - s_2)}$$

where

$$s_1 = -\alpha - \sqrt{\alpha^2 - \omega_n^2} \qquad \text{and} \qquad s_2 = -\alpha + \sqrt{\alpha^2 - \omega_n^2} \qquad (10.12)$$

are the poles of $\mathbf{H}(s)$.

For the case that $\omega_n > \alpha$—the underdamped case—s_1 and s_2 are complex conjugates that can be expressed as

$$s_1 = -\alpha - j\omega_d \qquad \text{and} \qquad s_2 = -\alpha + j\omega_d$$

where $\omega_d = \sqrt{\omega_n^2 - \alpha^2}$. The corresponding pole-zero plot is shown in Fig. 10.40(a). Since $\omega_d = \sqrt{\omega_n^2 - \alpha^2} \Rightarrow \omega_n = \sqrt{\alpha^2 + \omega_d^2}$, then the distance from a pole to the origin of the s-plane is ω_n.

If ω_n is held constant and α is decreased in value, then the poles of $\mathbf{H}(s)$ will move closer to the $j\omega$ axis. If we make $\alpha = 0$, then the poles will be located on the $j\omega$ axis of the s-plane at $s = \pm j\omega_n$.

Conversely, if ω_n is held constant and α is increased in value such that $\alpha = \omega_n$—the critically damped case—then both poles will be located on the negative real axis of the s-plane at $s = -\alpha$, as shown in Fig. 10.40(b).

Finally, if ω_n is held contant and α is increased further in value such that $\alpha > \omega_n$—the overdamped case—then the poles will be located on the negative real axis of the s-plane at $s = -\alpha \pm \sqrt{\alpha^2 - \omega_n^2}$, as shown in Fig. 10.40(c).

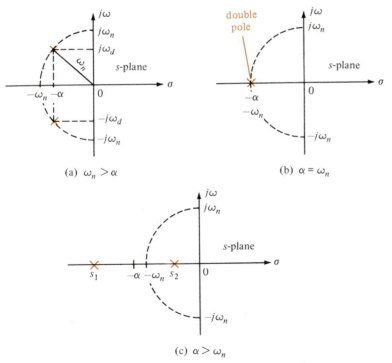

(a) $\omega_n > \alpha$

(b) $\alpha = \omega_n$

(c) $\alpha > \omega_n$

Fig. 10.40 Pole locations for $\mathbf{H}(s) = \omega_n^2/(s^2 + 2\alpha s + \omega_n^2)$.

DRILL EXERCISE 10.10

For the circuit given in Fig. 10.39, suppose that $L = 1$ H and $C = \frac{1}{25}$ F. Sketch the pole-zero plot for $\mathbf{H}(s) = \mathbf{V}_C/\mathbf{V}_1$ for the case that the value of R is (a) $0\,\Omega$, (b) $6\,\Omega$, (c) $8\,\Omega$, (d) $10\,\Omega$, and (e) $26\,\Omega$.
Answer: Poles—(a) $\pm j5$; (b) $-3 \pm j4$; (c) $-4 \pm j3$; (d) $-5, -5$; (e) $-1, -25$; zeros—none

As was demonstrated previously, a circuit having an input, say $\mathbf{V}_{in}e^{st}$, will have a forced response of the form $\mathbf{V}_o e^{st}$. Substituting these terms into the general form of the differential equation describing the circuit

$$a_n \frac{d^n v_o}{dt^n} + a_{n-1}\frac{d^{n-1}v_o}{dt^{n-1}} + \cdots + a_1 \frac{dv_o}{dt} + a_0 v_o = b_m \frac{d^m v_{in}}{dt^m} + \cdots + b_1 \frac{dv_{in}}{dt} + b_0 v_{in}$$

results in

$$(a_n s^n + a_{n-1}s^{n-1} + \cdots + a_1 s + a_0)\mathbf{V}_o e^{st}$$
$$= (b_m s^m + b_{m-1}s^{m-1} + \cdots + b_1 s + b_0)\mathbf{V}_{in}e^{st}$$

From this expression, we obtain the following general form of the transfer function $\mathbf{H}(s)$.

$$\mathbf{H}(s) = \frac{\mathbf{V}_o}{\mathbf{V}_{in}} = \frac{b_m s^m + b_{m-1}s^{m-1} + \cdots + b_1 s + b_0}{a_n s^n + a_{n-1}s^{n-1} + \cdots + a_1 s + a_0}$$

that is, $\mathbf{V}_o/\mathbf{V}_{in}$ is a ratio of polynomials in s with real coefficients.

A result from mathematics theory is that a polynomial with real coefficients can be factored into a product of quadratics of the form $as^2 + bs + c$, where a, b, and c are real numbers. From the quadratic formula, such a term can further be factored into $(s - s_1)(s - s_2)$, where

$$s_1 = \frac{-b + \sqrt{b^2 - 4ac}}{2a} \quad \text{and} \quad s_2 = \frac{-b - \sqrt{b^2 - 4ac}}{2a}$$

For the case that $b^2 \geq 4ac$, the numbers s_1 and s_2 are real. However, if $b^2 < 4ac$, then s_1 and s_2 are complex numbers and are conjugates. As a consequence of this, we can express the transfer function as

$$\mathbf{H}(s) = \frac{K(s - z_1)(s - z_2)\cdots(s - z_m)}{(s - p_1)(s - p_2)\cdots(s - p_n)}$$

where $z_1, z_2, \ldots, z_m$ are the zeros and $p_1, p_2, \ldots, p_n$ are the poles. The zeros and poles can be either real or complex, but complex zeros or poles occur in conjugate pairs.

For the case of distinct poles (the case of multiple poles will be discussed in Chapter 11), the natural response has the form

$$v_n(t) = A_1 e^{p_1 t} + A_2 e^{p_2 t} + \cdots + A_n e^{p_n t}$$

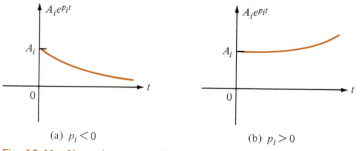

(a) $p_i < 0$ (b) $p_i > 0$

Fig. 10.41   Natural-response forms for a real pole.

If pole p_i is at the origin of the s-plane, that is, if $p_i = 0$, then the term in the natural response corresponding to it is $A_i e^0 = A_i$, a constant. If p_i is on the negative real axis or the positive real axis of the s-plane, then $A_i e^{p_i t}$ is a decaying exponential or increasing exponential, respectively, as shown in Fig. 10.41. If p_i is a complex number, then there is a pole $p_j = p_i^*$. As we have seen in Chapter 6, when $p_i = \sigma + j\omega$, the corresponding terms in the natural response can be combined in the form $A e^{\sigma t} \cos(\omega t + \theta)$. If the pair of conjugate poles is in the left half of the s-plane (i.e., $\sigma < 0$), this term is a damped sinusoid. If the pair is on the $j\omega$ axis ($\sigma = 0$), the term is a sinusoid. If the pair is in the right half of the s-plane, the term is an increasing sinusoid. These three cases are depicted in Fig. 10.42.

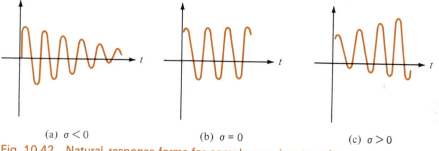

(a) $\sigma < 0$ (b) $\sigma = 0$ (c) $\sigma > 0$

Fig. 10.42   Natural-response forms for complex-conjugate poles.

As can be surmised from the above discussion, a circuit that has a stable operation does not have a network function with poles in the right half of the s-plane. In some applications, poles on the imaginary axis are undesirable, and only poles in the left half of the s-plane are allowable.

Graphical Determination of Frequency Responses

We have seen that the sinusoid $A \cos(\omega t + \theta)$ is a special case of the damped sinusoid $A e^{\sigma t} \cos(\omega t + \theta)$. We can obtain the former from the latter by setting $\sigma = 0$. In analyzing a circuit, using $s = \sigma + j\omega$ allows us to determine forced responses to damped sinusoids. If we set $\sigma = 0$ (that is, $s = j\omega$), we get the sinusoidal case.

Not only does the location of poles in the s-plane indicate the form of the natural response, but pole locations contribute to the shape of the frequency response. For example, the transfer function $\mathbf{H}(s) = \mathbf{V}_C/\mathbf{V}_1$ for the circuit shown in Fig. 10.39 on p. 482 is given by Equation (10.11) on p. 482. For the case of sinusoids, we set $s = j\omega$ and obtain Equation (10.3) on p. 455. But, we have already seen (Fig. 10.16 on p. 456) how the Bode plot for $\mathbf{H}(j\omega)$ given by Equation (10.3) changes for different relative values of α and ω_n. And, as indicated by Equation (10.12), the pole locations depend upon the values of α and ω_n.

We shall now present a graphical procedure for obtaining the frequency response of a transfer function by utilizing its pole-zero plot. This will indicate how the pole and zero locations influence the frequency response.

Suppose that s_0 is a complex number. Then s_0 is not only a point $s_0 = \sigma_0 + j\omega_0$ in the s-plane, it also represents the vector from the origin to the point $\sigma_0 + j\omega_0$, as shown in Fig. 10.43. Also shown is the vector s_1 from the origin to the point $\sigma_1 + j\omega_1$. If we place a vector s' directed from point s_0 to point s_1, then by vector addition, we have $s_0 + s' = s_1$. Thus $s' = s_1 - s_0$. We shall now use this result to graphically determine frequency responses.

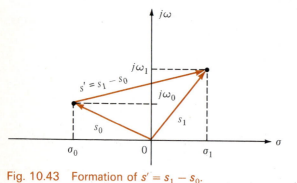

Fig. 10.43   Formation of $s' = s_1 - s_0$.

Given the transfer function

$$\mathbf{H}(s) = \frac{K(s - z_1)(s - z_2) \cdots (s - z_m)}{(s - p_1)(s - p_2) \cdots (s - p_n)}$$

for the sinusoidal case we set $s = j\omega$. Thus,

$$\mathbf{H}(j\omega) = \frac{K(j\omega - z_1)(j\omega - z_2) \cdots (j\omega - z_m)}{(j\omega - p_1)(j\omega - p_2) \cdots (j\omega - p_n)}$$

From the discussion above, $j\omega - p_i$ is the vector from pole p_i to the point $j\omega$ on the imaginary axis. Also, $j\omega - z_j$ is the vector from zero z_j to $j\omega$. Let us denote the former complex number by $D_i/\underline{\theta_i}$ and the latter by $N_j/\underline{\phi_j}$. Thus, we have

$$\mathbf{H}(j\omega) = \frac{K(N_1/\underline{\phi_1})(N_2/\underline{\phi_2})\cdots(N_m/\underline{\phi_m})}{(D_1/\underline{\theta_1})(D_2/\underline{\theta_2})\cdots(D_n/\underline{\theta_n})}$$

$$= \frac{KN_1N_2\cdots N_m}{D_1D_2\cdots D_n}\big/\underline{(\phi_1 + \phi_2 + \cdots + \phi_m - \theta_1 - \theta_2 - \cdots - \theta_n)}$$

In other words

$$|\mathbf{H}(j\omega)| = \frac{KN_1N_2\cdots N_m}{D_1D_2\cdots D_n}$$

and

$$\text{ang } \mathbf{H}(j\omega) = \phi_1 + \phi_2 + \cdots + \phi_m - \theta_1 - \theta_2 - \cdots - \theta_n$$

With these results we can graphically determine points for the amplitude and phase responses of the transfer function $\mathbf{H}(j\omega)$.

EXAMPLE 10.11

The transfer function

$$\mathbf{H}(s) = \frac{4(s+2)}{s^2 + 2s + 5} = \frac{4(s+2)}{(s+1-j2)(s+1+j2)}$$

has a zero at $s = -2$ and poles at $s = -1 + j2$ and $s = -1 - j2$. We can form $\mathbf{H}(j\omega)$ from $\mathbf{H}(s)$ simply by setting $s = j\omega$. Thus,

$$\mathbf{H}(j\omega) = \frac{4(j\omega + 2)}{(j\omega + 1 - j2)(j\omega + 1 + j2)} = \frac{4(2 + j\omega)}{(5 - \omega^2) + j2\omega}$$

To obtain the amplitude and phase responses of $\mathbf{H}(j\omega)$, we need to plot $|\mathbf{H}(j\omega)|$ and ang $\mathbf{H}(j\omega)$ versus ω, respectively. We can determine values for these plots graphically from the s-plane as follows:

Let $\omega = 1$ rad/s. Draw vectors from all the poles and zeros to $j\omega = j1$ on the imaginary axis, as shown in Fig. 10.44(a). The vector from pole p_1 to $j1$ is $(j1 - p_1) = \sqrt{2}/\underline{-45°}$, while the vector from pole p_2 to $j1$ is $(j1 - p_2) = \sqrt{10}/\underline{71.6°}$. The vector from zero z_1 to $j1$ is $(j1 - z_1) = \sqrt{5}/\underline{26.6°}$. Thus,

$$\mathbf{H}(j1) = \frac{4(\sqrt{5}/\underline{26.6°})}{(\sqrt{2}/\underline{-45°})(\sqrt{10}/\underline{71.6°})} = 2/\underline{0°}$$

from which, when $\omega = 1$ rad/s,

$$|\mathbf{H}(j\omega)| = 2 \quad \text{and} \quad \text{ang } \mathbf{H}(j\omega) = 0°$$

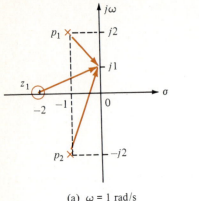

(a) $\omega = 1$ rad/s

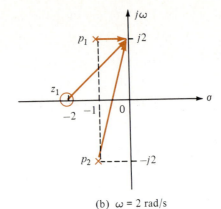

(b) $\omega = 2$ rad/s

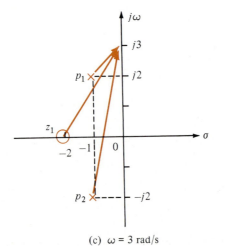

(c) $\omega = 3$ rad/s

Fig. 10.44   Determination of $|H(j\omega)|$ and ang $H(j\omega)$.

For $\omega = 2$ rad/s we get Fig. 10.44(b), and in this case we have

$$(j2 - p_1) = 1\underline{/0°} \qquad (j2 - p_2) = \sqrt{17}\underline{/76°} \qquad (j2 - z_1) = 2\sqrt{2}\underline{/45°}$$

and therefore

$$H(j2) = \frac{4(2\sqrt{2}\underline{/45°})}{(1\underline{/0°})(\sqrt{17}\underline{/76°})} = \frac{8\sqrt{34}}{17}\underline{/-31°} = 2.7\underline{/-31°}$$

Thus, when $\omega = 2$ rad/s,

$$|H(j\omega)| = 2.7 \qquad \text{and} \qquad \text{ang}\,H(j\omega) = -31°$$

For $\omega = 3$ rad/s we have the situation shown in Fig. 10.44(c), and

$$(j3 - p_1) = \sqrt{2}\underline{/45°} \qquad (j3 - p_2) = \sqrt{26}\underline{/78.7°} \qquad (j3 - z_1) = \sqrt{13}\underline{/56.3°}$$

and hence

$$\mathbf{H}(j3) = \frac{4(\sqrt{13}\underline{/56.3°})}{(\sqrt{2}\underline{/45°})(\sqrt{26}\underline{/78.7°})} = 2\underline{/-67.4°}$$

Thus, when $\omega = 3$ rad/s,

$$|\mathbf{H}(j\omega)| = 2 \quad \text{and} \quad \text{ang }\mathbf{H}(j\omega) = -67.4°$$

● SUMMARY

1. The frequency response of a network function consists of the amplitude response and the phase response.

2. The frequencies at which the amplitude response drops down to $1/\sqrt{2}$ of its maximum value are the half-power points.

3. The frequencies at which an impedance (or admittance) is purely real are the resonance frequencies of the impedance (or admittance).

4. The bandwidth and the quality factor are measures of the sharpness of an amplitude response.

5. The amplitude response is not necessarily maximum at a resonance frequency.

6. An impedance can be expressed as a function of the complex frequency s, as can other parameters such as the voltage transfer function.

7. The poles and zeros of a ratio of polynomials in s can be depicted in the s-plane with a pole-zero plot.

8. If there are no cancellations of common poles and zeros, the location of the poles of a transfer function indicate the form of the natural response.

9. The location of the poles and zeros of a transfer function determine the shape of its frequency response.

10. The pole-zero plot of a transfer function can be used to graphically determine the frequency response of the transfer function.

● PROBLEMS FOR CHAPTER 10

10.1 For the series RC circuit shown in Fig. P10.1, sketch the amplitude and phase responses for the transfer function $\mathbf{H}(j\omega) = \mathbf{V}_2/\mathbf{V}_1$, indicating the half-power frequency. What type of filter is this circuit?

10.2 For the series RC circuit given in Fig. P10.1, sketch the amplitude and phase

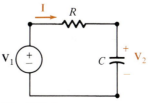

Fig. P10.1

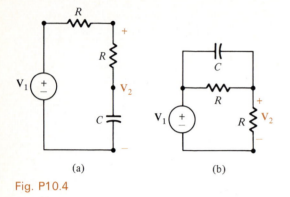

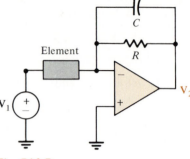

(a)   (b)

Fig. P10.4   Fig. P10.5

responses for $\mathbf{Y} = \mathbf{I}/\mathbf{V}_1$, indicating the half-power frequency.

10.3 For the series RL circuit given in Fig. DE10.1 (p. 445), sketch the amplitude and phase responses for (a) $\mathbf{H}(j\omega) = \mathbf{V}_R/\mathbf{V}_1$, and (b) $\mathbf{Y} = \mathbf{I}/\mathbf{V}_1$.

10.4 Sketch the amplitude response of $\mathbf{H}(j\omega) = \mathbf{V}_2/\mathbf{V}_1$ for each circuit shown in Fig. P10.4.

10.5 Sketch the amplitude response of $\mathbf{H}(j\omega) = \mathbf{V}_2/\mathbf{V}_1$ for the op-amp circuit shown in Fig. P10.5 when the element is (a) a resistor R, and (b) a capacitor C.

10.6 Repeat Problem 10.5 for the op-amp circuit shown in Fig. P10.6.

10.7 For the op-amp circuit shown in Fig. P10.7 sketch the amplitude response of $\mathbf{H}(j\omega) = \mathbf{V}_2/\mathbf{V}_1$, indicating the half-power frequencies.

10.8 For the op-amp circuit given in Fig. P10.7, interchange the Rs and the Cs, and repeat Problem 10.7.

10.9 Sketch the amplitude response of $\mathbf{H}(j\omega) = \mathbf{V}_2/\mathbf{V}_1$ for the circuit shown in Fig. P10.9.

10.10 Sketch the amplitude response of $\mathbf{H}(j\omega) = \mathbf{V}_2/\mathbf{V}_1$ for the circuit shown in Fig. P10.10.

10.11 Sketch the Bode plot for (a) $\mathbf{H}(j\omega) = K$, (b) $\mathbf{H}(j\omega) = j\omega$, and (c) $\mathbf{H}(j\omega) = 1/j\omega$.

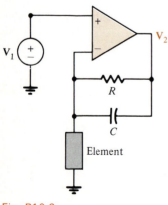

Fig. P10.6

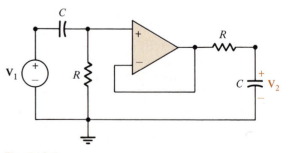

Fig. P10.7

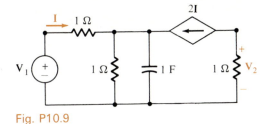

Fig. P10.9

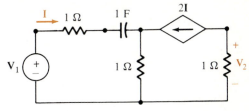

Fig. P10.10

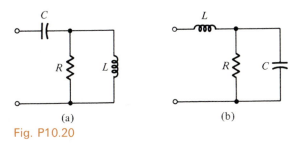

Fig. P10.14

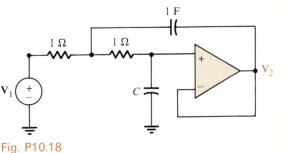

Fig. P10.18

10.12 For the series RLC circuit given in Fig. 10.13 (p. 453), let $\mathbf{V}_R$ be the voltage across the resistor R. Sketch the Bode plot for $\mathbf{H}(j\omega) = \mathbf{V}_R/\mathbf{V}_1$ when $R = 11\ \Omega$, $L = 1$ H, and $C = \frac{1}{10}$ F.

10.13 For the series RLC circuit given in Fig. 10.13 (p. 453), let $\mathbf{V}_L$ be the voltage across the inductor L. Sketch the Bode plot for $\mathbf{H}(j\omega) = \mathbf{V}_L/\mathbf{V}_1$ when $R = 11\ \Omega$, $L = 1$ H, and $C = \frac{1}{10}$ F.

10.14 Sketch the Bode plot of $\mathbf{H}(j\omega) = \mathbf{V}_2/\mathbf{V}_1$ for the RLC circuit shown in Fig. P10.14, given that $R = \frac{1}{11}\ \Omega$, $L = \frac{1}{10}$ H, and $C = 1$ F.

10.15 Sketch the amplitude-response portion of the Bode plot of $\mathbf{H}(j\omega) = \mathbf{V}_2/\mathbf{V}_1$ for the RLC circuit given in

Fig. P10.14 when $R = 10\ \Omega$, $L = 1$ H, and $C = 1$ F.

10.16 For the op-amp circuit shown in Fig. DE10.9 (p. 482), sketch the amplitude-response portion of the Bode plot of $\mathbf{H}(j\omega) = \mathbf{V}_2/\mathbf{V}_1$ when $C = \frac{1}{4}$ F.

10.17 Repeat Problem 10.16 for the case that $C = \frac{1}{400}$ F.

10.18 For the op-amp circuit shown in Fig. P10.18, sketch the amplitude-response portion of the Bode plot of $\mathbf{H}(j\omega) = \mathbf{V}_2/\mathbf{V}_1$ when $C = 1$ F.

10.19 Repeat Problem 10.18 for the case that $C = \frac{1}{400}$ F.

10.20 Find the resonance frequency for each of the circuits shown in Fig. P10.20.

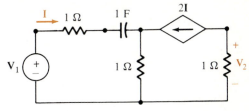

(a)

(b)

Fig. P10.20

10.21 For the circuit shown in Fig. P10.21, find the resonance frequency.

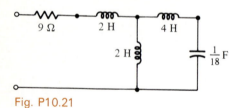

Fig. P10.21

10.22 Find the resonance frequency for the circuit shown in Fig. P10.22.

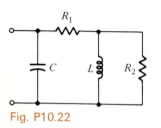

Fig. P10.22

10.23 Find the resonance frequency for the circuit shown in Fig. P10.23.

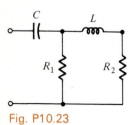

Fig. P10.23

10.24 For the circuit given in Fig. P10.22, interchange L and C and find the resonance frequency for the resulting circuit.

10.25 For the circuit given in Fig. P10.23, interchange L and C and find the resonance frequency for the resulting circuit.

10.26 Find the quality factor for the circuit shown in Fig. P10.26 given that $R = 6 \, \Omega$, $L = 2$ H, and $C = \frac{1}{36}$ F.

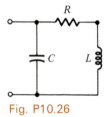

Fig. P10.26

10.27 Find the quality factor for the circuit shown in Fig. P10.27.

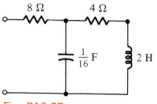

Fig. P10.27

10.28 Find the quality factor for the circuit given in Fig. P10.21 given that the resonance frequency is $\omega_r = 6/\sqrt{10}$ rad/s.

10.29 Figure 10.16 on p. 456 shows Bode plots of $\mathbf{H}(j\omega) = \mathbf{V}_2/\mathbf{V}_1$ for the series RLC circuit given in Fig. 10.13 (p. 453). Label each curve with the corresponding value of Q.

10.30 A 10-Ω resistor and a 2-H inductor are connected in series and $\omega = 50$ rad/s.

(a) What is the Q of this series connection?

(b) What parallel RL connection has the same admittance as the series connection at the given frequency?

(c) What is the Q of this parallel connection?

10.31 A 10-Ω resistor and a 2-H inductor are connected in parallel and $\omega = 50$ rad/s.

(a) What is the Q of this parallel connection?

(b) What series RL connection has the same impedance as the parallel connection at the given frequency?

(c) What is the Q of this series connection?

10.32 Consider the series connection of a resistance R_s and a reactance X_s and the parallel connection of a resistance R_p and a reactance X_p.

(a) Show that the admittance of the series connection is equal to the admittance of the parallel connection when

$$R_p = \frac{R_s^2 + X_s^2}{R_s}$$

$$X_p = \frac{R_s^2 + X_s^2}{X_s}$$

(b) Show that the quality factor Q_s of the series connection is equal to the quality factor Q_p of the parallel connection for the conditions given in (a).

10.33 Given the practical tank circuit in Fig. P10.26, if $R = 50\ \Omega$, $L = 50$ mH, and $C = 0.005\ \mu F$, approximate this circuit by a parallel RLC circuit. What is the quality factor of the parallel circuit?

10.34 Sketch the amplitude response (include the half-power frequencies) of the impedance of a parallel RLC circuit having $R = 2\ \Omega$, $L = 1$ H, and $C = \frac{1}{25}$ F, after it is magnitude-scaled by $K_m = 5 \times 10^3$ and frequency-scaled by $K_f = 10^5$. What are the scaled values of R, L, and C?

10.35 Given a series RLC circuit with $R = \frac{5}{3}\ \Omega$, $L = 5$ H, and $C = \frac{1}{25}$ F. Suppose the input is V and the output is V_C, the voltage across the capacitor. Sketch the amplitude response of V_C/V after the circuit is magnitude-scaled by $K_m = 300$ and frequency-scaled by $K_f = 10^6/15$. What are the scaled values of R, L, and C?

10.36 Suppose that $R = \frac{1}{20}\ \Omega$, $L = 5$ H, and $C = \frac{1}{2}$ F for the circuit given in Fig. P10.26. If the circuit is magnitude-scaled by $K_m = 10^3$ and frequency-scaled by $K_f = 10^5$, find the resulting values of R, L, and C.

10.37 What values of resistance, inductance, and capacitance, when magnitude-scaled by $K_m = 10^3$ and frequency-scaled by $K_f = 10^7$, will result in $R = 10$ kΩ, $L = 50\ \mu$H, and $C = 500$ pF?

10.38 The circuit shown in Fig. P10.38 is to be magnitude-scaled by $K_m = 2 \times 10^3$ and frequency-scaled by $K_f = 4 \times 10^5$. Determine all the resulting element values.

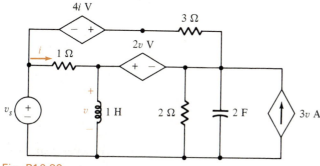

Fig. P10.38

10.39 Repeat Problem 10.38 for the op-amp circuit shown in Fig. DE10.8 (p. 477), given that $R_1 = 1\,\Omega$, $R_2 = 2\,\Omega$, and $C = 2$ F.

10.40 For the series RLC circuit shown in Fig. P10.40, suppose that $R = \frac{5}{3}\,\Omega$, $L = 5$ H, $C = \frac{1}{25}$ F, and $v_1(t) = 20e^{-6t}\cos 3t$ V. Find (a) $v_R(t)$, (b) $v_L(t)$, and (c) $v_C(t)$.

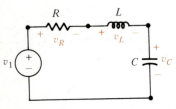

Fig. P10.40

10.41 Repeat Problem 10.40 for the case that $R = 2\,\Omega$, $L = \frac{1}{2}$ H, and $C = 2$ F.

10.42 For the circuit given in Fig. P10.14, suppose that $R = \frac{5}{3}\,\Omega$, $L = 5$ H, $C = \frac{1}{25}$ F, and $v_1(t) = 20e^{-6t}\cos 3t$ V. Find $v_C(t)$.

10.43 Find the Thévenin equivalent of the circuit shown in Fig. P10.43 given that $R_1 = 8\,\Omega$, $R_2 = 4\,\Omega$, $L = 2$ H, and $C = \frac{1}{16}$ F.

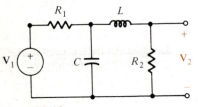

Fig. P10.43

10.44 For the circuit given in Fig. P10.43, suppose that $R_1 = 3\,\Omega$, $R_2 = 8\,\Omega$, $L = 1$ H, and C is replaced with another 1-H inductor. Find the Thévenin equivalent of the resulting circuit.

10.45 Find the Thévenin equivalent of the circuit shown in Fig. P10.45.

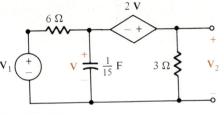

Fig. P10.45

10.46 Find the voltage transfer function V_2/V_1 for the circuit shown in Fig. P10.46.

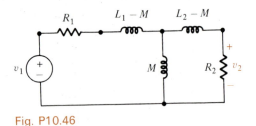

Fig. P10.46

10.47 For the series RLC circuit shown in Fig. P10.40, suppose that $R = \frac{5}{3}\,\Omega$, $L = 5$ H, and $C = \frac{1}{25}$ F. Draw the pole-zero plot for (a) $\mathbf{H}_R(s) = \mathbf{V}_R/\mathbf{V}_1$, (b) $\mathbf{H}_L(s) = \mathbf{V}_L/\mathbf{V}_1$, and (c) $\mathbf{H}_C(s) = \mathbf{V}_C/\mathbf{V}_1$.

10.48 Repeat Problem 10.47 for the case that $R = 2\,\Omega$, $L = \frac{1}{2}$ H, and $C = 2$ F.

10.49 Repeat Problem 10.47 for the case that $R = 2\,\Omega$, $L = 2$ H, and $C = 2$ F.

10.50 Draw the pole-zero plot of $\mathbf{H}(s) = \mathbf{V}_2/\mathbf{V}_1$ for the circuit described in Problem 10.43.

10.51 Draw the pole-zero plot of $\mathbf{H}(s) = \mathbf{V}_2/\mathbf{V}_1$ for the circuit described in Problem 10.44.

10.52 Draw the pole-zero plot of $\mathbf{H}(s) = \mathbf{V}_2/\mathbf{V}_1$ for the circuit described in Problem 10.45.

10.53 For the op-amp circuit given in Fig. DE10.9 (p. 482), draw the pole-zero plot of $\mathbf{H}(s) = \mathbf{V}_2/\mathbf{V}_1$ for the case that C is (a) 1 F, (b) $\frac{1}{4}$ F, and (c) $\frac{1}{16}$ F.

10.54 For the op-amp circuit given in Fig. P10.18, draw the pole-zero plot of $H(s) = V_2/V_1$ for the case that C is (a) $\frac{1}{2}$ F, (b) 1 F, and (c) 2 F.

10.55 A transfer function $H(s)$ has the pole-zero plot shown in Fig. P10.55. Find $H(s)$ given that (a) $H(0) = 2$, (b) $H(1) = 2$, (c) $H(-2) = 3$.

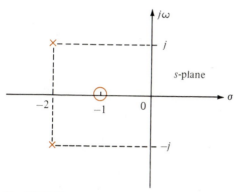

Fig. P10.55

10.56 Repeat Problem 10.55 given that there is an additional zero at $s = -3$.

10.57 Repeat Problem 10.55 for the case in which there is a double zero at $s = -1$.

10.58 Given the transfer function

$$H(s) = \frac{10(s + 1)}{s^2 + 4s + 5}$$

graphically determine the magnitude and angle of $H(s)$ for the case that (a) $s = j1$, (b) $s = j2$, and (c) $s = -2$.

10.59 Given the transfer function

$$H(s) = \frac{2(s + 1)}{s^2 + 5s + 6}$$

graphically determine the magnitude and angle of $H(j\omega)$ for the case that (a) $s = j1$, (b) $s = j2$, and (c) $s = j3$.

10.60 Repeat Problem 10.59 for

$$H(s) = \frac{s^2 + 4s + 5}{s^2 + 2s + 1}$$

CHAPTER 11

The Laplace Transform

● INTRODUCTION

The time-domain analysis of *RLC* circuits in general requires solving differential equations. For the case of a sinusoidal circuit (i.e., a circuit with a sinusoidal excitation or input), the need for writing and solving differential equations can be avoided by transforming the circuit to the frequency domain—that is, by employing the concepts of phasors and impedance (or admittance). So too, for damped-sinusoidal circuits can frequency-domain concepts be utilized, thereby eliminating the need to write and solve differential equations. However, frequency-domain analysis is not limited to circuits with either sinusoidal or damped-sinusoidal inputs. By employing a powerful mathematical tool—the Laplace transform—we can use frequency-domain techniques to analyze circuits that have any one of a wide variety of inputs. Although circuit inputs are assumed to be zero for $t < 0$, nonzero initial conditions can be accommodated with the circuit analysis.

Even though Laplace-transform techniques can be used to solve differential equations, in using the Laplace transform to analyze circuits, the writing of differential equations will not be required.

Not only does the Laplace transform have application to circuits, it also has application to various types of linear systems. By using simple linear-system elements such as integrators, adders, and scalers (amplifiers), more complicated linear systems (or circuits) can be realized or simulated—as is done with an analog computer.

11.1 DEFINITION AND PROPERTIES

An heuristic derivation of the Laplace transform can be presented by using concepts introduced in Chapters 13 and 14. However, such a derivation is not necessary for us to apply the Laplace transform at this time. Therefore, we shall now define the Laplace transform and postpone the discussion of its evolution until Chapter 14.

Given a function of time $f(t)$, we define its **Laplace transform**—designated either $\mathscr{L}[f(t)]$ or $\mathbf{F}(s)$—to be

$$\mathscr{L}[f(t)] = \mathbf{F}(s) = \int_0^\infty f(t)e^{-st}\,dt \tag{11.1}$$

where $s = \sigma + j\omega$. Because the lower limit of the integral in the definition of the Laplace transform is zero, the Laplace transform treats a function $f(t)$ as if $f(t) = 0$ for $t < 0$. Consequently, we will consider only such functions.

Although the lower limit on the above integral is $t = 0$, because of possible discontinuities at this point there may be situations where the use of $t = 0$ and $t = -\varepsilon$ (where $\varepsilon > 0$ is arbitrarily small) yield different results. Under this circumstance, we shall use $t = -\varepsilon$ (also denoted $t = 0^-$).

It can be shown that the **inverse Laplace transform** formula is given by

$$\mathscr{L}^{-1}[\mathbf{F}(s)] = f(t) = \frac{1}{2\pi j} \int_{c-j\infty}^{c+j\infty} \mathbf{F}(s)e^{st}\,ds$$

However, because the direct use of this formula requires some results from complex-variable theory, we shall avoid employing this integral. Instead, we shall form a table of Laplace transforms and the functions from which they come—and when we wish to find the inverse of a transform, we shall merely look up the inverse in the table.

EXAMPLE 11.1

It is a simple matter to determine the Laplace transform of a unit step function $u(t)$.

$$\mathscr{L}[u(t)] = \int_0^\infty u(t)e^{-st}\,dt = \int_0^\infty e^{-st}\,dt = -\frac{1}{s}e^{-st}\Big|_0^\infty = -\frac{1}{s}(0-1) = \frac{1}{s}$$

It is even simpler to determine the Laplace transform of an impulse function. By the sampling property of the impulse function,

$$\mathscr{L}[\delta(t)] = \int_0^\infty \delta(t)e^{-st}\,dt = \int_0^\infty \delta(t)e^{-0}\,dt = 1$$

Generalizing the step function to the exponential $e^{-at}u(t)$ for $a \geq 0$, we have

$$\mathscr{L}[e^{-at}u(t)] = \int_0^\infty e^{-at}u(t)e^{-st}\,dt = \int_0^\infty e^{-at}e^{-st}\,dt$$

$$= \frac{-1}{s+a}e^{-(s+a)t}\Big|_0^\infty = \frac{-1}{s+a}(0-1) = \frac{1}{s+a}$$

DRILL EXERCISE 11.1

Find the Laplace transform of $e^{-a(t-1)}u(t)$.

Answer: $\dfrac{e^a}{s+a}$

Although the Laplace transform of a function $f(t)$ can be obtained by using the defining integral [Equation (11.1)], sometimes it is more convenient to use some of the properties of this transform. We will now derive some of the more useful properties.

If $f(t) = f_1(t) + f_2(t)$, then

$$\mathscr{L}[f(t)] = \int_0^\infty f(t)e^{-st}\,dt = \int_0^\infty [f_1(t) + f_2(t)]e^{-st}\,dt$$

$$= \int_0^\infty [f_1(t)e^{-st} + f_2(t)e^{-st}]\,dt = \int_0^\infty f_1(t)e^{-st}\,dt + \int_0^\infty f_2(t)e^{-st}\,dt$$

$$= \mathscr{L}[f_1(t)] + \mathscr{L}[f_2(t)] \tag{11.2}$$

In other words, the Laplace transform of a sum of functions is equal to the sum of the transforms of the individual functions.

If K is a constant, then

$$\mathscr{L}[Kf(t)] = \int_0^\infty Kf(t)e^{-st}\,dt = K\int_0^\infty f(t)e^{-st}\,dt$$

$$= K\mathscr{L}[f(t)] \tag{11.3}$$

In other words, if a function is scaled by a constant, then the Laplace transform of the function is scaled by the same constant.

The properties of the Laplace transform given by Equations (11.2) and (11.3) collectively are referred to as the **linearity property** of the Laplace transform. We also say that the Laplace transform is a **linear transformation**.

EXAMPLE 11.2

Let us find the Laplace transform of

$$f(t) = 3(1 - e^{-2t})u(t)$$

Since we can express this function in the form

$$f(t) = (3 - 3e^{-2t})u(t) = 3u(t) - 3e^{-2t}u(t) = f_1(t) + f_2(t)$$

where

$$f_1(t) = 3u(t) \quad \text{and} \quad f_2(t) = -3e^{-2t}u(t)$$

then by the linearity property of the Laplace transform

$$\mathscr{L}[f(t)] = \mathscr{L}[3u(t)] + \mathscr{L}[-3e^{-2t}u(t)] = 3\mathscr{L}[u(t)] - 3\mathscr{L}[e^{-2t}u(t)]$$

$$= 3\left(\frac{1}{s}\right) - 3\left(\frac{1}{s+2}\right) = \frac{3}{s} - \frac{3}{s+2} = \frac{6}{s(s+2)}$$

DRILL EXERCISE 11.2

Find the Laplace transform of $(2 - 3e^{-10t} + e^{-30t})u(t)$.

Answer: $\dfrac{600}{s(s + 10)(s + 30)}$

Now recall Euler's formula

$$e^{j\theta} = \cos\theta + j\sin\theta \tag{11.4}$$

Replacing θ by $-\theta$, we get

$$e^{-j\theta} = \cos(-\theta) + j\sin(-\theta)$$

Since $\cos(-\theta) = \cos\theta$ and $\sin(-\theta) = -\sin\theta$, then

$$e^{-j\theta} = \cos\theta - j\sin\theta \tag{11.5}$$

By adding Equations (11.4) and (11.5), we get

$$\cos\theta = \frac{1}{2}(e^{j\theta} + e^{-j\theta}) \tag{11.6}$$

and subtracting Equation (11.5) from Equation (11.4), we obtain

$$\sin\theta = \frac{1}{2j}(e^{j\theta} - e^{-j\theta}) \tag{11.7}$$

These results can be used to find the Laplace transforms of sinusoids.

EXAMPLE 11.3

Given $f(t) = \cos\beta t\, u(t)$. Then

$$\mathscr{L}[\cos\beta t\, u(t)] = \mathscr{L}[\tfrac{1}{2}(e^{j\beta t} + e^{-j\beta t})u(t)] = \tfrac{1}{2}\mathscr{L}[e^{j\beta t}u(t) + e^{-j\beta t}u(t)]$$

$$= \tfrac{1}{2}\mathscr{L}[e^{j\beta t}u(t)] + \tfrac{1}{2}\mathscr{L}[e^{-j\beta t}u(t)]$$

Just as $\mathscr{L}[e^{-at}u(t)] = 1/(s + a)$, so too

$$\mathscr{L}[e^{-s_0 t}u(t)] = \frac{1}{s + s_0}$$

where s_0 is a complex number. Therefore,

$$\mathscr{L}[\cos\beta t\, u(t)] = \frac{1}{2}\left(\frac{1}{s - j\beta}\right) + \frac{1}{2}\left(\frac{1}{s + j\beta}\right) = \frac{1}{2}\frac{s + j\beta + s - j\beta}{(s - j\beta)(s + j\beta)} = \frac{s}{s^2 + \beta^2}$$

DRILL EXERCISE 11.3

Find the Laplace transform of $\sin\beta t\, u(t)$.

Answer: $\dfrac{\beta}{s^2 + \beta^2}$

Another property of the Laplace transform involves the derivative of a function. Specifically,

$$\mathscr{L}\left[\frac{df(t)}{dt}\right] = \int_0^\infty \frac{df(t)}{dt} e^{-st}\,dt = \int_0^\infty e^{-st}\frac{df(t)}{dt}\,dt$$

We may employ the formula for integration by parts

$$\int_a^b u\,dv = uv\Big|_a^b - \int_a^b v\,du$$

by selecting

$$u = e^{-st} \qquad \text{and} \qquad dv = \frac{df(t)}{dt}\,dt = df(t)$$

Then $du = -se^{-st}\,dt$ and $v = f(t)$. Thus,

$$\mathscr{L}\left[\frac{df(t)}{dt}\right] = e^{-at}f(t)\Big|_0^\infty - \int_0^\infty f(t)[-se^{-st}]\,dt$$

and, provided that $\lim_{t\to\infty} f(t)$ does not approach infinity at a rate equal to or higher than the exponential $e^{\sigma t}$, then

$$\mathscr{L}\left[\frac{df(t)}{dt}\right] = 0 - f(0) + s\int_0^\infty f(t)e^{-st}\,dt$$

$$= -f(0) + s\mathscr{L}[f(t)] = -f(0) + sF(s)$$

This result is known as the **differentiation property** of the Laplace transform.

EXAMPLE 11.4

Let us find the Laplace transform of $\sin \beta t\, u(t)$ by using the differentiation property.
Since

$$\frac{d[\sin \beta t\, u(t)]}{dt} = \beta \cos \beta t\, u(t)$$

then

$$\mathscr{L}\left(\frac{d[\sin \beta t\, u(t)]}{dt}\right) = \beta\mathscr{L}[\cos \beta t\, u(t)]$$

$$-\sin 0\, u(0) + s\mathscr{L}[\sin \beta t\, u(t)] = \beta\,\frac{s}{s^2 + \beta^2}$$

and therefore,

$$\mathscr{L}[\sin \beta t\, u(t)] = \frac{\beta}{s^2 + \beta^2}$$

DRILL EXERCISE 11.4

Use the differentiation property to find the Laplace transform of the unit ramp function $r(t) = tu(t)$.

Answer: $\dfrac{1}{s^2}$

We can apply the differentiation property to the second derivative of a function $f(t)$ as follows:

$$\mathscr{L}\left[\frac{d^2 f(t)}{dt^2}\right] = \mathscr{L}\left[\frac{d}{dt}\left(\frac{df(t)}{dt}\right)\right] = -\frac{df(0)}{dt} + s\mathscr{L}\left[\frac{df(t)}{dt}\right]$$

$$= -\frac{df(0)}{dt} + s[-f(0) + s\mathbf{F}(s)] = -\frac{df(0)}{dt} - sf(0) + s^2\mathbf{F}(s)$$

Extending this to the nth derivative, we get

$$\mathscr{L}\left[\frac{d^n f(t)}{dt^n}\right] = -\frac{d^{n-1}f(0)}{dt^{n-1}} - s\frac{d^{n-2}f(0)}{dt^{n-2}} - \cdots - s^{n-1}f(0) + s^n\mathbf{F}(s)$$

Note that $df(0)/dt$ is not the derivative of the constant $f(0)$, but is the notation for the derivative of $f(t)$ with t set equal to zero; that is,

$$\frac{df(0)}{dt} = \frac{df(t)}{dt}\bigg|_{t=0} \qquad \Rightarrow \qquad \frac{d^n f(0)}{dt^n} = \frac{d^n f(t)}{dt^n}\bigg|_{t=0}$$

DRILL EXERCISE 11.5

Find the Laplace transform of the parabola function $p(t) = t^2 u(t)$ by taking the second derivative of this function and using the differentiation property of the Laplace transform.

Answer: $\dfrac{2}{s^3}$

Having investigated the derivative of $f(t)$, let us consider its integral—that is, $\int_0^t f(t)\,dt$. If $\mathscr{L}[f(t)] = \mathbf{F}(s)$, then

$$\mathscr{L}\left[\int_0^t f(t)\,dt\right] = \mathscr{L}\left[\int_0^t f(x)\,dx\right] = \int_0^\infty \left[\int_0^t f(x)\,dx\right]e^{-st}\,dt$$

Now let

$$u = \int_0^t f(x)\,dx \qquad \text{and} \qquad dv = e^{-st}\,dt$$

Then

$$du = f(t)\,dt \qquad \text{and} \qquad v = -\frac{1}{s}e^{-st}$$

and

$$\mathscr{L}\left[\int_0^t f(t)\,dt\right] = \left[\int_0^t f(x)\,dx\right]\left[-\frac{1}{s}e^{-st}\right]\Big|_0^\infty - \int_0^\infty -\frac{1}{s}e^{-st}f(t)\,dt$$

If $\int_0^\infty f(x)\,dx$ does not approach infinity at a rate equal to or higher than the exponential $e^{\sigma t}$, then

$$\mathscr{L}\left[\int_0^t f(t)\,dt\right] = \left[\int_{0^-}^{0^-} f(x)\,dx\right]\left[\frac{1}{s}\right] + \frac{1}{s}\int_0^\infty f(t)e^{-st}\,dt$$

and since it is assumed that $f(t) = 0$ for $t < 0$, we have that

$$\mathscr{L}\left[\int_0^t f(t)\,dt\right] = \frac{1}{s}\mathbf{F}(s)$$

This result is known as the **integration property** of the Laplace transform.

EXAMPLE 11.5

The unit ramp function $r(t) = tu(t)$ is related to the unit step function $u(t)$ by

$$r(t) = tu(t) = \int_{-\infty}^t u(t)\,dt = \int_0^t u(t)\,dt$$

Thus,

$$\mathscr{L}[tu(t)] = \mathscr{L}\left[\int_0^t u(t)\,dt\right] = \frac{1}{s}\left(\frac{1}{s}\right) = \frac{1}{s^2}$$

DRILL EXERCISE 11.6

Use the fact that the parabola function $p(t) = t^2 u(t) = 2\int_{-\infty}^t r(t)\,dt$, where $r(t) = tu(t)$ is the unit ramp function, to find the Laplace transform of $p(t)$.

Answer: $\dfrac{2}{s^3}$

Another important property of the Laplace transform is obtained as follows: Suppose that $\mathbf{F}(s) = \mathscr{L}[f(t)]$. Then

$$\mathscr{L}[e^{-at}f(t)] = \int_0^\infty e^{-at}f(t)e^{-st}\,dt = \int_0^\infty f(t)e^{-(s+a)t}\,dt$$

$$= \mathbf{F}(s + a)$$

In other words, $\mathcal{L}[e^{-at}f(t)]$ can be obtained from $\mathcal{L}[f(t)]$—simply replace each s in $\mathcal{L}[f(t)]$ by $s + a$. This result is referred to as the **complex-translation property** of the Laplace transform.

EXAMPLE 11.6

Since $\mathcal{L}[u(t)] = \mathbf{F}(s) = 1/s$, then by the complex-translation property

$$\mathcal{L}[e^{-at}u(t)] = \mathbf{F}(s + a) = \frac{1}{s + a}$$

Furthermore,

$$\mathcal{L}[\cos \beta t\, u(t)] = \frac{s}{s^2 + \beta^2} \qquad \Rightarrow \qquad \mathcal{L}[e^{-\alpha t}\cos \beta t\, u(t)] = \frac{s + \alpha}{(s + \alpha)^2 + \beta^2}$$

Also,

$$\mathcal{L}[\sin \beta t\, u(t)] = \frac{\beta}{s^2 + \beta^2} \qquad \Rightarrow \qquad \mathcal{L}[e^{-\alpha t}\sin \beta t\, u(t)] = \frac{\beta}{(s + \alpha)^2 + \beta^2}$$

DRILL EXERCISE 11.7

Use the complex-translation property to find the Laplace transform of $te^{-at}u(t)$.

Answer: $\dfrac{1}{(s + a)^2}$

Given that $\mathcal{L}[f(t)] = \mathbf{F}(s)$, then

$$\frac{d\mathbf{F}(s)}{ds} = \frac{d}{ds}\int_0^\infty f(t)e^{-st}\,dt = \int_0^\infty f(t)\frac{d[e^{-st}]}{ds}\,dt$$

$$= \int_0^\infty f(t)[-te^{-st}]\,dt = -\int_0^\infty tf(t)e^{-st}\,dt = -\mathcal{L}[tf(t)]$$

Thus,

$$\mathcal{L}[tf(t)] = -\frac{d\mathbf{F}(s)}{ds} = -\frac{d}{ds}\{\mathcal{L}[f(t)]\}$$

and this is known as the **complex-differentiation property** of the Laplace transform. We now see that multiplication by t in the time domain corresponds to (minus) differentiation in the transform (frequency) domain.

EXAMPLE 11.7

Since $\mathcal{L}[e^{-at}u(t)] = 1/(s + a)$, then

$$\mathcal{L}[te^{-at}u(t)] = -\frac{d}{ds}\left(\frac{1}{s + a}\right) = \frac{1}{(s + a)^2}$$

Setting $a = 0$, we get

$$\mathscr{L}[tu(t)] = \frac{1}{s^2}$$

DRILL EXERCISE 11.8

Use the complex-differentiation property to find the Laplace transform of $t^2 e^{-at} u(t)$.

Answer: $\dfrac{2}{(s+a)^3}$

If $\mathscr{L}[f(t)] = \mathbf{F}(s)$, then for $a > 0$,

$$\mathscr{L}[f(t-a)u(t-a)] = \int_0^\infty f(t-a)u(t-a)e^{-st}\,dt = \int_a^\infty f(t-a)e^{-st}\,dt$$

Define the variable $x = t - a$. Then $dx = dt$, and $t = x + a$. Thus, $t = a \Rightarrow x = 0$, and $t = \infty \Rightarrow x = \infty$. Hence,

$$\mathscr{L}[f(t-a)u(t-a)] = \int_0^\infty f(x)e^{-s(x+a)}\,dt = e^{-sa}\int_0^\infty f(x)e^{-sx}\,dx$$

$$= e^{-sa}\mathbf{F}(s)$$

and this result is known as the **real-translation property** of the Laplace transform.

EXAMPLE 11.8

The Laplace transform of the function $f(t) = u(t) - u(t-a)$ can be determined as follows:

$$\mathscr{L}[f(t)] = \mathscr{L}[u(t) - u(t-a)] = \mathscr{L}[u(t)] - \mathscr{L}[u(t-a)]$$

$$= \frac{1}{s} - e^{-sa}\frac{1}{s} = \frac{1}{s}(1 - e^{-sa})$$

DRILL EXERCISE 11.9

Find the Laplace transform of $e^{-a(t-1)}u(t-1)$.

Answer: $\dfrac{e^{-s}}{s+a}$

Now suppose that $f(t)$ is a periodic or repetitive function for $t \geq 0$ and $f(t) = 0$ for $t < 0$. A sample of such a function is shown in Fig. 11.1 Since $f(t)$ is periodic for

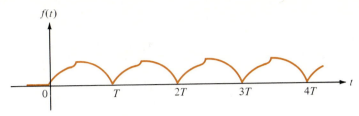

$f(t)$

Fig. 11.1   Function that is periodic for $t \geq 0$.

$t \geq 0$, it can be expressed as the sum of functions

$$f(t) = f_1(t) + f_2(t) + f_3(t) + \cdots$$

$$= \sum_{k=0}^{\infty} f_{k+1}(t)$$

where $f_{k+1}(t) = f_1(t - kT)$. The functions $f_1(t), f_2(t)$, and $f_3(t)$ are depicted in Fig. 11.2. We then have that

$$f(t) = \sum_{k=0}^{\infty} f_1(t - kT)$$

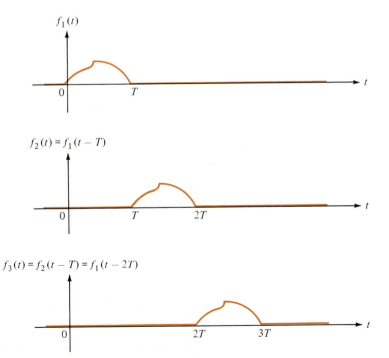

$f_1(t)$

$f_2(t) = f_1(t - T)$

$f_3(t) = f_2(t - T) = f_1(t - 2T)$

Fig. 11.2   Functions used to form $f(t)$.

Thus,

$$\mathcal{L}[f(t)] = \mathcal{L}\left[\sum_{k=0}^{\infty} f_1(t - kT)\right] = \sum_{k=0}^{\infty} \mathcal{L}[f_1(t - kT)] = \sum_{k=0}^{\infty} e^{-skT} \mathbf{F}_1(s)$$

where $\mathbf{F}_1(s) = \mathcal{L}[f_1(t)]$. Since $\mathbf{F}_1(s)$ is not dependent on k, then

$$\mathcal{L}[f(t)] = \mathbf{F}_1(s) \sum_{k=0}^{\infty} (e^{-sT})^k$$

But, the Taylor series expansion of the function $1/(1 - x)$ is given by

$$\frac{1}{1 - x} = 1 + x + x^2 + x^3 + \cdots = \sum_{k=0}^{\infty} x^k$$

Thus,

$$\mathcal{L}[f(t)] = \frac{\mathbf{F}_1(s)}{1 - e^{-sT}}$$

Thus, knowing the Laplace transform of $f_1(t)$—the function obtained from the first period of $f(t)$—it is a simple matter to determine the Laplace transform of the "periodic" function $f(t)$.

EXAMPLE 11.9
Let us determine the transform of the pulse train $f(t)$ shown in Fig. 11.3.

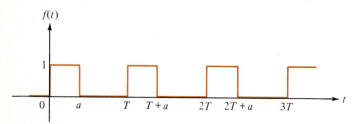

Fig. 11.3   Pulse train.

Since $f_1(t) = u(t) - u(t - a)$, from Example 11.8,

$$\mathbf{F}_1(s) = \frac{1}{s}(1 - e^{-sa}) \qquad \Rightarrow \qquad \mathbf{F}(s) = \frac{\mathbf{F}_1(s)}{1 - e^{-sT}} = \frac{1 - e^{-sa}}{s(1 - e^{-sT})}$$

Table 11.1 summarizes the most important properties of the Laplace transform and the transforms of frequently used functions.

Table 11.1 TABLE OF LAPLACE TRANSFORMS

$f(t)$	Property	$\mathbf{F}(s)$
$f(t)$	Definition	$\int_0^\infty f(t)e^{-st}\,dt$
$f_1(t) + f_2(t)$	Linearity	$\mathbf{F}_1(s) + \mathbf{F}_2(s)$
$Kf(t)$	Linearity	$K\mathbf{F}(s)$
$\dfrac{df(t)}{dt}$	Differentiation	$s\mathbf{F}(s) - f(0)$
$\dfrac{d^n f(t)}{dt^n}$	Differentiation	$s^n\mathbf{F}(s) - s^{n-1}f(0) - \cdots - \dfrac{d^{n-1}f(0)}{dt^{n-1}}$
$\int_0^t f(t)\,dt$	Integration	$\dfrac{1}{s}\mathbf{F}(s)$
$tf(t)$	Complex differentiation	$-\dfrac{d\mathbf{F}(s)}{ds}$
$e^{-at}f(t)$	Complex translation	$\mathbf{F}(s + a)$
$f(t-a)u(t-a)$	Real translation	$e^{-sa}\mathbf{F}(s)$
$f(t)$	Periodic function	$\dfrac{\mathbf{F}_1(s)}{1 - e^{-sT}}$
$\int_0^t x(\tau)h(t-\tau)\,d\tau$	Convolution	$\mathbf{H}(s)\mathbf{X}(s)$
$\delta(t)$		1
$u(t)$		$\dfrac{1}{s}$
$e^{-at}u(t)$		$\dfrac{1}{s + a}$
$\sin \beta t\, u(t)$		$\dfrac{\beta}{s^2 + \beta^2}$
$\cos \beta t\, u(t)$		$\dfrac{s}{s^2 + \beta^2}$
$e^{-\alpha t}\sin \beta t\, u(t)$		$\dfrac{\beta}{(s + \alpha)^2 + \beta^2}$
$e^{-\alpha t}\cos \beta t\, u(t)$		$\dfrac{s + \alpha}{(s + \alpha)^2 + \beta^2}$
$tu(t)$		$\dfrac{1}{s^2}$
$t^n u(t)$		$\dfrac{n!}{s^{n+1}}$
$te^{-at}u(t)$		$\dfrac{1}{(s + a)^2}$
$t^n e^{-at}u(t)$		$\dfrac{n!}{(s + a)^{n+1}}$

11.2 PARTIAL-FRACTION EXPANSIONS

A major application of the Laplace transform is in the solving of differential equations. Let us consider an example.

EXAMPLE 11.10

To determine the solution to the second-order differential equation

$$\frac{d^2x(t)}{dt^2} + 3\frac{dx(t)}{dt} + 2x(t) = 4e^{-3t}u(t)$$

subject to the initial conditions $x(0) = 2$ and $dx(0)/dt = -1$, take the Laplace transform of both sides of the equation. The result is the algebraic equation with complex coefficients

$$s^2\mathbf{X}(s) - sx(0) - \frac{dx(0)}{dt} + 3[s\mathbf{X}(s) - x(0)] + 2\mathbf{X}(s) = \frac{4}{s+3}$$

or

$$s^2\mathbf{X}(s) - 2s + 1 + 3s\mathbf{X}(s) - 6 + 2\mathbf{X}(s) = \frac{4}{s+3}$$

Thus,

$$(s^2 + 3s + 2)\mathbf{X}(s) = \frac{4}{s+3} + 2s + 5 \quad \Rightarrow \quad \mathbf{X}(s) = \frac{2s^2 + 11s + 19}{(s+1)(s+2)(s+3)}$$

This expression can be rewritten (we shall discuss the technique for accomplishing this step very soon) as follows:

$$\mathbf{X}(s) = \frac{5}{s+1} - \frac{5}{s+2} + \frac{2}{s+3}$$

From Table 11.1,

$$x(t) = (5e^{-t} - 5e^{-2t} + 2e^{-3t})u(t)$$

is the solution of the given differential equation subject to the boundary conditions stated.

DRILL EXERCISE 11.10

Find the solution to the second-order linear differential equation

$$\frac{d^2x(t)}{dt^2} + 40\frac{dx(t)}{dt} + 300x(t) = 600u(t)$$

subject to zero initial conditions, that is, $x(0) = 0$ and $dx(0)/dt = 0$. (*Hint*: Use Drill Exercise 11.2 on p. 499.)
Answer: $(2 - 3e^{-10t} + e^{-30t})u(t)$

The Laplace transform can be used not only to solve a single differential equation, but also to solve a set of simultaneous differential equations.

EXAMPLE 11.11

To solve the two simultaneous differential equations

$$2\frac{dx(t)}{dt} + 4x(t) + \frac{dy(t)}{dt} + 7y(t) = 5u(t)$$

$$\frac{dx(t)}{dt} + x(t) + \frac{dy(t)}{dt} + 3y(t) = 5\delta(t)$$

subject to the initial conditions $x(0) = 0$ and $y(0) = 0$, take the Laplace transform of both equations. The result is a pair of algebraic equations

$$2[s\mathbf{X}(s) - x(0)] + 4\mathbf{X}(s) + s\mathbf{Y}(s) - y(0) + 7\mathbf{Y}(s) = \frac{5}{s}$$

$$s\mathbf{X}(s) - x(0) + \mathbf{X}(s) + s\mathbf{Y}(s) - y(0) + 3\mathbf{Y}(s) = 5$$

which reduces to the pair of equations

$$(2s + 4)\mathbf{X}(s) + (s + 7)\mathbf{Y}(s) = \frac{5}{s}$$

$$(s + 1)\mathbf{X}(s) + (s + 3)\mathbf{Y}(s) = 5$$

which in matrix form is

$$\begin{bmatrix} 2s + 4 & s + 7 \\ s + 1 & s + 3 \end{bmatrix} \begin{bmatrix} \mathbf{X}(s) \\ \mathbf{Y}(s) \end{bmatrix} = \begin{bmatrix} \dfrac{5}{s} \\ 5 \end{bmatrix}$$

Forming determinants, we have

$$\Delta = \begin{vmatrix} 2s + 4 & s + 7 \\ s + 1 & s + 3 \end{vmatrix} = (2s + 4)(s + 3) - (s + 1)(s + 7) = s^2 + 2s + 5$$

$$\Delta_1 = \begin{vmatrix} \dfrac{5}{s} & s + 7 \\ 5 & s + 3 \end{vmatrix} = \frac{5}{s}(s + 3) - 5(s + 7) = \frac{-5s^2 - 30s + 15}{s}$$

$$\Delta_2 = \begin{vmatrix} 2s + 4 & \dfrac{5}{s} \\ s + 1 & 5 \end{vmatrix} = (2s + 4)5 - (s + 1)\frac{5}{s} = \frac{10s^2 + 15s - 5}{s}$$

By Cramer's rule, we get

$$\mathbf{X}(s) = \frac{\Delta_1}{\Delta} = \frac{-5s^2 - 30s + 15}{s(s^2 + 2s + 5)} \qquad \text{and} \qquad \mathbf{Y}(s) = \frac{\Delta_2}{\Delta} = \frac{10s^2 + 15s - 5}{s(s^2 + 2s + 5)}$$

By the discussion following immediately, $\mathbf{X}(s)$ and $\mathbf{Y}(s)$ can be rewritten as

$$\mathbf{X}(s) = \frac{3}{s} - \frac{8s + 36}{s^2 + 2s + 5} = \frac{3}{s} - \frac{8(s + 1)}{(s + 1)^2 + 2^2} - \frac{14(2)}{(s + 1)^2 + 2^2}$$

$$\mathbf{Y}(s) = \frac{-1}{s} + \frac{11s + 17}{s^2 + 2s + 5} = -\frac{1}{s} + \frac{11(s + 1)}{(s + 1)^2 + 2^2} + \frac{3(2)}{(s + 1)^2 + 2^2}$$

From Table 11.1,

$$x(t) = (3 - 8e^{-t}\cos 2t - 14e^{-t}\sin 2t)u(t)$$

and

$$y(t) = (-1 + 11e^{-t}\cos 2t + 3e^{-t}\sin 2t)u(t)$$

In the two preceding examples we encountered functions—in the form of ratios of polynomials in s—whose inverse transforms were desired. We obtained the inverses by expressing the function as a sum of simpler functions and then looking up the inverse transform of each term. This decomposition of a function into a sum of simpler functions is known as a **partial-fraction expansion**.

The process of taking a partial-fraction expansion will be broken up into three cases. In each case we shall assume that

$$\mathbf{F}(s) = \frac{\mathbf{N}(s)}{\mathbf{D}(s)}$$

where $\mathbf{N}(s)$ and $\mathbf{D}(s)$ are polynomials in s, and deg $\mathbf{N}(s) <$ deg $\mathbf{D}(s)$. The situation that deg $\mathbf{N}(s) \geq$ deg $\mathbf{D}(s)$ will be discussed immediately following.[†]

Case I: Simple Real Poles

Suppose that $\mathbf{F}(s)$ can be written as

$$\mathbf{F}(s) = \frac{\mathbf{N}(s)}{(s + \alpha)\mathbf{D}_1(s)}$$

where the real number $-\alpha$ is not a root of $\mathbf{D}_1(s)$. Then we can write $\mathbf{F}(s)$ as

$$\mathbf{F}(s) = \frac{K}{s + \alpha} + \mathbf{F}_1(s)$$

To determine K, multiply both sides of this equation by $s + \alpha$, which yields

$$(s + \alpha)\mathbf{F}(s) = K + (s + \alpha)\mathbf{F}_1(s)$$

$$\frac{\mathbf{N}(s)}{\mathbf{D}_1(s)} = K + (s + \alpha)\mathbf{F}_1(s)$$

[†] The degree of polynomial $\mathbf{P}(s)$ is denoted by deg $\mathbf{P}(s)$.

Setting $s = -\alpha$, we obtain a formula for K; that is,

$$K = (s + \alpha)\mathbf{F}(s)\Big|_{s=-\alpha} = \frac{\mathbf{N}(s)}{\mathbf{D}_1(s)}\Big|_{s=-\alpha} = \frac{\mathbf{N}(-\alpha)}{\mathbf{D}_1(-\alpha)}$$

The problem of finding the partial-fraction expansion of $\mathbf{F}(s)$ reduces to finding the partial-fraction expansion of $\mathbf{F}_1(s)$. Clearly, $\mathbf{F}_1(s) = \mathbf{F}(s) - K/(s + \alpha)$. If $\mathbf{F}_1(s)$ has a simple real pole, we can repeat the above process.

EXAMPLE 11.12

The function

$$\mathbf{X}(s) = \frac{2s^2 + 11s + 19}{(s + 1)(s + 2)(s + 3)}$$

was encountered in Example 11.10. Since this function has simple poles and the degree of the denominator is greater than the degree of the numerator, the partial-fraction expansion is

$$\mathbf{X}(s) = \frac{2s^2 + 11s + 19}{(s + 1)(s + 2)(s + 3)} = \frac{K_1}{s + 1} + \frac{K_2}{s + 2} + \frac{K_3}{s + 3}$$

where

$$K_1 = (s + 1)\mathbf{X}(s)\Big|_{s=-1} = \frac{2s^2 + 11s + 19}{(s + 2)(s + 3)}\Big|_{s=-1} = 5$$

$$K_2 = (s + 2)\mathbf{X}(s)\Big|_{s=-2} = \frac{2s^2 + 11s + 19}{(s + 1)(s + 3)}\Big|_{s=-2} = -5$$

$$K_3 = (s + 3)\mathbf{X}(s)\Big|_{s=-3} = \frac{2s^2 + 11s + 19}{(s + 1)(s + 2)}\Big|_{s=-3} = 2$$

Thus,

$$\frac{2s^2 + 11s + 19}{(s + 1)(s + 2)(s + 3)} = \frac{5}{s + 1} - \frac{5}{s + 2} + \frac{2}{s + 3}$$

and

$$x(t) = (5e^{-t} - 5e^{-2t} + 2e^{-3t})u(t)$$

DRILL EXERCISE 11.11

Use a partial-fraction expansion to find the inverse Laplace transform of

$$\mathbf{X}(s) = \frac{600}{s^3 + 40s^2 + 300s}$$

Answer: $(2 - 3e^{-10t} + e^{-30t})u(t)$

Case II: Simple Complex Poles

Since the complex roots of a polynomial with real coefficients always appear in conjugate pairs, suppose that $F(s)$ has the form

$$F(s) = \frac{N(s)}{(s + \alpha + j\beta)(s + \alpha - j\beta)D_1(s)}$$

where $-\alpha - j\beta$ and $-\alpha + j\beta$ are not roots of $D_1(s)$. Then we can write $F(s)$ as

$$F(s) = \frac{K}{s + \alpha + j\beta} + \frac{K^*}{s + \alpha - j\beta} + F_1(s)$$

where we determine K, and hence its complex conjugate K^*, as was done for the case of simple real roots. In other words,

$$K = (s + \alpha + j\beta)F(s)\Big|_{s = -\alpha - j\beta} = \frac{N(s)}{(s + \alpha - j\beta)D_1(s)}\Big|_{s = -\alpha - j\beta}$$

$$= \frac{N(-\alpha - j\beta)}{(-2j\beta)D_1(-\alpha - j\beta)}$$

Once K and K^* are determined, the corresponding two complex terms can be combined as follows: Suppose $K = a + jb$. Then $K^* = a - jb$, and

$$\frac{K}{s + \alpha + j\beta} + \frac{K^*}{s + \alpha - j\beta} = \frac{(a + jb)(s + \alpha - j\beta) + (a - jb)(s + \alpha + j\beta)}{(s + \alpha + j\beta)(s + \alpha - j\beta)}$$

$$= \frac{2a(s + \alpha)}{(s + \alpha)^2 + \beta^2} + \frac{2b\beta}{(s + \alpha)^2 + \beta^2}$$

EXAMPLE 11.13

In Example 11.11 we encountered the function

$$Y(s) = \frac{10s^2 + 15s - 5}{s(s^2 + 2s + 5)} = \frac{10s^2 + 15s - 5}{s(s + 1 + j2)(s + 1 - j2)}$$

which has the partial-fraction expansion

$$\frac{10s^2 + 15s - 5}{s(s + 1 + j2)(s + 1 - j2)} = \frac{K_0}{s} + \frac{K}{s + 1 + j2} + \frac{K^*}{s + 1 - j2}$$

where

$$K_0 = sY(s)\Big|_{s=0} = \frac{10s^2 + 15s - 5}{s^2 + 2s + 5}\Big|_{s=0} = -1$$

$$K = (s + 1 + j2)Y(s)\Big|_{s = -1 - j2} = \frac{10s^2 + 15s - 5}{s(s + 1 - j2)}\Big|_{s = -1 - j2}$$

$$= \frac{11}{2} + j\frac{3}{2} = a + jb$$

Thus,

$$\mathbf{Y}(s) = -\frac{1}{s} + \frac{11/2 + j3/2}{s + 1 + j2} + \frac{11/2 - j3/2}{s + 1 - j2} = -\frac{1}{s} + \frac{11(s + 1)}{(s + 1)^2 + 2^2} + \frac{3(2)}{(s + 1)^2 + 2^2}$$

and therefore

$$y(t) = (-1 + 11e^{-t}\cos 2t + 3e^{-t}\sin 2t)u(t)$$

DRILL EXERCISE 11.12

Find the inverse Laplace transform of

$$\mathbf{X}(s) = \frac{-5s^2 - 30s + 15}{s^3 + 2s^2 + 5s}$$

Answer: $(3 - 8e^{-t}\cos 2t - 14e^{-t}\sin 2t)u(t)$

In some cases, complex poles can be handled without the necessity of finding K (and hence, K^*) directly as discussed above. For instance, for the function $\mathbf{Y}(s)$ considered in the preceding example, we can write

$$\mathbf{Y}(s) = \frac{10s^2 + 15s - 5}{s(s^2 + 2s + 5)} = \frac{K_0}{s} + \mathbf{Y}_1(s)$$

where

$$K_0 = s\mathbf{Y}(s)\Big|_{s=0} = \frac{10s^2 + 15s - 5}{s^2 + 2s + 5}\Big|_{s=0} = -1$$

Thus,

$$\mathbf{Y}(s) = -\frac{1}{s} + \mathbf{Y}_1(s)$$

from which

$$\mathbf{Y}_1(s) = \frac{1}{s} + \mathbf{Y}(s) = \frac{1}{s} + \frac{10s^2 + 15s - 5}{s^2 + 2s + 5} = \frac{11s + 17}{s^2 + 2s + 5}$$

Therefore, we can write

$$\mathbf{Y}(s) = \frac{K_0}{s} + \mathbf{Y}_1(s) = -\frac{1}{s} + \frac{11s + 17}{s^2 + 2s + 5} = -\frac{1}{s} + \frac{11s + 17}{(s + 1)^2 + 2^2}$$

$$= -\frac{1}{s} + \frac{11s + 11 + 6}{(s + 1)^2 + 2^2} = -\frac{1}{s} + \frac{11(s + 1)}{(s + 1)^2 + 2^2} + \frac{3(2)}{(s + 1)^2 + 2^2}$$

as was obtained in Example 11.13.

Case III: Multiple Poles

Suppose that $F(s)$ has the form

$$F(s) = \frac{N(s)}{(s + s_0)^n D_1(s)}$$

where $-s_0$ is not a root of $D_1(s)$ and in general is complex. Then we can write $F(s)$ as

$$F(s) = \frac{K_1}{s + s_0} + \frac{K_2}{(s + s_0)^2} + \cdots + \frac{K_{n-1}}{(s + s_0)^{n-1}} + \frac{K_n}{(s + s_0)^n} + F_1(s)$$

Multiplying both sides of this equation by $(s + s_0)^n$ results in

$$(s + s_0)^n F(s) = K_1(s + s_0)^{n-1} + K_2(s + s_0)^{n-2} + \cdots$$
$$+ K_{n-1}(s + s_0) + K_n + (s + s_0)^n F_1(s)$$

Setting $s = -s_0$, we get

$$K_n = (s + s_0)^n F(s)\Big|_{s = -s_0}$$

To find K_{n-1}, after multiplication by $(s + s_0)^n$, take the derivative of both sides with respect to s. Then

$$\frac{d}{ds}\left[(s + s_0)^n F(s)\right] = (n - 1)K_1(s + s_0)^{n-2} + (n - 2)K_2(s + s_0)^{n-3} + \cdots$$

$$+ 2K_{n-2}(s + s_0) + K_{n-1} + 0 + (s + s_0)^n \frac{dF_1(s)}{ds}$$

$$+ n(s + s_0)^{n-1}F_1(s)$$

Setting $s = -s_0$ in this equation, we get

$$K_{n-1} = \frac{d}{ds}\left[(s + s_0)^n F(s)\right]\Big|_{s = -s_0}$$

Repeating this process,

$$2K_{n-2} = \frac{d^2}{ds^2}\left[(s + s_0)^n F(s)\right]\Big|_{s = -s_0} \quad \Rightarrow \quad K_{n-2} = \frac{1}{2}\frac{d^2}{ds^2}\left[(s + s_0)^n F(s)\right]\Big|_{s = -s_0}$$

In general, for $r = 0, 1, 2, \ldots, n - 1$,

$$K_{n-r} = \frac{1}{r!}\frac{d^r}{ds^r}\left[(s + s_0)^n F(s)\right]\Big|_{s = -s_0}$$

EXAMPLE 11.14

Let us determine the partial-fraction expansion of

$$F(s) = \frac{s - 2}{s(s + 1)^3} = \frac{K_0}{s} + \frac{K_1}{s + 1} + \frac{K_2}{(s + 1)^2} + \frac{K_3}{(s + 1)^3}$$

We have that

$$K_0 = sF(s)\Big|_{s=0} = \frac{s-2}{(s+1)^3}\Big|_{s=0} = -2$$

$$K_3 = (s+1)^3 F(s)\Big|_{s=-1} = \frac{s-2}{s}\Big|_{s=-1} = 3$$

$$K_2 = \frac{d}{ds}\left[(s+1)^3 F(s)\right]\Big|_{s=-1} = \frac{d}{ds}\left[\frac{s-2}{s}\right]\Big|_{s=-1} = \frac{2}{s^2}\Big|_{s=-1} = 2$$

$$K_1 = \frac{1}{2}\frac{d^2}{ds^2}\left[(s+1)^3 F(s)\right]\Big|_{s=-1} = \frac{1}{2}\frac{d}{ds}\left[\frac{2}{s^2}\right]\Big|_{s=-1} = -\frac{2}{s^3}\Big|_{s=-1} = 2$$

Thus,

$$F(s) = -\frac{2}{s} + \frac{2}{s+1} + \frac{2}{(s+1)^2} + \frac{3}{(s+1)^3}$$

From Table 11.1,

$$\mathcal{L}\left[\frac{t^n}{n!}e^{-at}u(t)\right] = \frac{1}{(s+a)^{n+1}}$$

Hence

$$f(t) = (-2 + 2e^{-t} + 2te^{-t} + \tfrac{3}{2}t^2 e^{-t})u(t)$$

DRILL EXERCISE 11.13

Find the inverse Laplace transform of

$$F(s) = \frac{1}{(s+1)(s+2)^2}$$

Answer: $[e^{-t} - (1+t)e^{-2t}]u(t)$

In the three cases of partial-fraction expansions discussed above, it was assumed that the degree of the denominator polynomial is greater than the degree of the numerator polynomial. For a situation in which this condition does not hold, divide the numerator by the denominator, and then express $F(s) = N(s)/D(s)$ as

$$F(s) = \frac{N(s)}{D(s)} = Q(s) + \frac{R(s)}{D(s)}$$

where $Q(s)$ is the quotient and $R(s)$ is the remainder. Long division (called the **Euclidean division algorithm**) guarantees that $\deg R(s) < \deg D(s)$. Thus, we can take a partial-fraction expansion of $R(s)/D(s)$ as described previously.

EXAMPLE 11.15

For the function

$$F(s) = \frac{2s^2 + s + 3}{(s + 1)(s + 2)} = \frac{2s^2 + s + 3}{s^2 + 3s + 2}$$

dividing the denominator into the numerator, we get the partial-fraction expansion

$$F(s) = 2 - \frac{5s + 1}{(s + 1)(s + 2)} = 2 + \frac{4}{s + 1} - \frac{9}{s + 2}$$

from which

$$f(t) = 2\,\delta(t) + (4e^{-t} - 9e^{-2t})u(t)$$

DRILL EXERCISE 11.14

Find the inverse Laplace transform of

$$F(s) = \frac{s^3}{(s + 1)(s + 2)^2}$$

Answer: $\delta(t) - \left[e^{-t} + 4(1 - 2t)e^{-2t}\right]u(t)$

In the previous discussion we learned how to take partial-fraction expansions algebraically. In addition, if $F(s)$ has simple poles, we can also take partial-fraction expansions graphically. For suppose that

$$F(s) = \frac{N(s)}{D(s)} = \frac{K(s - z_1)(s - z_2) \cdots (s - z_n)}{(s - p_1)(s - p_2) \cdots (s - p_m)}$$

where $m > n$ and the poles and zeros are, in general, complex. Taking a partial-fraction expansion of $F(s)$, we get

$$F(s) = \frac{K_1}{s - p_1} + \frac{K_2}{s - p_2} + \cdots + \frac{K_m}{s - p_m}$$

where

$$K_i = (s - p_i)F(s)\Big|_{s = p_i}$$

is called the **residue** of the ith pole. (The term "residue" is used only in conjunction with simple poles.) Thus,

$$K_i = \frac{K(p_i - z_1)(p_i - z_2) \cdots (p_i - z_n)}{(p_i - p_1) \cdots (p_i - p_{i-1})(p_i - p_{i+1}) \cdots (p_i - p_m)}$$

But, in the s-plane, $p_i - z_j$ is the vector from the jth zero to the ith pole; and $p_i - p_k$ is the vector from the kth pole to the ith pole. Thus,

$$K_i = \frac{K(N_{i1}\underline{/\phi_{i1}})(N_{i2}\underline{/\phi_{i2}}) \cdots (N_{in}\underline{/\phi_{in}})}{(M_{i1}\underline{/\theta_{i1}}) \cdots (M_{i,i-1}\underline{/\theta_{i,i-1}})(M_{i,i+1}\underline{/\theta_{i,i+1}}) \cdots (M_{im}\underline{/\theta_{im}})}$$

where

$$N_{ij} = \text{the magnitude of } p_i - z_j \qquad \phi_{ij} = \text{the angle of } p_i - z_j$$

$$M_{ik} = \text{the magnitude of } p_i - p_k \qquad \theta_{ik} = \text{the angle of } p_i - p_k$$

Therefore, from a pole-zero plot of $\mathbf{F}(s)$ we can determine the residues of the poles, and hence the partial-fraction expansion of $\mathbf{F}(s)$, by graphical means.

EXAMPLE 11.16

Consider the function

$$\mathbf{F}(s) = \frac{s^2 + 6s + 8}{s^3 + 2s^2 + 4s} = \frac{(s + 2)(s + 4)}{s(s + 1 + j\sqrt{3})(s + 1 - j\sqrt{3})}$$

which has the partial-fraction expansion

$$\mathbf{F}(s) = \frac{K_0}{s} + \frac{K_1}{s + 1 + j\sqrt{3}} + \frac{K_1^*}{s + 1 - j\sqrt{3}}$$

To determine K_0, draw vectors in the s-plane from each zero to the pole at the origin, as well as from each of the other poles to this pole. The result is shown in Fig. 11.4. Thus,

$$K_0 = \frac{(2\underline{/0°})(4\underline{/0°})}{(2\underline{/60°})(2\underline{/-60°})} = 2$$

To determine K_1, draw vectors from each zero to the pole at $s = -1 - j\sqrt{3}$, as well as from each of the other poles. The resulting picture is shown in Fig. 11.5 and

$$K_1 = \frac{(2\underline{/-60°})(\sqrt{12}\underline{/-30°})}{(2\underline{/-120°})(2\sqrt{3}\underline{/-90°})} = 1\underline{/120°} = -\frac{1}{2} + j\frac{\sqrt{3}}{2} = a + jb$$

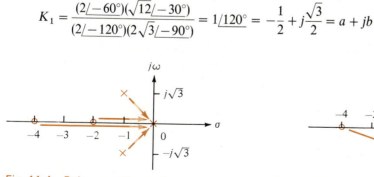

Fig. 11.4   Pole-zero plot used to determine K_0.

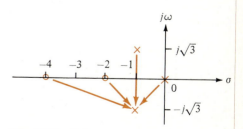

Fig. 11.5   Pole-zero plot used to determine K_1.

so

$$K_1^* = -\frac{1}{2} - j\frac{\sqrt{3}}{2} = a - jb$$

The resulting partial-fraction expansion

$$F(s) = \frac{2}{s} + \frac{-\frac{1}{2} + j\frac{\sqrt{3}}{2}}{s + 1 + j\sqrt{3}} + \frac{-\frac{1}{2} - j\frac{\sqrt{3}}{2}}{s + 1 - j\sqrt{3}} = \frac{2}{s} + \frac{-(s + 1)}{(s + 1)^2 + 3} + \frac{\sqrt{3}(\sqrt{3})}{(s + 1)^2 + 3}$$

and hence

$$f(t) = (2 - e^{-t}\cos\sqrt{3}t + \sqrt{3}e^{-t}\sin\sqrt{3}t)u(t)$$

11.3 APPLICATION TO CIRCUITS

Since the Laplace transform can be used to solve linear differential equations with constant coefficients, it can be employed to analyze linear, time-invariant circuits. One approach is to write the appropriate differential equations, and then take transforms. Even simpler is to take the transforms of individual components initially, and then apply Kirchhoff's laws and Ohm's law and proceed as before.

For a resistor having a value of R ohms, we know that

$$v(t) = Ri(t)$$

Taking the Laplace transform of both sides of this equation results in

$$\mathbf{V}(s) = R\mathbf{I}(s)$$

where $\mathbf{V}(s) = \mathcal{L}[v(t)]$ and $\mathbf{I}(s) = \mathcal{L}[i(t)]$. Defining the impedance $\mathbf{Z}_R(s)$ of the resistor to be the ratio of voltage transform to current transform, we get

$$\mathbf{Z}_R(s) = \frac{\mathbf{V}(s)}{\mathbf{I}(s)} = R$$

The circuit symbols of a resistor in the time domain and in the frequency (transform) domain are shown in Fig. 11.6(a) and (b), respectively.

For an inductor having a value of L henries,

$$v(t) = L\frac{di(t)}{dt}$$

(a) Time domain   (b) Frequency domain

Fig. 11.6   Resistor circuit symbols.

Taking the Laplace transform, we get

$$V(s) = L[sI(s) - i(0)] = LsI(s) - Li(0) \tag{11.8}$$

from which

$$I(s) = \frac{1}{Ls} V(s) + \frac{i(0)}{s} \tag{11.9}$$

For the case of zero initial conditions, $i(0) = 0$ and thus,

$$V(s) = LsI(s)$$

We then define the impedance $\mathbf{Z}_L(s)$ of the inductor to be the ratio of voltage transform to current transform when the initial current is zero. Thus,

$$\mathbf{Z}_L(s) = \frac{\mathbf{V}(s)}{\mathbf{I}(s)} = Ls$$

The time-domain circuit symbol for an inductor is shown in Fig. 11.7(a), while Fig. 11.7(b) shows the circuit symbol in the frequency domain when the initial current is zero. For the case that the initial current is not necessarily zero, the parallel connection shown in Fig. 11.7(c) models the frequency-domain description given by Equation (11.9). Note that if $i(0) = 0$, the model in Fig. 11.7(c) is equivalent to Fig. 11.7(b). Alternatively, the series connection shown in Fig. 11.7(d) also models an inductor in the frequency domain for the case that the initial current is not necessarily zero. This configuration arises from Equation (11.8).

For a capacitor having a value of C farads,

$$i(t) = C \frac{dv(t)}{dt}$$

so

$$\mathbf{I}(s) = C[s\mathbf{V}(s) - v(0)] = Cs\mathbf{V}(s) - Cv(0) \tag{11.10}$$

(a) Time domain

(b) Frequency domain—
zero initial current

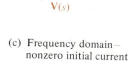
(c) Frequency domain—
nonzero initial current

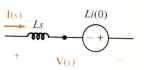
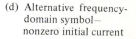
(d) Alternative frequency-
domain symbol—
nonzero initial current

Fig. 11.7 Inductor circuit symbols.

from which

$$V(s) = \frac{1}{Cs} I(s) + \frac{v(0)}{s} \qquad (11.11)$$

The impedance $\mathbf{Z}_C(s)$ of the capacitor (for zero initial voltage) is

$$\mathbf{Z}_C(s) = \frac{\mathbf{V}(s)}{\mathbf{I}(s)} = \frac{1}{Cs}$$

The circuit symbols for a capacitor in the time domain and the frequency domain, with zero and nonzero initial conditions, are shown in Fig. 11.8.

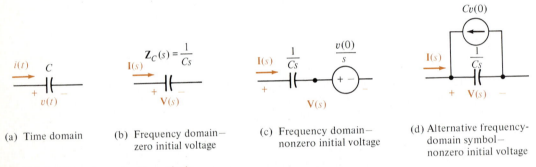

(a) Time domain   (b) Frequency domain—zero initial voltage   (c) Frequency domain—nonzero initial voltage   (d) Alternative frequency-domain symbol—nonzero initial voltage

Fig. 11.8 Capacitor circuit symbols.

Since we have the same expressions for the impedances of resistors, inductors, and capacitors as we had for the damped-sinusoidal case, we can use the same circuit analysis techniques—the difference being that we use the Laplace transforms of time functions rather than phasor representations.

In summary, an element (R, L, or C) can be modeled in the frequency domain by an impedance and an appropriate independent source. The relationship between voltage $\mathbf{V}(s)$, current $\mathbf{I}(s)$, and impedance $\mathbf{Z}(s)$ [or admittance $\mathbf{Y}(s)$] in each case is given by the general forms of Ohm's law:

$$\mathbf{V}(s) = \mathbf{Z}(s)\mathbf{I}(s) = \frac{\mathbf{I}(s)}{\mathbf{Y}(s)} \qquad \mathbf{I}(s) = \frac{\mathbf{V}(s)}{\mathbf{Z}(s)} = \mathbf{Y}(s)\mathbf{V}(s) \qquad \mathbf{Z}(s) = \frac{\mathbf{V}(s)}{\mathbf{I}(s)} = \frac{1}{\mathbf{Y}(s)}$$

EXAMPLE 11.17
Given that the series *RLC* circuit shown in Fig. 11.9(a) has zero initial conditions, let us find the step response $v(t)$. Figure 11.9(b) shows the circuit in the frequency domain. Of course, this circuit can be analyzed by using either mesh analysis or nodal

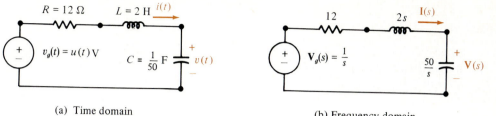

(a) Time domain

(b) Frequency domain

Fig. 11.9   A series *RLC* circuit.

analysis. However, even more simply, by voltage division we can write

$$\mathbf{V}(s) = \frac{50/s}{50/s + 2s + 12} \mathbf{V}_g(s) = \frac{50}{2s^2 + 12s + 50}\left(\frac{1}{s}\right)$$

or

$$\mathbf{V}(s) = \frac{25}{s(s^2 + 6s + 25)} = \frac{K_0}{s} + \mathbf{F}(s)$$

where

$$K_0 = s\mathbf{V}(s)\bigg|_{s=0} = \frac{25}{s^2 + 6s + 25}\bigg|_{s=0} = 1$$

Thus,

$$\mathbf{F}(s) = \mathbf{V}(s) - \frac{K_0}{s} = \frac{25}{s(s^2 + 6s + 25)} - \frac{1}{s} = \frac{-s - 6}{s^2 + 6s + 25}$$

Hence,

$$\mathbf{V}(s) = \frac{1}{s} - \frac{s + 6}{s^2 + 6s + 25} = \frac{1}{s} - \frac{s + 6}{(s + 3)^2 + 4^2}$$

$$= \frac{1}{s} - \frac{s + 3}{(s + 3)^2 + 4^2} - \frac{(3/4)(4)}{(s + 3)^2 + 4^2}$$

Therefore, from Table 11.1,

$$v(t) = u(t) - e^{-3t}\cos 4t\, u(t) - \tfrac{3}{4}e^{-3t}\sin 4t\, u(t)$$
$$= [1 - e^{-3t}(\cos 4t + \tfrac{3}{4}\sin 4t)]u(t)\ \text{V}$$

and this is the complete response (i.e., forced and natural responses).

For a linear circuit with zero initial conditions, if the input is scaled by a constant, then the response is scaled by the same constant. Thus, the response to $v_g(t) = \tfrac{2}{5}u(t)$ is

$$\tfrac{2}{5}v(t) = \tfrac{2}{5}u(t) - \tfrac{2}{5}e^{-3t}\cos 4t\, u(t) - \tfrac{3}{10}e^{-3t}\sin 4t\, u(t)\ \text{V}$$

(see Example 6.5 on p. 297).

DRILL EXERCISE 11.15

Given that the series RLC circuit shown in Fig. 11.9 has zero initial conditions, find the step response $v(t)$ and $i(t)$ for the case that $R = 5\ \Omega$, $L = \frac{1}{2}$ H, and $C = \frac{1}{8}$ F.

Answer: $(1 - \frac{4}{3}e^{-2t} + \frac{1}{3}e^{-8t})u(t)$ V; $\frac{1}{3}(e^{-2t} - e^{-8t})u(t)$ A

Having analyzed a circuit with zero initial conditions, let us now consider the case of a circuit with nonzero initial conditions.

EXAMPLE 11.18

Suppose that we wish to find $v(t)$ for the circuit shown in Fig. 11.10(a) subject to the initial condition $v(0) = 2$ V. In the frequency domain, the circuit is as shown in Fig. 11.10(b). Note that the voltage (transform) $\mathbf{V}(s)$ that is to be determined is the voltage across the series combination of a 1-F capacitor and a voltage source having a value of $v(0)/s = 2/s$.

By KCL at the node labeled $\mathbf{V}_1(s)$,

$$\mathbf{I}(s) + 2\mathbf{I}(s) = \frac{\mathbf{V}_1(s) - \mathbf{V}(s)}{5}$$

from which

$$3\mathbf{I}(s) = 3\left[\frac{-4/s - \mathbf{V}_1(s)}{3}\right] = \frac{\mathbf{V}_1(s) - \mathbf{V}(s)}{5}$$

Simplifying this expression, we get

$$6\mathbf{V}_1(s) - \mathbf{V}(s) = \frac{-20}{s} \tag{11.12}$$

Again, by KCL,

$$\frac{\mathbf{V}_1(s) - \mathbf{V}(s)}{5} = \frac{\mathbf{V}(s) - 2/s}{1/s}$$

from which

$$\mathbf{V}_1(s) - (1 + 5s)\mathbf{V}(s) = -10 \tag{11.13}$$

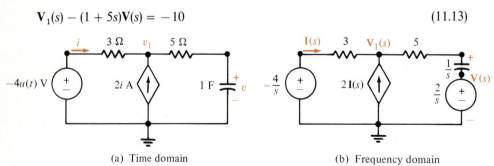

(a) Time domain   (b) Frequency domain

Fig. 11.10   Circuit with nonzero initial condition.

Combining Equation (11.12) and Equation (11.13) yields

$$\mathbf{V}(s) - 6(1 + 5s)\mathbf{V}(s) = \frac{20}{s} - 60 \qquad \Rightarrow \qquad \mathbf{V}(s) = \frac{2(s - 1/3)}{s(s + 1/6)} = \frac{-4}{s} + \frac{6}{s + 1/6}$$

Hence,

$$v(t) = -4u(t) + 6e^{-t/6}u(t) = (-4 + 6e^{-t/6})u(t) \text{ V}$$

(see Example 5.9 on p. 256).

(handwritten annotations in margin:)
$(-5 + 30s)V(s)$
$\frac{20}{s} - 60$ $20 - 60s$
$-30s - 5$ $-305^2/5s$

DRILL EXERCISE 11.16

For the parallel *RLC* circuit shown in Fig. DE11.16, suppose that $i(0) = -4$ A and $v(0) = 0$ V. Find $v(t)$ and $i(t)$ for the case that $R = 6\ \Omega$, $L = 7$ H, $C = \frac{1}{42}$ F, and $i_s(t) = 6u(t)$ A.

Answer: $84(e^{-t} - e^{-6t})u(t)$ V; $2(3 - 6e^{-t} + e^{-6t})u(t)$ A

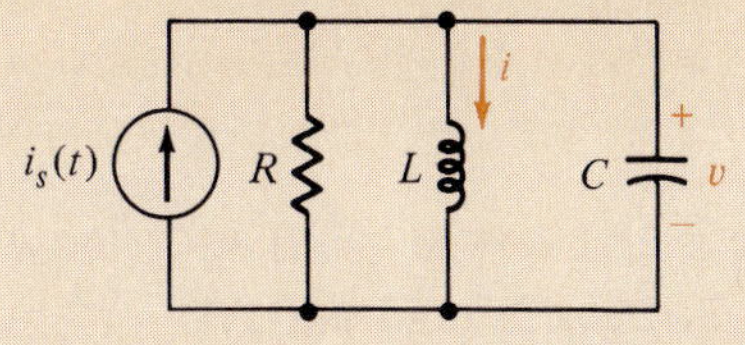

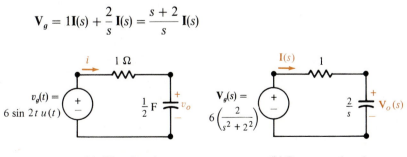

Fig. DE11.16

In Chapter 8 we saw how to find forced sinusoidal responses by using phasors. Let us now see an example of how to determine the complete response to a sinusoidal source (which is zero for $t < 0$) by using Laplace-transform techniques.

EXAMPLE 11.19

The circuit in Fig. 11.11(a) has a sinusoidal voltage excitation which begins at time $t = 0$. Figure 11.11(b) shows the frequency-domain representation of the circuit. By KVL,

$$\mathbf{V}_g = 1\mathbf{I}(s) + \frac{2}{s}\mathbf{I}(s) = \frac{s + 2}{s}\mathbf{I}(s)$$

(a) Time domain

(b) Frequency domain

Fig. 11.11   A sinusoidal circuit.

Thus,

$$\mathbf{I}(s) = \frac{s}{s+2}\mathbf{V}_g = \left(\frac{s}{s+2}\right)\left(\frac{12}{s^2+2^2}\right) = \frac{12s}{(s+2)(s^2+4)}$$

However,

$$\frac{12s}{(s+2)(s^2+4)} = \frac{K}{s+2} + \mathbf{F}(s) \quad \Rightarrow \quad K = \frac{12s}{s^2+4}\bigg|_{s=-2} = -3$$

Therefore,

$$\mathbf{F}(s) = \frac{12s}{(s+2)(s^2+4)} - \frac{K}{s+2} = \frac{12s}{(s+2)(s^2+4)} + \frac{3}{s+2} = \frac{3s+6}{s^2+4}$$

Hence,

$$\mathbf{I}(s) = -\frac{3}{s+2} + \frac{3s}{s^2+2^2} + \frac{3(2)}{s^2+2^2}$$

and the resulting current is

$$i(t) = -3e^{-2t}u(t) + 3\cos 2t\, u(t) + 3\sin 2t\, u(t) \text{ A}$$

This response is a complete response—the natural response is $i_n(t) = -3e^{-2t}u(t)$ A, and the forced response is $i_f(t) = 3\cos 2t\, u(t) + 3\sin 2t\, u(t) = 3\sqrt{2}\cos(2t - 45°)u(t)$ A.

If only the forced (steady-state) response is of interest,[†] for sinusoidal circuits Laplace-transform techniques can be avoided by taking the simpler phasor-analysis approach (see Example 8.6 on p. 367).

DRILL EXERCISE 11.17

For the series *RL* circuit shown in Fig. DE11.17, find the zero-state responses $i(t)$ and $v(t)$ given that $v_s(t) = (6\cos 2t - 8\sin 2t)u(t)$ V.

Answer: $(-2e^{-3t/2} + 2\cos 2t)u(t)$ A; $(6e^{-3t/2} - 8\sin 2t)u(t)$ V

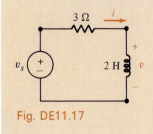

Fig. DE11.17

[†] The natural (transient) response is negligible after just a few time constants—the time constant is one-half second for this example.

Ramp, Step, and Impulse Functions

With the use of the Laplace transform, certain responses, such as impulse and ramp responses, can be obtained with relative ease directly rather than by first obtaining a step response and then differentiating it or integrating it.

EXAMPLE 11.20

Let us find the impulse responses $i_1(t)$ and $i_2(t)$ for the circuit shown in Fig. 11.12(a).

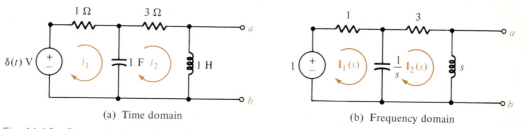

(a) Time domain   (b) Frequency domain

Fig. 11.12   Determination of impulse responses.

The frequency-domain representation of the given circuit is shown in Fig. 11.12(b). For mesh $\mathbf{I}_1(s)$, by KVL,

$$1\mathbf{I}_1(s) + \frac{1}{s}\left[\mathbf{I}_1(s) - \mathbf{I}_2(s)\right] = 1$$

from which

$$(s + 1)\mathbf{I}_1(s) - \mathbf{I}_2(s) = s \qquad (11.14)$$

For mesh $\mathbf{I}_2(s)$, by KVL,

$$\frac{1}{s}\left[\mathbf{I}_2(s) - \mathbf{I}_1(s)\right] + 3\mathbf{I}_2(s) + s\mathbf{I}_2(s) = 0$$

from which

$$\mathbf{I}_1(s) = (s^2 + 3s + 1)\mathbf{I}_2(s) \qquad (11.15)$$

Substituting this expression for $\mathbf{I}_1(s)$ into Equation (11.14) yields

$$(s + 1)(s^2 + 3s + 1)\mathbf{I}_2(s) - \mathbf{I}_2(s) = s$$

from which

$$\mathbf{I}_2(s) = \frac{1}{s^2 + 4s + 4} = \frac{1}{(s + 2)^2} \qquad \Rightarrow \qquad i_2(t) = te^{-2t}u(t) \text{ A}$$

In addition, from Equation (11.15)

$$\mathbf{I}_1(s) = \frac{s^2 + 3s + 1}{(s + 2)^2} = 1 - \frac{s + 3}{(s + 2)^2} = 1 - \frac{1}{s + 2} - \frac{1}{(s + 2)^2}$$

Thus,

$$i_1(t) = u(t) - e^{-2t}u(t) - te^{-2t}u(t) = \left[1 - (1 + t)e^{-2t}\right]u(t) \text{ A}$$

DRILL EXERCISE 11.18

For the circuit given in Fig. 11.12(a), change the value of the voltage source to $u(t)$ V and find the step responses $i_1(t)$ and $i_2(t)$ by using the results of Example 11.20 and the integration property of the Laplace transform.

Answer: $[\frac{1}{4} + (\frac{3}{4} + \frac{1}{2}t)e^{-2t}]u(t)$ A; $[\frac{1}{4} + (1 - \frac{1}{2}t)e^{-2t}]u(t)$ A

Having computed an impulse response directly, let us now determine the ramp response of a circuit.

EXAMPLE 11.21

Let us determine the ramp response $v_o(t)$ for the op-amp circuit shown in Fig. 11.13(a).

The frequency-domain representation of the given op-amp circuit is shown in Fig. 11.13(b). Since $r(t) = tu(t)$, then $\mathcal{L}[r(t)] = 1/s^2$. By KCL at node $\mathbf{V}_1(s)$,

$$\frac{\mathbf{V}_1(s) - 1/s^2}{1} + \frac{\mathbf{V}_1(s) - \mathbf{V}_o(s)}{1} + \frac{\mathbf{V}_1(s) - \mathbf{V}_o(s)}{1/s} = 0$$

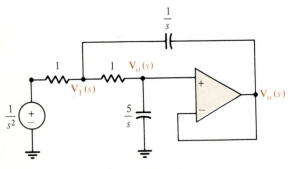

(a) Time domain

(b) Frequency domain

Fig. 11.13 Determination of ramp response.

from which

$$(s + 2)\mathbf{V}_1(s) - (s + 1)\mathbf{V}_o(s) = \frac{1}{s^2} \tag{11.16}$$

By voltage division, the voltage across the capacitor labeled $5/s$ is

$$\mathbf{V}_o(s) = \frac{5/s}{1 + 5/s}\,\mathbf{V}_1(s) = \frac{5}{s + 5}\,\mathbf{V}_1(s) \quad \Rightarrow \quad \mathbf{V}_1(s) = \frac{s + 5}{5}\,\mathbf{V}_o(s)$$

Substituting this expression for $\mathbf{V}_1(s)$ into Equation (11.16) yields

$$(s + 2)\frac{s + 5}{5}\,\mathbf{V}_o(s) - (s + 1)\mathbf{V}_o(s) = \frac{1}{s^2}$$

from which

$$\mathbf{V}_o(s) = \frac{5}{s^2(s^2 + 2s + 5)} = \frac{K_0}{s} + \frac{K_1}{s^2} + \mathbf{F}(s)$$

where

$$K_1 = \frac{5}{s^2 + 2s + 5}\bigg|_{s=0} = 1$$

$$K_0 = \frac{d}{ds}\left(\frac{5}{s^2 + 2s + 5}\right)\bigg|_{s=0} = \frac{-5(2s + 2)}{(s^2 + 2s + 5)^2}\bigg|_{s=0} = \frac{-10}{25} = -\frac{2}{5}$$

Thus,

$$\mathbf{F}(s) = \frac{5}{s^2(s^2 + 2s + 5)} + \frac{2/5}{s} - \frac{1}{s^2} = \frac{(2/5)(s + 2)}{s^2 + 2s + 5}$$

and

$$\mathbf{V}_o(s) = \frac{-2/5}{s} + \frac{1}{s^2} + \frac{(2/5)(s + 1)}{(s + 1)^2 + 2^2} + \frac{(1/5)(2)}{(s + 1)^2 + 2^2}$$

Hence, the ramp response is

$$v_o(t) = -\tfrac{2}{5}u(t) + tu(t) + \tfrac{2}{5}e^{-t}\cos 2t\,u(t) + \tfrac{1}{5}e^{-t}\sin 2t\,u(t)$$
$$= [-\tfrac{2}{5} + t + e^{-t}(\tfrac{2}{5}\cos 2t + \tfrac{1}{5}\sin 2t)]u(t)\ \text{V}$$

DRILL EXERCISE 11.19

For the op-amp circuit given in Fig. 11.13(a), change the value of the voltage source to $u(t)$ V and find the step response $v_o(t)$ by using the result of Example 11.21 and the differentiation property of the Laplace transform.

Answer: $[1 - e^{-t}(\cos 2t + \tfrac{1}{2}\sin 2t)]u(t)$ V

Thévenin's Theorem

In previous chapters, we have encountered Thévenin's theorem for resistive circuits, sinusoidal circuits, and damped-sinusoidal circuits. Now, with the use of the Laplace transform, we have the most general forms of this very important circuit theorem.

As we know, having identified a pair of terminals, a given circuit behaves as a single independent voltage source in series with an impedance. The problem of determining the Thévenin equivalent of a given circuit with respect to a pair of terminals amounts to finding the appropriate values of the independent voltage source and the impedance.

EXAMPLE 11.22

Figure 11.14(a) and (b) show a circuit in the time domain and the frequency domain, respectively. Let us determine the Thévenin equivalent of this circuit given that the initial conditions are zero.

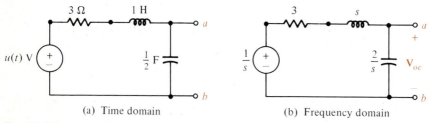

        (a) Time domain   (b) Frequency domain

Fig. 11.14   Given circuit.

First we find the open-circuit voltage V_{oc} between terminals a and b for the frequency-domain representation of the circuit [Fig. 11.14(b)].

By voltage division, we have that

$$V_{oc} = \frac{2/s}{2/s + s + 3}\left(\frac{1}{s}\right) = \frac{2}{s(s^2 + 3s + 2)} = \frac{2}{s(s+1)(s+2)} = \frac{1}{s} - \frac{2}{s+1} + \frac{1}{s+2}$$

Thus, the inverse Laplace transform of V_{oc} is

$$v_{oc}(t) = u(t) - 2e^{-t}u(t) + e^{-2t}u(t) = (1 - 2e^{-t} + e^{-2t})u(t) \text{ V}$$

To determine the Thévenin-equivalent (output) impedance Z_o, we set the independent voltage source in Fig. 11.14(b) to zero—that is, we replace the voltage source with a short circuit. The resulting circuit is shown in Fig. 11.15. Since this circuit does not contain a dependent source and the elements are connected in series and in parallel, we can appropriately combine impedances. By inspection we can write

$$Z_o = \frac{(2/s)(s+3)}{2/s + s + 3} = \frac{2(s+3)}{s^2 + 3s + 2}$$

Since impedance is a frequency-domain concept, we do not take the inverse Laplace transform of Z_o. Instead, we can "realize" or construct Z_o with an R, an L, and a C as shown in Fig. 11.16.

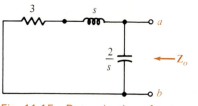

Fig. 11.15 Determination of output impedance Z_o.

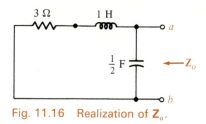

Fig. 11.16 Realization of Z_o.

The Thévenin equivalent of the given circuit is shown in the time domain in Fig. 11.17(a) and in the frequency domain in Fig. 11.17(b).

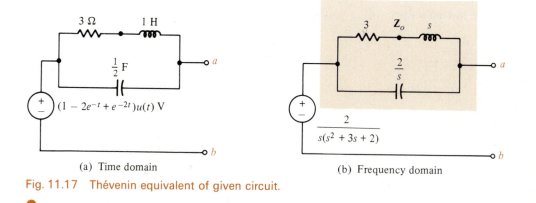

(a) Time domain

(b) Frequency domain

Fig. 11.17 Thévenin equivalent of given circuit.

DRILL EXERCISE 11.20

Find the Thévenin equivalent of the circuit given in Fig. 11.12 (p. 525).

Answer: $\dfrac{2}{(s+2)^2}; \dfrac{s(3s+4)}{(s+2)^2}$

11.4 APPLICATION TO LINEAR SYSTEMS

Suppose that the input to a linear system has a Laplace transform of $X(s)$, and suppose that the Laplace transform of the output, given that all the initial conditions are zero, is $Y(s)$. Then the **transfer function $H(s)$** of the system is defined to be

$$H(s) = \frac{Y(s)}{X(s)}$$

If the transfer function of a linear system is known, then when the input is specified, the output transform can be determined from the equation

$$\mathbf{Y}(s) = \mathbf{H}(s)\mathbf{X}(s)$$

Taking the inverse Laplace transform of $\mathbf{Y}(s)$ yields the corresponding output $y(t)$ in the time domain.

EXAMPLE 11.23

Given a simple low-pass filter with a voltage transfer function of

$$\mathbf{H}(s) = \frac{\mathbf{V}_2(s)}{\mathbf{V}_1(s)} = \frac{3}{s+3}$$

let us find the output voltage $v_2(t)$ given that the input voltage is $v_1(t) = 2e^{-3t}u(t)$ V.
Since

$$\mathbf{V}_1(s) = \mathcal{L}[2e^{-3t}u(t)] = \frac{2}{s+3}$$

then

$$\mathbf{V}_2(s) = \mathbf{H}(s)\mathbf{V}_1(s) = \left(\frac{3}{s+3}\right)\left(\frac{2}{s+3}\right) = \frac{6}{(s+3)^2}$$

and

$$v_2(t) = 6te^{-3t}u(t)\,\mathrm{V}$$

In this case, the forced and natural responses combine into the single term $6te^{-3t}u(t)$. This is a consequence of exciting the system at its pole; that is, the pole of $\mathbf{V}_1(s)$ is the same as the pole of $\mathbf{H}(s)$.

DRILL EXERCISE 11.21

A simple high-pass filter has a voltage transfer function of

$$\mathbf{H}(s) = \frac{\mathbf{V}_2(s)}{\mathbf{V}_1(s)} = \frac{3s}{s+3}$$

Find the output voltage $v_2(t)$ given that the input voltage is $v_1(t) = 2e^{-3t}u(t)$ V.
Answer: $6(1 - 3t)e^{-3t}u(t)$ V.

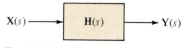

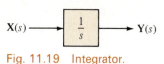

Fig. 11.18   Linear system.   Fig. 11.19   Integrator.

Let us represent a linear system (in the frequency domain) as shown in Fig. 11.18. Here $\mathbf{X}(s)$ is the Laplace transform of the input $x(t)$, and $\mathbf{Y}(s)$ is the Laplace transform of the output $y(t)$. The transfer function for the system is $\mathbf{H}(s) = \mathbf{Y}(s)/\mathbf{X}(s)$. One simple but important system is shown in Fig. 11.19. Since

$$\mathbf{Y}(s) = \frac{1}{s}\mathbf{X}(s) \quad \text{then} \quad y(t) = \mathscr{L}^{-1}\left[\frac{1}{s}\mathbf{X}(s)\right] = \int_0^t x(t)\,dt$$

That is, the output is the integral of the input. Thus, this system is an **integrator**.

By using integrators and two other simple components, we can "build" or "simulate" transfer functions and thereby simulate more complex linear systems. This is the essence of the analog computer.

One of the components is a **scaler**, or **amplifier**, whose output is the input multiplied by a constant A. This device is designated as shown in Fig. 11.20. The other component is an **adder**, whose output is the sum of its inputs. For the case of three inputs, an adder is depicted as in Fig. 11.21.

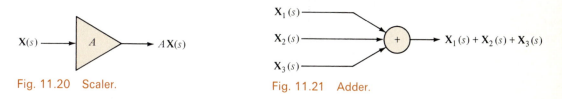

Fig. 11.20   Scaler.   Fig. 11.21   Adder.

One way to simulate the transfer function

$$\mathbf{H}(s) = \frac{\mathbf{Y}(s)}{\mathbf{X}(s)} = \frac{a_n s^n + a_{n-1}s^{n-1} + \cdots + a_1 s + a_0}{s^n + b_{n-1}s^{n-1} + \cdots + b_1 s + b_0}, \tag{11.17}$$

can be accomplished as follows:

Divide numerator and denominator of the transfer function by s^n. This yields

$$\frac{\mathbf{Y}(s)}{\mathbf{X}(s)} = \frac{a_n + a_{n-1}/s + \cdots + a_1/s^{n-1} + a_0/s^n}{1 + b_{n-1}/s + \cdots + b_1/s^{n-1} + b_0/s^n}$$

From this expression, we can write

$$\mathbf{Y}(s) = a_n\mathbf{X}(s) + \frac{a_{n-1}}{s}\mathbf{X}(s) + \cdots + \frac{a_1}{s^{n-1}}\mathbf{X}(s) + \frac{a_0}{s^n}\mathbf{X}(s)$$

$$- \frac{b_{n-1}}{s}\mathbf{Y}(s) - \cdots - \frac{b_1}{s^{n-1}}\mathbf{Y}(s) - \frac{b_0}{s^n}\mathbf{Y}(s)$$

and this can be realized by the diagram shown in Fig. 11.22.

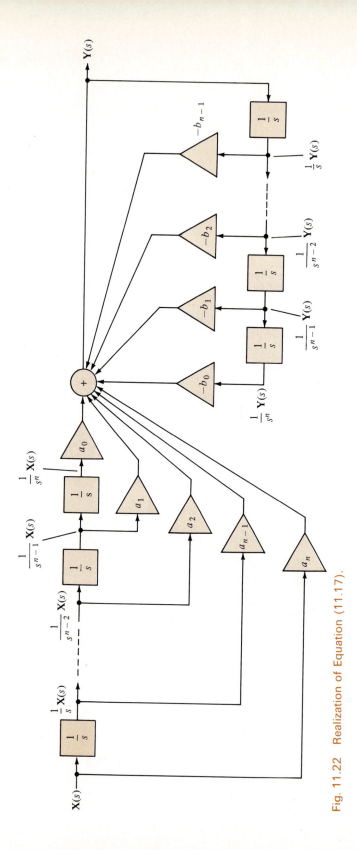

Fig. 11.22 Realization of Equation (11.17).

EXAMPLE 11.24
To simulate the transfer function

$$H(s) = \frac{4s^2 + 5s + 6}{s^2 + 2s + 3} \qquad (11.18)$$

first divide numerator and denominator by s^2. Thus,

$$\frac{Y(s)}{X(s)} = \frac{4 + 5/s + 6/s^2}{1 + 2/s + 3/s^2}$$

From this expression,

$$Y(s) = 4X(s) + \frac{5}{s}X(s) + \frac{6}{s^2}X(s) - \frac{2}{s}Y(s) - \frac{3}{s^2}Y(s)$$

Thus, the given transfer function can be simulated as shown in Fig. 11.23.

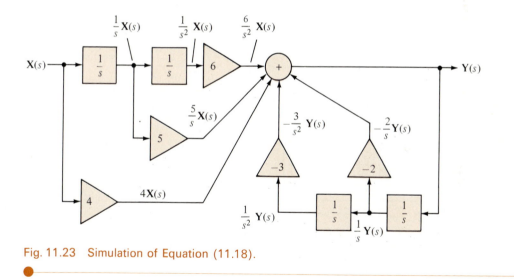

Fig. 11.23   Simulation of Equation (11.18).

Although Fig. 11.22 describes an obvious realization of the transfer function given by Equation (11.17), it is not the most economical realization. Specifically, the realization of Equation (11.17) shown in Fig. 11.24 employs n integrators, whereas Fig. 11.22 utilizes $2n$ integrators.

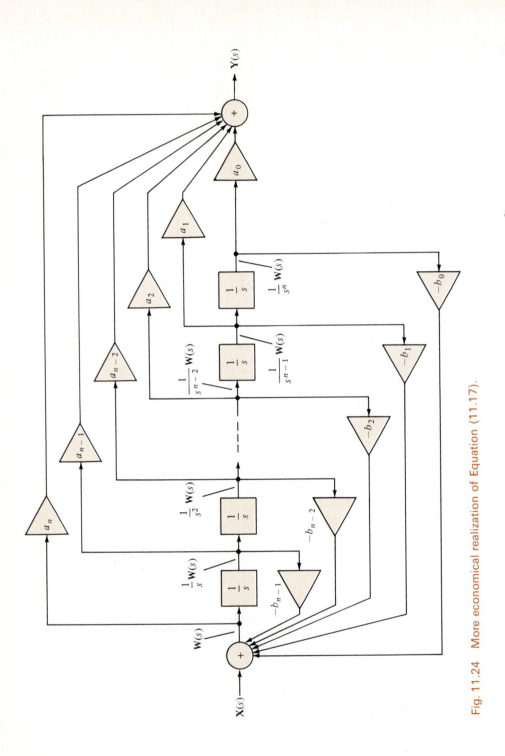

Fig. 11.24 More economical realization of Equation (11.17).

EXAMPLE 11.25

For the transfer function given by Equation (11.18), with respect to Fig. 11.24 we can identify the following:

$$n = 2 \qquad a_0 = 6 \qquad a_1 = 5 \qquad a_2 = 4 \qquad b_0 = 3 \qquad b_1 = 2$$

Therefore, Fig. 11.24 reduces to the diagram shown in Fig. 11.25.

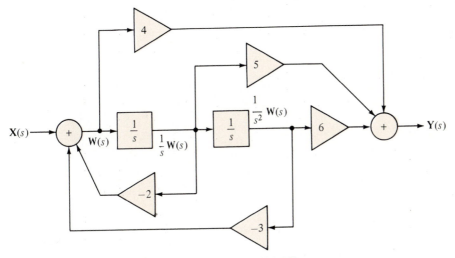

Fig. 11.25   Alternative simulation of Equation (11.18).

From Fig. 11.25, we have that

$$\mathbf{W}(s) = \mathbf{X}(s) - \frac{2}{s}\mathbf{W}(s) - \frac{3}{s^2}\mathbf{W}(s)$$

from which

$$\mathbf{W}(s) = \frac{s^2}{s^2 + 2s + 3}\mathbf{X}(s)$$

From Fig. 11.25, we also have that

$$\mathbf{Y}(s) = 4\mathbf{W}(s) + \frac{5}{s}\mathbf{W}(s) + \frac{6}{s^2}\mathbf{W}(s) = \frac{4s^2 + 5s + 6}{s^2}\mathbf{W}(s)$$

$$= \frac{4s^2 + 5s + 6}{s^2}\left[\frac{s^2}{s^2 + 2s + 3}\mathbf{X}(s)\right] = \frac{4s^2 + 5s + 6}{s^2 + 2s + 3}\mathbf{X}(s)$$

Thus, for Fig. 11.25,

$$\frac{\mathbf{Y}(s)}{\mathbf{X}(s)} = \frac{4s^2 + 5s + 6}{s^2 + 2s + 3}$$

Consider the linear system shown in Fig. 11.26. When the system is in the zero state,

$$\mathbf{Y}(s) = \mathbf{H}(s)\mathbf{X}(s) \tag{11.19}$$

For the case that the input is $x(t) = \delta(t)$, then $\mathbf{X}(s) = 1$ and

$$\mathbf{Y}(s) = \mathbf{H}(s)$$

Thus, the response to the unit impulse function $\delta(t)$ is

$$y(t) = \mathscr{L}^{-1}[\mathbf{Y}(s)] = \mathscr{L}^{-1}[\mathbf{H}(s)]$$

Define the function $h(t)$ by

$$h(t) = \mathscr{L}^{-1}[\mathbf{H}(s)]$$

For this reason, $h(t)$ is called the **impulse response** of the system.

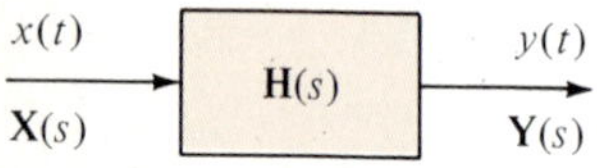

Fig. 11.26 Linear system.

The relationship between input and output transforms is a simple one: it is given by Equation (11.19). But what is the relationship between the input $x(t)$ and the output $y(t)$? It is not true that the output is the product of the input and impulse response; that is,

$$y(t) \neq h(t)x(t)$$

as you may be tempted to believe. The relationship is much more complicated. Let us now determine what the relationship is between $x(t)$, $y(t)$, and $h(t)$.

Since

$$\mathbf{X}(s) = \int_0^\infty x(t)e^{-st}\,dt = \int_0^\infty x(\tau)e^{-s\tau}\,d\tau$$

and

$$\mathbf{H}(s) = \int_0^\infty h(t)e^{-st}\,dt = \int_0^\infty h(\lambda)e^{-s\lambda}\,d\lambda$$

then from Equation (11.19), we have that

$$\mathbf{Y}(s) = \mathbf{H}(s)\int_0^\infty x(\tau)e^{-s\tau}\,d\tau = \int_0^\infty x(\tau)e^{-s\tau}\mathbf{H}(s)\,d\tau$$

$$= \int_0^\infty x(\tau)e^{-s\tau}\left[\int_0^\infty h(\lambda)e^{-s\lambda}\,d\lambda\right]d\tau = \int_0^\infty x(\tau)\left[\int_0^\infty h(\lambda)e^{-s(\lambda+\tau)}\,d\lambda\right]d\tau$$

In evaluating the integral in the brackets in the last term, define $t = \lambda + \tau$. Then $dt = d\lambda$ and $\lambda = t - \tau$. Furthermore, $\lambda = 0 \Rightarrow t = \tau$, while $\lambda = \infty \Rightarrow t = \infty$. Therefore, changing variables we get

$$\mathbf{Y}(s) = \int_0^\infty x(\tau) \left[\int_\tau^\infty h(t - \tau)e^{-st}\, dt \right] d\tau \tag{11.20}$$

The use of the Laplace transform implies that an input $x(t) = 0$ for $t < 0$. For a physical system, the resulting output must also have the property that it is $y(t) = 0$ for $t < 0$. (Such systems are said to be **causal**.) In particular, for a causal system since $\delta(t) = 0$ for $t < 0$, the response to the input $x(t) = \delta(t)$ must be zero for $t < 0$—that is, $h(t) = 0$ for $t < 0$.

As a consequence of this, $h(t - \tau) = 0$ for $t - \tau < 0$ (or $t < \tau$). Since τ varies between 0 and ∞, then

$$\int_0^\infty h(t - \tau)e^{-st}\, dt = \int_0^\tau h(t - \tau)e^{-st}\, dt + \int_\tau^\infty h(t - \tau)e^{-st}\, dt$$

$$= 0 + \int_\tau^\infty h(t - \tau)e^{-st}\, dt$$

Hence, Equation (11.20) becomes

$$\mathbf{Y}(s) = \int_0^\infty x(\tau) \left[\int_0^\infty h(t - \tau)e^{-st}\, dt \right] d\tau = \int_0^\infty \int_0^\infty x(\tau)h(t - \tau)e^{-st}\, d\tau\, dt$$

$$= \int_0^\infty \left[\int_0^\infty x(\tau)h(t - \tau)d\tau \right] e^{-st}\, dt = \int_0^\infty y(t)e^{-st}\, dt$$

Thus, we have that

$$y(t) = \int_0^\infty x(\tau)h(t - \tau)\, d\tau \tag{11.21}$$

Since $h(t - \tau) = 0$ for $t - \tau < 0$ (or $\tau > t$), we can rewrite Equation (11.21) as

$$y(t) = \int_0^t x(\tau)h(t - \tau)\, d\tau \tag{11.22}$$

When using the Laplace transform, it is assumed that a function $f(t) = 0$ for $t < 0$. Thus, interchanging the functions $x(t)$ and $h(t)$ results in the additional formula,

$$y(t) = \int_0^t h(\tau)x(t - \tau)\, d\tau \tag{11.23}$$

We refer to either Equation (11.22) or (11.23) as the **convolution integral**, and the process they describe is called **convolution**. Thus, we see that multiplication in the frequency domain corresponds to convolution in the time domain.

Evaluating the convolution integral is not complicated, but it can be quite subtle—it basically is a matter of bookkeeping. The form of bookkeeping, however, is often done in a graphical manner. The procedure will be illustrated with some examples.

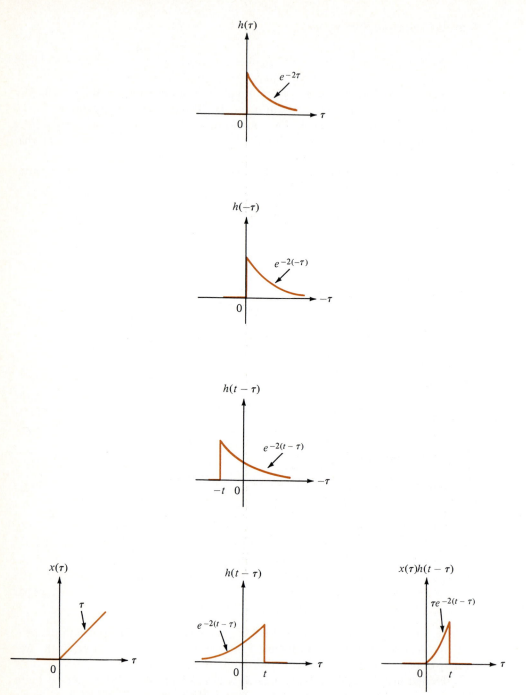

Fig. 11.27   Waveforms used for convolution.

EXAMPLE 11.26

The input $x(t) = tu(t)$ is applied to a system whose impulse response is $h(t) = e^{-2t}u(t)$. To determine the output by convolution, first sketch $x(\tau)$ versus τ and $h(\tau)$ versus τ. From $h(\tau)$ versus τ, we form $h(-\tau)$ versus $-\tau$, then $h(t - \tau)$ versus $-\tau$, and finally $h(t - \tau)$ versus τ. We then take the product $x(\tau)h(t - \tau)$ and integrate it with respect to τ to calculate $y(t)$. These steps are summarized in Fig. 11.27.

Therefore, for $0 \leq t < \infty$,

$$y(t) = \int_0^t x(\tau)h(t - \tau)\, d\tau = \int_0^t \tau e^{-2(t-\tau)}\, d\tau$$

$$= e^{-2t}\int_0^t \tau e^{2\tau}\, d\tau = e^{-2t}\left(\frac{1}{2}\tau e^{2\tau}\Big|_0^t - \int_0^t \frac{1}{2}e^{2\tau}\, d\tau\right)$$

$$= e^{-2t}\left(\frac{1}{2}te^{2t} - \frac{1}{4}e^{2t} + \frac{1}{4}\right) = \frac{t}{2} - \frac{1}{4} + \frac{1}{4}e^{-2t}$$

Since $y(t) = 0$ for $t < 0$ (the output is zero before the input is applied), we have that

$$y(t) = \left(\frac{t}{2} - \frac{1}{4} + \frac{1}{4}e^{-2t}\right)u(t)$$

which of course is the answer that is obtained when Laplace-transform techniques are used to determine $y(t)$.

DRILL EXERCISE 11.22

The impulse response of a system is $h(t) = 4e^{-5t}u(t)$. Use convolution to determine the output $y(t)$ when the input $x(t)$ is (a) $2e^{-3t}u(t)$ and (b) $2e^{-5t}u(t)$.
Answer: (a) $4(e^{-3t} - e^{-5t})u(t)$; (b) $8te^{-5t}u(t)$

In the preceding example, both the input and the impulse response are described by a single analytical expression for $0 \leq t < \infty$. When two or more expressions are required to describe either the input or the impulse response (or both), evaluating the convolution integral gets more involved.

EXAMPLE 11.27

Reconsider the system, whose impulse response is $h(t) = e^{-2t}u(t)$, given in Example 11.26. Suppose now that the input is changed to $x(t) = 2u(t) - 2u(t - 1)$. Then we have the function shown in Fig. 11.28. In this case, though, in evaluating the convolution integral the limits will not be the same for all values of t. In particular, for

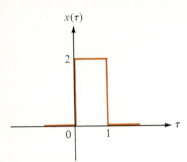

Fig. 11.28   Input to system.

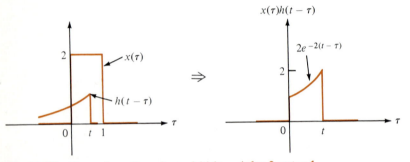

Fig. 11.29   Formation of product $x(\tau)h(t-\tau)$ for $0 \leq t < 1$.

$0 \leq t < 1$, we get the plots shown in Fig. 11.29. Thus,

$$y(t) = \int_0^t x(\tau)h(t-\tau)\,d\tau = \int_0^t 2e^{-2(t-\tau)}\,d\tau = 1 - e^{-2t}$$

However, for $1 \leq t < \infty$, we obtain the plots shown in Fig. 11.30. Therefore,

$$y(t) = \int_0^t x(\tau)h(t-\tau)\,d\tau = \int_0^1 2e^{-2(t-\tau)}\,d\tau = e^{-2(t-1)} - e^{-2t}$$

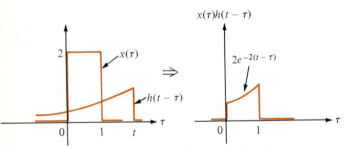

Fig. 11.30   Formation of product $x(\tau)h(t-\tau)$ for $1 \leq t < \infty$.

In summary, together with the fact that the output is zero before the input is applied, we have

$$y(t) = \begin{cases} 0 & \text{for} & -\infty < t < 0 \\ 1 - e^{-2t} & \text{for} & 0 \le t < 1 \\ e^{-2(t-1)} - e^{-2t} & \text{for} & 1 \le t < \infty \end{cases}$$

An alternative, but equivalent, expression for $y(t)$ is

$$y(t) = (1 - e^{-2t})u(t) - (1 - e^{-2(t-1)})u(t - 1)$$

This form for $y(t)$ is obtained directly when we solve the same problem with the use of Laplace transforms.

DRILL EXERCISE 11.23

The impulse response of a system is $h(t) = 4e^{-5t}u(t)$. Use convolution to determine the output $y(t)$ when the input is $x(t) = 2e^{-3t}[u(t) - u(t - 1)]$.
Answer: $4(e^{-3t} - e^{-5t})u(t) - 4(e^{-3t} - e^{-5t+2})u(t - 1)$

Let us now see the effect on the evaluation of the convolution integral when an input waveform is time delayed.

EXAMPLE 11.28

Again consider the system given in Example 11.26—that is, a system whose impulse response is $h(t) = e^{-2t}u(t)$. Suppose that the input is $x(t) = 2u(t - 1) - 2u(t - 2)$. For demonstration purposes, we shall find $y(t)$ by using the alternative form of the convolution integral. We get the functions shown in Fig. 11.31.

Thus, for $-1 \le t - 1 < 0$ (i.e., for $0 \le t < 1$),

$$x(t - \tau)h(\tau) = 0 \quad \Rightarrow \quad y(t) = \int_0^t x(t - \tau)h(\tau)\, d\tau = 0$$

For $0 \le t - 1 < 1$ (or $1 \le t < 2$), we obtain the plots shown in Fig. 11.32. We therefore have

$$y(t) = \int_0^t x(t - \tau)h(\tau)\, d\tau = \int_0^{t-1} 2e^{-2\tau}\, d\tau = 1 - e^{-2(t-1)}$$

For $1 \le t - 1 < \infty$ (or $2 \le t < \infty$), the plots are as shown in Fig. 11.33. Hence,

$$y(t) = \int_0^t x(t - \tau)h(\tau)\, d\tau = \int_{t-2}^{t-1} 2e^{-2\tau}\, d\tau = e^{-2(t-2)} - e^{-2(t-1)}$$

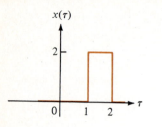

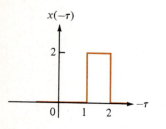

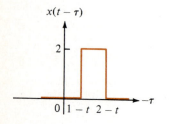

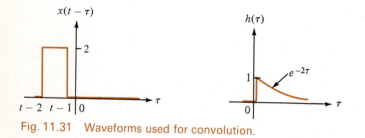

Fig. 11.31   Waveforms used for convolution.

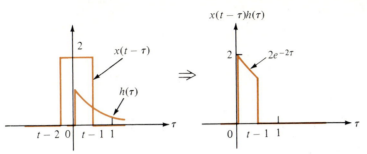

Fig. 11.32   Formation of product $x(t - \tau)h(\tau)$ for $1 \leq t < 2$.

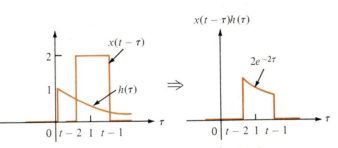

Fig. 11.33   Formation of product $x(t - \tau)h(\tau)$ for $2 \leq t < \infty$.

and therefore

$$y(t) = \begin{cases} 0 & \text{for} \quad -\infty < t < 1 \\ 1 - e^{-2(t-1)} & \text{for} \quad 1 \leq t < 2 \\ e^{-2(t-2)} - e^{-2(t-1)} & \text{for} \quad 2 \leq t < \infty \end{cases}$$

which can also be written in a single expression as

$$y(t) = (1 - e^{-2(t-1)})u(t - 1) - (1 - e^{-2(t-2)})u(t - 2)$$

Note that this response is equal to the response obtained in Example 11.27 delayed by 1 second. This is due to the fact that the system is time-invariant and the present input is the previous input delayed by 1 second. Thus we could have determined this response simply by inspection.

DRILL EXERCISE 11.24

The impulse response of a linear system is $h(t) = 4e^{-3t}u(t)$. Use convolution to determine the output $y(t)$ when the input is $x(t) = 2e^{-3t}[u(t - 1) - u(t - 2)]$.
Answer: $8(t - 1)e^{-3t}u(t - 1) - 8(t - 2)e^{-3t}u(t - 2)$

● SUMMARY

1. The Laplace transform is a linear transformation that can be used to solve linear differential equations and analyze linear circuits.

2. The inverse Laplace transform can be found by using a table of transforms and various transform properties, as well as partial-fraction expansions.

3. The impedance of an R-ohm resistor is R, of an L-henry inductor is Ls, and of a C-farad capacitor is $1/Cs$.

4. An inductor (or a capacitor) with a nonzero initial condition can be modeled by an independent source and an inductor (or capacitor) with a zero initial condition.

5. Circuit analysis using Laplace transforms results in complete (both forced and natural) responses.

6. Certain transfer functions can be simulated by using three types of devices: adders, scalers, and integrators.

7. Multiplication in the frequency domain corresponds to convolution in the time domain.

● PROBLEMS FOR CHAPTER 11

11.1 Find the Laplace transform of each of the following functions:
(a) $(2e^{-8t} - e^{-2t})u(t)$
(b) $(6 + 2e^{-6t} - 12e^{-t})u(t)$
(c) $(2 + 3t)e^{-2t}u(t)$
(d) $(\cos 4t - \sin 4t)e^{-3t}u(t)$

11.2 Find the Laplace transform of each of the following functions:
(a) $te^{-t}u(t - a)$
(b) $(t - a)e^{-\alpha(t-a)}u(t - a)$
(c) $\delta(t) + (a - b)e^{-bt}u(t)$
(d) $(t^3 + 1)e^{-2t}u(t)$

11.3 Repeat Problem 11.2 for the following:
(a) $\sin(\beta t - \phi)u(t)$
(b) $\cos(\beta t - \phi)u(t)$
(c) $e^{-\alpha t}\sin(\beta t - \phi)u(t)$
(d) $e^{-\alpha t}\cos(\beta t - \phi)u(t)$

11.4 Repeat Problem 11.2 for the following:
(a) $\cos(t - \pi/4)u(t - \pi/4)$
(b) $\cos(t - \pi/4)u(t)$
(c) $\sin t[u(t) - u(t - 2\pi)]$
(d) $\sin t[u(t) - u(t - \pi)]$

11.5 Find the Laplace transform of $|\sin \pi t|u(t)$.

11.6 Find the Laplace transform of the function shown in Fig. P11.6.

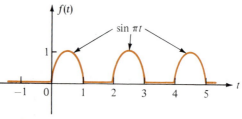

Fig. P11.6

11.7 Find the Laplace transform of the function shown in Fig. P11.7.

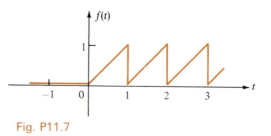

Fig. P11.7

11.8 Find the Laplace transform of each of the following functions:
(a) $\cos \alpha t \cos \beta t \, u(t)$
(b) $\sin \alpha t \cos \beta t \, u(t)$

11.9 Find the Laplace transform of each of the following functions:
(a) $\cos^2 \beta t \, u(t)$
(b) $\sin^2 \beta t \, u(t)$

11.10 Find the Laplace transform of each of the following functions:
(a) $(A_1 te^{-\alpha t} + A_2 e^{-\alpha t})u(t)$
(b) $(A_1 \cos \beta t + A_2 \sin \beta t)u(t)$
(c) $e^{-\alpha t}(A_1 \cos \beta t + A_2 \sin \beta t)u(t)$

11.11 Find the inverse Laplace transforms of the following functions:

(a) $\dfrac{6}{s(s + 1)(s + 3)}$

(b) $\dfrac{60(s + 4)}{s(s + 2)(s + 12)}$

11.12 Repeat Problem 11.11 for the following:

(a) $\dfrac{s + a}{s + b}$ (b) $\dfrac{s}{s + b}$

(c) $\dfrac{se^{-as}}{s + b}$ (d) $\dfrac{(s + a)e^{-as}}{s + b}$

11.13 Repeat Problem 11.11 for the following:

(a) $\dfrac{12s}{(s + 3)(s^2 + 9)}$ (b) $\dfrac{4(s^2 + 1)}{s(s^2 + 4)}$

(c) $\dfrac{20s}{(s^2 + 4)(s^2 + 3s + 2)}$

11.14 Repeat Problem 11.11 for the following:

(a) $\dfrac{6(s + 1)^3}{s^4}$ (b) $\dfrac{(s + 2)(s + 3)}{s(s + 1)^2}$

(c) $\dfrac{4(1 - e^{-2s})}{s^2(s + 2)}$

11.15 Use Laplace transforms to solve the differential equation

$$\frac{d^2x}{dt^2} + 7\frac{dx}{dt} + 6x = 36u(t)$$

subject to the initial conditions $x(0) = -4$ and $dx(0)/dt = 0$.

11.16 Repeat Problem 11.15 for

$$\frac{d^2x}{dt^2} + 3\frac{dx}{dt} + 2x = 20\cos 2t \, u(t)$$

subject to $x(0) = dx(0)/dt = 0$.

11.17 Use Laplace transforms to solve the simultaneous differential equations

$$\frac{dx}{dt} + 3x + y = 0$$

$$x - \frac{dy}{dt} - y = 0$$

subject to the initial conditions $x(0) = 1$ and $y(0) = 2$.

11.18 Repeat Problem 11.17 for

$$\frac{dx}{dt} + 3x + \frac{dy}{dt} = 30u(t)$$

$$\frac{dx}{dt} + 2\frac{dy}{dt} + 8y = 0$$

subject to $x(0) = y(0) = 0$.

11.19 Use the graphical evaluation of residues to find the inverse transforms of the functions given in Problem 11.11

11.20 Repeat Problem 11.19 for the functions given in Problem 11.13.

11.21 For the series *RLC* circuit shown in Fig. P11.21, find $v(t)$ and $i(t)$ given that $v(0) = 2$ V and $i(0) = 1$ A.

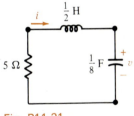

Fig. P11.21

11.22 For the parallel *RLC* circuit shown in Fig. P11.22, find $v(t)$ and $i(t)$ given that $v(0) = -0.14$ V and $i(0) = 1$ A.

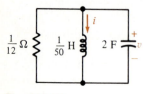

Fig. P11.22

11.23 For the series-parallel circuit shown in Fig. P11.23, find $v(t)$ and $i(t)$ given that $v(0) = 2$ V and $i(0) = 1$ A.

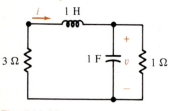

Fig. P11.23

11.24 Find the zero-state responses $v_C(t)$, $i_C(t)$, and $v_o(t)$ for the op-amp circuit shown in Fig. P11.24 given that $v_g(t) = u(t)$ V.

11.25 Repeat Problem 11.24 for the case that $v_g(t) = r(t)$ V.

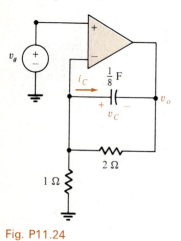

Fig. P11.24

11.26 Repeat Problem 11.24 for the case that $v_g(t) = e^{-2t}u(t)$ V.

11.27 Repeat Problem 11.24 for the case that $v_g(t) = (1 - e^{-4t})u(t)$ V.

11.28 Find the zero-state responses $v_C(t)$, $i_C(t)$, and $v_o(t)$ for the op-amp circuit shown in Fig. P11.28 given that $v_g(t) = u(t)$ V.

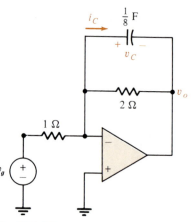

Fig. P11.28

11.29 Repeat Problem 11.28 for the case that $v_g(t) = \delta(t)$ V.

11.30 Repeat Problem 11.28 for the case that $v_g(t) = e^{-2t}u(t)$ V.

11.31 Repeat Problem 11.28 for the case that $v_g(t) = e^{-4t}u(t)$ V.

11.32 Find the step responses $v(t)$ and $i(t)$ for the circuit given in Fig. P5.3 (p. 268).

11.33 Find the step responses $i(t)$ and $v(t)$ for the circuit given in Fig. P5.8 (p. 268).

11.34 Find the step responses $v_C(t)$ and $v_o(t)$ for the op-amp circuit given in Fig. P5.10 (p. 268).

11.35 Find the step responses $v_C(t)$ and $v_o(t)$ for the op-amp circuit given in Fig. P5.12 (p. 268).

11.36 For the series *RLC* circuit given in Fig. 11.9 on p. 521, let $R = 2$ Ω, $L = 1$ H, and $C = 1$ F. Find $v(t)$ when $i(0) = \frac{1}{2}$ A and $v(0) = 0$ V.

11.37 For the op-amp circuit shown in Fig. P11.37, suppose that $v_C(0) = 4$ V. Find $v_o(t)$ given that
   (a) $v_g(t) = e^{-3t}u(t)$ V
   (b) $v_g(t) = \cos 2t\, u(t)$ V.

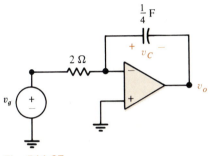

Fig. P11.37

11.38 Repeat Problem 11.37 for the circuit shown in Fig. P11.38.

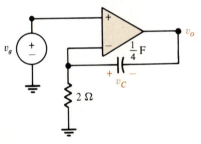

Fig. P11.38

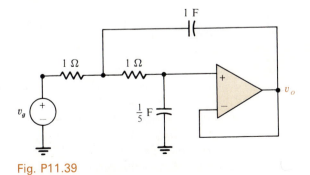

Fig. P11.39

11.39 Find the step response $v_o(t)$ for the op-amp circuit shown in Fig. P11.39.

11.40 For the op-amp circuit given in Fig. P11.39, change the value of the $\frac{1}{5}$-F capacitor to $\frac{25}{16}$ F, and find the zero-state response $v_o(t)$ for the case that $v_g(t) = 3u(t)$ V.

11.41 For the circuit shown in Fig. P11.41, find zero-state response $v(t)$ given that $R_1 = 1\,\Omega$, $R_2 = 3\,\Omega$, $L = 1$ H, $C = 1$ F, and $v_g(t) = u(t)$ V.

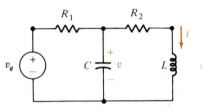

Fig. P11.41

11.42 Repeat Problem 11.41 for the case that $v_g(t) = \frac{4}{3}(1 - e^{-3t})u(t)$ V.

11.43 For the circuit shown in Fig. P11.41, find the zero-state response $i(t)$ given that $R_1 = 1\,\Omega$, $R_2 = 3.5\,\Omega$, $L = 1$ H, $C = 1$ F, and $v_g(t) = 3e^{-2t}u(t)$ V.

11.44 Repeat Problem 11.43 for the case that $R_1 = R_2 = 1\,\Omega$, $L = 1$ H, $C = 1$ F, and $v_g(t) = 2e^{-2t}u(t)$ V.

11.45 Find the zero-state response $v(t)$ for the RLC circuit shown in Fig. P11.45.

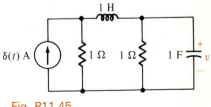

Fig. P11.45

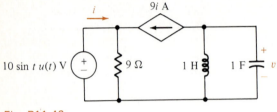

Fig. P11.46

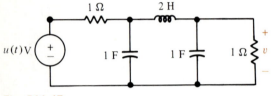

Fig. P11.47

11.46 Repeat Problem 11.45 for the circuit in Fig. P11.46.

11.47 Repeat Problem 11.45 for the circuit in Fig. P11.47.

11.48 Given that the capacitor is initially uncharged, determine the Thévenin equivalent of the circuit in Fig. P11.48.

11.49 The capacitors in the circuit shown in Fig. P11.49 are initially uncharged. Find the Thévenin equivalent of this circuit.

11.50 Repeat Problem 11.49 for the circuit shown in Fig. P11.50.

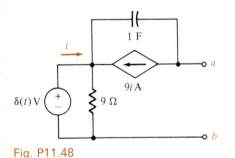

Fig. P11.48

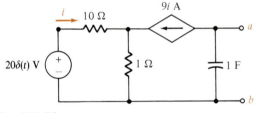

Fig. P11.50

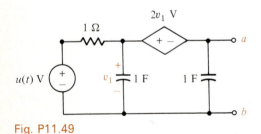

Fig. P11.49

11.51 Given that the transfer function of a linear system is $H(s) = 1/(s + 2)$, find the output $y(t)$ when the input $x(t)$ is
(a) $u(t)$
(b) $e^{-t}u(t)$
(c) $(1 - e^{-t})u(t)$
(d) $e^{-2t}u(t)$

11.52 Repeat Problem 11.51 for the case that $H(s) = s/(s + 2)$.

11.53 Given that $H(s) = (s - 1)/(s + 10)$ is the transfer function of a linear system, find the input $x(t)$ when the output $y(t)$ is

(a) $(-1 + 2e^{-t})u(t)$
(b) $(-2e^{-t} + 3e^{-2t})u(t)$
(c) $(1 - 11t)e^{-10t}u(t)$
(d) $(1 - 2t)e^{-t}u(t)$

11.54 Given that the input to a linear system is $x(t) = e^{-t}u(t)$, find the transfer function $\mathbf{H}(s)$ when the output $y(t)$ is

(a) $e^{-2t}u(t)$
(b) $\sin t\, u(t)$
(c) $e^{-t}\sin t\, u(t)$
(d) $te^{-t}u(t)$
(e) $(e^{-t} - e^{-2t})u(t)$

11.55 Repeat Problem 11.54 for the case that $x(t) = \cos t\, u(t)$.

11.56 Using integrators, amplifiers, and adder(s), simulate the transfer function

$$\mathbf{H}(s) = \frac{6s}{(s + 3)(s^2 + 9)}$$

in the form of (a) Fig. 11.22 on p. 532 and (b) Fig. 11.24 on p. 534.

11.57 Repeat Problem 11.56 for

$$\mathbf{H}(s) = \frac{12(s + 4)}{s(s + 2)(s + 12)}$$

11.58 Find the transfer function of the system shown in Fig. P11.58.

11.59 Find the transfer function of the system shown in Fig. P11.59.

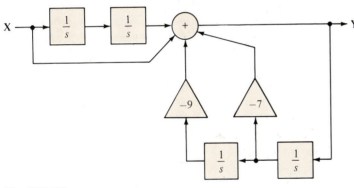

Fig. P11.58

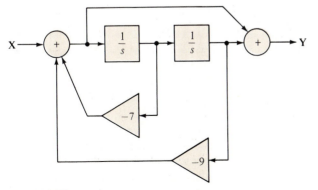

Fig. P11.59

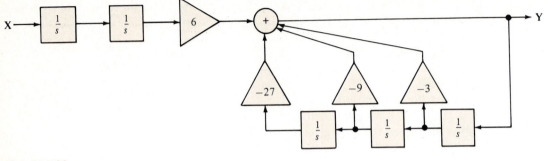

Fig. P11.60

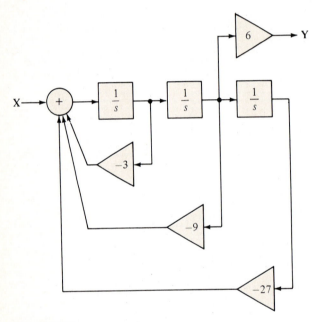

Fig. P11.61

11.60 Find the transfer function of the system shown in Fig. P11.60.

11.61 Find the transfer function of the system shown in Fig. P11.61.

11.62 A system has the transfer function

$$H(s) = \frac{s(s + 1)}{(s + 2)(s + 3)}$$

Find the input $x(t)$ that will result in the output

$$y(t) = e^{-t}u(t) - e^{-(t-2)}u(t - 2)$$

11.63 A system whose impulse response is $h(t) = \delta(t) - 11e^{-10t}u(t)$ has an output of $y(t) = (1 - 11t)e^{-10t}u(t)$. Find the input $x(t)$.

11.64 Find the impulse response of the system whose output is $y(t) = e^{-t}u(t)$ when the input is $x(t) = e^{-2t}u(t)$.

11.65 Use convolution to determine the output of a system whose impulse response is $h(t) = e^{-2t}u(t)$ and whose input is (a) $x(t) = e^{-t}u(t)$ and (b) $x(t) = 2u(t) - 2u(t - 1)$.

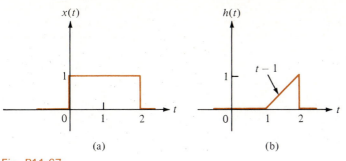

Fig. P11.67

11.66 Use convolution to find $y(t)$ when $h(t) = e^{-10t}u(t)$ and $x(t) = \delta(t) - 11e^{-10t}u(t)$.

11.67 Repeat Problem 11.66 for the functions shown in Fig. P11.67.

11.68 Repeat Problem 11.66 for
 (a) $h(t) = e^{-t}u(t)$, $x(t) = (1 - e^{-t})u(t)$
 (b) $h(t) = e^{-at}u(t)$, $x(t) = 2e^{-at}u(t)$.

11.69 Repeat Problem 11.66 for $h(t) = 2u(t) - 2u(t - 2)$ and $x(t) = \delta(t - 1) - \delta(t - 2)$.

11.70 Repeat Problem 11.66 for $h(t) = u(t) - 2u(t - 1) + u(t - 2)$ and $x(t) = 2u(t - 1) - 2u(t - 2)$.

CHAPTER **12**

Two-Port Networks

● **INTRODUCTION**

With the exception of the operational amplifier, we have been dealing almost exclusively with two-terminal circuit elements such as resistors, inductors, capacitors, and voltage and current sources. In this chapter we consider a new circuit element, the transformer, which is a four-terminal device that consists, in essence, of two inductors placed in physical proximity.

Transformers come in various sizes and have a variety of uses. Relatively small transformers are used in radios and televisions to couple amplifier stages, while larger transformers are used in the power-supply sections of these and numerous types of electronic equipment. Large, massive transformers are employed by electric utilities in the distribution of electric power.

Since a pair of terminals can be thought of as a "port," a four-terminal device or circuit is often referred to as a "two-port" network. Just as we could model a one-port network which contains no independent source as an impedance (or admittance), so can we characterize and model two-port networks—including the special case of a transformer.

12.1 TRANSFORMERS

We know that a current i flowing through a coil produces a magnetic field around the coil. If the current is time-varying, then so will be the resulting magnetic field. This magnetic field passes through the coil and in turn induces a voltage v across it.

The relationship between the voltage and the current is the familiar $v = L\,di/dt$, where L is the inductance of the coil. If there is a second coil near the first coil, the magnetic field also passes through the second coil and consequently induces a voltage across it as well. Under this circumstance, we say that the two coils are **magnetically coupled**.

Specifically, let us now consider the two inductors L_1 and L_2 shown in Fig. 12.1. For the case that $i_1 \neq 0$ and $i_2 = 0$, the voltage across inductor L_2 is

$$v_2(t) = M_{21}\frac{di_1(t)}{dt}$$

while if $i_1 = 0$ and $i_2 \neq 0$, then the voltage across inductor L_1 is

$$v_1(t) = M_{12}\frac{di_2(t)}{dt}$$

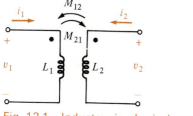

Fig. 12.1   Inductors in physical proximity.

We call M_{12} and M_{21} the **coefficients of mutual inductance** or **mutual inductance**, for short. As with the case of the **self-inductances** L_1 and L_2, the units of mutual inductance are henries. The dots shown in Fig. 12.1 indicate the phase relationship between the current in one inductor and the resulting voltage induced in the other inductor, and this can be stated as follows:

Given two magnetically coupled inductors, a current going into the dotted end of one results in an induced voltage across the second, where the dotted end of the second is positive ($+$). Alternatively, if the current in one inductor comes out of the dotted end, then the dotted end of the other is negative ($-$).

EXAMPLE 12.1

Given a pair of magnetically coupled inductors, suppose the current in one inductor is produced by a current source and the second inductor has no current through it. Then the voltage induced across the second inductor due to the current in the first inductor is depicted by the four cases shown in Fig. 12.2.

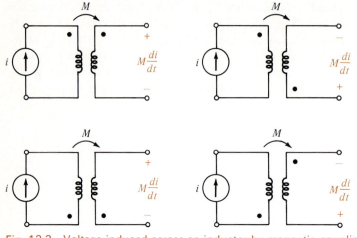

Fig. 12.2   Voltage induced across an inductor by magnetic coupling.

Returning now to the original pair of magnetically coupled inductors L_1 and L_2, having mutual inductances M_{12} and M_{21} (see Fig. 12.1), the general case is to have nonzero currents i_1 and i_2. By the principle of superposition, we then have

$$v_1(t) = L_1 \frac{di_1(t)}{dt} + M_{12} \frac{di_2(t)}{dt} \quad \text{and} \quad v_2(t) = M_{21} \frac{di_1(t)}{dt} + L_2 \frac{di_2(t)}{dt}$$

Although L_1 and L_2 need not be the same, we shall now see that $M_{12} = M_{21}$.

Suppose that the currents $i_1(t)$ and $i_2(t)$ are zero for $t < 0$. What is the energy required to bring these two currents, respectively, up to the positive constant values I_1 and I_2? There is more than one way to calculate this energy. One way is to have $i_1(t)$ go from 0 to I_1 between times $t = 0$ and $t = t_1$ while $i_2(t)$ remains at zero, and then have $i_2(t)$ go from 0 to I_2 between times $t = t_1$ and $t = t_2$ while $i_1(t)$ remains at I_1. These conditions are shown pictorially in Fig. 12.3.

The amount of energy required to reach this state is

$$w = \int_0^{t_2} v_1 i_1 \, dt + \int_0^{t_2} v_2 i_2 \, dt$$

$$= \int_0^{t_1} v_1 i_1 \, dt + \int_{t_1}^{t_2} v_1 i_1 \, dt + \int_0^{t_1} v_2 i_2 \, dt + \int_{t_1}^{t_2} v_2 i_2 \, dt$$

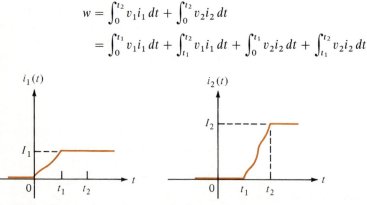

Fig. 12.3   Current through magnetically coupled inductors.

Looking at each of these four integrals individually, we find that the first integral is

$$\int_0^{t_1} v_1 i_1 \, dt = \int_0^{t_1} \left[L_1 \frac{di_1}{dt} + M_{12} \frac{di_2}{dt} \right] i_1 \, dt = \int_0^{t_1} L_1 i_1 \frac{di_1}{dt} \, dt + \int_0^{t_1} M_{12} i_1 \frac{di_2}{dt} \, dt$$

Since $di_2/dt = 0$ for $0 \le t < t_1$, then

$$\int_0^{t_1} v_1 i_1 \, dt = \int_{i_1(0)}^{i_1(t_1)} L_1 i_1 \, di_1 + \int_0^{t_1} 0 \, dt$$

But $i_1(0) = 0$ and $i_1(t_1) = I_1$. Thus,

$$\int_0^{t_1} v_1 i_1 \, dt = \int_0^{I_1} L_1 i_1 \, di_1 = \frac{1}{2} L_1 i_1^2 \Big|_0^{I_1} = \frac{1}{2} L_1 I_1^2$$

Since $i_2(t) = 0$ for $0 \le t \le t_1$, then the third integral is

$$\int_0^{t_1} v_2 i_2 \, dt = \int_0^{t_1} 0 \, dt = 0$$

The second integral is

$$\int_{t_1}^{t_2} v_1 i_1 \, dt = \int_{t_1}^{t_2} \left[L_1 \frac{di_1}{dt} + M_{12} \frac{di_2}{dt} \right] i_1 \, dt = \int_{t_1}^{t_2} L_1 i_1 \frac{di_1}{dt} \, dt + \int_{t_1}^{t_2} M_{12} i_1 \frac{di_2}{dt} \, dt$$

Since $di_1/dt = 0$ and $i_1(t) = I_1$ for $t_1 < t \le t_2$, then

$$\int_{t_1}^{t_2} v_1 i_1 \, dt = \int_{t_1}^{t_2} 0 \, dt + \int_{i_2(t_1)}^{i_2(t_2)} M_{12} I_1 \, di_2$$

But $i_2(t_1) = 0$ and $i_2(t_2) = I_2$, so

$$\int_{t_1}^{t_2} v_1 i_1 \, dt = \int_0^{I_2} M_{12} I_1 \, di_2 = M_{12} I_1 i_2 \Big|_0^{I_2} = M_{12} I_1 I_2$$

Finally, the fourth integral is

$$\int_{t_1}^{t_2} v_2 i_2 \, dt = \int_{t_1}^{t_2} \left[M_{21} \frac{di_1}{dt} + L_2 \frac{di_2}{dt} \right] i_2 \, dt = \int_{t_1}^{t_2} M_{21} i_2 \frac{di_1}{dt} \, dt + \int_{t_1}^{t_2} L_2 i_2 \frac{di_2}{dt} \, dt$$

Since $di_1/dt = 0$ for $t_1 < t \le t_2$, then

$$\int_{t_1}^{t_2} v_2 i_2 \, dt = \int_{t_1}^{t_2} 0 \, dt + \int_{i_2(t_1)}^{i_2(t_2)} L_2 i_2 \, di_2 = \int_0^{I_2} L_2 i_2 \, di_2 = \frac{1}{2} L_2 i_2^2 \Big|_0^{I_2} = \frac{1}{2} L_2 I_2^2$$

Summing these four integrals, we get

$$w = \tfrac{1}{2} L_1 I_1^2 + \tfrac{1}{2} L_2 I_2^2 + M_{12} I_1 I_2$$

An alternative way of obtaining the final currents, I_1 and I_2, is to first increase $i_2(t)$ and then $i_1(t)$. Doing so, as above, we get that the energy required is

$$w = \tfrac{1}{2} L_1 I_1^2 + \tfrac{1}{2} L_2 I_2^2 + M_{21} I_1 I_2$$

Since the preceding two expressions must be equal, we conclude that $M_{12} = M_{21}$, so we use the single symbol M for mutual inductance, as shown in Fig. 12.4.

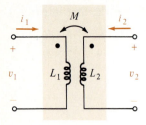

Fig. 12.4   Transformer.

We call such a four-terminal device a **transformer**. One side of the transformer is often called the **primary** winding and the other side is the **secondary** winding. The pair of equations describing this circuit element in the time domain is

$$v_1 = L_1 \frac{di_1}{dt} + M \frac{di_2}{dt}$$
$$v_2 = M \frac{di_1}{dt} + L_2 \frac{di_2}{dt}$$

(12.1)

In a manner similar to the energy discussion above, it can be shown that the energy stored in the transformer depicted in Fig. 12.4 is

$$w(t) = \tfrac{1}{2}L_1 i_1^2(t) + \tfrac{1}{2}L_2 i_2^2(t) + M i_1(t) i_2(t)$$

(12.2)

If the dot on either the primary or secondary (but not both) is moved to the other side, the expression becomes

$$w(t) = \tfrac{1}{2}L_1 i_1^2(t) + \tfrac{1}{2}L_2 i_2^2(t) - M i_1(t) i_2(t)$$

(12.3)

For an inductor L, in the time domain, $v = L\,di/dt$. For the case of sinusoids, $\mathbf{V} = j\omega L\mathbf{I}$, whereas, for the frequency domain in general (assuming zero initial conditions) $\mathbf{V} = Ls\mathbf{I}$. Just as for inductors, for the transformer we find, for the case of sinusoids, that

$$\mathbf{V}_1 = j\omega L_1 \mathbf{I}_1 + j\omega M \mathbf{I}_2$$
$$\mathbf{V}_2 = j\omega M \mathbf{I}_1 + j\omega L_2 \mathbf{I}_2$$

(12.4)

whereas, for the frequency domain in general (assuming zero initial conditions)

$$\mathbf{V}_1 = L_1 s\mathbf{I}_1 + Ms\mathbf{I}_2$$
$$\mathbf{V}_2 = Ms\mathbf{I}_1 + L_2 s\mathbf{I}_2$$

(12.5)

EXAMPLE 12.2
The sinusoidal circuit shown in Fig. 12.5(a) contains a transformer. The circuit is represented in the frequency domain in Fig. 12.5(b). Let us find $v_C(t)$ when $v(t) = 36\cos(3t - 60°)$ V. Let us also find the impedance seen by the source.

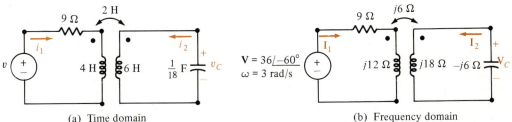

(a) Time domain   (b) Frequency domain

Fig. 12.5   Sinusoidal transformer circuit.

By KVL, we get

$$\mathbf{V} = 9\mathbf{I}_1 + j12\mathbf{I}_1 + j6\mathbf{I}_2 = (9 + j12)\mathbf{I}_1 + j6\mathbf{I}_2$$

(12.6)

and

$$0 = j6\mathbf{I}_1 + j18\mathbf{I}_2 - j6\mathbf{I}_2$$

(12.7)

From Equation (12.7),

$$\mathbf{I}_1 = -2\mathbf{I}_2$$

Substituting this into Equation (12.6) yields

$$\mathbf{V} = -2(9 + j12)\mathbf{I}_2 + j6\mathbf{I}_2 = -18\mathbf{I}_2 - j18\mathbf{I}_2 = -18(1 + j)\mathbf{I}_2$$

and thus

$$\mathbf{I}_2 = \frac{\mathbf{V}}{-18(1 + j)}$$

Since

$$\mathbf{V}_C = (-j6)(-\mathbf{I}_2) = \frac{j6\mathbf{V}}{-18(1 + j)}$$

$$= \frac{(6\underline{/90°})(36\underline{/-60°})}{(18\underline{/180°})(\sqrt{2}\underline{/45°})} = 6\sqrt{2}\underline{/-195°} = 8.49\underline{/165°}$$

then

$$v_C(t) = 8.49 \cos(3t + 165°) \text{ V}$$

For the more general frequency-domain representation shown in Fig. 12.6, by KVL,

$$\mathbf{V} = 9\mathbf{I}_1 + 4s\mathbf{I}_1 + 2s\mathbf{I}_2$$

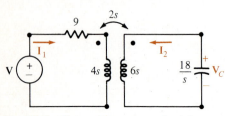

Fig. 12.6   General frequency-domain representation.

from which

$$\mathbf{V} = (9 + 4s)\mathbf{I}_1 + 2s\mathbf{I}_2 \qquad (12.8)$$

Also by KVL,

$$0 = 2s\mathbf{I}_1 + 6s\mathbf{I}_2 + \frac{18}{s}\mathbf{I}_2$$

from which

$$0 = s\mathbf{I}_1 + \left(3s + \frac{9}{s}\right)\mathbf{I}_2 \qquad (12.9)$$

From Equation (12.9),

$$\mathbf{I}_1 = -3\left(\frac{s^2 + 3}{s^2}\right)\mathbf{I}_2 \qquad (12.10)$$

Substituting Equation (12.10) into Equation (12.8) gives

$$\mathbf{V} = -3\left(\frac{s^2 + 3}{s^2}\right)(4s + 9)\mathbf{I}_2 + 2s\mathbf{I}_2$$

from which

$$\mathbf{V} = \frac{-(10s^3 + 27s^2 + 36s + 81)}{s^2}\mathbf{I}_2 \qquad (12.11)$$

Thus,

$$\mathbf{I}_2 = \frac{-s^2\mathbf{V}}{10s^3 + 27s^2 + 36s + 81}$$

From this equation and the fact that

$$V_C = \frac{18}{s}(-I_2)$$

we obtain the voltage transfer function

$$\frac{V_C}{V} = \frac{18s}{10s^3 + 27s^2 + 36s + 81}$$

Furthermore, from Equation (12.10),

$$I_2 = \frac{-s^2}{3(s^2 + 3)} I_1$$

which, when substituted into Equation (12.11) yields the impedance seen by the source

$$\frac{V}{I_1} = \frac{10s^3 + 27s^2 + 36s + 81}{3(s^2 + 3)}$$

DRILL EXERCISE 12.1

For the transformer circuit shown in Fig. DE12.1, suppose that $R_1 = 3\,\Omega$, $R_2 = 8\,\Omega$, $L_1 = 1$ H, $L_2 = 2$ H, and $M = 1$ H. Find $v_2(t)$ for the case that $v_g(t) = 3\cos 2t$ V.
Answer: $1.40\cos(2t + 35.54°)$ V

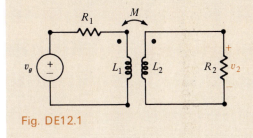

Fig. DE12.1

Although a transformer is in essence a pair of inductors that are magnetically coupled, when the bottom terminals are connected we can model such a device with circuit elements that are not magnetically coupled. Shown in Fig. 12.7 is a transformer

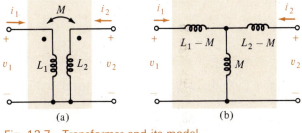

Fig. 12.7   Transformer and its model.

having mutual inductance M and a "T" connection of three inductors. Applying KVL to both circuits results in the same pair of equations—specifically, the equation-pair (12.1). Thus, the circuit given in (b) is a model of the transformer shown in (a). The "T-equivalent" circuit in (b) is only one possible model of a transformer.

EXAMPLE 12.3

For the transformer circuit shown in Fig. 12.5(a) on p. 557, $L_1 = 4$ H, $L_2 = 6$ H, and $M = 2$ H. Suppose that we connect the bottom two terminals. Since $L_1 - M = 2$ H and $L_2 - M = 4$ H, replacing the transformer by its T-equivalent, we get the time-domain circuit shown in Fig. 12.8(a). In the frequency domain the circuit is as shown in Fig. 12.8(b). By KVL,

$$\mathbf{V} = 9\mathbf{I}_1 + 2s\mathbf{I}_1 + 2s(\mathbf{I}_1 + \mathbf{I}_2) = (9 + 4s)\mathbf{I}_1 + 2s\mathbf{I}_2 \tag{12.8}$$

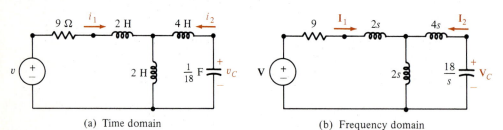

(a) Time domain   (b) Frequency domain

Fig. 12.8   Transformer circuit using T-equivalent circuit.

Also by KVL,

$$0 = 4s\mathbf{I}_2 + 2s(\mathbf{I}_1 + \mathbf{I}_2) + \frac{18}{s}\mathbf{I}_2$$

from which

$$0 = s\mathbf{I}_1 + \left(3s + \frac{9}{s}\right)\mathbf{I}_2 \tag{12.9}$$

Thus, we see that the circuit given in Fig. 12.8(b) yields Equations (12.8) and (12.9) just as the circuit in Fig. 12.6 did. However, for the circuit in Fig. 12.8(b), we do not have to be concerned with dots.

DRILL EXERCISE 12.2

Use the T-equivalent of a transformer to find $v_2(t)$ for the circuit shown in Fig. DE12.2 given that $v_g(t) = 3\cos 2t$ V.
Answer: $1.40\cos(2t + 35.54°)$ V

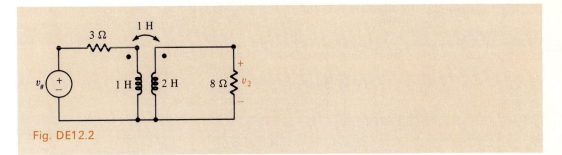

Fig. DE12.2

Another way to model a transformer without using magnetically-coupled elements is to employ dependent sources. In particular, the equation-pair (12.5) can be modeled as shown in Fig. 12.9. Unlike the T-equivalent circuit, this model can be utilized even when the bottom terminals of the transformer are not directly connected.

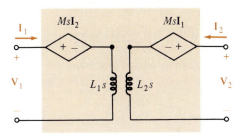

Fig. 12.9 Frequency-domain model of transformer.

Just as we could include nonzero initial conditions when modeling an inductor in the frequency domain (see Fig. 11.7 on p. 519), so too can we include the effects of nonzero initial conditions when modeling a transformer in the frequency domain. Specifically, given the transformer equation-pair (12.1), by taking Laplace transforms, we get

$$\mathbf{V}_1(s) = L_1[s\mathbf{I}_1(s) - i_1(0)] + M[s\mathbf{I}_2(s) - i_2(0)]$$
$$\mathbf{V}_2(s) = M[s\mathbf{I}_1(s) - i_1(0)] + L_2[s\mathbf{I}_2(s) - i_2(0)]$$

from which

$$\mathbf{V}_1(s) = L_1 s\mathbf{I}_1(s) + Ms\mathbf{I}_2(s) - [L_1 i_1(0) + Mi_2(0)]$$
$$\mathbf{V}_2(s) = Ms\mathbf{I}_1(s) + L_2 s\mathbf{I}_2(s) - [Mi_1(0) + L_2 i_2(0)]$$

(12.12)

The equation-pair (12.12) can be modeled as shown in Fig. 12.10.

Note that for the case of zero initial conditions—that is, $i_1(0) = i_2(0) = 0$—then the independent sources have a value of zero. Since a zero-valued voltage source is equivalent to a short circuit, for the case of zero initial conditions the model given in Fig. 12.10 reduces to the model shown in Fig. 12.9.

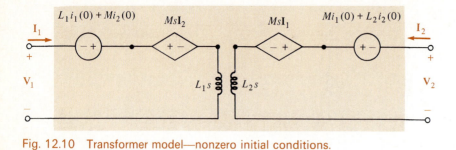

Fig. 12.10   Transformer model—nonzero initial conditions.

EXAMPLE 12.4

For the transformer circuit given in Fig. DE12.2 (p. 561, let us find $v_2(t)$ for $t \geq 0$ given that the initial conditions are $i_1(0) = i_2(0) = 1$ A and $v_g(t) = 1$ V for $t \geq 0$.

For the transformer model given in Fig. 12.10, the values of the dependent sources are

$$L_1 i_1(0) + M i_2(0) = 1(1) + 1(1) = 2 \quad \text{and} \quad M i_1(0) + L_2 i_2(0) = 1(1) + 2(1) = 3$$

Thus, the frequency-domain representation of the given transformer circuit is shown in Fig. 12.11. By KVL,

$$V_g = \frac{1}{s} = 3I_1 - 2 + sI_2 + sI_1 \quad \Rightarrow \quad (s+3)I_1 + sI_2 = \frac{1}{s} + 2$$

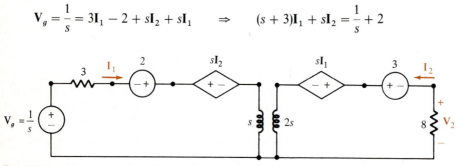

Fig. 12.11   Frequency-domain transformer circuit.

Also, by KVL

$$3 = sI_1 + 2sI_2 + 8I_2 \quad \Rightarrow \quad sI_1 + (2s + 8)I_2 = 3$$

Solving these two equations for I_2, we get

$$I_2 = \frac{s+8}{s^2 + 14s + 24} = \frac{s+8}{(s+2)(s+12)}$$

Thus,

$$V_2 = -8I_2 = \frac{-8(s+8)}{(s+2)(s+12)} = -\frac{4.8}{s+2} - \frac{3.2}{s+12}$$

Hence,

$$v_2(t) = -4.8e^{-2t} - 3.2e^{-12t} \quad \text{for} \quad t \geq 0$$

DRILL EXERCISE 12.3

For the transformer circuit described in Example 12.4, find $v_2(t)$ for $t \geq 0$ given the same initial conditions and $v_g(t) = t$ V for $t \geq 0$.

Answer: $\frac{1}{3} - 6e^{-2t} - \frac{7}{3}e^{-12t}$ V

12.2 THE IDEAL TRANSFORMER

The behavior of many transformers, especially those used in power systems, can be "idealized." This results in simplified voltage-current relationships and circuit models. These, then, can be employed to analyze circuits and obtain very accurate results. Therefore, we now proceed to develop and investigate the concept of an "ideal transformer."

Since the energy stored in a transformer is

$$w = \tfrac{1}{2}L_1 i_1^2 + \tfrac{1}{2}L_2 i_2^2 + M i_1 i_2 = \tfrac{1}{2}[L_1 i_1^2 + L_2 i_2^2] + M i_1 i_2$$

by completing the square, we get

$$w = \tfrac{1}{2}[(\sqrt{L_1} i_1 + \sqrt{L_2} i_2)^2 - 2\sqrt{L_1 L_2} i_1 i_2] + M i_1 i_2$$
$$= \tfrac{1}{2}(\sqrt{L_1} i_1 + \sqrt{L_2} i_2)^2 + (M - \sqrt{L_1 L_2}) i_1 i_2$$

Consider the case for which

$$\sqrt{L_1} i_1 + \sqrt{L_2} i_2 = 0$$

This occurs when

$$\sqrt{L_1} i_1 = -\sqrt{L_2} i_2 \quad \Rightarrow \quad i_2 = -\sqrt{\frac{L_1}{L_2}} \, i_1$$

and the resulting energy stored is given by

$$w = (M - \sqrt{L_1 L_2}) i_1 \left(-\sqrt{\frac{L_1}{L_2}} \, i_1 \right) = (\sqrt{L_1 L_2} - M) \left(\sqrt{\frac{L_1}{L_2}} \right) i_1^2$$

Since the energy stored is a nonnegative quantity, we must have that $0 \leq \sqrt{L_1 L_2} - M$, from which

$$\boxed{M \leq \sqrt{L_1 L_2}} \tag{12.13}$$

Thus, we have an upper bound for the mutual inductance M.

If we define the **coefficient of coupling** of a transformer, denoted by k, as

$$k = \frac{M}{\sqrt{L_1 L_2}}$$

then by inequality (12.13), we have that $0 \le k \le 1$.

The coupling coefficient k of a physical transformer is determined by a number of factors: the magnetic properties of the core on which the primary and secondary coils are wound; the number of turns of each coil; the coils' relative positions and their physical dimensions. If k is close to zero, we say that the coils are **loosely coupled**, and if k is close to one, we say that they are **tightly coupled**. Air-core transformers are typically loosely coupled, and iron-core transformers are usually tightly coupled. As a matter of fact, iron-core transformers can have coupling coefficients approaching unity.

Consider the case of a transformer with **perfect coupling**, that is, $k = 1$. We represent such a device as shown in Fig. 12.12. Since

$$\mathbf{V}_1 = j\omega L_1 \mathbf{I}_1 + j\omega M \mathbf{I}_2$$

then

$$\mathbf{I}_1 = \frac{\mathbf{V}_1 - j\omega M \mathbf{I}_2}{j\omega L_1} \tag{12.14}$$

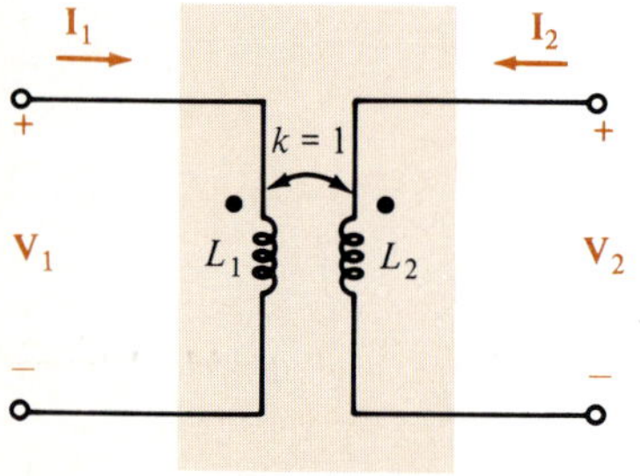

Fig. 12.12   Transformer with perfect coupling.

Also,

$$\mathbf{V}_2 = j\omega M \mathbf{I}_1 + j\omega L_2 \mathbf{I}_2 = j\omega M \left(\frac{\mathbf{V}_1 - j\omega M \mathbf{I}_2}{j\omega L_1} \right) + j\omega L_2 \mathbf{I}_2$$

$$= \frac{M \mathbf{V}_1}{L_1} - \frac{j\omega M^2 \mathbf{I}_2}{L_1} + j\omega L_2 \mathbf{I}_2$$

But for perfect coupling ($k = 1$), $M = \sqrt{L_1 L_2}$ so that

$$V_2 = \frac{\sqrt{L_1 L_2}\,V_1}{L_1} - \frac{j\omega L_1 L_2 I_2}{L_1} + j\omega L_2 I_2 = \sqrt{\frac{L_2}{L_1}}\,V_1 = N V_1$$

where $N = \sqrt{L_2/L_1}$.

Recall from freshman physics that inductance L is proportional to the square of the number of turns. Thus, the primary and secondary self-inductances are

$$L_1 = K N_1^2 \quad \text{and} \quad L_2 = K N_2^2$$

where N_1 and N_2 are the number of turns of the primary and the secondary, respectively. Thus,

$$N = \sqrt{\frac{L_2}{L_1}} = \sqrt{\frac{K N_2^2}{K N_1^2}} = \frac{N_2}{N_1}$$

so we call N the **turns ratio** of the transformer.

From Equation (12.14),

$$I_1 = \frac{V_1}{j\omega L_1} - \frac{M I_2}{L_1}$$

so that for perfect coupling

$$I_1 = \frac{V_1}{j\omega L_1} - \frac{\sqrt{L_1 L_2}\,I_2}{L_1}$$

$$= \frac{V_1}{j\omega L_1} - \sqrt{\frac{L_2}{L_1}}\,I_2 \qquad (12.15)$$

For the case that L_1 and L_2 approach infinity such that the turns ratio remains constant (along with perfect coupling), we say that the transformer is **ideal**. For an ideal transformer, Equation (12.15) becomes

$$I_1 = -N I_2 \quad \text{or} \quad I_2 = -\frac{I_1}{N}$$

As good coupling is achieved by transformers with iron cores, an ideal transformer is usually represented as shown in Fig. 12.13. Since the relationships between

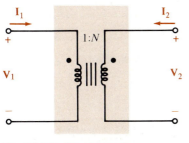

Fig. 12.13   Ideal transformer.

the voltages and the currents are given by the pair

$$\boxed{\begin{aligned} \mathbf{V}_2 &= N\mathbf{V}_1 \\ \mathbf{I}_2 &= -\mathbf{I}_1/N \end{aligned}}$$

(12.16)

we can model an ideal transformer by either of the two equivalent circuits shown in Fig. 12.14. For the circuit given in Fig. 12.14(a), clearly, we have that $\mathbf{V}_2 = N\mathbf{V}_1$ and $\mathbf{I}_1 = -N\mathbf{I}_2$, while for the circuit depicted in Fig. 12.14(b), $\mathbf{V}_1 = \mathbf{V}_2/N$ and $\mathbf{I}_2 = -\mathbf{I}_1/N$.

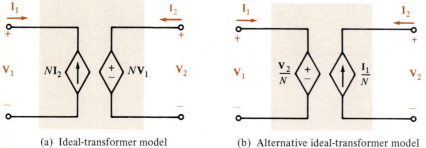

(a) Ideal-transformer model   (b) Alternative ideal-transformer model

Fig. 12.14   Models utilizing dependent sources.

The instantaneous power absorbed by the primary of an ideal transformer is $p_1 = v_1 i_1$, and that absorbed by the secondary is $p_2 = v_2 i_2$. Thus, the total instantaneous power absorbed by the transformer is

$$p = p_1 + p_2 = v_1 i_1 + v_2 i_2 = v_1 i_1 + (N v_1)\left(-\frac{i_1}{N}\right) = 0$$

Since the instantaneous power absorbed is zero, so is the average power, and, also, the energy stored must be zero. This fact can be confirmed from the formula for the energy stored in a transformer [Equation (12.2)] by using the relationships for perfect coupling $(M = \sqrt{L_1 L_2})$ and turns ratio $(N = \sqrt{L_2/L_1})$, along with the ideal transformer formulas. Consequently, we see that the ideal transformer is a lossless device.

EXAMPLE 12.5

Figure 12.15 depicts the equivalent circuit of a simple "class-A" transistor power amplifier. Let us calculate the voltage and power "gains" for this circuit.

By KVL,

$$\mathbf{V}_g = 750\mathbf{I} + 50(21\mathbf{I}) = 1800\mathbf{I} \quad \Rightarrow \quad \mathbf{I} = \frac{\mathbf{V}_g}{1800}$$

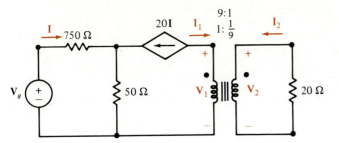

Fig. 12.15   Equivalent circuit of a power amplifier.

Since

$$\mathbf{I}_1 = -20\mathbf{I} = -20\left(\frac{\mathbf{V}_g}{1800}\right) = -\frac{\mathbf{V}_g}{90}$$

then

$$\mathbf{I}_2 = -\frac{\mathbf{I}_1}{1/9} = -9\mathbf{I}_1 = -9\left(-\frac{\mathbf{V}_g}{90}\right) = \frac{\mathbf{V}_g}{10}$$

Thus,

$$\mathbf{V}_2 = -20\mathbf{I}_2 = -20\left(\frac{\mathbf{V}_g}{10}\right) = -2\mathbf{V}_g$$

Therefore, the voltage transfer function $\mathbf{V}_2/\mathbf{V}_g$ is

$$\frac{\mathbf{V}_2}{\mathbf{V}_g} = -2$$

When the voltage transfer function is a real number, it is often called the **voltage gain**.
The instantaneous power supplied by the independent voltage source is

$$p_g = v_g i = v_g\left(\frac{v_g}{1800}\right) = \frac{v_g^2}{1800}$$

and the power absorbed by the 20-Ω load resistor is

$$p_2 = \frac{v_2^2}{20} = \frac{(-2v_g)^2}{10} = \frac{1}{5}v_g^2$$

Thus, the **power gain** p_2/p_g is

$$\frac{p_2}{p_g} = \frac{(1/5)v_g^2}{v_g^2/1800} = 360$$

DRILL EXERCISE 12.4

For the circuit given in Fig. 12.15, what turns ratio N yields a power gain of 810? What is the corresponding voltage gain?

Answer: $1/13.5; -3$

Impedance Matching

Consider the ideal-transformer circuit shown in Fig. 12.16. Since

$$\mathbf{V}_g = \mathbf{Z}_g \mathbf{I}_1 + \mathbf{V}_1 \tag{12.17}$$

and

$$\mathbf{V}_2 = -\mathbf{Z}_L \mathbf{I}_2 \tag{12.18}$$

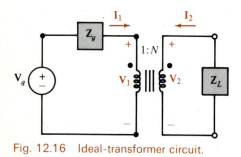

Fig. 12.16   Ideal-transformer circuit.

from Equation (12.16), Equation (12.18) becomes

$$N\mathbf{V}_1 = -\mathbf{Z}_L\left(-\frac{\mathbf{I}_1}{N}\right) \quad \Rightarrow \quad \mathbf{V}_1 = \frac{\mathbf{Z}_L}{N^2}\mathbf{I}_1$$

Substitution of this expression into Equation (12.17) yields

$$\mathbf{V}_g = \mathbf{Z}_g \mathbf{I}_1 + \frac{\mathbf{Z}_L}{N^2}\mathbf{I}_1$$

so that the impedance $\mathbf{V}_g/\mathbf{I}_1$ seen by the source is

$$\frac{\mathbf{V}_g}{\mathbf{I}_1} = \mathbf{Z}_g + \frac{\mathbf{Z}_L}{N^2} \tag{12.19}$$

which is $\mathbf{Z}_g$ in series with the load impedance $\mathbf{Z}_L$ scaled by the factor $1/N^2$. The term $\mathbf{Z}_L/N^2$ is often called the **reflected impedance**. We can also say that this term is the equivalent impedance **referred** to the primary side of the transformer.

From Equation (12.19),

$$\mathbf{I}_1 = \frac{\mathbf{V}_g}{\mathbf{Z}_g + \mathbf{Z}_L/N^2}$$

Therefore,

$$\mathbf{V}_2 = -\mathbf{Z}_L\mathbf{I}_2 = -\mathbf{Z}_L\left(-\frac{\mathbf{I}_1}{N}\right) = \frac{\mathbf{Z}_L}{N}\left(\frac{\mathbf{V}_g}{\mathbf{Z}_g + \mathbf{Z}_L/N^2}\right)$$

so

$$\mathbf{V}_2 = \frac{N\mathbf{Z}_L}{N^2\mathbf{Z}_g + \mathbf{Z}_L}\mathbf{V}_g$$

As an alternative approach, we can apply Thévenin's theorem to the circuit given in Fig. 12.16. First, we determine $\mathbf{V}_{oc}$ from the circuit shown in Fig. 12.17. Since $\mathbf{I}_2 = 0$, then

$$\mathbf{I}_1 = -N\mathbf{I}_2 = 0$$

and, by KVL,

$$\mathbf{V}_g = \mathbf{Z}_g\mathbf{I}_1 + \mathbf{V}_1 = \mathbf{V}_1$$

Thus,

$$\mathbf{V}_{oc} = \mathbf{V}_2 = N\mathbf{V}_1 = N\mathbf{V}_g$$

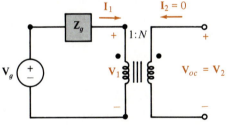

Fig. 12.17   Determination of open-circuit voltage.

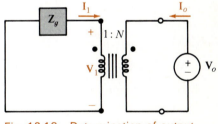

Fig. 12.18   Determination of output impedance.

To find the Thévenin-equivalent (output) impedance, set $\mathbf{V}_g = 0$ and take the ratio of $\mathbf{V}_o$ to $\mathbf{I}_o$ for the circuit shown in Fig. 12.18. Since

$$\mathbf{V}_1 = -\mathbf{Z}_g\mathbf{I}_1 = -\mathbf{Z}_g(-N\mathbf{I}_o) = N\mathbf{Z}_g\mathbf{I}_o$$

then

$$\mathbf{V}_o = N\mathbf{V}_1 = N(N\mathbf{Z}_g\mathbf{I}_o) = N^2\mathbf{Z}_g\mathbf{I}_o$$

Hence, the output impedance is

$$\mathbf{Z}_o = \frac{\mathbf{V}_o}{\mathbf{I}_o} = N^2\mathbf{Z}_g$$

Therefore, using Thévenin's theorem, we have the circuit shown in Fig. 12.19. By voltage division,

$$\mathbf{V}_2 = \frac{\mathbf{Z}_L}{\mathbf{Z}_L + N^2\mathbf{Z}_g}(N\mathbf{V}_g) = \frac{N\mathbf{Z}_L}{N^2\mathbf{Z}_g + \mathbf{Z}_L}\mathbf{V}_g$$

as was obtained above.

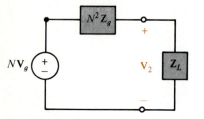

Fig. 12.19   Thévenin-equivalent circuit.

EXAMPLE 12.6

For the circuit given in Fig. 12.16, suppose that $\mathbf{Z}_g = 20$ kΩ and $\mathbf{Z}_L = 8$ Ω. Let us determine the value of the turns ratio N such that the 8-Ω load resistor absorbs maximum power.

Given the Thévenin-equivalent circuit shown in Fig. 12.19, we know that the load absorbs maximum power when the load resistance $\mathbf{Z}_L = R_L = 8$ Ω is equal to the output (Thevenin-equivalent) resistance $\mathbf{Z}_o = N^2\mathbf{Z}_g = 20,000N^2$, that is, when

$$20,000N^2 = 8$$

Solving this equation, we find that the turns ratio is

$$N = \tfrac{1}{50} = 0.02$$

In this example, we have used a transformer to "match" the 8-Ω load resistor to the 20-kΩ source resistance. When a transformer is used in such an application, it can be referred to as a **matching transformer**. Typically, this type of transformer is not designated by its turns ratio N, but rather by the impedances (resistances) it matches. Specifically, the transformer in this example could be called a "20-kΩ/8-Ω matching transformer."

DRILL EXERCISE 12.5

For the ideal-transformer circuit given in Fig. 12.17, suppose that the turns ratio is $N = 0.01$. Given that $\mathbf{Z}_g$ consists of an 80-kΩ resistor connected in series with a 0.0053-μF capacitor, what load will absorb maximum power at 500 Hz?
Answer: 8 Ω in series with 1.91 mH

12.3 TWO-PORT ADMITTANCE PARAMETERS

Such circuit elements as resistors, inductors, capacitors, and independent sources are two-terminal devices, which can be represented as shown in Fig. 12.20(a). More generally, an interconnection of circuit elements may have a single pair of terminals accessible as shown in Fig. 12.20(b). We can say that the two terminals constitute a **port**, and that the network is a **one-port network**. For the case that a one-port network contains no independent sources, it can be characterized by its impedance or admittance. For the case that independent sources are contained in a one-port network, it can be characterized by its Thévenin or Norton equivalent.

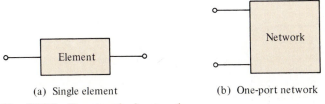

(a) Single element   (b) One-port network

Fig. 12.20   Two-terminal networks.

Now consider the situation where a network has two accessible pairs of terminals instead of one. Such a network, which is depicted in Fig. 12.21, is referred to as a **two-port network**. Just as a one-port network (or one-port, for short) can consist of a single element or many elements, so can a two-port network, or two-port. For example, a transformer is a simple two-port. So is the simple op-amp circuit shown in Fig. 12.22. In this case the device, the op amp, has three terminals, but one terminal is common to both ports.

Fig. 12.21   Two-port network.   Fig. 12.22   Op amp comprising two-port network.

In dealing with dependent sources, the assumption has been that such devices are two-terminal elements—that is, one-port networks. Technically, however, dependent sources are two-port networks. Figure 12.23 shows the two types of dependent current sources, while Fig. 12.24 depicts the two types of dependent voltage sources.

The characterization of two-port networks is both important and useful. Even a simple two-port consisting of a single bipolar junction transistor (BJT) is typically described in terms of its two-port characteristics.

In the following discussion, we shall consider two-ports that possibly contain dependent sources but do not contain independent sources. We begin by considering

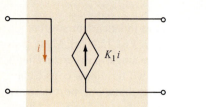
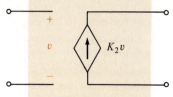

(a) Current dependent   (b) Voltage dependent

Fig. 12.23   Dependent current sources.

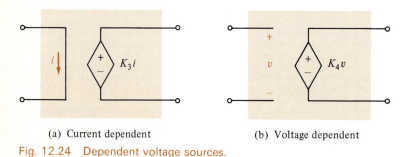

(a) Current dependent   (b) Voltage dependent

Fig. 12.24   Dependent voltage sources.

a two-port network (in the frequency domain) that has an independent voltage source applied to each port. This situation is depicted in Fig. 12.25.

Given the voltages V_1 and V_2, the currents I_1 and I_2 can be measured or, if the network is explicitly known, calculated. In either case I_1 and I_2 can be determined by means of the principle of superposition. For instance, that portion of I_1 due solely to V_1 is KV_1. Since KV_1 must have amperes as units, then K must have amperes/volts = siemens (or mhos) as units. In other words, K must be an admittance, say y_{11}. Similarly, the portion of I_1 due solely to V_2 is $y_{12}V_2$. Thus, by the principle of superposition, $I_1 = y_{11}V_1 + y_{12}V_2$. Using an analogous argument, we deduce that $I_2 = y_{21}V_1 + y_{22}V_2$.

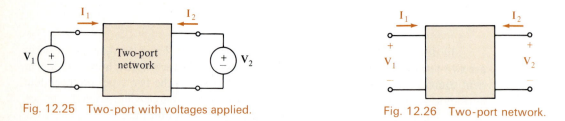

Fig. 12.25   Two-port with voltages applied.   Fig. 12.26   Two-port network.

Although the voltages V_1 and V_2 were produced by independent sources, the same results hold no matter how these voltages arise when the two-port is part of a larger circuit. In summary, we can describe the two-port network shown in Fig. 12.26

by the two equations

$$I_1 = y_{11}V_1 + y_{12}V_2 \qquad (12.20)$$

$$I_2 = y_{21}V_1 + y_{22}V_2 \qquad (12.21)$$

or by the single matrix equation

$$\begin{bmatrix} I_1 \\ I_2 \end{bmatrix} = \begin{bmatrix} y_{11} & y_{12} \\ y_{21} & y_{22} \end{bmatrix} \begin{bmatrix} V_1 \\ V_2 \end{bmatrix} \qquad (12.22)$$

From Equation (12.20), if we set $V_2 = 0$, then we have

$$y_{11} = \left. \frac{I_1}{V_1} \right|_{V_2 = 0}$$

(read $y_{11} = I_1/V_1$ with $V_2 = 0$). We can set $V_2 = 0$ by placing a short circuit across port 2 (the port with V_2 and I_2) as shown in Fig. 12.27. Similarly, we have

$$y_{12} = \left. \frac{I_1}{V_2} \right|_{V_1 = 0} \qquad y_{21} = \left. \frac{I_2}{V_1} \right|_{V_2 = 0} \qquad y_{22} = \left. \frac{I_2}{V_2} \right|_{V_1 = 0}$$

The admittance y_{21} also can be determined from the configuration shown in Fig. 12.27. The remaining two admittances, y_{12} and y_{22}, can be obtained from Fig. 12.28.

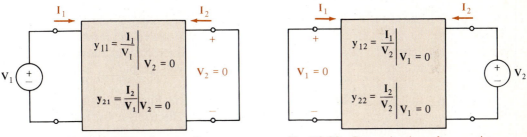

Fig. 12.27   Determination of y_{11} and y_{21}.

Fig. 12.28   Determination of y_{12} and y_{22}.

Because the admittances y_{11}, y_{12}, y_{21}, and y_{22} can be determined by short-circuiting one of the ports, they are called the **short-circuit admittance parameters** or **y parameters** of the two-port. If port 1 is considered the input and port 2 the output, then y_{11} is called the **short-circuit input admittance**, y_{22} is the **short-circuit output admittance**, and y_{12} and y_{21} are **short-circuit transfer admittances**.

EXAMPLE 12.7

Let us determine the short-circuit admittance parameters for the resistive two-port shown in Fig. 12.29.

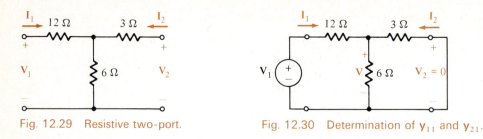

Fig. 12.29   Resistive two-port.   Fig. 12.30   Determination of y_{11} and y_{21}.

We can determine the short-circuit input admittance y_{11} and transfer admittance y_{21} from Fig. 12.30. Since the 3-Ω and 6-Ω resistors are connected in parallel, they form a 2-Ω resistance. Thus, by voltage division,

$$V = \frac{2V_1}{2 + 12} = \frac{V_1}{7}$$

and therefore

$$I_1 = \frac{V_1 - V}{12} = \frac{V_1 - (V_1/7)}{12} = \frac{V_1}{14} \quad \Rightarrow \quad y_{11} = \frac{I_1}{V_1}\bigg|_{V_2 = 0} = \frac{1}{14}\,\text{S}$$

Also,

$$I_2 = \frac{V_2 - V}{3} = \frac{0 - (V_1/7)}{3} = -\frac{V_1}{21} \quad \Rightarrow \quad y_{21} = \frac{I_2}{V_1}\bigg|_{V_2 = 0} = -\frac{1}{21}\,\text{S}$$

Don't get upset because y_{21} is a negative quantity. Although the input admittance y_{11} is in this case the admittance of the connection of three positive-valued resistors, the transfer admittance is the ratio of a current at one port to the voltage at another. The term "admittance" is used because the ratio is current to voltage, but y_{21} is not the admittance of a particular port.

To find y_{12} and y_{22}, we short-circuit port 1, as shown in Fig. 12.31. In this case, the parallel combination of the 6-Ω and 12-Ω resistors is effectively a 4-Ω resistance. Thus, by voltage division,

$$V = \frac{4V_2}{4 + 3} = \frac{4}{7}V_2$$

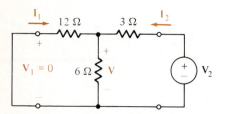

Fig. 12.31   Determination of y_{12} and y_{22}.

Thus

$$\mathbf{I}_1 = \frac{\mathbf{V}_1 - \mathbf{V}}{12} = \frac{0 - (4/7)\mathbf{V}_2}{12} = -\frac{\mathbf{V}_2}{21} \quad \Rightarrow \quad \mathbf{y}_{12} = \frac{\mathbf{I}_1}{\mathbf{V}_2}\bigg|_{\mathbf{V}_1 = 0} = -\frac{1}{21}\ \text{S}$$

and

$$\mathbf{I}_2 = \frac{\mathbf{V}_2 - \mathbf{V}}{3} = \frac{\mathbf{V}_2 - (4/7)\mathbf{V}_2}{3} = \frac{\mathbf{V}_2}{7} \quad \Rightarrow \quad \mathbf{y}_{22} = \frac{\mathbf{I}_2}{\mathbf{V}_2}\bigg|_{\mathbf{V}_1 = 0} = \frac{1}{7}\ \text{S}$$

DRILL EXERCISE 12.6

Find the short-circuit admittance parameters for the two-port network shown in Fig. DE12.6.
Answer: $\frac{1}{8}$ S; $\frac{1}{8}$ S; $-\frac{1}{16}$ S; $\frac{3}{16}$ S

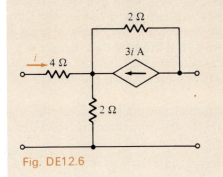

Fig. DE12.6

Having seen an example of a resistive two-port in a "T" configuration (Fig. 12.29), let us now consider a "π" network consisting of arbitrary admittances $\mathbf{Y}_a$, $\mathbf{Y}_b$, and $\mathbf{Y}_c$ as shown in Fig. 12.32.

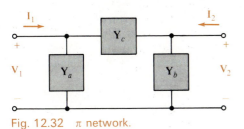

Fig. 12.32 π network.

In order to obtain $\mathbf{y}_{11}$ and $\mathbf{y}_{21}$, we place a short circuit across port 2. From the viewpoint of port 1, $\mathbf{Y}_a$ and $\mathbf{Y}_c$ are then in parallel. Thus,

$$\mathbf{y}_{11} = \mathbf{Y}_a + \mathbf{Y}_c$$

Since the short circuit across $\mathbf{Y}_b$ means that the voltage across $\mathbf{Y}_b$ is zero and that therefore there is no current through $\mathbf{Y}_b$, by current division we have that

$$\mathbf{I}_2 = -\frac{\mathbf{Y}_c}{\mathbf{Y}_c + \mathbf{Y}_a}\mathbf{I}_1 \quad \Rightarrow \quad \mathbf{I}_2 = -\mathbf{Y}_c\left(\frac{\mathbf{I}_1}{\mathbf{Y}_a + \mathbf{Y}_c}\right)$$

But since (when there is a short circuit across port 2)

$$\mathbf{I}_1 = \mathbf{y}_{11}\mathbf{V}_1 = (\mathbf{Y}_a + \mathbf{Y}_c)\mathbf{V}_1 \quad \Rightarrow \quad \frac{\mathbf{I}_1}{\mathbf{Y}_a + \mathbf{Y}_c} = \mathbf{V}_1$$

then

$$\mathbf{I}_2 = -\mathbf{Y}_c\mathbf{V}_1 \quad \Rightarrow \quad \mathbf{y}_{21} = -\mathbf{Y}_c$$

Similarly, we can obtain

$$\mathbf{y}_{12} = -\mathbf{Y}_c \quad \text{and} \quad \mathbf{y}_{22} = \mathbf{Y}_b + \mathbf{Y}_c$$

Note that for this circuit, as in the previous one (Fig. 12.29), $\mathbf{y}_{12} = \mathbf{y}_{21}$. This is not sheer luck, but is due to a special property. Resistors, inductors, and capacitors are elements that are "bilateral"; that is, they can be placed in a circuit in either direction and the result will be the same. A circuit that contains only bilateral elements is known as a **bilateral network**. For such a two-port it can be shown that $\mathbf{y}_{12} = \mathbf{y}_{21}$. Yet there are two-ports containing nonbilateral elements, such as dependent sources, that also have this property. We say that any two-port having the property that $\mathbf{y}_{12} = \mathbf{y}_{21}$ is a **reciprocal network**.

In the foregoing discussion we had a reciprocal network (Fig. 12.32) consisting of three arbitrary admittances $\mathbf{Y}_a$, $\mathbf{Y}_b$, and $\mathbf{Y}_c$. Having determined the short-circuit admittance parameters in terms of these admittances, we find that

$$\mathbf{y}_{11} + \mathbf{y}_{12} = \mathbf{Y}_a \qquad \mathbf{y}_{22} + \mathbf{y}_{12} = \mathbf{Y}_b \qquad -\mathbf{y}_{12} = \mathbf{Y}_c$$

Hence, given an arbitrary reciprocal two-port, we can model it with the π-equivalent network shown in Fig. 12.33. For the T-connected, resistive two-port given in Fig. 12.29,

$$\mathbf{y}_{11} + \mathbf{y}_{12} = \tfrac{1}{14} + (-\tfrac{1}{21}) = \tfrac{1}{42}\ \text{S}$$

$$\mathbf{y}_{22} + \mathbf{y}_{12} = \tfrac{1}{7} + (-\tfrac{1}{21}) = \tfrac{2}{21}\ \text{S}$$

$$-\mathbf{y}_{12} = \tfrac{1}{21}\ \text{S}$$

so its π-equivalent circuit is as shown in Fig. 12.34.

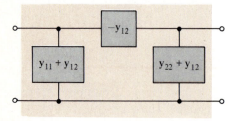

Fig. 12.33 π-equivalent network.

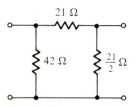

Fig. 12.34 π-equivalent of circuit in Fig. 12.29.

The π-equivalent circuit shown in Fig. 12.33 can be used for reciprocal two-ports. For nonreciprocal two-ports, as well as reciprocal two-ports, we can use the equivalent circuit shown in Fig. 12.35 which employs two voltage-dependent current sources. Applying KCL at ports 1 and 2, we get Equations (12.20) and (12.21), respectively, on p. 573.

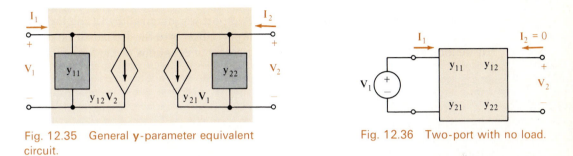

Fig. 12.35   General **y**-parameter equivalent circuit.

Fig. 12.36   Two-port with no load.

Knowing the short-circuit admittance parameters (**y** parameters) of a given two-port, we can express other parameters of the two-port in terms of the **y** parameters. For example, let us find the voltage transfer function $\mathbf{V}_2/\mathbf{V}_1$ with no load connected to port 2, as shown in Fig. 12.36. Although we can replace the two-port by its equivalent circuit, since Equations (12.20) and (12.21) describe the two-port regardless of what is connected to it, setting $\mathbf{I}_2 = 0$ we get, from Equation (12.21),

$$0 = \mathbf{y}_{21}\mathbf{V}_1 + \mathbf{y}_{22}\mathbf{V}_2 \quad \Rightarrow \quad \frac{\mathbf{V}_2}{\mathbf{V}_1} = -\frac{\mathbf{y}_{21}}{\mathbf{y}_{22}}$$

For the case that port 2 is terminated with a 1-Ω resistor, as shown in Fig. 12.37, we have

$$\mathbf{V}_2 = -1\mathbf{I}_2 \quad \Rightarrow \quad \mathbf{I}_2 = -\mathbf{V}_2$$

Substituting this into Equation (12.21) we obtain

$$-\mathbf{V}_2 = \mathbf{y}_{21}\mathbf{V}_1 + \mathbf{y}_{22}\mathbf{V}_2 \quad \Rightarrow \quad \frac{\mathbf{V}_2}{\mathbf{V}_1} = \frac{-\mathbf{y}_{21}}{1 + \mathbf{y}_{22}}$$

It may be that some or all of the **y** parameters of a two-port do not exist. Consider the two-port shown in Fig. 12.38. In order to calculate $\mathbf{y}_{11}$ and $\mathbf{y}_{21}$, a short

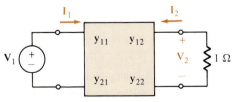

Fig. 12.37   Two-port with 1-Ω load.

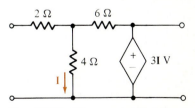

Fig. 12.38   Two-port which has no **y** parameters.

circuit is placed across port 2. This means that $3\mathbf{I} = 0$, and hence $\mathbf{I} = 0$. However, a nonzero voltage applied to port 1 implies that $\mathbf{I} \neq 0$. The apparent paradox indicates that no solution exists, and consequently, neither does $\mathbf{y}_{11}$ and $\mathbf{y}_{21}$. The same conclusion can be drawn about $\mathbf{y}_{12}$ and $\mathbf{y}_{22}$ if you attempt to determine these parameters.

12.4 OTHER TWO-PORT PARAMETERS

Our development of the **y** parameters of a two-port was obtained by letting the port voltages be the independent variables and the port currents be the dependent variables. If we look at the converse situation, we get a pair of equations of the form

$$\mathbf{V}_1 = \mathbf{z}_{11}\mathbf{I}_1 + \mathbf{z}_{12}\mathbf{I}_2 \qquad (12.23)$$

$$\mathbf{V}_2 = \mathbf{z}_{21}\mathbf{I}_1 + \mathbf{z}_{22}\mathbf{I}_2 \qquad (12.24)$$

which can be written as the single matrix equation

$$\begin{bmatrix} \mathbf{V}_1 \\ \mathbf{V}_2 \end{bmatrix} = \begin{bmatrix} \mathbf{z}_{11} & \mathbf{z}_{12} \\ \mathbf{z}_{21} & \mathbf{z}_{22} \end{bmatrix} \begin{bmatrix} \mathbf{I}_1 \\ \mathbf{I}_2 \end{bmatrix} \qquad (12.25)$$

Given a two-port network, we can determine the impedances $\mathbf{z}_{11}$ and $\mathbf{z}_{21}$ by open-circuiting port 2 as shown in Fig. 12.39. From Equations (12.23) and (12.24)

$$\mathbf{z}_{11} = \left.\frac{\mathbf{V}_1}{\mathbf{I}_1}\right|_{\mathbf{I}_2=0} \qquad \text{and} \qquad \mathbf{z}_{21} = \left.\frac{\mathbf{V}_2}{\mathbf{I}_1}\right|_{\mathbf{I}_2=0}$$

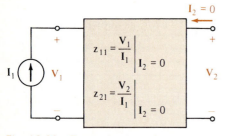

Fig. 12.39 Determination of $\mathbf{z}_{11}$ and $\mathbf{z}_{21}$.

respectively. Similarly, applying a current source $\mathbf{I}_2$ at port 2 and open-circuiting port 1 ($\mathbf{I}_1 = 0$), we easily obtain

$$\mathbf{z}_{12} = \left.\frac{\mathbf{V}_1}{\mathbf{I}_2}\right|_{\mathbf{I}_1=0} \qquad \text{and} \qquad \mathbf{z}_{22} = \left.\frac{\mathbf{V}_2}{\mathbf{I}_2}\right|_{\mathbf{I}_1=0}$$

From the fact that the impedances $\mathbf{z}_{11}$, $\mathbf{z}_{12}$, $\mathbf{z}_{21}$, and $\mathbf{z}_{22}$ can be determined by open-circuiting one of the ports, they are called the **open-circuit impedance parameters** or **z parameters** of the two-port. If port 1 is considered the input and port 2 the output, then $\mathbf{z}_{11}$ is called the **open-circuit input impedance**, $\mathbf{z}_{22}$ is the **open-circuit output impedance**, and $\mathbf{z}_{12}$ and $\mathbf{z}_{21}$ are open-circuit transfer impedances.

EXAMPLE 12.8

Let us find the **z** parameters for the resistive π network shown in Fig. 12.40.

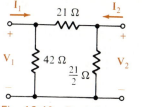

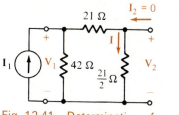

Fig. 12.40   Resistive two-port network.

Fig. 12.41   Determination of z_{11} and z_{21}.

We determine z_{11} and z_{21} from the configuration shown in Fig. 12.41. Since the 21-Ω and $\frac{21}{2}$-Ω resistors are in series, they form a $\frac{63}{2}$-Ω resistance. This in turn is in parallel with 42 Ω. Thus,

$$z_{11} = \frac{42(63/2)}{42 + (63/2)} = 18\ \Omega$$

Of course, $z_{11} = V_1/I_1$ can also be obtained by using mesh or nodal analysis.

One way to obtain $z_{21} = V_2/I_1$ is by using current division to determine **I**. Since

$$I = \frac{42}{42 + (63/2)}\,I_1 = \frac{4}{7}\,I_1$$

then

$$V_2 = \tfrac{21}{2}\,I = 6I_1 \qquad \Rightarrow \qquad z_{21} = 6\ \Omega$$

We can find z_{12} and z_{22} from the circuit shown in Fig. 12.42. In this case,

$$I = \frac{21/2}{(21/2) + 63}\,I_2 = \frac{1}{7}\,I_2$$

and

$$V_1 = 42I = 6I_2 \qquad \Rightarrow \qquad z_{12} = 6\ \Omega$$

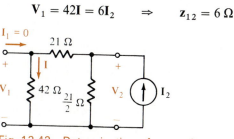

Fig. 12.42   Determination of z_{12} and z_{22}.

Also,

$$z_{22} = \frac{(21/2)63}{(21/2) + 63} = 9\ \Omega$$

DRILL EXERCISE 12.7

Find the z parameters for the two-port given in Fig. DE12.6 on p. 575.
Answer: $6\,\Omega$; $-4\,\Omega$; $2\,\Omega$; $4\,\Omega$

Note that in the preceding example that $\mathbf{z}_{12} = \mathbf{z}_{21}$. Since the network is obviously bilateral, and hence reciprocal, then $\mathbf{y}_{12} = \mathbf{y}_{21}$. Does this imply that $\mathbf{z}_{12} = \mathbf{z}_{21}$?

Return now to Equation (12.22) on p. 573. By Cramer's rule, we have

$$\mathbf{V}_1 = \frac{\begin{vmatrix} \mathbf{I}_1 & \mathbf{y}_{12} \\ \mathbf{I}_2 & \mathbf{y}_{22} \end{vmatrix}}{\begin{vmatrix} \mathbf{y}_{11} & \mathbf{y}_{12} \\ \mathbf{y}_{21} & \mathbf{y}_{22} \end{vmatrix}} = \frac{\mathbf{y}_{22}}{\Delta_\mathbf{y}}\mathbf{I}_1 - \frac{\mathbf{y}_{12}}{\Delta_\mathbf{y}}\mathbf{I}_2 \qquad \mathbf{V}_2 = \frac{\begin{vmatrix} \mathbf{y}_{11} & \mathbf{I}_1 \\ \mathbf{y}_{21} & \mathbf{I}_2 \end{vmatrix}}{\begin{vmatrix} \mathbf{y}_{11} & \mathbf{y}_{12} \\ \mathbf{y}_{21} & \mathbf{y}_{22} \end{vmatrix}} = \frac{\mathbf{y}_{11}}{\Delta_\mathbf{y}}\mathbf{I}_2 - \frac{\mathbf{y}_{21}}{\Delta_\mathbf{y}}\mathbf{I}_1$$

where $\Delta_\mathbf{y} = \mathbf{y}_{11}\mathbf{y}_{22} - \mathbf{y}_{12}\mathbf{y}_{21}$.

Comparing these two expressions with Equations (12.23) and (12.24) on p. 578, we conclude that

$$\mathbf{z}_{11} = \frac{\mathbf{y}_{22}}{\Delta_\mathbf{y}} \qquad \mathbf{z}_{12} = \frac{-\mathbf{y}_{12}}{\Delta_\mathbf{y}} \qquad \mathbf{z}_{21} = \frac{-\mathbf{y}_{21}}{\Delta_\mathbf{y}} \qquad \mathbf{z}_{22} = \frac{\mathbf{y}_{11}}{\Delta_\mathbf{y}}$$

Thus if $\mathbf{y}_{12} = \mathbf{y}_{21}$, then $\mathbf{z}_{12} = \mathbf{z}_{21}$, and vice versa. Furthermore, we see that if the **y** parameters of a two-port have been determined, the above relationships can be used to obtain the **z** parameters.

For the two-port given in Fig. 12.40 on p. 579, we previously determined (see Fig. 12.34 on p. 576) that

$$\mathbf{y}_{11} = \tfrac{1}{14}\,\text{S} \qquad \mathbf{y}_{12} = -\tfrac{1}{21}\,\text{S} = \mathbf{y}_{21} \qquad \mathbf{y}_{22} = \tfrac{1}{7}\,\text{S}$$

Hence,

$$\Delta_\mathbf{y} = \mathbf{y}_{11}\mathbf{y}_{22} - \mathbf{y}_{12}\mathbf{y}_{21} = (\tfrac{1}{14})(\tfrac{1}{7}) - (-\tfrac{1}{21})^2 = \tfrac{1}{126}$$

so

$$\mathbf{z}_{11} = \frac{\mathbf{y}_{22}}{\Delta_\mathbf{y}} = \frac{1/7}{1/126} = 18\,\Omega \qquad \mathbf{z}_{12} = \frac{-\mathbf{y}_{12}}{\Delta_\mathbf{y}} = \frac{1/21}{1/126} = 6\,\Omega = \mathbf{z}_{21}$$

$$\mathbf{z}_{22} = \frac{\mathbf{y}_{11}}{\Delta_\mathbf{y}} = \frac{1/14}{1/126} = 9\,\Omega$$

which verify the results of Example 12.8.

Having seen an example of a resistive π network, let us now consider the T network consisting of arbitrary impedances $\mathbf{Z}_a$, $\mathbf{Z}_b$, and $\mathbf{Z}_c$ as shown in Fig. 12.43. In order to obtain $\mathbf{z}_{11}$ and $\mathbf{z}_{21}$, we leave port 2 open-circuited. Then, clearly,

$$\mathbf{z}_{11} = \mathbf{Z}_a + \mathbf{Z}_c$$

Since $\mathbf{I}_2 = 0$, then

$$\mathbf{V}_2 = \mathbf{Z}_c\mathbf{I}_1 \qquad \Rightarrow \qquad \mathbf{z}_{21} = \mathbf{Z}_c$$

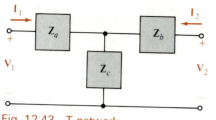

Fig. 12.43   T network.

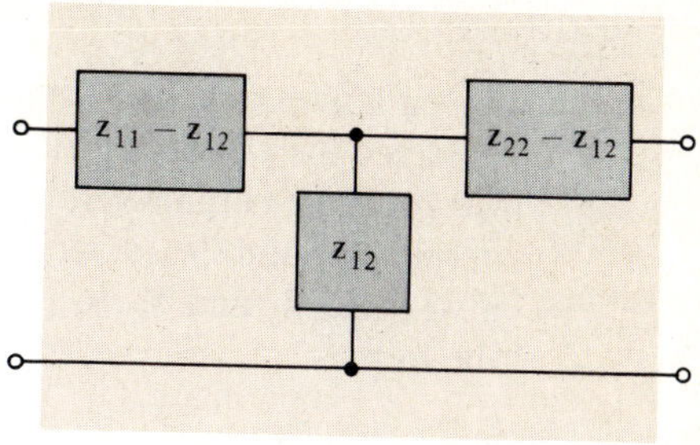

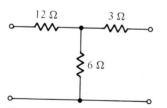

Fig. 12.44   T-equivalent network.

Similarly,

$$\mathbf{z}_{12} = \mathbf{Z}_c \quad \text{and} \quad \mathbf{z}_{22} = \mathbf{Z}_b + \mathbf{Z}_c$$

From the $\mathbf{z}$ parameters of this reciprocal two-port, we have

$$\mathbf{z}_{11} - \mathbf{z}_{12} = \mathbf{Z}_a \qquad \mathbf{z}_{22} - \mathbf{z}_{12} = \mathbf{Z}_b \qquad \mathbf{z}_{12} = \mathbf{Z}_c$$

Thus, we can deduce that a reciprocal two-port can be modeled by the T-equivalent network shown in Fig. 12.44. For the resistive π network given in Fig. 12.40, we have

$$\mathbf{z}_{11} - \mathbf{z}_{12} = 18 - 6 \; = 12 \; \Omega$$

$$\mathbf{z}_{22} - \mathbf{z}_{12} = 9 - 6 = 3 \; \Omega$$

$$\mathbf{z}_{12} = 6 \; \Omega$$

and therefore its T-equivalent circuit is as shown in Fig. 12.45.

Fig. 12.45   T-equivalent of circuit in Fig. 12.40.

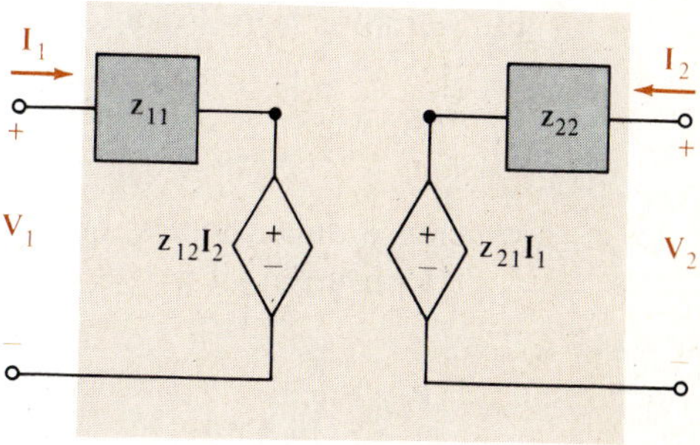

Fig. 12.46   General $\mathbf{z}$-parameter equivalent circuit.

A general equivalent circuit of a two-port, whether reciprocal or not, whose $\mathbf{z}$ parameters are $\mathbf{z}_{11}$, $\mathbf{z}_{12}$, $\mathbf{z}_{21}$, and $\mathbf{z}_{22}$ is shown in Fig. 12.46. To verify that this configuration indeed yields Equations (12.23) and (12.24) on p. 578, we need only apply KVL at ports 1 and 2.

As with the case of $\mathbf{y}$ parameters, there are special cases of two-ports for which the $\mathbf{z}$ parameters do not exist (are undefined).

Hybrid Parameters

Given a two-port, by selecting the port voltages to be the independent variables, we obtained the **y** parameters; by selecting the port currents as the independent variables, we got the **z** parameters. However, there is no reason why we can't pick the voltage at one port and the current at the other to be the independent variables. For example, if we select $\mathbf{I}_1$ and $\mathbf{V}_2$ to be the independent variables, we get a pair of equations of the form

$$\mathbf{V}_1 = \mathbf{h}_{11}\mathbf{I}_1 + \mathbf{h}_{12}\mathbf{V}_2 \tag{12.26}$$

$$\mathbf{I}_2 = \mathbf{h}_{21}\mathbf{I}_1 + \mathbf{h}_{22}\mathbf{V}_2 \tag{12.27}$$

which can be written as the single matrix equation

$$\begin{bmatrix} \mathbf{V}_1 \\ \mathbf{I}_2 \end{bmatrix} = \begin{bmatrix} \mathbf{h}_{11} & \mathbf{h}_{12} \\ \mathbf{h}_{21} & \mathbf{h}_{22} \end{bmatrix} \begin{bmatrix} \mathbf{I}_1 \\ \mathbf{V}_2 \end{bmatrix} \tag{12.28}$$

Since the independent variables are mixed (one current and one voltage), we refer to these parameters as the **hybrid** or **h parameters** of the two-port. It is in terms of these parameters that bipolar junction transistors (BJTs) are typically described.

If we set $\mathbf{V}_2 = 0$ (short-circuit port 2), then from Equation (12.26),

$$\mathbf{h}_{11} = \left. \frac{\mathbf{V}_1}{\mathbf{I}_1} \right|_{\mathbf{V}_2 = 0}$$

which is called the **short-circuit input impedance** and consequently has ohms as units. Furthermore, from Equation (12.27),

$$\mathbf{h}_{21} = \left. \frac{\mathbf{I}_2}{\mathbf{I}_1} \right|_{\mathbf{V}_2 = 0}$$

which is a dimensionless quantity called the **short-circuit forward current gain**.

Conversely, if we set $\mathbf{I}_1 = 0$ (open circuit port 1), then from Equation (12.26),

$$\mathbf{h}_{12} = \left. \frac{\mathbf{V}_1}{\mathbf{V}_2} \right|_{\mathbf{I}_1 = 0}$$

which is a dimensionless quantity called the **open-circuit reverse voltage gain**. Finally, from Equation (12.27),

$$\mathbf{h}_{22} = \left. \frac{\mathbf{I}_2}{\mathbf{V}_2} \right|_{\mathbf{I}_1 = 0}$$

which is called the **open-circuit output admittance**, and its units are siemens (or mhos).

In transistor applications, the symbols $\mathbf{h}_{11}, \mathbf{h}_{21}, \mathbf{h}_{12}, \mathbf{h}_{22}$ are replaced by $\mathbf{h}_i, \mathbf{h}_f, \mathbf{h}_r, \mathbf{h}_o$, respectively, to denote input, forward, reverse, output.

EXAMPLE 12.9

Let us calculate the **h** parameters for the T network shown in Fig. 12.45. We calculate h_{11} from Fig. 12.47. Instead of writing mesh or node equations, note that the 3-Ω and 6-Ω resistors in parallel are effectively 2 Ω, and this in turn is in series with 12 Ω. Thus,

$$h_{11} = 12 + 2 = 14 \, \Omega$$

We can also determine h_{21} from this circuit. By current division,

$$-I_2 = \frac{6}{6+3} I_1 \quad \Rightarrow \quad h_{21} = -\frac{2}{3}$$

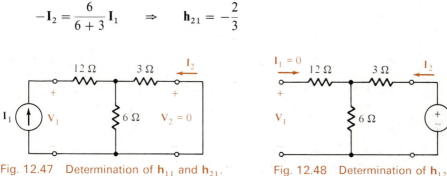

Fig. 12.47   Determination of h_{11} and h_{21}.

Fig. 12.48   Determination of h_{12} and h_{22}.

We can determine h_{12} and h_{22} from the circuit shown in Fig. 12.48. In this case we have that

$$I_2 = \frac{V_2}{3+6} \quad \Rightarrow \quad h_{22} = \frac{1}{9} \, S$$

and

$$V_1 = 6I_2 = 6\left(\frac{V_2}{9}\right) \quad \Rightarrow \quad h_{12} = \frac{2}{3}$$

DRILL EXERCISE 12.8

Find the **h** parameters for the two-port network given in Fig. DE12.6 on p. 575.
Answer: $8 \, \Omega; 1, \frac{1}{2}, \frac{1}{4} \, S$

Note that, for the reciprocal network given in Fig. 12.45, $h_{12} \neq h_{21}$. But is there a relationship between these two parameters for reciprocal networks?

From Equation (12.24) on p. 578, we have

$$I_2 = \frac{V_2 - z_{21}I_1}{z_{22}} \tag{12.29}$$

Substituting this into Equation (12.23) on p. 578, we get

$$V_1 = z_{11}I_1 + z_{12}\left(\frac{V_2 - z_{21}I_1}{z_{22}}\right) = \left(z_{11} - \frac{z_{12}z_{21}}{z_{22}}\right)I_1 + \frac{z_{12}}{z_{22}}V_2$$

$$= \frac{\Delta_z}{z_{22}}I_1 + \frac{z_{12}}{z_{22}}V_2$$

where $\Delta_z = z_{11}z_{22} - z_{12}z_{21}$. Comparing this result with Equation (12.26), we conclude that

$$h_{11} = \frac{\Delta_z}{z_{22}} \qquad h_{12} = \frac{z_{12}}{z_{22}}$$

In addition, from Equation (12.29), we have

$$I_2 = \frac{V_2 - z_{21}I_1}{z_{22}} = -\frac{z_{21}}{z_{22}}I_1 + \frac{1}{z_{22}}V_2$$

Comparing this result with Equation (12.27), we conclude that

$$h_{21} = -\frac{z_{21}}{z_{22}} \qquad h_{22} = \frac{1}{z_{22}}$$

Thus, for a reciprocal network ($z_{12} = z_{21}$), we see that $h_{12} = -h_{21}$, and vice versa.

A general equivalent circuit of a two-port whose **h** parameters are known is shown in Fig. 12.49. To verify that this equivalent circuit yields Equations (12.26) and (12.27), we need only apply KVL at port 1 and KCL at port 2.

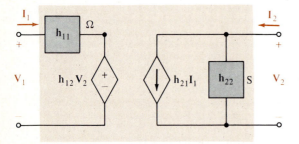

Fig. 12.49   General **h**-parameter equivalent circuit.

EXAMPLE 12.10

A two-port consisting of a transistor is terminated with a 10-kΩ resistor, as shown in Fig. 12.50. Typical **h** parameters are $h_{11} = 1$ kΩ, $h_{12} = 2.5 \times 10^{-4}$, $h_{21} = 50$, and $h_{22} = 25\ \mu S \Rightarrow 1/h_{22} = 40$ kΩ. By KCL,

$$50I_1 + \frac{V_2}{40,000} + \frac{V_2}{10,000} = 0 \qquad \Rightarrow \qquad 2 \times 10^6 I_1 + 5V_2 = 0$$

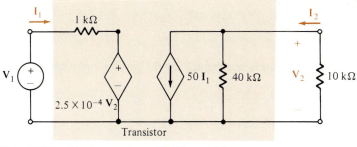

Fig. 12.50 Single transistor (BJT) amplifier.

But

$$I_1 = \frac{V_1 - 2.5 \times 10^{-4}V_2}{1000}$$ (12.30)

and substituting this expression into the previous one, we get

$$2000[V_1 - 2.5 \times 10^{-4}V_2] + 5V_2 = 0$$

from which the voltage gain is

$$\frac{V_2}{V_1} = -444.44$$

The input impedance is obtained from Equation (12.30):

$$I_1 = \frac{V_1 + (2.5 \times 10^{-4})(\tfrac{4}{9} \times 10^3)V_1}{1000} = \frac{1}{900} V_1$$

Hence, the impedance seen by the independent voltage source is

$$\frac{V_1}{I_1} = 900 \ \Omega$$

DRILL EXERCISE 12.9

For the transistor amplifier given in Fig. 12.50, remove the 10-kΩ load resistance and find the output impedance of the amplifier.
Answer: 80 kΩ

Some other two-port parameters are the **g parameters**, which are defined by the pair of equations

$$I_1 = g_{11}V_1 + g_{12}I_2$$
$$V_2 = g_{21}V_1 + g_{22}I_2$$

The corresponding matrix form is

$$\begin{bmatrix} I_1 \\ V_2 \end{bmatrix} = \begin{bmatrix} g_{11} & g_{12} \\ g_{21} & g_{22} \end{bmatrix} \begin{bmatrix} V_1 \\ I_2 \end{bmatrix}$$

The **transmission** or **ABCD parameters** are defined by the pair of equations

$$V_1 = AV_2 - BI_2$$
$$I_1 = CV_2 - DI_2$$

The corresponding matrix form is

$$\begin{bmatrix} V_1 \\ I_1 \end{bmatrix} = \begin{bmatrix} A & B \\ C & D \end{bmatrix} \begin{bmatrix} V_2 \\ -I_2 \end{bmatrix}$$

The appearance of the minus signs in the defining equations for the transmission parameters results in a special property for these parameters. Specifically, consider the **cascade connection** of two-ports shown in Fig. 12.51, and let us calculate the transmission parameters for the resulting two-port network.

For the individual two-ports, we have that

$$\begin{bmatrix} V_1' \\ I_1' \end{bmatrix} = \begin{bmatrix} A' & B' \\ C' & D' \end{bmatrix} \begin{bmatrix} V_2' \\ -I_2' \end{bmatrix} \quad \text{and} \quad \begin{bmatrix} V_1'' \\ I_1'' \end{bmatrix} = \begin{bmatrix} A'' & B'' \\ C'' & D'' \end{bmatrix} \begin{bmatrix} V_2'' \\ -I_2'' \end{bmatrix}$$

Since $V_1' = V_1$, $I_1' = I_1$, $V_1'' = V_2'$, $I_1'' = -I_2'$, $V_2'' = V_2$, and $I_2'' = I_2$, these matrix equations can be written as

$$\begin{bmatrix} V_1 \\ I_1 \end{bmatrix} = \begin{bmatrix} A' & B' \\ C' & D' \end{bmatrix} \begin{bmatrix} V_2' \\ -I_2' \end{bmatrix} \quad \text{and} \quad \begin{bmatrix} V_2' \\ -I_2' \end{bmatrix} = \begin{bmatrix} A'' & B'' \\ C'' & D'' \end{bmatrix} \begin{bmatrix} V_2 \\ -I_2 \end{bmatrix}$$

Combining these, we get

$$\begin{bmatrix} V_1 \\ I_1 \end{bmatrix} = \begin{bmatrix} A' & B' \\ C' & D' \end{bmatrix} \begin{bmatrix} A'' & B'' \\ C'' & D'' \end{bmatrix} \begin{bmatrix} V_2 \\ -I_2 \end{bmatrix} = \begin{bmatrix} A & B \\ C & D \end{bmatrix} \begin{bmatrix} V_2 \\ -I_2 \end{bmatrix}$$

Thus, we deduce that

$$\begin{bmatrix} A & B \\ C & D \end{bmatrix} = \begin{bmatrix} A' & B' \\ C' & D' \end{bmatrix} \begin{bmatrix} A'' & B'' \\ C'' & D'' \end{bmatrix}$$

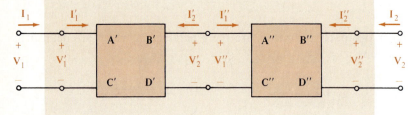

Fig. 12.51   Cascade connection of two-ports.

and we see that when two-ports are cascaded, the matrix of the transmission parameters for the resulting two-port is equal to the product of the matrices of the transmission parameters for the individual two-ports.

When two-ports are connected in different ways, the appropriate two-port parameters can be combined simply to yield the parameters for the resulting two-ports (see Problems 12.67–12.70).

Table 12.1 summarizes the conversion formulas for the five types of two-port parameters that we have discussed.

Table 12.1 CONVERSION OF TWO-PORT PARAMETERS

Two-Port Parameters	In terms of				
	y	**z**	**g**	**h**	**ABCD**
y	$y_{11} \quad y_{12}$ $y_{21} \quad y_{22}$	$\dfrac{z_{22}}{\Delta_z} \quad -\dfrac{z_{12}}{\Delta_z}$ $-\dfrac{z_{21}}{\Delta_z} \quad \dfrac{z_{11}}{\Delta_z}$	$\dfrac{\Delta_g}{g_{22}} \quad \dfrac{g_{12}}{g_{22}}$ $-\dfrac{g_{21}}{g_{22}} \quad \dfrac{1}{g_{22}}$	$\dfrac{1}{h_{11}} \quad -\dfrac{h_{12}}{h_{11}}$ $\dfrac{h_{21}}{h_{11}} \quad \dfrac{\Delta_h}{h_{11}}$	$\dfrac{D}{B} \quad -\dfrac{\Delta}{B}$ $-\dfrac{1}{B} \quad \dfrac{A}{B}$
z	$\dfrac{y_{22}}{\Delta_y} \quad -\dfrac{y_{12}}{\Delta_y}$ $-\dfrac{y_{21}}{\Delta_y} \quad \dfrac{y_{11}}{\Delta_y}$	$z_{11} \quad z_{12}$ $z_{21} \quad z_{22}$	$\dfrac{1}{g_{11}} \quad -\dfrac{g_{12}}{g_{11}}$ $\dfrac{g_{21}}{g_{11}} \quad \dfrac{\Delta_g}{g_{11}}$	$\dfrac{\Delta_h}{h_{22}} \quad \dfrac{h_{12}}{h_{22}}$ $-\dfrac{h_{21}}{h_{22}} \quad \dfrac{1}{h_{22}}$	$\dfrac{A}{C} \quad \dfrac{\Delta}{C}$ $\dfrac{1}{C} \quad \dfrac{D}{C}$
g	$\dfrac{\Delta_y}{y_{22}} \quad \dfrac{y_{12}}{y_{22}}$ $-\dfrac{y_{21}}{y_{22}} \quad \dfrac{1}{y_{22}}$	$\dfrac{1}{z_{11}} \quad -\dfrac{z_{12}}{z_{11}}$ $\dfrac{z_{21}}{z_{11}} \quad \dfrac{\Delta_z}{z_{11}}$	$g_{11} \quad g_{12}$ $g_{21} \quad g_{22}$	$\dfrac{h_{22}}{\Delta_h} \quad -\dfrac{h_{12}}{\Delta_h}$ $-\dfrac{h_{21}}{\Delta_h} \quad \dfrac{h_{11}}{\Delta_h}$	$\dfrac{C}{A} \quad -\dfrac{\Delta}{A}$ $\dfrac{1}{A} \quad \dfrac{B}{A}$
h	$\dfrac{1}{y_{11}} \quad -\dfrac{y_{12}}{y_{11}}$ $\dfrac{y_{21}}{y_{11}} \quad \dfrac{\Delta_y}{y_{11}}$	$\dfrac{\Delta_z}{z_{22}} \quad \dfrac{z_{12}}{z_{22}}$ $-\dfrac{z_{21}}{z_{22}} \quad \dfrac{1}{z_{22}}$	$\dfrac{g_{22}}{\Delta_g} \quad -\dfrac{g_{12}}{\Delta_g}$ $-\dfrac{g_{21}}{\Delta_g} \quad \dfrac{g_{11}}{\Delta_g}$	$h_{11} \quad h_{12}$ $h_{21} \quad h_{22}$	$\dfrac{B}{D} \quad \dfrac{\Delta}{D}$ $-\dfrac{1}{D} \quad \dfrac{C}{D}$
ABCD	$-\dfrac{y_{22}}{y_{21}} \quad -\dfrac{1}{y_{21}}$ $-\dfrac{\Delta_y}{y_{21}} \quad -\dfrac{y_{11}}{y_{21}}$	$\dfrac{z_{11}}{z_{21}} \quad \dfrac{\Delta_z}{z_{21}}$ $\dfrac{1}{z_{21}} \quad \dfrac{z_{22}}{z_{21}}$	$\dfrac{1}{g_{21}} \quad \dfrac{g_{22}}{g_{21}}$ $\dfrac{g_{11}}{g_{21}} \quad \dfrac{\Delta_g}{g_{21}}$	$-\dfrac{\Delta_h}{h_{21}} \quad -\dfrac{h_{11}}{h_{21}}$ $-\dfrac{h_{22}}{h_{21}} \quad -\dfrac{1}{h_{21}}$	$A \quad B$ $C \quad D$
	$\Delta_y = y_{11}y_{22}$ $\quad - y_{12}y_{21}$	$\Delta_z = z_{11}z_{22}$ $\quad - z_{12}z_{21}$	$\Delta_g = g_{11}g_{22}$ $\quad - g_{12}g_{21}$	$\Delta_h = h_{11}h_{22}$ $\quad - h_{12}h_{21}$	$\Delta = AD - BC$

● SUMMARY

1. A transformer is obtained by placing two inductors in physical proximity.

2. An ideal transformer has perfect coupling and infinite self-inductances.

3. The energy stored in an ideal transformer is zero.

4. A one-port network containing no independent sources can be described by its impedance or admittance.

5. A two-port network containing no independent sources may be described by certain two-port parameters.

6. A two-port for which $\mathbf{y}_{12} = \mathbf{y}_{21}$ (equivalently, $\mathbf{z}_{12} = \mathbf{z}_{21}$ or $\mathbf{h}_{12} = -\mathbf{h}_{21}$) is a reciprocal network.

● PROBLEMS FOR CHAPTER 12

12.1 Consider the sinusoidal transformer circuit given in Fig. 12.5 (p. 557).
  (a) Find the impedance seen by the source.
  (b) Find the energy stored in the transformer at time $t = 0$.

12.2 Consider the sinusoidal transformer circuit in Fig. 12.5 (p. 557). Find the reasonance frequency.

12.3 Repeat Problem 12.1 for the transformer circuit shown in Fig. P12.3, where $v(t) = 36\cos(3t - 60°)$ V.

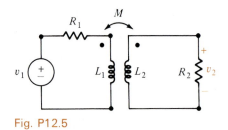

Fig. P12.5

12.6 Find the voltage transfer function $\mathbf{H}(s) = \mathbf{V}_2/\mathbf{V}_1$ for the transformer circuit in Fig. P12.6.

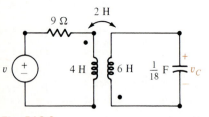

Fig. P12.3

12.4 For the circuit given in Fig. P12.3, find $v_C(t)$ when $v(t) = 36\cos(3t - 60°)$ V.

12.5 Find the voltage transfer function $\mathbf{H}(s) = \mathbf{V}_2/\mathbf{V}_1$ for the transformer circuit shown in Fig. P12.5.

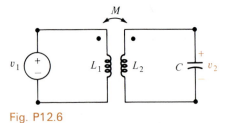

Fig. P12.6

12.7 Consider the transformer circuit given in Fig. P12.6.
  (a) Find the impedance seen by the source.
  (b) Find a formula for the resonance frequency.

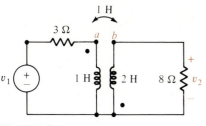

Fig. P12.8

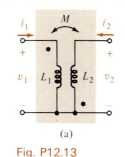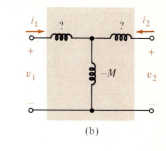

(a)   (b)

Fig. P12.13

12.8 Consider the transformer circuit shown in Fig. P12.8.
  (a) Find the voltage transfer function $\mathbf{H}(s) = \mathbf{V}_2/\mathbf{V}_1$.
  (b) Find the impedance seen by the source.

12.9 For the circuit given in Fig. P12.8, the 8-Ω resistor is the load. Replace the remainder of the circuit by its Thévenin equivalent, and then find $\mathbf{H}(s) = \mathbf{V}_2/\mathbf{V}_1$.

12.10 For the transformer circuit given in Fig. P12.8, place a 1-F capacitor between nodes a and b, and find $\mathbf{V}_2/\mathbf{V}_1$.

12.11 Find the voltage transfer function $\mathbf{H}(s) = \mathbf{V}_2/\mathbf{V}_1$ for the circuit in Fig. P12.11.

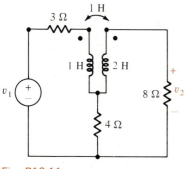

Fig. P12.11

12.12 For the circuit given in Problem 12.11 replace the 4-Ω resistor with a 1-F capacitor, and repeat the problem.

12.13 Given the transformer circuit in Fig. P12.13(a), what inductance values should be chosen in order to make the circuit in (b) the T-equivalent of (a)?

12.14 Use the result obtained in Problem 12.13 to solve Problem 12.8.

12.15 Verify that the circuit in Fig. P12.15 is a π-equivalent circuit of a transformer by expressing v_1 and v_2 in terms of i_1, i_2, L_1, L_2, and M.

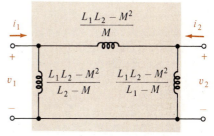

Fig. P12.15

12.16 For the sinusoidal transformer circuit given in Fig. 12.5 (p. 557), use the π-equivalent circuit shown in Fig. P12.15 to determine $v_C(t)$.

12.17 Consider the ideal-transformer circuit shown in Fig. P12.17.
  (a) What is the impedance seen by the voltage source?
  (b) What is the voltage gain $\mathbf{V}_2/\mathbf{V}_g$?
  (c) To what value should the 16-Ω load resistance be changed such that it will absorb maximum power?

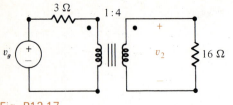

Fig. P12.17

12.18 For the circuit given in Fig. P12.17, assume a turns ratio of $1:N$. What value of N will result in the 16-Ω load resistor absorbing the maximum amount of power?

12.19 Repeat Problem 12.17 for the ideal-transformer circuit in Fig. P12.19, where the 8-Ω resistor is the load.

12.20 Consider the admittance shown in Fig. P12.20.
   (a) Find the resonance frequency.
   (b) Find the quality factor.
   (c) Find the bandwidth.

12.21 For the admittance given in Problem 12.20, interchange the inductor and the capacitor; then repeat the problem.

12.22 Consider the impedance indicated in Fig. P12.22.
   (a) Find the resonance frequency.
   (b) Find the quality factor.
   (c) Find the bandwidth.

12.23 For the impedance given in Problem 12.22, interchange the inductor and the capacitor; then repeat the problem.

12.24 Find the voltage transfer function $H(s) = V_C/V_g$ for the circuit shown in Fig. P12.22 when $R = 2\,\Omega$, $L = 3$ H, $C = \frac{1}{4}$ F, and $N = 5$.

12.25 For the circuit given in Fig. P12.22, find $v_C(t)$ when $R = 2\,\Omega, L = 2$ H, $C = 2$ F, $N = \frac{1}{10}$, and (a) $v_g(t) = 10\cos 5t$, (b) $v_g(t) = 10\cos 10t$ V.

12.26 Find $v(t)$ for the circuit in Fig. P12.26.

12.27 For the power amplifier given in Fig. 12.15 (p. 567), use an equivalent circuit

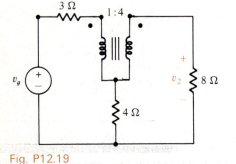

Fig. P12.19

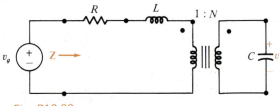

Fig. P12.22

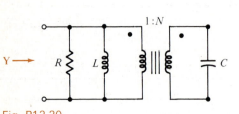

Fig. P12.20

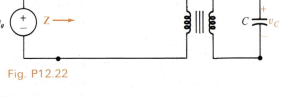

Fig. P12.26

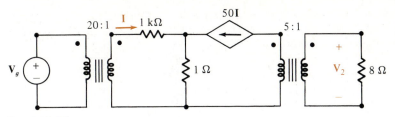

Fig. P12.28

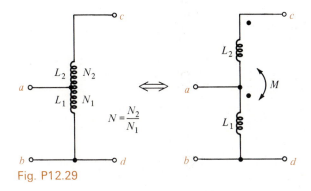

Fig. P12.29

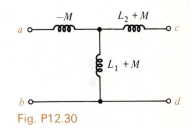

Fig. P12.30

of the ideal transformer to determine the power gain p_2/p_g.

12.28 Figure P12.28 represents the equivalent circuit of a simple "class-B" transistor power amplifier.

(a) Find the voltage gain $\mathbf{V}_2/\mathbf{V}_g$.

(b) If p_g is the power supplied by the voltage source and p_2 is the power absorbed by the 8-Ω load resistor, find the power gain p_2/p_g.

12.29 If a coil with $N_1 + N_2$ turns is "tapped," what results is known as an **autotransformer**. This connection is shown, along with its equivalent circuit, in Fig. P12.29. Place a capacitor C between terminals c and d, and assume that the autotransformer has perfect coupling $(k = 1)$. Show that the admittance between terminals a and b is $sC(1 + N)^2 + 1/L_1 s$.

12.30 Verify that the autotransformer given in Problem 12.29 can be modeled by

the equivalent circuit shown in Fig. P12.30.

12.31 For the autotransformer given in Problem 12.29, place a capacitor C between terminals a and b. Assuming perfect coupling, show that the admittance between terminals c and d is $sC/(1 + N)^2 + 1/Ls$, where $L = L_1 + L_2 + 2M$.

12.32 Find the resonance frequency for the admittance given in (a) Problem 12.29 and (b) Problem 12.31.

12.33 Find the **y** parameters for the resistive two-port T network in Fig. P12.33.

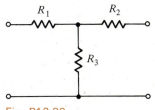

Fig. P12.33

12.34 Find the π-equivalent of the two-port given in Fig. P12.33. Compare your results with the Y-Δ transformation studied previously (see p. 424).

12.35 Determine whether or not the transformer circuit in Fig. P12.35 is a reciprocal network.

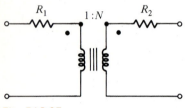

Fig. P12.35

12.36 Repeat Problem 12.35 for the transformer shown in Fig. P12.36.

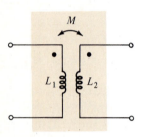

Fig. P12.36

12.37 Find the **y** parameters for the π network in Fig. P12.37.

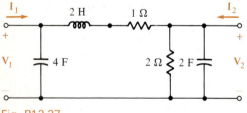

Fig. P12.37

12.38 For the circuit shown in Fig. P12.37, given that $\mathbf{I}_2 = 0$, (a) find $\mathbf{V}_2/\mathbf{V}_1$ and (b) change the 2-Ω resistor to 3 Ω and find $\mathbf{V}_2/\mathbf{V}_1$.

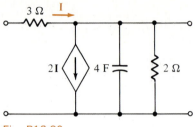

Fig. P12.39

12.39 Determine whether or not the two-port shown in Fig. P12.39 is a reciprocal network.

12.40 Repeat Problem 12.39 for the circuit in Fig. P12.40.

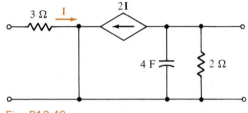

Fig. P12.40

12.41 Find the values of the dependent voltage sources so that the circuit shown in Fig. P12.41 is the equivalent circuit of a two-port having the **y** parameters $\mathbf{y}_{11}, \mathbf{y}_{12}, \mathbf{y}_{21}, \mathbf{y}_{22}$.

12.42 For an arbitrary two-port network, find an expression for the impedance

$$\frac{\mathbf{V}_1}{\mathbf{I}_1}\bigg|_{\mathbf{I}_2=0}$$

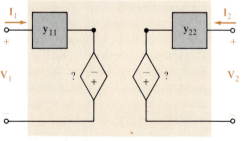

Fig. P12.41

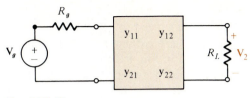

Fig. P12.43

in terms of the **y** parameters of the two-port.

12.43 For the network shown in Fig. P12.43, find V_2/V_g given that $y_{11} = 3$ S, $y_{12} = -1$ S, $y_{21} = 20$ S, $y_{22} = 2$ S, $R_g = 1$ Ω, and $R_L = 0.1$ Ω.

12.44 Repeat Problem 12.43 for the case that $y_{11} = y_{22} = 0.5$ S, $y_{12} = y_{21} = -1$ S, $R_g = 0.4$ Ω, and $R_L = 10$ Ω.

12.45 In the circuit in Fig. P12.45, z_{11}, z_{12}, z_{21}, and z_{22} are impedances. Find the **y** parameters for this two-port.

12.46 Find the **y** parameters for the two-port shown in Fig. P12.46, which contains an operational amplifier.

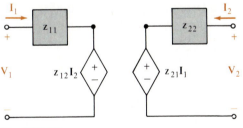

Fig. P12.45

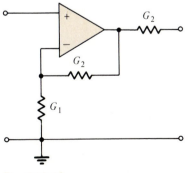

Fig. P12.46

12.47 Repeat Problem 12.46 for the op-amp circuit in Fig. P12.47.

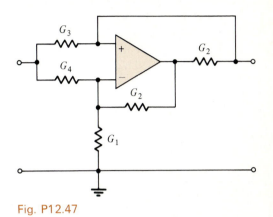

Fig. P12.47

12.48 Find the **z** parameters for the resistive two-port π network shown in Fig. P12.48.

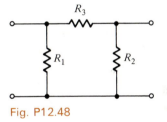

Fig. P12.48

12.49 Find the T-equivalent of the two-port given in Fig. P12.48. Compare your results with the Δ-Y transformation studied previously (see p. 424).

12.50 Find the **z** parameters of the T network shown in Fig. P12.50.

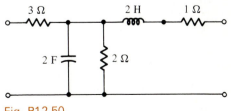

Fig. P12.50

12.51 Find the **z** parameters of the two-port given in Fig. P12.39.

12.52 Find the **z** parameters of the two-port given in Fig. P12.40.

12.53 A two-port network has **z** parameters z_{11}, z_{12}, z_{21}, and z_{22}. Find the **y** parameters of this two-port in terms of the **z** parameters.

12.54 Given a two-port network, find

$$\left.\frac{V_2}{V_1}\right|_{I_2=0}$$

in terms of the **z** parameters of the two-port.

12.55 A two-port network is terminated with a 1-Ω load resistor. Find an expression for V_2/V_1 in terms of the two-port's **z** parameters.

12.56 Find the values of the dependent current sources so that the circuit shown in Fig. P12.56 is the equivalent circuit of a two-port having the **z** parameters z_{11}, z_{12}, z_{21}, z_{22}.

12.57 For the network shown in Fig. P12.57, find V_2/V_g given that $z_{11} = 2\ \Omega$, $z_{12} = 3\ \Omega = z_{21}$, and $z_{22} = 3\ \Omega$.

12.58 Repeat Problem 12.57 for the case that z_{21} is changed to $z_{21} = 5\ \Omega$.

12.59 Find the **h** parameters of the two-port shown in Fig. P12.59.

12.60 Consider a two-port network whose **y** parameters are y_{11}, y_{12}, y_{21}, and y_{22}. Express the **h** parameters of this network in terms of its **y** parameters.

12.61 Given a two-port network, find an expression for

$$\left.\frac{V_2}{V_1}\right|_{I_2=0}$$

in terms of the network's **h** parameters.

12.62 A two-port network is terminated with a 1-Ω load resistor. Find an expression for V_2/V_1 in terms of the **h** parameters of the two-port.

12.63 The two-port given in Fig. P12.57 has **h** parameters $h_{11} = 2\ \Omega$, $h_{12} = 0.6$, $h_{21} = 4$, and $h_{22} = 0.5$ S. Find V_2/V_g.

12.64 Find the **g** parameters for the π network given in Fig. P12.59.

12.65 Draw an equivalent circuit for a two-port described by its **g** parameters.

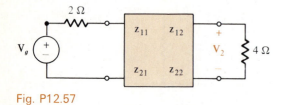

Fig. P12.56

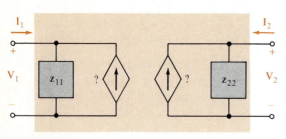

Fig. P12.57

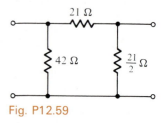

Fig. P12.59

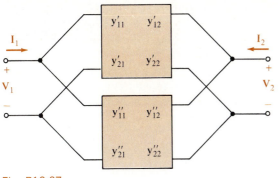

Fig. P12.67

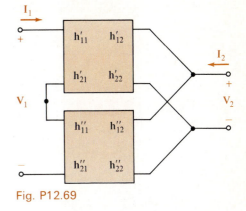

Fig. P12.69

12.66 A two-port network is terminated with a 1-Ω load resistor. Find an expression for V_2/V_1 in terms of its transmission parameters.

12.67 Figure P12.67 shows a parallel-parallel connection of two-ports. Find the **y** parameters of the resulting two-port in terms of the **y** parameters of the individual two-ports.

12.68 Figure P12.68 shows a series-series connection of two-ports. Find the **z** parameters of the resulting two-port in terms of the **z** parameters of the individual two-ports.

12.69 Figure P12.69 shows a series-parallel connection of two-ports. Find the **h** parameters of the resulting two-port in terms of the **h** parameters of the individual two-ports.

12.70 Figure P12.70 shows a parallel-series connection of two-ports. Find the **g** parameters of the resulting two-port in terms of the **g** parameters of the individual two-ports.

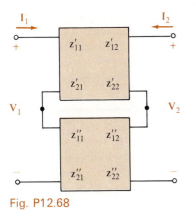

Fig. P12.68

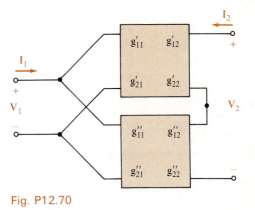

Fig. P12.70

CHAPTER 13

Fourier Series

● INTRODUCTION

Previously we mentioned that the sinusoid is a very important function. In this chapter we shall discuss a major reason why: A repetitive or periodic function is equal to a (probably infinite) sum of sinusoids! As a consequence of the linearity property of linear circuits, this result—known as Fourier's theorem—means that circuits with nonsinusoidal inputs that are periodic can be analyzed with sinusoidal phasor techniques.

A periodic function can be expressed as a sum of sinusoids. Such a sum, known as the Fourier series representation or Fourier series of the function, can be either trigonometric or exponential in form. It is the latter form that suggests a generalization, known as the Fourier transform, that enables us to analyze circuits having inputs that are nonperiodic.

We start this chapter by stating (without proof) Fourier's theorem. Next we discuss the direct approach for obtaining the trigonometric form of the Fourier series representation of a periodic function. When speaking of the trigonometric Fourier series, we can use one of two forms; one consists of sines and cosines, whereas the other consists of sinusoids with phase angles. We then see how to determine the response of a circuit to a periodic function by using the Fourier series representation of the function, the principle of superposition, and sinusoidal circuit analysis. By using symmetry properties of certain functions we then discuss the subject of reducing the work required for determining the Fourier series representations of these functions. Furthermore, we see that it may be quite a bit simpler to find the Fourier series representation of a function by utilizing one of its derivatives rather than dealing directly with the function. The key to this shortcut is the impulse function and its sampling property. Finally, we use Euler's formula to develop the complex or exponential form of the Fourier series. Although less intuitive (since complex sinusoids are less intuitive than real sinusoids), this form is more compact than the trigonometric form. More important, though, we shall see in the next chapter how the exponential form can be extended to the concept of the Fourier transform, which allows the analysis of circuits whose inputs are nonperiodic.

13.1 THE TRIGONOMETRIC FOURIER SERIES

We begin by considering functions that have a very special property—periodicity.

A function $f(t)$ is said to be **periodic** if there exists a positive, real number T such that

$$f(t + T) = f(t)$$

for all t. If $f(t)$ is periodic, then we say that T is the **period** of $f(t)$.

According to this definition, if $f(t)$ is periodic with period T, it is also periodic with period $2T$ (or $3T$, or $4T$, etc.). However, when it is stated that the periodic function $f(t)$ has period T, the usual implication is that there is no positive $T' < T$ for which $f(t)$ is periodic.

EXAMPLE 13.1

For the function $f(t) = \sin \omega t$, since

$$\sin \omega \left(t + \frac{2\pi}{\omega} \right) = \sin(\omega t + 2\pi) = \sin \omega t \qquad \text{for all} \quad t$$

then $\sin \omega t$ is periodic, with period $T = 2\pi/\omega$.

Similarly, $\cos \omega t$ and $\cos(\omega t + \phi)$ are periodic and have period $T = 2\pi/\omega$. Furthermore, since

$$e^{j\omega(t + 2\pi/\omega)} = e^{j\omega t + j2\pi} = e^{j\omega t}e^{j2\pi} = e^{j\omega t} \qquad \text{for all} \quad t$$

then $e^{j\omega t}$ is periodic, with period $T = 2\pi/\omega$.

From this example, it should be clear that sinusoids are periodic functions. What may not be clear is the remarkable result that "any" periodic function (exceptions are certain types of exotic functions that are rarely, if ever, encountered) can be expressed as a sum of sinusoids of appropriate amplitudes and frequencies. This result, known as Fourier's theorem,[†] can be summarized as follows.

[†] Named for the French mathematician Joseph Fourier (1768–1830).

Fourier's Theorem

Given the real function $f(t)$, which is periodic with period T seconds, there exist real numbers $a_0, a_1, b_1, a_2, b_2, a_3, b_3, \ldots$ such that

$$f(t) = a_0 + a_1 \cos \omega_0 t + b_1 \sin \omega_0 t + a_2 \cos 2\omega_0 t + b_2 \sin 2\omega_0 t$$
$$+ a_3 \cos 3\omega_0 t + b_3 \sin 3\omega_0 t + \cdots \tag{13.1}$$

or

$$f(t) = a_0 + \sum_{n=1}^{\infty} (a_n \cos n\omega_0 t + b_n \sin n\omega_0 t) \tag{13.2}$$

where $\omega_0 = 2\pi/T$ radians per second is called the **fundamental frequency** or **first harmonic** of $f(t)$. The frequency $n\omega_0$ is called the **nth harmonic**. The above formula (either form) is known as the **trigonometric Fourier series** of $f(t)$. The constants a_0, $a_1, b_1, a_2, b_2, a_3, b_3, \ldots$ are called the **(trigonometric) Fourier coefficients** of $f(t)$.

Although the proof of Fourier's theorem is beyond the scope of this book, the application is not. The problem therefore is, given a periodic function $f(t)$, what is its Fourier series representation? In other words, how are the Fourier coefficients determined and what are they?

In order to answer these questions, we shall need to employ some trigonometric properties. It is a matter of elementary integral calculus to show for $\omega_0 = 2\pi/T$ that

$$\int_0^T \sin \omega_0 t \, dt = 0 \qquad \text{and} \qquad \int_0^T \cos \omega_0 t \, dt = 0$$

Although the above integrations are performed over the period from 0 to T, the same results are obtained when the integrations are performed over an arbitrary period, say from t_1 to $t_1 + T$, for any t_1.

Furthermore, it is not much more involved to verify the more general results

$$\int_0^T \sin n\omega_0 t \, dt = 0 \tag{13.3}$$

and

$$\int_0^T \cos n\omega_0 t \, dt = 0 \tag{13.4}$$

for all $n = 1, 2, 3, \ldots$. Again, when the integrations are performed over any interval of T seconds, the same results are obtained.

By using the trigonometric identity $\sin A \cos B = \frac{1}{2}[\sin(A + B) + \sin(A - B)]$, it can be shown for $n = 1, 2, 3, \ldots$ and $m = 1, 2, 3, \ldots$ that

$$\int_0^T \sin m\omega_0 t \cos n\omega_0 t \, dt = 0 \tag{13.5}$$

Furthermore, with the use of $\cos A \cos B = \frac{1}{2}[\cos(A + B) + \cos(A - B)]$, it follows that

$$\int_0^T \cos m\omega_0 t \cos n\omega_0 t \, dt = \begin{cases} 0 & \text{for} \quad m \neq n \\ \dfrac{T}{2} & \text{for} \quad m = n \end{cases} \tag{13.6}$$

Finally, with $\sin A \sin B = \frac{1}{2}[\cos(A - B) - \cos(A + B)]$, it follows that

$$\int_0^T \sin m\omega_0 t \sin n\omega_0 t \, dt = \begin{cases} 0 & \text{for} \quad m \neq n \\ \dfrac{T}{2} & \text{for} \quad m = n \end{cases} \tag{13.7}$$

Returning to the Fourier series, Equation (13.2), integrating both sides of this equation over a period yields

$$\int_0^T f(t) \, dt = \int_0^T \left[a_0 + \sum_{n=1}^{\infty} (a_n \cos n\omega_0 t + b_n \sin n\omega_0 t) \right] dt \tag{13.8}$$

But since the integral of a sum is the sum of the integrals,

$$\int_0^T f(t) \, dt = \int_0^T a_0 \, dt + \sum_{n=1}^{\infty} \left[\int_0^T a_n \cos n\omega_0 t \, dt + \int_0^T b_n \sin n\omega_0 t \, dt \right] \tag{13.9}$$

But, from Equations (13.4) and (13.3), the two integrals inside the summation vanish. The result is

$$\int_0^T f(t) \, dt = a_0 \int_0^T dt = a_0 t \Big|_0^T = a_0 T$$

from which

$$a_0 = \frac{1}{T} \int_0^T f(t) \, dt \tag{13.10}$$

Thus, we have a formula for the Fourier coefficient a_0—called the **average value** of $f(t)$ or the **dc component** of $f(t)$. The limits on the integral can be replaced with any interval of T seconds.

Suppose now that in the formula for the Fourier series, both sides are first multiplied by the factor $\cos m\omega_0 t$ and then integrated with respect to t. Then

$$\int_0^T f(t) \cos m\omega_0 t \, dt = \int_0^T \left[a_0 + \sum_{n=1}^{\infty} (a_n \cos n\omega_0 t + b_n \sin n\omega_0 t) \right] \cos m\omega_0 t \, dt$$

$$= \int_0^T a_0 \cos m\omega_0 t \, dt + \sum_{n=1}^{\infty} \left[\int_0^T a_n \cos n\omega_0 t \cos m\omega_0 t \, dt \right.$$

$$\left. + \int_0^T b_n \sin n\omega_0 t \cos m\omega_0 t \, dt \right]$$

From Equations (13.4), (13.6), and (13.5), on the right-hand side of this equation the first integral is zero for all $m = 1, 2, 3, \ldots$, the second integral is zero for $m \neq n$ and equal to $a_n(T/2)$ when $m = n$, and the third integral is zero for all $m = 1, 2, 3, \ldots$ and $n = 1, 2, 3, \ldots$. Thus,

$$\int_0^T f(t) \cos m\omega_0 t \, dt = a_n\left(\frac{T}{2}\right) \qquad \text{for} \quad n = m$$

Hence,

$$a_n = \frac{2}{T} \int_0^T f(t) \cos n\omega_0 t \, dt \qquad \text{for} \quad n = 1, 2, 3, \ldots \tag{13.11}$$

is a formula for the coefficient a_n; the limits of integration can be over an arbitrary period as well.

By multiplying both sides of the Fourier series formula by $\sin m\omega_0 t$ and integrating with respect to t, in a similar manner we obtain the formula

$$b_n = \frac{2}{T} \int_0^T f(t) \sin n\omega_0 t \, dt \qquad \text{for} \quad n = 1, 2, 3, \ldots \tag{13.12}$$

where the integral can be over an arbitrary period as well.

EXAMPLE 13.2

The periodic function shown in Fig. 13.1 is known as a half-wave rectified sine wave. For this function $T = 2$ s. Thus, $\omega_0 = 2\pi/T = \pi$ rad/s. The dc component is

$$a_0 = \frac{1}{T} \int_0^T f(t) \, dt = \frac{1}{2}\left[\int_0^1 f(t) \, dt + \int_1^2 f(t) \, dt\right] = \frac{1}{2}\left[\int_0^1 \sin \pi t \, dt + 0\right] = \frac{1}{\pi}$$

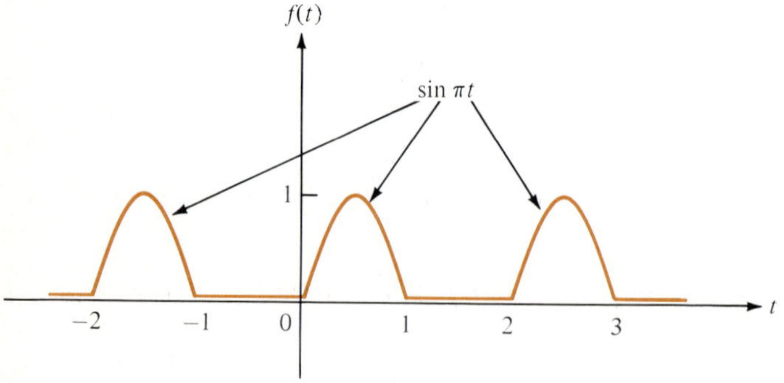

Fig. 13.1   Half-wave rectified sine wave.

In addition,

$$a_n = \frac{2}{T} \int_0^T f(t) \cos n\omega_0 t \, dt = \frac{2}{T} \left[\int_0^1 f(t) \cos n\omega_0 t \, dt + \int_1^2 f(t) \cos n\omega_0 t \, dt \right]$$

$$= \frac{2}{2} \int_0^1 \sin \pi t \cos n\pi t \, dt = \int_0^1 \frac{1}{2} [\sin \pi(1 + n)t + \sin \pi(1 - n)t] \, dt$$

For $n = 1$, we get

$$a_1 = \int_0^1 \frac{1}{2} \sin 2\pi t \, dt = \frac{1}{2} \left(\frac{-1}{2\pi} \cos 2\pi t \right) \Big|_0^1 = 0$$

For $n = 2, 3, 4, \ldots$,

$$a_n = \frac{1 - \cos(1 + n)\pi}{2\pi(1 + n)} + \frac{1 - \cos(1 - n)\pi}{2\pi(1 - n)}$$

Since for n even ($n = 2, 4, 6, \ldots$), $n + 1$ and $n - 1$ are odd, then

$$\cos(1 + n)\pi = -1 \qquad \text{and} \qquad \cos(1 - n)\pi = \cos(n - 1)\pi = -1$$

so

$$\cos(1 + n)\pi = \cos(1 - n)\pi$$

and since for n odd ($n = 3, 5, 7, \ldots$), $n + 1$ and $n - 1$ are even, then

$$\cos(1 + n)\pi = \cos(n - 1)\pi = \cos(1 - n)\pi = 1$$

Therefore,

$$a_n = \frac{1 - \cos(1 + n)\pi}{2\pi(1 + n)} + \frac{1 - \cos(1 + n)\pi}{2\pi(1 - n)}$$

or

$$a_n = \frac{1 - \cos(1 + n)\pi}{\pi(1 + n)(1 - n)} = \frac{1 - \cos(1 + n)\pi}{\pi(1 - n^2)} \qquad \text{for} \quad n = 2, 3, 4, \ldots$$

Next,

$$b_n = \frac{2}{T} \int_0^T f(t) \sin n\omega_0 t \, dt = \int_0^1 \sin \pi t \sin n\pi t \, dt$$

$$= \int_0^1 \frac{1}{2} [\cos \pi(1 - n)t - \cos \pi(1 + n)t] \, dt$$

For the case $n = 1$, we get

$$b_1 = \int_0^1 \frac{1}{2} [1 - \cos 2\pi t] \, dt = \frac{1}{2} \int_0^1 dt - \frac{1}{2} \int_0^1 \cos 2\pi t \, dt$$

$$= \frac{1}{2} t \Big|_0^1 - \frac{1}{2} \left(\frac{1}{2\pi} \sin 2\pi t \right) \Big|_0^1 = \frac{1}{2}$$

For $n = 2, 3, 4, \ldots,$

$$b_n = \frac{\sin(1-n)\pi}{2\pi(1-n)} - \frac{\sin(1+n)\pi}{2\pi(1+n)}$$

But

$$\sin(1-n)\pi = \sin(1+n)\pi = 0$$

so

$$b_n = 0 \quad \text{for} \quad n = 2, 3, 4, \ldots$$

Thus, the trigonometric Fourier series for $f(t)$ is

$$f(t) = a_0 + \sum_{n=1}^{\infty} (a_n \cos n\omega_0 t + b_n \sin n\omega_0 t)$$

$$= \frac{1}{\pi} + \sum_{n=2}^{\infty} \frac{1 - \cos(1+n)\pi}{\pi(1-n^2)} \cos n\pi t + \frac{1}{2} \sin \pi t$$

Writing the first few terms in this sum we have

$$f(t) = \frac{1}{\pi} + \frac{1}{2} \sin \pi t - \frac{2}{3\pi} \cos 2\pi t - \frac{2}{15\pi} \cos 4\pi t - \frac{2}{35\pi} \cos 6\pi t - \cdots$$

$$= 0.32 + 0.5 \sin \pi t - 0.21 \cos 2\pi t - 0.04 \cos 4\pi t - 0.02 \cos 6\pi t - \cdots$$

Therefore, the half-wave rectified sine wave is composed of a dc component, a sinusoid having the fundamental frequency, and sinusoids whose frequencies are the even harmonics. In order to get an idea of the relative amount of the components constituting $f(t)$, we can plot the magnitude of each sinusoid (the dc component is a sinusoid of zero frequency) versus frequency. Such a plot is shown in Fig. 13.2.

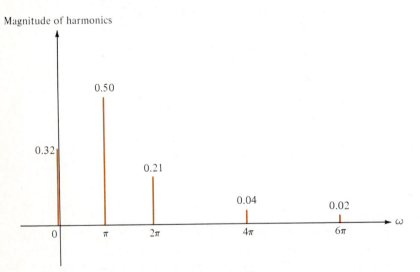

Fig. 13.2 Plot of harmonic magnitude versus frequency.

DRILL EXERCISE 13.1

Find the trigonometric Fourier series of the function $f(t)$ shown in Fig. DE13.1.

Answer: $-\dfrac{1}{2} - \dfrac{2}{\pi} \sin \pi t - \dfrac{2}{3\pi} \sin 3\pi t - \dfrac{2}{5\pi} \sin 5\pi t - \dfrac{2}{7\pi} \sin 7\pi t - \cdots$

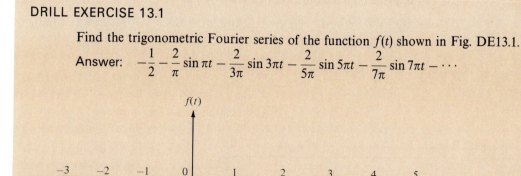

Fig. DE13.1

In Example 13.2, the nth harmonic component of $f(t)$ consists either entirely of a sine or a cosine, but not both. Thus, the magnitude of the nth harmonic component is equal to the amplitude of the corresponding sinusoid.

In general, however, the nth term in the summation of the Fourier series is

$$a_n \cos n\omega_0 t + b_n \sin n\omega_0 t$$

Since this can be rewritten as

$$A_n \cos(n\omega_0 t + \phi_n)$$

where

$$A_n = \sqrt{a_n^2 + b_n^2} \qquad \text{and} \qquad \phi_n = -\tan^{-1} \frac{b_n}{a_n}$$

then the amplitude of the nth harmonic (component) is $\sqrt{a_n^2 + b_n^2}$.

Consequently, an alternative form of the trigonometric Fourier series is

$$f(t) = a_0 + \sum_{n=1}^{\infty} A_n \cos(n\omega_0 t + \phi_n)$$

In Example 13.2, the plot of the magnitude of the harmonics versus frequency is the same as a plot of the amplitude A_n of the harmonics versus frequency, which we shall call the **amplitude spectrum** of $f(t)$. In a similar vein, we can plot the phase angle ϕ_n of the harmonics versus frequency. Such a plot is called the **phase spectrum** of $f(t)$. The amplitude and phase spectra constitute the **frequency spectrum** of $f(t)$. Despite this definition, people often refer to the amplitude spectrum alone as the frequency spectrum, for in many situations phase is not an important factor.

For the preceding example, we can write $f(t)$ as

$$f(t) = 0.32 + 0.5\cos(\pi t - 90°) + 0.21\cos(2\pi t - 180°) + 0.04\cos(4\pi t - 180°)$$
$$+ 0.02\cos(6\pi t - 180°) + \cdots$$

Thus, a plot of the phase spectrum of $f(t)$ is shown in Fig. 13.3.

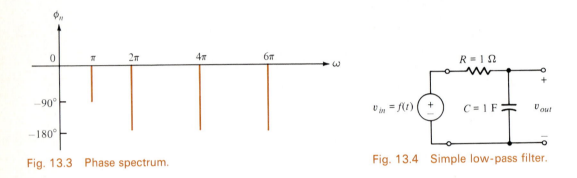

Fig. 13.3   Phase spectrum.

Fig. 13.4   Simple low-pass filter.

A Circuit Application

Suppose now that the function $f(t)$ given in Example 13.2 is a voltage that is the input to the series RC network shown in Fig. 13.4.

Since

$$v_{in} = \frac{1}{\pi} + \frac{1}{2}\sin \pi t + \sum_{n=2}^{\infty} a_n \cos n\pi t = v_0 + v_1 + \sum_{n=2}^{\infty} v_n$$

then by the property of linearity,

$$v_{out} = v_0^1 + v_1^1 + \sum_{n=2}^{\infty} v_n^1$$

where v_i^1 is the output when the input is v_i.

Using phasors and voltage division,

$$\mathbf{V}_{out} = \frac{1/j\omega C}{(1/j\omega C) + R}\mathbf{V}_{in} = \frac{1}{1 + j\omega RC}\mathbf{V}_{in} = \frac{1}{1 + j\omega}\mathbf{V}_{in} = \frac{\mathbf{V}_{in}}{\sqrt{1 + \omega^2}/\tan^{-1}\omega}$$

The response to the input

$$\mathbf{V}_0 = \frac{1}{\pi} \quad (\omega = 0) \quad \text{is} \quad \mathbf{V}_0^1 = \frac{1}{1 + j0}\left(\frac{1}{\pi}\right) = \frac{1}{\pi}$$

(Remember that a capacitor is an open circuit to dc, and therefore, for the dc part, the output voltage equals the input voltage.) The phasor representation of the first harmonic is

$$\mathbf{V}_1 = \tfrac{1}{2}/{-90°} \quad (\omega = \pi \text{ rad/s})$$

The response (in phasor form) to this input is

$$\mathbf{V}_1^1 = \frac{(1/2)\underline{/-90°}}{\sqrt{1+\pi^2}\,\underline{/\tan^{-1}\pi}} = \frac{1}{2\sqrt{1+\pi^2}}\,\underline{/(-90° - \tan^{-1}\pi)} = 0.15\,\underline{/-162.3°}$$

The nth harmonic ($n \geq 2$) of the input is

$$\mathbf{V}_n = a_n\underline{/0°} = a_n \qquad (\omega = n\pi \text{ rad/s})$$

and its response is

$$\mathbf{V}_n^1 = \frac{a_n}{\sqrt{1+(n\pi)^2}\,\underline{/\tan^{-1}(n\pi)}} = \frac{a_n}{\sqrt{1+(n\pi)^2}}\,\underline{/-\tan^{-1}(n\pi)}$$

Hence, the output voltage is

$$v_{out} = \frac{1}{\pi} + 0.15\cos(\pi t - 162.3°) + \sum_{n=2}^{\infty} \frac{a_n}{\sqrt{1+(n\pi)^2}}\cos[n\pi t - \tan^{-1}(n\pi)]$$

Writing the first two nonzero terms in the summation, we get

$$v_{out} = 0.32 + 0.15\cos(\pi t - 162.3°) - 0.033\cos(2\pi t - 81°)$$
$$- 0.0034\cos(4\pi t - 85.4°) - \cdots$$

The amplitude spectrum of v_{out} is shown in Fig. 13.5. Note that the entire dc component of the input appears at the output. However, only 30 percent of the first harmonic reaches the output, only about 14 percent of the second harmonic, and so on. In the expression for v_{out} we see that the RC circuit diminishes the amount of higher harmonics (second and above) by the factor $1/\sqrt{1+(n\pi)^2}$. Such a circuit is an example of a low-pass filter.

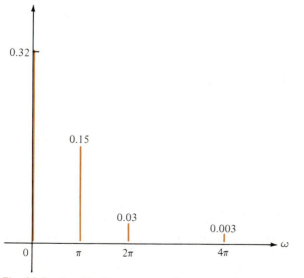

Fig. 13.5 Amplitude spectrum of output voltage.

13.2 FUNCTIONAL SYMMETRY

Having seen a use for the Fourier series, let us return to the problem of determining the Fourier series of a periodic function $f(t)$. Needless to say, this can be accomplished by substituting the expression for $f(t)$ into the formulas for a_0, a_n, and b_n. However, for even some rather innocuous-looking functions, an inordinate amount of calculation may result. Fortunately, it is often possible to take shortcuts by using different mathematical operations and properties. To begin with, we define the following:

A function $f(t)$ is said to be an **even function**, or simply **even**, if

$$f(-t) = f(t) \qquad \text{for all} \quad t$$

From the definition, it is apparent that an even function is one whose plot is symmetrical around the vertical axis.

As an example, the function $f(t) = t^2$ is an even function. Since $\cos(-\theta) = \cos\theta$, the function $f(t) = \cos\omega t$ is an even, periodic function of t.

We shall now see how to reduce the amount of work required to determine the Fourier series of an even, periodic function.

In the formula for the coefficient a_n [Equation (13.11) on p. 600], let us select the period of integration to be $-T/2$ to $T/2$. Then

$$a_n = \frac{2}{T} \int_{-T/2}^{T/2} f(t) \cos n\omega_0 t \, dt$$

$$= \frac{2}{T} \int_{-T/2}^{0} f(t) \cos n\omega_0 t \, dt + \frac{2}{T} \int_{0}^{T/2} f(t) \cos n\omega_0 t \, dt$$

Replacing t by $-t$ in the first integral yields

$$a_n = \frac{2}{T} \int_{-T/2}^{0} f(-t) \cos n\omega_0(-t) \, d(-t) + \frac{2}{T} \int_{0}^{T/2} f(t) \cos n\omega_0 t \, dt$$

Since $\cos n\omega_0(-t) = \cos(-n\omega_0 t) = \cos n\omega_0 t$, $d(-t) = -dt$, and

$$\int_{-T/2}^{0} d(-t) = -\int_{T/2}^{0} dt = \int_{0}^{T/2} dt$$

then

$$a_n = \frac{2}{T} \int_{0}^{T/2} f(-t) \cos n\omega_0 t \, dt + \frac{2}{T} \int_{0}^{T/2} f(t) \cos n\omega_0 t \, dt$$

If $f(t)$ is even, then $f(-t) = f(t)$, and thus

$$\boxed{a_n = \frac{4}{T} \int_{0}^{T/2} f(t) \cos n\omega_0 t \, dt \qquad \text{for} \quad f(t) \text{ even}}$$

Therefore, the coefficient a_n can be determined by integrating over half a period; but this half-period must be the interval from $t = 0$ to $t = T/2$.

Although this is possibly time-saving, the significant result about even periodic functions deals with the coefficient b_n. From Equation (13.12) on p. 600,

$$b_n = \frac{2}{T} \int_{-T/2}^{T/2} f(t) \sin n\omega_0 t \, dt$$

$$= \frac{2}{T} \int_{-T/2}^{0} f(t) \sin n\omega_0 t \, dt + \frac{2}{T} \int_{0}^{T/2} f(t) \sin n\omega_0 t \, dt$$

Again, replacing t by $-t$ in the first integral, since $\sin n\omega_0(-t) = \sin(-n\omega_0 t) = -\sin n\omega_0 t$, then

$$b_n = -\frac{2}{T} \int_{0}^{T/2} f(-t) \sin n\omega_0 t \, dt + \frac{2}{T} \int_{0}^{T/2} f(t) \sin n\omega_0 t \, dt$$

If $f(t)$ is an even function, then $f(-t) = f(t)$ and

$$b_n = 0 \qquad \text{for} \quad n = 1, 2, 3, \ldots$$

These results can also be justified intuitively. Since the cosine function is even, a sum of cosines will also be even. However, the sine function is not even, so the addition of sine components will yield a function that is not even.

EXAMPLE 13.3

For the "square-wave" function shown in Fig. 13.6, the period is $T = 2$ s. Thus $\omega_0 = 2\pi/T = \pi$ rad/s. Let us determine the Fourier series for this function.

In a manner similar to that described for a_n, we can also show that for an even function

$$a_0 = \frac{2}{T} \int_{0}^{T/2} f(t) \, dt$$

Since $f(t)$ is even,

$$a_0 = \frac{2}{2} \int_{0}^{1} f(t) \, dt = \int_{0}^{1/2} 1 \, dt + \int_{1/2}^{1} -1 \, dt = \frac{1}{2} - \frac{1}{2} = 0$$

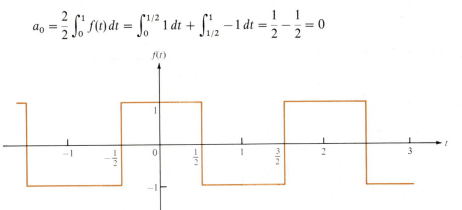

Fig. 13.6   Square-wave function.

Also,

$$a_n = \frac{4}{T} \int_0^{T/2} f(t) \cos n\omega_0 t \, dt = 2 \int_0^1 f(t) \cos n\pi t \, dt$$

$$= 2 \left[\int_0^{1/2} \cos n\pi t \, dt + \int_{1/2}^1 - \cos n\pi t \, dt \right] = \frac{4}{n\pi} \sin \frac{n\pi}{2}$$

Furthermore, since $f(t)$ is an even function,

$$b_n = 0 \quad \text{for} \quad n = 1, 2, 3, \ldots$$

Thus,

$$f(t) = a_0 + \sum_{n=1}^{\infty} (a_n \cos n\omega_0 t + b_n \sin n\omega_0 t) = \sum_{n=1}^{\infty} \frac{4}{n\pi} \sin \frac{n\pi}{2} \cos n\pi t$$

Writing out the first few terms of the series, we get

$$f(t) = \frac{4}{\pi} \cos \pi t - \frac{4}{3\pi} \cos 3\pi t + \frac{4}{5\pi} \cos 5\pi t - \frac{4}{7\pi} \cos 7\pi t + \cdots$$

$$= 1.27 \cos \pi t - 0.42 \cos 3\pi t + 0.25 \cos 5\pi t - 0.18 \cos 7\pi t + \cdots$$

DRILL EXERCISE 13.2

Find the Fourier series of the pulse train shown in Fig. DE13.2.

Answer: $0.67 + 0.276 \cos \dfrac{2\pi}{3} t - 0.138 \cos \dfrac{4\pi}{3} t + 0.069 \cos \dfrac{8\pi}{3} t$

$- 0.055 \cos \dfrac{10\pi}{3} t + \cdots$

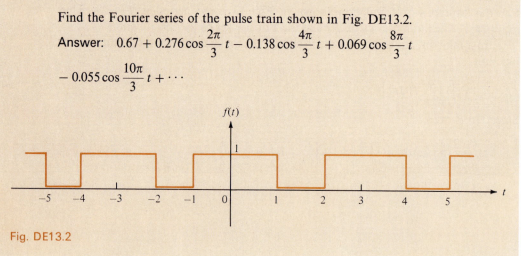

Fig. DE13.2

In addition to even function symmetry, we have the following definition: A function $f(t)$ is said to be an **odd function**, or simply **odd**, if

$$f(-t) = -f(t) \quad \text{for all} \quad t$$

From this definition, we see that the plot of an odd function is antisymmetrical around the vertical axis. That is, if the reflection of the positive portion of the plot is inverted, then the negative portion is obtained.

As an example, the function $f(t) = t^3$ is odd, as is the function $f(t) = t$. Since $\sin(-\theta) = -\sin\theta$, then the function $f(t) = \sin\omega t$ is also an odd function.

In a manner almost identical to that done for even functions, it can be shown that when $f(t)$ is an odd function,

$$a_n = \frac{2}{T}\int_{-T/2}^{T/2} f(t)\cos n\omega_0 t\, dt = 0 \qquad \text{for} \quad n = 1, 2, 3, \dots$$

and

$$b_n = \frac{4}{T}\int_{0}^{T/2} f(t)\sin n\omega_0 t\, dt \qquad \text{for} \quad f(t) \text{ odd}$$

Furthermore,

$$a_0 = \frac{1}{T}\int_{-T/2}^{T/2} f(t)\, dt = \frac{1}{T}\int_{-T/2}^{0} f(t)\, dt + \frac{1}{T}\int_{0}^{T/2} f(t)\, dt$$

$$= \frac{1}{T}\int_{-T/2}^{0} f(-t)\, d(-t) + \frac{1}{T}\int_{0}^{T/2} f(t)\, dt$$

$$= \frac{1}{T}\int_{0}^{T/2} f(-t)\, dt + \frac{1}{T}\int_{0}^{T/2} f(t)\, dt$$

and, since $f(-t) = -f(t)$,

$$a_0 = -\frac{1}{T}\int_{0}^{T/2} f(t)\, dt + \frac{1}{T}\int_{0}^{T/2} f(t)\, dt = 0$$

for an odd function.

EXAMPLE 13.4

Consider another square-wave function, as shown in Fig. 13.7. Inspection reveals that it is an odd function, and thus we can determine its Fourier series representation as was done for the even square-wave function $f(t)$ given in Fig. 13.6. However, using

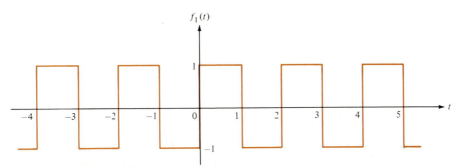

Fig. 13.7   Odd square-wave function.

the fact that $f_1(t) = f(t - 1/2)$, we have

$$f_1(t) = \frac{4}{\pi} \cos \pi \left(t - \frac{1}{2} \right) - \frac{4}{3\pi} \cos 3\pi \left(t - \frac{1}{2} \right)$$

$$+ \frac{4}{5\pi} \cos 5\pi \left(t - \frac{1}{2} \right) - \frac{4}{7\pi} \cos 7\pi \left(t - \frac{1}{2} \right) + \cdots$$

$$= \frac{4}{\pi} \cos \left(\pi t - \frac{\pi}{2} \right) - \frac{4}{3\pi} \cos \left(3\pi t - \frac{3\pi}{2} \right)$$

$$+ \frac{4}{5\pi} \cos \left(5\pi t - \frac{5\pi}{2} \right) - \frac{4}{7\pi} \cos \left(7\pi t - \frac{7\pi}{2} \right) + \cdots$$

$$= 1.27 \sin \pi t + 0.42 \sin 3\pi t + 0.25 \sin 5\pi t + 0.18 \sin 7\pi t + \cdots$$

DRILL EXERCISE 13.3

Find the Fourier series of the square-wave function given in Fig. 13.7 (p. 609) without using the results of Example 13.3.
Answer: $1.27 \sin \pi t + 0.42 \sin 3\pi t + 0.25 \sin 5\pi t + 0.18 \sin 7\pi t + \cdots$

Note that for the square waves in Figs. 13.6 and 13.7, the Fourier series representations contain only odd harmonics. This fact is due to another type of symmetry that both functions have.

A periodic function $f(t)$ having period T is said to be **half-wave symmetric** if

$$f \left(t - \frac{T}{2} \right) = -f(t) \qquad \text{for all} \quad t$$

If a plot of $f(t)$ is shifted half a period and then inverted, the original plot is recovered.

For a periodic function $f(t)$,

$$a_n = \frac{2}{T} \int_{-T/2}^{T/2} f(t) \cos n\omega_0 t \, dt$$

$$= \frac{2}{T} \int_{-T/2}^{0} f(t) \cos n\omega_0 t \, dt + \frac{2}{T} \int_{0}^{T/2} f(t) \cos n\omega_0 t \, dt$$

For the first integral, define the new variable $x = t + T/2$. Thus, $t = x - T/2$, and $dt = dx$. Therefore,

$$\frac{2}{T} \int_{-T/2}^{0} f(t) \cos n\omega_0 t \, dt = \frac{2}{T} \int_{0}^{T/2} f \left(x - \frac{T}{2} \right) \cos n\omega_0 \left(x - \frac{T}{2} \right) dx$$

$$= \frac{2}{T} \int_{0}^{T/2} f \left(x - \frac{T}{2} \right) \left[\cos n\omega_0 x \cos \frac{n\omega_0 T}{2} + \sin n\omega_0 x \sin \frac{n\omega_0 T}{2} \right] dx$$

Since

$$\cos \frac{n\omega_0 T}{2} = \cos n \frac{2\pi}{T} \frac{T}{2} = \cos n\pi$$

$$\sin \frac{n\omega_0 T}{2} = \sin n \frac{2\pi}{T} \frac{T}{2} = \sin n\pi = 0 \qquad \text{for} \quad n = 1, 2, 3, \dots$$

we have that

$$\frac{2}{T} \int_{-T/2}^{0} f(t) \cos n\omega_0 t \, dt = \frac{2}{T} \int_{0}^{T/2} f\left(x - \frac{T}{2}\right) \cos n\omega_0 x \cos n\pi \, dx$$

$$= \frac{2}{T} \cos n\pi \int_{0}^{T/2} f\left(x - \frac{T}{2}\right) \cos n\omega_0 x \, dx$$

$$= \frac{2}{T} \cos n\pi \int_{0}^{T/2} f\left(t - \frac{T}{2}\right) \cos n\omega_0 t \, dt$$

Substituting this into the expression for a_n given above, we get

$$a_n = \frac{2}{T} \cos n\pi \int_{0}^{T/2} f\left(t - \frac{T}{2}\right) \cos n\omega_0 t \, dt + \frac{2}{T} \int_{0}^{T/2} f(t) \cos n\omega_0 t \, dt$$

If $f(t)$ is a half-wave symmetric function, then $f(t - T/2) = -f(t)$, and

$$a_n = \frac{2}{T} \cos n\pi \int_{0}^{T/2} -f(t) \cos n\omega_0 t \, dt + \frac{2}{T} \int_{0}^{T/2} f(t) \cos n\omega_0 t \, dt$$

$$= (1 - \cos n\pi) \frac{2}{T} \int_{0}^{T/2} f(t) \cos n\omega_0 t \, dt$$

Since

$$(1 - \cos n\pi) = \begin{cases} 2 & \text{for} \quad n = 1, 3, 5, \dots \\ 0 & \text{for} \quad n = 2, 4, 6, \dots \end{cases}$$

then for a half-wave symmetric function,

$$a_n = \begin{cases} \dfrac{4}{T} \displaystyle\int_{0}^{T/2} f(t) \cos n\omega_0 t \, dt & \text{for} \quad n \text{ odd} \\[4mm] 0 & \text{for} \quad n \text{ even} \end{cases}$$

Similarly, we can show that

$$b_n = \begin{cases} \dfrac{4}{T} \displaystyle\int_{0}^{T/2} f(t) \sin n\omega_0 t \, dt & \text{for} \quad n \text{ odd} \\[4mm] 0 & \text{for} \quad n \text{ even} \end{cases}$$

In other words, a half-wave symmetric function contains only odd harmonics.

The Use of Derivatives

For functions possessing even, odd, and half-wave symmetries we can use the results given previously to eliminate some of the work required to determine the Fourier series. In addition, we shall now discuss a time-saving technique that can be applied to many types of functions—including functions not having any of the symmetries mentioned above. This technique usually employs the sampling property of impulse functions in the evaluations of integrals.

Now suppose that the periodic function $f(t)$ has the trigonometric Fourier series representation

$$f(t) = a_0 + \sum_{n=1}^{\infty} (a_n \cos n\omega_0 t + b_n \sin n\omega_0 t)$$

where T is the period of $f(t)$ and $\omega_0 = 2\pi/T$. Taking the derivative of this equation, since the derivative of a sum equals the sum of the derivatives, we get

$$\frac{df(t)}{dt} = 0 + \sum_{n=1}^{\infty} (-n\omega_0 a_n \sin n\omega_0 t + n\omega_0 b_n \cos n\omega_0 t)$$

or

$$f'(t) = \sum_{n=1}^{\infty} (n\omega_0 b_n \cos n\omega_0 t - n\omega_0 a_n \sin n\omega_0 t) \tag{13.13}$$

But since $f(t)$ is periodic with period T, its derivative $f'(t)$ must be periodic with period T. Therefore, $f'(t)$ has a Fourier series representation

$$f'(t) = a_0' + \sum_{n=1}^{\infty} (a_n' \cos n\omega_0 t + b_n' \sin n\omega_0 t) \tag{13.14}$$

where $\omega_0 = 2\pi/T$. Comparing Equations (13.13) and (13.14), we have that

$$a_0' = 0 \qquad a_n' = n\omega_0 b_n \qquad b_n' = -n\omega_0 a_n$$

Thus, if we know the Fourier coefficients of $f'(t)$, it is a simple matter to determine the Fourier coefficients of $f(t)$—with the exception of a_0. Of course, the coefficients a_n' and b_n' can be obtained from the formulas

$$a_n' = \frac{2}{T} \int_{-T/2}^{T/2} f'(t) \cos n\omega_0 t \, dt \qquad b_n' = \frac{2}{T} \int_{-T/2}^{T/2} f'(t) \sin n\omega_0 t \, dt$$

Again, the limits of integration can be changed to any interval constituting one period.

EXAMPLE 13.5

Consider the "sawtooth" waveform shown in Fig. 13.8. Since $T = 1$ s, then $\omega_0 = 2\pi/T = 2\pi$ rad/s. Also,

$$a_0 = \frac{1}{T} \int_0^T f(t) \, dt = \frac{1}{1} \int_0^1 t \, dt = \left. \frac{t^2}{2} \right|_0^1 = \frac{1}{2}$$

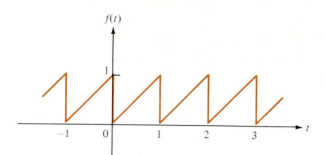

Fig. 13.8   Sawtooth waveform.

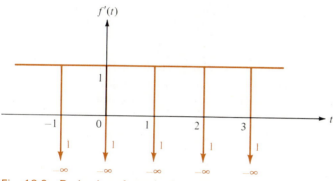

Fig. 13.9   Derivative of sawtooth waveform.

Instead of determining a_n and b_n directly, let us take the derivative of $f(t)$. The result is shown in Fig. 13.9. Thus

$$a_n' = \frac{2}{T} \int_{-T/2}^{T/2} f'(t) \cos n\omega_0 t \, dt$$

$$n\omega_0 b_n = \frac{2}{1} \int_{-1/2}^{1/2} [1 - \delta(t)] \cos n\omega_0 t \, dt$$

$$n(2\pi)b_n = 2 \int_{-1/2}^{1/2} \cos n(2\pi)t \, dt - 2 \int_{-1/2}^{1/2} \delta(t) \cos n(2\pi)t \, dt$$

$$2\pi n b_n = \frac{2}{2\pi n} \sin 2\pi n t \Big|_{-1/2}^{1/2} - 2 \cos n(2\pi)0 = 0 - 2$$

from which

$$b_n = -\frac{1}{n\pi}$$

Also,

$$b_n' = \frac{2}{T} \int_{-T/2}^{T/2} f'(t) \sin n\omega_0 t \, dt$$

and, as above,

$$-2\pi n a_n = \frac{2}{2\pi n}\cos 2\pi nt \Big|_{-1/2}^{1/2} - 2\sin n(2\pi)0 = \frac{2}{2\pi n}\left[\cos n\pi - \cos(-n\pi)\right] - 0$$

from which

$$a_n = 0$$

Thus,

$$f(t) = \frac{1}{2} + \sum_{n=1}^{\infty}\left(-\frac{1}{n\pi}\right)\sin 2n\pi t$$

or

$$f(t) = \frac{1}{2} - \frac{1}{\pi}\sin 2\pi t - \frac{1}{2\pi}\sin 4\pi t - \frac{1}{3\pi}\sin 6\pi t - \frac{1}{4\pi}\sin 8\pi t - \cdots$$

$$= 0.5 - 0.32\sin 2\pi t - 0.16\sin 4\pi t - 0.11\sin 6\pi t - 0.08\sin 8\pi t - \cdots$$

The fact that $a_n = 0$ is not surprising for the following reason. Although $f(t)$ is not an odd function, $f_1(t) = f(t) - \frac{1}{2}$ is. Thus, there are no cosine terms in the Fourier series of $f_1(t)$. Consequently, the series representation of $f(t) = f_1(t) + \frac{1}{2}$ also contains no cosine terms; that is, $a_n = 0$.

DRILL EXERCISE 13.4

Find the Fourier series of the function $f(t)$ shown in Fig. DE13.4 by using the derivative of $f(t)$.

Answer: $0.5 + 0.405\cos \pi t + 0.045\cos 3\pi t + 0.016\cos 5\pi t + 0.008\cos 7\pi t + \cdots$

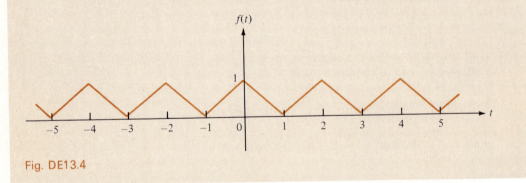

Fig. DE13.4

In Example 13.5, the coefficients a'_n and b'_n were determined by using the limits $t = -\frac{1}{2}$ to $t = \frac{1}{2}$ s. Suppose instead that the limits used go from $t = 0$ to $t = 1$ s. Under this circumstance, one may be tempted to include the impulse at $t = 0$ and the impulse at $t = 1$ s in the appropriate integral. However, to verify that this is not the case, simply subtract an arbitrarily small positive quantity, say ε, from both limits.

The resulting limits, $t = -\varepsilon$ and $t = 1 - \varepsilon$, indicate that the impulse at $t = 0$ is included in an integral, but the one at $t = 1$ s is not.

One additional point. It was indicated that when the formulas (not based on one of the symmetries) were being used, the integral limits were irrelevant provided that the interval was one period. When different periods are used for the same coefficient, however, the results will be apparently different formulas. But although these formulas appear different, they are equivalent; that is plugging the same value of n in both formulas will yield the same number.

Suppose now that we take the second derivative of the Fourier series representation of $f(t)$. Then

$$f''(t) = \frac{d^2 f(t)}{dt^2} = \sum_{n=1}^{\infty} [-(n\omega_0)^2 a_n \cos n\omega_0 t - (n\omega_0)^2 b_n \sin n\omega_0 t] \tag{13.15}$$

But since $f(t)$ is periodic, so is $f''(t)$; and the series representation of $f''(t)$ is

$$f''(t) = a_0'' + \sum_{n=1}^{\infty} (a_n'' \cos n\omega_0 t + b_n'' \sin n\omega_0 t) \tag{13.16}$$

Comparing Equations (13.15) and (13.16), and from the fomulas for the Fourier coefficients, we have

$$a_0'' = 0$$

$$-(n\omega_0)^2 a_n = a_n'' = \frac{2}{T} \int_{-T/2}^{T/2} f''(t) \cos n\omega_0 t \, dt$$

and

$$-(n\omega_0)^2 b_n = b_n'' = \frac{2}{T} \int_{-T/2}^{T/2} f''(t) \sin n\omega_0 t \, dt$$

where $\omega_0 = 2\pi/T$ and the integrations can equally be performed over an arbitrary period.

Therefore, knowing the coefficients a_n'' and b_n'' of $f''(t)$, it is a simple matter to determine a_n and b_n, the coefficients of $f(t)$.

This approach can be extended to higher-order derivatives.

EXAMPLE 13.6

Consider the triangular waveform shown in Fig. 13.10. Since $T = 2$ s, then $\omega_0 = 2\pi/T = \pi$ rad/s. Also,

$$a_0 = \frac{1}{T} \int_{-1/2}^{3/2} f(t) \, dt = \frac{1}{2} \int_{-1/2}^{1/2} 2t \, dt + \frac{1}{2} \int_{1/2}^{3/2} (-2t + 2) \, dt = 0$$

This result can be obtained by inspection when one sees that $f(t)$ is an odd function.

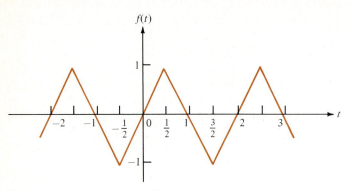

Fig. 13.10   Triangular waveform.

It would take a few pages of messy calculations to determine expressions for a_n and b_n by directly using their formulas—try it and see! However, by taking derivatives, the complexity of the solution can be reduced significantly. First we form $f'(t)$ as shown in Fig. 13.11.

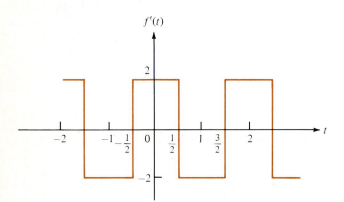

Fig. 13.11   Derivative of triangular waveform.

To get $f''(t)$ we take the derivative of $f'(t)$. The result is shown in Fig. 13.12. Since $f''(t)$ is an odd function, then

$$-(n\omega_0)^2 a_n = a_n'' = 0 \quad \Rightarrow \quad a_n = 0$$

which is to be expected since $f(t)$ is also an odd function. Furthermore,

$$b_n'' = \frac{4}{T} \int_0^{T/2} f''(t) \sin n\omega_0 t\, dt$$

$$-(n\omega_0)^2 b_n = \frac{4}{2} \int_0^1 -4\delta\left(t - \frac{1}{2}\right) \sin n\omega_0 t\, dt$$

$$-(n\pi)^2 b_n = 2\left[-4 \sin n\pi \left(\frac{1}{2}\right)\right] \quad \Rightarrow \quad b_n = \frac{8}{(n\pi)^2} \sin \frac{n\pi}{2}$$

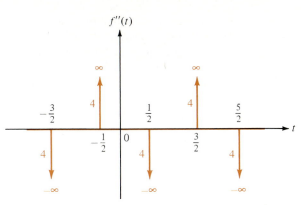

Fig. 13.12   Second derivative of triangular waveform.

Thus, for the original function,

$$f(t) = \sum_{n=1}^{\infty} \frac{8}{(n\pi)^2} \sin \frac{n\pi}{2} \sin n\pi t = \frac{8}{\pi^2} \sum_{n=1}^{\infty} \frac{\sin(n\pi/2)}{n^2} \sin n\pi t$$

Writing the first few terms in the series, we have

$$f(t) = \frac{8}{\pi^2} \sin \pi t - \frac{8}{9\pi^2} \sin 3\pi t + \frac{8}{25\pi^2} \sin 5\pi t - \frac{8}{49\pi^2} \sin 7\pi t + \cdots$$

$$= 0.81 \sin \pi t - 0.09 \sin 3\pi t + 0.032 \sin 5\pi t - 0.017 \sin 7\pi t + \cdots$$

Note that because

$$\sin \frac{n\pi}{2} = 0 \qquad \text{for} \quad n = 2, 4, 6, \ldots$$

$f(t)$ contains no even harmonics. This is a consequence of the fact that $f(t)$, as well as its derivatives, is a half-wave symmetric function.

DRILL EXERCISE 13.5

Find the Fourier series of the function $f(t)$ given in Fig. DE13.4 (p. 614) by using the second derivative of $f(t)$.

Answer: $0.5 + 0.405 \cos \pi t + 0.045 \cos 3\pi t + 0.016 \cos 5\pi t + 0.008 \cos 7\pi t + \cdots$

Upon inspection of the foregoing example, we see that $f(t)$ is an odd function, its derivative $f'(t)$ is an even function, and its derivative $f''(t)$ is again an odd function. This results from the fact that the derivative of an even periodic function is odd, and vice versa. Since an even periodic function consists only of cosines (and possibly a constant), the derivative of such a function will be composed only of sines and thus must be an odd function. Conversely, since an odd periodic function consists only of sines, its derivative will be composed only of cosines; thus, it must be an even function (with no dc component). Implicit in this argument is the fact that a sum of even functions is again even, and the sum of odd functions is again odd. (See Problem 13.10.)

In the next example we shall see a more subtle use of derivatives for the purpose of obtaining the Fourier series representation of a periodic function.

EXAMPLE 13.7

Reconsider the half-wave rectified sine wave given by Fig. 13.13. Again $T = 2\,\text{s} \Rightarrow \omega_0 = 2\pi/T = \pi$ rad/s. In Example 13.2 on p. 600, we saw that $a_0 = 1/\pi$. Taking the derivative of $f(t)$ results in the waveform shown in Fig. 13.14, whereas the second derivative of $f(t)$ is shown in Fig. 13.15. But note—and this is the crux of the matter—that the second derivative $f''(t)$ contains the function $f(t)$. Specifically, for the interval $0 \le t < 2\,\text{s}$, we have

$$f''(t) = \pi\delta(t) + \pi\delta(t-1) - \pi^2 f(t)$$

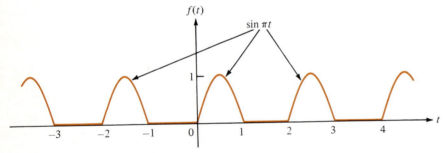

Fig. 13.13   Half-wave rectified sine wave.

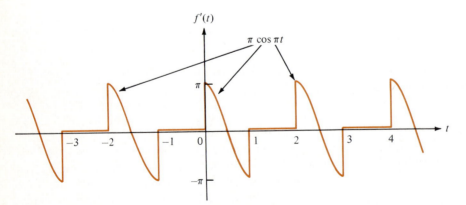

Fig. 13.14   Derivative of half-wave rectified sine wave.

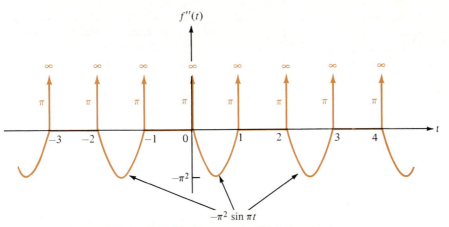

Fig. 13.15   Second derivative of half-wave rectified sine wave.

Thus,

$$a_n'' = \frac{2}{T} \int_0^T f''(t) \cos n\omega_0 t \, dt$$

$$-(n\omega_0)^2 a_n = \frac{2}{T} \int_0^T \left[\pi\delta(t) + \pi\delta(t-1) - \pi^2 f(t) \right] \cos n\omega_0 t \, dt$$

$$-(n\pi)^2 a_n = \pi \cos n\pi(0) + \pi \cos n\pi(1) + \frac{2}{T} \int_0^T - \pi^2 f(t) \cos n\omega_0 t \, dt$$

$$= \pi(1 + \cos n\pi) - \pi^2 \left(\frac{2}{T} \int_0^T f(t) \cos n\omega_0 t \, dt \right)$$

But

$$\frac{2}{T} \int_0^T f(t) \cos n\omega_0 t \, dt = a_n$$

Hence,

$$-(n\pi)^2 a_n = \pi(1 + \cos n\pi) - \pi^2 a_n \qquad \Rightarrow \qquad a_n = \frac{1 + \cos n\pi}{\pi(1 - n^2)}$$

as was obtained before for $n = 2, 3, 4, \ldots$. But for $n = 1$, $a_n = 0/0$—which is un-defined. By L'Hôpital's rule,[†] however,

$$a_1 = \lim_{n \to 1} a_n = \lim_{n \to 1} \frac{\dfrac{d}{dn}(1 + \cos n\pi)}{\dfrac{d}{dn}\pi(1 - n^2)} = \lim_{n \to 1} \frac{-\pi \sin n\pi}{-2n\pi} = 0$$

[†] Named for the French mathematician Guillaume François Antoine de L'Hôpital (1661–1704).

Continuing,

$$b_n'' = \frac{2}{T} \int_0^T f''(t) \sin n\omega_0 t \, dt$$

$$-(n\omega_0)^2 b_n = \frac{2}{T} \int_0^1 \left[\pi\delta(t) + \pi\delta(t-1) - \pi^2 f(t)\right] \sin n\pi t \, dt$$

and, as above,

$$-(n\pi)^2 b_n = \pi \sin n\pi(0) + \pi \sin n\pi(1) - \pi^2 b_n$$

from which

$$b_n = \frac{\sin n\pi}{\pi(1 - n^2)} \quad \Rightarrow \quad b_n = 0 \quad \text{for} \quad n = 2, 3, 4, \ldots$$

When $n = 1$, $b_n = 0/0$, and therefore, by L'Hôpital's rule

$$b_1 = \lim_{n\to 1} b_n = \lim_{n\to 1} \frac{\dfrac{d}{dn}\sin n\pi}{\dfrac{d}{dn}\pi(1-n^2)} = \lim_{n\to 1} \frac{\pi\cos n\pi}{-2n\pi} = \frac{\cos \pi}{-2} = \frac{1}{2}$$

as we obtained in Example 13.2.

DRILL EXERCISE 13.6

Find the Fourier coefficients a_0, a_n, and b_n for the function $f(t)$ shown in Fig. DE13.6 by using the derivative of $f(t)$.

Answer: $1 - e^{-1}$; $\dfrac{2(1 - e^{-1})}{1 + (2n\pi)^2}$; $\dfrac{4n\pi(1 - e^{-1})}{1 + (2n\pi)^2}$

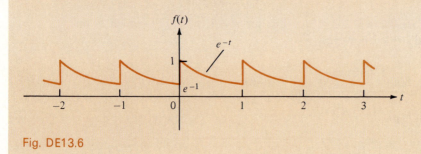

Fig. DE13.6

13.3 THE COMPLEX FOURIER SERIES

Although the trigonometric Fourier series is a relatively intuitive concept (we can picture sines and cosines in our minds), by using an alternative series representation known as the **exponential** or **complex Fourier series** we can (1) mathematically shorten the series representation and (2) generalize the concept to the Fourier transform, which will enable us to deal with nonperiodic functions.

The key equation in the development of the complex Fourier series is Euler's formula. From

$$e^{j\theta} = \cos\theta + j\sin\theta \tag{13.17}$$

replacing θ by $-\theta$, we get

$$e^{-j\theta} = \cos\theta - j\sin\theta \tag{13.18}$$

Adding Equations (13.17) and (13.18), we obtain

$$\cos\theta = \frac{e^{j\theta} + e^{-j\theta}}{2} \tag{13.19}$$

On the other hand, subtracting Equation (13.18) from Equation (13.17) results in

$$\sin\theta = \frac{e^{j\theta} - e^{-j\theta}}{2j} \tag{13.20}$$

Suppose now that $f(t)$ is a periodic function having period T and the trigonometric Fourier series representation given by

$$f(t) = a_0 + \sum_{n=1}^{\infty} (a_n \cos n\omega_0 t + b_n \sin n\omega_0 t)$$

where $\omega_0 = 2\pi/T$. Then, by Equations (13.19) and (13.20),

$$f(t) = a_0 + \sum_{n=1}^{\infty} \left[a_n \left(\frac{e^{jn\omega_0 t} + e^{-jn\omega_0 t}}{2} \right) + b_n \left(\frac{e^{jn\omega_0 t} - e^{-jn\omega_0 t}}{2j} \right) \right]$$

$$= a_0 + \sum_{n=1}^{\infty} \left[\left(\frac{a_n}{2} + \frac{b_n}{2j} \right) e^{jn\omega_0 t} + \left(\frac{a_n}{2} - \frac{b_n}{2j} \right) e^{-jn\omega_0 t} \right]$$

$$= a_0 + \sum_{n=1}^{\infty} \frac{a_n - jb_n}{2} e^{jn\omega_0 t} + \sum_{n=1}^{\infty} \frac{a_n + jb_n}{2} e^{-jn\omega_0 t}$$

If we define $m = -n$, then $n = -m$ and

$$f(t) = a_0 + \sum_{n=1}^{\infty} \frac{a_n - jb_n}{2} e^{jn\omega_0 t} + \sum_{-m=1}^{\infty} \frac{a_{-m} + jb_{-m}}{2} e^{jm\omega_0 t}$$

But, from Equation (13.11) on p. 600,

$$a_{-m} = \frac{2}{T} \int_0^T f(t) \cos(-m)\omega_0 t \, dt = \frac{2}{T} \int_0^T f(t) \cos m\omega_0 t \, dt = a_m$$

Similarly, $b_{-m} = -b_m$. But

$$\sum_{-m=1}^{\infty} = \sum_{m=-1}^{-\infty} = \sum_{m=-\infty}^{-1}$$

Thus,

$$f(t) = a_0 + \sum_{n=1}^{\infty} \frac{a_n - jb_n}{2} e^{jn\omega_0 t} + \sum_{m=-\infty}^{-1} \frac{a_m - jb_m}{2} e^{jm\omega_0 t}$$

$$= a_0 + \sum_{n=1}^{\infty} \frac{a_n - jb_n}{2} e^{jn\omega_0 t} + \sum_{n=-\infty}^{-1} \frac{a_n - jb_n}{2} e^{jn\omega_0 t}$$

Now define the coefficient c_n by

$$c_0 = a_0 \quad \text{and} \quad c_n = \frac{a_n - jb_n}{2} \quad \text{for all} \quad n \neq 0$$

Then

$$f(t) = \sum_{n=-\infty}^{\infty} c_n e^{jn\omega_0 t} \tag{13.21}$$

where $\omega_0 = 2\pi/T$. This is the complex Fourier series representation of $f(t)$. In other words, we can express $f(t)$ as a sum of complex exponentials. Note the simple form of this series representation. But, if we first have to calculate a_n and b_n in order to find c_n, this representation would not be any simpler to determine. Fortunately, we can derive a formula for obtaining c_n directly. This is done as follows.

From the definition of c_n,

$$c_n = \frac{1}{2}(a_n - jb_n) = \frac{1}{2}\left(\frac{2}{T}\int_0^T f(t) \cos n\omega_0 t \, dt - j\frac{2}{T}\int_0^T f(t) \sin n\omega_0 t \, dt\right)$$

$$= \frac{1}{2}\left(\frac{2}{T}\int_0^T f(t)(\cos n\omega_0 t - j\sin n\omega_0 t) \, dt\right)$$

By Euler's formula,

$$c_n = \frac{1}{T}\int_0^T f(t) e^{-jn\omega_0 t} \, dt \tag{13.22}$$

which is a formula for c_n. Note that if $n = 0$, we obtain

$$c_0 = \frac{1}{T}\int_0^T f(t)e^0 \, dt = \frac{1}{T}\int_0^T f(t) \, dt = a_0$$

and thus the formula for c_n is valid for all n. Again, in the formula for c_n the integration can be performed over any period, not only from $t = 0$ to $t = T$; different periods will result in equivalent expressions for c_n.

For the trigonometric Fourier series, a_n and b_n are coefficients of sinusoids—respectively, of cosines and sines having nonnegative frequencies. The nth harmonic ($n \neq 0$) of $f(t)$ is a sinusoid with amplitude $\sqrt{a_n^2 + b_n^2}$, and a plot of $\sqrt{a_n^2 + b_n^2}$ along with $|a_0|$ is the amplitude spectrum of $f(t)$. On the other hand, for the complex Fourier series, c_n is the coefficient of a complex exponential—called a **complex sinusoid** (recall Euler's formula). Furthermore, since n takes on values from $-\infty$ to ∞, these complex sinusoids have negative frequencies as well as nonnegative frequencies.

Since for $n \neq 0$, $c_n = \frac{1}{2}(a_n - jb_n)$, then

$$|c_n| = \tfrac{1}{2}\sqrt{a_n^2 + b_n^2}$$

Thus, we see that the magnitude of c_n is equal to half of the amplitude of the nth harmonic of $f(t)$. In addition,

$$c_{-n} = \tfrac{1}{2}(a_{-n} - jb_{-n})$$

But, we have seen that $a_{-n} = a_n$ and $b_{-n} = -b_n$, so

$$c_{-n} = \tfrac{1}{2}(a_n + jb_n) = c_n^*$$

Therefore,

$$|c_{-n}| = \tfrac{1}{2}\sqrt{a_n^2 + b_n^2} = |c_n|$$

which accounts for the other half of the amplitude of the nth harmonic of $f(t)$. In other words, $|c_n| + |c_{-n}| = \sqrt{a_n^2 + b_n^2}$. Also, since $c_0 = a_0$, then $|c_0| = |a_0|$.

For these reasons, a plot of $|c_n|$ versus ω is called the **complex amplitude spectrum** of $f(t)$. A plot of the angle of c_n versus ω is called the **complex phase spectrum** of $f(t)$. These two spectra constitute the **complex frequency spectrum** of $f(t)$.

EXAMPLE 13.8

Let us find the complex Fourier series of the pulse train given in Fig. 13.16, where the period is T and $\omega_0 = 2\pi/T$.

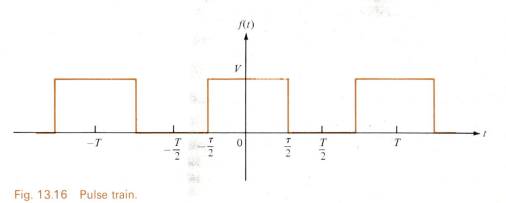

Fig. 13.16   Pulse train.

From the formula for c_n,

$$c_n = \frac{1}{T} \int_{-T/2}^{T/2} f(t) e^{-jn\omega_0 t}\, dt = \frac{1}{T} \int_{-\tau/2}^{\tau/2} V e^{-jn\omega_0 t}\, dt = \frac{V}{T} \frac{-e^{-jn\omega_0 t}}{jn\omega_0}\bigg|_{-\tau/2}^{\tau/2}$$

$$= \frac{V}{jn\omega_0 T}\left(e^{jn\omega_0\tau/2} - e^{-jn\omega_0\tau/2}\right) = \frac{V\tau}{T}\frac{\sin(n\omega_0\tau/2)}{n\omega_0\tau/2} = \frac{V\tau}{T}\frac{\sin(n\pi\tau/T)}{n\pi\tau/T}$$

Thus,

$$f(t) = \sum_{n=-\infty}^{\infty} \frac{V\tau}{T}\frac{\sin(n\pi\tau/T)}{n\pi\tau/T} e^{j2n\pi t/T}$$

In determining the complex amplitude spectrum of $f(t)$, we use the fact that c_n is the product of a constant and a function of the form $(\sin x)/x$. A plot of this well-known function, called the **sinc function** and designated sinc(x), is shown in Fig. 13.17. As a consequence, the complex amplitude spectrum of $f(t)$ is given by Fig. 13.18. Note

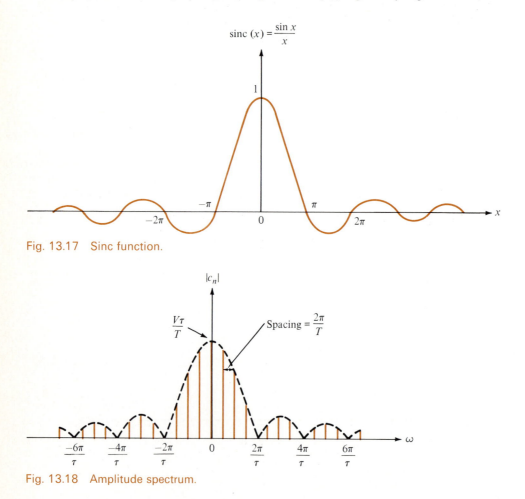

Fig. 13.17 Sinc function.

Fig. 13.18 Amplitude spectrum.

that the pulse width τ determines the sharpness of the sinc(x) envelope of the spectrum—the narrower the pulse width, the broader the envelope and hence the more harmonics of large magnitudes comprise $f(t)$. Also, note that if the period increases (pulse repetition rate decreases), then the spacing between the harmonics decreases. In the limit as the period approaches infinity (the repetition rate goes to zero), the discrete spectrum becomes a continuous spectrum.

DRILL EXERCISE 13.7

Find the complex Fourier series of the function shown in Fig. DE13.7.

Answer: $\dfrac{1}{2} + \dfrac{j}{\pi}e^{-j\pi t} - \dfrac{j}{\pi}e^{j\pi t} + \dfrac{j}{3\pi}e^{-j3\pi t} - \dfrac{j}{3\pi}e^{j3\pi t} + \cdots$

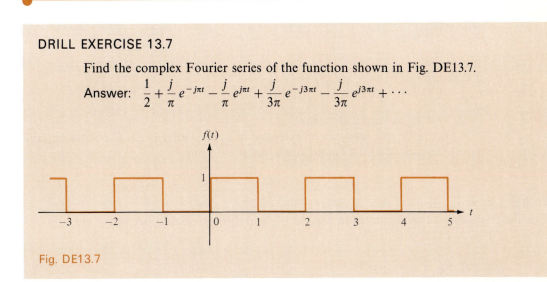

Fig. DE13.7

If $f(t)$ is a periodic function having period T with a complex Fourier series representation

$$f(t) = \sum_{n=-\infty}^{\infty} c_n e^{jn\omega_0 t}$$

where $\omega_0 = 2\pi/T$ and

$$c_n = \frac{1}{T} \int_{-T/2}^{T/2} f(t)e^{-jn\omega_0 t}\, dt$$

then, taking the derivative of $f(t)$, we get

$$f'(t) = \frac{df(t)}{dt} = \sum_{n=-\infty}^{\infty} jn\omega_0 c_n e^{jn\omega_0 t}$$

But, since $f'(t)$ is also periodic, with period T, it has a complex Fourier series representation

$$f'(t) = \sum_{n=-\infty}^{\infty} c'_n e^{jn\omega_0 t}$$

Comparing this equation with the one preceding it, and by the formula for the complex Fourier series coefficients, we have

$$jn\omega_0 c_n = c'_n = \frac{1}{T}\int_{-T/2}^{T/2} f'(t)e^{-jn\omega_0 t}\,dt$$

Thus, knowing c'_n, it is a simple matter to determine c_n.

Continuing to the second derivative,

$$f''(t) = \frac{d^2 f(t)}{dt^2} = \sum_{n=-\infty}^{\infty} -(n\omega_0)^2 c_n e^{jn\omega_0 t} \qquad \text{and} \qquad f''(t) = \sum_{n=-\infty}^{\infty} c''_n e^{jn\omega_0 t}$$

implies that

$$-(n\omega_0)^2 c_n = c''_n = \frac{1}{T}\int_{-T/2}^{T/2} f''(t)e^{-jn\omega_0 t}\,dt$$

Thus, from c''_n we can easily obtain c_n.

Of course, this idea can be extended to higher-order derivatives, and an arbitrary period can be used for the limits of the integrals.

EXAMPLE 13.9

For the triangular waveform given in Fig. 13.10 on p. 616, its second derivative is shown in Fig. 13.12 on p. 617. Thus,

$$c''_n = \frac{1}{T}\int_{-T/2}^{T/2} f''(t)e^{-jn\omega_0 t}\,dt$$

$$-(n\omega_0)^2 c_n = \frac{1}{2}\int_{-1}^{1}\left[4\delta\left(t+\frac{1}{2}\right) - 4\delta\left(t-\frac{1}{2}\right)\right]e^{-jn\omega_0 t}\,dt$$

$$-(n\pi)^2 c_n = \frac{4e^{jn\pi/2} - 4e^{-jn\pi/2}}{2}$$

from which

$$c_n = -\frac{4j}{(n\pi)^2}\,\frac{e^{jn\pi/2} - e^{-jn\pi/2}}{2j} = -\frac{4j}{(n\pi)^2}\sin\frac{n\pi}{2}$$

Since $c_n = a_n/2 - jb_n/2$, we have that

$$a_n = 0 \qquad \text{for} \quad n \neq 0$$

and

$$\frac{b_n}{2} = \frac{4}{(n\pi)^2}\sin\frac{n\pi}{2} \qquad \Rightarrow \qquad b_n = \frac{8}{(n\pi)^2}\sin\frac{n\pi}{2}$$

which agrees with the answer obtained in Example 13.6.

To find c_0, we use the fact that $c_0 = a_0$. As was shown in Example 13.6 on p. 615, $a_0 = 0 = c_0$.

DRILL EXERCISE 13.8

Find the complex Fourier series of the function $f(t)$ given in Fig. DE13.4 (p. 614).
Answer: $0.5 + 0.203e^{-j\pi t} + 0.203e^{j\pi t} + 0.023e^{-j3\pi t} + 0.023e^{j3\pi t} + \cdots$

● SUMMARY

1. A periodic function $f(t)$ with period T has the trigonometric Fourier series representation

$$f(t) = a_0 + \sum_{n=1}^{\infty} (a_n \cos n\omega_0 t + b_n \sin n\omega_0 t)$$

where $\omega_0 = 2\pi/T$. The formulas for a_0, a_n, and b_n are on pp. 599 and 600.

2. An alternative trigonometric Fourier series representation is

$$f(t) = a_0 + \sum_{n=1}^{\infty} A_n \cos(n\omega_0 t + \phi_n)$$

where $A_n = \sqrt{a_n^2 + b_n^2}$ and $\phi_n = -\tan^{-1}(b_n/a_n)$.

3. The frequency spectrum of $f(t)$ consists of two discrete spectra. The amplitude spectrum is a plot of A_n (along with a_0) versus frequency. The phase spectrum is a plot of ϕ_n versus frequency.

4. A circuit's (forced) response to a periodic function $f(t)$ is found by expressing $f(t)$ as a sum of sinusoids (its Fourier series representation), finding the response to each individual sinusoid, and then summing all the individual responses.

5. The trigonometric Fourier series of an even periodic function contains no sine terms. The Fourier series of an odd function contains no cosine terms and has an average value of zero. A half-wave symmetric function contains only odd harmonics. (The dc term is the zero harmonic and thus is even.)

6. The derivative $f'(t)$ of a function $f(t)$ having period T also has period T. The Fourier coefficients of $f'(t)$ are often easier to calculate than the coefficients of $f(t)$. If we know the coefficients of $f'(t)$, it is extremely easy to determine the coefficients of $f(t)$—except for a_0.

7. A periodic function can also be expressed as a sum of complex sinusoids: the exponential Fourier series representation is

$$f(t) = \sum_{n=-\infty}^{\infty} c_n e^{jn\omega_0 t}$$

where $\omega_0 = 2\pi/T$. The formula for c_n is on p. 622.

● *PROBLEMS FOR CHAPTER 13*

13.1 (a) Find the Fourier series representation of the function shown in Fig. P13.1.
 (b) Plot the amplitude spectrum for this function.

13.2 Repeat Problem 13.1 for the function shown in Fig. P13.2.

13.3 Repeat Problem 13.1 for the full-wave rectified sine wave in Fig. P13.3.

13.4 Repeat Problem 13.1 for the function shown in Fig. P13.4.

13.5 Repeat Problem 13.1 for the function shown in Fig. P13.5.

13.6 Repeat Problem 13.1 for the function shown in Fig. P13.6.

13.7 Repeat Problem 13.1 for the function shown in Fig. P13.7.

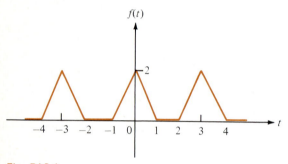

Fig. P13.1

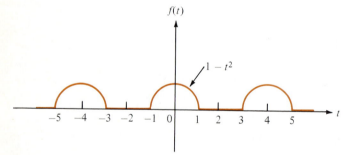

Fig. P13.2

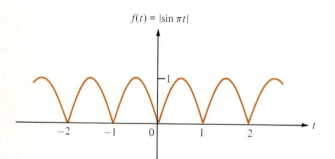

Fig. P13.3

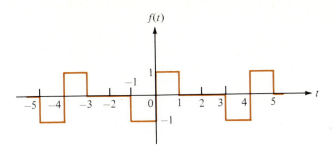

Fig. P13.4

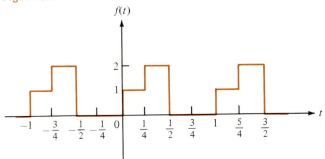

Fig. P13.5

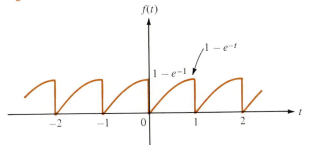

Fig. P13.6

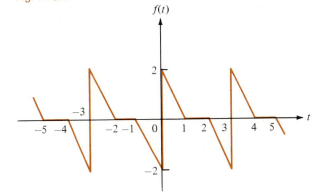

Fig. P13.7

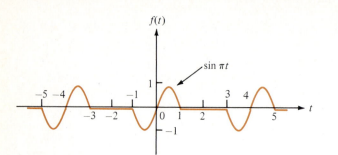

Fig. P13.8

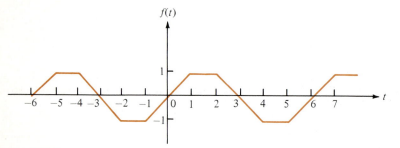

Fig. P13.9

13.8 Repeat Problem 13.1 for the function shown in Fig. P13.8.

13.9 Repeat Problem 13.1 for the function shown in Fig. P13.9.

13.10 (a) Show that the sum of two even functions is an even function.

    (b) Show that the sum of two odd functions is an odd function.

    (c) Show that the product of two even functions is an even function.

(d) Show that the product of two odd functions is an even function.

(e) Show that the product of an odd function and an even function is an odd function.

13.11 Show that the amplitude spectra of the periodic functions $f(t)$ and $f(t-a)$ are the same.

13.12 Use the Fourier series of the half-wave rectified sine wave given in Fig. 13.1 on p. 600 to find the Fourier series

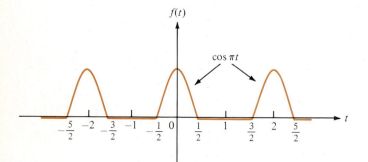

representation of the function shown in Fig. P13.12.

13.13 Use the Fourier series of the triangular waveform given in Fig. 13.10 on p. 616 to find the Fourier series representation of the function shown in Fig. P13.13.

13.14 Use the Fourier series of the sawtooth waveform given in Fig. 13.8 on p. 613 to find the Fourier series representation of the function shown in Fig. P13.14.

13.15 Suppose that the half-wave rectified sine wave given in Fig. 13.1 on p. 600 is the input voltage $v_1(t)$ to the circuit shown in Fig. P13.15.

(a) Find the amplitude spectrum of the output voltage $v_2(t)$.

(b) The output $v_2(t)$ is approximately what function?

13.16 Repeat Problem 13.15 for the case that $v_1(t)$ is the function given in Fig. 13.8 on p. 613.

13.17 Repeat Problem 13.15 for the case that $v_1(t)$ is the function given in Fig. P13.5.

13.18 Use Equation (13.19) on p. 621 to determine the complex Fourier series representation of $f(t) = 5\cos 7t$. Plot the complex amplitude spectrum of $f(t)$.

13.19 Repeat Problem 13.18 for $f(t) = 5\sin 7t$, using Equation (13.20) on p. 621.

13.20 Repeat Problem 13.18 for $f(t) = 5\cos(7t - \pi/2)$.

13.21 Suppose that $f(t)$ is an even periodic function. Show that

$$c_n = \frac{2}{T} \int_0^{T/2} f(t) \cos n\omega_0 t \, dt$$

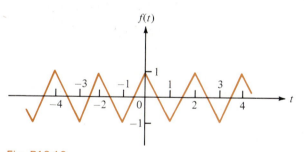

Fig. P13.13

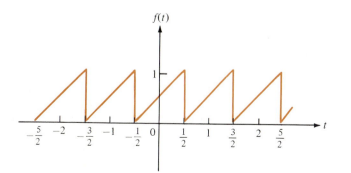

Fig. P13.14

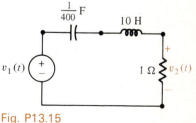

Fig. P13.15

13.22 Suppose that $f(t)$ is an odd periodic function. Show that

$$c_n = \frac{-j2}{T} \int_0^{T/2} f(t) \sin n\omega_0 t \, dt$$

13.23 Find the complex Fourier series for the function given in Fig. P13.1. (Do not use a_n and b_n determined previously to calculate c_n.)

13.24 Repeat Problem 13.23 for the function given in Fig. P13.2.

13.25 Repeat Problem 13.23 for the function given in Fig. P13.3.

13.26 Repeat Problem 13.23 for the function given in Fig. P13.4.

13.27 Repeat Problem 13.23 for the function given in Fig. P13.5.

13.28 Repeat Problem 13.23 for the function given in Fig. DE13.6 on p. 620.

13.29 Repeat Problem 13.23 for the function given in Fig. P13.7.

13.30 Repeat Problem 13.23 for the function given in Fig. P13.8.

CHAPTER 14

The Fourier Transform

● INTRODUCTION

We have seen that for a periodic function $f(t)$ having period T, we can represent $f(t)$ as a sum of sinusoids—for ordinary sinusoids we have the trigonometric Fourier series, and for complex sinusoids we have the exponential Fourier series.

Although periodic functions are very important, so are nonperiodic functions. We can extend the concept of a series representation of $f(t)$ to the case of a nonperiodic function by considering such a function to be periodic with period $T = \infty$.

We begin this chapter with the heuristic development of the Fourier transform pair of integrals. One of these, the Fourier transform, takes a function of time $f(t)$ and converts or transforms it into a function of frequency $\mathbf{F}(j\omega)$. The other, the inverse Fourier transform, takes the function of frequency $\mathbf{F}(j\omega)$ and transforms it back into the function of time $f(t)$. We see that both of these tranforms are linear transformations.

We then determine the Fourier transforms of a number of important functions of time and, as in the case of Fourier series, may utilize the operation of time differentiation to simplify the computations required to find transforms. We also derive Parseval's theorem, which gives us an integral equation relating $f(t)$ and $\mathbf{F}(j\omega)$. It is this relation that gives us an important physical interpretation in terms of energy of the Fourier transform. More important, we see how to use the Fourier transform to describe and analyze systems and circuits. By transforming circuits to the frequency domain (i.e., taking Fourier transforms) we get a circuit analysis problem that can be handled algebraically, as is done for Laplace transforms. Fourier-transform techniques allow us to deal with circuits and systems which have inputs that are nonzero for $t < 0$. On the other hand, Laplace transforms may be used when initial conditions and inputs (for $t \geq 0$) are known—knowledge of how the initial conditions are established, or what the values of inputs are for $t < 0$, may or may not be specified.

14.1 THE FOURIER INTEGRAL

To begin with, let $f(t)$ be periodic, with period T. Then the complex Fourier series representation is

$$f(t) = \sum_{n=-\infty}^{\infty} c_n e^{jn\omega_0 t}$$

where $\omega_0 = 2\pi/T$ and

$$c_n = \frac{1}{T} \int_{-T/2}^{T/2} f(t) e^{-jn\omega_0 t}\, dt = \frac{1}{T} \int_{-T/2}^{T/2} f(x) e^{-jn\omega_0 x}\, dx$$

Substituting this into the series representation of $f(t)$ yields

$$f(t) = \sum_{n=-\infty}^{\infty} \left[\frac{1}{T} \int_{-T/2}^{T/2} f(x) e^{-jn\omega_0 x}\, dx \right] e^{jn\omega_0 t}$$

Since $\omega_0 = 2\pi/T$, then $1/T = \omega_0/2\pi$ and

$$f(t) = \sum_{n=-\infty}^{\infty} \left[\frac{1}{2\pi} \int_{-T/2}^{T/2} f(x) e^{-jn\omega_0 x}\, dx \right] e^{jn\omega_0 t} \omega_0$$

If we let T get large, then the quantity $\Delta\omega$ defined by $\omega_0 = 2\pi/T = \Delta\omega$ gets small, and

$$f(t) = \sum_{n=-\infty}^{\infty} \left[\frac{1}{2\pi} \int_{-T/2}^{T/2} f(x) e^{-jn\Delta\omega x}\, dx \right] e^{jn\Delta\omega t} \Delta\omega$$

As $T \to \infty$, then $\Delta\omega \to d\omega$ and the discrete harmonics $n\omega_0$ become a continuous frequency variable, say ω; that is, $n\omega_0 = n\Delta\omega \to \omega$. Furthermore, the discrete sum $\sum_{n=-\infty}^{\infty}$ becomes the continuous sum $\int_{-\infty}^{\infty}$. Thus, in the limit, the preceding equation becomes

$$f(t) = \int_{-\infty}^{\infty} \frac{1}{2\pi} \left[\int_{-\infty}^{\infty} f(x) e^{-j\omega x}\, dx \right] e^{j\omega t}\, d\omega$$

and, by changing variables for the integral in the brackets,

$$f(t) = \frac{1}{2\pi} \int_{-\infty}^{\infty} \left[\int_{-\infty}^{\infty} f(t) e^{-j\omega t}\, dt \right] e^{j\omega t}\, d\omega$$

which has the form

$$f(t) = \frac{1}{2\pi} \int_{-\infty}^{\infty} \mathbf{F}(j\omega) e^{j\omega t}\, d\omega \qquad\qquad (14.1)$$

where

$$\mathbf{F}(j\omega) = \int_{-\infty}^{\infty} f(t)e^{-j\omega t}\,dt \qquad (14.2)$$

The function $\mathbf{F}(j\omega)$ is called the **Fourier transform** of $f(t)$. The Fourier transform of the function $f(t)$ is often denoted $\mathscr{F}[f(t)]$; that is,

$$\mathscr{F}[f(t)] = \mathbf{F}(j\omega)$$

Equation (14.1) is a formula for obtaining $f(t)$ from the transform $\mathbf{F}(j\omega)$. Thus, this integral is called the **inverse Fourier transform** of $\mathbf{F}(j\omega)$, denoted $\mathscr{F}^{-1}[\mathbf{F}(j\omega)]$; that is,

$$\mathscr{F}^{-1}[\mathbf{F}(j\omega)] = f(t)$$

Equations (14.1) and (14.2) are known as the **Fourier transform pair**.

EXAMPLE 14.1

The function $f(t)$ shown in Fig. 14.1 consists of a single pulse having width τ and height V. From the Fourier transform formula,

$$\mathbf{F}(j\omega) = \int_{-\infty}^{\infty} f(t)e^{-j\omega t}\,dt = \int_{-\tau/2}^{\tau/2} Ve^{-j\omega t}\,dt = -\frac{V}{j\omega}e^{-j\omega t}\Big|_{-\tau/2}^{\tau/2}$$

$$= \frac{2V}{\omega}\left[\frac{e^{j\omega\tau/2} - e^{-j\omega\tau/2}}{2j}\right] = \frac{2V}{\omega}\left(\frac{\omega\tau}{2}\right)\left(\frac{\sin(\omega\tau/2)}{\omega\tau/2}\right)$$

$$= V\tau\,\frac{\sin(\omega\tau/2)}{\omega\tau/2} = V\tau\,\text{sinc}\left(\frac{\omega\tau}{2}\right)$$

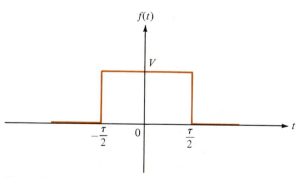

Fig. 14.1   Single pulse.

DRILL EXERCISE 14.1

Find the Fourier transform of the function $f(t)$ shown in Fig. DE14.1.
Answer: $2(1 - \cos \omega)/j\omega$

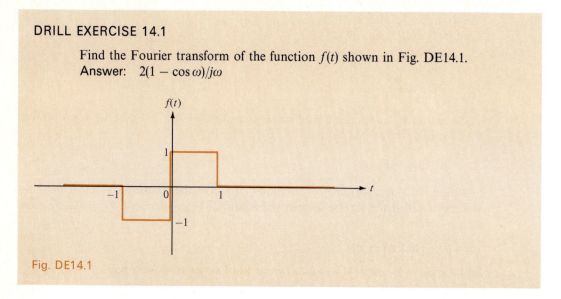

Fig. DE14.1

We have determined the frequency spectrum for a train of pulses of width τ and height V (see Example 13.8 on p. 623) and found that, as the period of this pulse train approaches infinity, the frequency spectrum becomes continuous.

For the case of Fourier transforms, the **amplitude spectrum** of $f(t)$ is the plot of $|F(j\omega)|$ versus ω, and the **phase spectrum** is the plot of the angle of $F(j\omega)$ versus frequency. These two spectra constitute the **frequency spectrum** of $f(t)$. Quite often the amplitude spectrum alone is referred to as the frequency spectrum.

In the preceding example, the Fourier transform $F(j\omega)$ is the product of a constant and a sinc function, and the (amplitude portion of the) frequency spectrum is shown in Fig. 14.2. For the case of a periodic function, the discrete amplitude spectrum signifies the amplitudes (for the trigonometric case) or the magnitudes (for the complex case) of the sinusoids comprising the function. However, for a nonperiodic

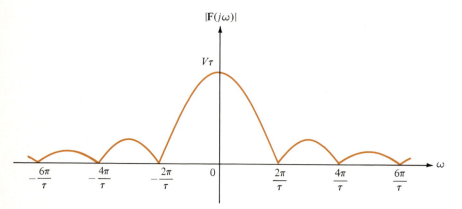

Fig. 14.2   Amplitude spectrum of function in Fig. 14.1.

function, the frequency spectrum is continuous and no longer signifies the amplitudes or magnitudes of sinusoids.

In order to obtain an interpretation of the frequency spectrum, we proceed as follows:

$$\mathbf{F}(j\omega) = \int_{-\infty}^{\infty} f(t)e^{-j\omega t}\,dt = \int_{-\infty}^{\infty} f(t)(\cos \omega t - j \sin \omega t)\,dt$$

$$= \int_{-\infty}^{\infty} f(t)\cos \omega t\,dt - j\int_{-\infty}^{\infty} f(t)\sin \omega t\,dt$$

Replacing ω by $-\omega$, we get

$$\mathbf{F}(-j\omega) = \int_{-\infty}^{\infty} f(t)\cos(-\omega)t\,dt - j\int_{-\infty}^{\infty} f(t)\sin(-\omega)t\,dt$$

$$= \int_{-\infty}^{\infty} f(t)\cos \omega t\,dt + j\int_{-\infty}^{\infty} f(t)\sin \omega t\,dt$$

and for real functions $f(t)$,

$$\mathbf{F}(-j\omega) = \mathbf{F}^*(j\omega)$$

where $\mathbf{F}^*(j\omega)$ is the complex conjugate of $\mathbf{F}(j\omega)$.

We also obtain

$$\int_{-\infty}^{\infty} f^2(t)\,dt = \int_{-\infty}^{\infty} f(t)[f(t)]\,dt = \int_{-\infty}^{\infty} f(t)\left[\frac{1}{2\pi}\int_{-\infty}^{\infty} \mathbf{F}(j\omega)e^{j\omega t}\,d\omega\right]dt$$

$$= \frac{1}{2\pi}\int_{-\infty}^{\infty}\int_{-\infty}^{\infty} f(t)\mathbf{F}(j\omega)e^{j\omega t}\,d\omega\,dt$$

$$= \frac{1}{2\pi}\int_{-\infty}^{\infty} \mathbf{F}(j\omega)\left[\int_{-\infty}^{\infty} f(t)e^{j\omega t}\,dt\right]d\omega$$

$$= \frac{1}{2\pi}\int_{-\infty}^{\infty} \mathbf{F}(j\omega)\left[\int_{-\infty}^{\infty} f(t)e^{-j(-\omega)t}\,dt\right]d\omega$$

$$= \frac{1}{2\pi}\int_{-\infty}^{\infty} \mathbf{F}(j\omega)\mathbf{F}(-j\omega)\,d\omega = \frac{1}{2\pi}\int_{-\infty}^{\infty} \mathbf{F}(j\omega)\mathbf{F}^*(j\omega)\,d\omega$$

But if $c = a + jb$, then

$$cc^* = (a + jb)(a - jb) = a^2 + b^2 = |c|^2$$

Thus,

$$\boxed{\int_{-\infty}^{\infty} f^2(t)\,dt = \frac{1}{2\pi}\int_{-\infty}^{\infty} |\mathbf{F}(j\omega)|^2\,d\omega}$$

This result is known as **Parseval's theorem.**[†]

[†] Named for the French mathematician Marc-Antoine Parseval-Deschenes.

If $f(t)$ is the voltage across or current through a 1-Ω resistor, then

$$\int_{-\infty}^{\infty} f^2(t)\, dt$$

is the energy absorbed by the resistor. Thus, we can think of $|\mathbf{F}(j\omega)|^2$—the square of the amplitude spectrum of $f(t)$—as the energy density or energy per unit bandwidth (J/Hz) of $f(t)$.

Transforms of Important Functions

Before we apply Fourier-transform techniques to electric circuits, let us determine the transforms of various important functions.

Given a unit impulse function $\delta(t - a)$, then

$$\mathscr{F}[\delta(t - a)] = \int_{-\infty}^{\infty} \delta(t - a)e^{-j\omega t}\, dt$$

and, by the sampling property of an impulse function,

$$\mathscr{F}[\delta(t - a)] = e^{-j\omega a}$$

For the special case $a = 0$,

$$\mathscr{F}[\delta(t)] = 1$$

The amplitude spectrum of the impulse function is obtained from

$$|\mathscr{F}[\delta(t - a)]| = |e^{-j\omega a}| = |\cos \omega a - j \sin \omega a| = \sqrt{\cos^2 \omega a + \sin^2 \omega a} = 1$$

Since the amplitude spectrum (and hence, energy density) of an impulse function is constant, the energy content of an impulse function is infinite! This explains why impulse functions cannot be physically realized.

Since

$$\mathscr{F}[\delta(t - a)] = e^{-j\omega a} \quad \Rightarrow \quad \mathscr{F}^{-1}[e^{-j\omega a}] = \delta(t - a)$$

then from the inverse Fourier transform formula [Equation (14.1) on p. 634],

$$\frac{1}{2\pi} \int_{-\infty}^{\infty} e^{-j\omega a}e^{j\omega t}\, d\omega = \delta(t - a) = \frac{1}{2\pi} \int_{-\infty}^{\infty} e^{j\omega(t - a)}\, d\omega$$

Thus,

$$\int_{-\infty}^{\infty} e^{j\omega(t - a)}\, d\omega = 2\pi\delta(t - a)$$

For the case $a = 0$,

$$\int_{-\infty}^{\infty} e^{j\omega t}\, d\omega = 2\pi\delta(t)$$

Interchanging variables, we also have

$$\int_{-\infty}^{\infty} e^{j\omega t}\, dt = 2\pi\delta(\omega)$$

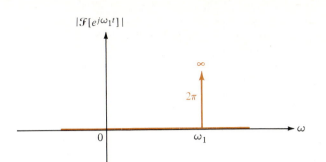

Fig. 14.3   Amplitude spectrum of $e^{j\omega_1 t}$.

We use this result to determine the Fourier transform of a complex sinusoid of frequency ω_1 as follows:

$$\mathcal{F}[e^{j\omega_1 t}] = \int_{-\infty}^{\infty} e^{j\omega_1 t}e^{-j\omega t}\,dt = \int_{-\infty}^{\infty} e^{j(\omega_1 - \omega)t}\,dt = 2\pi\delta(\omega_1 - \omega)$$

But since an impulse function is zero everywhere except where its argument is zero, $\delta(\omega_1 - \omega) = \delta(\omega - \omega_1)$. Thus,

$$\mathcal{F}[e^{j\omega_1 t}] = 2\pi\delta(\omega - \omega_1)$$

The amplitude spectrum of $e^{j\omega_1 t}$ is therefore as shown in Fig. 14.3. By setting $\omega_1 = 0$, we have the special case

$$\mathcal{F}[e^{j0}] = 2\pi\delta(\omega - 0) \quad \Rightarrow \quad \mathcal{F}[1] = 2\pi\delta(\omega)$$

Suppose that $f(t) = f_1(t) + f_2(t)$. Then

$$\mathcal{F}[f_1(t) + f_2(t)] = \int_{-\infty}^{\infty} [f_1(t) + f_2(t)]e^{-j\omega t}\,dt$$

$$= \int_{-\infty}^{\infty} f_1(t)e^{-j\omega t}\,dt + \int_{-\infty}^{\infty} f_2(t)e^{-j\omega t}\,dt = \mathcal{F}[f_1(t)] + \mathcal{F}[f_2(t)]$$

Also,

$$\mathcal{F}[Kf(t)] = \int_{-\infty}^{\infty} Kf(t)e^{-j\omega t}\,dt = K\int_{-\infty}^{\infty} f(t)e^{-j\omega t}\,dt = K\mathcal{F}[f(t)]$$

Because of these two properties, we say that the Fourier transform is a **linear transformation**.

By the property of linearity of the Fourier transform,

$$\mathcal{F}[K] = 2\pi K\delta(\omega)$$

Now we can use linearity to determine the Fourier transform of a sinusoid of frequency ω_1. By Equation (13.19) on p. 621,

$$\mathcal{F}[\cos \omega_1 t] = \mathcal{F}\left[\frac{e^{j\omega_1 t} + e^{-j\omega_1 t}}{2}\right] = \frac{1}{2}\mathcal{F}[e^{j\omega_1 t}] + \frac{1}{2}\mathcal{F}[e^{-j\omega_1 t}]$$

$$= \pi\delta(\omega - \omega_1) + \pi\delta(\omega + \omega_1)$$

The amplitude spectrum of $\cos \omega_1 t$ is shown in Fig. 14.4.

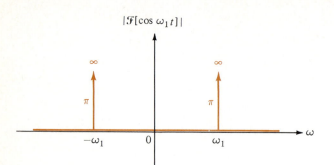

Fig. 14.4   Amplitude spectrum of $\cos \omega_1 t$.

To find the Fourier transform of $e^{-at}u(t)$, where $a > 0$, we can proceed as follows:

$$\mathcal{F}[e^{-at}u(t)] = \int_{-\infty}^{\infty} e^{-at}u(t)e^{-j\omega t}\, dt = \int_{0}^{\infty} e^{-(j\omega + a)t}\, dt = \frac{-1}{j\omega + a}\, e^{-j\omega t}e^{-at}\Big|_{0}^{\infty}$$

But $e^{-j\omega t}$ is a complex number whose magnitude is unity. Thus, since

$$\lim_{t \to \infty} e^{-at} = 0$$

then

$$\mathcal{F}[e^{-at}u(t)] = \frac{-1}{j\omega + a}\, [0 - 1] = \frac{1}{j\omega + a}$$

From the function $e^{-at}u(t)$, by setting $a = 0$ we get a unit step function $u(t)$. This may lead us to believe that the Fourier transform of $u(t)$ is $1/j\omega$. However, because $\int_{-\infty}^{\infty} f(t)\, dt$ is not finite when $f(t) = u(t)$, this conclusion cannot be justified. Such a problem does not arise when $f(t)$ is the **signum function**, designated sgn(t), which is

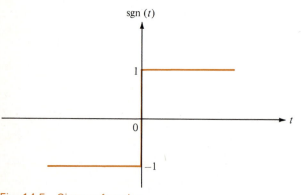

Fig. 14.5   Signum function.

defined by

$$\text{sgn}(t) = \begin{cases} -1 & \text{for} \quad t < 0 \\ 1 & \text{for} \quad t \geq 0 \end{cases} = -1 + 2u(t)$$

A sketch of this function is shown in Fig. 14.5. However,

$$\mathcal{F}[\text{sgn}(t)] = \int_{-\infty}^{\infty} \text{sgn}(t)e^{-j\omega t}\,dt = \int_{-\infty}^{0} -1e^{-j\omega t}\,dt + \int_{0}^{\infty} 1e^{-j\omega t}\,dt$$

which cannot be evaluated. Therefore consider the function $f(t)$ shown in Fig. 14.6, in which $a > 0$. In this case,

$$\mathcal{F}[f(t)] = \int_{-\infty}^{\infty} f(t)e^{-j\omega t}\,dt = \int_{-\infty}^{0} -e^{at}e^{-j\omega t}\,dt + \int_{0}^{\infty} e^{-at}e^{-j\omega t}\,dt$$

$$= \frac{-1}{a - j\omega}\,e^{(a-j\omega)t}\Big|_{-\infty}^{0} + \frac{-1}{a + j\omega}\,e^{-(a+j\omega)t}\Big|_{0}^{\infty}$$

$$= -\frac{1}{a - j\omega} + \frac{1}{a + j\omega} = \frac{-2j\omega}{a^2 + \omega^2}$$

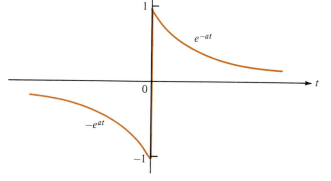

Fig. 14.6   Function whose limit is signum function.

Therefore,

$$\lim_{a \to 0} f(t) = \text{sgn}(t) \quad \Rightarrow \quad \mathcal{F}[\text{sgn}(t)] = \lim_{a \to 0} \frac{-2j\omega}{a^2 + \omega^2} = \frac{-2j}{\omega} = \frac{2}{j\omega}$$

Since

$$\text{sgn}(t) = -1 + 2u(t) \quad \Rightarrow \quad u(t) = \tfrac{1}{2} + \tfrac{1}{2}\text{sgn}(t)$$

then

$$\mathscr{F}[u(t)] = \mathscr{F}\left[\frac{1}{2} + \frac{1}{2}\,\text{sgn}(t)\right] = \mathscr{F}\left[\frac{1}{2}\right] + \frac{1}{2}\mathscr{F}[\text{sgn}(t)]$$

$$= \left(\frac{1}{2}\right)2\pi\delta(\omega) + \frac{1}{2}\left(\frac{2}{j\omega}\right) = \pi\delta(\omega) + \frac{1}{j\omega}$$

Given the periodic function $f(t)$ having period T, its complex Fourier series representation is

$$f(t) = \sum_{n=-\infty}^{\infty} c_n e^{jn\omega_0 t}$$

where $\omega_0 = 2\pi/T$ and c_n are the complex Fourier coefficients. Then

$$\mathscr{F}[f(t)] = \int_{-\infty}^{\infty} \left(\sum_{n=-\infty}^{\infty} c_n e^{jn\omega_0 t}\right) e^{-j\omega t}\, dt = \sum_{n=-\infty}^{\infty} \left(\int_{-\infty}^{\infty} c_n e^{jt(n\omega_0 - \omega)}\, dt\right)$$

$$= \sum_{n=-\infty}^{\infty} c_n 2\pi\delta(n\omega_0 - \omega) = \sum_{n=-\infty}^{\infty} 2\pi c_n \delta(\omega - n\omega_0)$$

Thus, the Fourier transform of a periodic function is a sum of impulses whose values are determined by the complex Fourier series coefficients.

14.2 THE USE OF DERIVATIVES

A technique for determining the Fourier transform of a function $f(t)$ by employing its derivative(s)—as was done for Fourier series—is based on the following derivation: Given a function $f(t)$, then

$$\mathscr{F}[f'(t)] = \mathscr{F}\left[\frac{df(t)}{dt}\right] = \int_{-\infty}^{\infty} \frac{df(t)}{dt}\, e^{-j\omega t}\, dt$$

For integration by parts,

$$\int_a^b u\, dv = uv\Big|_a^b - \int_a^b v\, du$$

If we let

$$u = e^{-j\omega t} \qquad \text{and} \qquad dv = \frac{df(t)}{dt}\, dt = df(t)$$

then

$$du = -j\omega e^{-j\omega t}\, dt \qquad \text{and} \qquad v = f(t)$$

and

$$\mathscr{F}[f'(t)] = e^{-j\omega t} f(t)\Big|_{-\infty}^{\infty} - \int_{-\infty}^{\infty} f(t)[-j\omega e^{-j\omega t}]\, dt$$

For the case in which $\lim_{t \to -\infty} f(t) = \lim_{t \to \infty} f(t) = 0$, we have

$$\mathscr{F}[f'(t)] = j\omega \int_{-\infty}^{\infty} f(t)e^{-j\omega t} \, dt$$

or

$$\boxed{\mathscr{F}\left[\frac{df(t)}{dt}\right] = j\omega \mathscr{F}[f(t)] = j\omega \mathbf{F}(j\omega)}$$

Reapplying this result, we obtain

$$\mathscr{F}[f''(t)] = \mathscr{F}\left[\frac{d^2 f(t)}{dt^2}\right] = (j\omega)^2 \mathbf{F}(j\omega)$$

and, in general,

$$\mathscr{F}\left[\frac{d^n f(t)}{dt^n}\right] = (j\omega)^n \mathbf{F}(j\omega)$$

EXAMPLE 14.2

To find the Fourier transform of the function $f(t) = te^{-at}u(t)$, take the derivative of $f(t)$. Thus,

$$\frac{df(t)}{dt} = \frac{d}{dt}\left[te^{-at}u(t)\right] = t\frac{d}{dt}\left[e^{-at}u(t)\right] + e^{-at}u(t)$$

$$= t[e^{-at}\delta(t) - ae^{-at}u(t)] + e^{-at}u(t)$$

$$= te^{-at}\delta(t) - ate^{-at}u(t) + e^{-at}u(t)$$

$$= 0\delta(t) - af(t) + e^{-at}u(t) = -af(t) + e^{-at}u(t)$$

Taking the Fourier transform, since $\lim_{t \to -\infty} f(t) = \lim_{t \to \infty} f(t) = 0$, we obtain

$$j\omega \mathbf{F}(j\omega) = -a\mathbf{F}(j\omega) + \frac{1}{j\omega + a}$$

from which

$$\mathbf{F}(j\omega) = \frac{1}{(j\omega + a)^2} = \mathscr{F}\left[te^{-at}u(t)\right]$$

DRILL EXERCISE 14.2

Find the Fourier transform of $f(t) = t^2 e^{-at} u(t)$.

Answer: $\dfrac{2}{(j\omega + a)^3}$

EXAMPLE 14.3

Given the function $f(t)$ shown in Fig. 14.7. Since $\lim\limits_{t \to -\infty} f(t) = \lim\limits_{t \to \infty} f(t) = 0$, we can apply the differentiation property developed above.

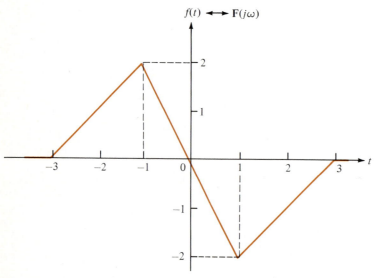

Fig. 14.7   Given function.

The derivative of $f(t)$ is shown in Fig. 14.8. Taking the second derivative, we get the function shown in Fig. 14.9. Since

$$f''(t) = \delta(t + 3) - 3\delta(t + 1) + 3\delta(t - 1) - \delta(t - 3)$$

then

$$(j\omega)^2 F(j\omega) = e^{j\omega 3} - 3e^{j\omega 1} + 3e^{-j\omega 1} - e^{-j\omega 3}$$

$$-\omega^2 F(j\omega) = 2j\left(\frac{e^{j3\omega} - e^{-j3\omega}}{2j}\right) - 2j\left(\frac{3e^{j\omega} - 3e^{-j\omega}}{2j}\right)$$

from which

$$F(j\omega) = \frac{2j}{\omega^2}(3\sin\omega - \sin 3\omega)$$

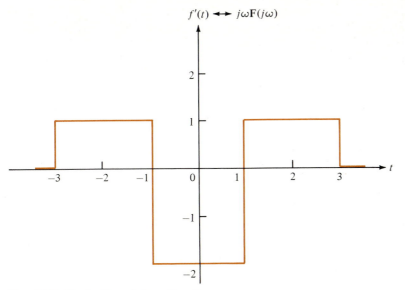

Fig. 14.8   Derivative of given function.

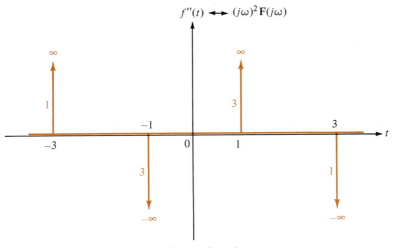

Fig. 14.9   Second derivative of given function.

DRILL EXERCISE 14.3

Find the Fourier transform of the function $f(t)$ given in Fig. DE14.1 (p. 636) by using the derivative of $f(t)$.

Answer: $2(1 - \cos\omega)/j\omega$

If you don't appreciate the differentation property of the Fourier transform by now, try to find $\mathbf{F}(j\omega)$ for the function in the previous example by directly substituting $f(t)$ into the Fourier transform formula.

A more subtle use of the differentiation property is shown in the following example.

EXAMPLE 14.4

Consider the function shown in Fig. 14.10, whose first and second derivatives are shown in Figs. 14.11 and 14.12, respectively.

Since

$$f''(t) = -\delta(t + \pi) + \delta(t - \pi) - f(t)$$

then

$$(j\omega)^2 \mathbf{F}(j\omega) = -e^{j\omega\pi} + e^{-j\omega\pi} - \mathbf{F}(j\omega)$$

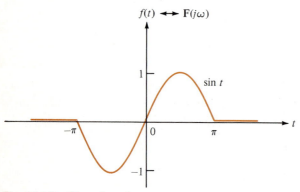

$$f(t) \longleftrightarrow F(j\omega)$$

Fig. 14.10   Given function.

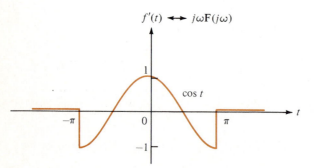

$$f'(t) \longleftrightarrow j\omega F(j\omega)$$

Fig. 14.11   Derivative of given function.

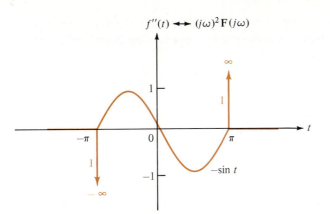

Fig. 14.12   Second derivative of given function.

from which

$$\mathbf{F}(j\omega) = \frac{-e^{j\omega\pi} + e^{-j\omega\pi}}{1 - \omega^2} = \frac{2j(e^{j\omega\pi} - e^{-j\omega\pi})}{(\omega^2 - 1)(2j)} = \frac{2j\sin\pi\omega}{\omega^2 - 1}$$

DRILL EXERCISE 14.4

Find the Fourier transform of the function shown in Fig. DE14.4.

Answer: $\dfrac{2\pi}{\pi^2 - \omega^2}\cos\dfrac{\omega}{2}$

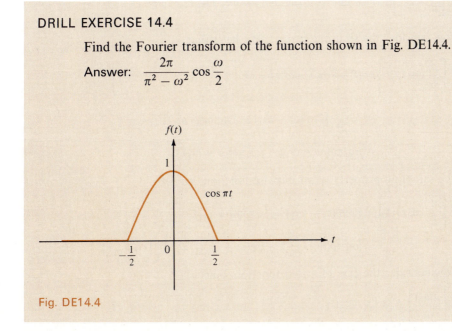

Fig. DE14.4

We have just seen that taking the derivative in the time domain corresponds to multiplication by $j\omega$ in the frequency domain. The proof presented was for functions $f(t)$ having the property that

$$\lim_{t \to \pm \infty} f(t) = 0$$

However, for some other functions not having this property (e.g., a sinusoid or a step function) it is also true that

$$\mathscr{F}\left[\frac{d}{dt}f(t)\right] = j\omega\mathscr{F}[f(t)]$$

To demonstrate this fact, consider the complex sinusoid $e^{j\omega_1 t}$. We have that

$$\mathscr{F}\left[\frac{d}{dt}e^{j\omega_1 t}\right] = \mathscr{F}[j\omega_1 e^{j\omega_1 t}] = j\omega_1 \mathscr{F}[e^{j\omega_1 t}]$$

$$= j\omega_1[2\pi\delta(\omega - \omega_1)] = 2\pi j\omega_1\delta(\omega - \omega_1)$$

However, by the sampling property of the impulse function,

$$2\pi j\omega_1\delta(\omega - \omega_1) = 2\pi j\omega\delta(\omega - \omega_1)$$

Thus,

$$\mathscr{F}\left[\frac{d}{dt}e^{j\omega_1 t}\right] = 2\pi j\omega\delta(\omega - \omega_1) = j\omega[2\pi\delta(\omega - \omega_1)] = j\omega\mathscr{F}[e^{j\omega_1 t}]$$

Now consider the sinusoid $\cos\omega_1 t$. We have that

$$\mathscr{F}\left[\frac{d}{dt}\cos\omega_1 t\right] = \mathscr{F}[-\omega_1\sin\omega_1 t] = \mathscr{F}\left[-\frac{\omega_1}{2j}(e^{j\omega_1 t} - e^{-j\omega_1 t})\right]$$

$$= -\frac{\omega_1}{2j}[2\pi\delta(\omega - \omega_1) - 2\pi\delta(\omega + \omega_1)]$$

$$= j\omega_1\pi\delta(\omega - \omega_1) - j\omega_1\pi\delta(\omega + \omega_1)$$

Using the sampling property of an impulse function, we get

$$\mathscr{F}\left[\frac{d}{dt}\cos\omega_1 t\right] = j\omega\pi\delta(\omega - \omega_1) + j\omega\pi\delta(\omega + \omega_1)$$

$$= j\omega[\pi\delta(\omega - \omega_1) + \pi\delta(\omega + \omega_1)] = j\omega\mathscr{F}[\cos\omega_1 t]$$

Now consider the case of a step function. Since

$$\mathscr{F}\left[\frac{du(t)}{dt}\right] = \mathscr{F}[\delta(t)] = 1$$

and

$$j\omega \mathscr{F}\left[u(t)\right] = j\omega\left[\frac{1}{j\omega} + \pi\delta(\omega)\right] = 1 + j\omega\pi\delta(\omega) = 1 + 0\delta(\omega) = 1$$

then

$$\mathscr{F}\left[\frac{du(t)}{dt}\right] = j\omega\mathscr{F}\left[u(t)\right]$$

In essence, we shall only be considering functions that have the property that

$$\mathscr{F}\left[\frac{df(t)}{dt}\right] = j\omega\mathscr{F}\left[f(t)\right]$$

We have previously seen that

$$\mathscr{F}\left[e^{-at}u(t)\right] = \frac{1}{j\omega + a}$$

where a is a positive real number. The same result holds when a is a complex number with a positive real part. Using this fact, we get

$$\mathscr{F}\left[e^{-\alpha t}\sin\omega_1 t\, u(t)\right]$$

$$= \mathscr{F}\left[e^{-\alpha t}\left(\frac{e^{j\omega_1 t} - e^{-j\omega_1 t}}{2j}\right)u(t)\right] = \frac{1}{2j}\mathscr{F}\left[e^{-(\alpha - j\omega_1)t}u(t) - e^{-(\alpha + j\omega_1)t}u(t)\right]$$

$$= \frac{1}{2j}\left[\frac{1}{j\omega + (\alpha - j\omega_1)} - \frac{1}{j\omega + (\alpha + j\omega_1)}\right]$$

$$= \frac{1}{2j}\left(\frac{2j\omega_1}{(j\omega)^2 + 2\alpha j\omega + \alpha^2 + \omega_1^2}\right) = \frac{\omega_1}{(j\omega + \alpha)^2 + \omega_1^2}$$

In a similar manner we can show that

$$\mathscr{F}\left[e^{-\alpha t}\cos\omega_1 t\, u(t)\right] = \frac{j\omega + \alpha}{(j\omega + \alpha)^2 + \omega_1^2}$$

It can be shown that

$$\mathscr{F}\left[\sin\omega_1 t\, u(t)\right] = \frac{\omega_1}{(j\omega)^2 + \omega_1^2} + \frac{j\pi}{2}\left[\delta(\omega + \omega_1) - \delta(\omega - \omega_1)\right]$$

$$\mathscr{F}\left[\cos\omega_1 t\, u(t)\right] = \frac{j\omega}{(j\omega)^2 + \omega_1^2} + \frac{\pi}{2}\left[\delta(\omega - \omega_1) + \delta(\omega + \omega_1)\right]$$

A number of common Fourier transforms are summarized in Table 14.1.

Table 14.1 TABLE OF FOURIER TRANSFORMS

$f(t)$	$F(j\omega)$
$\dfrac{1}{2\pi}\displaystyle\int_{-\infty}^{\infty} F(j\omega)e^{j\omega t}\,d\omega$	$\displaystyle\int_{-\infty}^{\infty} f(t)e^{-j\omega t}\,dt$
$\delta(t)$	1
$\delta(t-a)$	$e^{-j\omega a}$
K	$2\pi K\delta(\omega)$
$e^{j\omega_1 t}$	$2\pi\delta(\omega-\omega_1)$
$\cos\omega_1 t$	$\pi\delta(\omega-\omega_1)+\pi\delta(\omega+\omega_1)$
$\sin\omega_1 t$	$j\pi\delta(\omega+\omega_1)-j\pi\delta(\omega-\omega_1)$
$e^{-\alpha t}u(t)$	$\dfrac{1}{j\omega+\alpha}$
$\mathrm{sgn}(t)$	$\dfrac{2}{j\omega}$
$u(t)$	$\dfrac{1}{j\omega}+\pi\delta(\omega)$
$\cos\omega_1 t\, u(t)$	$\dfrac{j\omega}{(j\omega)^2+\omega_1^2}+\dfrac{\pi}{2}\big[\delta(\omega-\omega_1)+\delta(\omega+\omega_1)\big]$
$\sin\omega_1 t\, u(t)$	$\dfrac{\omega_1}{(j\omega)^2+\omega_1^2}+\dfrac{j\pi}{2}\big[\delta(\omega+\omega_1)-\delta(\omega-\omega_1)\big]$
$e^{-\alpha t}\cos\omega_1 t\, u(t)$	$\dfrac{j\omega+\alpha}{(j\omega+\alpha)^2+\omega_1^2}$
$e^{-\alpha t}\sin\omega_1 t\, u(t)$	$\dfrac{\omega_1}{(j\omega+\alpha)^2+\omega_1^2}$
$f_1(t)+f_2(t)$	$F_1(j\omega)+F_2(j\omega)$
$Kf(t)$	$KF(j\omega)$
$\dfrac{df(t)}{dt}$	$j\omega F(j\omega)$
$f(t-a)$	$e^{-j\omega a}F(j\omega)$
$e^{-\alpha t}f(t)$	$F(j\omega+\alpha)$
$e^{j\omega_1 t}f(t)$	$F(j[\omega-\omega_1])$
$te^{-\alpha t}u(t)$	$\dfrac{1}{(j\omega+\alpha)^2}$
$u(t+a)-u(t-a)$	$2a\left(\dfrac{\sin a\omega}{a\omega}\right)$
$\displaystyle\int_{-\infty}^{\infty} f_1(\tau)f_2(t-\tau)\,dt$	$F_1(j\omega)F_2(j\omega)$
$f_1(t)f_2(t)$	$\dfrac{1}{2\pi}\displaystyle\int_{-\infty}^{\infty} F_1(j\lambda)F_2(j[\omega-\lambda])\,d\lambda$

14.3 APPLICATION OF THE FOURIER TRANSFORM

Suppose that we have a linear time-invariant system with input $x(t)$ and output $y(t)$, as shown in Fig. 14.13, which is described by a linear differential equation with constant coefficients. If the initial conditions are zero, in general we have that

$$A_n \frac{d^n y}{dt^n} + A_{n-1} \frac{d^{n-1} y}{dt^{n-1}} + \cdots + A_1 \frac{dy}{dt} + A_0 y$$

$$= B_m \frac{d^m x}{dt^m} + B_{m-1} \frac{d^{m-1} x}{dt^{m-1}} + \cdots + B_1 \frac{dx}{dt} + B_0 x$$

$x(t) \longrightarrow \boxed{} \longrightarrow y(t)$

Fig. 14.13   Linear system.

If we take the Fourier transform of both sides of this equation, we obtain

$$(j\omega)^n A_n Y(j\omega) + (j\omega)^{n-1} A_{n-1} Y(j\omega) + \cdots + j\omega A_1 Y(j\omega) + A_0 Y(j\omega)$$
$$= (j\omega)^m B_m X(j\omega) + \cdots + j\omega B_1 X(j\omega) + B_0 X(j\omega)$$

or

$$[(j\omega)^n A_n + (j\omega)^{n-1} A_{n-1} + \cdots + j\omega A_1 + A_0] Y(j\omega)$$
$$= [(j\omega)^m B_m + (j\omega)^{m-1} B_{m-1} + \cdots + j\omega B_1 + B_0] X(j\omega)$$

Thus,

$$Y(j\omega) = \frac{(j\omega)^m B_m + \cdots + j\omega B_1 + B_0}{(j\omega)^n A_n + \cdots + j\omega A_1 + A_0} X(j\omega)$$

or

$$\boxed{Y(j\omega) = H(j\omega) X(j\omega)}$$

where $H(j\omega)$ is called the **system function** or **transfer function** of the system. We therefore have that

$$\boxed{H(j\omega) = \frac{Y(j\omega)}{X(j\omega)}}$$

Note that if we know the system function and the transform of the input, it is a simple matter to determine the transform of the output; by taking the inverse transform, we get the output.

Suppose that the input is $x(t) = \delta(t)$. Then

$$\mathbf{X}(j\omega) = 1$$

Thus,

$$\mathbf{Y}(j\omega) = \mathbf{H}(j\omega)\mathbf{X}(j\omega) = \mathbf{H}(j\omega)$$

and the output is

$$y(t) = \mathscr{F}^{-1}[\mathbf{Y}(j\omega)] = \mathscr{F}^{-1}[\mathbf{H}(j\omega)] = h(t)$$

Therefore $h(t)$, the inverse transform of the system function, is called the **impulse response** of the system.

EXAMPLE 14.5

Given a system whose impulse response is $h(t) = 2e^{-t}u(t)$, let us determine the step response.

Since

$$\mathbf{X}(j\omega) = \mathscr{F}[u(t)] = \pi\delta(\omega) + \frac{1}{j\omega} \qquad \text{and} \qquad \mathbf{H}(j\omega) = \mathscr{F}[h(t)] = \frac{2}{j\omega + 1}$$

then

$$\mathbf{Y}(j\omega) = \mathbf{H}(j\omega)\mathbf{X}(j\omega) = \frac{2}{j\omega + 1}\left[\pi\delta(\omega) + \frac{1}{j\omega}\right]$$

$$= \frac{2\pi}{j\omega + 1}\delta(\omega) + \frac{2}{(j\omega)(j\omega + 1)} = 2\pi\delta(\omega) + \frac{2}{(j\omega)(j\omega + 1)}$$

Just as we showed that the Fourier transform is linear, we can show that the inverse transform is also. Thus,

$$\mathscr{F}^{-1}[\mathbf{F}_1(j\omega) + \mathbf{F}_2(j\omega)] = \mathscr{F}^{-1}[\mathbf{F}_1(j\omega)] + \mathscr{F}^{-1}[\mathbf{F}_2(j\omega)]$$

and

$$\mathscr{F}^{-1}[K\mathbf{F}(j\omega)] = K\mathscr{F}^{-1}[\mathbf{F}(j\omega)]$$

Thus,

$$y(t) = \mathscr{F}^{-1}[2\pi\delta(\omega)] + \mathscr{F}^{-1}\left[\frac{2}{(j\omega)(j\omega + 1)}\right]$$

The inverse transform of the first term is 1. To obtain the inverse transform of the second term we can take a partial-fraction expansion as is done for Laplace transforms. In other words, we can write

$$\frac{2}{(j\omega)(j\omega + 1)} = \frac{K_1}{j\omega} + \frac{K_2}{j\omega + 1}$$

where

$$K_1 = \frac{2}{j\omega + 1}\bigg|_{j\omega = 0} = \frac{2}{1} = 2 \qquad \text{and} \qquad K_2 = \frac{2}{j\omega}\bigg|_{j\omega = -1} = \frac{2}{-1} = -2$$

Thus,

$$\frac{2}{(j\omega)(j\omega + 1)} = \frac{2}{j\omega} - \frac{2}{j\omega + 1}$$

and

$$\mathscr{F}^{-1}\left[\frac{2}{(j\omega)(j\omega + 1)}\right] = \mathscr{F}^{-1}\left[\frac{2}{j\omega}\right] - \mathscr{F}^{-1}\left[\frac{2}{j\omega + 1}\right] = \text{sgn}(t) - 2e^{-t}u(t)$$

Hence, the step response is

$$y(t) = 1 + \text{sgn}(t) - 2e^{-t}u(t) = 2u(t) - 2e^{-t}u(t) = 2(1 - e^{-t})u(t)$$

DRILL EXERCISE 14.5

A linear system has an impulse response of $h(t) = 3e^{-3t}u(t)$. Find the input $x(t)$ which results in an output of $y(t) = 3(e^{-3t} - e^{-4t})u(t)$.

Answer: $e^{-4t}u(t)$

Convolution

For the case that $x(t)$ is not an impulse function, knowing the impulse response $h(t)$ we can determine the output without resorting to transforms. To obtain this result, we proceed as follows:

From the fact that

$$Y(j\omega) = H(j\omega)X(j\omega)$$

and

$$X(j\omega) = \int_{-\infty}^{\infty} x(t)e^{-j\omega t}\, dt = \int_{-\infty}^{\infty} x(\tau)e^{-j\omega \tau}\, d\tau$$

we have

$$Y(j\omega) = H(j\omega)\int_{-\infty}^{\infty} x(\tau)e^{-j\omega \tau}\, d\tau = \int_{-\infty}^{\infty} x(\tau)e^{-j\omega \tau}H(j\omega)\, d\tau$$

$$= \int_{-\infty}^{\infty} x(\tau)e^{-j\omega \tau}\left[\int_{-\infty}^{\infty} h(\lambda)e^{-j\omega \lambda}\, d\lambda\right] d\tau = \int_{-\infty}^{\infty} x(\tau)\left[\int_{-\infty}^{\infty} h(\lambda)e^{-j\omega(\lambda + \tau)}\, d\lambda\right] d\tau$$

In evaluating the integral in the brackets, let $t = \lambda + \tau$. Then $dt = d\lambda$, and $\lambda = t - \tau$. Thus, $\lambda = -\infty \Rightarrow t = -\infty$, and $\lambda = \infty \Rightarrow t = \infty$. Therefore, changing variables, we get

$$Y(j\omega) = \int_{-\infty}^{\infty} x(\tau) \left[\int_{-\infty}^{\infty} h(t-\tau)e^{-j\omega t} \, dt \right] d\tau = \int_{-\infty}^{\infty} \int_{-\infty}^{\infty} x(\tau)h(t-\tau)e^{-j\omega t} \, d\tau \, dt$$

$$= \int_{-\infty}^{\infty} \left[\int_{-\infty}^{\infty} x(\tau)h(t-\tau) \, d\tau \right] e^{-j\omega t} \, dt = \int_{-\infty}^{\infty} y(t)e^{-j\omega t} \, dt$$

Thus, we deduce that

$$y(t) = \int_{-\infty}^{\infty} x(\tau)h(t-\tau) \, d\tau$$

If we interchange the roles of $x(t)$ and $h(t)$, in a similar manner we can obtain

$$y(t) = \int_{-\infty}^{\infty} h(\tau)x(t-\tau) \, d\tau$$

Each of these last two integrals describes a process called **convolution**, and therefore each is called the **convolution integral**. This process (the evaluation of the integral) enables us to determine the output from the input and the impulse response without taking transforms. Thus, we see that multiplication in the frequency (or transform) domain corresponds to convolution in the time domain.

Although the evaluation of the convolution integral is not difficult, it can be quite subtle as was shown in the chapter on Laplace transforms. However, for the very special case that either the impulse response $h(t)$ or the input $x(t)$ is an impulse function, the convolution integral is easily evaluated by using the sampling property of an impulse function.

EXAMPLE 14.6

Suppose that $x(t) = 3\delta(t-4)$ is the input to a system whose impulse response is $h(t) = 2e^{-5t}u(t)$. Then the output is

$$y(t) = \int_{-\infty}^{\infty} x(\tau)h(t-\tau) \, d\tau = \int_{-\infty}^{\infty} [3\delta(\tau-4)][2e^{-5(t-\tau)}u(t-\tau)] \, d\tau$$

$$= \int_{-\infty}^{\infty} [\delta(\tau-4)][6e^{-5(t-\tau)}u(t-\tau)] \, d\tau$$

and by the sampling property of an impulse function

$$y(t) = 6e^{-5(t-4)}u(t-4)$$

This result is by no means surprising, for if $2e^{-5t}u(t)$ is the impulse response [i.e., the response to an input of $\delta(t)$], then by linearity the response to $3\delta(t)$ is $6e^{-5t}u(t)$. Furthermore, because of the time-invariance property, the response to $3\delta(t-4)$ is $6e^{-5(t-4)}u(t-4)$.

Also note that

$$y(t) = \int_{-\infty}^{\infty} h(\tau)x(t-\tau)\,d\tau = \int_{-\infty}^{\infty} [2e^{-5\tau}u(\tau)][3\delta(t-\tau-4)]\,d\tau$$

$$= \int_{-\infty}^{\infty} [6e^{-5t}u(\tau)][\delta(t-\tau-4)]\,d\tau$$

and by the sampling property (since the variable of integration is τ, the impulse function is nonzero when $\tau = t - 4$), we get that

$$y(t) = 6e^{-5(t-4)}u(t-4)$$

as was obtained above.

● ──────────

Filters

Since

$$\mathbf{Y}(j\omega) = \mathbf{H}(j\omega)\mathbf{X}(j\omega) \qquad \Rightarrow \qquad |\mathbf{Y}(j\omega)| = |\mathbf{H}(j\omega)\mathbf{X}(j\omega)| = |\mathbf{H}(j\omega)|\,|\mathbf{X}(j\omega)|$$

then the amplitude spectrum of the output function is the product of the amplitude spectrum of the input function and $|\mathbf{H}(j\omega)|$, which we call the **amplitude response** of the system.

The system function $\mathbf{H}(j\omega)$ of a linear system is equal to the Fourier transform of the system's impulse response $h(t)$, and for a physical linear system $h(t)$ is a real function of time. As a consequence of these facts, it is not difficult to show that the amplitude response of a physical linear system is an even function of ω (see Problem 14.16). Therefore, in the following discussions, when plotting $|\mathbf{H}(j\omega)|$ versus ω, we will show only nonnegative values of ω since the plot for negative values of ω is just the mirror reflection (around the vertical axis) of the plot for positive values of ω.

Consider the system whose amplitude response is shown in Fig. 14.14. Mathematically, we can write

$$|\mathbf{H}(j\omega)| = \begin{cases} 1 & \text{for} \quad 0 \le \omega \le \omega_c \\ 0 & \text{for} \quad \omega_c < \omega < \infty \end{cases}$$

If the input to this system is the real function $x(t)$, then the amplitude spectrum of $x(t)$ is an even function of ω. Thus, the amplitude spectrum of the output is also an even function of ω, and for nonnegative values of ω, is given by

$$|\mathbf{Y}(j\omega)| = |\mathbf{H}(j\omega)|\,|\mathbf{X}(j\omega)| = \begin{cases} |\mathbf{X}(j\omega)| & \text{for} \quad 0 \le \omega \le \omega_c \\ 0 & \text{for} \quad \omega_c < \omega < \infty \end{cases}$$

Hence this system passes that portion of the input below the frequency ω_c, but stops that portion above ω_c. We call the frequency band $0 \le \omega \le \omega_c$ the **pass band** and $\omega_c < \omega < \infty$ the **stop band**. Since it is the low frequencies that are passed and the high frequencies that are not passed, we call such a system a **low-pass filter**. Because all of the frequencies in the pass band are passed equally and all the frequencies in the stop band are completely stopped, this low-pass filter is said to be **ideal**.

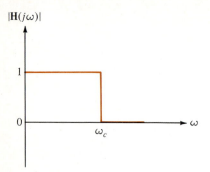

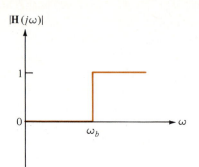

Fig. 14.14 Amplitude response of ideal low-pass filter.

Fig. 14.15 Amplitude response of ideal high-pass filter.

The amplitude response of an **ideal high-pass filter** is shown in Fig. 14.15. In this case the stop band is the frequency band $0 \leq \omega < \omega_b$ and the pass band is $\omega_b \leq \omega < \infty$. The amplitude response of an **ideal bandpass filter** is shown in Fig. 14.16. In this case the pass band consists of the interval $\omega_1 \leq \omega \leq \omega_2$, whereas $0 \leq \omega < \omega_1$ and $\omega_2 < \omega < \infty$ are both stop bands.

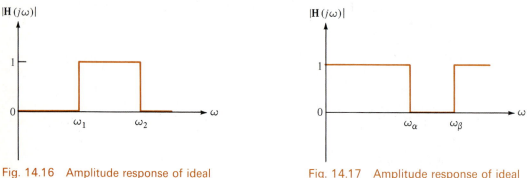

Fig. 14.16 Amplitude response of ideal bandpass filter.

Fig. 14.17 Amplitude response of ideal band-elimination filter.

Another type of filter is an **ideal band-elimination** (or **rejection**) **filter**.[†] The amplitude response of such a filter is seen in Fig. 14.17. The stop band is $\omega_\alpha < \omega < \omega_\beta$, whereas $0 \leq \omega \leq \omega_\alpha$ and $\omega_\beta \leq \omega < \infty$ are both pass bands.

14.4 APPLICATION TO CIRCUITS

In order to apply Fourier transforms to circuits, first consider a resistor [Fig. 14.18(a)]. Since

$$v(t) = Ri(t)$$

[†] Also called a **trap**.

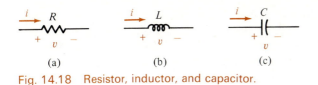

Fig. 14.18   Resistor, inductor, and capacitor.

then taking the Fourier transform yields

$$\mathbf{V}(j\omega) = R\mathbf{I}(j\omega)$$

Defining impedance to be the ratio of the voltage transform to the current transform, the impedance of the resistor $\mathbf{Z}_R(j\omega)$ is therefore

$$\mathbf{Z}_R(j\omega) = \frac{\mathbf{V}(j\omega)}{\mathbf{I}(j\omega)} = R$$

For an inductor [Fig. 14.18(b)], since

$$v(t) = L\frac{di(t)}{dt} \qquad \Rightarrow \qquad \mathbf{V}(j\omega) = Lj\omega\mathbf{I}(j\omega)$$

then

$$\mathbf{Z}_L(j\omega) = \frac{\mathbf{V}(j\omega)}{\mathbf{I}(j\omega)} = j\omega L$$

In addition, for a capacitor [Fig. 14.18(c)], since

$$i(t) = C\frac{dv(t)}{dt} \qquad \Rightarrow \qquad \mathbf{I}(j\omega) = Cj\omega\mathbf{V}(j\omega)$$

then

$$\mathbf{Z}_C(j\omega) = \frac{\mathbf{V}(j\omega)}{\mathbf{I}(j\omega)} = \frac{1}{j\omega C}$$

For each of the elements described above, we have the three forms of Ohm's law:

$$\mathbf{Z}(j\omega) = \frac{\mathbf{V}(j\omega)}{\mathbf{I}(j\omega)} \qquad \mathbf{V}(j\omega) = \mathbf{Z}(j\omega)\mathbf{I}(j\omega) \qquad \mathbf{I}(j\omega) = \frac{\mathbf{V}(j\omega)}{\mathbf{Z}(j\omega)}$$

Thus, we see that we get the same expressions for the impedances of resistors, capacitors, and inductors as was obtained for phasors (the sinusoidal case). In addition, the expressions describing transformers are the same as for phasors. Hence, we can employ the circuit analysis techniques we used previously for sinusoidal circuits—the difference being that instead of phasors, we use Fourier transforms.

EXAMPLE 14.7

Let us find the system function and the impulse response for the circuit shown in Fig. 14.19(a).

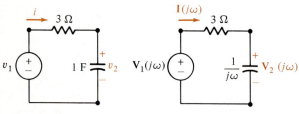

    (a) Time domain   (b) Frequency domain

Fig. 14.19   Circuit for Example 14.7.

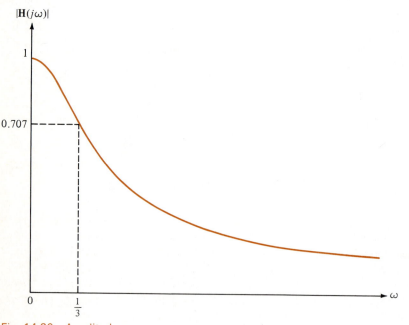

Fig. 14.20   Amplitude response.

The circuit is represented in the frequency domain by Fig. 14.19(b). By voltage division,

$$\mathbf{V}_2(j\omega) = \frac{1/j\omega}{(1/j\omega) + 3} \mathbf{V}_1(j\omega) = \frac{1}{1 + 3j\omega} \mathbf{V}_1(j\omega)$$

Thus, the system function is given by

$$\mathbf{H}(j\omega) = \frac{\mathbf{V}_2(j\omega)}{\mathbf{V}_1(j\omega)} = \frac{1/3}{j\omega + 1/3}$$

For very small values of ω the value of $|\mathbf{H}(j\omega)|$ is approximately unity (when $\omega = 0$ then $|\mathbf{H}(j\omega)| = 1$), whereas for very large values of ω the value of $|\mathbf{H}(j\omega)|$ is very small. A plot (for nonnegative values of ω) of the amplitude response is shown in Fig. 14.20. (Note that the half-power frequency is $\frac{1}{3}$ rad/s.) Thus, we see that the circuit is a (nonideal) low-pass filter.

The impulse response is

$$h(t) = \mathscr{F}^{-1}[\mathbf{H}(j\omega)] = \tfrac{1}{3}e^{-t/3}u(t) \text{ V}$$

that is, this is the output $v_2(t)$ when the input is $v_1(t) = \delta(t)$ V.

DRILL EXERCISE 14.6

Find the impulse response for the circuit shown in Fig. DE14.6 given that $R = 3 \, \Omega$, $L = 2$ H, and $C = \frac{1}{18}$ F.

Answer: $6(1 - 3t)e^{-3t}u(t)$ V

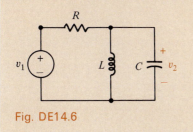

Fig. DE14.6

Laplace transforms can be employed when initial conditions (either zero or nonzero) are known and inputs are given for $t \geq 0$. This is not the case for Fourier transforms—the initial conditions must be zero. However, when inputs are specified for $t < 0$ as well as $t \geq 0$, we may directly utilize Fourier-transform techniques. In particular, we can use Fourier transforms to determine zero-input responses for circuits with independent sources whose values are zero for $t \geq 0$. Furthermore, we can also employ Fourier transforms to determine complete responses to inputs that are nonzero for all t.

EXAMPLE 14.8

Let us find $v_2(t)$ for the op-amp circuit shown in Fig. 14.21(a) given that $R_1 = 2\,\Omega$, $R_2 = 5\,\Omega$, $C = \frac{1}{20}$ F, and $v_1(t) = 4 - 4u(t)$ V. Figure 14.21(b) shows the frequency-domain representation of the op-amp circuit. Let's abbreviate $\mathbf{V}_1(j\omega)$ by $\mathbf{V}_1$ and $\mathbf{V}_2(j\omega)$ by $\mathbf{V}_2$.

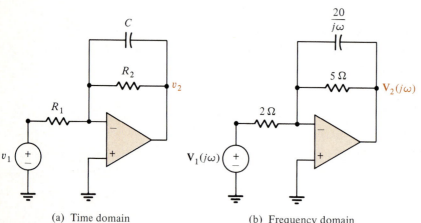

(a) Time domain   (b) Frequency domain

Fig. 14.21   Op-amp circuit.

By KCL,

$$\frac{\mathbf{V}_1}{2} + \frac{\mathbf{V}_2}{5} + \frac{\mathbf{V}_2}{20/j\omega} = 0$$

from which

$$\frac{\mathbf{V}_2}{5} + \frac{j\omega \mathbf{V}_2}{20} = -\frac{\mathbf{V}_1}{2} \quad \Rightarrow \quad \mathbf{V}_2 = -\frac{10}{j\omega + 4}\,\mathbf{V}_1$$

Since $v_1(t) = 4 - 4u(t)$ V, then

$$\mathbf{V}_1(j\omega) = 4[2\pi\delta(\omega)] - 4\left[\frac{1}{j\omega} + \pi\delta(\omega)\right] = 4\pi\delta(\omega) - \frac{4}{j\omega}$$

Thus,

$$\mathbf{V}_2(j\omega) = -\frac{10}{j\omega + 4}\left[4\pi\delta(\omega) - \frac{4}{j\omega}\right] = -\frac{40\pi\delta(\omega)}{j\omega + 4} + \frac{40}{j\omega(j\omega + 4)}$$

$$= -10\pi\delta(\omega) + \frac{10}{j\omega} - \frac{10}{j\omega + 4} = -5[2\pi\delta(\omega)] + 5\left[\frac{2}{j\omega}\right] - \frac{10}{j\omega + 4}$$

Hence,

$$v_2(t) = -5 + 5\,\text{sgn}(t) - 10e^{-4t}u(t) = -5 + 5[-1 + 2u(t)] - 10e^{-4t}u(t)$$
$$= -10 + 10u(t) - 10e^{-4t}u(t) = -10 + 10(1 - e^{-4t})u(t) \text{ V}$$

(see Example 5.5 on p. 231).

DRILL EXERCISE 14.7

For the op-amp circuit shown in Fig. DE14.7, find $v_2(t)$ given that $R_1 = 2\,\Omega$, $R_2 = 5\,\Omega$, $C = \frac{1}{20}$ F, and $v_1(t) = 4 - 4u(t)$ V.
Answer: $14 - 14u(t) + 10e^{-4t}u(t)$ V

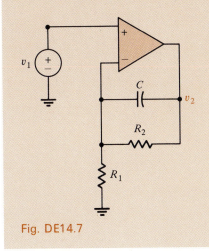

Fig. DE14.7

EXAMPLE 14.9

For the circuit shown in Fig. 14.22(a), let us find $v_2(t)$ for all t given that $v_1(t) = 2 - 6u(t)$ V.

The frequency-domain representation of the given circuit is shown in Fig. 14.22(b). By KCL,

$$\mathbf{I} + 2\mathbf{I} = \frac{\mathbf{V} - \mathbf{V}_2}{5} = 3\mathbf{I}$$

$$\frac{\mathbf{V} - \mathbf{V}_2}{5} = 3\frac{\mathbf{V}_1 - \mathbf{V}}{3} = \mathbf{V}_1 - \mathbf{V}$$

from which

$$6\mathbf{V} - \mathbf{V}_2 = 5\mathbf{V}_1 \tag{14.3}$$

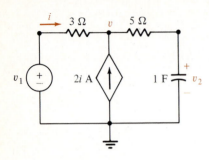

(a) Time domain

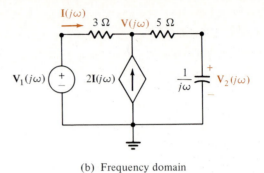

(b) Frequency domain

Fig. 14.22   Circuit for Example 14.9.

Also, by KCL,

$$\frac{V - V_2}{5} = \frac{V_2}{1/j\omega} = j\omega V_2$$

from which

$$V - V_2 = j\omega 5 V_2 \qquad \Rightarrow \qquad V = (1 + j\omega 5)V_2$$

Substituting this into Equation (14.3) yields

$$6(1 + j\omega 5)V_2 - V_2 = 5V_1$$

from which

$$V_2 = \frac{1}{1 + j\omega 6} V_1 = \frac{1/6}{j\omega + 1/6} V_1$$

Since $v_1(t) = 2 - 6u(t)$ V, then

$$V_1(j\omega) = 2[2\pi\delta(\omega)] - 6\left[\frac{1}{j\omega} + \pi\delta(\omega)\right] = -2\pi\delta(\omega) - \frac{6}{j\omega}$$

and

$$V_2(j\omega) = \frac{1/6}{j\omega + 1/6}\left[-2\pi\delta(\omega) - \frac{6}{j\omega}\right] = -\frac{\pi\delta(\omega)/3}{j\omega + 1/6} - \frac{1}{j\omega(j\omega + 1/6)}$$

$$= -2\pi\delta(\omega) - \frac{6}{j\omega} + \frac{6}{j\omega + 1/6}$$

Thus,

$$v_2(t) = -1 - 3\,\text{sgn}(t) + 6e^{-t/6}u(t) = -1 - 3[-1 + 2u(t)] + 6e^{-t/6}u(t)$$

$$= 2 - 6u(t) + 6e^{-t/6}u(t) = 2 - 6(1 - e^{-t/6})u(t) \text{ V}$$

(see Example 5.9 on p. 256 and Example 11.18 on p. 522).

DRILL EXERCISE 14.8

For the *RLC* circuit given in Fig. DE14.6 (p. 659), suppose that $R = 1\,\Omega$, $L = 2$ H, and $C = \frac{1}{2}$ F. Find $v_2(t)$ when $v_1(t) = 1 - 2u(t)$ V.
Answer: $-4te^{-t}u(t)$ V

The formula for the Fourier transform of $f(t)$ is

$$\mathcal{F}[f(t)] = \mathbf{F}(j\omega) = \int_{-\infty}^{\infty} f(t)e^{-j\omega t}\,dt$$

When certain functions (e.g., a step function) are substituted into this formula, it cannot be evaluated, since $e^{-j\omega t}$ has no limit as $t \to \infty$. However,

$$\lim_{t \to \infty} e^{-\sigma t}e^{-j\omega t} = \lim_{t \to \infty} e^{-(\sigma + j\omega)t} = 0$$

when $\sigma > 0$. If we define the complex variable $s = \sigma + j\omega$ and assume that $f(t) = 0$ for $t < 0$, then we get the Laplace transform of $f(t)$. Specifically,

$$\mathcal{L}[f(t)] = \mathbf{F}(s) = \int_{0}^{\infty} f(t)e^{-st}\,dt$$

and, as we have seen, this transformation allows for the inclusion of initial conditions when determining responses for $t \geq 0$.

● SUMMARY

1. The frequency spectrum of $f(t)$ consists of two continuous spectra. The amplitude spectrum is a plot of the magnitude of the Fourier transform of $f(t)$ versus frequency, and the phase spectrum is a plot of the angle of the Fourier transform versus frequency.

2. An energy relationship between a function and its Fourier transform is given by Parseval's theorem.

3. The Fourier transform is a linear transformation that can be used to analyze circuits.

4. The use of Fourier transforms for circuit analysis results in the notion of impedance consistent with sinusoidal (phasor) analysis.

5. Multiplication of Fourier transforms corresponds to the convolution of the corresponding time functions.

● PROBLEMS FOR CHAPTER 14

14.1 Find the Fourier transform of $f(t) = \sin \omega_1 t$.

14.2 Find the Fourier transform of the function shown in Fig. P14.2.

14.3 Find the Fourier transform of the function shown in Fig. P14.3.

14.4 Find the Fourier transform of the function shown in Fig. P14.4.

14.5 Find the Fourier transform of the function shown in Fig. P14.5.

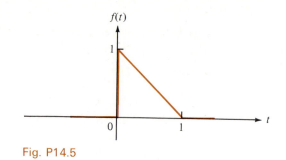

Fig. P14.5

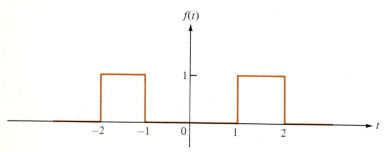

Fig. P14.2

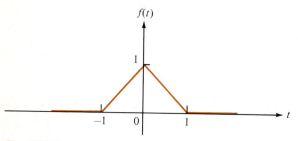

Fig. P14.3

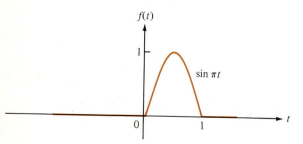

Fig. P14.4

14.6 Given that $\mathscr{F}[f(t)] = \mathbf{F}(j\omega)$, show that

$$\mathscr{F}[f(t - a)] = e^{-j\omega a}\mathbf{F}(j\omega)$$

This result is known as the **real translation property** of the Fourier transform.

14.7 Use the property given in Problem 14.6 to find the Fourier transform of

$$f(t) = Vu\left(t + \frac{\tau}{2}\right) - Vu\left(t - \frac{\tau}{2}\right)$$

14.8 Find the Fourier transform of

$$f(t) = \cos(\omega_1 t - \phi)$$
$$= \cos \omega_1\left(t - \frac{\phi}{\omega_1}\right)$$

14.9 Suppose that $f(t)$ is an even function. Show that

$$\mathbf{F}(j\omega) = 2\int_0^\infty f(t)\cos \omega t \, dt$$

14.10 Use the result given in Problem 14.9 to find the Fourier transform of the function shown in Fig. P14.10.

14.11 Suppose that $f(t)$ is an odd function. Show that

$$\mathbf{F}(j\omega) = -2j\int_0^\infty f(t)\sin \omega t \, dt$$

14.12 Use the result given in Problem 14.11 to find the Fourier transform of the function shown in Fig. 14.7 (p. 644).

14.13 Given that $\mathscr{F}[f(t)] = \mathbf{F}(j\omega)$, show that

$$\mathscr{F}[e^{-\alpha t}f(t)] = \mathbf{F}(j\omega + \alpha)$$

That is, given $\mathbf{F}(j\omega)$—the Fourier transform of $f(t)$—then the Fourier transform of $e^{-\alpha t}f(t)$ can be obtained from $\mathbf{F}(j\omega)$ by replacing $j\omega$ with $j\omega + \alpha$. The constant α can be real or complex. This result is known as the **complex-translation property** of the Fourier transform.

14.14 (a) Show that

$$\mathscr{F}[e^{j\omega_1 t}f(t)] = \mathbf{F}(j[\omega - \omega_1])$$

This result is known as the **frequency-translation property**.

(b) Show that

$$\mathscr{F}[(\cos \omega_1 t)f(t)] =$$
$$\tfrac{1}{2}\mathbf{F}(j[\omega - \omega_1]) + \tfrac{1}{2}\mathbf{F}(j[\omega + \omega_1])$$

This property is referred to as **modulation**.

14.15 Suppose that the amplitude spectrum of $f(t)$ is as shown in Fig. P14.15.
(a) Sketch the amplitude spectrum of $e^{j\omega_c t}f(t)$ for the case that $\omega_c > \omega_B$.
(b) Sketch the amplitude spectrum of $(\cos \omega_c t)f(t)$ for the case that $\omega_c > \omega_B$.

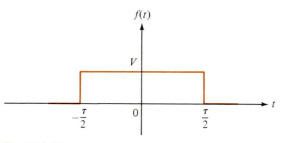

Fig. P14.10

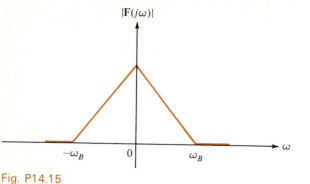

Fig. P14.15

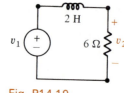

Fig. P14.19

14.16 Suppose that $f(t)$ is a real function.
  (a) Show that $|\mathbf{F}(j\omega)|$ is an even function of ω. (It's for this reason that amplitude spectra of real functions can be plotted for nonnegative values of ω; the negative side of the plot is just the mirror reflection of the positive side.)
  (b) Show that the angle of $\mathbf{F}(j\omega)$ is an odd function of ω.

14.17 Suppose that the voltage across a 1-Ω resistor is $v(t) = te^{-at}u(t)$ V.
  (a) What is the total energy absorbed by the resistor?
  (b) What percent of this energy is in the frequency band $-a \leq \omega \leq a$?

  Hint: $\int \dfrac{d\omega}{(\omega^2 + a^2)^2} =$

  $$\dfrac{\omega}{2a^2(\omega^2 + a^2)} + \dfrac{1}{2a^2} \int \dfrac{d\omega}{\omega^2 + a^2}$$

14.18 Given that $\mathbf{F}(j\omega)$ is the Fourier transform of $f(t)$. In the expression $\mathbf{F}(j\omega)$, replacing ω by t results in a time function $F(jt)$, which may be complex. In the expression $f(t)$, replacing t by ω results in a function $\mathbf{f}(\omega)$. Show that
  (a) $\mathscr{F}[F(jt)] = 2\pi f(-\omega)$

  (b) $\mathscr{F}^{-1}[\mathbf{f}(\omega)] = \dfrac{1}{2\pi} F(-jt)$

These results are known as the **symmetry property** of the Fourier transform.

14.19 For the circuit in Fig. P14.19, the input is $v_1(t)$ and the output is $v_2(t)$.
  (a) Find the system function for this network.
  (b) Find the impulse response.
  (c) Sketch the amplitude response.
  (d) What type of filter is this circuit?

14.20 Repeat Problem 14.19 for the circuit shown in Fig. P14.20.

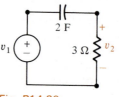

Fig. P14.20

14.21 Repeat Problem 14.19 for the circuit shown in Fig. P14.21.

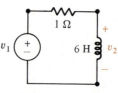

Fig. P14.21

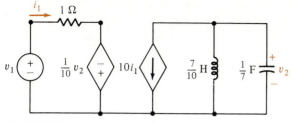

Fig. P14.23

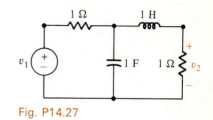

Fig. P14.27

14.22 Repeat Problem 14.19 for the op-amp circuit shown in Fig. 14.21(a) (p. 660).

14.23 Repeat Problem 14.19 for the circuit in Fig. P14.23.

14.24 Find the impulse response for the circuit in Fig. P14.24.

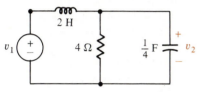

Fig. P14.24

14.25 For the op-amp circuit given in Fig. DE14.7 (p. 661), the input is $v_1(t)$ and the output is $v_2(t)$. Find the impulse response.

14.26 For the circuit shown in Fig. P14.26, the input is $v_1(t)$ and the output is $v_2(t)$. Find the impulse response.

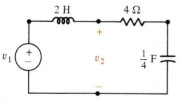

Fig. P14.26

14.27 Find the impulse response of the circuit shown in Fig. P14.27.

14.28 Find the impulse response for the transformer circuit in Fig. P14.28.

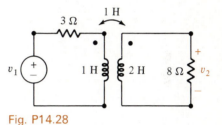

Fig. P14.28

14.29 For the circuit shown in Fig. P14.29, the input is the current $i(t) = \text{sgn}(t)$ A. Find the output voltage $v(t)$.

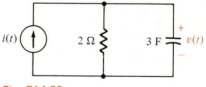

Fig. P14.29

14.30 Given a linear system with impulse response $h(t)$ and output $y(t)$, find the corresponding input $x(t)$ for the following cases:

(a) $h(t) = e^{-at}u(t)$,
$y(t) = e^{-at}\sin \omega_1 t\, u(t)$

(b) $h(t) = e^{-at}\cos \omega_1 t\, u(t)$,
$y(t) = e^{-at}u(t)$

(c) $h(t) = (e^{-at} + e^{-bt})u(t)$,
$y(t) = e^{-at}u(t)$

(d) $h(t) = e^{-at}u(t)$,
$y(t) = \cos \omega_1 t\, u(t)$

14.31 Given a linear system with input $x(t)$ and output $y(t)$, find the impulse response for the following cases:

(a) $x(t) = e^{-at} \sin \omega_1 t \, u(t)$,
$y(t) = te^{-at}u(t)$

(b) $x(t) = e^{-at} \cos \omega_1 t \, u(t)$,
$y(t) = e^{-at} \sin \omega_1 t \, u(t)$

(c) $x(t) = (e^{-at} + e^{-bt})u(t)$,
$y(t) = te^{-at}u(t)$

(d) $x(t) = e^{-at}u(t)$, $y(t) = \sin \omega_1 t \, u(t)$

14.32 Given the system function of an ideal low-pass filter

$$\mathbf{H}(j\omega) = u(\omega + \omega_c) - u(\omega - \omega_c)$$

use the fact that

$$\mathscr{F}[u(t + a) - u(t - a)] = 2a\left(\frac{\sin a\omega}{a\omega}\right)$$

and the symmetry property (see Problem 14.18) of the Fourier transform to determine the impulse response $h(t)$. Sketch this function. Why is it not possible to construct a device having this impulse response?

Matrices and Determinants

A rectangular array of numbers having n rows and m columns, written as

$$\begin{bmatrix} a_{11} & a_{12} & a_{13} & \cdots & a_{1m} \\ a_{21} & a_{22} & a_{23} & \cdots & a_{2m} \\ a_{31} & a_{32} & a_{33} & \cdots & a_{3m} \\ \vdots & \vdots & \vdots & & \vdots \\ a_{n1} & a_{n2} & a_{n3} & \cdots & a_{nm} \end{bmatrix}$$

is called an **$n \times m$ matrix**. Note that the number in the ith row and jth column of the matrix is denoted by a_{ij}. We say that two $n \times m$ matrices are **equal** if all their corresponding entries are equal.

Given that two matrices are the same dimension (i.e., they are both $n \times m$ matrices), we can define their addition as follows:

Suppose that **A** and **B** are both $n \times m$ matrices, where a_{ij} and b_{ij} are the respective entries in row i and column j. Then the **sum** of **A** and **B**, denoted **A** + **B**, is the $n \times m$ matrix whose entry in row i and column j is $a_{ij} + b_{ij}$, for all $i = 1, 2, \ldots, n$ and $j = 1, 2, \ldots, m$. In other words, the sum of two matrices is the matrix obtained by adding the corresponding entries.

EXAMPLE A.1

Let **A** and **B** be the following 2×3 matrices:

$$\mathbf{A} = \begin{bmatrix} 3 & 0 & -1 \\ 4 & -2 & -7 \end{bmatrix} \quad \text{and} \quad \mathbf{B} = \begin{bmatrix} 1 & 2 & 3 \\ -4 & 5 & -6 \end{bmatrix}$$

Then we have

$$\mathbf{A} + \mathbf{B} = \begin{bmatrix} 3+1 & 0+2 & -1+3 \\ 4-4 & -2+5 & -7-6 \end{bmatrix} = \begin{bmatrix} 4 & 2 & 2 \\ 0 & 3 & -13 \end{bmatrix}$$

Note that as a consequence of ordinary arithmetic, it is true in general for two $n \times m$ matrices $\mathbf{A}$ and $\mathbf{B}$ that

$$\mathbf{A} + \mathbf{B} = \mathbf{B} + \mathbf{A}$$

In other words, matrix addition is **commutative**.

It is not only possible, but desirable, to multiply matrices. However, multiplication is a more complicated process than addition. To begin with, to take the matrix product $\mathbf{AB}$, where $\mathbf{A}$ is an $n \times m$ matrix, it is required that $\mathbf{B}$ be an $m \times p$ matrix. (We can have that $p = n$ or $p = m$ or neither.)

Suppose that $\mathbf{A}$ is an $n \times m$ matrix and $\mathbf{B}$ is an $m \times p$ matrix. We can define multiplication as follows:

Let $\mathbf{C}$ be equal to the **product** of $\mathbf{A}$ and $\mathbf{B}$; that is, $\mathbf{C} = \mathbf{AB}$. If the ith row of $\mathbf{A}$ is

$$a_{i1} \quad a_{i2} \quad a_{i3} \quad \cdots \quad a_{im}$$

and the jth column of $\mathbf{B}$ is

$$b_{1j}$$
$$b_{2j}$$
$$b_{3j}$$
$$\vdots$$
$$b_{mj}$$

then the entry in row i and column j of $\mathbf{C}$ is

$$c_{ij} = a_{i1}b_{1j} + a_{i2}b_{2j} + a_{i3}b_{3j} + \cdots + a_{im}b_{mj}$$

Note that $\mathbf{C}$ is an $n \times p$ matrix.

EXAMPLE A.2

Suppose that $\mathbf{A}$ is a 2×3 matrix and $\mathbf{B}$ is a 3×1 matrix as follows:

$$\mathbf{A} = \begin{bmatrix} 3 & 0 & -1 \\ 4 & -2 & -7 \end{bmatrix} \quad \text{and} \quad \mathbf{B} = \begin{bmatrix} 2 \\ -2 \\ 0 \end{bmatrix}$$

Then $\mathbf{C} = \mathbf{AB}$ is the following 2×1 matrix:

$$\mathbf{C} = \mathbf{AB} = \begin{bmatrix} 3 & 0 & -1 \\ 4 & -2 & -7 \end{bmatrix} \begin{bmatrix} 2 \\ -2 \\ 0 \end{bmatrix} = \begin{bmatrix} (3)(2) + (0)(-2) + (-1)(0) \\ (4)(2) + (-2)(-2) + (-7)(0) \end{bmatrix} = \begin{bmatrix} 6 \\ 12 \end{bmatrix}$$

Note that in this case we cannot even form the product $\mathbf{BA}$.

In general, for matrix multiplication, $\mathbf{AB} \neq \mathbf{BA}$. In other words, matrix multiplication is not commutative in general.

Having defined matrix equivalence, addition, and multiplication, we are able to now talk about the concept of a matrix equation. First, consider the following set of simultaneous linear equations:

$$a_{11}x_1 + a_{12}x_2 + \cdots + a_{1m}x_m = b_1$$
$$a_{21}x_1 + a_{22}x_2 + \cdots + a_{2m}x_m = b_2$$
$$\vdots \qquad\qquad\qquad \vdots \qquad \vdots$$
$$a_{n1}x_1 + a_{n2}x_2 + \cdots + a_{nm}x_m = b_n$$

As a consequence of the definitions of matrix equivalence, addition, and multiplication, we can alternatively represent this set of equations in matrix form as

$$
\begin{bmatrix}
a_{11} & a_{12} & \cdots & a_{1m} \\
a_{21} & a_{22} & \cdots & a_{2m} \\
\vdots & \vdots & & \vdots \\
a_{n1} & a_{n2} & \cdots & a_{nm}
\end{bmatrix}
\begin{bmatrix}
x_1 \\
x_2 \\
\vdots \\
x_m
\end{bmatrix}
=
\begin{bmatrix}
b_1 \\
b_2 \\
\vdots \\
b_n
\end{bmatrix}
$$

which is the matrix equation

$$\mathbf{AX} = \mathbf{B}$$

where

$$
\mathbf{A} =
\begin{bmatrix}
a_{11} & a_{12} & \cdots & a_{1m} \\
a_{21} & a_{22} & \cdots & a_{2m} \\
\vdots & \vdots & & \vdots \\
a_{n1} & a_{n2} & \cdots & a_{nm}
\end{bmatrix}
\qquad
\mathbf{X} =
\begin{bmatrix}
x_1 \\
x_2 \\
\vdots \\
x_m
\end{bmatrix}
\qquad
\mathbf{B} =
\begin{bmatrix}
b_1 \\
b_2 \\
\vdots \\
b_n
\end{bmatrix}
$$

We have seen the difficulty of solving a set of n simultaneous equations. However, to solve the simple equation

$$\mathbf{AX} = \mathbf{B}$$

for $\mathbf{X}$, we need only "divide" both sides of the equation by $\mathbf{A}$. Since we are dealing with a matrix equation, though, ordinary division will not suffice. Thus, we shall require the use of a few more new concepts.

We sometimes refer to an $n \times n$ matrix as a **square matrix**. Given a square matrix, the entries $a_{11}, a_{22}, a_{33}, \ldots, a_{nn}$ comprise the **diagonal** of the matrix. The $n \times n$ matrix in which all the diagonal entries are 1 and all the nondiagonal entries are 0 is called the **identity** or **unit matrix** and is denoted by $\mathbf{I}$.

Note that for any $n \times m$ matrix $\mathbf{A}$, it is true that

$$\mathbf{AI} = \mathbf{A}$$

where $\mathbf{I}$ is the $m \times m$ identity matrix, and

$$\mathbf{IA} = \mathbf{A}$$

where $\mathbf{I}$ is the $n \times n$ identity matrix. Specifically, if $\mathbf{A}$ is a square $n \times n$ matrix, then

$$\mathbf{AI} = \mathbf{IA} = \mathbf{A}$$

where $\mathbf{I}$ is the $n \times n$ identity matrix. Actually, for any $m \times n$ matrix $\mathbf{A}$ it is true that

$$\mathbf{AI} = \mathbf{IA} = \mathbf{A}$$

but it should be understood that two different dimensions of identity matrices appear in this equation.

Given an $n \times n$ matrix $\mathbf{A}$, then an $n \times n$ matrix, denoted $\mathbf{A}^{-1}$, is said to be the **inverse** of $\mathbf{A}$ if

$$\mathbf{AA}^{-1} = \mathbf{A}^{-1}\mathbf{A} = \mathbf{I}$$

Furthermore, only a square matrix can have an inverse, and not every square matrix may have an inverse.

The **transpose** of a matrix $\mathbf{A}$ is denoted $\mathbf{A}^t$ and is the matrix obtained from $\mathbf{A}$ by interchanging its rows with its columns. In other words, if a_{ij} is in row i and column j of $\mathbf{A}$, then a_{ij} is in row j and column i of $\mathbf{A}^t$.

EXAMPLE A.3

The following are examples of matrices and their transposes:

$$\mathbf{A}_1 = \begin{bmatrix} 3 & 0 & -1 \\ 4 & 1 & 2 \end{bmatrix} \qquad \mathbf{A}_1^t = \begin{bmatrix} 3 & 4 \\ 0 & 1 \\ -1 & 2 \end{bmatrix}$$

$$\mathbf{A}_2 = \begin{bmatrix} 2 \\ -1 \\ 3 \end{bmatrix} \qquad \mathbf{A}_2^t = \begin{bmatrix} 2 & -1 & 3 \end{bmatrix}$$

$$\mathbf{A}_3 = \begin{bmatrix} 1 & -1 & 0 \\ 2 & 5 & 7 \\ 8 & -3 & 3 \end{bmatrix} \qquad \mathbf{A}_3^t = \begin{bmatrix} 1 & 2 & 8 \\ -1 & 5 & -3 \\ 0 & 7 & 3 \end{bmatrix}$$

Let us now discuss how to determine whether or not a square matrix has an inverse, and how to determine what that inverse is. For once we have done this, given a set of n simultaneous equations in n unknowns, written in matrix form as

$$\mathbf{AX} = \mathbf{B}$$

we can multiply both sides of this equation by $\mathbf{A}^{-1}$ to obtain

$$\mathbf{A}^{-1}\mathbf{AX} = \mathbf{A}^{-1}\mathbf{B}$$

$$\mathbf{IX} = \mathbf{A}^{-1}\mathbf{B}$$

$$\mathbf{X} = \mathbf{A}^{-1}\mathbf{B}$$

which is the solution.

Our first step is to introduce the concept of a "determinant." The **determinant** of a square matrix **A** is a number that is assigned to the matrix by the rule that is discussed below:

Given the square matrix

$$\mathbf{A} = \begin{bmatrix} a_{11} & a_{12} & a_{13} & \cdots & a_{1n} \\ a_{21} & a_{22} & a_{23} & \cdots & a_{2n} \\ \vdots & \vdots & \vdots & & \vdots \\ a_{n1} & a_{n2} & a_{n3} & \cdots & a_{nn} \end{bmatrix}$$

we denote the determinant of **A** by any of the three equivalent ways:

$$\det \mathbf{A} = \Delta_{\mathbf{A}} = \begin{vmatrix} a_{11} & a_{12} & a_{13} & \cdots & a_{1n} \\ a_{21} & a_{22} & a_{23} & \cdots & a_{2n} \\ \vdots & \vdots & \vdots & & \vdots \\ a_{n1} & a_{n2} & a_{n3} & \cdots & a_{nn} \end{vmatrix}$$

Note: The determinant of a 1×1 matrix $\mathbf{A} = [a_{11}]$ is simply the single entry; that is

$$|a_{11}| = a_{11}$$

The **minor** of entry a_{ij} is the determinant of the matrix which is obtained from **A** by eliminating the ith row and jth column. The minor of a_{ij} is denoted by $\det \mathbf{A}_{ij}$. The **cofactor** of a_{ij} is denoted by c_{ij} and is defined as

$$c_{ij} = (-1)^{i+j} \det \mathbf{A}_{ij}$$

We calculate a determinant as follows: Pick either any row or any column. If row i is selected, then

$$\det \mathbf{A} = a_{i1}c_{i1} + a_{i2}c_{i2} + \cdots + a_{in}c_{in}$$

If column j is selected, then

$$\det \mathbf{A} = a_{1j}c_{1j} + a_{2j}c_{2j} + \cdots + a_{nj}c_{nj}$$

In either case, the same number is obtained.

Because of the frequent appearance of 2×2 and 3×3 matrices in this book, let us develop formulas for calculating the corresponding determinants.

Suppose that

$$\mathbf{A} = \begin{bmatrix} a_{11} & a_{12} \\ a_{21} & a_{22} \end{bmatrix}$$

and suppose that we calculate the determinant of **A** by selecting the first column. We then have

$$\det \mathbf{A} = a_{11}(-1)^{1+1}|a_{22}| + a_{21}(-1)^{2+1}|a_{12}|$$
$$= a_{11}a_{22} - a_{21}a_{12}$$

A simple way to remember this formula is to make an "X" inside the determinant, as shown in Fig. A.1, to indicate that the products $a_{11}a_{22}$ and $a_{21}a_{12}$ are formed. In addition, the signs associated with these products can be remembered as shown in Fig. A.2. For example,

$$\begin{vmatrix} 1 & -2 \\ 4 & 6 \end{vmatrix} = (1)(6) - (4)(-2) = 6 + 8 = 14$$

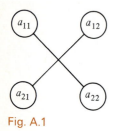

Fig. A.1

Fig. A.2

For a 3×3 matrix

$$\mathbf{A} = \begin{bmatrix} a_{11} & a_{12} & a_{13} \\ a_{21} & a_{22} & a_{23} \\ a_{31} & a_{32} & a_{33} \end{bmatrix}$$

let us select the first row. Then

$$\det \mathbf{A} = a_{11}(-1)^{1+1}\begin{vmatrix} a_{22} & a_{23} \\ a_{32} & a_{33} \end{vmatrix} + a_{12}(-1)^{1+2}\begin{vmatrix} a_{21} & a_{23} \\ a_{31} & a_{33} \end{vmatrix} + a_{13}(-1)^{1+3}\begin{vmatrix} a_{21} & a_{22} \\ a_{31} & a_{32} \end{vmatrix}$$

$$= a_{11}(a_{22}a_{33} - a_{32}a_{23}) - a_{12}(a_{21}a_{33} - a_{31}a_{23}) + a_{13}(a_{21}a_{32} - a_{31}a_{22})$$

$$= a_{11}a_{22}a_{33} - a_{11}a_{32}a_{23} - a_{12}a_{21}a_{33} + a_{12}a_{31}a_{23} + a_{13}a_{21}a_{32} - a_{13}a_{31}a_{22}$$

$$= a_{11}a_{22}a_{33} + a_{12}a_{31}a_{23} + a_{13}a_{21}a_{32} - (a_{11}a_{32}a_{23} + a_{12}a_{21}a_{33} + a_{13}a_{31}a_{22})$$

At first glance it may appear that this formula is just too long to commit to memory. However, if you can remember the pattern associated with the three positively signed terms, which is shown in Fig. A.3, and the pattern associated with the three negatively signed terms, which is shown in Fig. A.4, then in effect you have remembered the formula. For example,

$$\begin{vmatrix} 2 & -3 & -7 \\ 5 & 1 & 0 \\ -8 & 2 & 7 \end{vmatrix} = (2)(1)(7) + (-3)(-8)(0) + (-7)(5)(2)$$

$$- [(2)(2)(0) + (-3)(5)(7) + (-7)(-8)(1)]$$

$$= 14 + 0 - 70 - [0 - 105 + 56] = -56 + 49 = -7$$

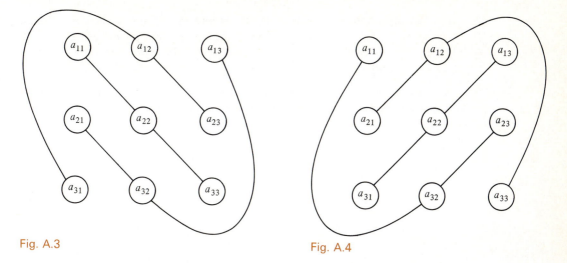

Fig. A.3   Fig. A.4

Unfortunately, there is no simple formula for the determinant of an $n \times n$ matrix, where n is larger than 3.

Having discussed the concept of the determinant of a square matrix $\mathbf{A}$, we can now determine whether or not $\mathbf{A}$ has an inverse, and if so, what it is. We begin by stating a classical result from linear algebra: A square matrix $\mathbf{A}$ has an inverse if and only if $\det \mathbf{A} \neq 0$.

Given that $\det \mathbf{A} \neq 0$, form the matrix $\mathbf{B}$, where b_{ij}, the entry in row i and column j, is defined (recalling that c_{ij} is the cofactor of a_{ij}) as

$$b_{ij} = \frac{c_{ij}}{\det \mathbf{A}}$$

Then the inverse of $\mathbf{A}$ is equal to the transpose of $\mathbf{B}$; that is,

$$\mathbf{A}^{-1} = \mathbf{B}^t$$

Now that we know how to take matrix inverses, it is a routine matter to solve a set of n simultaneous linear equations having n unknowns. We simply write the equations in the matrix form

$$\mathbf{AX} = \mathbf{B}$$

Then, if $\det \mathbf{A} \neq 0$, we multiply both sides of the equation by $\mathbf{A}^{-1}$ to obtain the unique solution

$$\mathbf{X} = \mathbf{A}^{-1}\mathbf{B}$$

If $\det \mathbf{A} = 0$, then there is no unique solution of the equations.

We have just seen that we can solve a set of simultaneous equations for all the unknowns by utilizing the inverse of a matrix. However, this can be accomplished without the necessity of first calculating an inverse. The technique for doing this is known as **Cramer's rule**, which can be stated as follows:

CRAMER'S RULE

Given a set of simultaneous, linear equations written in matrix form as AX = B, let $\Delta = \det A$. Define Δ_i to be the determinant of the matrix that is obtained by replacing the ith column of A with the column forming B. Then

$$x_i = \frac{\Delta_i}{\Delta}$$

EXAMPLE A.4

For the matrix equation of the form **AX = B** given by

$$\begin{bmatrix} 1 & -2 \\ 4 & 6 \end{bmatrix} \begin{bmatrix} x_1 \\ x_2 \end{bmatrix} = \begin{bmatrix} 28 \\ 21 \end{bmatrix}$$

we have

$$\Delta = \det \mathbf{A} = \begin{vmatrix} 1 & -2 \\ 4 & 6 \end{vmatrix} = 14$$

Replacing the first column of **A** by the column forming **B**, we get

$$\Delta_1 = \begin{vmatrix} 28 & -2 \\ 21 & 6 \end{vmatrix} = 168 + 42 = 210$$

Thus,

$$x_1 = \frac{\Delta_1}{\Delta} = \frac{210}{14} = 15$$

In addition, we have

$$\Delta_2 = \begin{vmatrix} 1 & 28 \\ 4 & 21 \end{vmatrix} = 21 - 112 = -91 \quad \Rightarrow \quad x_2 = \frac{\Delta_2}{\Delta} = \frac{-91}{14} = -\frac{13}{2}$$

For the matrix equation

$$\begin{bmatrix} 2 & -3 & -7 \\ 5 & 1 & 0 \\ -8 & 2 & 7 \end{bmatrix} \begin{bmatrix} x_1 \\ x_2 \\ x_3 \end{bmatrix} = \begin{bmatrix} 5 \\ -2 \\ 1 \end{bmatrix}$$

we have seen that

$$\Delta = \begin{vmatrix} 2 & -3 & -7 \\ 5 & 1 & 0 \\ -8 & 2 & 7 \end{vmatrix} = -7$$

Since

$$\Delta_1 = \begin{vmatrix} 5 & -3 & -7 \\ -2 & 1 & 0 \\ 1 & 2 & 7 \end{vmatrix} = 35 + 0 + 28 - (-7 + 0 + 42) = 28$$

we have

$$x_1 = \frac{\Delta_1}{\Delta} = \frac{28}{-7} = -4$$

Furthermore,

$$\Delta_2 = \begin{vmatrix} 2 & 5 & -7 \\ 5 & -2 & 0 \\ -8 & 1 & 7 \end{vmatrix} = -28 + 0 - 35 - (-112 + 0 + 175) = -126$$

and thus

$$x_2 = \frac{\Delta_2}{\Delta} = \frac{-126}{-7} = 18$$

Finally,

$$\Delta_3 = \begin{vmatrix} 2 & -3 & 5 \\ 5 & 1 & -2 \\ -8 & 2 & 1 \end{vmatrix} = 2 - 48 + 50 - (-40 - 8 - 15) = 67$$

and therefore

$$x_3 = \frac{\Delta_3}{\Delta} = \frac{67}{-7} = -\frac{67}{7}$$

SPICE

Linear circuits can be described by linear equations. We can perform circuit analysis by writing the equations that characterize a particular circuit and then finding the solutions to these equations. Throughout this book, we have studied techniques to analyze different types of linear circuits.

The digital computer is a very useful tool when it comes to the analysis of circuits. A computer can be programmed to solve a set of simultaneous algebraic equations, thereby eliminating the drudgery of hand calculations. Furthermore, a computer must be used in order to do the numerical calculations discussed in Chapter 7.

In addition to using a computer to solve equations, there are computer programs available which will perform circuit analysis. The most well-known circuit-analysis software is the Simulation Program with Integrated-Circuit Emphasis—SPICE, for short. SPICE does not require that circuit equations be written. Instead, a circuit is described by a data file which is read by the program, and SPICE analyzes that circuit.

In order to run SPICE, we first create an "input" file which contains statements that describe the circuit and what types of analyses and printouts to perform. Such statements are called **element statements** and **control statements**, respectively. If no analysis statement is made, SPICE will automatically perform a dc analysis of the given circuit. The final statement of the file is the statement ".END".

SPICE is available not only for mainframe and minicomputers, but there are also versions for personal computers. We will now proceed to discuss how to use SPICE by specifying how a circuit should be described for SPICE, and the types of analyses that it can perform.

B.1 CIRCUIT DESCRIPTION

A circuit to be analyzed has to be described in a manner that is acceptable to SPICE. Furthermore, a circuit has to be composed of certain types of electric-circuit elements. For SPICE, circuits can consist of resistors, inductors, capacitors, independent sources (both voltage and current), dependent current sources (both current-dependent and voltage-dependent), and dependent voltage sources (both current-dependent and voltage-dependent). In addition, circuits can contain transformers, transmission lines, and the four most common semiconductor devices: diodes, bipolar junction transistors (BJTs), junction field-effect transistors (JFETs), and metal-oxide semiconductor field-effect transistors (MOSFETs).

To describe a given circuit, first the nodes are labeled $0, 1, 2, 3, \ldots, n$. The node labeled 0 is the reference (or ground) node. After the nodes have been labeled, we specify the nodes of each element. Let us now indicate some of the various element statements for SPICE. In the following discussions, the sequence XXXXXXX represents an alphanumeric string of from one to seven characters.

Resistors

The general form of a **resistor** specification is

```
RXXXXXXX N1 N2 VALUE
```

where RXXXXXXX designates a resistor, N1 and N2 are the nodes of the resistor (node order is irrelevent for resistors), and VALUE is the resistance in ohms—this number can be either positive or negative, but not zero. As an example, the specification

```
R1 3 5 27
```

indicates that resistor R1 is connected between nodes 3 and 5, and it has a value of 27 ohms. Another example is

```
RL 10 0 1K
```

and this indicates that resistor RL is connected between node 10 and the reference node, and the value of RL is 1000 ohms. When expressing the values of resistors or other circuit elements, in addition to the ordinary decimal form, we can use either the symbolic form or the exponential form of the value as indicated in the following table.

Table B.1 SPICE SYMBOLS

Value	Symbolic Form	Exponential Form
10^{-15}	F	1E–15
10^{-12}	P	1E–12
10^{-9}	N	1E–9
10^{-6}	U	1E–6
10^{-3}	M	1E–3
10^{3}	K	1E3
10^{6}	MEG	1E6
10^{9}	G	1E9
10^{12}	T	1E12

Independent Constant Voltage Sources

The specification for an **independent constant (dc) voltage source** has the general form

```
VXXXXXXX N+ N- DC VALUE
```

where VXXXXXXX designates a voltage source, N+ is the positive node of the voltage source, N− is the negative node, DC indicates a constant value, and VALUE is the constant voltage in volts. As an example, the specification

```
VS 1 0 DC 6
```

indicates that there is a 6-V independent voltage source (battery) connected between node 1 and the reference node.

EXAMPLE B.1

Before we look at any more element specifications, let us analyze a simple dc resistive circuit with SPICE. Consider the circuit shown in Fig. B.1 (see Fig. 1.41 on p. 25). Here the nodes of the circuit have been labeled 0, 1, 2, 3. Let us call the input file VOLDIV.CIR. The contents of this file are:

```
V1 3 0 DC 28
R1 3 1 5
R2 1 0 4
R3 1 2 1
R4 2 0 3
.END
```

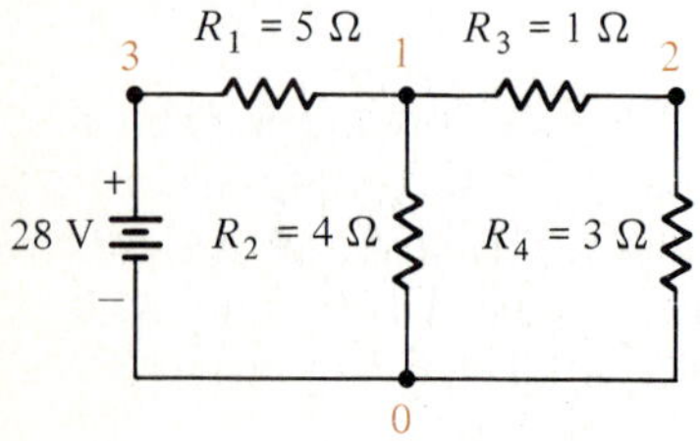

Fig. B.1

When SPICE is run, since no type of analysis is specified, it will automatically perform a dc analysis. The resulting output file, call it VOLDIV.OUT, will contain the following:

```
NODE  VOLTAGE          NODE  VOLTAGE          NODE  VOLTAGE
(  1)  8.0000          (  2)  6.0000          (  3) 28.0000
```

This indicates that the voltage at node 1 (with respect to the reference) is 8 V, the voltage at node 2 is 6 V, and the voltage at node 3 is 28 V.

Independent Constant Current Sources

The specification for an **independent constant current source** has the general form

```
IXXXXXXX N+ N- DC VALUE
```

where IXXXXXXX designates a current source, the current source's arrow is directed from node $N+$ to node $N-$, DC indicates a constant value, and VALUE is the constant current in amperes.

Voltage-Dependent Sources

The general form for a **voltage-dependent** (or **voltage-controlled**) **voltage source** is

```
EXXXXXXX N+ N- NC+ NC- VALUE
```

where $N+$ is the positive node of the source, $N-$ is the negative node, $NC+$ is the positive node of the dependent (or controlling) voltage, $NC-$ is the negative node of the dependent voltage, and VALUE is the "value" of the dependent source—in particular, if the dependent source is labeled kv, then k is the value (dimensionless) of the source.

The general form for a **voltage-dependent** (or **voltage-controlled**) **current source** is

```
GXXXXXXX N+ N- NC+ NC- VALUE
```

where the current source's arrow is directed from node $N+$ to node $N-$, $NC+$ is the positive node of the dependent (or controlling) voltage, $NC-$ is the negative node of the dependent voltage, and VALUE is the "value" of the dependent source—specifically, if the dependent source is labeled kv, then k is the value (in siemens or mhos) of the source.

EXAMPLE B.2

Consider the circuit shown in Fig. B.2 (see Fig. 2.12 on p. 66). The following is the input file for this circuit:

```
V1 0 1 DC 1
V2 3 4 DC .5
I1 0 4 DC 2
E1 3 2 1 2 3
R1 1 2 .25
R2 0 2 1
R3 0 3 .125
R4 2 4 .5
.END
```

The resulting output file contains the following results:

NODE VOLTAGE	NODE VOLTAGE	NODE VOLTAGE	NODE VOLTAGE
(1) -1.0000	(2) -2.0000	(3) 1.0000	(4) .5000

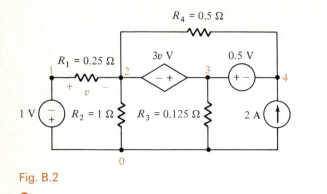

Fig. B.2

In addition to the node voltages, by including an .OP statement, SPICE will also provide the values of the currents through the independent voltage sources and the total power dissipation by all of the independent-source elements. Also determined is the voltage across and the current through each dependent voltage source and the current through each dependent current source. For the SPICE program given in Example B.2, if we add the control statement

```
.OP
```

then the output also contains the following:

```
VOLTAGE SOURCE CURRENTS

NAME       CURRENT

V1          4.000D+00

V2          3.000D+00

TOTAL POWER DISSIPATION   -4.50D+00 WATTS

VOLTAGE-CONTROLLED VOLTAGE SOURCES

                E1
V-SOURCE    3.00
I-SOURCE   -1.10E+01
```

Note that the letter D is used instead of the exponential symbol E for the values of currents through independent voltage sources and total power dissipation.

Operational Amplifiers

Since an ideal operational amplifier is modeled by a voltage-dependent voltage source (see Fig. 3.1 on p. 104), we can create an element statement for an op amp. Specifically, the general form for an **operational amplifier** will be

```
EXXXXXXX NOUT O NIN+ NIN- A
```

where NOUT is the output node, NIN+ is the noninverting-input node, NIN− is the inverting-input node, and A is the gain of the op amp. For an ideal op amp, A is infinite—therefore, to have a good approximation of an ideal op amp, make the gain a very large positive number.

EXAMPLE B.3

For the op-amp circuit shown in Fig. B.3, we have the following input file:

```
VS  1  0  DC  .1
R1  1  2  1K
R2  3  0  1K
R3  3  4  10K
R4  2  4  20K
E1  4  0  3  2  1E10
.END
```

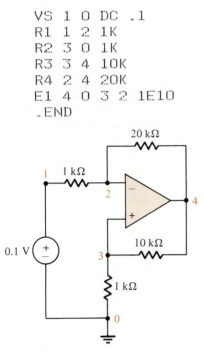

Fig. B.3

The resulting output file contains the following:

```
NODE  VOLTAGE       NODE  VOLTAGE       NODE  VOLTAGE       NODE  VOLTAGE
(   1)   .1000      (   2)   .2000      (   3)   .2000      (   4)  2.2000
```

Current-Dependent Sources

In order to analyze circuits with current-dependent sources, SPICE requires a slight modification of a given circuit. In particular, we must insert an independent voltage source having a value of zero volts (i.e., a short circuit) in the circuit such that the dependent (or controlling) current flows through this source (its name is designated by VNAM) from the positive side to the negative side.

The general form for a **current-dependent** (or **current-controlled**) **current source** is

```
FXXXXXXX  N+  N−  VNAM  VALUE
```

where the arrow of the current source is directed from node $N+$ to node $N-$ and VALUE is the "value" of the dependent source—specifically, if the dependent source is labeled *ki*, then *k* is the value (dimensionless) of the dependent source.

The general form for a **current-dependent** (or **current-controlled**) **voltage source** is

```
HXXXXXXX  N+  N-  VNAM  VALUE
```

where $N+$ is the positive node of the source, $N-$ is the negative node of the source, VNAM designates the name of the zero-valued independent voltage source through which the dependent (or controlling) current flows (from the positive side to the negative side), and VALUE is the "value" of the dependent source—specifically, if the dependent source is labeled *ki*, then *k* is the value (in ohms) of the dependent source.

B.2 TRANSFER FUNCTIONS AND TRANSIENT ANALYSIS

As mentioned above, when no type of analysis is specified, SPICE will automatically perform a dc analysis. This type of analysis will determine all of the node voltages for a given circuit. By using the appropriate control statement, we can also have SPICE perform a dc analysis which, in addition to calculating node voltages, will calculate a specific transfer function (gain) as well as the input and output resistances for a circuit. This statement has the form

```
.TF  OUTVAR  INSRC
```

where OUTVAR is the output variable and INSRC is the input source. An output variable can be either the voltage between any pair of nodes or the current through an independent voltage source. Specifically, V(N1, N2) is the voltage between nodes N1 and N2 (with the $+$ at node N1 and the $-$ at node N2). If the comma and N2 are omitted, then node N2 is assumed to be the reference node. The notation I(VXXXXXXX) designates the current flowing through voltage source VXXXXXXX from the positive side to the negative side.

EXAMPLE B.4

For the circuit shown in Fig. B.4 (see Fig. 2.8 on p. 58), suppose that we have the following input file:

```
I1 0 1 DC 1M
VCUR 1 2
R1 1 0 75
R2 2 3 150
R3 3 0 25
R4 3 4 15K
R5 0 4 1.5K
F1 4 3 VCUR 50
.TF V(4) I1
.END
```

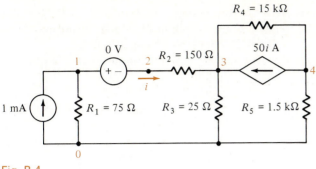

Fig. B.4

In this case, since the circuit contains a current-dependent current source, then the dependent current must go through a zero-valued independent voltage source—let us call it VCUR. Since no value for VCUR is specified, then it has a default value of zero. Such a voltage source, which is equivalent to a short circuit, is placed in series with the 150-ohm resistor. The control statement .TF indicates that V(4) is the output variable, and SPICE will calculate the transfer function V(4)/I1, the (input) resistance seen by the independent current source, and the output resistance (between nodes 4 and 0). The output file for this circuit contains the following:

```
NODE VOLTAGE          NODE VOLTAGE          NODE VOLTAGE          NODE VOLTAGE
(  1) 0.0709          (  2) 0.0709          (  3) 0.0628          (  4) -3.6875

V(4)/I1                                            =  -3.687D+03
INPUT RESISTANCE AT I1                             =   7.094D+01
OUTPUT RESISTANCE AT V(4)                          =   1.475D+03
```

Inductors and Capacitors

The general form for an **inductor** is

    LXXXXXXX N+ N- VALUE <IC=INCOND>

where N+ is the positive node, N- is the negative node, and VALUE is the inductance in henries. The brackets ⟨ ⟩ indicate that the enclosed term is optional. In this case, the optional term IC = INCOND is the initial condition of the inductor. If none is specified, then the initial condition is set to zero, and the node polarities are irrelevent. If the initial condition is nonzero, then the initial current goes through the inductor from the positive node to the negative node.

The general form for a **capacitor** is

    CXXXXXXX N+ N- VALUE <IC=INCOND>

where N+ is the positive node, N- is the negative node, and VALUE is the capacitance in farads. In this case, the optional term is the initial condition of the capacitor.

If none is specified, then the initial condition is set to zero, and the node polarities are irrelevent. If the initial condition is nonzero, then node N+ is the positive plate of the capacitor, and node N− is the negative plate of the capacitor.

Knowing the element statements for inductors and capacitors, we are now in a position to use SPICE to determine zero-input responses. To perform such transient analyses, we will use the .TRAN statement. SPICE does not give us an analytical expression, but rather gives us a printout or a plot (or both) of a circuit variable. Thus, along with a .TRAN statement, we will also use either a .PRINT or a .PLOT statement.

The general form of a .TRAN statement is

```
.TRAN TSTEP TSTOP <TSTART> <UIC>
```

where TSTEP is the printing or plotting increment and TSTOP is the final time. Specifying the initial time with TSTART is optional—if TSTART is omitted, it is assumed to be zero. If the circuit to be analyzed has nonzero initial conditions, the term UIC is included in the .TRAN statement.

The general form of a .PRINT statement for transient analysis is

```
.PRINT TRAN OV1 <OV2 ... OV8>
```

where OV1, OV2, ..., OV8 are output variables. This statement indicates, that it is possible to print out anywhere from one to eight output variables for a given circuit.

The general form of the .PLOT statement for transient analysis is

```
.PLOT TRAN OV1 <OV2 ... OV8>
```

This statement will plot from one to eight output variables, and will also print the first variable listed.

EXAMPLE B.5

Consider the zero-input circuit shown in Fig. B.5 (see Fig. 7.5 on p. 325). Suppose that the initial conditions for this circuit are:

$$i_1(0) = 0 \text{ A} \qquad i_2(0) = 1 \text{ A} \qquad v(0) = -2 \text{ V}$$

For the following input file:

```
R1 0 1 1
R2 0 3 1
C1 2 0 2 IC=-2
L1 1 2 1
L2 2 3 1 IC=1
.TRAN .1 10 UIC
.PLOT TRAN V(3)
.END
```

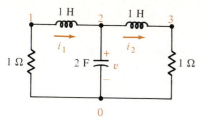

Fig. B.5

the output variable is taken to be the voltage at node 3. The resulting plot (and printout, too) is as shown in Fig. 7.6 (p. 326).

In order to perform a transient analysis due to a nonzero input, we must use an independent source whose value is time-dependent. SPICE has an independent-source function, called a PULSE function, which enables us to obtain step responses for circuits. The general form of this function is

PULSE(V1 V2 TD TR TF PW PER)

where the parameters are indicated in Fig. B.6. When using this function, we must specify the "initial value" V1 and the "pulsed value" V2. If any other parameter is omitted or set to zero, it is given a default value. The "delay time" TD has a default value of 0. The "rise time" TR and "fall time" TF have default values of TSTEP, while the "pulse width" PW and the "period" PER have default values of TSTOP. (TSTEP and TSTOP are the printing increment and final time, respecitvely, of the associated .TRAN statement.)

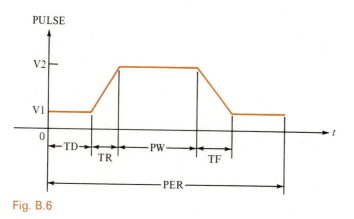

Fig. B.6

In order to make a pulse function approximate a unit step function, we make V1 zero, V2 unity, TD zero, TR very small, and omit the remaining parameters, thereby incorporating their default values.

EXAMPLE B.6

Consider the circuit shown in Fig. B.7 (see Fig. 7.11 on p. 333). The following is an input file to print out points of the step response every 0.1 s from $t = 0$ to $t = 10$ s:

```
VS  1  0  PULSE(0  1  0  1F)
R1  1  3  1
R2  0  2  1
L1  2  3  2
C1  0  3  1
C2  0  2  1
.TRAN  .1  10
.PLOT  TRAN  V(2)
.END
```

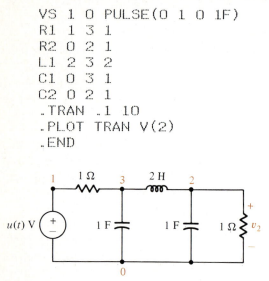

Fig. B.7

To approximate a step function, we have made the rise time TR of the pulse very small—in this case, TR = 1 Fs. A plot of the output voltage $v_2(t)$ versus t is similar to the plot shown in Fig. 7.12 on p. 334.

B.3 SINUSOIDAL ANALYSIS

In addition to dc analysis and transient analysis, SPICE will also perform sinusoidal or ac analysis.

The general form of an **independent ac (sinusoidal) voltage source** is

```
VXXXXXXX  N+  N-  AC  <ACMAG  <ACPHASE>>
```

where VXXXXXXX designates a voltage source, N+ is the positive node of the source, N− is the negative node of the source, AC indicates a sinusoidal source, ACMAG is the ac magnitude (i.e., the amplitude of the sinusoid), and ACPHASE is the ac phase (i.e., the phase angle of the sinusoid). If ACMAG is omitted, then a value of unity is assumed. If ACPHASE is omitted, then a value of zero is assumed.

The general form of an **independent ac current source** is

```
IXXXXXXX  N+  N-  AC  <ACMAG  <ACPHASE>>
```

where IXXXXXXX designates a current source, the current source's arrow is directed from node N+ to node N−, and the terms AC, ACMAG, and ACPHASE are as described above.

To use SPICE to analyze a sinusoidal circuit for a given frequency, we use the following control statement:

```
.AC LIN 1 FREQ FREQ
```

where FREQ is the sinusoidal frequency in hertz. The significance of the terms "LIN" and "1" will be discussed shortly.

Unlike dc analysis, SPICE will not automatically print out the values of the ac node voltages. Instead, we must specify which variables are to be listed with a .PRINT statement. The general form of a .PRINT statement for ac analysis is

```
.PRINT AC OV1 <OV2 ... OV8>
```

where the voltage output variables are designated VM—magnitude, VP—phase, VR—real part, VI—imaginary part, and VDB—$20 \log_{10}$ (magnitude). To specify current output variables, replace V by I in these designations.

EXAMPLE B.7

Consider the sinusoidal circuit shown in Fig. B.8 (see Fig. 8.31 on p. 381).

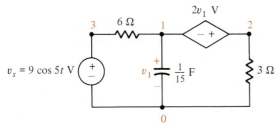

Fig. B.8

The following input file can be used to determine the node voltages and the independent-source current:

```
VS 3 0 AC 9
R1 1 3 6
R2 0 2 3
C1 0 1 6.667E-2
E1 2 1 1 0 2
.AC LIN 1 .7958 .7958
.PRINT AC VM(1) VP(1) VM(2) VP(2) IM(VS) IP(VS)
.END
```

The resulting output file contains the following:

```
   FREQ           VM(1)             VP(1)
7.958E-01    1.236E+00       -1.595E+01

    VM(2)          VP(2)           IM(VS)           IP(VS)
3.709E+00    -1.595E+01     1.303E+00     -1.775E+02
```

Thus, we have the following phasors:

$$\mathbf{V}_1 = 1.236\underline{/-15.95°} \qquad \mathbf{V}_2 = 3.709\underline{/-15.95°} \qquad \mathbf{I}_s = 1.303\underline{/-177.5°}$$

In addition to single-frequency analysis, SPICE can also perform ac circuit analysis for a frequency range. Frequency can have a decade variation, an octave variation, or a linear variation. Thus, the control statement takes one of three forms:

```
.AC DEC ND FSTART FSTOP
```

where DEC indicates a decade variation of frequency, and ND is the number of points per decade.

```
.AC OCT NO FSTART FSTOP
```

where OCT indicates an octave variation of frequency, and NO is the number of points per octave.

```
.AC LIN NP FSTART FSTOP
```

where LIN indicates a linear variation of frequency, and NP is the number of points.

In all three cases above, FSTART is the starting frequency, and FSTOP is the final frequency.

To print or plot the resulting ac output, respectively, we use the following control statements:

```
.PRINT AC OV1 <OV2 ... OV8>
.PLOT AC OV1 <OV2 ... OV8>
```

where the output variables are as described in the preceding ac print statement (p. 689).

EXAMPLE B.8

For the simple low-pass filter shown in Fig. B.9(a), the input file

```
V1 1 0 AC
R1 1 2 4
C1 0 2 .04
.AC LIN 100 .01 4
.PLOT AC VM(2) VP(2)
.END
```

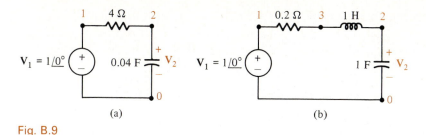

Fig. B.9

will yield a plot of the magnitude of the capacitor voltage versus frequency (in hertz) and a plot of the phase of the capacitor voltage versus frequency. Both plots use the same frequency axis, and the frequency variation is linear ranging from 0.01 to 4 Hz. (We cannot use 0 as the starting frequency for an .AC control statement.) Both magnitude and phase plots are composed of 100 points. Since the voltage-source element statement does not specify a magnitude and a phase, they are assumed to be 1 and 0, respectively. Therefore, the magnitude and phase plots are the same as the amplitude and phase responses, respectively, for the circuit transfer function V_2/V_1.

For the circuit shown in Fig. B.9(b), the input file

```
V1 1 0 AC
R1 1 3 .2
L1 2 3 1
C1 0 2 1
.AC DEC 50 .016 .4
.PLOT AC VDB(2)
.END
```

will yield a plot of $20 \log_{10}|V_2|$ versus frequency, where the frequency variation from 0.016 to 0.4 Hz has 50 points per decade. Since the input voltage has unity magnitude and zero phase, then the resulting plot is the amplitude-response portion of the Bode plot for the transfer function V_2/V_1.

Transformers

The general form of a (nonideal) **transformer**, that is, magnetically coupled (mutual) inductors, is

```
KXXXXXXX LYYYYYYY LZZZZZZZ VALUE
```

where XXXXXXX, YYYYYYY, ZZZZZZZ are alphanumeric strings of from one to seven characters, LXXXXXXX and LYYYYYYY are the self-inductances of the transformer (each self-inductance is also listed separately with its own element statement), and VALUE is the coefficient of coupling of the transformer. In particular, if a transformer has self-inductances L_1 and L_2, and mutual inductance M, then the coefficient of coupling is $k = M/\sqrt{L_1 L_2}$. The value of the coefficient of coupling (VALUE) is a number that must be greater than zero and less than or equal to one. The "dots" of the transformer correspond to the positive nodes of the self-inductances.

EXAMPLE B.9

For the transformer circuit shown in Fig. B.10 (see Fig. 12.5 on p. 557), we have the following input file:

```
V1 1 0 AC 36 -60
R1 1 2 9
C1 0 3 .05556
K1 L1 L2 .4082
L1 2 0 4
L2 3 0 6
.AC LIN 1 .4775 .4775
.PRINT AC VM(3) VP(3)
.END
```

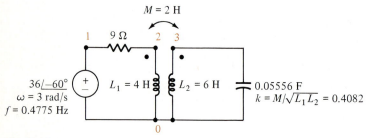

Fig. B.10

The resulting output file contains the following:

```
     FREQ        VM(3)        VP(3)
   4.775E-01    8.481E+00    1.650E+02
```

This corresponds to the phasor $\mathbf{V}_3 = 8.481\underline{/165°}$.

Fourier Series

SPICE can perform a trigonometric Fourier-series analysis of a function as part of a transient analysis. The general form of the control statement is

```
.FOUR FREQ OV1 <OV2 OV3 ...>
```

where FREQ is the fundamental frequency in hertz, and OV1, OV2, OV3,... are output variables for which the Fourier series is desired. The analysis is performed over the interval of time from TSTOP − 1/FREQ to TSTOP, where TSTOP is the final time for the associated .TRAN statement.

The form of the Fourier series is[†]

$$f(t) = a_0 + \sum_{n=1}^{\infty} A_n \sin(n\omega_0 t + \theta_n)$$

where $\omega_0 = 2\pi$ FREQ. SPICE determines the average value (dc component) a_0 and the amplitudes (or Fourier components) and phase angles for the first nine harmonics.

In addition to the independent-source PULSE function, SPICE has an independent-source SIN function whose general form is

```
SIN(VO VA FREQ TD THETA)
```

The corresponding functional form is

$$\text{VO} \qquad \text{for } 0 \le t < \text{TD}$$

$$\text{VO} + \text{VA}\, e^{-\text{THETA}(t - \text{TD})} \sin(2\pi \text{FREQ}[t - \text{TD}]) \qquad \text{for TD} \le t \le \text{TSTOP}$$

where VO is the offset, VA is the amplitude, and FREQ is the frequency in hertz. The default values for the delay TD and the damping factor THETA are zero.

EXAMPLE B.10

Let us use SPICE to determine the Fourier series of the function shown in Fig. B.11(a). Such a function can be obtained from the SIN function by setting VO = 0, VA = 1, FREQ = 0.5, TD = 1, and THETA = 0. We can use the resulting SIN function to describe the source in a simple circuit such as the one shown in Fig. B.11(b), and then perform a transient analysis. Adding the appropriate .FOUR statement to the SPICE input file, we get the desired Fourier series. For example, the following:

```
VS 1 0 SIN(0 1 .5 1)
R1 1 0 1
.TRAN .01 2
.FOUR .5 V(1)
.END
```

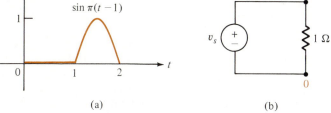

(a)   (b)

Fig. B.11

[†] We may obtain the form of the Fourier series given on p. 603 by using the fact that $\phi_n = \theta_n - 90°$ for $n = 1, 2, 3, \ldots$.

results in an output file which contains:

```
FOURIER COMPONENTS OF TRANSIENT RESPONSE V(1)

DC COMPONENT =    3.183D-01
```

HARMONIC NO	FREQUENCY (HZ)	FOURIER COMPONENT	PHASE (DEG)
1	5.000D-01	5.000D-01	-179.982
2	1.000D+00	2.123D-01	-90.000
4	2.000D+00	4.248D-02	-90.000
6	3.000D+00	1.824D-02	-90.000
8	4.000D+00	1.015D-02	-90.000

Another independent-source function is the PWL (piecewise linear) function whose general form is

```
PWL (T1 V1 <T2 V2 T3 V3 ...>)
```

where each pair TN, VN signifies that the value of the source is VN at time TN. The value of the source in the interval $TN < t < T(N + 1)$ is determined by using linear interpolation on the values VN and $V(N + 1)$.

EXAMPLE B.11
The function shown in Fig. B.12 (see Fig. 13.10 on p. 616) can be characterized by the PWL function with T1 = 0, V1 = 0, T2 = 0.5, V2 = 1, T3 = 1.5, V3 = −1, T4 = 2,

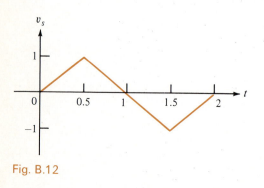

Fig. B.12

and V4 = 0. For the circuit given in Fig. B.11(b), the following input file

```
VS 1 0 PWL(0 0 .5 1 1.5 -1 2 0)
R1 1 0 1
.TRAN .01 2
.FOUR .5 V(1)
.END
```

yields an output file that contains:

HARMONIC NO	FREQUENCY (HZ)	FOURIER COMPONENT	PHASE (DEG)
1	5.000D-01	8.105D-01	0.000
3	1.500D+00	9.003D-02	180.000
5	2.500D+00	3.239D-02	0.000
7	3.500D+00	1.651D-02	180.000
9	4.500D+00	9.974D-03	0.000

There is much more to SPICE than has been covered in this appendix, which is intended to serve as an introduction to the subject. For more details on this topic, see the *User's Guide* for the version of SPICE that is being employed.

Answers to Selected Problems

CHAPTER 1

1.2 (a) 0 V, (b) 5 V, (c) 0 V, (d) -5 V, (e) 0 V

1.5 $3\pi \cos \pi t$ A

1.7 (a) 0 V, (b) 1 V, (c) -1 V, (d) -0.5 V, (e) 0 V

1.10 (a) $-\frac{1}{3}$ A, (b) $\frac{8}{9}$ A, (c) $-\frac{11}{9}$ A, (d) $-\frac{7}{9}$ A, (e) $-\frac{7}{9}$ A

1.12 (a) 4 A, (b) $-\frac{3}{4}e^{-2t}$ A, (c) $-18 \sin 2t$ V, (d) $-e^{-t} \cos 5t$ V

1.14 (a) 2 Ω, (b) 6 Ω, (c) 3 Ω, (d) 6 Ω

1.16 (a) 3 A, (b) 0 A, (c) -3 A

1.18 $\frac{5}{3}$ A, $\frac{10}{3}$ A, $\frac{20}{9}$ A, $-\frac{10}{9}$ A

1.20 -12 A, -8 A, -18 A, -6 A

1.23 $-\frac{1}{6} \cos 2t$ V

1.25 (a) $v = -6$ V, (b) any value of v is permissible,
(c) both a series and a parallel connection

1.28 (a) -2 A, (b) 0 V, (c) 2 A, 36 V, (d) -4 A, 15 V, 13 V

1.31 (a) $-\frac{3}{2}$ A, -3 V, 3 V, (b) -1 A, -4 V, 2 V

1.33 $\frac{2}{3}$ A, 2 V

1.35 (a) 16 V, (b) 24 V, (c) 32 V, (d) $\frac{8}{3}$ Ω

1.37 (a) $\frac{3}{2}$ Ω, (b) $\frac{21}{17}$ Ω, $\frac{54}{41}$ Ω

1.39 (a) 2 A, (b) 0 A, (c) -2 A

1.42 (a) 9 V, (b) -9 V

1.44 (a) $v = 4v_g$, (b) $v_2 = 2v_1$

1.46 (a) 5 A, (b) 0 Ω

1.48 (a) 8 V, (b) ∞

1.50 (a) 70 Ω, (b) 30 Ω, (c) 49

1.52 1.154 W, 0.111 W, -1.331 W, 0.066 W

1.55 (a) -18 W, 9 W, -36 W, 18 W, 27 W

(b) 18 W, 9 W, -72 W, 18 W, 27 W

CHAPTER 2

2.2 (a) -1 V, 1 V, -2 V, (b) -1 A, 4 A, -3 A, 2 A

2.4 (a) 1 V, 2 V, 3 V, (b) -1 A, 4 A, -3 A, 2 A

2.6 10 V, 6 V, 4 V

2.8 (a) 8 V, 6 V, 2 V, -2 V, (b) 24 A, (c) 3 S

2.10 4 V, 1.5 V, 2.5 V, 3.5 V

2.12 (a) 4 V, -6 V, -12 V, (b) 6 A, (c) $\frac{2}{3}$ Ω

2.14 (a) 0 V, -6 V, -12 V, (b) 0 V, (c) 0 Ω

2.16 (a) 12 V, 6 V, 8 V, 2 V, (b) 4 A, (c) 3 Ω

2.17 (a) $-h_f/R_L/[h_i + (h_i h_o - h_f h_r)R_L]$

(b) $[h_i + (h_i h_o - h_f h_r)R_L]/(1 + h_o R_L)$

2.19 (a) 30.96, (b) 43.22 Ω

2.24 (a) 4 A, (b) 0 A

2.26 (a) 2.25 Ω, (b) 0 V

2.28 1.2 V, -0.4 V, -2 V

2.30 10 V, 4 V, 6 V

2.32 $\frac{2}{3}$ Ω

2.34 7 Ω

2.36 Same as Problem 2.17

2.38 (a) -51.98, (b) 1309.6 Ω

2.40 0.75 A, -0.15 A, 0.9 A, 2 Ω

2.42 $-\frac{1}{6}$ A, $\frac{1}{2}$ A, $\frac{2}{3}$ A, $\frac{2}{3}$ Ω

2.44 1 A, 0.5 A, -0.25 A, 0.25 A, 3 Ω

CHAPTER 3

3.2 (a) 2.2 V, (b) -0.66 mW

3.4 $-R$

3.6 $(1 + R_L/R_1)R_s$

3.8 (a) $(1 + R_2/R_L)v_s$, (b) $-R_1/R_2$

3.10 $-\frac{2}{3}$

3.12 $11v_b - 21v_a$

3.14 -1.8

3.16 6

3.18 2 A

3.20 -9 V, 5 V

3.22 0.96 V

3.24 6 V

3.26 (a) $\frac{28}{5}$ V, $\frac{26}{5}$ Ω, (b) $\frac{7}{9}$ A

3.28 (a) 12 V, 4 Ω, (b) 2 A

3.30 (a) 8.7 V, 3.35 Ω, (b) 2 A

3.32 $-\frac{5}{9}$ V, $\frac{7}{18}$ Ω

3.34 -18 V, -4 Ω

3.36 -4 V, 0 Ω

3.38 $-(R_2/R_1)v_s$, R_2

3.40 2.5 Ω

3.42 (a) $\frac{112}{29}$ A, $\frac{29}{9}$ Ω, (b) 2 A

3.44 (a) $-\frac{7}{9}$ A, 2 Ω, (b) $-\frac{2}{9}$ A

3.46 (a) 0.76 A, 3.92 Ω, (b) 0.25 A

3.48 3 A, 3 Ω

3.50 4.5 A, -4 Ω

3.52 $-v_s/R_1$, R_2

3.54 0 A, 3 Ω

3.57 2 A, ∞

3.59 2 Ω, 0.302 W

3.61 3 Ω, 6.75 W

3.64 -9 V, 5 V

3.66 6 V

3.68 3 A, 3 V

CHAPTER 4

4.2 (a) 0 for $-\infty < t < 0$, $2e^{-2t}$ for $0 \le t < \infty$

(b) 0 for $-\infty < t < 0$, e^{-2t} for $0 \le t < \infty$

(c) 0 for $-\infty < t < 0$, 1 for $0 \le t < \infty$

4.4 (a) 0 for $-\infty < t < 0$, 1 for $0 \le t < 1$, -1 for $1 \le t < 2$, 0 for $2 \le t < \infty$

(b) 0 for $-\infty < t < 0$, $2t$ for $0 \le t < 1$, $-2(t-2)$ for $1 \le t < 2$,
    0 for $2 \le t < \infty$

(c) 0 for $-\infty < t < 0$, $2t + 1$ for $0 \le t < 1$, $-2t + 3$ for $1 \le t < 2$,
    0 for $2 \le t < \infty$

4.6 0 for $-\infty < t < 0$, 2 for $0 \le t < 1$, 0 for $1 \le t < \infty$

0 for $-\infty < t < 0$, t^2 for $0 \le t < 1$, 1 for $1 \le t < \infty$

0 for $-\infty < t < 0$, $2t^2$ for $0 \le t < 1$, 2 for $1 \le t < \infty$

0 for $-\infty < t < 0$, $2t$ for $0 \le t < 1$, 2 for $1 \le t < \infty$

0 for $-\infty < t < 0$, $2t + 2$ for $0 \le t < 1$, 2 for $1 \le t < \infty$

4.8 0 for $-\infty < t < 0$, 1 for $0 \le t < 1$, 0 for $1 \le t < \infty$

0 for $-\infty < t < 0$, $\frac{1}{2}t^2$ for $0 \le t < 1$, $\frac{1}{2}$ for $1 \le t < \infty$

0 for $-\infty < t < 0$, $\frac{1}{2}$ for $0 \le t < 1$, 0 for $1 \le t < \infty$

0 for $-\infty < t < 0$, $\frac{1}{2}$ for $0 \le t < 1$, 0 for $1 \le t < \infty$

0 for $-\infty < t < 0$, $t + \frac{1}{2}$ for $0 \le t < 1$, 1 for $1 \le t < \infty$

4.10 0 for $-\infty < t < 0$, $3t$ for $0 \le t < 1$, $-3t + 6$ for $1 \le t < 2$, 0 for $2 \le t < \infty$

0 for $-\infty < t < 0$, 1 for $0 \le t < 1$, -1 for $1 \le t < 2$, 0 for $2 \le t < \infty$

0 for $-\infty < t < 0$, $3t - 1$ for $0 \le t < 1$, $-3t + 5$ for $1 \le t < 2$,
0 for $2 \le t < \infty$

4.12 (a) 0 for $-\infty < t < 0$, $e^{-t/2}$ for $0 \le t < \infty$
(b) 0 for $-\infty < t < 0$, $1 - e^{-t/2}$ for $0 \le t < \infty$
(c) 0 for $-\infty < t < 0$, 1 for $0 \le t < \infty$

4.14 0 for $-\infty < t < 0$, 2 for $0 \le t < 1$, 0 for $1 \le t < \infty$
0 for $-\infty < t < 0$, t^2 for $0 \le t < 1$, 1 for $1 \le t < \infty$
0 for $-\infty < t < 0$, 2 for $0 \le t < 1$, 0 for $1 \le t < \infty$
0 for $-\infty < t < 0$, 1 for $0 \le t < 1$, 0 for $1 \le t < \infty$
0 for $-\infty < t < 0$, $t + 1$ for $0 \le t < 1$, 1 for $1 \le t < \infty$

4.16 0 for $-\infty < t < 0$, 2 for $0 \le t < 1$, 0 for $1 \le t < \infty$
0 for $-\infty < t < 0$, 2 for $0 \le t < 1$, 0 for $1 \le t < \infty$
0 for $-\infty < t < 0$, 1 for $0 \le t < 1$, 0 for $1 \le t < \infty$
0 for $-\infty < t < 0$, 1 for $0 \le t < 1$, 0 for $1 \le t < \infty$
0 for $-\infty < t < 0$, $-t$ for $0 \le t < 1$, -1 for $1 \le t < \infty$

4.18 0 for $-\infty < t < 0$, -2 for $0 \le t < 1$, 0 for $1 \le t < \infty$
0 for $-\infty < t < 0$, -2 for $0 \le t < 1$, 0 for $1 \le t < \infty$
0 for $-\infty < t < 0$, -1 for $0 \le t < 1$, 0 for $1 \le t < \infty$
0 for $-\infty < t < 0$, -1 for $0 \le t < 1$, 0 for $1 \le t < \infty$
0 for $-\infty < t < 0$, $-t - 1$ for $0 \le t < 1$, -1 for $1 \le t < \infty$

4.20 0 for $-\infty < t < 0$, 2 for $0 \le t < 1$, 0 for $1 \le t < \infty$
0 for $-\infty < t < 0$, 2 for $0 \le t < 1$, 0 for $1 \le t < \infty$
0 for $-\infty < t < 0$, 1 for $0 \le t < 1$, 0 for $1 \le t < \infty$
0 for $-\infty < t < 0$, t for $0 \le t < 1$, 1 for $1 \le t < \infty$
0 for $-\infty < t < 0$, $t + 1$ for $0 \le t < 1$, 1 for $1 \le t < \infty$

4.23 (a) $r(t) - r(t - 1)$, (b) $-r(t) + 3r(t - 1) - 2r(t - 2)$,
(c) $2r(t) - 4r(t - 1) - 2u(t - 1) + 2r(t - 2) + 2u(t - 2)$,
(d) $2r(t) - 4u(t - 1) - 2r(t - 2)$

4.25 (a) $-r(t) + 3r(t - 1) - 2r(t - 2)$ A,
(b) $-u(t) + 3u(t - 1) - 2u(t - 2)$ V,
(c) $-\frac{1}{2}u(t) + \frac{3}{2}u(t - 1) - u(t - 2)$ A,
(d) $-\frac{1}{2}u(t) - r(t) + \frac{3}{2}u(t - 1) + 3r(t - 1) - u(t - 2) - 2r(t - 2)$ A

4.27 (a) $r(t) - r(t - 1)$ V, (b) $2u(t) - 2u(t - 1)$ A,
(c) $u(t) - u(t - 1)$ V, (d) $r(t) + u(t) - r(t - 1) - u(t - 1)$ V

4.29 (a) $r(t) - r(t - 1)$ V, (b) $-2u(t) + 2u(t - 1)$ A,
(c) $-u(t) + u(t - 1)$ V, (d) $-u(t) + u(t - 1)$ V,
(e) $-r(t) - u(t) + r(t - 1) + u(t - 1)$ V

4.31 $2u(t) - 4\delta(t - 1) - 2u(t - 2)$ V

4.33 (a) $-u(t - 1) + r(t - 2) - r(t - 4) - u(t - 4)$ A,
(b) $-\delta(t - 1) + u(t - 2) - u(t - 4) - \delta(t - 4)$ V,
(c) $-\frac{1}{2}\delta(t - 1) + \frac{1}{2}u(t - 2) - \frac{1}{2}u(t - 4) - \frac{1}{2}\delta(t - 4)$ A,
(d) $-\frac{1}{2}\delta(t - 1) - u(t - 1) + \frac{1}{2}u(t - 2) + r(t - 2) - \frac{3}{2}u(t - 4) - r(t - 4)$
$\qquad\qquad\qquad\qquad\qquad\qquad\qquad - \frac{1}{2}\delta(t - 4)$ A

4.35 (a) $2\delta(t) - 2\delta(t - 1)$ A, (b) $\delta(t) - \delta(t - 1)$ V, (c) $-u(t) + u(t - 1)$ V

4.37 (a) $2\delta(t) - 2\delta(t - 1)$ A, (b) $\delta(t) - \delta(t - 1)$ V,
(c) $\delta(t) + u(t) - \delta(t - 1) - u(t - 1)$ V

4.39 $\frac{1}{4}t^2$ V for $1 \le t < 2$ s, 1 V for $2 \le t < \infty$

4.41 $u(t) - 3u(t-1) + 2u(t-2)$ V, $3r(t) - 9r(t-1) + 6r(t-2)$ A

4.43 (a) $u(t) - u(t-1)$ V, (b) $\delta(t) - \delta(t-1)$ V, (c) $r(t) - r(t-1)$ V,
(d) $u(t) + \delta(t) + r(t) - u(t-1) - \delta(t-1) - r(t-1)$ V

4.45 (a) $2u(t) - 2u(t-1)$ A, (b) $r(t) - r(t-1)$ V, (c) $-r(t) + r(t-1)$ V

4.47 (a) $2u(t) - 2u(t-1)$ A, (b) $r(t) - r(t-1) + u(t) - u(t-1)$ V,
(c) $-r(t) + r(t-1) - u(t) + u(t-1)$ V

4.53 1.875 H

4.55 $v_1 = u(t)$ V, $3\dfrac{d}{dt}(v_2 - v_1) + \dfrac{1}{4}\displaystyle\int_{-\infty}^{t} v_2 \, dt + \dfrac{v_2}{5} - r(t) = 0$

4.59 $i_1 = u(t)$ A, $3\dfrac{d}{dt}(i_2 - i_1) + \dfrac{1}{4}\displaystyle\int_{-\infty}^{t} i_2 \, dt + \dfrac{i_2}{5} - r(t) = 0$

4.67 (a) 3 A, (b) -6 V, (c) -3 A/s, (d) 6 V/s

4.69 (a) 6 V, (b) -12 A, (c) -6 V/s, (d) 12 A/s

4.71 (a) -6 V, (b) 3 A, (c) 0 A, (d) 1.5 V/s, (e) -0.75 A/s

4.73 (a) 2 A, (b) -8 V, (c) -8 A/s, (d) 16 A/s

4.75 (a) 10 V, (b) -2 A, (c) -20 V/s, (d) -5 A/s

4.77 (a) 30 V, (b) -5 A, (c) -120 V/s, (d) 20 A/s

4.79 (a) 1 A, (b) 1 V, (c) 0 V, (d) -2 A, (e) -2 V/s, (f) 0 A/s, (g) -2 V/s,
(h) 2 A/s

CHAPTER 5

5.2 $-\frac{50}{3}e^{-t}u(t)$ V, $\frac{10}{3} - \frac{10}{3}(1 - e^{-t})u(t)$ A

5.4 $-\frac{104}{15}e^{-t/5}u(t)$ V, $\frac{13}{3} - \frac{13}{3}(1 - e^{-t/5})u(t)$ A

5.6 $30 - 30(1 - e^{-4t})u(t)$ V, $-5e^{-4t}u(t)$ A

5.8 $3 - 3(1 - e^{-t})u(t)$ A, $-9e^{-t}u(t)$ V

5.10 $4 - 4(1 - e^{-t})u(t)$ V, $6 - 6(1 - e^{-t})u(t)$ V

5.12 $8 - 8(1 - e^{-3t})u(t)$ V, $-6 + 6(1 - e^{-3t})u(t)$ V

5.14 $9 + 3(e^{-4t} + 2e^{-t} - 3)u(t)$ V, $-e^{-t}u(t)$ A

5.16 $9 + 9(e^{-4t} - 2e^{-t/2} - 1)u(t)$ V, $3 + 3(e^{-t/2} - 1)u(t)$ A

5.18 $\frac{2}{3} - \frac{2}{3}(1 - e^{-t/12})u(t)$ A, $4 - \frac{4}{3}(1 - e^{-t/12})u(t)$ V

5.20 $4 - 4(1 - e^{-2t})u(t) + (0.0733e^{-3(t-2)} - 4e^{-2t})u(t-2)$ V,
$-1.33e^{-2t}u(t) + (1.33e^{-2t} - 0.0366e^{-3(t-2)})u(t-2)$ A

5.22 $\frac{2}{3}(1 - e^{-4t})u(t)$ V, $\frac{1}{3}e^{-4t}u(t)$ A

5.24 $\frac{11}{15}(1 - e^{-5t})u(t)$ V, $\frac{11}{18}e^{-5t}u(t)$ A

5.26 $\frac{1}{3}e^{-t/9}u(t)$ A, $(1 - e^{-t/9})u(t)$ V

5.28 $4(1 - e^{-t})u(t)$ V, $6(1 - e^{-t})u(t)$ V

5.30 $2(1 - e^{-2t})u(t)$ V, $3(1 - e^{-2t})u(t)$ V

5.32 $(1 - e^{-t/3RC})u(t)$ V

5.34 $\dfrac{L}{R}(1 - e^{-Rt/2L})u(t)$ A

5.36 $-2 + \frac{8}{3}(1 - e^{-4t})u(t)$ V

5.38 $3 - \frac{10}{3}(1 - e^{-t})u(t)$ A, $-10e^{-t}u(t)$ V

5.40 $5 + 5(1 - e^{-9t})u(t)$ V, $\frac{9}{4}e^{-9t}u(t)$ A

5.42 $8 + 16(1 - e^{-t})u(t)$ V, $\frac{16}{7}e^{-t}u(t)$ A

5.44 (a) $\frac{1}{2}e^{-3t}u(t)$ A, (b) $\delta(t) - 3e^{-3t}u(t)$ V, (c) $\delta(t) - 2e^{-3t}u(t)$ V

5.47 (a) $2(1 - e^{-4t})u(t)$ V, (b) $e^{-4t}u(t)$ A

5.49 (a) $6te^{-3t}u(t)$ A, (b) $(-36t + 12)e^{-3t}u(t)$ V, (c) $(-24t + 12)e^{-3t}u(t)$ V

5.51 (a) $4(e^{-2t} - e^{-4t})u(t)$ V, (b) $(-e^{-2t} + 2e^{-4t})u(t)$ A,
(c) $4(-e^{-2t} + e^{-4t})u(t)$ V

5.53 (a) $(-2 + 8te^{-4t} + 2e^{-4t})u(t)$ V, (b) $-4te^{-4t}u(t)$ A,
(c) $(3 - 8te^{-4t} - 3e^{-4t})u(t)$ V

CHAPTER 6

6.1 $1 - (1 + \frac{5}{8}e^{-3t} - \frac{13}{8}e^{-t})u(t)$ V, $1 - (1 - \frac{15}{2}e^{-3t} + \frac{13}{2}e^{-t})u(t)$ A

6.4 $1 - (1 + \frac{1}{2}e^{-6t} - \frac{3}{2}e^{-2t})u(t)$ V, $\frac{1}{2}(e^{-6t} - e^{-2t})u(t)$ A

6.6 $2 - 2(1 - e^{-2t}\cos 2t)u(t)$ A, $2 - 2[1 - \sqrt{2}e^{-2t}\cos(2t - \pi/4)]u(t)$ V

6.9 $3 - 3(1 + e^{-4t} - 2e^{-2t})u(t)$ A, $3(e^{-4t} - e^{-2t})u(t)$ V

6.10 $4 - 4(1 - e^{-2t}\cos 2t)u(t)$ A, $4 - 4[1 - \sqrt{2}e^{-2t}\cos(2t - \pi/4)]u(t)$ V

6.12 $2 - [2 - (t + 2)e^{-t}]u(t)$ A, $1 - [1 - (t + 1)e^{-t}]u(t)$ V

6.14 $2 - 2(1 - e^{-t/2}\cos\frac{1}{2}t)u(t)$ A, $2e^{-t/2}\cos(\frac{1}{2}t - 3\pi/2)u(t)$ V

6.16 $2 - 2[1 - (t + 1)e^{-t}]u(t)$ V, $-2te^{-t}u(t)$ A

6.18 $\dfrac{d^2v_2}{dt^2} + \left(\dfrac{1}{R_1C_1} + \dfrac{1}{R_2C_1} + \dfrac{1}{R_2C_2}\right)\dfrac{dv}{dt} + \dfrac{1}{R_1R_2C_1C_2}v = 0$

6.20 $70(e^{-2t} - e^{-5t})u(t)$ V

6.22 $2 - (2 + e^{-3t/2} - 3e^{-t/2})u(t)$ V

6.24 $3 - (6 + 2e^{-8t} - 8e^{-2t})u(t)$ V, $2(e^{-8t} - e^{-2t})u(t)$ A

6.26 $1 - 2(1 - te^{-t} - e^{-t})u(t)$ A, $-4te^{-t}u(t)$ V

6.27 $r(t) - (\frac{7}{6} + \frac{1}{30}e^{-6t} - \frac{6}{5}e^{-t})u(t)$ A

6.29 $[4.8 - 5e^{-4t}\cos(3t - 0.284)]u(t)$ A

6.31 $2(e^{-2t} + te^{-t} - e^{-t})u(t)$ V

6.33 $\left[-2 + \dfrac{4}{\sqrt{3}}e^{-t}\cos\left(\sqrt{3}t - \dfrac{\pi}{6}\right)\right]u(t)$ V

6.35 $(2e^{-3t} - 4e^{-2t} + 2e^{-t})u(t)$ V

6.37 $\frac{1}{4}(1 - 2te^{-2t} - e^{-2t})u(t)$ A, $\frac{1}{4}(3 - 2te^{-2t} - 3e^{-2t})u(t)$ V

6.39 $70(e^{-5t} - e^{-2t})u(t)$ V

6.41 $e^{-t}\sin t\, u(t)$ V

6.43 $\frac{4}{3}[e^{-8t} + (6t - 1)e^{-2t}]u(t)$ V

CHAPTER 7

7.3 $\dfrac{d}{dt}\begin{bmatrix} i_1 \\ i_2 \end{bmatrix} = \begin{bmatrix} -R_1/L_1 & -R_1/L_1 \\ -R_1/L_2 & -(R_1 + R_2)/L_2 \end{bmatrix}\begin{bmatrix} i_1 \\ i_2 \end{bmatrix}$

7.5 $\dfrac{d}{dt}\begin{bmatrix} i_L \\ v \end{bmatrix} = \begin{bmatrix} 0 & \frac{10}{7} \\ -7 & -7 \end{bmatrix}\begin{bmatrix} i_L \\ v \end{bmatrix}$

7.7 $\dfrac{d}{dt}\begin{bmatrix} i_L \\ v_1 \\ v_2 \end{bmatrix} = \begin{bmatrix} 0 & 1/L & -1/L \\ -1/C_1 & -1/RC_1 & 0 \\ 1/C_2 & -3/RC_2 & 0 \end{bmatrix} \begin{bmatrix} i_L \\ v_1 \\ v_2 \end{bmatrix}$

7.10 $\dfrac{d}{dt}\begin{bmatrix} i_1 \\ i_2 \\ v_1 \\ v_2 \end{bmatrix} = \begin{bmatrix} -R/L_1 & R/L_1 & -1/L_1 & 0 \\ R/L_2 & -R/L_2 & 1/L_2 & -1/L_2 \\ 1/5C_1 & -1/5C_1 & 0 & 0 \\ 4/5C_2 & 1/5C_2 & 0 & 0 \end{bmatrix} \begin{bmatrix} i_1 \\ i_2 \\ v_1 \\ v_2 \end{bmatrix}$

7.16 $\dfrac{d}{dt}\begin{bmatrix} i \\ v \end{bmatrix} = \begin{bmatrix} 0 & -\frac{1}{2} \\ 4 & -1 \end{bmatrix}\begin{bmatrix} i \\ v \end{bmatrix} + \begin{bmatrix} \frac{1}{2} \\ 0 \end{bmatrix}u(t)$

7.19 $\dfrac{d}{dt}\begin{bmatrix} i \\ v \end{bmatrix} = \begin{bmatrix} -3 & -1 \\ 1 & -1 \end{bmatrix}\begin{bmatrix} i \\ v \end{bmatrix} + \begin{bmatrix} 1 \\ 0 \end{bmatrix}u(t)$

7.22 $\dfrac{d}{dt}\begin{bmatrix} i_L \\ v \end{bmatrix} = \begin{bmatrix} 0 & \frac{10}{7} \\ -7 & -7 \end{bmatrix}\begin{bmatrix} i_L \\ v \end{bmatrix} + \begin{bmatrix} 0 \\ -70 \end{bmatrix}u(t)$

7.25 $\dfrac{d}{dt}\begin{bmatrix} v_1 \\ v_2 \end{bmatrix} = \begin{bmatrix} -3 & -3 \\ -1 & -2 \end{bmatrix}\begin{bmatrix} v_1 \\ v_2 \end{bmatrix} + \begin{bmatrix} 1 \\ 0 \end{bmatrix}v_s$

7.28 $\dfrac{d}{dt}\begin{bmatrix} i \\ v_1 \\ v_2 \end{bmatrix} = \begin{bmatrix} 0 & \frac{1}{2} & -\frac{1}{2} \\ -1 & -1 & 0 \\ 1 & 0 & -1 \end{bmatrix}\begin{bmatrix} i \\ v_1 \\ v_2 \end{bmatrix} + \begin{bmatrix} 0 \\ 1 \\ 0 \end{bmatrix}v_s$

7.36 $\dfrac{d}{dt}\begin{bmatrix} i_1 \\ i_2 \end{bmatrix} = \begin{bmatrix} -4 & \frac{8}{3} \\ 4 & -\frac{20}{3} \end{bmatrix}\begin{bmatrix} i_1 \\ i_2 \end{bmatrix} + \begin{bmatrix} \frac{2}{3} \\ \frac{4}{3} \end{bmatrix}v_s$

7.38 $\dfrac{d}{dt}\begin{bmatrix} i_L \\ v \end{bmatrix} = \begin{bmatrix} -\frac{24}{37} & -\frac{66}{37} \\ \frac{27}{37} & -\frac{9}{37} \end{bmatrix}\begin{bmatrix} i_L \\ v \end{bmatrix} + \begin{bmatrix} \frac{60}{37} \\ -\frac{12}{37} \end{bmatrix}v_s$

CHAPTER 8

8.2 $8.314\cos(\sqrt{3}t - 60°)$ V, leads by $43.9°$

8.4 $-1.2\cos 2t + 2.4\sin 2t$ V, $1.2\cos 2t + 3.6\sin 2t$ A, lags by $26.57°$

8.6 $3\cos t$ V, in phase

8.8 $\frac{16}{15}(e^{-4t} - e^{-t} + \frac{3}{2}\sin 2t)u(t)$ V

8.10 $3(te^{-t} - e^{-t} + \cos t)u(t)$ V

8.11 (a) $8.06e^{j60.26°}$, (c) $3.61e^{j123.7°}$, (e) $4e^{j0°}$, (g) $7e^{j90°}$

8.12 (b) $-1 + j1.732$, (d) $-3.46 - j2$, (f) $-j$, (h) -2

8.13 (a) $4.60 + j4.96$, (c) $1.5 - j2.60$

8.14 (b) $5.0\cos(\omega t - 23.08°)$, (d) $2.95\cos(\omega t + 16.35°)$

8.15 (a) $j12$, (c) $5 + j5\sqrt{3}$

8.17 (b) $2.22e^{j123.69°}$, (d) $20.62e^{j104.04°}$, (f) $5.66e^{-j21.87°}$, (h) $17.0e^{j0°}$

8.18 (b) $-1.23 + j1.85$, (d) $-5.0 + j20.0$, (f) $5.25 - j2.11$, (h) 17

8.19 (b) 0

8.21 $8.314\cos(\sqrt{3}t - 60°)$ V, leads by $43.9°$

8.23 $2.68\cos(2t - 116.57°)$ V, $3.79\cos(2t - 71.57°)$ A, lags by $26.57°$

8.25 $3\cos t$ V, in phase

8.27 (a) $6\sqrt{2}\cos(3t + 165°)$ V, (b) $9 + j9$ Ω

8.29 (a) $\cos(2t - 90°) = \sin 2t$ V, (b) $3.2 + j1.6$ Ω

8.31 (a) $1.88 - j0.22\ \Omega$, (b) $1\ \Omega$, (c) $0.4 + j1.2\ \Omega$

8.34 $2.77\cos(\sqrt{3}t - 60°)$ A

8.35 $6\sqrt{2}\underline{/165°}$ V, $0.5 - j9.5\ \Omega$

8.37 $\cos(2t - 90°) = \sin 2t$ V

8.39 $6.8\underline{/30°}$ A, $6.8\underline{/-90°}$ A

8.41 (a) $5.88\cos(2t + 78.7°)$ V, (b) $1.15 - j0.23\ \Omega$

8.43 (a) $6.91 - j0.30\ \Omega$, (c) $3.20 - j0.40\ \Omega$

8.45 (a) $0.219\cos(5t - 146.9°)$ V, (b) $0.5 - j0.2\ \Omega$

8.47 $2\sqrt{2}\cos(4t + 45°)$ V

CHAPTER 9

9.2 -588 mW, 470.6 mW, 0 W, 0 W, 117.6 mW

9.4 -8.0 W, 7.5 W, 0 W, 0 W, 0.5 W

9.7 -7.76 W, 7.76 W, 0.60 W, 0 W, 0 W, -0.60 W

9.9 (a) 601.41 W, 601.41 W, 601.41 W, (b) 601.41 W, 1202.81 W

9.12 1 mW, 2 mW, 2.25 mW

9.14 (a) 4.5 mW, 9 mW, 10.125 mW, (c) 2.5 mW, 5 mW, 5.625 mW

9.16 (a) 0.5, 0.707

9.18 8.16 mW, 5.51 mW, 0.012 mW, 294 mW

9.20 $4\ \Omega$, 3 H

9.22 (a) 0, $-90°$, (b) leading, (c) $3.49\ \mu$F

9.25 236.55 V rms

9.26 (a) $13.06\underline{/-2.53°}$ A, (b) 0.999, (c) lagging

9.28 (a) $0.686\underline{/-31°}$ VA, (b) 0.686 VA, (c) 0.86 leading

9.31 (a) $36\sqrt{2}$ VA, (b) 36 VA, 24 VA, 6 VA, 12 VA, 6 VA, (c) no

9.33 (a) 881.7 W, 826.6 W, (b) 826.2 W, 777.9 W

9.36 $7.348\underline{/-42.71°}$ A, $7.348\underline{/-162.71°}$ A, $7.348\underline{/77.29°}$ A, 1943.8 W

9.39 $9.49\underline{/-29.24°}$ A, $15.21\underline{/-148.1°}$ A, $13.50\underline{/70.0°}$ A, 3494.9 W

9.41 $48.37\underline{/-29.74°}$ A, $48.37\underline{/-149.74°}$ A, $48.37\underline{/-90.26°}$ A, 9360 W

9.43 (a) $31.87 + j19.75\ \Omega$, (b) $17.5\ \mu$F

9.46 881.7 W, 826.6 W

9.47 601.41 W, 1202.81 W

9.51 1892.1 W, 1600.8 W

CHAPTER 10

10.2 $1/RC$

10.4 (a) $1/\sqrt{2}RC$, (b) $\sqrt{2}/RC$

10.7 $0.414/RC$, $2.414/RC$

10.10 half-power frequency is 0.25 rad/s

10.19 Plot given in Fig. 10.16 which is labeled $\alpha = 0.05\ \omega_n$,

10.21 $6/\sqrt{10}$ rad/s

10.22 $\dfrac{R_2}{R_1 + R_2}\sqrt{\dfrac{1}{LC} - \dfrac{R_1^2}{L^2}}$

10.25 $\dfrac{R_1}{R_1 + R_2} \sqrt{\dfrac{1}{LC} - \dfrac{1}{R_1^2 C^2}}$

10.28 4.22

10.31 (a) 0.1, (b) 9.9 Ω, 19.8 mH, (c) 0.1

10.34 175 krad/s, 1.425 Mrad/s, 10 kΩ, 50 mH, 80 pF

10.36 50 Ω, 50 mH, 0.005 μF

10.38 2 kΩ, 4 kΩ, 6 kΩ, 5 mH, 0.0025 μF, 1.5 mv, 8 ki

10.40 (a) $0.97e^{-6t}\cos(3t - 157.17°)$ V,
   (b) $19.52e^{-6t}\cos(3t - 3.73°)$ V, (c) $2.17e^{-6t}\cos(3t + 49.4°)$ V

10.43 $\dfrac{4V_1}{s^2 + 4s + 12}, \dfrac{4(s^2 + 2s + 8)}{s^2 + 4s + 12}$

10.46 $\dfrac{R_2 Ms}{(L_1 L_2 - M^2)s^2 + (L_1 R_2 + L_2 R_1)s + R_1 R_2}$

10.48 (a) poles: -3.73, -0.268; zero at origin
   (b) poles: -3.73, -0.268; double zero at origin
   (c) poles: -3.73, -0.268; no (finite) zeros

10.50 poles: $-2 - j2\sqrt{2}$, $-2 + j2\sqrt{2}$; no (finite) zeros

10.53 (a) poles: -1.866, -0.134; no (finite) zeros
   (b) double pole at -1; no (finite) zeros
   (c) poles: $-1 - j\sqrt{3}$, $-1 + j\sqrt{3}$; no (finite) zeros

10.55 (a) $\dfrac{10(s + 1)}{s^2 + 4s + 5}$, (b) $\dfrac{10(s + 1)}{s^2 + 4s + 5}$, (c) $\dfrac{-3(s + 1)}{s^2 + 4s + 5}$

10.58 (a) $2.5\underline{/0°}$, (b) $2.77\underline{/-19.45°}$, (c) $10\underline{/180°}$

CHAPTER 11

11.2 (a) $\dfrac{as + a + 1}{(s + 1)^2} e^{-a(s+1)}$, (b) $\dfrac{e^{-as}}{(s + \alpha)^2}$, (c) $\dfrac{s + a}{s + b}$, (d) $\dfrac{s^3 + 6s^2 + 12s + 14}{(s + 2)^4}$

11.4 (a) $\dfrac{se^{-s\pi/4}}{s^2 + 1}$, (b) $\dfrac{1}{\sqrt{2}}\left(\dfrac{s + 1}{s^2 + 1}\right)$, (c) $\dfrac{1 - e^{-2\pi s}}{s^2 + 1}$, (d) $\dfrac{1 + e^{-\pi s}}{s^2 + 1}$

11.6 $\dfrac{(1 + e^{-s})\pi}{(1 - e^{-2s})(s^2 + \pi^2)}$

11.8 (a) $\dfrac{s(s^2 + \alpha^2 + \beta^2)}{s^4 + 2(\alpha^2 + \beta^2)s^2 + (\alpha^2 - \beta^2)^2}$, (b) $\dfrac{\alpha(s^2 + \alpha^2 - \beta^2)}{s^4 + 2(\alpha^2 + \beta^2)s^2 + (\alpha^2 - \beta^2)^2}$

11.10 (a) $\dfrac{A_1 s + \alpha A_1 + A_2}{(s + \alpha)^2}$, (b) $\dfrac{A_1 s + A_2 \beta}{s^2 + \beta^2}$, (c) $\dfrac{A_1 s + A_1 \alpha + A_2 \beta}{(s + \alpha)^2 + \beta^2}$

11.12 (a) $\delta(t) + (a - b)e^{-bt}u(t)$, (b) $\delta(t) - be^{-bt}u(t)$,
   (c) $\delta(t - a) + (a - b)e^{-b(t-a)}u(t - a)$

11.14 (a) $(6 + 18t + 9t^2 + t^3)u(t)$, (b) $(6 - 5e^{-t} - 2te^{-t})u(t)$,
   (c) $(-1 + 2t + e^{-2t})u(t) - [-1 + 2(t - 2) + e^{-2(t-2)}]u(t - 2)$

11.16 $(5e^{-2t} - 4e^{-t} - \cos 2t + 3\sin 2t)u(t)$

11.18 $(10 - 6e^{-2t} - 4e^{-12t})u(t)$, $3(e^{-12t} - e^{-2t})u(t)$

11.20 (a) $(-2e^{-3t} + 2\cos 3t + 2\sin 2t)u(t)$, (b) $(1 + 3\cos 2t)u(t)$,
(c) $(5e^{-2t} - 4e^{-t} - \cos 2t + 3\sin 2t)u(t)$

11.22 $-\frac{1}{50}e^{-3t}(7\cos 4t + \sin 4t)$ V for $t \geq 0$, $e^{-3t}(\cos 4t - \sin 4t)$ A for $t \geq 0$

11.24 $-2(1 - e^{-4t})u(t)$ V, $-e^{-4t}u(t)$ A, $(3 - 2e^{-4t})u(t)$ V

11.26 $4(e^{-4t} - e^{-2t})u(t)$ V, $(e^{-2t} - 2e^{-4t})u(t)$ A, $(5e^{-2t} - 4e^{-4t})u(t)$ V

11.29 $8e^{-4t}u(t)$ V, $\delta(t) - 4e^{-4t}u(t)$ A, $-8e^{-4t}u(t)$ V

11.31 $8te^{-4t}u(t)$ V, $(1 - 4t)e^{-4t}u(t)$ A, $-8te^{-4t}u(t)$

11.32 $\frac{11}{15}(1 - e^{-5t})u(t)$ V, $\frac{11}{18}e^{-5t}u(t)$ A

11.34 $4(1 - e^{-t})u(t)$ V, $6(1 - e^{-t})u(t)$ V

11.37 (a) $-\frac{14}{3} + \frac{2}{3}e^{-3t}$ V for $t \geq 0$, (b) $-4 - \sin 2t$ V for $t \geq 0$

11.39 $(1 - e^{-t}\cos 2t - \frac{1}{2}e^{-t}\sin 2t)u(t)$ V

11.42 $(1 - e^{-2t} - 2te^{-2t})u(t)$ V

11.45 $e^{-t}\sin t\, u(t)$ V

11.47 $\left(\dfrac{1}{2} - \dfrac{1}{2}e^{-t} - \dfrac{1}{\sqrt{3}}\, e^{-t/2}\sin\dfrac{\sqrt{3}}{2}t\right)u(t)$ V

11.49 $-\dfrac{1}{s}$, -1

11.52 (a) $e^{-2t}u(t)$, (b) $(2e^{-2t} - e^{-t})u(t)$, (c) $(e^{-t} - e^{-2t})u(t)$, (d) $(1 - 2t)e^{-2t}u(t)$

11.54 (a) $\dfrac{s+1}{s+2}$, (b) $\dfrac{s+1}{s^2+1}$, (c) $\dfrac{s+1}{s^2+2s+2}$, (d) $\dfrac{1}{s+1}$, (e) $\dfrac{1}{s+2}$

11.58 $\dfrac{s^2+1}{s^2+7s+9}$

11.60 $\dfrac{6s}{s^3+3s^2+9s+27}$

11.63 $e^{-10t}u(t)$

11.65 $(e^{-t} - e^{-2t})u(t)$

11.67 0 for $0 \leq t < 1$, $\frac{1}{2}(t-1)^2$ for $1 \leq t < 2$, $\frac{1}{2}$ for $2 \leq t < 3$,
$-\frac{1}{2}(t-2)(t-4)$ for $3 \leq t < 4$, 0 for $4 \leq t < \infty$

11.69 $2u(t-1) - 2u(t-2) - 2u(t-3) + 2u(t-4)$

CHAPTER 12

12.3 (a) $9 + j9\ \Omega$, (b) 0.94 J

12.5 $\dfrac{R_2 Ms}{(L_1 L_2 - M^2)s^2 + (R_1 L_2 + R_2 L_1)s + R_1 R_2}$

12.7 (a) $j\omega L_1 + \dfrac{j\omega^3 M^2 C}{1 - \omega^2 L_2 C}$, (b) $\sqrt{\dfrac{L_1}{(L_1 L_2 - M^2)C}}$, $\dfrac{1}{\sqrt{L_2 C}}$

12.10 $\dfrac{8s(4s^2 - 3s - 1)}{11s^3 + 121s^2 + 14s + 24}$

12.12 $\dfrac{8(s^2 + 1)}{s^3 + 14s^2 + 25s + 11}$

12.14 $v_1 = L_1\dfrac{di_1}{dt} + M\dfrac{di_2}{dt}$, $v_2 = M\dfrac{di_1}{dt} + L_2\dfrac{di_2}{dt}$

12.16 $6\sqrt{2}\cos(3t + 165°)$ V

12.18 2.31

12.20 (a) $1/N\sqrt{LC}$, (b) $NR\sqrt{C/L}$, (c) $1/N^2RC$

12.22 (a) $1/N\sqrt{LC}$, (b) $\sqrt{L/C}/NR$, (c) R/L

12.25 $0.33\cos(10t - 172.4°)$ V

12.27 698.2

12.32 (a) $1/(1 + N)\sqrt{L_1C}$, (b) $(1 + N)/\sqrt{LC}$

12.34 $\dfrac{R_2}{R_1R_2 + R_1R_3 + R_2R_3}, \dfrac{R_1}{R_1R_2 + R_1R_3 + R_2R_3}, \dfrac{R_3}{R_1R_2 + R_1R_3 + R_2R_3}$

12.36 Reciprocal

12.38 (a) $\dfrac{2}{8s^2 + 6s + 3}$, (b) $\dfrac{3}{12s^2 + 8s + 4}$

12.40 Not reciprocal

12.42 $\dfrac{y_{22}}{y_{11}y_{22} - y_{12}y_{21}}$

12.44 3.125

12.46 $0, 0, -(G_1 + G_2), G_2$

12.49 $\dfrac{R_1R_3}{R_1 + R_2 + R_3}, \dfrac{R_2R_3}{R_1 + R_2 + R_3}, \dfrac{R_1R_2}{R_1 + R_2 + R_3}$

12.51 $\dfrac{24s + 5}{8s + 1}, \dfrac{2}{8s + 1}, -\dfrac{2}{8s + 1}, \dfrac{2}{8s + 1}$

12.53 $z_{22}/\Delta_z, -z_{12}/\Delta_z, -z_{21}/\Delta_z, z_{11}/\Delta_z$

12.55 $\dfrac{z_{21}}{z_{11} + z_{11}z_{22} - z_{12}z_{21}}$

12.58 1.538

12.60 $1/y_{11}, -y_{12}/y_{11}, y_{21}/y_{11}, (y_{11}y_{22} - y_{12}y_{21})/y_{11}$

12.62 $\dfrac{h_{21}}{h_{12}h_{21} - h_{11}(1 + h_{22})}$

12.66 $1/(A + B)$

12.68 $z'_{11} + z''_{11}, z'_{12} + z''_{12}, z'_{21} + z''_{21}, z'_{22} + z''_{22}$

CHAPTER 13

13.1 $0.67 + 0.91\cos\dfrac{2\pi}{3}t + 0.23\cos\dfrac{4\pi}{3}t + 0.057\cos\dfrac{8\pi}{3}t + 0.036\cos\dfrac{10\pi}{3}t + \cdots$

13.3 $0.64 - 0.42\cos 2\pi t - 0.085\cos 4\pi t - 0.036\cos 6\pi t - 0.02\cos 8\pi t - \cdots$

13.5 $0.75 + 1.01\cos(2\pi t - 108.4°) + 0.318\cos(4\pi t + 90°) +$
$$0.336\cos(6\pi t - 71.6°) + \cdots$$

13.7 $0.747\sin\dfrac{2\pi}{3}t + 0.768\sin\dfrac{4\pi}{3}t + 0.285\sin\dfrac{8\pi}{3}t + 0.276\sin\dfrac{10\pi}{3}t +$
$$0.171\sin\dfrac{14\pi}{3}t + \cdots$$

13.9 $1.05 \sin \dfrac{\pi}{3} t - 0.042 \sin \dfrac{5\pi}{3} t + 0.021 \sin \dfrac{7\pi}{3} t - 0.009 \sin \dfrac{11\pi}{3} t + \cdots$

13.12 $0.32 + 0.5 \cos \pi t + 0.21 \cos 2\pi t - 0.04 \cos 4\pi t + 0.02 \cos 6\pi t -$
$$0.01 \cos 8\pi t + \cdots$$

13.15 (a) 0, 0.0052, 0.162, 0.00043, 0.00011, (b) $0.162 \cos(2\pi t - 140.3°)$ V

13.18 $2.5e^{-j7t} + 2.5e^{j7t}$

13.23 $0.667 + 0.456e^{-j2\pi t/3} + 0.456e^{j2\pi t/3} + 0.114e^{-j4\pi t/3} + 0.114e^{j4\pi t/3} + \cdots$

13.25 $0.637 + 0.212e^{-j2\pi t} - 0.212e^{j2\pi t} - 0.0424e^{-j4\pi t} - 0.0424e^{j4\pi t} - \cdots$

13.27 $0.75 + \dfrac{1}{2\pi}(-1 + j3)e^{-j2\pi t} - \dfrac{1}{2\pi}(1 + j3)e^{j2\pi t} - j\dfrac{1}{2\pi} e^{-j4\pi t} + j\dfrac{1}{2\pi} e^{j4\pi t} + \cdots$

13.29 $j0.373e^{-j2\pi t/3} - j0.373e^{j2\pi t/3} + j0.384e^{-j4\pi t/3} - j0.384e^{j4\pi t/3} + \cdots$

CHAPTER 14

14.2 $2(\sin 2\omega - \sin \omega)/\omega$

14.5 $\dfrac{1}{j\omega} + \dfrac{1}{\omega^2}(1 - e^{-j\omega})$

14.7 $V\tau \dfrac{\sin(\omega\tau/2)}{\omega\tau/2}$

14.10 $V\tau \dfrac{\sin(\omega\tau/2)}{\omega\tau/2}$

14.12 $\dfrac{j2}{\omega^2}(3 \sin \omega - \sin 3\omega)$

14.17 (a) $\dfrac{1}{4a^3}$, (b) 81.83%

14.19 (a) $3/(j\omega + 3)$, (b) $3e^{-3t}u(t)$, (d) low-pass filter

14.21 (a) $j\omega/(j\omega + \frac{1}{6})$, (b) $\delta(t) - \frac{1}{6}e^{-t/6}u(t)$, (c) high-pass filter

14.24 $\dfrac{4}{\sqrt{7}} e^{-t/2} \sin \dfrac{\sqrt{7}}{2} t\, u(t)$

14.26 $2e^{-t} \cos t\, u(t)$

14.28 $1.6(6e^{-12t} - e^{-2t})u(t)$

14.30 (a) $\omega_1 e^{-at} \cos \omega_1 t\, u(t)$, (c) $\frac{1}{2}\delta(t) + \dfrac{b-a}{4} e^{-(a+b)t/2}u(t)$

14.31 (b) $\omega_1 e^{-at}u(t)$, (d) $\omega_1 \cos \omega_1 t\, u(t) + a \sin \omega_1 t\, u(t)$

Index